Basic Writings *of* George Washington

Basic Writings

of

George Washington

Edited, with an Introduction
and Notes, by
SAXE COMMINS

RANDOM HOUSE · NEW YORK

FIRST PRINTING

*For their encouragement and aid thanks are due
Professor Henry Steele Commager of Columbia University
and Colonel Joseph I. Greene, Infantry, Retired.*

Contents

Part One
THE COLONIAL PERIOD

v

Part Two

THE REVOLUTIONARY PERIOD

vi

vii

viii

ix

Part Three
THE PRESIDENCY

Introduction

This single-volume compilation of 242 items was derived from approximately 17,000 documents collected in the Bicentennial Commission's thirty-nine-volume edition of *The Writings of George Washington*. Published by authority of Congress, with the sponsorship of the then President of the United States, Herbert Hoover, and a distinguished group of scholars and statesmen, the vast undertaking was under the general editorial direction of John C. Fitzpatrick. Superseding the two other notable collections made by Jared Sparks in 1834-1837 in twelve volumes and by Worthington C. Ford in 1889-1893 in fourteen volumes, the Bicentennial Edition includes everything known or newly discovered, up to the time the last volume went to press in 1941, of whatever Washington wrote or had attributed to him. The Diaries, also edited by John C. Fitzpatrick, were issued in four volumes in 1925 by the Mount Vernon Ladies' Association of the Union.

That hitherto-unknown letters, general orders, proclamations, addresses, instructions, appointments, memoranda and missing portions of the Diaries may be discovered in the future remains a possibility, but the likelihood of finding new revelations of the character and career of Washington is scant. His life and work have been revealed by more historical studies and biographies, laudatory and critical, than have been devoted to any other American, with the exception of Abraham Lincoln, in the annals of the nation.

To our best knowledge, no single-volume edition of Washington's significant writings is available. This gleaning from the field reaped by many scholars may, therefore, become the means by which a new generation can learn in essence the main events and the contending principles in the struggle for the founding of the Republic entirely from the point of view of Washington's role in that drama.

His forty-six years of commanding activity, from his twenty-first year until his death at sixty-seven, encompass the formative period of the nation. In his person is symbolized its growth from a colonial dependency through the eight years of revolutionary upheaval to constitutional statehood. The national character, it can be said retrospectively, took a sharp impress from his convictions and his qualities of personality. To present those convictions and that personality in his own words and to offer a historic panorama of the time in which they made themselves felt is this book's reason for being.

In order to bring the events in their proper succession and Washington's responses to them within a convenient form, selections from his surviving writings have been made in three general categories. The first embraces the Colonial Period and traces Washington's development from the time he went to fight the French and Indians in the vicinity of what is now Pittsburgh to his conversion to the cause which dominated his whole mind and spirit for the rest of his life: Independence. The second, and necessarily the largest section, the Revolutionary Period, begins with his appointment as Commander in Chief and carries through the War of Independence to the day he resigned his commission and sought the tranquillity of retirement in Mount Vernon. Finally, Part Three, which bears the title of The Presidency, includes his activities as a landed proprietor, as the presiding officer of the Constitutional Convention, his two terms as Chief Executive and, in the end, his retirement and death.

Manifestly, within the limited scope of this volume the omissions must by far exceed the inclusions. To offer the writings Washington committed to paper before he came of age would be to squander valuable space for a sampling of his juvenilia. These effusions might be of academic interest for the rhetorical style fashionable among colonial youths at the middle of the eighteenth century, but they bear little relationship to the development of the soldier, the commander and the statesman.

It is hardly germane to its purposes to perpetuate the record of Washington's numerous communications, asking for kettles and salt for the Army, complaining about his troubles with his teeth, listing minor appointments, ordering punishments for negligible infractions and the like minutiae which so often demanded his attention. Deliberately the selections were made for this volume so that they would convey a continuous, chronological history of the more meaningful aspects of Washington's participation in decisive events from the time he was twenty-one years old, when his military career began.

Washington wrote or had written for him what he himself could observe. Because his information was frequently second and third hand, many oblique references occur throughout his papers. He could not be everywhere during the eight years of war and the equal number of years of his two Administrations. But for his direction of the siege of Boston during the early stages of the conflict and his shift to Yorktown during its later phases, he was, so to speak, confined, though constantly moving, between the Hudson and Delaware Rivers in the States of New York, New Jersey and Pennsylvania. Thus many events of tremendous consequence in the Revolution and hence in his military career took place while he was not present. When Ticonderoga fell and the expedition to Quebec under Benedict Arnold failed, he was absent. He did not participate in the Battle of Saratoga, the Indian campaigns, the naval engagements, the fighting in the South around Charleston, Savannah, Richmond, Portsmouth, or in the defense against the destructive raids the British made on Connecticut. So inadequate were communications then, that, when the General Peace between Great Britain and America was signed in Paris, he did not learn of the Treaty until more than two months after the event. Shortly before the Constitutional Convention was summoned, Washington heard only in circuitous fashion about Shays' Rebellion and merely referred to it as "these commotions."

In order to explain absences and omissions and to maintain a simple continuity, a connective tissue of Notes has been supplied. There is one for each document, unless a succession of items covers a single episode, as in the treason of Benedict

Arnold. One Note in this instance suffices for the events that led to the discovery of his treachery, his escape and Major André's execution.

The Notes are prepared with the utmost brevity. Their aim is to provide such background as is considered necessary to clarify a cryptic allusion or a historic event in which Washington did not participate directly. They are neither critical nor controversial, but try to be factual and precise in accordance with the consensus of authoritative historians. They permit Washington to speak for himself without, it is hoped, obtrusive interruptions.

Above all, the Notes, when read with the documents, re-affirm the most conspicuous feature of Washington's character: his steadfastness of purpose.

From the time he espoused the cause of Independence through all the years and vicissitudes which followed, he never wavered in his single-minded devotion to that faith. In the disaster at Brooklyn Heights, the heartbreaking retreat across New Jersey, the winter of despair at Valley Forge, the endless desertions from his army, the betrayal by Benedict Arnold (a cruel blow to his judgment of a man), the factionalism of Congress, the anxieties over the Constitution and the slow ratification by the States, he was sustained by an unshakable conviction that total independence was beyond compromise—and inevitable.

Washington's simplicity of belief became a heroic obduracy. He certainly was, for example, too forthright with himself to harbor any illusions about his gifts as a writer. He was entirely without literary pretensions. His spelling, although it improved somewhat in later life, was almost by ear. The documents, as given here, retain his quaint orthographical habits.

That many of them were written by his aides-de-camp and secretaries under his dictation or supervision is well known. A long succession of secretaries lent their hands to the writing or copying of the formidable number of communications which were sent out over Washington's signature. Among the most notable of these assistants were Stephen Moylan, Tench Tilghman, Edmund Randolph, Alexander Hamilton, Joseph Reed,

Jonathan Trumbull, James McHenry, David Humphreys, Caleb Gibbs and others of like distinction.

How much Alexander Hamilton contributed to the writing partnership has been argued for almost a century and a half. Particularly has the question of the authorship of The Farewell Address, by far Washington's most famous utterance historically, been under violent dispute. The facts of the preparation of this document are discussed in the proper place, but here it is sufficient to say that in the four-way collaboration of Washington, Madison, Jay and Hamilton, the ideas and most of the language were Washington's. Addenda, emendations and editorial commentary were no doubt suggested by his advisers. The evidence that Washington created the document is to be found in a letter he wrote to Madison more than four years before the speech was delivered. He then outlined in substance the ideas, if not the final form, of The Farewell Address.

Subsequent Presidents, as is generally recognized, have had addresses and other papers prepared for them. These writings have remained undisputed as their own in the public record. What is important is that Washington dominated the content and was completely responsible for the letter and spirit of everything written by his aides for his signature. Naturally, there is no dispute among historians about the letters and other documents written in his own hand, of which many survive.

To convey in broad outline the main events of the critical first half century of America in the making, as perceived at the time by Washington himself, is the only purpose of this book. It presumes to make little, if any, attempt at interpretation. It does, however, try to bring into sharper focus, by judicious selection, a self-portrait of a man of action and to arrange some significant details, by way of background, of the world in which he lived.

SAXE COMMINS

May, 1948

Part One

THE
COLONIAL
PERIOD

JOURNEY TO THE FRENCH COMMANDANT

*At the age of twenty-one, George Washington, then adjutant
for the southern district of Virginia, was directed by Governor
Robert Dinwiddie to deliver a warning to the French that their
use of Ohio lands, to which the British claimed prior rights,
would not be tolerated. The Ohio Company protested to the
Governor, who, incidentally, was a stockholder, against the
hostile behavior of the French and their Indian allies. Washington's letters while on this mission, from the time he was commissioned until he was summoned to Alexandria on March 20,
1754, record his experiences and observations in the vicinity of
what is now Pittsburgh.*

Wednesday, October 31, 1753

I was commissioned and appointed by the Honourable
Robert Dinwiddie, Esq; Governor, &c., of Virginia, to visit and
deliver a letter to the Commandant of the French forces on
the Ohio, and set out on the intended Journey the same day:
The next, I arrived at Fredericksburg, and engaged Mr. Jacob
Vanbraam, to be my French interpreter; and proceeded with
him to Alexandria, where we provided Necessaries. From
thence we went to Winchester, and got Baggage, Horses, &c;
and from thence we pursued the new Road to Wills-Creek,*
where we arrived the 14th of November.

Here I engaged Mr. Gist to pilot us out, and also hired four
others as Servitors, Barnaby Currin and John Mac-Quire, Indian Traders, Henry Steward, and William Jenkins; and in
company with those persons, left the Inhabitants the Day following.

The excessive Rains and vast Quantity of Snow.

---

* Now Cumberland, Md.

3

November 22, 1753

As I got down before the Canoe, I spent some time in viewing the Rivers, and the Land in the Fork;† which I think extremely well situated for a Fort, as it has the absolute Command of both Rivers. The Land at the Point is 20 or 25 Feet above the common Surface of the Water; and a considerable Bottom of flat, well-timbered land all around it, very convenient for Building: The Rivers are each a Quarter of a Mile, or more, across, and run here very near at right Angles: Aligany bearing N.E. and Monongahela S.E. The former of these two is a very rapid and swift running Water; the other deep and still, without any perceptible Fall.

About two Miles from this, on the South East Side of the river, at the Place where the Ohio Company intended to erect a Fort, lives Shingiss, king of the Delawares: We called upon him, to invite him to Council at the Loggs-Town.

As I had taken a good deal of Notice Yesterday of the Situation at the Forks, my Curiosity led me to examine this more particularly, and I think it greatly inferior, either for Defence or Advantages; especially the latter: For a Fort at the Forks would be equally well situated on the Ohio, and have the entire command of the Monongahela; which runs up to our Settlements and is extremely well designed for Water Carriage, as it is of a deep still Nature. Besides a fort at the Fork might be built at a much less Expence, than at the other Place.

Nature has well contrived this lower Place, for Water Defence; but the Hill whereon it must stand being about a Quarter of a Mile in Length, and then descending gradually on the Land Side, will render it difficult and very expensive, to make a sufficient Fortification there.—The whole Flat upon the Hill must be taken-in, the Side next the Descent made extremely high, or else the Hill itself cut away: Otherwise, the Enemy may raise Batteries within that Distance without being exposed to a single Shot from the Fort.

† The present site of Pittsburgh, at the junction of the Monongahela and Allegheny Rivers.

SPEECH TO INDIANS AT LOGSTOWN

Intended to win the Six Nations' aid in the campaign against the French and those Indians allied to them, this speech was delivered to the Half-King, a chief who owed allegiance to the Six Nations and acted as their representative. It has the merit of being brief and direct and certainly is free of those rhetorical flourishes which characterized Washington's few juvenile writings

November 26, 1753

We met in Council at the Long-House, about 9 o'clock, where I spoke to them as follows:

Brothers, I have called you together in Council by order of your Brother, the Governor of Virginia, to acquaint you, that I am sent, with all possible Dispatch, to visit, and deliver a Letter to the French Commandant, of very great Importance to your Brothers, the English; and I dare say, to you their Friends and Allies.

I was desired, Brothers, by your Brother the Governor, to call upon you, the Sachems of the Nations, to inform you of it, and to ask your Advice and Assistance to proceed to the nearest and best Road to the French. You see, Brothers, I have gotten thus far on my Journey.

His Honour likewise desired me to apply to you for some of your young Men, to conduct and provide Provisions for us on our Way; and be a safe-guard against those French Indians who have taken up the hatchet against us. I have spoken thus particularly to you Brothers, because his Honour our Governor treats you as good Friends and Allies; and holds you in great Esteem. To confirm what I have said, I give you this String of Wampum.

JOURNEY TO THE FRENCH COMMANDANT
(Continued)

The Indian town to which Washington refers here was Venango, situated at the junction of French Creek and the Allegheny River. A hardy campaigner from the beginning of his military career, Washington always records as facts the changes and chances of an expedition; nothing is set down to dramatize obstacles overcome or to suggest the immemorial complaints of the soldier.

December 4, 1753

This is an old Indian Town, situated at the Mouth of French Creek on Ohio; and lies near N. about 60 miles from the Loggs-Town, but more than 70 the Way we were obliged to go.

We found the French Colours hoisted at a House from which they had driven Mr. John Frazier, an English Subject. I immediately repaired to it, to know where the Commander resided. There were three Officers, one of whom, Capt. Joncaire, informed me, that he had the Command of the Ohio: But that there was a General Officer at the near Fort, where he advised me to apply for an Answer. He invited us to sup with them; and treated us with the greatest Complaisance.

The Wine, as they dosed themselves pretty plentifully with it, soon banished the Restraint which at first appeared in their Conversation; and gave a Licence to their Tongues to reveal their sentiments more freely.

They told me, That it was their absolute Design to take possession of the Ohio, and by G—— they would do it: For that altho' they were sensible the English could raise two Men for their one; yet they knew their Motions were too slow and dilatory to prevent any Undertaking of theirs. They pretend to have an undoubted Right to the River, from a Discovery made by one La Salle 60 Years ago; and the Rise of this Expedition is, to prevent our settling on the River or Waters of it, as they had heard of some Families moving-out in Order thereto.

December 11, 1753

At 11 o'Clock we set out for the Fort, and were prevented from arriving there till the 11th by excessive Rains, Snows, and bad Travelling, through many Mires and Swamps. These we were obliged to pass, to avoid crossing the Creek, which was impossible, either by fording or rafting, the Water was so high and rapid.

December 12, 1753

I prepared early to wait upon the Commander, and was received and conducted to him by the second Officer in Command. I acquainted him with my Business, and offered my Commission and Letter: Both of which he desired me to keep till the Arrival of Monsieur Riparti Captain, at the next Fort, who was sent for and expected every Hour.

This Commander is a Knight of the military Order of St. Lewis, and named Legardeur de St. Pierre. He is an elderly Gentleman, and has much the Air of a Soldier. He was sent over to take the Command immediately upon the Death of the late General, and arrived here about seven Days before me.

At 2 o'Clock the Gentleman who was sent for arrived, when I offered the Letter, &c, again; which they received, and adjourned into a private Apartment for the Captain to translate, who understood a little English. After he had done it, the Commander desired I would walk-in, and bring my Interpreter to peruse and correct it; which I did.

13th. The chief Officers retired, to hold a Council of War; which gave me an Opportunity of taking the Dimensions of the Fort, and making what Observations I could.

December 15, 1753

The Commandant ordered a plentiful Store of Liquor, Provision, &c., to be put on Board our Canoe; and appeared to be extremely complaisant, though he was exerting every Artifice which he could invent to set our own Indians at Variance with us, to prevent their going 'till after our Departure. Presents, Rewards, and every Thing which could be suggested by him or his Officers.—I can't say that ever in my Life I suffered so much Anxiety as I did in this Affair:

December 16, 1753

We had a tedious and very fatiguing Passage down the Creek. Several Times we had like to have been staved against Rocks; and many Times were obliged all Hands to get out and remain in the Water Half an Hour or more, getting over the Shoals. At one Place the Ice had lodged and made it impassable by Water; therefore we were obliged to carry our Canoe across a Neck of Land, a quarter of a Mile over. We did not reach Venango, till the 22d, where we met with our Horses.

December 23, 1753

Our Horses were now so weak and feeble, and the Baggage so heavy (as we were obliged to provide all the Necessaries which the Journey would require) that we doubted much their performing it; therefore myself and others (except the Drivers, who were obliged to ride) gave up our Horses for Packs, to assist along with the Baggage. I put myself in an Indian walking Dress, and continued with them three Days, till I found there was no Probability of their getting home in any reasonable Time. The Horses grew less able to travel every Day; the Cold increased very fast; and the Roads were becoming much worse by a deep Snow, continually freezing: Therefore as I was uneasy to get back, to make Report of my Proceedings to his Honour, the Governor, I determined to prosecute my Journey the nearest Way through the Woods, on Foot.

Accordingly I left Mr. Vanbraam in Charge of our Baggage: with Money and Directions to Provide Necessaries from Place to Place for themselves and Horses, and to make the most convenient Dispatch in Travelling.

I took my necessary Papers; pulled off my Cloaths; and tied myself up in a Match Coat. Then with Gun in Hand and Pack at my Back, in which were my Papers and Provisions, I set-out with Mr. Gist, fitted in the same Manner, on Wednesday the 26th.

The Day following, just after we had passed a Place called the Murdering-Town (where we intended to quit the Path, and steer across the Country for Shannapins Town) we fell in with a Party of French Indians, who had lain in Wait for us. One of them fired at Mr. Gist or me, not 15 steps off, but fortunately missed. We took this Fellow into Custody, and kept him till about 9 o'clock at Night; Then let him go, and walked all the remaining Part of the Night without making any Stop; that we might get the Start, so far, as to be out of the Reach of their Pursuit the next Day, since we were well assured they would follow our Tract as soon as it was light. The next Day we continued travelling till quite dark, and got to the River about two Miles above Shannapins. We expected to have found the River frozen, but it was not, only about 50 Yards from each Shore; The Ice I suppose had broken up above, for it was driving in vast Quantities.

There was no Way for getting over but on a Raft; Which we set about with but one poor Hatchet, and finished just after Sun-setting. This was a whole Day's Work. Then set off; But before we were Half Way over, we were jammed in the Ice, in such a Manner that we expected every Moment our Raft to sink, and ourselves to perish. I put-out my setting Pole to try to stop the Raft, that the Ice might pass by; when the Rapidity of the Stream threw it with so much Violence against the Pole, that it jerked me out into ten Feet Water: but I fortunately saved myself by catching hold of one of the Raft Logs. Notwithstanding all our Efforts we could not get the Raft to either

Shore; but were obliged, as we were near an Island, to quit our Raft and make to it.

The Cold was so extremely severe, that Mr. Gist had all his Fingers, and some of his Toes frozen; but the water was shut up so hard, that we found no Difficulty in getting-off the Island, on the Ice, in the Morning, and went to Mr. Frazier's.

January 1, 1754

Tuesday the 1st Day of January, we left Mr. Frazier's House, and arrived at Mr. Gist's at Monongahela the 2d, where I bought a Horse, Saddle, etc: the 6th we met 17 Horses loaded with Materials and Stores, for a Fort at the Forks of Ohio, and the Day after some Families going out to settle: This Day we arrived at Wills Creek, after as fatiguing a Journey as it is possible to conceive, rendered so by excessive bad Weather. From the first Day of December to the 15th, there was but one Day on which it did not rain or snow incessantly: and throughout the whole Journey we met with nothing but one continued Series of cold wet Weather, which occasioned very uncomfortable Lodgings: especially after we had quitted our Tent, which was some Screen from the Inclemency of it.

On the 11th I got to Belvoir: where I stopped one Day to take necessary Rest; and then set out and arrived at Williamsburgh the 16th; when I waited upon his Honour the Governor with the Letter I had brought from the French Commandant; and to give an Account of the Success of my Proceedings.

January 17, 1754

The French are now coming from their Forts on Lake Erie and on the Creek to Venango to Erect another Fort. And from thence they design to the Forks of Monongehele and to the Logs Town, and so to continue down the River building at the most convenient places in order to prevent our Settlements &ca.

N.B. A Little below Shanapins Town in the Fork is the place

where we are going immediately to Build a Fort as it commands the Ohio and Monongehele.

To GOVERNOR DINWIDDIE

The problem of feeding, paying and clothing his troops was to harass Washington from the beginning of his career as an officer through all of the Revolutionary War. It confronted him in the Indian campaign, but in this instance his concern was for a mere twenty-five men.

Alexandria, March 9, 1754

HONBLE. SIR: In my last by Mr. Stuart, I slightly mentioned the objection many had against Enlisting (to wit) not knowing who was to be pay Master or the times for payment: It is now grown a pretty general Clamour, and some of those, who were amongst the first Enlisters, being needy, and knowing it to be usual for His Majesty's Soldiers to be paid once a Week, or at most every Fortnight, are very importunate to receive their Due: I have soothed and quieted them as much as possible, under pretence of receiving your Honour's Instructions in this particular at the arrival of the Colonel.

I have increased my number of Men to abt. 25, and dare venture to say, I should have had several more, if the excessive bad weather did not prevent their meeting agreeable to their Officer's Commands.

We daily Experience the great necessity for Cloathing the Men, as we find the generality of those, who are to be Enlisted, are of those loose, Idle Persons, that are quite destitute of House, and Home, and, I may truly say, many of them of Cloaths; which last, renders them very incapable of the necessary Service, as they must unavoidably be expos'd to inclement weather in their Marches, &c., and can expect no other, than to encounter almost every difficulty, that's incident to a Soldier's Life. There is many of them without Shoes, others want Stockings, some are without Shirts, and not a few that have Scarce

a Coat, or Waistcoat to their Backs; In short, they are as illy
provided as can well be conceiv'd, but I really believe every
Man of them, for their own Credits sake, is willing to be
Cloathed at their own Expense. They are perpetually teazing
me to have it done, but I am not able to advance the money
provided there was no risque in it, which there certainly is, and
too great for me to run; tho' it would be nothing to the Country, as a certain part of their pay might be deducted and appropriated to that use: Mr. Carlyle, or any of the merchants
here, would furnish them with proper necessarys, if there was
a certainty of any part of their pay stopt to reimburse the
Expense. But I must here in time put a kirb to my requests,
and remember that I ought not to be too importunate; otherwise I shall be as troublesome to your Honour, as the Soldiers
are to me: there is nothing but the necessity of the thing could
urge me to be thus free, but I shall no more exagerate this
affair to your Honour, as I am well assured, whatever you
think for the Benefit or good of the Expedition, you will cause
to have done.

[V.H.S.]

To RICHARD CORBIN

*Washington's desire to achieve a rank commensurate with
his responsibilities led him to seek the influence of Richard
Corbin, member of the Governor's Council.*

March, 1754

DEAR SIR: In a conversation with you at Green Spring,
you gave me some room to hope for a commission above that
of major, and to be ranked among the chief officers of this expedition. The command of the whole forces is what I neither
look for, expect, nor desire; for I must be impartial enough to
confess, it is a charge too great for my youth and inexperience
to be entrusted with. Knowing this, I have too sincere a love
for my country, to undertake that which may tend to the preju-

dice of it. But if I could entertain hopes, that you thought me worthy of the post of lieutenant-colonel, and would favor me so far as to mention it at the appointment of officers, I could not but entertain a true sense of the kindness.

I flatter myself, that, under a skilful commander, or man of sense (whom I most sincerely wish to serve under), with my own application and diligent study of my duty, I shall be able to conduct my steps without censure, and, in time, render myself worthy of the promotion, that I shall be favored with now. I am, &c.

To GOVERNOR DINWIDDIE

Prophetic of his major care as Commander in Chief of the Revolutionary armies is Washington's first reference to "managing a number of self-willed, ungovernable people." Here is early evidence of the indomitable will by which the recalcitrance of his troops was overcome.

Alexandria, March 20, 1754

SIR: I was favored with your letter by Mr. Stewart, enclosing a lieutenant-colonel's commission, and I hope my future behaviour will sufficiently testify the true sense I have of this kindness.

At present there are about seventy-five men at Alexandria, near fifty of whom I have enlisted. The others have been sent by Messrs. Polson, Mercer, and Waggener to this place. Very few officers have repaired hither yet, which has occasioned a fatiguing time to me, in managing a number of self-willed, ungovernable people. I shall implicitly obey your commands, and march out with all expedition. Major Carlyle is now preparing wagons for the conveyance of provisions, which till now could not move, on account of the heavy roads.

I doubt not but your Honor has been informed before this of Mr. Vanbraam's ill success in Augusta, by the express, who was sent from thence for that purpose.

Major Muse's promotion, and Messrs. Rose and Bently's declining, will occasion a want of officers; in which case I would beg leave to mention Mr. Vanbraam for a command, who is the oldest lieutenant, and an experienced soldier. Unless the officers come in, I shall be obliged to appoint him to that office, till I have your Honor's further directions. It would be conferring a very great obligation on him, were you to confirm the appointment. I verily believe his behaviour would not render him displeasing to you. I have given Captain Stephen orders to be in readiness to join us at Winchester with his company, as they were already in that neighbourhood, and raised there.

I have nothing further to add at present, but my sincere thanks for the indulgent favors I have met with, and I am &c.

To WILLIAM FAIRFAX

William Fairfax was a member of the King's Council in Virginia and for a time its President. An emigré to the colonies in the early part of the eighteenth century, he became the founder of the distinguished Fairfax family of Virginia.

Alexandria, March 22, 1754

Dr. Sir: I wrote to you in Frederick not knowing your Intention of going to Stafford, desiring that all your Men &c. might be in readiness to march by the middle or last of next week at furthest for Ohio: I have just receiv'd the Governor's Orders (which was sent upon the arrival of Captn Trent's express) to dispatch with all expedition thither, with the men already raiz'd and such Officers as I see proper: therefore, I shall do myself the Honour of calling upon you for one; I expect several others up this Day, together with three Sloops from York James River, and Eastern Shore with recruits; those who cannot be in readiness to go, are to stay and march with

Coln. Frye* who is to bring out the remainder of the Men,
Artillery &c. I shou'd be glad you wou'd repair to Alexandria
imediately upon the receipt of this in your way to Winchester
that we may consult on proper Means.

P. S. I suppose you have read or heard of the Governor's
command requiring all officers to be and appear at Alexandria
the 20th inst.

JOURNAL OF MARCH TOWARD THE OHIO

*Captured by the French at Fort Necessity, all the original
notes of the march toward the Ohio were translated and published in France. They were edited to justify the French occupation of the Ohio region. The memoranda were cut in some
places and amplified in others and so changed and twisted as
to make it seem that the French had come to this region as
liberators.*

March 31, 1754

On the 31st March, I received from his Honour a Lieutenant Colonel's Commission in the Virginia Regiment, whereof
Joshua Fry, Esquire, was Colonel, dated the 15th, with Orders
to take the troops, which were at that time quartered at Alexandria under my command, and to march with them towards the
Ohio, there to aid Captain Trent in building Forts, and in
defending the possessions of his Majesty against the attempts
and hostilities of the French.

April the 2d. Every Thing being ready, we began our march
according to our Orders, the 2d of April, with two Companies

---

* Col. Joshua Fry. He had been put in command of this expedition by
Governor Dinwiddie, with instructions to build forts and hold the Ohio
country against the French. He died May 31 from an accidental fall from
his horse, and the actual management of the expedition devolved upon
Washington.

of Foot, commanded by Captain Peter Hog, and Lieutenant Jacob Vanbraam, five subalterns, two Sergeants, six Corporals, one Drummer, and one hundred and twenty soldiers, one Surgeon, one Swedish Gentleman, who was a volunteer, two wagons, guarded by one Lieutenant, Sergeant, Corporal and twenty-five Soldiers.

We left Alexandria on Tuesday noon and pitched our tents about four miles from Cameron, having marched six miles.

SPEECH TO THE INDIANS AT WILLS CREEK

This speech, and several others in like vein, was also translated and published in the French version of Washington's Journal. "Conotocarious," the name by which Washington signed himself, was one the Indians conferred upon him. It means "devourer of villages."

April 23, 1754

To the Half-King, and the Chiefs and Warriors of the Shawanese and Loups our Friends and Brethren. I received your speech by Brother Bucks who came to us with the two young men six days after their departure from you. We return you our greatest thanks and our hearts burn with love and affection towards you, in gratitude for your steadfast attachment to us, as also your friendly speech, and your wise counsels. This young man will inform you where he found a small part of our army, making towards you, clearing the roads for a great number of our warriors, who are ready to follow us, with our great guns, our ammunition and provisions. I cannot delay letting you know the thoughts of our hearts, I send you back this young man, with this speech, to acquaint you therewith, and the other young man I have sent to the Governor of Virginia, to deliver him your speech and your wampum, and to be an eyewitness of the preparations we are making, to come in all haste to assist you, whose interest is as dear to us as our lives. We know the character of the treacherous French, and our conduct shall plainly show you how much we have it at heart. I shall not be satisfied if I do not see you before all our forces are met together at the Fort which is in our way, wherefore, I desire with the greatest earnestness, that you and Scruneyattha, or one of you, should come as soon as possible to meet us on the road, and to assist us in council. To assure you of the sincerity of my speech, and of the good will we bear you, I present you with these strings of wampum, that you may remember how much I am your Friend and Brother. Signed Go Washington Conotocarious.

To GOVERNOR DINWIDDIE

Punctilious in making his reports, the youthful commander inserts a paragraph in which he seeks approval from the Governor, whose indifference made the expedition more trying than it should have been. The rest of the letter, however, shows how acutely Washington perceived the strategic necessity of winning over some of the Indian tribes, how carefully he calculated his need for supplies and how tactfully he informed Dinwiddie of his letters to other Governors on the progress of the campaign.

Will's Creek, April 25, 1754

SIR: Captain Trent's ensign, Mr. Ward, has this day arrived from the Fork of the Monongahela, and brings the disagreeable account, that the fort, on the 17th instant, was surrendered at the summons of Monsieur Contrecœur to a body of French, consisting of upwards of one thousand men, who came from Venango with eighteen pieces of cannon, sixty batteaux, and three hundred canoes. They gave him liberty to bring off all his men and working-tools, which he accordingly did the same day.

Immediately upon this information I called a council of war, to advise on proper measures to be taken in this exigency. A copy of their resolves, with the proceedings, I herewith enclose by the bearer, whom I have continued express to your Honor for more minute intelligence.

Mr. Ward has the summons with him, and a speech from the Half-King, which I also enclose, with the wampum. He is accompanied by one of the Indians mentioned therein, who were sent to see where we were, what was our strength, and to know the time to expect us out. The other young man I have prevailed upon to return to the Half-King with the following speech.

I hope my proceedings in these affairs will be satisfactory to your Honor, as I have, to the utmost of my knowledge, consulted the interest of the expedition and good of my country; whose rights, while they are asserted in so just a cause, I will defend to the last remains of life.

Hitherto the difficulties I have met with in marching have been greater, than I expect to encounter on the Ohio, when possibly I may be surrounded by the enemy, and these difficulties have been occasioned by those, who, had they acted as becomes every good subject, would have exerted their utmost abilities to forward our just designs. Out of seventy-four wagons impressed at Winchester, we got but ten after waiting a week, and some of those so badly provided with teams, that the soldiers were obliged to assist them up the hills, although it was known they had better teams at home. I doubt not that in some points I may have strained the law; but I hope, as my sole motive was to expedite the march, I shall be supported in it, should my authority be questioned, which at present I do not apprehend, unless some busybody intermeddles.

Your Honor will see by the resolves in council, that I am destined to the Monongahela with all the diligent despatch in my power. We will endeavour to make the road sufficiently good for the heaviest artillery to pass, and when we arrive at Red-stone Creek, fortify ourselves as strongly as the short time will allow. I doubt not that we can maintain a possession there, till we are reinforced, unless the rising of the waters shall admit the enemy's cannon to be conveyed up in canoes, and then I flatter myself we shall not be so destitute of intelligence, as not to get timely notice of it, and make a good retreat.

I hope you will see the absolute necessity for our having, as soon as our forces are collected, a number of cannon, some of heavy metal, with mortars and grenadoes to attack the French, and put us on an equal footing with them.

Perhaps it may also be thought advisable to invite the Cherokees, Catawbas, and Chickasaws to march to our assistance, as we are informed that six hundred Chippewas and Ottawas are marching down Scioto Creek to join the French, who are coming up the Ohio. In that case I would beg leave to recommend their being ordered to this place first, that a peace may be concluded between them and the Six Nations; for I am informed by several persons, that, as no good harmony subsists between them, their coming first to the Ohio may create great disorders, and turn out much to our disadvantage.

As I had opportunities I wrote to the governors of Maryland and Pennsylvania, acquainting them with these advices, and enclosed the summons and Indian speech, which I hope you will not think me too forward in doing. I considered that the Assembly of Maryland was to sit in five days, that the Pennsylvania Assembly is now sitting, and that, by giving timely notice, something might be done in favor of this expedition, which now requires all the force we can muster.

By the best information I can get, I much doubt whether any of the Indians will be in to treat in May. Are the Indian women and children, if they settle amongst us, to be maintained at our expense? They will expect it.

To GOVERNOR DINWIDDIE

Governor Dinwiddie's response to Washington's appeal was to urge him to continue on his mission and count on the rewards of success and the Governor's own generosity in taking notice of his merit. The mere mention of discontent was considered unreasonable and pernicious by His British Majesty's representative in Virginia.

Great Crossing of the Youghiogany, May 18, 1754

SIR: I am heartily concerned, that the officers have such real cause to complain of the Committee's resolves; and still more to find my inclinations prone to second their just grievances.

I have endeavoured, as far as I was able, to see in the best light I could the trifling advantages that may accrue; yet nothing prevents their throwing down their commissions (with gratitude and thanks to your Honor, whose good intentions of serving us we are all well assured of) but the approaching danger, which has too far engaged their honor to recede till other officers are sent in their room, or an alteration made regarding their pay, during which time they will assist with their best endeavours voluntarily, that is, without receiving the gratuity allowed by the resolves of the Committee.

Giving up my commission is quite contrary to my intention. Nay, I ask it as a greater favor, than any amongst the many I have received from your Honor, to confirm it to me. But let me serve voluntarily; then I will, with the greatest pleasure in life, devote my services to the expedition without any other reward, than the satisfaction of serving my country; but to be slaving dangerously for the shadow of pay, through woods, rocks, mountains—I would rather prefer the great toil of a daily laborer, and dig for a maintenance, provided I were reduced to the necessity, than serve upon such ignoble terms; for I really do not see why the lives of his Majesty's subjects in Virginia should be of less value, than of those in other parts of his American dominions; especially when it is well known, that we must undergo double their hardship.

I could enumerate a thousand difficulties that we have met with, and must expect to meet with, more than other officers who have almost double our pay; but as I know you reflect on these things, and are sensible of the hardships we must necessarily encounter, it would be needless to enlarge.

Besides, as I have expatiated fully (and, perhaps, too warmly) in a letter to Colonel Fairfax, who, I suppose, will accompany you to Winchester, upon the motives that occasion these my resolves, I shall not trouble you with them; for the subject leads me too far when I engage in it.

Another thing resolved by the Committee is, that only one sergeant and one corporal be allowed to a company; with whom it is as much impossible to do the necessary duty, as it is to conquer kingdoms with my handful of men.

Upon the whole, I find so many clogs upon the expedition, that I quite despair of success; nevertheless, I humbly beg it, as a particular favor, that your Honor will continue me in the post I now enjoy, the duty whereof I will most cheerfully execute as a volunteer, but by no means upon the present pay.

I hope what I have said will not be taken amiss; for I really believe, were it as much in your power, as it is your inclination, we should be treated as gentlemen and officers, and not have annexed to the most trifling pay, that ever was given to English officers, the glorious allowance of soldier's diet—a pound of pork, with bread in proportion, per day. Be the consequence what it will, I am determined not to leave the regiment, but to be amongst the last men that quit the Ohio, even if I serve as a private volunteer, which I greatly prefer to the establishment we are now upon. I am, &c.

SPEECH TO THE HALF-KING

The result of this speech was something less than Washington expected. Some Indians arrived, with their families, and became more of a hindrance than a help. Later they added to his burdens by complaining that he failed in his promises, and in the end, when Fort Necessity was besieged, they deserted altogether.

Youghiogheny River, May 19, 1754

I despatched the young Indian who had returned with Mr Ward, to the Half-King, with the following speech.

To the Half-King, &c. My Brethren, It gives me great pleasure, to learn that you are marching to assist me with your counsels; be of good courage, my brethren, and march vigorously towards your brethren the English; for fresh forces will soon join them, who will protect you against your treacherous enemy the French. I must send My friends to you, that they acquaint you with an agreeable speech which the Governor of Virginia has sent to you: He is very sorry for the bad usage you have received. The swollen streams do not permit us to come to you quickly, for that reason I have sent this young man to invite you to come and meet us: he can tell you many things that he has seen in Virginia, and also how well he was received by the most prominent men; they did not treat him as the French do your people who go to their Fort; they refuse them provisions; this man has had given him all that his heart could wish; for the confirmation of all this, I here give you a Belt of Wampum.

JOURNAL

This is Washington's own record of his baptism of fire. It is the first of many times that he exposed himself to open fighting. This engagement in the woods lasted fifteen minutes and the first of the ten Frenchmen to be killed was Jumonville, their leader, whose death was to plague Washington afterward. The battle itself was the result of two armed scouting parties coming upon each other without intention and firing away at sight. When the smoke cleared, Washington had all he could do to prevent the Indians from killing the twenty-one prisoners and adding their scalps to the ten they had already accounted for.

May 27, 1754

About eight in the Evening I received an express from the Half-King, who informed me, that as he was coming to join us, he had seen along the road, the tracks of two men, which he had followed, till he was brought to a low obscure place; that he thought the whole Party of French was hidden there.

That very moment I sent out forty men, and ordered my ammunition to be put in a place of safety, fearing it to be a Stratagem of the French to attack our Camp: I left a guard to defend it and with the rest of my men, set out in a heavy rain, and in a night as dark as pitch, along a path scarce broad enough for one man; we were sometime fifteen or twenty minutes out of the path, before we could come to it again, and we would often strike against each other in the darkness: All night long we continued our route, and on the 28th, about sun-rise, we arrived at the Indian Camp, where, after holding a council with the Half-King, we concluded to attack them together; so we sent out two men to discover where they were, as also their position, and what sort of ground was therabout; after which, we prepared to surround them marching one after the other, Indian fashion: We had advanced pretty near to them, as we thought, when they discovered us; I ordered my company to fire; my fire was supported by that of Mr. Waggoner, and my company and his, received the whole fire of the French, during the greater part of the action, which only lasted a quarter of an hour, before the enemy were routed.

We killed Mr. de Jumonville, the Commander of the party, as also nine others; we wounded one, and made twenty-one prisoners, among whom were M. la Force, M. Drouillon, and two cadets. The Indians scalped the dead, and took away the greater part of their Arms, after which we marched on with the prisoners under guard, to the Indian camp, where again I held a council with the Half-King; and there informed him, that the Governor was desirous to see him, and was expecting him at Winchester; he answered that, he could not go just then, as his People were in too imminent a danger from the French, whom they had attacked; that he must send runners to all the allied nations, inviting them to take up the Hatchet. He sent a young Delaware Indian to the Delaware Nation, and gave him also a French scalp to carry to them. This man desired to have a part of the presents which were allotted to them, but the remaining part he said might be kept for another opportunity. He said he would go to his own family, and to several others, and bring them to Mr. Gist's, whither he desired me to send men and horses to assist them in coming to our camp. After this I marched on with the prisoners. They had informed me that they had been sent with a summons to order me to retire—A plausible pretence to discover our camp, and to obtain knowledge of our forces and our situation! It was so clear that they had come to reconnoitre what we were that I admired their assurance, when they told me they were come as an Embassy; their instructions were to get what knowledge they could of the roads, rivers, and of all the Country as far as the Potowmack. And instead of coming as an Embassador, publicly, and in an open manner, they came secretly, and sought after the most hidden retreats, more fit for deserters than for Embassadors; they encamped there and remained hidden for whole days together, at a distance of not more than five miles from us; they sent spies to reconnoiter our camp; the whole body turned back 2 miles; they sent the two messengers mentioned in the instructions to inform M. de Contrecœur of the place where we were, and of our disposition, that he might send his detachments to inforce the summons as soon as it should be given.

Besides, an Embassador has princely attendants, whereas this was only a simple petty French officer; an Embassador has no need of spies, his person being always sacred: and since their intention was so good, why did they tarry two days, five miles distance from us, without acquainting me with the summons, or at least, with something that related to the Embassy? That alone would be sufficient to excite the strongest suspicions, and we must to do them the justice to say, that as they wanted to hide themselves, they could not have picked out better places than they had done.

The summons is so insolent, and savors so much of Gasconnade, that if it had been brought openly by two men, it would have been an excessive Indulgence to have suffered them to return.

It was the opinion of the Half-King in this case that their intentions were evil, and that it was a pure pretence; that they had never intended to come to us otherwise than as enemies; and if we had been such fools as to let them go, they would never have helped us to take any other Frenchmen.

They say they called to us as soon as they had discovered us;

which is an absolute falsehood for I was then marching at the head of the company going towards them and can positively affirm, that, when they first saw us, they ran to their arms, without calling; as I must have heard them had they so done.

To JOHN AUGUSTINE WASHINGTON

The letters which George Washington wrote to his brothers, John Augustine and Lund, during his entire military career convey his observations and feelings with less reservation than he exercised in almost any of his other writings. Referring to the frequently quoted "I heard the bullets whistle, and, believe me, there is something charming in the sound," Washington Irving, in his Life of Washington, *condones this display of youthful heroics by explaining: "He was, indeed, but twenty-two years when he said it; it was just after his first battle; he was flushed with success, and was writing to a brother."*

Camp At Great Meadow, May 31, 1754

Since my last arrived at this place, where three days ago we had an engagement with the French, that is, a party of our men with one of theirs. Most of our men were out upon other detachments, so that I had scarcely 40 men remaining under my command, and about 10 or 12 Indians; nevertheless we obtained a most signal victory. The battle lasted about 10 or 15 minutes, with sharp firing on both sides, till the French gave ground and ran, but to no great purpose. There were 12 killed of the French, among whom was Mons. de Jumonville, their commander, and 21 taken prisoners, among whom are Mess. La Force and Drouillon, together with two cadets. I have sent them to his honour the Governor, at Winchester, under a guard of 20 men, conducted by Lieutenant West. We had but one man killed, and two or three wounded. Among the wounded on our side was Lieutenant Waggener, but no danger, it is hoped, will ensue. We expect every hour to be attacked by superior force, but, if they forbear one day longer, we shall be prepared for them. We have already got entrenchments, are

about a pallisado which I hope will be finished to-day. The
Mingoes have struck the French and I hope will give a good
blow before they have done. I expect 40 odd of them here tonight, which, with out fort and some reinforcements from Col.
Fry, will enable us to exert our noble courage with spirit.

P. S. I fortunately escaped without any wound, for the right
wing, where I stood, was exposed to and received all the enemy's fire, and it was the part where the man was killed, and the
rest wounded. I heard the bullets whistle, and, believe me,
there is something charming in the sound.

To GOVERNOR DINWIDDIE

*The fullness of Lieutenant Colonel Washington's report is
in effect a disguised rebuke and protest against Governor Dinwiddie's indifference to the plight of the members of the Indian
expedition. Pleas for provisions and reinforcements and all
requests for definition of rank and responsibility had been ignored. The division of command irked Washington and drove
him to one of the few expressions of despair to be found in his
letters of this period: "God knows when we shall be able to do
anything for to deserve better of our Country."*

•

June 12, 1754

We have been extremely ill used by Major Carlyle's
deputies, which I am heartily sorry for, since he is a gentleman
so capable of the business himself, and has taken so much pains
to give satisfaction. He, I believe, has been deceived, and we
have suffered by those under him, and by those who have contracted for provisions. We have been six days without flour,
and there is none upon the road for our relief that we know of,
though I have by repeated expresses given him timely notice.
We have not provisions of any sort enough in camp to serve us
two days. Once before we should have been four days without
provisions, if Providence had not sent a trader from the Ohio

to our relief, for whose flour I was obliged to give twenty-one shillings and eight pence per hundred.

In a late letter to Major Carlyle, I have complained of the tardiness of his deputies. I likewise desired, that suitable stores of ammunition might be sent up speedily, for till that is done we have it not in our power to attempt any advantageous enterprise; but must wait its arrival at Red-stone, for which I shall set off the moment provisions arrive to sustain us on the march. Major Carlyle mentioned a contract he had made with Mr. Croghan for flour, likewise Mr. Croghan's offer of furnishing more if required. I have therefore desired to have all that Mr. Croghan can furnish.

The Indians are drawing off from the River daily, one of whom last night brought news of Monacatoocha. He went from Logstown about five nights ago with the French scalps, and four hatchets, with which he intended to visit the four tribes of Indians between this and Lake Erie, and present to each tribe a scalp and hatchet, and at the same time acquaint them that it was expected, as the English and Six Nations had hand-in-hand struck the French, they would join our forces. This messenger likewise says, that Monacatoocha was determined not only to counsel with the chiefs of those tribes, but with their great warriors also, which is customary in these cases, and was to return as soon as possible, which he imagined would be in fifteen days; but in case he should not return in that time, he left orders for the Indians at Logstown to set off for Red-stone Creek, so that they all would meet at Red-stone to join their brothers the English. He also desired there might be no attack made against the French fort, till he should return, by which time he hoped all the forces would be gathered, and then they would make a general attack together, and gain a complete victory at once.

The Half-King has sent messengers to other places for warriors, who are to meet us also at Red-stone Creek. Besides these, he has sent two messengers, by the advice of Mr. Croghan, Mr. Montour, and myself, one to invite the Shawanese to come and receive one of their men, who was imprisoned in Carolina, and to counsel with us, and the other to the Delawares for the same purpose, as we hear both these nations have accepted the hatchet against us. This report was first brought by an Indian sent from Logstown to the Half-King, and since confirmed by nine French deserters, who arrived at our camp to-day. These men farther say, that the fort at the Fork is completed, and proof against any attempts, but with bombs, on the land side. There were not above five hundred men in it, when they left it, but they suppose by this time two hundred more are arrived. Nine hundred were ordered to follow them, who might be expected in fourteen or fifteen days.

I was as much disappointed when I met these persons to-day, as ever I was in my life. By misunderstanding the scouts that brought me intelligence, that is, mistaking ninety for nine, I marched out at the head of one hundred and thirty men (the major part of the effective men in the regiment), full with the hope of procuring another present of French prisoners for your Honor. Judge then my disappointment at meeting nine only, and those coming for protection. I guarded against all casualties, that might happen to the camp, and ordered Major Muse to repair into the fort, and erect the small swivels for the defence of the place, which he could do in an hour's time.

Agreeably to your desire I shall here mention the names of the gentlemen, who are to be promoted. Lieutenant George Mercer will worthily succeed to a captaincy. Captain Vanbraam has acted as captain ever since we left Alexandria. He is an experienced, good officer, and very worthy of the command he has enjoyed. Mr. James Towers is the oldest ensign, for whom you will please to send a lieutenancy. To Captain Stephen I have already given a major's commission, finding one blank among Colonel Fry's papers. If merit, Sir, will entitle a gentlemen to your notice, Mr. Peyrouny may justly claim a share of your favor. His conduct has been governed by the most consummate prudence, and all his actions have sufficiently testified his readiness to serve his country, which I really believe he looks upon Virginia to be. He was sensibly chagrined, when I acquainted him with your pleasure, of giving him an ensigncy. This he had twelve years ago, and long since commanded a company. He was prevailed on by Colonel Fry, when he left Alexandria, to accept the former commission, and

assist my detachment, as I had very few officers, till we all met
on the Ohio, which commission he would now have resigned,
and returned to Virginia, but for my great dissuasion to the
contrary. I have promised to solicit your Honor to appoint
him adjutant, and continue him ensign, which will induce a
very good officer to remain in the regiment. The office of adjutant, Sir, is most necessary to a regiment, in distributing the
daily orders, receiving all reports, and seeing orders executed.
In short, an adjutant is an indispensable officer. Should you be
pleased to indulge me in the request, I shall look upon it in a
very particular light, as I think the personal merit of the gentlemen, his knowledge of military duty, and his activity will
render him highly worthy of the favor. An ensign is still wanting, whom I hope you will send, if you know of any one suitable for the office. A young man in the camp, who came with
Captain Lewis, has solicited, but I am yet ignorant of his character and qualities. He is a volunteer, and recommended by
Captain Lewis.

In a letter by Mr. Ward, you acquainted me, that you had
given orders to Colonel Fry to examine into the proceedings of
Captain Trent, and his lieutenant, Frazier, by a court-martial.
I shall be glad if you will repeat your orders and instructions to
me, or rather to Colonel Innes; for an officer cannot be tried by
those of his own regiment only, but has a right to be heard in a
general court-martial. Captain Trent's behaviour has been very
tardy, and has convinced the world of what they before suspected, his great timidity. Lieutenant Frazier, though not altogether blameless, is much more excusable, for he would not
accept of the commission, till he had a promise from his captain, that he should not reside at the fort, nor visit it above
once a week, or as he saw necessary.

Queen Aliquippa desired that her son, who is really a great
warrior, might be taken into council, as he was declining and
unfit for business, and that he should have an English name
given him. I therefore called the Indians together by the advice of the Half-King, presented one of the medals, and desired him to wear it in remembrance of his great father, the
King of England, and called him by the name of Colonel Fairfax, which he was told signified the first of the council. This

gave him great pleasure. I was also informed, that an English name would please the Half-King, which made me presume to give him that your Honor, and call him Dinwiddie; interpreted in their language, the head of all. I am, &c.

P.S. These deserters corroborate what the others said and we suspected. LaForce's party were sent out as spies, and were to show that summons if discovered, or overpowered, by a superior party of ours. They say the commander was blamed for sending so small a party.

Since writing the aforegoing, Captain Mackay, with the Independent Company, has arrived, whom I take to be a very good sort of a gentleman. For want of proper instructions from your Honor, I am much at a loss to know how to act, or proceed in regard to his company. I made it my particular study to receive him (as it was your desire) with all the respect and politeness, that were due to his rank, or that I was capable of showing; and I do not doubt from his appearance and behaviour, that a strict intimacy will ensue, when matters shall be put in a clear light. But at present, I assure you, they will rather impede the service, than forward it; for, as they have commissions from the King, they look upon themselves as a distinct body, and will not incorporate and do duty with our men, but keep separate guards, and encamp separately. I have not offered to control Captain Mackay in any thing, nor showed that I claimed a superior command, except in giving the parole and countersign, which must be the same in an army consisting of different nations, to distinguish friends from foes. He knows the necessity of this yet does not think he is to receive it from me. Then who is to give it? Am I to issue these orders to a company? Or is an independent captain to prescribe rules to the Virginia regiment? This is the question. But its absurdity is obvious.

It now behooves you, Sir, to lay your absolute commands on one or the other to obey. This is indispensably necessary, for nothing clashes more with reason, than to conceive our small bodies can act distinctly, without having connexion with one another, and yet be serviceable to the public. I do not doubt that Captain Mackay is an officer of sense, and I dare say will do the best for the service; but, Sir, two commanders are so incompatible, that we cannot be as useful to one another, or the public, as we ought; and I am sincerely sorry, that he has arrived before your instructions by Colonel Innes, who I doubt not will be fully authorized how to act. But as we have no news of Colonel Innes, I have, in the mean time, desired Major Carlyle to send this by an immediate express to you, who, I hope, will satisfy these doubts.

Captain Mackay and I have lived in the most perfect harmony since his arrival, and have reasoned on this calmly; and, I believe, if we should occasion to exert our whole force, we shall do as well as divided authority can do. We have not had the least warmth of dispute. He thinks you have not a power to give commissions, that will command him. If so, I can very confidently say, that his absence would tend to the public advantage. I have been particularly careful of discovering no foolish desire of commanding him, neither have I intermeddled with his company in the least, or given any directions concerning it, except on these General the Word, Countersign, and place to repair to in case of an Alarm, none of which he thinks he sh'd receive. I have testified to him in the most serious manner the pleasure I sh'd take in consulting and advising with him upon all occasions, and I am very sensible, with him we shall never differ when your Honour decides this, which I am convinced your own just discernment and consideration will make appear, the impossibility of a Med'm. The nature of the thing will not allow of it.

It must be known who is to Command before orders will be observed, and I am very confident your Honour will see the absurdity and consider the Effects of Capt. Mackay's having the direction of the Regiment, for it would certainly be the hardest thing in Life if we are to do double and trible duty, and neither be entitled to the Pay or Rank of Soldiers. That the first Column of the Virginia Regiment has done more for the Interest of the Expedition than any other Company or Corps that will hereafter arrive, will be obvious to them all. This, Hon'ble Sir, Capt. Mackay did not hesitate one moment to allow since he has seen the Work we have done upon the Roads &c. We shall part tomorrow. I shall continue my March to Red Stone, while the Company remains here; but this, Sir,

I found absolutely necessary for the Publick Interest. Capt. Mackay says, that it is not in his power to oblige his Men to work upon the Road, unless he will engage them a Shilling Sterling a Day, which I would not choose to do; and to suffer them to March at their ease, whilst our faithful Soldiers are laboriously employed, carry's an air of such distinction that it is not to be wondered at if the poor fellows were to declare the hardship of it. He also declares to me that this is not particular to his Company only, but that no Soldiers subject to Martial law can be obliged to do it for less. I, therefore, shall continue to compleat the work we have begun with my poor fellows; we shall have the whole credit, as none others have assisted. I hope from what has been said your honour will see the necessity of giving your speedy orders on this head, and I am sensible you will consider the Evil tendency that will accompany Captn. Mackay's com[mandin]g for I am sorry to observe this is what we always hoped to enjoy; the Rank of Officers, which to me, Sir, is much dearer than the Pay.

Captn. Mackay brought none of the Cannon, very little Ammunition, about 5 Days allowance of Flour, and 60 Beeves. Since I have spun a letter to this enormous size, I must go a little further and beg your Honour's patience to peruse it. I am much grieved to find our Stores so slow advancing. God knows when we shall [be] able to do any thing for to deserve better of our Country. I am etc.

The Contents of this Letter is a profound Secret.

JOURNAL

SPEECH TO THE INDIANS

These speeches failed to impress the Indians. When they had the choice between the strength of the French and the weakness of the British, they could not be swayed by wampum and promises. In the meantime, the French were advancing from Fort Duquesne, and the English decided to retreat to Wills Creek. They got only as far as Fort Necessity, an exposed stockade in the Great Meadows. Within two days the French troops appeared, and in that time the Indians, upon whom Washington had counted, disappeared. The French, numbering 700, began their attack on July 3rd. The English losses were about one-third of the garrison, and the following day, after a parley, Fort Necessity was surrendered. One of the articles of the capitulation agreement, to which Washington had to submit, was an admission that Jumonville had been "assassinated" in the engagement of May 28th.

On the march to Red Stone, June 18, 1754

BRETHREN: We are very glad to see you, and sorry that you are disquieted by such reports that: The English intend to injure you, or any of your allies; this report we know must have been forged by the French, who are always treacherous, and asserting the greatest falsehoods whenever they think they will turn out to their advantage; they speak well, promise fine things, but all from the lips only; whilst their heart is corrupt, and full of venomous poison. You have been their children and they have done everything for you, but they no sooner thought themselves strong enough than they returned to their natural pride and drove you off from your lands, declaring you had no right on the Ohio. The English, your real friends, are too generous to think of ever using the Six Nations, their faithful allies, in such a manner; after you had gone to the Governors of Virginia and Pennsylvania they (at your repeated request) sent an army to maintain your rights; to put you again in possession of your lands, and to take care of your wives and children, to dispossess the French, to maintain your rights and to secure the whole country for you; for these very ends are the English arms now employed; it is for the safety of your wives and your children that we are fighting; and as this is the only motive of our conduct we cannot reasonably doubt of being joined by the rest of your forces to oppose the common enemy. Those who will not join us shall be answerable for whatever may be the consequence, we only desire your brethren to choose the side which seems most acceptable to them. The Indians of the Six Nations are those who have the most interest in this war,

for them it is that we fight.; and it would greatly trouble me
to do them the least harm; we have engaged in this war to assist
and protect you; our arms are open to receive you and our
hands ready to feed your families during the war. The Governor of Virginia has often desired that they might be sent to
him that he may see them in person, feed and clothe them according to their own desire; but as you could not decide to
send them to him, we are ready to share all our provisions with
you, in a friendly manner and to take such measures and give
such orders that enough shall be brought to maintain your
wives and children. Such conduct will evidently prove how
much more the English love and esteem their faithful allies the
Six Nations, than the French do; as we have drawn the sword
in your cause and in your defence, hesitate no longer, delay
not a moment, but put all your wives and children under our
protection, and they shall find plenty of provisions; in the
meanwhile set your young men and your warriors to sharpening their hatchets, to join and unite with us vigorously in our
battles. The present, my Brethren, which I offer you is not so
considerable as I could wish, but I expect in a short time, a
quantity of goods, which are to be at my disposal, to reward
those who shall have shown themselves brave and active on this
occasion; I shall, moreover recompense them most generously.
Be of good Courage, my brethren, deliver your Country and
secure it to your children; let me know the thoughts of your
Hearts on this affair, that I may give an account of your sentiments to your great Friend and Brother, the Governor of Virginia. To assure you of my sincerity and esteem I present you
this belt of wampum.

June 20, 1754

The Council still continued.
When the Delawares knew that they were suspected of being in the French Interest, they demanded the Reason why
they had been sent for, and what they should tell the French at
their Return.
I answered them, it was to let them understand, that we were

to come at their reiterated requests to assist them with Sword in Hand; that we intended to put them in the Possession of those Lands which the French had taken from them.

And as they had often demanded our Assistance, as our ancient and faithful Allies, I invited them to come and place themselves under our Protection, together with their Women and Children.

On the march to Red Stone, June 21, 1754

Met very early, and I spoke first to the Delawares in the following manner.

Brethren; By your open and generous conduct on this occasion you have made yourself dearer to us than ever; we return you our thanks, that you did not go to Venango, when the French first invited you there; their treating you in such a childish manner, as we perceive they do, raises in us a just and strong resentment. They call you their children, and speak to you as if you were children in reality and had no more understanding than such. Consider well my brethren, and compare all their speeches, and you will find that all it tends to, is to tell you, I am going to open your eyes, to unstop your ears and such like words to no purpose, and only proper to amuse children. You also observe brethren that if they deliver a speech, or make a promise, and confirm it with a belt, they imagine it binds them no longer than they think it consistent with their interest to stand to it. They have given one example of it; and I will point it out to you, in the leap which they say they have made over the barrier which you had set for them; which ought to stir you up, my Brethren, to just anger, and cause you to embrace the favourable opportunity that we offer you, as we are come at your request, to assist you, and by means of which, you may make them leap back again with more speed than they advanced. (A string of wampum.) The French are continually telling you not to give heed to ill reports that are told you concerning them, who are your fathers. If they did not know in their very hearts, how richly they deserve it on account of their injustice to you, why should they suspect that they are accused?

Why should they take so much care to forewarn you, in order
to hinder you from believing what is told you concerning them?
As to what they say of us, our conduct alone will answer in our
behalf. Examine the truth yourselves. You know the roads leading to our habitations, you have lived amongst us, you can
speak our language; but in order to refute whatever may be
said against us and to assure you of our brotherly love; we once
more invite your old men, your wives and your children, to
take refuge under our protection and in our arms, in order to
be plentifully fed, whilst your warriors and young men join
with ours and espouse together the common cause. (A string of
wampum.) Brethren we thank you with all our hearts, for having declared unto us your resolution of accomplishing the engagements which you entered into at the treaty of Logstown
and we can do no otherwise than praise your generous conduct
with regard to your Grandsons the Shawanese; it gives us infinite pleasure. We are greatly obliged for the advice given you
by Onondaga, charging you to hold fast the chain of friendship by which we are bound; I dare say, that, had he known,
how nearly you were interested in this war, or that it was for
love of you, and at your request, that we have taken up arms, he
would have ordered you to declare and to act immediately
against the common enemy of the Six Nations. In order to assure you of my affection, and to confirm the truth of what I
have said, I present you with two great strings of wampum.

June 21, 1754

Immediately after the Council was over, notwithstanding all that Mr. Montour could do to dissuade them, the Delawares as also the Half-King, and all the other Indians returned
to the Great Meadows; but though we had lost them, I still had
spies of our own people, to prevent any surprise. As I was told
that if I sent a belt of wampum and a speech, it might bring
back the Half-King and his young men, I sent the following
speech by Mr. Croghan:

'Tis but lately since we were assembled together; we were sent
here by your Brother the Governor of Virginia, at your own Request

in Order to succour you, and fight for your Cause; wherefore my Brethren, I must require that you and your young Men come to join and encamp with us, that we may be ready to receive our Brother Monacatoocha, whom I daily expect; That this Request may have its desired Effect, and make a suitable Impression upon your Minds I present you with this String of Wampum.

To THOMAS LEE

At the request of Thomas Lee, once President of the Virginia Council, Washington made the following observations on the navigability of the Potomac River. Thirty years later his interest in navigable routes from the west to the Virginia tidewater was to be resumed with great energy and was to be continued through his two terms in office as President.

August, 1754

SIR: Your desire, added to my own curiosity engaged me the last time I was in Frederick to return down by Water to discover the Navigation of Potomack; the following are the observations I made thereupon in that Trip. From the mouth of Paterson's Creek to the begg. of Shannondoah Falls there is no other obstacle than the shallowness of the Water to prevent Craft from passing. The first of those Falls is also even and shallow but swift and continues so with interruptions of Rocks to what is known by the Spout wch. is a mile and half; from this their is Rocky swift and very uneven water for near 6 Miles, in which distance there are 4 Falls, the first of which is tolerably clear of Rocks but shallow yet may be much amended by digging a Channel on the Maryland side abt. 2 Miles from this, and ½ Mile below the Mouth of Shannondoah is what they call the Spout, which is the great (and indd. almost the only) difficulty of the whole it has a considerable Fall the water being confined shoots with great Rapidity and what adds much to the difficulty is the bottom being exceeding Rocky occasions a Rippling so prodigious that none but boats or large Canoes can pass. The canoe I was in wh'ch was not small had near sunk having received much water on both sides and at the hd. Their may be a passage also got round this also upon the Maryland shoar that Vessels may be hald up after removing some Rocks which a moderate expence may accomplish. One of the other two Falls is swift and ugly not much unlike the Spout but when the River is higher than ordinary a passage may be had round a small Island on the Other side which passage may be greatly improved. abt. 8 miles below this there is another Fall which is very easy and passable and abt. 2 Miles from that is a cluster of small Islands with many Rocks and swift water which renders the passage somewhat precarious. From this to the Seneca Fall the Water is as smooth and even as can be desir'd, with scarcely any perceptable Fall. The Seneca Fall is easily pass'd in two places and Canoes may continue within two Miles of the Gt. Falls but further it is not possible therefore the *trouble and expence* of going up Seneca Falls will not be adiquite to the expence and trouble [and] will not answer the Charges as all Carriages for the benefits of a good Road are oblig'd to pass Difficult Bridge from whence it is but 8 Miles to the Landing place at the Sugarland Island and is 5 Miles to the Lowest landing that can be h'd below the afores'd Falls of Seneca. Thus Sir as far as I was capable, have I given you an acct. of the Conveniences and inconveniences that attend the Navigation of Potomack fr'm the Fall up, which I doubt but you will readily concur with me in judging it more convenient least expensive and I may further say by much the most expeditious way to the Country. There is but one objection that can obviate this Carriage and that is the Scarcity of water in the best season of the year for this kind of conveyance.

To GOVERNOR DINWIDDIE

When Washington returned with the remnants of his troops from the debacle at Fort Necessity, Governor Dinwiddie issued one contradictory order after another. The last straw came when he reorganized the Virginia Regiment and reduced the

*rank of all officers above captain. Washington promptly re-
signed and for four months devoted himself to his Mount Vernon estate. The British Major General Edward Braddock was
then organizing the campaign for the capture of Fort Duquesne
that was to come to such grief. On May 10, 1755, Washington
was named Braddock's aide-de-camp. The march from Fort
Cumberland began on June 7th, and it was marked by one
failure after another until it ended in disaster. Though stricken
by fever and carried a good portion of the way in a covered
wagon, Washington persisted in staying with his regiment to
the bitter end. The French and Indians were everywhere in the
forests and finally attacked from all sides. Although they outnumbered the enemy, Braddock's forces fell into panic and
were slaughtered. Braddock himself was wounded in the breast
and died three days later. Taking command, Washington, sick
as he was, managed to bring the survivors back to Fort Cumberland. His own reference to his participation indicates the fury
of the action: "I luckily escap'd with't a wound tho' I had four
Bullets through my Coat and two Horses shot under me." The
disaster at the Monongahela stirred the colonists and made
Washington's name known far beyond Virginia for the first
time.*

Fort Cumberland, July 18, 1755

HONBL. SIR: As I am favour'd with an oppertunity, I
shou'd think myself excusable was I to omit giv'g you some acct.
of our late Engagem't with the French on the Monongahela the
9th. Inst.

We continued our March from Fort Cumberland to Frazier's
(which is within 7 Miles of Duquisne) with't meet'g with any
extraordinary event, hav'g only a stragler or two picked up by
the French Indians. When we came to this place, we were attack'd (very unexpectedly I must own) by abt. 300 French and
Ind'ns; Our numbers consisted of abt. 1300 well arm'd Men,
chiefly Regular's, who were immediately struck with such a
deadly Panick, that nothing but confusion and disobedience of
order's prevail'd amongst them: The Officer's in gen'l behav'd

with incomparable bravery, for which they greatly suffer'd, there being near 60 kill'd and wound'd. A large proportion, out of the number we had! The Virginian Companies behav'd like Men and died like Soldiers; for I believe out of the 3 Companys that were there that day, scarce 30 were left alive: Captn. Peyrouny and all his Officer's, down to a Corporal, were kill'd; Captn. Polson shar'd almost as hard a Fate, for only one of his Escap'd: In short the dastardly behaviour of the English Soldier's expos'd all those who were inclin'd to do their duty to almost certain Death; and at length, in despight of every effort to the contrary, broke and run as Sheep before the Hounds, leav'g the Artillery, Ammunition, Provisions, and, every individual thing we had with us a prey to the Enemy; and when we endeavour'd to rally them in hopes of regaining our invaluable loss, it was with as much success as if we had attempted to have stop'd the wild Bears of the Mountains. The Genl. was wounded behind in the shoulder, and into the Breast, of w'ch he died three days after; his two Aids de Camp were both wounded, but are in a fair way of Recovery; Colo. Burton and Sir Jno. St. Clair are also wounded, and I hope will get over it; Sir Peter Halket, with many other brave Officers were kill'd in the Field. I luckily escap'd with't a wound tho' I had four Bullets through my Coat and two Horses shot under me. It is suppose that we left 300 or more dead in the Field; about that number we brought of wounded; and it is imagin'd (I believe with great justice too) that two thirds of both [?]* received their shott from our own cowardly English Soldier's who gather'd themselves into a body contrary to orders 10 or 12 deep, wou'd then level, Fire and shoot down the Men before them.

I tremble at the consequences that this defeat may have upon our back settlers, who I suppose will all leave their habitations unless there are proper measures taken for their security.

Colo. Dunbar, who commands at present, intends so soon as his Men are recruited at this place, to continue his March to Phila. into Winter Quarters: so that there will be no Men left here unless it is the poor remains of the Virginia Troops, who survive and will be too small to guard our Frontiers. As Captn. Orme is writg. to your honour I doubt not but he will

* Two words missing.

give you a circumstantial acct. of all things, which will make it needless for me to add more than that I am, etc.

To WARNER LEWIS

Washington's commission as Commander in Chief of the Virginia forces was dated and signed by Governor Dinwiddie on August 14, 1755, but for reasons of petty economy his pay did not begin until September 1st. His instructions began with an accusation against the French as invaders of British land on the Ohio and continued with the stipulation that the Virginia Regiment should comprise sixteen companies; that the Indians should be won over with goods and presents; that morality and virtue should be taught the troops and that they should be punished for drunkenness and swearing. It is interesting to examine Washington's views on command offered on the very day, unknown to him, his commission was being signed.

Mount Vernon, August 14, 1755

DEAR SIR: After returning the most sincere and grateful thanks for your kind condolence on my late indisposition; and for the too generous, and give me leave further to say, partial opinion you have entertain'd of my ability's; I must express my concern for not having it in my power to meet you, and other Friends, who have signified their desire of seeing me (in Williamsburg). Your Letter only came to hand at nine last Night, and you inform me of the Assembly breaking up the latter end of the Week, which allows a time too short to perform a journey of 160 miles distance particularly by a person in my weak and feeble condition altho' I am happily recover'd from the low ebb to w'ch I was reduced by a sickness of near 5 Weeks continuance. Had I got timely notice, I wou'd have attempted the ride by slow and easy journeys, if it had been only for the satisfaction of seeing my Friends, who I flatter myself from what you say, are kind enough to sympathise in my good, and evil Fortunes.

The Chief Reason (next to indisposition) that prev'd me from coming down to this Assembly was a determination not to offer myself, and that determination proceeded from the following Reason's. 1st. a belief that I cou'd not get a command upon such terms as I shou'd care to accept; as I must confess I never will quit my Family, injure my Fortune, and (above all) impair my health to run the risque of such Changes and Vicissitudes as I have done; but shall now expect, if I am employ'd again, to have something certain again, was I to have the command, I shou'd insist upon somethings which ignorance and inexperience made me overlook before, particularly that of having the Officers in some measure appointed *with* my advice, and with my concurrence; for I must say, I think a commanding Officer not hav'g this liberty appear's to me to be one of the strangest thing in Life, when it is well known how much the conduct and bravery of an Officer influences the Men; how much a Commanding Officer is answerable for the behaviour of the inferiour Officer's; and how much his good or ill success in time of action depends upon the conduct of each particular Officer; especially in this kind of Fighting, where being dispers'd, each and every of them at that immediate time, has greater liberty to misbehave than if he were regularly, and compactly drawn up under the Eyes of their superior Officer's. However on the other hand, how little credit is given to a Commander, who perhaps after a defeat, in relating the cause justly lays the blame on some individual whose cowardly behav'r betray'd the whole to ruin; how little does the World consider the Circumstances, and how apt are mankind to level their vindictive Censures against the unfortunate Chief, who perhaps merited least of the blame. Does it not appear then that the appointing of Officers is a thing of the utmost consequence; a thing that shou'd require the greatest circumspection; ought it to be left to blind chance? or what is still worse, to a forced partiality? Shou'd it not be left to a Man whose powers and what is still dearer, whose honour depends upon their good Examples.

There are necessary Officer's yet wanting, which no Provision have been made for. A small Military Chest is so absolutely necessary, that it is impossible to do without, nor no Man can conduct an affair of this kind who has it not. These things I shou'd expect, was I appointed.

But, besides all these, I had other Reasons wh'h with'd me f'm offering. I believe our Circumstances are now to that unhappy Dilemma that no Man can gain any Honour by conduct'g our Forces at this time, but rather loose in his reputation; for I am very confid't the progress must be slow for want of conveniences to transport our Provisions &c. over the Mountains and this chiefly occasion'd, by the late ill treatm't of the Waggoner's and Horse driver's, who have rec'd little for their Lab'r and noth'g for their lost Hors's and Wag'ns; w'ch will be an infallible mean's of prevent'g all from assist'g that are not oblig'd; so that I am truly sensible, whoever undertakes it will meet with such insurmountable obstacles that he will be soon look'd upon in the very light of an idle, indolent body, have his conduct censured and perhaps meet with opprobious abuse, when it is as much out of his power to avoid these delays as to com'd the rag'g Seas in a Storm. Seeing these things in the above light that I did, had no small influence upon me, as I was pretty much assur'd I shou'd loose what at present constitutes the chief part of my happiness, i. e. the esteem and notice the Country has been pleas'd to honour me with.

It is possible you may infer from what I have said that my intention's is to decline at all events, but my meaning is entirely different: I was determin'd not to offer, because to solicit the Command and at the same time to make my proposals I thought wou'd look a little incongruous, and to carry a face of too much self sufficiency, as if I imagin'd there were none other's equally (if not more) capable of conducting the affair than myself; But if the command shou'd be offer'd the case is then alter'd as I am at liberty to make such objection's as my Reason and my small experience have pointed out. I hope you'll make my Comp's to all inquiring F'ds. I am Dr. Warner Y'r etc.

GENERAL INSTRUCTIONS FOR THE RECRUITING OFFICERS OF THE VIRGINIA REGIMENT

Washington's practical sense, his passion for detail and his constant regard for the welfare of his troops are apparent in the many sets of instructions written by him. Typical of his concern for his recruits, their equipment, training and discipline is the following:

Williamsburg, September 3, 1755

First; That each Captain shall, by beat of Drum or otherwise, Raise Thirty men; Each Lieutenant Eighteen; and each Ensign, Twelve men.

Secondly: That each Captain shall appoint proper Persons to act as non-commissioned Officers, during their Recruiting Service: But those non-commissioned Officers, so appointed, are not to be confirmed, 'till approved of by me, or a Field Officer for that purpose.

Thirdly: That no Officer shall list any Men under Sixteen, or above Fifty years of age: Nor are they to list men under five feet four Inches high, unless they are well made, strong, and active; then, and in that case, they will be received.

Neither are they to list any men who have old Sores upon their legs, or who are subject to Fits; which will be inspected into by the Surgeons, upon their arrival at Quarters: and such as are found to come under these Articles, will be discharged; and the Officers have no allowance made.

Fourthly: That, when each Recruiting Officer has listed his Complement of Men, he is immediately to repair to the Place of Rendezvouz; which I hope, and expect, will be by the first day of October next: but if in case the whole should not be complete by that time; it is then my Orders, that each Captain shall forthwith send one of his Subalterns with all the Recruits, to the quarters assigned him, and remain with the other Subaltern to complete his Company, with all imaginable Diligence.

There will be a Field Officer to receive, review, and examine the Recruits that are brought in; who will have power to reject and discharge, such as come under the above Articles.

Fifthly: That, for each Recruit that is passed by such Field Officer, the Officer who Listed him, shall receive two Pistoles, and an allowance of eight-pence per Day for Subsistance, from the day of his attestation, to the day of his being received into the Regiment.

Sixthly: That all Recruits, so soon as they are Listed, are to take the Oaths provided for that purpose; which is to be attested by the Magistrate who administered them.

Their Stature, Complexion, and so forth, is to be taken also, and entered by the Recruiting Officer in a Book kept for that purpose.

Seventhly: That no Officer shall bring in any charge against his Men for Necessaries; Each man being to receive full Clothing, on his arrival at the place of Rendezvous.

Lastly: That when you are on the Recruiting Service, and on your March; you are to observe the same good Order and Discipline, as in Camp or in Quarters; and you are to conform yourself, in every respect, to the Rules and Articles of War. Given under my hand etc. . . .

To ENSIGN DENNIS McCARTHY

Washington's warning to an overzealous recruiting officer provides further evidence of his attention to minutiae, his military ethics and his willingness to tolerate and forgive an initial error.

November 22, 1755

I am very sorry you have given me occasion to complain of your conduct in Recruiting; and to tell you, that the methods and unjustifiable means you have practised, are very unacceptable, and have been of infinitely prejudice to the Service: of this I am informed by many Gentlemen, as well as by all the

Officers who were ordered to recruit in these parts: and am further assured, that it is next to an impossibility to get a man where you have been; such terror have you occasioned by forcibly taking, confining and torturing those, who would not voluntarily enlist. These proceedings not only cast a slur upon your own Character, but reflect dishonour upon mine; as giving room to conjecture, that they have my concurrence for their source. I must therefore acquaint you, that such Behaviour in an Officer would shake his Commission! Let it then be a warning to you, who I still hope, erred more through inadvertence than design; for which reason, I shall forget the past, in sanguine hopes of what is to come. I am &c.

To GOVERNOR DINWIDDIE

Here Washington provides Governor Dinwiddie with a faithful résumé of the military situation and covers such a diversity of subjects as the need for salt, kettles and clothing, more recruits, better commissary services, a mutiny bill, the apprehension of deserters, etc., etc.

Alexandria, December 5, 1755

HONBLE. SIR: I have sent the bearer, Captain John Mercer (who has accompts. to settle with the Committee), to the treasurer for the balance of that ten thousand pounds; and to acquaint your Honour, that, meeting with letters at Fredericksburg, as I returned from Williamsburg, informing me that all was peaceable above, and that nothing was so immediately wanting as salt. I got what I could at that place, and hastened on here to engage more; to receive the recruits expected in; and to wait the arrival of the vessel with arms, &c., from James River, in order to forward them up with the greater despatch. The vessel is not yet arrived.

I have impatiently expected to hear the result of your Honour's letter to General Shirley; and wish that the delays may not prove ominous. In that case, I shall not know how to act;

for I can never submit to the command of Captain Dagworthy, since you have honoured me with the command of the Virginia regiment, &c.

The country has sustained inconceivable losses by delaying the commissaries at Williamsburg: Many of the Carolina beeves are dead, through absolute poverty; and the chief part of them too poor to slaughter. We are at a loss how to act, for want of the mutiny bill; and should be obliged to your Honour, if you will have fifty or a hundred printed, and sent by the bearer. There is a clause in that bill, which if you are not kind enough to obviate it, will prevent entirely the good intention of it: i. e., delaying the execution of sentences, until your Honour shall be made acquainted with the proceedings of the court. This, at times when there is the greatest occasion for examples, will be morally impossible (I mean, while we are on our march; perhaps near the Ohio,) when none but strong parties can pass with safety: at all times it must be attended with great expense, trouble and inconveniency. This I represented to Colonel Corbin, and some other gentlemen of the Council, when I was down; who said that that objection to the Bill would be removed, by your Honour's giving blank warrants, to be filled up as occasion should require. This would effectually remedy all those evils, and put things in their proper channel.

We suffer greatly for want of kettles: those sent from below being tin, are of short duration. We shall also, in a little time, suffer as much for the want of clothing; none can be got in these parts; those which Major Carlyle and Dalton contracted to furnish, we are disappointed off. Shoes and stockings we have, and get more if wanted, but nothing else. I should be glad your Honor would direct what is to be done in these cases; and that you would be kind enough to desire the treasurer to send some part of the money in gold and silver: were this done, we might often get necessaries for the regiment in Maryland, or Pennsylvania, when they cannot be had here. But with our money it is impossible; our paper not passing there.

The recruiting service goes on extremely slow. Yesterday being a day appointed for rendezvousing at this place, there came in ten officers with twenty men only. If I had any other than paper money, and you approved of it; I would send to

Pennsylvania and the borders of Carolina: I am confident, men might be had there. Your Honor never having given any particular directions about the provisions; I should be glad to know, whether you would have more laid in than what will serve for twelve hundred men; that I may give orders accordingly.

As I cannot now conceive, that any great danger can be apprehended at Fort Cumberland this winter; I am sensible, that my constant attendance there, cannot be so serviceable as riding from place to place, making the proper dispositions, and seeing that all our necessaries are forwarded up with despatch. I therefore think it advisable to inform your Honour of it, hoping that it will correspond with your own opinion.

I forgot to mention when I was down, that Mr. Livingston, the Fort Major, was appointed adjutant to our regiment: I knew of none else whose long servitude in a military way, had qualified better for the office; he was appointed the 17th of September.

Captain Mercer's pay as aid-de-camp seems yet doubtful; I should be glad if your Honour would fix it; so is Captain Stewart's. If Captain Stewart's is encreased, I suppose all the officers belonging to the light-horse will expect to have theirs augmented also. Colonel Stephens, in a late letter, discovered an inclination to go to the Creek and Cherokee Indians this winter. I told him where to apply, if he had any such thoughts. I believe, on so useful a business, he might be spared until the spring. If your Honor think proper to order the act of Assembly for apprehending deserters, and against harbouring them, to be published every Sunday in each parish church, until the people were made acquainted with the law, it would have a very good effect. The commonalty in general err more through ignorance than design. Few of them are acquainted that such a law exists: and there is no other certain way of bringing it to their knowledge. There are a great many of the men that did once belong to our companies, deserted from the regiments into which they were draughted, that would now gladly return, if they could be sure of indemnity. If your Honor would be kind enough to intimate this to General Shirley, or the colonels of those regiments, it would be of service to us: without leave, we dare not receive them. I am, &c.

To GOVERNOR DINWIDDIE

Indian warfare, with its dependence on cunning and stealth, requires new strategy. Here Washington recommends a chain of forts for defense, the concentration of population in townships and ever-stronger armed forces.

Winchester, April 7, 1756

HONBLE. SIR; I arrived here yesterday, and think it advisable to despatch an express (notwithstanding I hear two or three are already sent down) to inform you of the unhappy situation of affairs on this quarter. The enemy have returned in greater numbers, committed several murders not far from Winchester, and even are so daring as to attack our forts in open day, as your Honor may see by the enclosed letters and papers. Many of the inhabitants are in a miserable situation by their losses, and so apprehensive of danger, that, I believe, unless a stop is put to the depredations of the Indians, the Blue Ridge will soon become our frontier.

I find it impossible to continue on to Fort Cumberland, until a body of men can be raised, in order to do which I have advised with Lord Fairfax, and other officers of the militia, who have ordered each captain to call a private muster, and to read the exhortation enclosed (for orders are no longer regarded in this county), in hopes that this expedient may meet with the wished-for success. If it should, I shall, with such men as are ordered from Fort Cumberland to join these, scour the woods and suspected places, in all the mountains, valleys, &c. on this part of our frontiers; and doubt not but I shall fall in with the Indians and their *more* cruel associates! I hope the present emergency of affairs, assisted by such good news as the Assembly may by this time have received from England, and the

Commissioners, will determine them to take vigorous measures for their own and country's safety, and no longer depend on an uncertain way of raising men for their own protection. However absurd it may appear, it is nevertheless certain, that five hundred Indians have it more in their power to annoy the inhabitants, than ten times their number of regulars. For besides the advantageous way they have of fighting in the woods, their cunning and craft are not to be equalled, neither their activity and indefatigable sufferings. They prowl about like wolves, and, like them, do their mischief by stealth. They depend upon their dexterity in hunting and upon the cattle of the inhabitants for provisions. For which reason, I own, I do not think it unworthy the notice of the legislature to compel the inhabitants (if a general war is likely to ensue, and things to continue in this unhappy situation for any time), to live in townships, working at each other's farms by turns, and to drive their cattle into the thick settled parts of the country. Were this done, they could not be cut off by small parties, and large ones could not subsist without provisions.

It seemed to be the sentiment of the House of Burgesses when I was down, that a chain of forts should be erected upon our frontiers, for the defence of the people. This expedient, in my opinion, without an inconceivable number of men, will never answer their expectations.

I doubt not but your Honor has had a particular account of Major Lewis's unsuccessful attempt to get to the Shawanese Town. It was an expedition, from the length of the march, I own, I always had little expectation of, and often expressed my uneasy apprehensions on that head. But since they are returned, with the Indians that accompanied them, I think it would be a very happy step to prevail upon the latter to proceed as far as Fort Cumberland. It is in their power to be of infinite use to us; and without Indians, we shall never be able to cope with those cruel foes to our country.

I would therefore beg leave to recommend in a very earnest manner, that your Honor would send an express to them immediately for this desirable end. I should have done it myself, but was uncertain whether it might prove agreeable or not. I also hope your Honour will order Major Lewis to secure his guides, as I understand he attributes all his misfortunes to their misconduct. Such offences as those should meet with adequate punishment, else we may ever be misled by designing villains. I am your Honor's, &c.

Since writing the above, Mr. Pearis, who commanded a party as per enclosed list, is returned, who relates, that, upon the North River, he fell in with a small body of Indians which he engaged, and, after a dispute of half an hour, put them to flight. Monsieur Douville, commander of the party, was killed and scalped, and his instructions found about him, which I enclose. We had one man killed, and two wounded. Mr. Pearis sends the scalp by Jenkins; and I hope, although it is not an Indian's, they will meet with an adequate reward at least, as the monsieur's is of much more consequence. The whole party jointly claim the reward, no person pretending solely to assume the merit.

Your Honor may in some measure penetrate into the daring designs of the French by their instructions, where orders are given to burn, if possible, our magazine at Conococheague, a place that is in the midst of a thickly settled country.

I have ordered the party there to be made as strong as time and our present circumstances will afford, for fear they should attempt to execute the orders of Dumas. I have also ordered up an officer and twenty recruits to assist Joseph Edwards, and the people on those waters. The people of this town are under dreadful apprehensions of an attack, and all the roads between this and Fort Cumberland are much infested. As I apprehend you will be obliged to draft men, I hope care will be taken that none are chosen but active, resolute men—men, who are practised to arms, and are marksmen.

I also hope that a good many more will be taken than what are requisite to complete our numbers to what the Assembly design to establish; as many of those we have got are really in a manner unfit for duty; and were received more through necessity than choice; and will very badly bear a re-examination. Another thing I would beg leave to recommend; and that is, that such men as are drafted, should be only taken for a time, by which means we shall get better men, and which will in all probability stay with us.

To GOVERNOR DINWIDDIE

Moved by Washington's frantic appeal, Governor Dinwiddie ordered out half of the militia, but overlooked one detail: he made no provision for feeding them. Reinforcements, under these circumstances, were of little help, and again Washington had to fall back on defensive tactics. Meanwhile settlers were leaving their farms and turning back eastward, thus once more dashing Washington's hopes for the development of the western country.

Winchester, April 22, 1756

HONBLE. SIR: This encloses several letters, and the minutes of a council of war, which was held upon the receipt of them. Your Honor may see to what unhappy straits the distressed inhabitants as well as I, am reduced. I am too little acquainted, Sir, with pathetic language, to attempt a description of the people's distresses, though I have a generous soul, sensible of wrongs, and swelling for redress. But what can I do? If bleeding, dying! would glut their insatiate revenge, I would be a willing offering to savage fury, and die by inches to save a people! I see their situation, know their danger, and participate their sufferings, without having it in my power to give them further relief, than uncertain promises. In short, I see inevitable destruction in so clear a light, that, unless vigorous measures are taken by the Assembly, and speedy assistance sent from below, the poor inhabitants that are now in forts, must unavoidably fall, while the remainder of the country are flying before the barbarous foe. In fine, the melancholy situation of the people, the little prospect of assistance, the gross and scandalous abuses cast upon the officers in general, which is reflecting upon me in particular, for suffering misconducts of such extraordinary kinds, and the distant prospects, if any, that I can see, of gaining honor and reputation in the service, are motives which cause me to lament the hour, that gave me a commission, and would induce me, at any other time than this of imminent danger, to resign without one hesitating moment, a command, which I never expect to reap either honor or benefit from; but, on the contrary, have almost an absolute certainty of incurring displeasure below, while the murder of poor innocent babes and helpless families may be laid to my account here!

The supplicating tears of the women, and moving petitions from the men, melt me into such deadly sorrow, that I solemnly declare, if I know my own mind, I could offer myself a willing sacrifice to the butchering enemy, provided that would contribute to the people's ease.

Lord Fairfax has ordered men from the adjacent counties, but when they will come, or in what numbers, I cannot pretend to determine. If I may judge from the success we have met with here, I have but little hopes, as three days' incessant endeavours have produced but twenty men.

I have too often urged my opinion for vigorous measures, therefore I shall only add, that, besides the accounts you will receive in the letters, we are told from all parts, that the woods appear to be alive with Indians, who feast upon the fat of the land. As we have not more than a barrel or two of powder at this place, the rest being at Fort Cumberland, I could wish your Honor would send up some. I have wrote to Alexandria and Fredericksburg, desiring that two barrels may be sent from each place, but whether there is any at either, I know not. I have sent orders to Captain Harrison to be diligent on the waters where he is posted, and to use his utmost endeavours to protect the people; and, if possible, to surprise the enemy at their sleeping-places. Ashby's letter is a very extraordinary one. The design of the Indians was only, in my opinion, to intimidate him into a surrender. For which reason I have wrote him word, that if they do attack him, he must defend that place to the last extremity, and when he is bereft of hope, then to lay a train to blow up the fort, and retire by night to Cumberland. A small fort, which we have at the mouth of Patterson's Creek, containing an officer and thirty men guarding stores, was attacked smartly by the French and Indians; and were as warmly received, upon which they retired. Our men at present are dispersed into such small bodies, guarding the people and public stores, that we are not able to make, or even form a body. I am your Honor's, &c.

ADVERTISEMENT

To help allay the settlers' fears, Washington issued the following public notice, urging the farmers to return to their plantations and promising protection by the militia. Actually the settlers feared the soldiers quite as much as they did the Indians, and the advertisement persuaded few of them to return. When the Indians finally gave up their forays and the militia was discharged after the harvest season, the settlers turned westward again.

Winchester, May, 1756

Whereas I have great reason to believe, the Dangers apprehended from the French and Indian incursions are now pretty much over; none of them being seen or heard of for sometime past; and having certain advice of several parties of them returning over the Alleghany mountains. I take this method of informing and persuading those unfortunate people who were obliged to abandon their Plantation, of their security and necessity to return again. Numbers of the Militia being already, and more will be very soon, so posted and dispersed around the Frontiers. Building Forts, scouting, scouring and pattrolling the woods; that the least appearance of the Enemy will soon be discovered and every necessary measure taken to repel them, and defend the Inhabitants from any danger or trouble. It is to be hoped, that people will pay regard to this notice; if their own interest or the public good can be motives to prevail with them to return and take care of their cattle and Crops. As they will be so well guarded and defended, that with good assistance, they may for the future live in the greatest security and peace.

To THE EARL OF LOUDOUN

John, Earl of Loudoun, was appointed Commander in Chief of the British Forces in North America and Governor of the Colony of Virginia. His arrival in America encouraged Washington in the belief that he would receive some measure of aid for his plan for an offensive campaign which would have as its object the capture of Fort Duquesne. Robert Dinwiddie, still in favor of defensive strategy, had the ear of the new Governor and was more influential than a mere colonel in the field. Washington tried, but failed, to win by a personal appearance more support for his regiment and advancement for himself. All he could accomplish was to gain consent to a withdrawal from Fort Cumberland.

January, 1757

MY LORD: The posture of affairs in this quarter is really melancholy, and the prospect was rendered more gloomy while there appeared no hopes of amendment; but, from the presence of your Lordship at this time in the Dominion, we conceive hopes of seeing these threatening clouds dispelled.

The sums of money, my Lord, which have been granted by this colony to carry on war, have been very considerable; and to reflect to what little purpose is matter of great concern, and will seem surprising to those, who are not acquainted with the causes, and the confusion with which all our affairs have hitherto been conducted, owing to our having no fixed object, or pursuing any regular system, or plan of operation.

As I have studied with attention and care the nature of the service in which we are engaged, have been engaged therein from the beginning of the present broils, and have been an eyewitness to all the movements and various proceedings, I beg leave to offer a concise and candid account of our circumstances to your Lordship; from which many errors may be discovered, that merit redress in a very high degree.

It was not until it was too late, we discovered that the French were on the Ohio; or rather, that we could be persuaded they came there with a design to invade his Majesty's dominions. Nay, after I was sent out in December, 1753, and brought undoubted testimony even from themselves of their avowed design, it was yet thought a fiction, and a scheme to promote the interest of a private company, even by some who had a share in the government. These unfavorable surmises caused great delay in raising the first men and money, and gave the active enemy time to take possession of the Fork of Ohio (which they now call Duquesne), before we were in sufficient strength to advance thither, which has been the chief source of all our past and present misfortunes. For by this means (the French getting between us and our Indian allies) they fixed those in their interests, who were wavering, and obliged the others to neutrality, 'till the unhappy defeat of his (late) Excellency General Braddock.

The troops under Colonel Dunbar going into quarters in July, and the inactivity of the neighbouring colonies, and the incapacity of this, conspired to give the French great room to exult, and the Indians little reason to expect a vigorous offensive war on our side, and induced the other, which promised the greatest show of protection. This is an undeniable fact, and that all of the Indians did not forsake the English interest, 'till three months after the battle of Monongahela, but actually waited to see what measures would be concerted to regain our losses, and afford them the protection we had but too liberally promised them.

Virginia, it is true, was not inactive all this time: On the contrary, voted a handsome supply for raising men to carry on the war, or, more properly, to defend herself; matters being reduced to this extremity for want of assistance. But even in this she signally failed, arising, I apprehend, from the following causes:

The men first levied to repel the enemy marched for Ohio the beginning of April, 1754, without tents, without clothes, in short, without any conveniences to shelter them, (in that remarkably cold and wet season,) from the inclemency of the weather, and to make the service tolerably agreeable. In this state did they, notwithstanding, continue, till the battle of the Meadows, in July following, never receiving in all that space any subsistence; and were very often under the greatest straits and difficulties for want of provisions.

These things were productive of great murmurings and discontent, and rendered the service so distasteful to the men, that, not being paid immediately upon coming in, they thought themselves bubbled, and that no reward for their services was ever intended. This caused great desertion; and the deserters, spreading over the country, recounting their sufferings and want of pay (which rags and poverty sufficiently testified) fixed in the mind of the populace such horrid impressions of the hardships they had encountered, that no arguments could remove these prejudices, or facilitate the recruiting service.

This put the Assembly upon enacting a law to impress vagrants, which added to our difficulties, for, compelling these abandoned miscreants into the service, they embraced every opportunity to effect their escape, gave a loose to their vicious principles, and invented the most unheard-of stories to palliate desertion and gain compassion; in which they not only succeeded, but obtained protection also. So that it was next to impossible, after this, to apprehend deserters, while the civil officers rather connived at their escape, than aided in securing them.

Thus were affairs situated, when we were ordered, in September, 1755, to recruit our force to twelve hundred men. 'T is easy therefore to conceive, under these circumstances, why we did not fulfil the order, especially when the officers were not sufficiently allowed for this arduous task. We continued, however, using our endeavours until March following, without much success.

The Assembly, meeting about that time, came to a resolution of augmenting our numbers to fifteen hundred men, by drafting the militia, (who were to continue in the service until December *only*,) and by a clause in the act exempting all those, who should pay ten pounds, our numbers were very little increased, one part of the people paying that sum, and many of the poorer sort absconding. This was not the only pernicious clause in the act for the funds arising from these forfeitures were thrown into the treasury; whereas, had they been deposited in proper hands for recruiting, the money might have turned to good account. But a greater grievance than either of these was restraining the forces from marching out of the colony, or acting offensively, and ordering them to build forts, and garrison them, along our frontiers (of more than three hundred miles in extent.) How equal they or any like number are to the task, and how repugnant a defensive plan is to the true interest and welfare of the colony, I submit to any judge to determine who will consider the following particulars.

First, that erecting forts at greater distances than fifteen or eighteen miles, or a day's march asunder, and garrisoning them with less than eighty or a hundred men, is not answering the intention; because, if they are at a greater distance from each other, it is inconvenient for the soldiers to scout between, and it gives the enemy full scope to make their incursions without being discovered, until they have fallen on the inhabitants and committed a ravage. And, after they are discovered, the time required in assembling troops from forts more distant, prevents a pursuit being made in time, and allows the enemy to escape without danger into a country so mountainous, and full of swamps hollow ways covered with woods. Then, to garrison them with less than eighty or a hundred men, the number is too small to afford detachments, but what are very liable to be cut off by the enemy, whose numbers in this close country can scarcely be known till they are proved. Indian parties are generaly intermixed with some Frenchmen, and are so dexterous at skulking, that their spies, lying about these small forts for some days and taking a prisoner, make certain discoveries of the strength of the garrison; and then, upon observing a scouting party coming out, will first cut it off, and afterwards attempt the fort. Instances of this have lately happened.

Secondly, our frontiers are of such extent, that if the enemy were to make a formidable attack on one side, before the troops on the other could get to their assistance, they might overrun the country; and it is not improbable, if they had a design upon one part, they would make a feint upon the other.

Thirdly, what it must cost the country to build these forts, and to remove stores and provisions into them; and

Fourthly, and lastly where and when this expense will end? For we may be assured, if we do not endeavour to remove the cause, we shall be as liable to the same incursions seven years hence as now; indeed more so. Because, if the French are allowed to possess those lands in peace, they will have the entire command of the Indians, and grow stronger in their alliance; while we, by our defensive schemes and pusillanimous behaviour, will exhaust our treasury, reduce our strength, and become the contempt of these savage nations, who are every day enriching themselves with the plunder and spoils of our people.

It will evidently appear from the whole tenor of my conduct, but more especially from reiterated representations, how strongly I have urged the Governor and Assembly to pursue different measures, and to convince them, by all the reasons I was capable of offering, of the impossibility of covering so extensive a frontier from Indian incursions, without more force than Virginia *can* maintain. I have endeavoured to demonstrate, that it would require fewer men to remove the cause, than to prevent the effects, while the cause subsists. This, notwithstanding, as I before observed, was the measure adopted, and the plan under which we have acted for eight months past, with the disagreeable reflection of doing no essential service to our country, gaining honor to ourselves, or reputation to our regiment. However, under these disadvantageous restraints I must beg leave to say, that the regiment has not been inactive; on the contrary, it has performed a vast deal of work, and has been very alert in defending the people, which will appear by observing, that, notwithstanding we are more contiguous to the French and their Indian allies, and more exposed to their frequent incursions, than any of the neighbouring colonies, we have not lost half the inhabitants, which others have done, but considerably more soldiers in their defence. For in the course of this campaign, since March, I mean, (as we have had but one constant campaign, and continued scene of action, since we first entered the service), our troops have been engaged in upwards of twenty skirmishes, and we have had near an hundred men killed and wounded, from a small regiment dispersed over the country, and acting upon the defensive, as ours is by order. This, I conceive, will not appear inconsiderable to those, who are in the least degree acquainted with the nature of this service, and the posture of our affairs; however it may to chimney-corner politicians, who are thirsting for news, and expecting by every express to hear in what manner Fort Duquesne was taken, and the garrison led away captive by our small numbers; altho' we are restrained from making the attempt, were our hopes of success ever so rational!

The next things, I shall beg leave to mention, is our military laws and regulations.

The first men raised, if I rightly remember, were under no law; if any, the military law, which was next of kin to it. But under this we remained a short time, and, instilling notions into the soldiers, who knew no better, that they were governed by the articles of war, we felt little inconveniences; and the next campaign we were joined by the regulars, and made subject to their laws. After the regulars left us, the Assembly, as I before mentioned, passed an act in September following to raise twelve hundred men, and, in order (I suppose) to improve upon the act of Parliament, prepared a military code of their own, but such a one as no military discipline could be preserved by while it existed. This being represented by the most pressing and repeated remonstrances, induced the Assembly to pass a bill in October following, for one year only, making mutiny and desertion death, but took no cognizance of many other crimes, equally punishable by act of Parliament. So that no officer, or soldier, accused of cowardice, holding correspondence with the enemy, quitting a post, or sleeping upon it, and many other crimes of a capital dye, or pernicious tendency, could be legally tried. Neither was there any provision made for quartering or billeting of soldiers, impressing wagons, &c., &c.

But that which contributed the most towards rendering this law inconvenient and absurd, and at the same time to demonstrate that the Assembly fully intended to prevent any enterprise of their troops out of the colony, was a clause forbidding any courts-martial to sit out of it; by which means all proceedings held at Fort Cumberland (in Maryland) were illegal, and we were obliged to remove to Virginia for trial of offenders, or act contrary to law, and lie open to prosecution. How then were we to behave upon a march perhaps fifty, eighty, or an hundred miles distant? These circumstances concurring to render the law ineffectual, induced me again to recommend an amendment, which I did with all the force and energy of argument I was master of. But no regard has hitherto been paid to my remonstrances. To what cause it is owing, I know not, unless to short sittings and hurry of business; for I can conceive of no reason upon earth, why the Assembly should be against instituting rules for the regulation of their forces, which long experience in established armies has fully evinced the necessity of. But, to cut short the account, we are under no government at all, to speak properly. Indeed, there is a jumble of laws that have little meaning or design in them, but to conspire to make the command intricate, precarious in supporting authority, and not to offend the civil powers, who, tenacious of liberty, and prone to censure and condemn all proceedings which are not strictly lawful, not considering what cases may arise to render them necessary.

Another grievance, which this act subjects us to, is the method prescribed to pay for deserters. Many of our deserters are apprehended in Maryland and Pennsylvania, and, for the sake of reward, are brought to the regiment; instead thereof they receive certificate only, that they are entitled to two hundred weight of tobacco. This certificate is to be given into a Court of Claims, they refer it to the Assembly; and there it may lie perhaps two or three years before it is paid. This causes great dissatisfaction, and the ill-disposed to aid, rather than prevent, the escape of soldiers.

No regular provision is established for the maimed and wounded, which is a discouraging reflection, and grievously complained of. The soldiers justly observe, that the result of bravery is often a broken leg, arm, or incurable wound; and when they are disabled, and no longer fit for service, they are discharged, and reduced to the necessity of begging from door to door, or perish thro' indigence. It is true, no instance of this kind hath yet appeared; on the contrary, the Assembly have dealt generously by those unfortunate soldiers, who have met with this fate. But then, this provision is not established, nor in any wise compulsory, and a man may suffer in the interval of their sitting.

After giving this short and genuine account of our military laws, and then observing that these laws are expired, I conceive there need but few arguments to prove the difficulty of keeping soldiers under proper discipline, who know they are not (legally) punishable for the most atrocious crimes. When this happens to be the case, as it is ours at present, how is it to be wondered at, if mutiny, desertion, and all other irregularities should creep into the camp, or garrison? more especially if we consider that hard duty, want of clothes and almost every necessary that renders a soldier's life comfortable and easy, are strong incentives, and, to go further, when these in *themselves* intolerable grievances are set to view in the most glaring point of light by a person, who, lost to all sense of honor and virtue, (and building, I am sorry to say, upon a proclamation inviting the deserters from the Virginia Regiment to enlist into the Royal American Regiment,) hath made use of every artifice to represent the fatigues and hardships of this service, and the ease and conveniences of the other, to seduce them from their duty.

Want of clothing may be esteemed another principal grievance, which our soldiers have labored under. In the first twelve months of their service they received no clothing; but in March, 1754, they were presented each with a suit made of thin, sleazy cloth without lining, and flannel waistcoats of an inferior sort. After that no others were sent for (and two pence stoppages drawn from every man's pay, recruits not excepted,) until repeated complaints and remonstrances from me, enforced in June last by a representation of many gentlemen of the Assembly, (who had formed an association, and saw the disagreeable situation of the soldiers,) induced the Committee, to whom those addresses were presented, to send for clothing, &c. These were to have been here by the middle of October, but no advice is received of them yet, which gives the soldiers some pretence to suspect they are deceived. And it is owing to this irregular pay, and the causes aforementioned, that their late disobedience ought to be ascribed. For I can truly say, and confidently assert, that no soldiers ever were under better command than these were before.

Perhaps it may be asked, by gentlemen not thoroughly acquainted with the nature of our service, why the officers do not see that their men's pay is more properly applied? In answer I must beg leave to observe, that, after the soldiers have appropriated a part for purchasing reasonable and fit necessaries, the remainder is barely sufficient to keep them in shoes, owing, in the first place, to the very great consumption the service occasions, and, in the next, to the exorbitant price, which this article bears. I have known a soldier go upon command with a new pair of shoes, which shoes perhaps have stood from seven shillings and sixpence to ten shillings, and return back without any; so much do they wear in wading creeks, fording rivers, clambering mountains covered with rocks, &c.

As great a grievance as any I have mentioned is yet unnoticed, *i. e.,* the militia under their present regulation. A representation of this matter comes better and more properly from others; yet my zeal for the service and my interest in the welfare of my country, have influenced me to touch slightly on some things relative to their conduct, as I cannot enter deeply into the causes that produce them.

When they come into service it is with the utmost difficulty they are prevailed upon to take measures for self-defence, much less for the protection of the inhabitants; But indolent and careless, and always unguarded, are liable to be surprized. By this means Vass's fort was taken (and the garrison destroyed, and Dickinson's was on the point of sharing the same fate).

To set forth all the reasons that can contribute to render the militia of little use, and to point out all the causes which combine to make our service infinitely hard and disagreeable, would swell these observations into a volume, and require time, and a more able pen than mine. But there are yet some things that require to be spoken to the ill-judged economy that is shown in raising of men. We are either insensible of danger, till it breaks upon our heads, or else, thro' mistaken notions of economy, evade the expence, till the blow is struck, and then run into an extreme of raising militia. These, after an age, as it were, is spent in assembling them, come up, make a noise for a time, oppress the inhabitants, and then return, leaving the frontiers unguarded as before. Notwithstanding former experience convinces us, if reason did not, that the French and Indians are watching their opportunity, when we are lulled into fatal security and are unprepared to resist an attack, to muster their force to invade the country, and by ravaging one part terrify another, and then retreat when our militia assemble, repeating the stroke as soon as they are dispersed, sending down parties in the intermedium to discover our motions, procure intelligence, and sometimes to divert our troops. Such an invasion we may expect in March, if measures to prevent it are neglected, as they hitherto have been.

The want of tools occasions insurmountable difficulties in carrying on our works, either offensive or defensive. Cartridge-paper is an article not to be met with in Virginia. And now, before I sum up the whole, I must beg leave to add, my unwearied endeavours are inadequately rewarded. The orders I receive are full of ambiguity. I am left, like a wanderer in a wilderness, to proceed at hazard. I am answerable for consequences, and blamed, without the privilege of defence. This, my Lord, I beg leave to declare to your Lordship, is at present my situation. Therefore, it is not to be wondered at, if, under such peculiar circumstances, I should be sicken'd in a service, which promises so little of a soldier's reward. I have long been satisfied of the impossibility of continuing in this service, without loss of honor. Indeed, I was fully convinced of it before I accepted the command the second time, (seeing the cloudy prospect that stood before me;) and did for this reason reject the offer, (until I was ashamed any longer to refuse,) not caring to expose my character to public censure. But the solicitations of the country overcame my objections, and induced me to accept it.

Another reason of late has continued me in it until now, and that is, the dawn of hope that arose, when I heard your Lordship was destined by his Majesty for the important command of his armies in America, and appointed to the government of his dominion of Virginia. Hence it was, that I drew my hopes, and fondly pronounced your Lordship our patron. Altho' I had not the honor to be known to your Lordship, your Lordship's name was familiar to my ear, on account of the important services performed to his Majesty in other parts of the world. Do not think, my Lord, that I am going to flatter; notwithstanding I have exalted sentiments of your Lordship's character and respect your rank, it is not my intention to adulate. My nature is open and honest and free from guile!

We have, my Lord, ever since our defeat at the Meadows, and, behaviour under his Excellency General Braddock, been tantalized, nay, bid to expect most sanguinely a better establishment, and have waited in tedious expectation of seeing this accomplished. The Assembly, it is true, have, I believe, done every thing in their power to bring this about; first, by soliciting his Honor, the Lieutenant-Governor, to address his Majesty; and next, by addressing his Majesty themselves in favor of their regiment. What success these addresses have met with, I am yet a stranger to.

With regard to myself, I cannot forbear adding, that, had his Excellency General Braddock survived his unfortunate defeat, I should have met with preferment agreeable to my wishes. I had his promise to that purpose, and I believe that gentleman was too sincere and generous to make unmeaning offers, where no favors were asked. General Shirley was not unkind in his promises, but he has gone to England. I do not know, my Lord, in what light this short and disinterested relation may be received by your Lordship; but with the utmost candor and submission it is offered. It contains no misrepresentations, nor aggravated relation of facts, nor unjust reflections.

Virginia is a country young in war, and, till the breaking out of these disturbances, has remained in the most profound and tranquil peace, ne'er studying war nor warfare. It is not, therefore, to be imagined, that she can fall into proper measures at once. All that can be expected at her hands she cheerfully offers, the sinews of war, and these only want your Lordship's ability and experience to be properly applied and directed.

It is for this reason I have presumed to lay this information before your Lordship, that, if there be any thing in it which appears worthy of redress, and your Lordship will condescend to point out the way it may be obtained.

And now, my Lord, how to apologize to your Lordship, for assuming a freedom, which must (at any rate) give you trouble, I know not, unless an affectionate zeal to serve my country, steady attachment to her interests, the *honor* of arms, and crying grievances she is struggling under, will plead an excuse, till I am so happy as to have an opportunity of testifying how much I admire your Lordship's character, and with what profound respect I have the honor to be, &c.

To THE RIGHT HON'BLE JOHN, EARL OF LOUDOUN: GENERAL AND COMMANDER IN CHIEF OF ALL HIS MAJESTYS FORCES IN NORTH AMERICA; AND GOVERNOR AND COMMANDER IN CHIEF OF HIS MAJESTYS MOST ANTIENT COLONY AND DOMINION OF VIRGINIA

February, 1757

WE, the Officers of the Virginia Regiment, beg leave to congratulate your Lordship on your safe arrival in America; and to express the deep sense We have of His Majestys great WISDOM and paternal care for His Colonies, in sending your Lordship to their protection at this critical Juncture. WE likewise beg leave to declare our singular satisfaction and sanguine hopes, on your Lordships immediate appointment over our Colony; as it in a more especial manner Entitles Us to your Lordships patronage.

FULL of hopes that a perfect Union of the Colonies will be brought about by your Lordships Wisdom and Authority; and big with expectations of seeing the extravagant insolence of an insulting, subtile and inhumane Enemy Restrained; and of having it in Our power to take our desired Revenge.

WE humbly represent to Your Lordship, that WE were the first Troops in Action on the Continent, on occasion of the present Broils, and that by several Engagements and continual Skirmishes with the Enemy, We have to our cost acquired a knowledge of them, and of their crafty and cruel practises: Which WE are ready to testify with the greatest chearfulness and Resolution, whenever We are so happy as to be honored with the Execution of your Lordships Commands.

To COLONEL JOHN STANWYX

Still under a divided command and committed to defensive strategy, the troops under Washington fretted through the spring and summer. Plagued by desertions, inadequate support in men and supplies, Washington wrote to Colonel John Stanwyx, commander of the middle and southern departments: "To think of defending a frontier as ours is of more than three hundred and fifty miles' extent, with only seven hundred men, is vain and idle, especially when that frontier lies more contiguous to the enemy than any other."

Fort Loudoun, October 8, 1757

DEAR SIR: I am favored with an opportunity by Mr. Livingston, to acknowledge the receipt of your agreeable favor of the 19th ultimo; and to inform you of a very extraordinary affair, which has happened at this place, namely, the desertion of our quartermaster. This infamous fellow, as he has proved himself, after having disposed, in a clandestine manner, of many of our regimental stores, being called upon to settle his accounts (not that I, or any officer in the regiment, had the least suspicion of the scene of roguery he was carrying on), pretended, that he could not come to an exact settlement without going to Alexandria, where some of the stores yet lay. Several of our soldiers deserting at the same time, (being the time when Lt. Campbell called upon you) he was sent in pursuit of them, which (for we had no doubt of his honest intentions) afforded him the desired opportunity of making his escape. He was ordered too to take Alexandria in his return. His villainy was not laid open, before his departure, and was at last only accidentally discovered. This person John Hamilton had been several years a sergeant in one of his Majesty's regiments, in which character he served three years under me. During that time he gave such signal proofs of his bravery and good behavior, as bound me, in honor and gratitude, to do something for him. And I therefore got him promoted to be quartermaster, as he was acquainted with the duty, and capable, (I thought,) of discharging it.

We have had several visitations from the enemy, and much mischief done, since my last to you. About the 17th ultimo there were upwards of twenty persons killed only twelve miles from this garrison, and notwithstanding I sent a strong detachment from hence to pursue them, and ordered the passes of the mountains to be waylaid by commands from other places, yet we were not able to meet with these savages.

On Friday se'nnight, a body of near or not quite a hundred fell upon the inhabitants along the great road between this place and Pennsylvania, got fifteen more. The mischief would have been much greater, had not an officer and twenty men of the regiment, who were then out, fallen in with and engaged the enemy. Finding, however, that his party was overpowered, and like to be surrounded, he retreated to a stockade, not far distant, in which they were besieged for three hours; but the firing communicated an alarm from one habitation to another, by which means most of the families were timely apprised of their danger, and happily got safe off. Our party killed one Indian (whose scalp they obtained) and wounded several others.

I exert every means in my power to protect a much distressed country, but it is a task too arduous. To think of defending a frontier as ours is, of more than three hundred and fifty miles' extent, with only seven hundred men, is vain and idle, especially when that frontier lies more contiguous to the enemy than any other. I am, and have for a long time been, fully convinced, that, if we continue to pursue a defensive plan, the country must be inevitably lost.

You will be kind enough, Sir, to excuse the freedom with which I deliver my sentiments, and believe me to be, (for I really am,) with unfeigned truth and regard, your most obedient, humble servant.

N. B. These constant alarms and perpetual movements of the soldiers of this garrison, have almost put a stop to the progress of the public works at this place.

To GOVERNOR DINWIDDIE

The last letter written to Governor Dinwiddie still pleads for help in the campaign. Sick and discouraged, Washington developed an alarming case of dysentery and fever and was ordered home to Mount Vernon by his physician, Dr. Craik. Convalescence during more than four months brought him back to robust health.

Fort Loudoun, November 5, 1757

SIR: Duty to my Country, and his Majesty's interest, indispensably requires, that I again trouble your Honor on the subject of Indian affairs here; which have been impeded and embarrassed by such a train of mismanagement, as a continuance of which must inevitably produce the most melancholy consequences.

The sincere disposition the Cherokees have betrayed to espouse our cause heartily has been demonstrated beyond the most distant doubt; and, if rewarded in the manner in which that laudable and meritorious disposition entitles them to, wou'd, in all human probability, soon effect a favorable change in the present (apparently) desperate situation of this poor, unhappy part of his Majesty's dominions.

But, in the stead of meeting with that great encouragement, which the esential services of that brave people undoubtedly merit, several of them, after having undergone the rudest toils and fatigues of an excessively long march, destitute of all the conveniences and almost necessaries of life, and, (to give us still more convincing proofs of their strong attachment to our interest) in that very situation went to war, and in the way behaved nobly (from which we reaped a signal advantage,) and when they returned here, with an enemy's scalp, baggage and other trophies of honor, they must have gone home without any kind of reward or thanks, or even provisions to support them on their march, justly fired with the highest resentment for their mal-treatment, had not I and my officers strained a point, procured them some things, of which they were in absolute want, and made it the object of our care, in various respects, to please them.

Another party of those Indians since very opportunely arrived to our assistance, at the very juncture the enemy made an irruption into this settlement, pursued their tracks, came up with three of them, two of whom they scalped, and wounded the third. They are now returned from this pursuit, and are nearly in the same situation with those abovementioned. I applied to Captain Gist in their behalf, and told him I must represent the matter to your Honor. But he assures me that he has neither goods to reward them, money to procure them, or even an interpreter, which totally incapacitates him for doing any kind of service. If so (which I have no reason to doubt) it is surprising, that any man shou'd be entrusted with the negotiating of such important affairs, and not be possessed of the means to accomplish the undertaking. By which he, and several others, who received high pay from Virginia, are not only rendered useless, but our interests with those Indians is at the brink of destruction. Whenever a party of them arrive here, they immediately apply to me; but I have neither any thing to give them, nor any right to do it. Nor is there anybody to inform them to what these and their other disappointments is owing; which reduces me to such a dilemma, as I wou'd most gladly be extricated from.

I must likewise beg leave to mention to your Honor once more the vast hardships, many of the people groan under here, having been so long kept out of the money, which the country owes them on account of the Indians. When I proposed going down to Williamsburgh, many of them brought their accounts to me, which I intended (had you given me liberty,) to have laid before your Honor. I mention this circumstance, not with any view of being employed in examining and paying off those accounts, (which for many reasons I can by no means undertake,) but in hope that your Honor will be pleased to give directions to and denominate some person for that purpose, for the neglect of which so many poor people greatly suffer. I am, &c.

To MRS. MARTHA CUSTIS

This is one of the few letters to Martha Washington that have been preserved.

July 20, 1758

We have begun our march for the Ohio. A courier is starting for Williamsburg, and I embrace the opportunity to send a few words to one whose life is now inseparable from mine. Since that happy hour when we made our pledges to each other, my thoughts have been continually going to you as another Self. That an all-powerful Providence may keep us both in safety is the prayer of your ever faithful and affectionate friend.

To MRS. GEORGE WILLIAM FAIRFAX

Because of its ambiguity, this letter to Sally Cary Fairfax has made historians speculate with considerable relish whether it was for Sally Fairfax or Martha Custis that Colonel Washington declared himself with eighteenth-century courtliness "a votary of love."

Camp at Fort Cumberland, September 12, 1758

DEAR MADAM: Yesterday I was honored with your short but very agreeable favor of the first inst. How joyfully I catch at the happy occasion of renewing a correspondence which I feared was disrelished on your part, I leave to time, that never failing expositor of all things, and to a monitor equally faithful in my own breast, to testify. In silence I now express my joy; silence, which in some cases, I wish the present, speaks more intelligently than the sweetest eloquence.

If you allow that any honor can be derived from my opposition to our present system of management, you destroy the merit of it entirely in me by attributing my anxiety to the animating prospect of possessing Mrs. Custis, when—I need not tell you, guess yourself. Should not my own Honor and country's welfare be the excitement? 'Tis true, I profess myself a votary of love. I acknowledge that a lady is in the case, and further I confess that this lady is known to you. Yes, Madame, as well as she is to one who is too sensible of her charms to deny the Power whose influence he feels and must ever submit to. I feel the force of her amiable beauties in the recollection of a thousand tender passages that I could wish to obliterate, till I am bid to revive them. But experience, alas! sadly reminds me how impossible this is, and evinces an opinion which I have long entertained, that there is a Destiny which has the control of our actions, not to be resisted by the strongest efforts of Human Nature.

You have drawn me, dear Madame, or rather I have drawn myself, into an honest confession of a simple Fact. Misconstrue not my meaning; doubt it not, nor expose it. The world has no business to know the object of my Love, declared in this manner to you, when I want to conceal it. One thing above all things in this world I wish to know, and only one person of your acquaintance can solve me that, or guess my meaning. But adieu to this till happier times, if I ever shall see them. The hours at present are melancholy dull. Neither the rugged toils of war, no the gentler conflict of A——— B———s,* is in my choice. I dare believe you are as happy as you say, I wish I was happy also. Mirth, good humor, ease of mind, and—what else? —cannot fail to render you so and consummate your wishes.

If one agreeable lady could almost wish herself a fine gentleman for the sake of another, I apprehend that many fine gentlemen will wish themselves finer e'er Mrs. Spotswood is possest. She has already become a reigning toast in this camp, and many there are in it who intend (fortune favoring) to

---

* "Assembly Balls" are probably the words intended.—*Ford.*

make honorable scars speak the fullness of their merit, and be a messenger of their Love to Her.

I cannot easily forgive the unseasonable haste of my last express, if he deprived me thereby of a single word you intended to add. The time of the present messenger is, as the last might have been, entirely at your disposal. I can't expect to hear from my friends more than this once before the fate of the expedition will some how or other be determined. I therefore beg to know when you set out for Hampton, and when you expect to return to Belvoir again. And I should be glad also to hear of your speedy departure, as I shall thereby hope for your return before I get down. The disappointment of not seeing your family would give me much concern. From any thing I can yet see 'tis hardly possible to say when we shall finish. I don't think there is a probability of it till the middle of November. Your letter to Captain Gist I forwarded by a safe hand the moment it came to me. His answer shall be carefully transmitted.

Col. Mercer, to whom I delivered your message and compliments, joins me very heartily in wishing you and the Ladies of Belvoir the perfect enjoyment of every happiness this world affords. Be assured that I am, dear Madame, with the most unfeigned regard, your most obedient and most obliged humble servant.

N. B. Many accidents happening (to use a vulgar saying) between the cup and the lip, I choose to make the exchange of carpets myself, since I find you will not do me the honor to accept mine.

To FRANCIS FAUQUIER

Through the spring, summer and fall of 1758, the campaign against Fort Duquesne continued with many discouragements and reversals. The end came on November 25th, when the French set fire to the stronghold which for five years had been Washington's objective. Upon taking possession, the British renamed it Fort Pitt. The entire expedition was now over and peace negotiations were begun with the Delaware and other Indian tribes on the Ohio River. Brigadier General George

Washington could now retire from the Virginia Regiment, return to Mount Vernon and, on January 6, 1759, marry Mrs. Martha Custis.

Camp, at Fort Duquesne, November 28, 1758

HONBLE. SIR: I have the pleasure to inform you, that Fort Duquesne, or the ground rather on which it stood, was possessed by his Majesty's troops on the 25th instant. The enemy, after letting us get within a day's march of the place, burned the fort, and ran away (by the light of it) at night, going down the Ohio by water, to the number of about five hundred men, from our best information. The possession of this fort has been matter of great surprise to the whole army, and we cannot attribute it to more probable causes, than those of weakness, want of provisions, and desertion of their Indians. Of these circumstances we were luckily informed by three prisoners, who providentially fell into our hands at Loyal Hannan, at a time when we despaired of proceeding, and a council of war had determined, that it was not advisable to advance beyond the place above mentioned this season, but the information above caused us to march on without tents or baggage, and with a light train of artillery only, with which we have happily succeeded. It would be tedious, and I think unnecessary, to relate every trivial circumstance, that has happened since my last. To do this, if needful, shall be the employment of a leisure hour, when I have the pleasure to pay my respects to your Honor.

The General purposes to wait here a few days to settle matters with the Indians, and then all the troops, (except a sufficient garrison which will I suppose be left here, to secure the possession) will march to their respective governments. I therefore give your Honor this early notice of it, that your directions relative to those of Virginia may meet me timely on the road. I cannot help premising, in this place, the hardships the troops have undergone, and the naked condition they now are in, in order that you may judge if it is not necessary that they should have some little recess from fatigue, and time to provide themselves with necessaries, for at present they are destitute of every comfort of life. If I do not get your orders to the contrary, I shall march the troops under my command directly to Winchester; from whence they may then be disposed of, as you shall afterwards direct.

General Forbes desires me to inform you, that he is prevented, by a multiplicity of different affairs, from writing to you so fully now, as he would otherwise have done, and from enclosing you a copy of a letter which he has written to the commanding officer stationed on the communication from hence to Winchester, &c. relative to the Little Carpenter's conduct, (a chief of the Cherokees). But that, the purport of that letter was to desire, they would deprive him of the use of arms and ammunition, and escort him from one place to another, to prevent his doing any mischief to the inhabitants, allowing him provisions only. His behavior, the General thought, rendered this measure necessary.

This fortunate, and, indeed, unexpected success of our arms will be attended with happy effects. The Delawares are suing for peace, and I doubt not that other tribes on the Ohio will follow their example. A trade, free, open, and upon equitable terms, is what they seem much to stickle for, and I do not know so effectual a way of riveting them to our interest, as sending out goods immediately to this place for that purpose. It will, at the same time, be a means of supplying the garrison with such necessaries as may be wanted; and, I think, those colonies, which are as greatly interested in the support of this place as Virginia is, should neglect no means in their power to establish and support a strong garrison here. Our business, (wanting this) will be but half finished; while, on the other hand, we obtain a firm and lasting peace, if this end is once accomplished.

General Forbes is very assiduous in getting these matters settled upon a solid basis, and has great merit (which I hope will be rewarded) for the happy issue which he has brought our affairs to, infirm and worn down as he is. At present I have nothing further to add, but the strongest assurances of my being your Honor's most obedient and most humble servant.

To ROBERT CARY & COMPANY, MERCHANTS, LONDON

Of incidental interest, this list of household goods to be imported from London suggests the scale of living at Mount Vernon in 1759.

Williamsburg, May 1, 1759

GENTLN. The Inclos'd is the Ministers Certificate of my Marriage with Mrs. Martha Custis, properly as I am told, Authenticated, You will therefore for the future please to address all your Letters which relate to the Affairs of the late Danl. Parke Custis Esqr. to me, as by Marriage I am entitled to a third part of that Estate, and Invested likewise with the care of the other two thirds by a Decree of our Genl. Court which I obtain'd in order to strengthen the Power I before had in consequence of my Wifes Administration.

I have many Letters of yours in my possession unanswered but at present this serves only to advise you of the above Change and at the same time to acquaint you that I shall continue to make you the same Consignments of Tobo. as usual, and will endeavour to encrease it in proportion as I find myself and the Estate benefitted thereby.

The Scarcity of the last years Crop, and the high prices of Tobo. consequent thereupon wou'd in any other Case, have induc'd me to sell the Estates Crop (which indeed is only 16 Hhds.) in the Country but for a present, and I hope small advantage only I did not care to break the Chain of Corrispondance that had so long subsisted, and therefore have, according to your desire, given Captn. Talman an offer of the whole.

On the otherside is an Invoice of some Goods which I beg of you to send me by the first Ship bound either to Potomack or Rappahannock, as I am in immediate want of them. Let them be Insur'd, and in case of Accident reshipp'd witht. Delay; direct for me at Mount Vernon Potomack River Virginia; the former is the name of my Seat the other of the River on which 'tis Situated. I am, &c.

INVOICE OF SUNDRY GOODS TO BE SHIP'D BY ROBT. CARY, ESQ., AND COMPANY FOR THE USE OF GEORGE WASHINGTON—VIZ:

May, 1759

1 Tester Bedstead 7½ feet pitch, with fashionable bleu or bleu and White Curtains to suit a Room lind w't the Ireld. paper.—

Window Curtains of the same for two Windows; with either Papier Maché Cornish to them, or Cornish cover'd with the Cloth.

1 fine Bed Coverlid to match the Curtains. 4 Chair bottoms of the same; that is, as much Covring suited to the above furniture as will go over the seats of 4 Chairs (which I have by me) in order to make the whole furniture of this Room uniformly handsome and genteel.

1. Fashionable Sett of Desert Glasses, and Stands for Sweet Meats Jellys &ca. together with Wash Glasses and a proper Stand for these also.—

2 Setts of Chamber, or Bed Carpets—Wilton.

4. Fashionable China Branches, & Stands, for Candles.

2 Neat fire Screens

50 lbs Spirma Citi Candles

6 Carving knives and Forks—handles of Stain'd Ivory and bound with Silver.

A pretty large Assortment of Grass Seeds—amongst which let there be a good deal of Lucerne & St. Foin, especially the former, also a good deal of English, or bleu Grass Clover Seed I have.—

1 Large, neat, and easy Couch for a Passage.

50 yards of best Floor Matting.—

2 pair of fashionable mixd, or Marble Cold. Silk Hose.

6 pr. of finest Cotton Ditto.

6 pr. of finest thread Ditto

6 pr. of midling Do. to cost abt. 5/.

6 pr. Worsted Do of ye best sorted—2 pr of w'ch. to be White.
N.B. All the above Stockings to be long, and tolerably large.

1 piece of finest and most fashionable Stock Tape.

1 Suit of Cloaths of the finest Cloth, & fashionable colour made
by the Inclos'd measure.—

The newest, and most approv'd Treatise of Agriculture—besides this, send me a small piece in Octavo—call'd a New
System of Agriculture, or a Speedy Way to grow Rich.

Longley's Book of Gardening.—

Gibson, upon Horses the latest Edition in Quarto—

Half a dozn. pair of Men's neatest Shoes and Pumps, to be
made by one Didsbury on Colo. Baylors Last; but a little
larger than this and to have high Heels.

6 pr. Mens riding Gloves rather large than the middle size.

One neat Pocket Book, capable of receiving Memorandoms &
small Cash Accts. to be made of Ivory, or any thing else that
will admit of cleaning.—

Fine Soft Calf Skin for a pair of Boots—

Ben leathr. for Soles.

Six Bottles of Greenhows Tincture.

Order from the best House in Madeira a Pipe of the best Old
Wine, and let it be Secur'd from Pilferers.

To FRANCIS DANDRIDGE

*Washington disappeared from public life, except as an obscure member of the Virginia House of Burgesses, to become
the fox-hunting squire of Mount Vernon who devoted his
energies to the acquisition of more and more land, the supervision of his slaves, indentured servants and hired hands, and
the cultivation and disposition of the crops of his plantation.
As he grew wealthier and more independent, the separation
of his interests from the Mother Country widened. The enactment by Parliament of taxation on the American colonies
stirred resentment, and the Stamp Act particularly was regarded as an unconstitutional violation of liberty. In his letter
to Francis Dandridge, an uncle of Martha Washington who*

lived in England, the retired soldier and man of property saw in the Stamp Act many evil consequences, chief of which would be a lessening of trade and a virtual stoppage of the courts of justice.

Mount Vernon, September 20, 1765

SIR: If you will permit me after six years silence, the time I have been married to your Niece, to pay my respects to you in this Epistolary way I shall think myself happy in beginning a corrispondance which cannot but be attended with pleasure on my side.

I should hardly have taken the liberty Sir, of Introducing myself to your acquaintance in this manner, and at this time, least you shoud think my motives for doing of it arose from sordid views had not a Letter which I receivd sometime this Summer from Robt. Cary & Co. given me Reasons to believe that such an advance on my side would not be altogether disagreeable on yours before this I rather apprehended that some disgust at the News of your Nieces Marriage with me, and why I coud not tell, might have been the cause of your silence upon that event, and discontinuing a corrispodance which before then you had kept up with her; but if I could only flatter myself, that you woud in any wise be entertaind with the few occurances that it might be in my power to relate from hence I shoud endeavour to attone for my past remisness, in this respect, by future punctuality.

At present few things are under notice of my observation that can afford you any amusement in the recital. The Stamp Act Imposed on the Colonies by the Parliament of Great Britain engrosses the conversation of the Speculative part of the Colonists, who look upon this unconstitutional method of Taxation as a direful attack upon their Liberties, and loudly exclaim against the Violation; what may be the result of this and some other (I think I may add) ill judged Measures, I will not undertake to determine; but this I may venture to affirm, that the advantage accrueing to the Mother Country will fall greatly short of the expectations of the Ministry; for certain it is, our whole Substance does already in a manner flow to Great Britain and that whatsoever contributes to lessen our Importation's must be hurtful to their Manufacturers. And the Eyes of our People, already beginning to open, will perceive, that many Luxuries which we lavish our substance to Great Britain for, can well be dispensd with whilst the necessaries of Life are (mostly) to be had within ourselves. This consequently will introduce frugality, and be a necessary stimulation to Industry. If Great Britain therefore Loads her Manufactures with heavy Taxes, will it not facilitate these Measures? they will not compel us I think to give our Money for their exports, whether we will or no, and certain I am none of their Traders will part from them without a valuable consideration. Where then is the Utility of these Restrictions?

As to the Stamp Act, taken in a single view, one, and the first bad consequences attending it I take to be this. Our Courts of Judicature must inevitably be shut up; for it is impossible (or next of kin to it) under our present Circumstances that the Act of Parliam't can be complyd with were we ever so willing to enforce the execution; for not to say, which alone woud be sufficient, that we have not Money to pay the Stamps, there are many other Cogent Reasons to prevent it; and if a stop be put to our judicial proceedings I fancy the Merchants of G. Britain trading to the Colonies will not be among the last to wish for a Repeal of it.

I live upon Potomack River in Fairfax County, about ten Miles below Alexandria and many Miles distant from any of my Wifes Relations; who all reside upon York River, and who we seldom see more than once a year, not always that. My wife who is very well and Master and Miss Custis (Children of her former Marriage) all join in making a tender of their Duty and best respects to yourself and the Aunt. My Compliments to your Lady I beg may also be made acceptable and that you will do me the justice to believe that I am, etc.

Sent by Captn. Jno. Johnstown

To GEORGE MASON

George Mason, the noted Virginia constitutionalist, was a neighbor of the Washingtons on the Potomac. Ever since Washington had expressed his first mild protest against the Stamp Act, which had been repealed, he continued to advance progressively but cautiously to consideration of the whole question of the infringement of American liberty. Petitions to the crown and appeals to Parliament having been unavailing, boycott of the trade and manufactures of the Mother Country won his approval. Step by step Washington moved toward a conviction of the righteousness of total independence, and, once arrived at, it became the unswerving principle which dominated every subsequent act of his revolutionary career.

Mount Vernon, April 5, 1769

DEAR SIR: Herewith you will receive a letter and Sundry papers which were forwarded to me a day or two ago by Doctor Ross of Bladensburg. I transmit them with the greater pleasure, as my own desire of knowing your sentiments upon a matter of this importance exactly coincides with the Doctors inclinations.

At a time when our lordly Masters in Great Britain will be satisfied with nothing less than the deprication of American freedom, it seems highly necessary that some thing shou'd be done to avert the stroke and maintain the liberty which we have derived from our Ancestors; but the manner of doing it to answer the purpose effectually is the point in question.

That no man shou'd scruple, or hesitate a moment to use a-ms in defence of so valuable a blessing, on which all the good and evil of life depends; is clearly my opinion; yet A-ms I wou'd beg leave to add, should be the last resource; the denier resort. Addresses to the Throne, and remonstrances to parliament, we have already, it is said, proved the inefficacy of; how far then their attention to our rights and priviledges is to be

81

awakened or alarmed by starving their Trade and manufactures, remains to be tryed.

The northern Colonies, it appears, are endeavouring to adopt this scheme. In my opinion it is a good one, and must be attended with salutary effects, provided it can be carried pretty generally into execution; but how far it is practicable to do so, I will not take upon me to determine. That there will be difficulties attending the execution of it every where, from clashing interests, and selfish designing men (ever attentive to their own gain, and watchful of every turn that can assist their lucrative views, in preference to any other consideration) cannot be denied; but in the Tobacco Colonies where the Trade is so diffused, and in a manner wholly conducted by Factors for their principals at home, these difficulties are certainly enhanced, but I think not insurmountably increased, if the Gentlemen in their several Counties wou'd be at some pains to explain matters to the people, and stimulate them to a cordial agreement to purchase none but certain innumerated Articles out of any of the Stores after such a period, not import nor purchase any themselves. This, if it did not effectually withdraw the Factors from their Importations, wou'd at least make them extremely cautious in doing it, as the prohibited Goods could be vended to none but the non-associator, or those who wou'd pay no regard to their association; both of whom ought to be stigmatized, and made the objects of publick reproach.

The more I consider a Scheme of this sort, the more ardently I wish success to it, because I think there are private, as well as public advantages to result from it; the former certain, however precarious the other may prove; for in respect to the latter I have always thought that by virtue of the same power (for here alone the authority derives) which assume's the right of Taxation, they may attempt at least to restrain our manufactories; especially those of a public nature; the same equity and justice prevailing in the one case as the other, it being no greater hardship to forbid my manufacturing, than it is to order me to buy Goods of them loaded with Duties, for the express purpose of raising a revenue. But as a measure of this sort will be an additional exertion of arbitrary power, we cannot be worsted I think in putting it to the Test. On the other hand, that the

Colonies are considerably indebted to Great Britain, is a truth universally acknowledged. That many families are reduced, almost, if not quite, to penury and want, from the low ebb of their fortunes, and Estates daily selling for the discharge of Debts, the public papers furnish but too many melancholy proofs of. And that a scheme of this sort will contribute more effectually than any other I can devise to immerge the Country from the distress it at present labours under, I do most firmly believe, if it can be generally adopted. And I can see but one set of people (the Merchants excepted) who will not, or ought not, to wish well to the Scheme; and that is those who live genteely and hospitably, on clear Estates. Such as these were they, not to consider the valuable object in view, and the good of others, might think it hard to be curtail'd in their living and enjoyments; for as to the penurious Man, he saves his money, and he saves his credit, having the best plea for doing that, which before perhaps he had the most violent struggles to refrain from doing. The extravagant and expensive man has the same good plea to retrench his Expences. He is thereby furnished with a pretext to live within bounds, and embraces it, prudence dictated œconomy to him before, but his resolution was too weak to put in practice; for how can I, says he, who have lived in such and such a manner change my method? I am ashamed to do it; and besides such an alteration in the system of my living, will create suspicions of a decay in my fortune, and such a thought the World must not harbour; I will e'en continue my course: till at last the course discontinues the Estate, a sale of it being the consequence of his perseverance in error. This I am satisfied is the way that many who have set out in the wrong tract, have reasoned, till ruin stares them in the face. And in respect to the poor and needy man, he is only left in the same situation he was found; better I might say, because as he judges from comparison his condition is amended in proportion as it approaches nearer to those above him.

Upon the whole therefore, I think the Scheme a good one, and that it ought to be tryed here, with such alterations as the exigency of our circumstances render absolutely necessary; but how, and in what manner to begin the work, is a matter worthy of consideration, and whether it can be attempted with propriety, or efficacy (further than a communication of sentiments to one another) before May, when the Court and Assembly will meet together in Williamsburg, and a uniform plan can be concerted, and sent into the different counties to operate at the same time, and in the same manner every where, is a thing I am somewhat in doubt upon, and shou'd be glad to know your opinion of. I am Dr. Sir, etc.

CATALOGUE OF BOOKS FOR MASTER CUSTIS

The classical flavor of this list of books, with no relief in the way of novels or even of contemporary writings, indicates the sternness of Washington's views on the education of his stepson, then fifteen years of age. It is of passing interest to observe that such eighteenth-century writers as Voltaire, Rousseau, Montesquieu, Pope, Johnson, Swift, Sterne, Fielding, Smollett, Addison, Berkeley and Kant, to mention the famous only, are totally ignored.

July 25, 1769

Pub: Terent Apri Comod:, Editio Ricard: Bentleii, Cantab
Am Edi'n of Horace
All Ciceros Works; a very neat Editn. by the Forlis's of Glasgow in 20 12 mo. Vol.
Titi Livii Patavin: Historian Libri Edit Rudimanni 4 vols.
M Valin: Martialis, and Aliorum Epigrammate.
Hugo Grotius de vertitate Xtiana Religionis.
Græcæ Grammatices Rudiments, in Unum Scholie Westmonasterensis
Gr. Test an elegant Edn. printed for R Urie in Glasgow
Dawson's Lexicon to the Gr'k Test't
Græcæ Gramatices Rudimenta &ca. by Thoms. Stackhouse AM 8vo.
Origin, and structure of the Greek Tongue by Gregory Sharpe L. L. D.
De Verbis Mediis L. Kusteri I Clerici, I Clarkii, and E Schmidii

Commentationes Auxit Suamg adjicit Christ: Wolfe to be sold by Vaillant

Clavis Homerica, Editis recentissima

Harwoods liberal Translation of the N: T: with his Introductory Observ'ns to the Study of the Scriptures

Blackwells Sacred Classics, 2 vols.

Sharpes Arguments in defence of Christianity 2 vols.

Gerards Dissertations on subjects relatg. to the Evidens. of Xtianity

Oswalds Appeal to Common Sense in behalf of Religion

Squire on Indifference for Religion

Ferguson on the Histy. of Civil Society

Beccerias Essay on Crimes and Punishmts.

Dodsleys Collection of English Poetry

Vision's in Verse by Doctr. Cotton

The Amuranth, or a Collection of Religious Poems

Thompson Works

Milton's Works the Editn. by Baskerville

A Genl. History of the World by Grey and Guthrie

Baron Hombergs Introduction to Genl. Histry. translated by Dr. Sharpe

Humes History of England the 4th. Edtn.

Mrs McCauley's Do*

Hookes Roman History, 10 vol.

Kennets Roman Antiquities

Potters Greek Antiquities

A good Collection of Voyages and Travles

Matho, or Cosmotheoria Puerilis

Burgs Dignity of Human Nature

Watts's Logick

Fishers Arithmetick

Rolling Method of Studying the Belles Lettres

Steels Christian Hero

Burgs Art of Speaking

History of England in a Series of Letters from a Nobleman to his Son.

Martins Philsopl. Grammer

Robertson's History of Scotland

* Mrs. Catherine Macaulay's *History of England* in eight volumes.

Tookes Pantheon
Wells Geographia Classica
Recueil des Auteurs Francois

To REVEREND JONATHAN BOUCHER

Washington's general ideas on education are outlined in this letter to Reverend Jonathan Boucher, tutor to his stepson, John Parke Custis. "A knowledge of books," Washington insists, "is the basis upon which other knowledge is to be built . . . it is men and things more than books . . ."

Mount Vernon, July 9, 1771

DEAR SIR: From several concurring causes, which exist at this moment, the eve of my departure for Williamsburg, I have both my head and my hands too full of business to allow me time to write more than a hasty ill digested Letter; This, however, I shall attempt to do in answer to yours of the 4th. Inst.

In my last I informed you (as well as I can recollect the contents of the letter) that the friends (I do not confine myself to the relations only) of Mr. Custis, were divided in their opinions, of the propriety of his travelling, not because they thought advantages would not result from it, but on account of the expense, as he would commence his tour with so heavy a charge, as you thought sufficient to induce you to accompany him, which would at once anticipate half his income; for his estate is of that kind, which rather comes under the denomination of a large than a profitable one. He has it is true a good deal of land and a great many slaves, but the former is more to be esteemed for the situation than the quality, being indifferent and much worn, so that large crops cannot be made from them. These doubtful opinions was sufficient cause, I observed in my last for me to be circumspect in my conduct, as I had another tribunal to account to besides that in my own breast, for the part I was to act on this occasion. For you cannot but know, that every farthing, which is expended in behalf of this young gentleman, must undergo the inspection of the General

Court, in their examination of my guardianship accounts, and that it would be imprudent in me to permit him to launch into any uncommon or expensive pursuits, (especially at a time when a heavy and expensive chancery suit is instituted against his estate,) without first knowing whether such an expence would be approved by those, who had a constitutional right to judge of the expediency or propriety of the measure.

These are the reasons why I said in my last letter, that my own inclinations were still as strong as ever for Mr. Custis's pursuing his travelling scheme, provided the Court should approve of the expense (I did not want their opinion of the utility of travelling) and provided also that it should appear, when his judgment is a little more matured, that he is desirous of undertaking this tour upon a plan of improvement, rather than a vague desire of gratifying an idle curiosity, or spending his money; for by the bye, if his mother does not speak her own sentiments, rather than his, he is lukewarm in the scheme; and I cannot help giving it as my opinion, that his education, from what I have understood of his improvement (however advanced it may be for a youth of his age) is by no means ripe enough for a travelling tour; not that I think his becoming a mere scholar is a desirable education for a gentleman; but I conceive a knowledge of books is the basis upon which other knowledge is to be built; and that it is men and things more than books he is to be acquainted with by travelling. At present, however well versed he may be in the principles of the Latin language (which is not to be wondered at, as he began the study of it as soon as he could speak), he is unacquainted with several of their classical authors, which might be useful to him to read. He is ignorant of Greek (the advantages of learning which I do not pretend to judge of), knows nothing of French, which is absolutely necessary to him as a traveller; little or nothing acquainted with arithmetic, and totally ignorant of the mathematics; than which, so much of it at least as relates to surveying, nothing can be more essentially necessary to any man possessed of a large landed estate, the bounds of some part or other of which are always in controversy.

Now, whether he has time between this and next spring to acquire a sufficient knowledge of these, or so much of them as are requisite, I leave you to judge; and whether a boy of seventeen years old, which will be his age next November can have any just notions of the end and design of travelling? I have already given it as my opinion, that it would be precipitating this event, unless he was to go immediately to the university for a couple of years, and in which case he could see nothing of America; which might be a disadvantage to him, as it is to be expected that every man, who travels with a view of observing the laws and customs of other countries, should be able to give some description of the situation and government of his own.

Upon the whole, it is impossible for me at this time to give a more decisive answer, however strongly inclined I may be to put you upon an absolute certainty in this affair, than I have done; and I should think myself wanting in candor, if I concealed any circumstances from you, which leads me to fear, that there is a possibility, if not a probability, that the whole design may be totally defeated; and therefore I add, that before I ever thought myself at liberty to encourage this plan, I judged it highly reasonable and necessary, that his mother should be consulted. I laid your first letter and proposals before her, and desired that she would ponderate well, before she resolved, as an unsteady behavior might be a disadvantage to you. Her determination was, that, if it appeared to be his inclination to undertake this tour, and it should be adjudged for his benefit, she would not oppose it, whatever pangs it might give her to part with him. This declaration she still adheres to, but in so faint a manner, that I think, what with her fears and his indifference, it will soon be declared that he has no inclination to go, the consequence of which is too obvious to be mentioned. I do not say that this will be the case; I cannot speak positively. But as this is the result of my own reflections upon the matter, I thought it but fair to communicate them to you.

Several causes, I believe, have concurred to make her view his departure, (as the time approaches) with more reluctance than she expected. The unhappy situation of her daughter has in some degree fixed her eyes upon him as her only hope. Add to this the doubts of her friends, &c., to what I have already said, I can only add, that my warmest wishes are to see him prosecute a plan, at a proper period, which I am sure must redound to his advantage, and that nothing shall be wanted on my part to aid and assist him in it. In the event of his going, I should think myself highly favoured, and him much honored, by Governor Eden's letters of introduction. Such, with others that might be procured, could not fail of having their advantages.

You will please to make my compliments to Mr. Dulany, and assure him, that I have not the least vestige of a house at the Frederic Springs, otherwise it should have been, if unengaged, much at his service. The two seasons I spent there was in a house of Mr. Mercer's.

I scarce know what answer to give to the papers you transmitted to me as an executor of the will of Col. Thos. Colvill, deceased. The affairs of that estate are unhappily involved with John Semple, to whom Colo. Colvill in his life time sold a tract of land in Maryland, called Merryland, for I think £2600 sterling and from whom we can neither get the money nor land. Till this matter is settled the executors are unable to pay off the Legacies in this country, consequently can answer no demands of the residuary legatees in England, who only come in for the surplusage if any there be. I believe there will be more than sufficient to discharge the debts and legacies here, but the overplus will be trifling. I am, &c.

To REVEREND JONATHAN BOUCHER

The earliest and most familiar of the many portraits of Washington was painted by Charles Willson Peale, a former maker of saddles, coaches and watches and one-time student under John Singleton Copley and Benjamin West. The fee paid the artist was £18.4 plus £13 each for three miniatures, or a total of £57.4. Dressed in the uniform of a Virginia colonel, Washington is represented as more youthful than he actually appeared at forty when he posed for this picture.

Mount Vernon, May 21, 1772

DR. SIR: Inclination having yielded to Importunity, I am now contrary to all expectations under the hands of Mr. Peale; but in so grave—so sullen a mood—and now and then under the influence of Morpheus, when some critical strokes are making, that I fancy the skill of this Gentleman's Pencil, will be put to it, in describing to the World what manner of man I am. I have no doubt of Mr. Peale's meeting with very good Incouragement in a Tour to Williamsburg; for having mentioned him to some Gentlemen at our Court, they seem desirous of employing him in his way down.

Your excuse for denying us the pleasure of your company, with Governor Eden and Lady, tho not strictly warranted by Scripture, is nevertheless highly admissable, and I sincerely congratulate you upon the prospect of happiness; as I think there is a fair Field of it opening to your view, from the judiciousness of your choice—Whether Mrs. Washington ever stretches as far as Annapolis or not, we shall certainly take some very early opportunity of making your acquaintance on this occasion.

To BENEDICT CALVERT

Washington, the ever-watchful guardian of John Parke Custis, takes the occasion of his stepson's proposal to Eleanor Calvert to address her father on the consequences of marriage in haste. The wedding took place ten months to the day after this letter was written.

Mount Vernon, April 3, 1773

DEAR SIR: I am now set down to write to you on a Subject of Importance, and of no small embarrassment to me. My Son in Law and Ward, Mr. Custis, has, as I have been informed, paid his Addresses to your Second Daughter, and having made some progress in her Affections has required her in Marriage. How far a union of this Sort may be agreeable to you, you best can tell, but I should think myself wanting in Candor was I not to acknowledge, that, Miss Nellie's amiable qualifications stands confess'd at all hands; and that, an alliance with your Family, will be pleasing to his.

This acknowledgment being made you must permit me to add Sir, that at this, or in any short time, his youth, inexperience, and unripened Education, is; and will be insuperable obstacles in my eye, to the completion of the Marriage. As his Guardian, I conceive it to be my indispensable duty (to endeavor) to carry him through a regular course of Education, many branches of which, sorry I am to add, he is totally deficient of; and to guard his youth to a more advanced age before an Event, on which his own Peace and the happiness of another is to depend, takes place; not that I have any doubt of the warmth of his Affections, nor, I hope I may add, any fears of a change in them; but at present, I do not conceive that he is capable of bestowing that due attention to the Important consequences of a marriage State, which is necessary to be done by those, who are Inclin'd to enter into it; and of course, am unwilling he should do it till he is. If the Affection which they have avowd for each other is fixd upon a Solid Basis, it will receive no diminution in the course of two or three years, in which time he may prosecute his Studies, and thereby render himself more deserving of the Lady, and useful to Society; If unfortunately, (as they are both young) there should be an abatement of Affection on either side, or both, it had better precede, than follow after, Marriage.

Delivering my Sentiments thus, will not, I hope, lead you into a belief that I am desirous of breaking off the Match; to postpone it, is all I have in view; for I shall recommend it to the young Gentleman with the warmth that becomes a man of honour, (notwithstanding he did not vouchsafe to consult either his Mother or me, on the occasion) to consider himself as much engaged to your Daughter as if the indissoluble Knot was tied; and, as the surest means of effecting this, to stick close to his Studies, (in which I flatter myself you will join me) by which he will, in a great measure, avoid those little Flirtations with other Girls which may, by dividing the Attention, contribute not a little to divide the Affection.

It may be expected of me perhaps to say something of Fortune, But, to discend to particulars, at this time, may seem rather premature. In general therefore I shall inform you that Mr. Custis's Estate consists of about 15,000 Acres of Land, good part of it adjoining to the City of Williamsburg, and none 40 Miles from it; several Lotts in the said City; between two and three hundred Negroes; and about Eight or ten thousand Pounds upon Bond, and in the hands of his Merchants. This Estate he now holds Independent of his Mother's Dower, which will be an acquisition to it at her Death, and upon the whole such an one as you will readily acknowledge ought to entitle him to a handsome Portion in a Wife; But, as I should never require a Child of my own to make a Sacrifice of himself to Interest, so, neither do I think it incumbent on me to recommend it as a Guardian; but as I know you are full able, I should hope, and expect, if we were now upon the point of Settling these Preliminaries, that you would also be willing to do something genteel by your Daughter.

At all times when you, Mrs. Calvert, or the young Ladies can make it convenient to favor us with a visit we should be happy in seeing you at this place. Mrs. Washington and Miss Custis join me in respectful Compliments and I am, dear Sir, etc.

To BURWELL BASSETT

The death of Martha Parke Custis (Patsy), stepdaughter of George Washington, at the age of sixteen was a tragic blow. Washington's relationship to the two Custis children could not have been more devoted had they been his own. Patsy had suffered from epilepsy and every treatment known at the time was tried to no avail.

Mount Vernon, June 20, 1773

DEAR SIR: It is an easier matter to conceive, than to describe the distress of this Family; especially that of the unhappy Parent of our Dear Patsy Custis, when I inform you that yesterday removed [*sic*] the Sweet Innocent Girl Entered into a more happy and peaceful abode than any she has met with in the afflicted Path she hitherto has trod.

She rose from Dinner about four o'clock in better health and spirits than she appeared to have been in for some time; soon after which she was seized with one of her usual Fits, and expired in it, in less than two minutes without uttering a word, a groan, or scarce a sigh. This sudden, and unexpected blow, I scarce need add has almost reduced my poor Wife to the lowest ebb of Misery; which is encreas'd by the absence of her son, (whom I have just fixed at the College in New York from whence I returned the 8th Inst) and want of the balmy consolation of her Relations; which leads me more than ever to wish she could see them, and that I was Master of Arguments powerful enough to prevail upon Mrs. Dandridge to make this place her entire and absolute home. I should think as she lives a lonesome life (Betsy being married) it might suit her well, and be agreeable, both to herself and my Wife, to me most assuredly it would.

I do not purpose to add more at present, the end of my writing being only to inform you of this unhappy change.

Our Sincere Affections are offered to Mrs. Bassett, Mrs. Dandridge, and all other Friends, and I am very sincerely

To GEORGE MUSE

The Squire of Mount Vernon, aroused to anger, speaks his mind to a claimant for lands to which, apparently, he was not entitled.

Mount Vernon, January 29, 1774

Sir: Your impertinent Letter of the 24th. ulto., was delivered to me yesterday by Mr. Smith. As I am not accustomed to receive such from any Man, nor would have taken the same language from you personally, without letting you feel some marks of my resentment; I would advise you to be cautious in writing me a second of the same tenour; for though I understand you were drunk when you did it, yet give me leave to tell you, that drunkness is no excuse for rudeness; and that, but for your stupidity and sottishness you might have known, by attending to the public Gazettes, (particularly Rinds of the 14th. of January last) that you had your full quantity of ten thousand acres of Land allowed you; that is, 9073 acres in the great Tract of 51,302 acres, and the remainder in the small tract of 927 acres; whilst I wanted near 500 acres of my quantity, Doctr. Craik of his, and almost every other claimant little or much of theirs. But suppose you had really fallen short 73 acres of your 10,000, do you think your superlative merit entitles you to greater indulgences than others? or that I was to make it good to you, if it did? when it was at the option of the Governor and Council to have allowed you but 500 acres in the whole, if they had been inclin'd so to do. If either of these should happen to be your opinion, I am very well convinced you will stand singular in it; and all my concern is, that I ever engag'd in behalf of so ungrateful and dirty a fellow as you are. But you may still stand in need of my assistance, as I can inform you that your affairs, in respect to these Lands, do not stand upon so solid a basis as you may imagine, and this you may take by way of hint; as your coming in for any, much less a full share may still be a disputed point, by a Gentleman who is not in this Country at this time, and who is exceedingly dissatisfied therewith. I wrote to you [him?] a few days ago concerning the other distribution, proposing an easy method of dividing our Lands; but since I find in what temper you are, I am sorry I took the trouble of mentioning the Land, or your name in a Letter, as I do not think you merit the least assistance from G: Washington.

To GEORGE WILLIAM FAIRFAX

Washington's account of the Virginia Resolutions is preceded by a statement concerning the rental of Belvoir and ends with details of the conveyance of the "Bloomery Tract," an iron works, omitted here because these observations are not germane to the development of his ideas on independence. The section of his letter to George William Fairfax preserved here expresses the colonists' and his own views on taxation without consent, the invasion of rights and privileges by the Mother Country, the stoppage of courts of justice and the scarcity of circulating cash due to England's despotic policy toward America.

Williamsburg, June 10, 1774

. . . Our Assembly met at this place the 4th. Ulto. according to Proragation, and was dissolved the 26th. for entering into a resolve of which the Inclosd is a Copy, and which the Govr. thought reflected too much upon his Majesty, and the British Parliament to pass over unnoticed; this Dissolution was as sudden as unexpected for there were other resolves of a much more spirited nature ready to be offerd to the House wch. would have been unanimously adopted respecting the Boston Port Bill as it is calld but were withheld till the Important business of the Country could be gone through. As the case stands the assembly sat In 22 day's for nothing, not a Bill being [   ] from the rising of the Court to the day of the Dissolution and came either to advise, or [   ] the Measure. The day after this Event the Members convend themselves at the Raleigh Tavern and enterd into the Inclosd Association which being followed two days after by an Express from Boston accompanied by the Sentiments of some Meetings in our Sister Colonies to the Northwd. the proceedings mentioned in the Inclos'd Papers were had thereupon and a general meeting requested of all the late Representatives in this City on the first of August when it is hopd, and expected that some vigorous [and effectual] meas-

ures will be effectually adopted to obtain that justice which is
denied to our Petitions and Remonstrances [and Prayers]; in
short the Ministry may rely on it that Americans will never be
tax'd without their own consent that the cause of Boston the
despotick Measures in respect to it I mean now is and ever will
be considered as the cause of America (not that we approve
their conduct in destroyg. the Tea) and that we shall not suffer
ourselves to be sacrificed by piece meals though god only knows
what is to become of us, threatned as we are with so many
hoverg. evils as hang over us at present; having a cruel and
blood thirsty Enemy upon our Backs, the Indians, between
whom and our Frontier Inhabitants many Skirmishes have
happnd, and with whom a general War is inevitable whilst
those from whom we have a right to seek protection are endeavouring by every piece of Art and despotism to fix the
Shackles of Slavery upon us. This Disolution which it is said
and believd, will not be followed by an Election till Instructions are receivd from the Ministry has left us without the
means of Defence except under the old Militia Invasion Laws
which are by no means adequate to the exigency's of the Country for from the best Accts. we have been able to get, there is a
confederacy of the Western, and Southern Indian's formd
against us and our Settlements over the Alligany Mountains indeed in Hampshire, Augusta &ca. are in the utmost Consternation and distress in short since the first Settlemt. of this Colony
the Minds of People in it never were more disturbd, or our
Situation so critical as at present; arising as I have said before
from an Invasion of our Rights and Priviledges by the Mother
Country; and our lives and properties by the Savages whilst
Cruel Frost succeeded by as cruel a drought contributed not a
little to our unhappy Situation, tho it is now thought the Injury done to wheat by the frost is not so great as was at first
apprehended; the present opinion being that take the Country
through half crops will be made; to these may be added and a
matter of no small moment they are that a total stop is now put
to our Courts of Justice (for want of a Fee Bill, which expird
the 12th. of April last) and the want of Circulating Cash
amongst Us; for shameful it is that the meeting of Merchants
which ought to have been at this place the 25th. of April, never

happend till Eight about 10 [days] ago, and I believe will break up in a manner very dissatisfactory to every one if not injurious to their Characters. . . .

To BRYAN FAIRFAX

The following three letters set forth with a feeling of outrage Washington's political views as they relate to Britain's disdainful attitude toward the colonies, her arbitrary assumption of the right to taxation, her attacks on the liberty and property of the people of Boston, her deprivation of the Massachusetts Bay charter and her determination to transport colonists for trial. Slow to indignation, Washington is now moving rapidly to the severance of his last ties of loyalty to England.

Mount Vernon, July 4, 1774

DEAR SIR: John* has just delivered to me your favor of yesterday, which I shall be obliged to answer in a more concise manner, than I could wish, as I am very much engaged in raising one of the additions to my house, which I think (perhaps it is fancy) goes on better whilst I am present, than in my absence from the workmen.

I own to you, Sir, I wished much to hear of your making an open declaration of taking a poll for this county, upon Colonel West's publicly declining last Sunday; and I should have written to you on the subject, but for information then received from several gentlemen in the churchyard, of your having refused to do so, for the reasons assigned in your letter; upon which, as I think the country never stood more in need of men of abilities and liberal sentiments than now, I entreated several gentlemen at our church yesterday to press Colonel Mason to take a poll, as I really think Major Broadwater, though a good man, might do as well in the discharge of his domestic concerns, as in the capacity of a legislator. And therefore I again express my wish, that either you or Colonel Mason would offer.

* John Alton.

I can be of little assistance to either, because I early laid it down as a maxim not to propose myself, and solicit for a second.

As to your political sentiments, I would heartily join you in them, so far as relates to a humble and dutiful petition to the throne, provided there was the most distant hope of success. But have we not tried this already? Have we not addressed the Lords, and remonstrated to the Commons? And to what end? Did they deign to look at our petitions? Does it not appear, as clear as the sun in its meridian brightness, that there is a regular, systematic plan formed to fix the right and practice of taxation upon us? Does not the uniform conduct of Parliament for some years past confirm this? Do not all the debates, especially those just brought to us, in the House of Commons on the side of government, expressly declare that America must be taxed in aid of the British funds, and that she has no longer resources within herself? Is there any thing to be expected from petitioning after this? Is not the attack upon the liberty and property of the people of Boston, before restitution of the loss to the India Company was demanded, a plain and self-evident proof of what they are aiming at? Do not the subsequent bills (now I dare say acts), for depriving the Massachusetts Bay of its charter, and for transporting offenders into other colonies or to Great Britain for trial, where it is impossible from the nature of the thing that justice can be obtained, convince us that the administration is determined to stick at nothing to carry its point? Ought we not, then, to put our virtue and fortitude to the severest test?

With you I think it a folly to attempt more than we can execute, as that will not only bring disgrace upon us, but weaken our cause; yet I think we may do more than is generally believed, in respect to the non-importation scheme. As to the withholding of our remittances, that is another point, in which I own I have my doubts on several accounts, but principally on that of justice; for I think, whilst we are accusing others of injustice, we should be just ourselves; and how this can be, whilst we owe a considerable debt, and refuse payment of it to Great Britain, is to me inconceivable. Nothing but the last extremity, I think, can justify it. Whether this is now come, is the question.

I began with telling you, that I was to write a short letter.

My paper informs me I have done otherwise. I shall hope to see you to-morrow, at the meeting of the county in Alexandria, when these points are to be considered. I am, dear Sir, your most obedient and humble servant.

To BRYAN FAIRFAX

Mount Vernon, July 20, 1774

DEAR SIR: Your letter of the 17th was not presented to me till after the resolutions (which were adjudged advisable for this county to come to) had been revised, altered, and corrected in the committee; nor till we had gone into a general meeting in the court-house, and my attention necessarily called every moment to the business that was before it. I did, however, upon receipt of it (in that hurry and bustle) hastily run it over, and handed it round to the gentlemen on the bench of which there were many; but, as no person present seemed in the least disposed to adopt your sentiments, as there appeared a perfect satisfaction and acquiescence in the measures proposed (except from a Mr. Williamson, who was for adopting your advice literally, without obtaining a second voice on his side), and as the gentlemen, to whom the letter was shown, advised me not to have it read, as it was not like to make a convert, and repugnant (some of them thought) to the very principle we were contending for, I forbore to offer it otherwise than in the manner above mentioned; which I shall be sorry for, if it gives you any dissatisfaction in not having your sentiments read to the county at large, instead of communicating them to the first people in it, by offering them the letter in the manner I did.

That I differ very widely from you, in respect to the mode of obtaining a defeat [repeal] of the acts so much and so justly complained of, I shall not hesitate to acknowledge; and that this difference in opinion may probably proceed from the different constructions we put upon the conduct and intention of the ministry may also be true; but, as I see nothing, on the one hand, to induce a belief that the Parliament would embrace a favorable opportunity of repealing acts, which they go on with great rapidity to pass, and in order to enforce their tyrannical system; and, on the other, I observe, or think I observe, that government is pursuing a regular plan at the expense of law and justice to overthrow our constitutional rights and liberties, how can I expect any redress from a measure, which has been ineffectually tried already? For, Sir, what is it we are contending against? Is it against paying the duty of three pence per pound on tea because burthensome? No, it is the right only, we have all along disputed, and to this end we have already petitioned his Majesty in as humble and dutiful manner as subjects could do. Nay, more, we applied to the House of Lords and House of Commons in their different legislative capacities, setting forth, that, as Englishmen, we could not be deprived of this essential and valuable part of a constitution. If, then, as the fact really is, it is against the right of taxation that we now do, and (as I before said) all along have contended, why should they suppose an exertion of this power would be less obnoxious now than formerly? And what reasons have we to believe, that they would make a second attempt, while the same sentiments filled the breast of every American, if they did not intend to enforce it if possible?

The conduct of the Boston people could not justify the rigor of their measures, unless there had been a requisition of payment and refusal of it; nor did that measure require an act to deprive the government of Massachusetts Bay of their charter, or to exempt offenders from trial in the place where offences were committed, as there was not, nor could not be, a single instance produced to manifest the necessity of it. Are not all these things self evident proofs of a fixed and uniform plan to tax us? If we want further proofs, do not all the debates in the Huse of Commons serve to confirm this? And has not General Gage's conduct since his arrival (in stopping the address of his Council, and publishing a proclamation more becoming a Turkish bashaw, than an English governor, declaring it treason to associate in any manner by which the commerce of Great Britain is to be affected) exhibited an unexampled testimony of the most despotic system of tyranny, that ever was practised in a free government? In short, what further proofs are wanted to satisfy one of the designs of the ministry, than their own acts, which are uniform and plainly tending to the same point, nay, if I mistake not, avowedly to fix the right of taxation? What hope then from petitioning, when they tell us, that now or never is the time to fix the matter? Shall we, after this, whine and cry for relief, when we have already tried it in vain? Or shall we supinely sit and see one province after another fall a prey to despotism? If I was in any doubt, as to the right which the Parliament of Great Britain had to tax us without our consent, I should most heartily coincide with you in opinion, that to petition, and petition only, is the proper method to apply for relief; because we should then be asking a favor, and not claiming a right, which, by the law of nature and our constitution, we are, in my opinion, indubitably entitled to. I should even think it criminal to go further than this, under such an idea; but none such I have. I think the Parliament of Great Britain hath no more right to put their hands into my pocket, without my consent, than I have to put my hands into yours for money; and this being already urged to them in a firm, but decent manner, by all the colonies, what reason is there to expect any thing from their justice?

As to the resolution for addressing the throne, I own to you, Sir, I think the whole might as well have been expunged. I expect nothing from the measure, nor should my voice have accompanied it, if the non-importation scheme was intended to be retarded by it; or I am convinced, as much as I am of my existence, that there is no relief but in their distress; and I think, at least I hope, that there is public virtue enough left among us to deny ourselves every thing but the bare necessaries of life to accomplish this end. This we have a right to do, and no power upon earth can compel us to do otherwise, till they have first reduced us to the most abject state of slavery that ever was designed for mankind. The stopping our exports would, no doubt, be a shorter cut than the other to effect this purpose; but if we owe money to Great Britain, nothing but the last necessity can justify the non-payment of it; and, therefore, I have great doubts upon this head, and wish to see the other method first tried, which is legal and will facilitate these payments.

I cannot conclude without expressing some concern, that I

should differ so widely in sentiment from you, in a matter of such great moment and general import; and should much distrust my own judgment upon the occasion, if my nature did not recoil at the thought of submitting to measures, which I think subversive of every thing that I ought to hold dear and valuable, and did I not find, at the same time, that the voice of mankind is with me.

I must apologize for sending you so rough a sketch of my thoughts upon your letter. When I looked back, and saw the length of my own, I could not, as I am also a good deal hurried at this time, bear the thoughts of making off a fair copy. I am, &c.

To BRYAN FAIRFAX

Mount Vernon, August 24, 1774

DEAR SIR: Your letter of the 5th instant came to this place, forwarded by Mr. Ramsay, a few days after my return from Williamsburg, and I delayed acknowledging it sooner, in the hopes that I should find time, before I began my other journey to Philadelphia, to answer it fully, if not satisfactorily; but, as much of my time has been engrossed since I came home by company, by your brother's sale and the business consequent thereupon, in writing letters to England, and now in attending to my own domestic affairs previous to my departure as above, I find it impossible to bestow so much time and attention to the subject matter of your letter as I could wish to do, and therefore, must rely upon your good nature and candor in excuse for not attempting it. In truth, persuaded as I am, that you have read all the political pieces, which compose a large share of the *Gazette* at this time, I should think it, but for your request, a piece of inexcusable arrogance in me, to make the least essay towards a change in your political opinions; for I am sure I have no new lights to throw upon the subject, or any other arguments to offer in support of my own doctrine, than what you have seen; and could only in general add, that an innate spirit of freedom first told me, that the measures, which administration hath for some time been, and now are most violently pursuing, are repugnant to every principle of natural justice; whilst much abler heads than my own hath fully convinced me, that it is not only repugnant to natural right, but subversive of the laws and constitution of Great Britain itself, in the establishment of which some of the best blood in the kingdom hath been spilt. Satisfied, then, that the acts of a British Parliament are no longer governed by the principles of justice, that it is trampling upon the valuable rights of Americans, confirmed to them by charter and the constitution they themselves boast of, and convinced beyond the smallest doubt, that these measures are the result of deliberation, and attempted to be carried into execution by the hand of power, is it a time to trifle, or risk our cause upon petitions, which with difficulty obtain access, and afterwards are thrown by with the utmost contempt? Or should we, because heretofore unsuspicious of design, and then unwilling to enter into disputes with the mother country, go on to bear more, and forbear to enumerate our just causes of complaint? For my own part, I shall not undertake to say where the line between Great Britain and the colonies should be drawn; but I am clearly of opinion, that one ought to be drawn, and our rights clearly ascertained. I could wish, I own, that the dispute had been left to posterity to determine, but the crisis is arrived when we must assert our rights, or submit to every imposition, that can be heaped upon us, till custom and use shall make us as tame and abject slaves, as the blacks we rule over with such arbitrary sway.

I intended to have wrote no more than an apology for not writing; but I find I am insensibly running into a length I did not expect, and therefore shall conclude with remarking, that, if you disavow the right of Parliament to tax us (unrepresented as we are) we only differ in respect to the mode of opposition, and this difference principally arises from your belief, that they—the Parliament, I mean—want a decent opportunity to repeal the acts; whilst I am as fully convinced, as I am of my own existence, that there has been a regular, systematic plan formed to enforce them, and that nothing but unanimity in the colonies (a stroke they did not expect) and firmness, can prevent it. It seems from the best advices from Boston, that General Gage is exceedingly disconcerted at the quiet and steady conduct of the people of the Massachusetts Bay, and at the measures pursuing by the other governments; as I dare say he expected to have forced those oppressed people into compliance, or irritated them to acts of violence before this, for a more colorable pretense of ruling that and the other colonies with a high hand. But I am done.

I shall set off on Wednesday next for Philadelphia, whither, if you have any commands, I shall be glad to oblige you in them; being, dear Sir, with real regard, &c.

P. S. Pray what do you think of the Canada Bill?

To CAPTAIN ROBERT MACKENZIE

Robert MacKenzie, who had served as a captain in the Virginia Regiment under Washington, was offended by the behavior of the people of Boston toward their British rulers. He contended that their rebellious citizens-in-arms left General Gage no other recourse but to suppress them by force. In their defense, Washington here argues in substance that violence begets violence and that the colonists had been driven to desperate measures by the tyrannical acts of Parliament. Prophetically he says: ". . . more blood will be spilt on this occasion, if the ministry are determined to push matters to extremity, than history has ever yet furnished instances of in the annals of North America, and such a vital wound given to the peace of this great country, as time itself cannot cure, or eradicate the remembrance of."

Philadelphia, October 9, 1774

DEAR SIR: Your letter of the 13th. ultimo from Boston gave me pleasure, as I learnt thereby, that you were well, and might be expected at Mount Vernon in your way to or from James River, in the course of the winter.

When I have said this, permit me with the freedom of a friend (for you know I always esteemed you) to express my sorrow, that fortune should place you in a service, that must fix curses to the latest posterity upon the diabolical contrivers, and, if success (which, by the by, is impossible) accompanies it, execrations upon all those, who have been instrumental in the execution.

I do not mean by this to insinuate, that an officer is not to discharge his duty, even when chance, not choice, has placed him in a disagreeable situation; but I conceive, when you condemn the conduct of the Massachusetts people, you reason from effects, not causes; otherwise you would not wonder at a people, who are every day receiving fresh proofs of a systematic assertion of an arbitrary power, deeply planned to overturn the laws and constitution of their country, and to violate the most essential and valuable rights of mankind, being irritated, and with difficulty restrained from acts of the greatest violence and intemperance. For my own part, I confess to you candidly, that I view things in a very different point of light to the one in which you seem to consider them; and though you are led to believe by venal men, for such I must take the liberty of calling those new-fangled counsellors, which fly to and surround you, and all others, who, for honorary or pecuniary gratifications, will lend their aid to overturn the constitution, and introduce a system of arbitrary government, although you are taught, I say, by discoursing with such men, to believe, that the people of Massachusetts are rebellious, setting up for independency, and what not, give me leave, my good friend, to tell you, that you are abused, grossly abused, and this I advance with a degree of confidence and boldness, which may claim your belief, having better opportunities of knowing the real sentiments of the people you are among, from the leaders of them, in opposition to the present measures of the administration, than you have from those whose business it is, not to disclose truths, but to misrepresent facts in order to justify as much as possible to the world their own conduct; for give me leave to add, and I think I can announce it as a fact, that it is not the wish or interest of that government, or any other upon this continent, separately or collectively, to set up for independency; but this you may at the same time rely on, that none of them will ever submit to the loss of those valuable rights and privileges, which are essential to the happiness of every free state, and without which, life, liberty, and property are rendered totally insecure.

These, Sir, being certain consequences, which must naturally result from the late acts of Parliament relative to America in general, and the government of Massachusetts Bay in particular, is it to be wondered at, I repeat, that men, who wish to avert the impending blow, should attempt to oppose it in its progress, or prepare for their defence, if it cannot be diverted? Surely I may be allowed to answer in the negative; and again give me leave to add as my opinion, that more blood will be spilt on this occasion, if the ministry are determined to push matters to extremity, than history has ever yet furnished instances of in the annals of North America, and such a vital wound given to the peace of this great country, as time itself cannot cure, or eradicate the remembrance of.

But I have done. I was involuntarily led into a short discussion of this subject by your remarks on the conduct of the Boston people, and your opinion of their wishes to set up for independency. I am as well satisfied as I can be of my existence that no such thing is desired by any thinking man in all North America; on the contrary, that it is the ardent wish of the warmest advocates for liberty, that peace and tranquility, upon constitutional grounds, may be restored, and the horrors of civil discord prevented.

I am very glad to hear that my friend Stewart was well when you left London. I have not had a letter from him these five years, nor heard of him I think for two. I wish you had mentioned his employment, poor Mercer! I often hear from him; much cause has he, I fear, to lament his having fallen into the accursed state of attendance and dependance. I remain with very great esteem, dear Sir.

To GEORGE WILLIAM FAIRFAX

The Battle of Lexington brought home to Washington the full realization that the alternative between fighting and sub-

*mitting to tyranny had finally to be faced. No virtuous man, he
here insists, can hesitate in such a choice.*

Philadelphia, May 31, 1775

DEAR SIR: Since my last (dated about the first of April) I
have received from Mr. Craven Peyton the Sum of £193.6.10
(as you may see by the enclosed Account) with which, and the
Balance of the former Money, I now remit you the following
Bills; to wit, One drawn by Mr. Thomas Contee on Mr. Mollison, for £40 Sterling, and another drawn by Lyonel Bradstreet
on Mr. William Tippell of London for the like Sum (indorsed
by Mr. Contee; the strongest assurances being given me, that
they are both good) Mr. Contee is Mr. Mollison's principal
Factor, or Agent, in Maryland, and is besides a Man of property
himself; but notwithstanding this, the times are so ticklish, that
there is no such thing as answering for the payment of Bills.
You must therefore, either take the chance of receiving bad
ones, or suffer your Money to lay dead.

I have also, since my coming to this place, purchased a Bill
from Messieurs Willing and Morris of £161.5.10 Sterling,
which will, I believe, for I have not a state of our Account with
me, about Balance it. With the Copy of Mr. Peyton's Account,
you will receive a List of the Rents which he collected since last
settlement; and these, as I have not been favoured with a Line
from you, since your Letter of June, is all I recollect at present
worth communicating relative to your business.

Before this Letter can reach you, you must, undoubtedly,
have received an Account of the engagement in the Massachusetts Bay between the Ministerial Troops (for we do not, nor
cannot yet prevail upon ourselves to call them the King's
Troops) and the Provincials of that Government; But as you
may not have heard how that affair began, I inclose you the
several Affidavits that were taken after the Action.

General Gage acknowledges, that the detachment under
Lieutenant Colonel Smith was sent out to destroy private property; or, in other Words, to destroy a Magazine which self pres-

ervation obliged the Inhabitants to establish. And he also confesses, in effect at least, that his Men made a very precipitate retreat from Concord, notwithstanding the reinforcement under Lord Piercy, the last of which may serve to convince Lord Sandwich (and others of the same sentiment) that the Americans will fight for their Liberties and property, however pusilanimous, in his Lordship's Eye, they may appear in other respects.

From the best Accounts I have been able to collect of that affair; indeed from every one, I believe the fact, stripped of all colouring, to be plainly this, that if the retreat had not been as precipitate as it was (and God knows it could not well have been more so) the Ministerial Troops must have surrendered, or been totally cut off: For they had not arrived in Charlestown (under cover of their Ships) half an hour, before a powerful body of Men from Marblehead and Salem were at their heels, and must, if they had happened to have been up one hour sooner, inevitably intercepted their retreat to Charlestown. Unhappy it is though to reflect, that a Brother's Sword has been sheathed in a Brother's breast, and that, the once happy and peaceful plains of America are either to be drenched with Blood, or Inhabited by Slaves. Sad alternative! But can a virtuous Man hesitate in his choice?

Part Two

THE REVOLUTIONARY PERIOD

ACCEPTANCE OF APPOINTMENT AS GENERAL AND COMMANDER IN CHIEF

Washington's commission as General and Commander in Chief was ordered by Congress and signed by its President, John Hancock. The official document is dated Philadelphia, June 19, 1775, and thus postdates Washington's acceptance by three days. This seeming anticipation of the event is accounted for by the time required after the appointment for the drafting and engraving of the actual certificate.

June 16, 1775

MR. PRESIDENT: Tho' I am truly sensible of the high Honour done me in this Appointment, yet I feel great distress from a consciousness that my abilities and Military experience may not be equal to the extensive and important Trust: However, as the Congress desires I will enter upon the momentous duty, and exert every power I Possess In their Service for the Support of the glorious Cause: I beg they will accept my most cordial thanks for this distinguished testimony of their Approbation.

But lest some unlucky event should happen unfavourable to my reputation, I beg it may be remembered by every Gentn in the room, that I this day declare with the utmost sincerity, I do not think my self equal to the Command I am honoured with.

As to pay, Sir, I beg leave to Assure the Congress that as no pecuniary consideration could have tempted me to have accepted this Arduous employment [at the expence of my domestt. ease and happiness] I do not wish to make any proffit from it: I will keep an exact Account of my expences; those I doubt not they will discharge and that is all I desire.

To MRS. MARTHA WASHINGTON

Among the few personal letters addressed to her which Mrs. Washington did not destroy is this expression of the new Commander in Chief's feelings two days after his acceptance of his commission. Its tone is solemn and determined. Hardly an ardent letter, it nonetheless conveys a pang at parting and a certain reluctance about taking the field after seventeen years of retirement from military life.

Philadelphia, June 18, 1775

My Dearest: I am now set down to write to you on a subject, which fills me with inexpressible concern, and this concern is greatly aggravated and increased, when I reflect upon the uneasiness I know it will give you. It has been determined in Congress, that the whole army raised for the defence of the American cause shall be put under my care, and that it is necessary for me to proceed immediately to Boston to take upon me the command of it.

You may believe me, my dear Patsy, when I assure you, in the most solemn manner that, so far from seeking this appointment, I have used every endeavor in my power to avoid it, not only from my unwillingness to part with you and the family, but from a consciousness of its being a trust too great for my capacity, and that I should enjoy more real happiness in one month with you at home, than I have the most distant prospect of finding abroad, if my stay were to be seven times seven years. But as it has been a kind of destiny, that has thrown me upon this service, I shall hope that my undertaking it is designed to answer some good purpose. You might, and I suppose did perceive, from the tenor of my letters, that I was apprehensive I could not avoid this appointment, as I did not pretend to intimate when I should return. That was the case. It was utterly out of my power to refuse this appointment, without exposing my character to such censures, as would have reflected dishonor upon myself, and given pain to my friends. This, I am sure, could not, and ought not, to be pleasing to you, and must have lessened me considerably in my own esteem. I shall rely, therefore, confidently on that Providence, which has heretofore preserved and been bountiful to me, not doubting but that I shall return safe to you in the fall. I shall feel no pain from the toil or the danger of the campaign; my unhappiness will flow from the uneasiness I know you will feel from being left alone. I therefore beg, that you will summon your whole fortitude, and pass your time as agreeably as possible. Nothing will give me so much sincere satisfaction as to hear this, and to hear it from your own pen. My earnest and ardent desire is, that you would pursue any plan that is most likely to produce content, and a tolerable degree of tranquillity; as it must add greatly to my uneasy feelings to hear, that you are dissatisfied or complaining at what I really could not avoid.

As life is always uncertain, and common prudence dictates to every man the necessity of settling his temporal concerns, while it is in his power, and while the mind is calm and undisturbed, I have, since I came to this place (for I had not time to do it before I left home) got Colonel Pendleton to draft a will for me, by the directions I gave him, which will I now enclose. The provision made for you in case of my death will, I hope, be agreeable.

I shall add nothing more, as I have several letters to write, but to desire that you will remember me to your friends, and to assure you that I am, with the most unfeigned regard, my dear Patsy, your affectionate, &c.

To BURWELL BASSETT

With genuine modesty and a true understanding of the realities Washington writes to Colonel Burwell Bassett of his reluctance to give up the serene existence at Mount Vernon for the hazards of command. He even refers to the political motives back of his selection and hints at the penalty of failure. With complete candor he balances his belief in the justice of the cause, close attention to its prosecution and the strictest integrity against his untried abilities and lack of experience.

Philadelphia, June 19, 1775

DEAR SIR: I am now Imbarked on a tempestuous Ocean, from whence perhaps, no friendly harbour is to be found. I have been called upon by the unanimous Voice of the Colonies to the Command of the Continental Army. It is an honour I by no means aspired to. It is an honour I wished to avoid, as well from an unwillingness to quit the peaceful enjoyment of my Family, as from a through conviction of my own Incapacity and want of experience in the conduct of so momentous a concern; but the partiallity of the Congress, added to some political motives, left me without a choice. May God grant, therefore, that my acceptance of it, may be attended with some good to the common cause, and without Injury (from want of knowledge) to my own reputation. I can answer but for three things, a firm belief of the justice of our Cause, close attention in the prosecution of it, and the strictest Integrity. If these cannot supply the place of Ability and Experience, the cause will suffer, and more than probable my character along with it, as reputation derives its principal support from success; but it will be remembered, I hope, that no desire or insinuation of mine, placed me in this situation. I shall not be deprived therefore of a comfort in the worst event if I retain a consciousness of having acted to the best of my judgment.

I am at liberty to tell you that the Congress in committee (which will I dare say, be agreed to when reported) have consented to a Continental Currency, and have ordered two million of Dollars to be struck for payment of the Troops, and other expenses arising from our defence, as also that 15,000 Men are voted as a Continental Army, which will I dare say be augmented as more Troops are Imbarked and Imbarking for America than was expected at the time of passing that vote. As to other Articles of Intelligence I must refer you to the Gazettes as the Printers pick up every thing that is stirring in that way.

The other Officers in the higher departments are not yet fixed, therefore I cannot give you their names. I set out tomorrow for Boston, where I shall always be glad to hear from you. My best wishes attend Mrs. Bassett, Mrs. Dandridge, and all our relations and friends. In great haste, as I have many Letters to write, and other business to do. I remain with the sincerest regards, Dear Sir, &c.

P. S. I must entreat you and Mrs. Bassett if possible to visit at Mt. Vernon, as also my Wife's other friends. I could wish you to take her down, as I have no expectation of returning till Winter and feel great uneasiness at her lonesome situation. I have sent my Chariot and Horses back.

To THE CAPTAINS OF SEVERAL INDEPENDENT COMPANIES IN VIRGINIA

On the eve of his departure for Boston, Washington bade farewell to his old comrades-in-arms of the Virginia Regiment. Again he disclaims any special qualifications for the task and again adverts to the political motives of Congress in appointing him. These, in historical perspective, were to bind the South to the North and satisfy both the planters and the merchants.

Philadelphia, June 20, 1775

GENTLEMEN: I am now about to bid adieu to the companies under your respective commands, at least for a while. I have launched into a wide and extensive field, too boundless for my abilities, and far, very far, beyond my experience. I am called, by the unanimous voice of the Colonies, to the command of the Continental army; an honor I did not aspire to; and honor I was solicitous to avoid, upon a full conviction of my inadequacy to the importance of the service. The partiality of the Congress, however, assisted by a political motive, rendered my reasons unavailing, and I shall to-morrow set out for the camp near Boston.

I have only to beg of you, therefore, before I go (especially as you did me the honor to put your companies under my direction, and know not how soon you may be called upon in Virginia for an exertion of your military skill) by no means to relax in the discipline of your respective companies. I have the honor to be, etc.

To MRS. MARTHA WASHINGTON

The battle of Bunker Hill had been fought on June 17th and word of the defeat, which in effect was a triumph and was acclaimed as such by the colonists, reached Washington when he was twenty miles out of Philadelphia on his way by slow stages to New York and Boston. Just before his cavalcade left Philadelphia, he wrote a last note to his wife.

Philadelphia, June 23, 1775

MY DEAREST: As I am within a few minutes of leaving this city, I would not think of departing from it with out dropping you a line, especially as I do not know whether it may be in my power to write again till I get to the camp at Boston. I go fully trusting in that providence, which has been more bountiful to me than I deserve and in full confidence of a happy meeting with you some time in the fall. I have no time to add more as I am surrounded with company to take leave of me. I return an unalterable affection for you which neither time or distance can change my best love to Jack and Nelly and regard for the rest of the family; conclude me with the utmost truth and Sincerity, Yr. entire.

To THE PRESIDENT OF CONGRESS

The newly appointed Commander in Chief left Philadelphia on June 23rd. His destination was Cambridge, Mass., by way of Trenton, New Brunswick, Newark, Hoboken, N. J.; New York City, Kingsbridge, New Rochelle, N. Y.; New Haven,

Hartford, Wethersfield, Conn.; Springfield, Worcester and Watertown, Mass.

New York, June 24 [25], 1775

GENTLEMEN: The Rain on Friday Afternoon and Saturday the Advice of several Gentlemen of the Jerseys' and this City, by no Means to cross Hudsons River at the lower Ferry and some other Occurrences too trivial to mention (which happened on the Road) prevented my arrival at this place until the Afternoon of this day. In the morning, after giving General Schuyler such Orders, as, from the result of my Inquiry into matters here, appear necessary, I shall set out on my Journey to the Camp at Boston and shall proceed with all the dispatch in my Power.

Powder is so essential an Article that I cannot help again repeating the necessity of a supply. The Camp at Boston, from the best Accounts I can get from thence, is but very poorly supplied. At this place they have scarce any. how they are provided in General Wooster's Camp I have not been able yet to learn.

Governor Tryon is arrived and General Schuyler directed to advise you of the line of Conduct he moves in. I fear it will not be very favourable to the American Cause. I have only to add that I am with the greatest respect and regard, etc.

To MAJOR GENERAL PHILIP SCHUYLER

Washington's first orders to one of his generals includes a warning against the Governor of New York, William Tryon, who was fiercely antagonistic to the cause of Independence. The inhabitants of New York were largely anti-Revolutionary, and they gave strong support to their royalist Governor. On the day of Washington's arrival in New York City an embarrassing contretemps was averted. Tryon was due to land from England just as Washington was approaching the city. Fortunately, the General arrived in the afternoon and was accorded full military honors. When Tryon reached the city in the evening his recep-

tion took place at eight. It was a repeat performance, with the oratory this time in praise of the Crown.

New York, June 25, 1775

Sir: You are to take upon you the Command of all the Troops destined for the New York Department, and see that the Orders of the Continental Congress are carried into Execution, with as much Precision and Exactness as possible. For your better Government therein you are herewith furnished with a Copy of the Instructions given to me by that Hon'e Body. Such Parts thereof as are within the Line of your Duty, you will please to pay particular Attention to. Delay no Time in occupying the several Posts, recommended by the Provincial Congress of this Colony, and putting them in a fit Posture, to answer the End designed: neither delay any Time in securing the Stores, which are or ought to have been removed from this City by Order of the Continental Congress. Keep a watchful Eye upon Governor Tryon, and if you find him directly or indirectly, attempting any Measures inimical to the common Cause, use every Means in your Power to frustrate his Designs. It is not in my Power, at this Time, to point out the Mode by which this End is to be accomplished; but if forcible Measures are judged necessary, (respecting the Person of the Governor) I should have no Difficulty in ordering of it, if the Continental Congress was not sitting; but as this is the Case, the seizing of a Governor quite a new Thing and of exceeding great Importance, I must refer you to that Body for Direction, in Case His Excelly. the Governor should make any Move towards increasing the Strength of the Tory Party, or in arming them against the Cause we are embarked in. In like Manner watch the Movements of the Indian Agent (Col. Guy Johnston) and prevent, as far as you can, the Effect of his Influence to our Prejudice with the Indians. Obtain the best Information you can of the Temper and Disposition of those People, and also of the Canadians, that a proper Line may be mark'd out to conciliate their good Opinion, or facilitate any future Operation.

The Posts on Lake Champlain, &c., you will please to have

properly supplied with Provisions and Ammunition, and this I am persuaded you will aim at doing, on the best Terms, to prevent our good Cause from sinking under a heavy Load of Expence.

You will be pleased also to make regular Returns to me, once a Month and to the Continental Congress, and oftener as Occurrences may require, of the Forces under your Command, of your Provisions Stores &c. and give me the earliest Advices of every Piece of Intelligence; which you shall judge of Importance to be speedily known. Your own good Sense must govern in all Matters not particularly pointed out, as I do not wish to circumscribe you within narrow Limits. I remain with great Regard, etc.

To THE NEW YORK LEGISLATURE

In the Tory stronghold of New York, Washington, with consummate tact, promises the re-establishment of peace and harmony between the Mother Country and the colonies when the issues of the war are settled. Here, for the first time, he enunciates the famous principle that the soldier is, above all, the citizen.

June 26, 1775

GENTLEMEN: At the same time that with you I deplore the unhappy necessity of such an Appointment, as that with which I am now honoured, I cannot but feel sentiments of the highest gratitude for this affecting Instance of distinction and Regard.

May your every wish be realized in the success of America, at this important and interesting Period; and be assured that the every exertion of my worthy Colleagues and myself will be equally extended to the re-establishment of Peace and Harmony between the Mother Country and the Colonies, as to the fatal, but necessary, operations of War. When we assumed the Soldier, we did not lay aside the Citizen; and we shall most

sincerely rejoice with you in that happy hour when the establishment of American Liberty, upon the most firm and solid
foundations, shall enable us to return to our Private Stations
in the bosom of a free, peaceful and happy Country. I am etc.

ANSWER TO AN ADDRESS
OF THE MASSACHUSETTS LEGISLATURE

*Escorted by a deputation which met him at Springfield,
Washington, accompanied by General Charles Lee, entered
Cambridge on July 2nd to a thunderous reception. On the following day he took formal command of the army and began to
inform himself on the strength and disposition of the contending forces. In his reply to the Massachusetts Legislature's welcome to the province, Washington candidly admits that as yet
he knows little about the state of the army he has undertaken
to lead.*

July 4, 1775

Gentlemen: Your kind congratulations on my appointment and arrival, demand my warmest acknowledgments, and
will ever be retained in grateful remembrance.

In exchanging the enjoyments of domestic life for the duties
of my present honorable but arduous station, I only emulate
the virtue and public spirit of the whole province of the Massachusetts Bay, which, with a firmness and patriotism without
example in modern history, have sacrificed all the comforts of
social and political life, in support of the rights of mankind,
and the welfare of our common country. My highest ambition
is to be the happy instrument of vindicating those rights, and
to see this devoted province again restored to peace, liberty, and
safety.

The short space of time, which has elapsed since my arrival,
does not permit me to decide upon the state of the army. The
course of human affairs forbids an expectation that troops
formed under such circumstances should at once possess the

order, regularity, and discipline of veterans. Whatever deficiencies there may be, will, I doubt not, soon be made up by the activity and zeal of the officers, and the docility and obedience of the men. These qualities, united with their native bravery and spirit, will afford a happy presage of success, and put a final period to those distresses, which now overwhelm this once happy country.

I most sincerely thank you, Gentlemen, for your declaration of readiness at all times to assist me in the discharge of the duties of my station. They are so complicated and extended, that I shall need the assistance of every good man, and lover of his country. I therefore repose the utmost confidence in your aid.

In return for your affectionate wishes to myself, permit me to say, that I earnestly implore the divine Being, in whose hands are all human events, to make you and your constituents as distinguished in private and public happiness, as you have been by ministerial oppression, and private and public distress.

GENERAL ORDERS

The first of the General Orders to the army, like all the others which were to be issued with great frequency through the eight years of the Revolutionary War, indicates Washington's scrupulous concern for details, whether dealing with appointments, ordnance, supplies, discipline, hygiene, furloughs, or court-martial, while always stressing the cause of Independence. The Parole and Countersign were changed almost daily as passwords to distinguish friend from foe.

Head Quarters, Cambridge, July 4, 1775

Parole Abington. Countersign Bedford.

Exact returns to be made by the proper Officers of all the Provisions Ordnance, Ordnance Stores, Powder, Lead working Tools of all kinds, Tents, Camp Kettles, and all other Stores under their respective care, belonging to the Armies at Roxbury and Cambridge. The commanding Officer of each Regiment to make a return of the number of blankets wanted to compleat every Man with one at least.

The Hon: Artemus Ward, Charles Lee, Philip Schuyler, and Israel Putnam Esquires are appointed Major Generals of the American Army, and due obedience is to be paid them as such. The Continental Congress not having compleated the appointments of the other officers in said army nor had sufficient time to prepare and forward their Commissions; any officer is to continue to do duty in the Rank and Station he at present holds, until further orders.

Thomas Mifflin Esqr: is appointed by the General one of his Aid-de-Camps. Joseph Reed Esqr. is in like manner appointed Secretary to the General, and they are in future to be consider'd and regarded as such.

The Continental Congress having now taken all the Troops of the several Colonies, which have been raised, or which may be hereafter raised for the support and defence of the Liberties of America; into their Pay and Service. They are now the Troops of the UNITED PROVINCES of North America; and it is hoped that all Distinctions of Colonies will be laid aside; so that one and the same Spirit may animate the whole, and the only Contest be, who shall render, on this great and trying occasion, the most essential service to the Great and common cause in which we are all engaged.

It is required and expected that exact discipline be observed, and due Subordination prevail thro' the whole Army, as a Failure in these most essential points must necessarily produce extreme Hazard, Disorder and Confusion; and end in shameful disappointment and disgrace.

The General most earnestly requires, and expects, a due observance of those articles of war, established for the Government of the army, which forbid profane cursing, swearing and drunkeness; And in like manner requires and expects, of all Officers, and Soldiers, not engaged on actual duty, a punctual attendance on divine Service, to implore the blessings of heaven upon the means used for our safety and defence.

All Officers are required and expected to pay diligent Attention to keep their Men neat and clean; to visit them often at their quarters, and inculcate upon them the necessity of cleanliness, as essential to their health and service. They are particularly to see, that they have Straw to lay on, if to be had, and to make it known if they are destitute of this article. They are also to take care that Necessarys be provided in the Camps and frequently filled up to prevent their being offensive and unhealthy. Proper Notice will be taken of such Officers and Men, as distinguish themselves by their attention to these necessary duties.

The commanding Officer of each Regiment is to take particular care that not more than two Men of a Company be absent on furlough at the same time, unless in very extraordinary cases.

Col. Gardner is to be buried to morrow at 3, O'Clock, P. M. with the military Honors due to so brave and gallant an Officer, who fought, bled and died in the Cause of his country and mankind. His own Regiment, except the company at Malden, to attend on this mournful occasion. The places of those Companies in the Lines on Prospect Hill, to be supplied by Col. Glovers regiment till the funeral is over.

No Person is to be allowed to go to Fresh-water pond a fishing or on any other occasion as there may be danger of introducing the small pox into the army.

It is strictly required and commanded that there be no firing of Cannon or small Arms from any of the Lines, or elsewhere, except in case of necessary, immediate defence, or special order given for that purpose.

All Prisoners taken, Deserters coming in, Persons coming out of Boston, who can give any Intelligence; any Captures of any kind from the Enemy, are to be immediately reported and brought up to Head Quarters in Cambridge.

Capt. Griffin is appointed Aide-de-Camp to General Lee and to be regarded as such.

The Guard for the security of the Stores at Watertown, is to be increased to thirty men immediately.

A Serjeant and six men to be set as a Guard to the Hospital, and are to apply to Doctor Rand.

Complaint having been made against John White Quarter Master of Col. Nixon's Regmt. for misdemeanors in drawing out Provisions for more Men than the Regiment consisted of; a Court Martial consisting of one Captain and four Subalterns is ordered to be held on said White, who are to enquire, determine and report.

GENERAL ORDERS

Within a few days of his arrival in Cambridge, Washington was made acutely aware of the deficiencies of the army under his command. Discipline was at low ebb; straggling, negligence, casual shifts from one regiment to another, disdain of orders, petty thievery were all too common. First acquaintance with actual conditions was followed without hesitation by rigorous attempts to bring a kind of order out of the chaos.

Head Quarters, Cambridge, July 7, 1775

Parole Dorchester. Countersign Exeter.

It is with inexpressible Concern that the General upon his first Arrival in the army, should find an Officer sentenced by a General Court-Martial to be cashier'd for Cowardice. A Crime of all others, the most infamous in a Soldier, the most injurious to an Army, and the last to be forgiven; inasmuch as it may, and often does happen, that the Cowardice of a single Officer may prove the Distruction of the whole Army: The General therefore (tho' with great Concern, and more especially, as the Transaction happened before he had the Command of the Troops) thinks himself obliged for the good of the service, to approve the Judgment of the Court-Martial with respect to Capt. John Callender, who is hereby sentenced to be cashiered. Capt. John Callender is accordingly cashiered and dismiss'd from all farther service in the Continental Army as an Officer.

The General having made all due inquiries, and maturely consider'd this matter is to led to the above determination not only from the particular Guilt of Capt. Callender, but the fatal Consequences of such Conduct to the army and to the cause of america.

He now therefore most earnestly exhorts Officers of all Ranks to shew an example of Bravery and Courage to their men; assuring them that such as do their duty in the day of Battle, as brave and good Officers, shall be honor'd with every mark of distinction and regard; their names and merits made known to the General Congress and all America: while on the other hand, he positively declares that every Officer, be his rank what it may, who shall betray his Country, dishonour the Army and his General, by basely keeping back and shrinking from his duty in any engagement; shall be held up as an infamous Coward and punish'd as such, with the utmost martial severity; and no Connections, Interest or Intercessions in his behalf will avail to prevent the strict execution of justice.

Capt. Scotts and Capt. Styler's Company's from New Hampshire, are to be incorporated, or added to Col. Sergants Regiment, agreeable to the application made for that purpose. No Officer or Soldier posted in the Lines for the defence of them, on Prospect Hill, on Winter Hill, or elsewhere, are upon any account to sleep out of their encampment or leave it at night. The Troops from New Hampshire are particularly requir'd to attend to this Order, from their particular Circumstances of situation.

No Soldier, belonging to these Post's or elsewhere, to be suffered to straggle at a distance from their respective parade, on any pretence, without leave from his Officers: As an unguarded Hour, may prove fatal to the whole army, and to the noble Cause in which we are engaged. The Importance of which, to every man of common understanding must inspire every good Officer and Soldier, with the noblest Ardour and strictest attention, least he should prove the fatal Instrument of our ruin.

The Adjutant General is required, to make a return as quick as possible of the Troops in Cambridge, their number and the duty they do.

Complaints having been made with respect to the Bread, as being sour and unwholesome; the Quarter Master General is hereby directed to enquire into the matter and report upon it: At the same time to inform the Bakers that if any Complaints are made, and they shall be found just, they will be most severely punished.

The Guards on the Roads leading to Bunker's Hill, are ordered not to suffer any person to pass them, unless an Officer is sent down from the Lines to order it, or they will be severely punished.

The General has great Reason; and is highly displeased, with the Negligence and Inattention of those Officers, who have placed as Centries at the out-posts, Men with whose Character they are not acquainted. He therefore orders, that for the future, no Man shall be appointed to those important Stations, who is not a Native of this Country, or has a Wife, or Family in it, to whom he is known to be attached. This Order is to be consider'd as a standing one and the Officers are to pay obedience to it at their peril.

A Complaint of the most extraordinary kind, having been made to the General, that Soldiers inlisted in one Regiment, have been seduced to reinlist into others, by Agents employed for that purpose under the specious promises of money, or leave of absence from the Army, a procedure so subversive of all order, discipline, and of the very Existance of the army, cannot be forgiven, the strictest Orders are therefore given against such practices, and the General most earnestly declares, that if any Agent or Soldier, shall hereafter be found so offending, he will punish them with the utmost severity.

A General Court Martial having sat upon William Pattin and reported, that no Evidence appeared against him, to support the Charge; the General defers his decision upon the Report, untill farther consideration. In the meantime, the Adjutant General is ordered to wait on Col. Ward, by whom the Prisoner was confin'd and learn from him upon whose complaint and what Witnesses, there are to support it.

A regimental Court Martial is ordered to sit to morrow 10 oClock, on Samuel Bartlett of the Company late Capt. Callenders, and Col. Gridley's Regiment, confin'd for "abusive behaviour."

A General Court Martial to sit to morrow, 10 oClock A. M. for the Trial of Thomas Danieby, charged with "stealing", each of the above Prisoners to have Notice to day, and the Witnesses in like manner order'd to attend.

In order that all the sick and wounded in the Army may be provided for, and taken Care of in the best way and manner possible: It is order'd that when any Officer or Soldier is so ill, either by a Wound, or otherwise, that the Surgeon of the Regt. to which he belongs finds he cannot be properly taken care of in such Regt. such Surgeon shall send him to the Camp Hospital to which they belong, with a Certificate of the Man's Name, the Company to which he belongs, and in that case the Surgeon of the Hospital shall receive said sick and wounded and in case such Hospital shall be too full, in that case the Surgeon of said Hospital shall send such of his patients, as may be removed with safety, to the Hospital at Water-town, with the like Certificate as above, on which the Surgeon of Water-town Hospital is to receive, and take care of him.

To THE MASSACHUSETTS LEGISLATURE

One of Washington's major problems in regard to the militia was due to an unwillingness to call men who were engaged in bringing in the harvest. The Committees of Congress to which he here refers were responsible for safety and supplies and were authorized to confer directly with the Commander in Chief. The fewer than 14,500 men in the entire army actually outnumbered the enemy in and around Boston, but the advantages of position, equipment and discipline were overwhelmingly on the side of the British.

Head Quarters, Cambridge, July 10, 1775

SIR: After much difficulty and delay, I have procured such Returns of the State of the Army as will enable us to form a Judgment of its Strength. It is with great Concern I find it far inadequate to our General expectations and the Duties that may be required of it; the Number of Men fit for Duty in the

Forts Raised in this Province, including all the out Posts & Artillery does not amount to 9,000; The Troops raised in the other Colonies are more Complete; but yet fall Short of their Establishment; so that, upon the whole, I cannot Estimate the Present Army at more than 14,500 Men Capable of Duty; I have the Satisfaction to find the Troops, both in Camp & Quarters, very healthy; so that the Deficiency must arise from the Regiments never having been filled up to the Establishment & the Number of Men on Furlough; But the former is by much the most Considerable; Under all these Circumstances, I, yesterday, called a Council of War, and, Inclosed, I send you an Extract of our Determination, so far as they Respect the Province of Massachusetts Bay. Your own Prudence will suggest the Necessity of Secrecy on this Subject, as we have the utmost Reason to believe the Enemy suppose our Numbers much greater than they are; an Error which it is not our Interest to remove.

The great extent of our Lines and the uncertainty which may be the Point of Attack, added to the Necessity of immediate Support, have induced me to order that Horses ready Saddled should be kept at Several Posts, in order to bring the most early Intelligence of any Movement of the Enemy; For this Purpose, I should be glad that 10 Horses might be provided as soon as possible. As I am informed the Congress purposes to rise immediately, I should be glad to know what Committees are left, or upon whom the executive Business devolves. I have the honor, etc.

To THE PRESIDENT OF CONGRESS

While making recommendations to Congress, Washington here appraises the British strength in the vicinity of Boston and lists the disadvantages with which he is confronted. He elsewhere estimated that in the Battle of Bunker Hill on June 17th, a fortnight before his arrival on the scene, the Continental Army had lost 145 killed and missing and 304 wounded. According to the most reliable accounts, the British paid for their doubtful victory with a loss of 1,054 out of a detachment of 2,000.

Camp at Cambridge, July 10, 1775

SIR: I arrived safely at this place on the 3d instant;—
after a Journey attended with a good deal of Fatigue and retarded by necessary attentions to the successive Civilties which
accompanied me in my whole route. Upon my arrival I immediately visited the several Posts occupied by our Troops, and
as soon as the Weather permitted, reconnoitred those of the
Enemy. I found the latter strongly entrenching on Bunkers Hill
about a mile from Charlestown, and advanced about half a mile
from the place of the last Action, with their Centries advanced
about 150 Yards on this side the narrowest part of the neck
leading from this place to Charles Town. Their floating Batteries lay in Mystick River, near their Camp, and a twenty Gun
Ship below the Ferry place between Boston and Charles Town.
They have also a Battery on Copse Hill, on the Boston side,
which much annoyed our Troops in the late Attack. Upon
Roxbury Neck they are also deeply entrenched and strongly
fortified. Their advanced Guard 'till last Saturday, occupied
Brown's Houses, about a Mile from Roxbury Meeting House
and twenty rods from their Lines: But at that time a party from
General Thomas's Camp surprized the Guard, drove them in
and burnt the Houses.

The Bulk of their Army commanded by General Howe, lays
on Bunker's Hill, and the remainder on Roxbury neck, except
the light Horse, and a few Men in the Town of Boston. On our
side we have thrown up Intrenchments on Winter and Prospect
Hills, the Enemy's Camp in full view, at the distance of little
more than a mile. Such intermediate points, as would admit
a Landing, I have since my arrival taken care to strengthen
down to Sewall's Farms where a strong Intrenchment has been
thrown up. At Roxbury General Thomas has thrown up a
Strong Work on the Hill, about two hundred Yards above the
Meeting House, which with the Brokenness of the Ground and
Rocks, have made the Pass very secure. The Troops raised in
New Hampshire with a Regiment from Rhode Island occupy
Winter Hill. A Part of those from Connecticut under General

Putnam are on Prospect Hill. The Troops in this Town are entirely of the Massachusetts: The remainder of the Rhode Island Men, at Sewalls Farm. Two Regiments of Connecticut and nine of the Massachusetts are at Roxbury. The residue of the Army, to the Number of about seven hundred, are posted in several small Towns along the Coasts, to prevent the depredations of the Enemy: Upon the whole I think myself authorized to say, that considering the great extent of Line and the nature of the Ground, we are as well secured, as could be expected in so short a time and under the disadvantages we labour. These consist in a Want of Engineers to construct proper Works and direct the Men; a Want of Tools and a sufficient Number of Men to man the Works in case of an Attack. You will observe by the Proceedings of the Council of War, which I have the Honor to enclose, that it is our unanimous Opinion to hold and defend these Works, as long as possible. The Discouragement it would give the Men and its contrary Effect on the Ministerial Troops thus to abandon our Incampment in their Face, formed with so much Labour and expence; added to the certain Destruction of a considerable and valuable extent of Country, and the uncertainty of finding a place in all respects so capable of making a stand are leading reasons for this Determination. At the same time we are very sensible of the Difficulties which attend the Defence of Lines of so great extent, and the Dangers which may ensue from such a Division of the Army.

My earnest Wishes to comply with the Instructions of the Congress in making an early and complete return of the State of the Army, has led into an involuntary delay of addressing you, which has given me much concern. Having given Orders for that purpose immediately upon my arrival, and not then so well apprized of the imperfect Obedience which had been paid to those of like nature from General Ward, I was led from day to day to expect they would come and therefore detained the messenger. They are not so complete as I could wish, but much allowance is to be made for inexperience in Forms and Liberties which had been taken (not given) on this subject. These reasons I flatter myself will no longer exist and of consequence more regularity and exactness in future prevail. This, with a necessary attention to the Lines, the movements of the

Ministerial Troops and our immediate security, must be my apoligy, which I beg you to lay before the Congress, with the utmost duty and respect.

We labour under great Disadvantages for want of Tents, for tho' they have been help'd by a collection of Sails from the Sea-port Towns, the Number is yet far short of our Necessities. The Colleges and Houses of this Town are necessarily occupied by the Troops, which affords another reason for keeping our present Station: But I most sincerely wish the whole Army was properly provided to take the Field, as I am well assured, that besides greater Expedition and activity in case of alarm, it would highly conduce to health and discipline. As meterials are not to be had here, I would beg leave to recommend the pro-curing a farther supply from Philadelphia, as soon as possible.

I should be extremely dificient in Gratitude as well as Justice, if I did not take the first Opportunity to acknowledge the Readiness and attention which the Congress and different com-mittees have shewn, to make every thing as convenient and agreeable as possible. But there is a vital and enherent Prin-ciple of delay incompatible with Military service in transacting Business, through such various and different channels. I esteem it my Duty therefore to represent the Inconvenience that must unavoidably ensue from a dependence on a number of Persons for supplies, and submit it to the consideration of the Congress, whether the public service will not be best promoted by ap-pointing a Commissary General for these purposes:

We have a very remarkable instance of the preference of such a mode in the Establishment of Connecticut, as their Troops are extremely well provided under the direction of Mr. Trum-bull, and he has at different Times assisted others with various Articles; should my sentiments happily coincide with those of the Congress, I beg leave to recommend Colonel Trumbull as a very proper person for this department. In the Arrangement of Troops collected under such circumstances, and upon the Spur of immediate necessity, several appointments have been ommitted, which appear to me indispensably necessary for the good Government of the Army, particularly a Quarter Master General, A Commissary of Musters and a Commissary of Ar-tillery. These I must particularly recommend to the Notice &

Provision of the Honorable Congress. I find myself already much embarrassed for want of a Military Chest; these embarrass ments will encrease every day, I must therefore most earnestly request that money may be forwarded to me as soon as possible. The want of this most necessary Article, will I fear, produce great Inconveniences if not prevented by an early attention.

I find the Army in general and particularly the Troops raised in Massachusetts Bay very difficient in necessary Clothing: Upon Inquiry it appears there is no Probability of Obtaining any supplies in this Quarter; upon the best consideration of this matter, I am able to form, I am of Opinion that a number of hunting Shirts, not less than 10,000, would in a great Degree remove the difficulty in the cheapest and quickest manner. I know nothing so trivial in a speculative View, that in Practice would have a happy Tendency to unite the men and abolish those Provincial distinctions which lead to Jealousy and Dissatisfaction. In a former part of my Letter I mentioned the want of Engineers. I can hardly express the Disappointment I have experienced on this Subject; the Skill of those we have being very imperfect and confined to the mere manual exercise of cannon, whereas the war in which we are engaged, requires a Knowledge comprehending the Duties of the Field and Fortifications. If any Persons possessed of these Qualifications are to be found in the Southern Colonies, it would be of great Public Service to forward them with all expedition. Upon the Article of Ammunition, I must re-echo the former complaints on this Subject; we are so exceedingly destitute that our Artillery will be of little use without a supply both large and seasonable; what we have, must be reserved for the small Arms and that managed with the utmost Frugality. I am very sorry to observe that the appointments of General Officers in the Provinces of Massachusetts and Connecticut have not corresponded with the wishes and Judgment of either the Civil or Military. The great Dissatisfaction expressed on this Subject and the apparent Danger of throwing the whole Army into the utmost Disorder, together with the strong Representations made by the Provincial Congress, have induced me to retain the Commissions in my hands until the pleasure of the Continental Congress should be farther known, except General Putnam's which was given the Day I came to the Camp and before I was apprized of these disgusts. In such a Step, I must beg the Congress will do me the Justice to believe that I have been actuated solely by a regard to the Public Good.

I have not, nor could have any private Attachments, every Gentleman in Appointment was a Stranger to me but from Character: I must therefore rely upon the candour and Indulgence of Congress; for their most favourable construction of my Conduct in this particular. General Spencer's disgust was so great at General Putnam's promotion, that he left the Army without visiting me or making known his Intention in any respect.

General Pomeroy had also retired before my Arrival, occasioned as is said by some Disappointment from the Provincial Congress. General Thomas is much esteemed and most earnestly desired to continue in the service, and as far as my Opportunities have enabled me to judge, I must join in the general Opinion, that he is an able good officer and his Resignation would be a public Loss. The postponing him to Pomroy and Heath, whom he has commanded, would make his continuance very difficult and probably operate on his mind, as the like circumstance did on that of Spencer.

The State of the Army you will find ascertained, with tolerable Precision, in the Returns which accompany this Letter. Upon finding the Number of Men to fall so far short of the Establishment and below all Expectation, I immediately called a Council of the General Officers, whose opinion as to the mode of filling up the regiments and providing for the present Exigency, together with the best Judgment we are able to form of the Ministerial Troops, I have the Honor of inclosing. From the Number of Boys, Deserters and Negroes which have inlisted in this Province, I entertain some doubts whether the Number required, can be raised here; and all the General Officers agree, that no Dependance can be put on the Militia for a continuance in Camp, or Regularity and Discipline during the short time they may stay. This unhappy and devoted Province has been so long in a State of Anarchy, and the Yoke of Ministerial Oppression so heavily laid, that great allowances are to be made for their Troops collected under such circumstances; The Defficiencies in their numbers, their Discipline and Stores can only lead to this conclusion, that their Spirit has exceeded their Strength. But at the same time I would humbly submit to the Congress, the Propriety of making some further Provision of men from the other Colonies. If these Regiments should be completed to their Establishment, the dismission of those who are unfit for Duty, on account of their Age and Character, would occasion a considerable Reduction, and at all events, they have been inlisted upon such Terms, that they may be dismissed when other Troops arrive: But should my apprehens'ons be realized, and the Regiments here not be filled up, the public Cause would suffer by an absolute Dependance upon so doubtful an Event, unless some Provision is made against such a Disappointment. It requires no Military Skill to judge of the Difficulty of introducing Discipline and Subordination into an Army while we have the Enemy in View and are in daily expectation of an attack, but it is of so much Importance, that every Effort will be made to this End, which Time and circumstances will admit. In the mean Time I have the Pleasure of observing, that there are Materials for a good Army, a great Number of Men, able Bodied, Active, Zealous in the Cause and of unquestionable Courage.

I am now Sir, to acknowledge the receipt of your Favor of the 28th June, enclosing the Resolutions of Congress of the 27th and a Copy of a Letter from the Committee of Albany, to all which I shall pay due Attention. General Gates and General Sullivan have both arrived in good Health.

My best Abilities are at all Times devoted to the Service of my Country, but I feel the Weight, variety and Importance of my present Duties too sensibly, not to wish a more immediate and frequent communication with the Congress. I fear it may often happen, in the Course of our present Operations, that I shall need the Assistance and Direction from them which Time and Distance will not allow me to receive. Since writing the above, I have to acknowledge your Favor of the 4th instant by Fessenden, and the receipt of the Commission and Articles of War. Among the other returns I have also sent one of our killed, wounded and missing in the late Action, but have been

able to procure no certain Account of the Loss of the Ministerial Troops, my best Intelligence fixes it at 500 killed and 700
wounded; but it is no more than Conjecture the utmost pains
being taken, to conceal their Loss.

Having ordered the Commanding Officer at Roxbury to give
me the earliest Intelligence of every Motion of the Enemy, by
Land or Water, discoverable from the Heights of his Camp, I
this instant, as I was closing my Letter received the enclosed
from his Brigade Major. The Design of this Motion I know
not; it may be to make a Diversion somewhere along the Coast;
it may be for New York, or it may be practised as a Deception
on Us. I thought it not improper however to mention the Matter to you: I have done the same to the Commanding Officer
at New York, and I shall let it be known by the Committee of
Safety here, that the Intelligence may be communicated, as they
see best, to the Sea Coast of this Government. I have the Honor,
etc.

To RICHARD HENRY LEE

*Richard Henry Lee had acted as a delegate to the Virginia
Convention at Williamsburg. Later, at the General Congress
in Carpenter's Hall in Philadelphia, he drafted a memorial to
the inhabitants of the British colonies, imploring their aid for
Independence. Here Washington mentions 14,000 men fit for
duty, whereas to counter the more rapid mobility of the enemy,
it was essential to have available a much larger force than the
British, who had the advantage of position and could take the
initiative at any time or place of their choosing.*

Camp at Cambridge, July 10, 1775

DEAR SIR: I was exceeding glad to receive a letter from
you, as I always shall be whenever it is convenient; though perhaps my hurry, till such time as matters are drawn a little out
of the chaos they appear in at present, will not suffer me to

write you such full and satisfactory answers, or give such clear and precise accounts of our situation and views, as I could wish, or you might expect. After a journey, a good deal retarded, principally by the desire of the different townships through which I travelled of showing respect to the general of your armies, I arrived here on this day week; since which I have been laboring with as much assiduity by fair and threatening means, to obtain returns of our strength in this camp and Roxbury and their dependencies, as a man could do, and never have been able to accomplish the matter till this day; and now, I will not answer for the correctness of them, although I have sent several of the regimental returns back more than once to have mistakes rectified.

I do not doubt but the Congress will think me very remiss in not writing to them sooner; but you may rely on it yourself, and I beg you to assure them, that it has never been in my power till this day to comply with their orders. Could I have conceived, that what ought, and, in a regular army, would have been done in an hour, would employ eight days, I should have sent an express on the second morning after I arrived, with a general account of things; but expecting in the morning to receive the returns in the evening, and in the evening surely to find them in the morning, and at last getting them full of imperfections, I have been drilled on from day to day, till I am ashamed to look back at the time, which has elapsed since my arrival here. You will perceive by the returns, that we have but about sixteen thousand effective men in all this department, whereas, by the accounts which I received from even the first officers in command, I had no doubt of finding between eighteen and twenty thousand; out of these there are only fourteen thousand fit for duty. So soon as I was able to get this state of the army, and came to the knowledge of our weakness, I immediately summoned a council of war, the result of which you will see, as it is enclosed to the Congress. Between you and me, I think we are in an exceedingly dangerous situation, as our numbers are not much larger than we suppose those of the enemy to be, from the best accounts we are able to get. They are situated in such a manner, as to be drawn to any point of attack, without our having an hour's previous notice of it, if the General will keep his own counsel; whereas we are obliged to be guarded at all points, and know not where, with precision to look for them.

I should not, I think, have made choice of the present posts, in the first instance, although I believe the communication between the town and country could not have been so well cut off without them; and, as much labor has been bestowed in throwing up lines, and making redoubts; as Cambridge, Roxbury, and Watertown must be immediately exposed to the mercy of the enemy, were we to retreat a little further into the country; as it would give a general dissatisfaction to this colony, dispirit our own people, and encourage the enemy, to remove at this time to another place; we have for these reasons resolved in council to maintain our ground if we can. Our lines on Winter and Prospect Hills, and those of the enemy on Bunker's Hill, are in full view of each other, a mile distant, our advance guards much nearer, and the sentries almost near enough to converse; at Roxbury and Boston Neck it is the same. Between these, we are obliged to guard several of the places at which the enemy may land. They have strongly fortified, or will fortify in a few days, their camps and Bunker's Hill; after which, and when their newly landed troops have got a little refreshed, we shall look for a visit, if they mean, as we are told they do, to come out of their lines. Their great command of artillery, and adequate stores of powder, give them advantages, which we have only to lament the want of.

The abuses in this army, I fear, are considerable, and the new modelling of it, in the face of an enemy, from whom we every hour expect an attack, is exceedingly difficult and dangerous. If things therefore should not turn out as the Congress would wish, I hope they will make proper allowances. I can only promise and assure them, that my whole time is devoted to their service, and that as far as my judgment goes, they shall have no cause to complain. I need not tell you, that this letter is written in much haste; the fact will sufficiently appear from the face of it. I thought a hasty letter would please you better than no letter, and, therefore, I shall offer no further apology, but assure you, that, with sincere regard for my fellow laborers with you, and Dr. Shippen's family, I am, dear Sir, your most affectionate servant.

GENERAL ORDERS

Because his troops were without uniforms, Washington devised means of identification by the use of varicolored ribbons. His emphasis on cleanliness as a safeguard for the health of the army and these first steps toward creating an elementary kind of discipline suggest the magnitude of his task in modeling an effective force out of the odds and ends of recruits under his command.

Head Quarters, Cambridge, July 14, 1775

Parole Hallifax. Countersign Inverness.

As the Health of any Army principally depends upon Cleanliness; it is recommended in the strongest manner, to the Commanding Officer of Corps, Posts and Detachments, to be strictly diligent, in ordering the Necessarys to be filled up once a Week, and new ones dug; the Streets of the encampments and Lines to be swept daily, and all Offal and Carrion, near the camp, to be immediately burned: The Officers commanding in Barracks, or Quarters, to be answerable that they are swept every morning, and all Filth and Dirt removed from about the houses. Next to Cleanliness, nothing is more conducive to a Soldiers health, than dressing his provisions in a decent and proper manner. The Officers commanding Companies should therefore daily inspect the Camp Kitchen, and see the Men dress their Food in a wholesome way.

The Commanding Officers in those parts of the Lines and Redoubts, where the Pikes are placed, will order the Quarter Masters of Corps, to see the pikes greas'd twice a week; they are to be answerable also that the pikes are kept clean, and always ready and fit for service.

The General observing great remissness, and neglect, in the several Guards in and about the Camp, orders the Officers commanding any Guard to turn out his Guard immediately upon the near Approach of the Commander in Chief or any of the General Officers, and upon passing the Guard; The Commander in Chief is to be received with rested Arms; the Officer to salute, and the Drums to beat a march: The Majors General with rested Arms, the Officer to salute and the Drums to beat two Ruffles; The Brigadiers General with rested Arms, the Officer to salute and the Drums to beat one Ruffle. There being something awkward, as well as improper, in the General Officers being stopp'd at the out-posts; ask'd for passes by the Sentries, and obliged often to send for the Officer of the Guard (who it sometimes happens is as much unacquainted with the Persons of the Generals, as the Private Men) before they can pass in or out: It is recommended to both Officers and Men to make themselves acquainted with the persons of all the Officers in General Command, and in the mean time to prevent mistakes: The General Officers and their Aids-de-Camp, will be distinguished in the following manner.

The Commander in Chief by a light blue Ribband, wore across his breast, between his Coat and Waistcoat.

The Majors and Brigadiers General, by a Pink Ribband wore in the like manner.

The Aids-de-Camp by a green ribband.

The Court Martial of which Col. Ward is Presdt. is dissolved.

Daniel Carmiele, Soldier in Col. Patterson's Regiment, tried for "Disobedience of orders, for reinlisting and taking advance Money twice over, and for Drunkenness" is found guilty of the several Charges, and ordered to be whipt on the bare back, with 30 Lashes, and discharged from the army. The General approves the Sentense and orders it to be executed to morrow morning, at the head of the Regiment he belongs to.

To THE PRESIDENT OF CONGRESS

Through the eight years of war, Washington was handicapped by lack of information concerning the strength, movements and intentions of the enemy. An intelligence service was totally lacking and casual spies were unreliable. Only occasionally does he mention the inadequacy of his foreknowledge of British plans, but he constantly pleads for more and more reinforcements and a better system of recruiting.

Camp at Cambridge, July 20, 1775

SIR: Since I did myself the Honor of Addressing you the 14th instant I have received Advice from Governor Trumbull, that the Assembly of that Colony had voted and that they are now raising Two Regiments of 700 men each, to join this Army, in consequence of an Application from the Provincial Congress of Massachusetts Bay. The Rhode Island Assembly has also made an Augmentation for this purpose; these Reinforcements with the Rifle men who are daily expected and such recruits as may come in, to fill up the Regiments here, will I apprehend, compose an Army sufficiently strong to oppose any Force which can be brought against us at present. I am very sensible that the heavy expence necessarily attendant upon the Campaign will call for the utmost Frugality and care, and would therefore, if possible, avoid inlisting one unnecessary man. As this is the first certain Account of the destination of these new raised Troops, I thought proper to communicate my Sentiments as early as possible, least the Congress should Act upon my Letter of the 10th and raise Troops in the Southern Colonies, which in my present Judgment may be dispens'd with.

In these 8 days past there have been no Movements in either Camp of any consequence: On our side we have continued the Works without any Intermission, and they are now so far advanced as to leave us little to apprehend on that Score. On the side of the Enemy, they have also been very industrious in finishing their Lines both on Bunker's Hill and Roxbury Neck. In this interval also their Transports have arrived from New York and they have been employed in landing and Stationing their Men. I have been able to collect no certain Account of the Numbers arrived, but the inclosed Letter, wrote th'o not signed by Mr. Sheriff Lee and delivered me by Captain Darby, who went express with an Account of the Lexington Battle, will enable us to form a pretty accurate Judgment. The increase of

Tents and Men in the Town of Boston is very obvious, but all my Accounts from thence agree, that there is a great Mortality, occasioned by the Want of Vegetables and fresh meat; and their Loss in the late Battle at Charles Town (from the few recoveries of their Wounded) is greater than first supposed. The State of the Inhabitants detained in Boston is very distressing, they are equally destitute of the comfort of fresh Provisions and many are so reduced in their circumstances, as to be unable to supply themselves with Salt: Such Fish as the Soldiery leave, is their principal support. Added to all this, such Jealousy and Suspicion prevails that they can scarcely speak or even look, without exposing themselves to some Species of Military Execution.

I have not been able from any Intelligence I have received, to form any certain Judgment of the future Operations of the Enemy. Some Times I have suspected an Intention of detaching part of their Army to some part of the Coast, as they have been building a number of Flat Bottomed Boats capable of holding 200 Men each. But from their Works and the Languge held at Boston there is reason to think they expect an attack from us and are principally engaged in preparing against it. I have ordered all the Whale Boats for many miles along the Coast to be collected and some of them are employed every Night to watch the motion of the Enemy by water, in order to guard as much as possible against any surprize.

Upon my Arrival and since, some Complaints have been preferr'd against Officers for Cowardice in the late Action on Bunkers Hill; tho' there were several strong Circumstances and a very general opinion against them, none have been condemn'd except a Captain Callender of the Artillery who was immediately cashier'd. I have been sorry to find it an uncontradicted Truth, that the principal failure of Duty that day, was in the Officers, tho' many of them distinguished themselves by their gallant Behaviour, but the Soldiers generally shew'd great Spirit and Resolution.

Next to the more immediate and pressing Duties of putting our Lines in as secure a State as possible, attending to the Movements of the Enemy, and gaining Intelligence; my great concern is to establish Order, Regularity & Discipline, without which our Numbers would embarass us and in case of an Action, general confusion must infallibly ensue.

In order to this I propose to divide the Army into three Divisions, at the Head of each will be a General Officer, these Divisions to be again subdivided into Brigades, under their respective Brigadiers; but the difficulty arising from the Arrangement of General Officers and waiting the further Proceedings of the Congress on this Subject has much retarded my progress in this most necessary Work. I should be very happy to receive their final Commands, as any Determination would enable me to proceed in my Plan. General Spencer returned to the Camp two days ago and has agreed to serve under Putnam, rather than leave the Army entirely. I have heard nothing from General Pomroy; should he wholly retire I apprehend it will be necessary to supply his place as soon as possible. General Folsom proposed also to retire.

In addition to the Officers mentioned in mine of the 10th instant, I would humbly propose that some Provision should be made for a Judge Advocate and Provoost Marshall; the Necessity of the first Appointment was so great, that I was Obliged to nominate a Mr. Tudor who was well recommended to me and now executes the Office under an Expectation of receiving Captains Pay. An allowance in my Opinion scarcely adequate to the Services in New raised Troops, where there are Courts Martial every Day. However as that is the proportion in the regular Army and he is contented, there will be no necessity of an Addition.

I must also renew my request as to Money, and the Appointment of a Pay Master, I have forbore urging Matters of this Nature, from my Knowledge of the many important concerns which engage the Attention of the Congress; but as I find my difficulties thicken every day, I make no Doubt suitable regard will be paid to a necessity of this kind. The Inconvenience of borrowing such sums, as are constantly requisite must be too plain for me to enlarge on and is a situation from which I should be very happy to be relieved. Upon the best consideration of the Appointment of the several Officers of Commissary General, Muster Master General, Quarter Master General and Pay Master General, Commissary of Artillery &c.; I am clearly of Opinion that they not only conduce to Order, Dispatch and Discipline, but that is a Measure of Oeconomy. The Delay, the Waste, and unpunishable Neglect of Duty arising from these Offices being in commission in several Hands, evidently shew that the Public Expence must be finally enhanced. I have experienced the Want of these Officers, in completing the returns of Men, Ammunition and Stores, the latter are yet very imperfect from the Number of Hands in which they are dispersed.

I have enclosed the last Weekly return, which is more accurate than the former, and hope in a little time we shall be perfectly regular in this, as well as some other necessary Branches of Duty. I have made Inquiry with respect to the Establishment of the Hospital and find it in a very unsetled Condition. There is no Principal Director, or any Subordination among the Surgeons; of consequence Disputes and Contentions have arisen and must continue until it is reduced to some System. I could wish that it was immediately taken into consideration as the Lives and Health of both Officers and Soldiers so much depend upon a due regulation of this Department. I have been particularly attentive to the least Symptoms of the Small Pox, hitherto we have been so fortunate, as to have every Person removed so soon, as not only to prevent any Communication, but any Apprehension or Alarm it might give in the Camp. We shall continue the utmost Vigilance against this most dangerous Enemy.

In an Army properly organized, there are sundry Officers of an Inferiour kind, such as Waggon Master, Master Carpenter &ca. but I doubt whether my Powers are sufficiently extensive for such Appointments; if it is thought proper to repose such a Trust in me, I shall be governed in the Discharge of it, by a strict regard to Oeconomy and the public Interest.

My Instructions from the Honorable Congress, direct that no Troops are to be disbanded without their express directions, nor to be recruited to more than double the number of the Enemy.

Upon this Subject I beg leave to represent, that unless the Regiments of this Province are more successful in recruiting, than I have reason to expect, a reduction of some of them will be highly necessary, as the Public is put to the whole expence of an Establishment of Officers, while the real Strength of the Regiment, which consists in the Rank and file, is defective. In case of such a Reduction, doubtless some of the Privates and all the Officers would return Home, but many of the former would go into the remaining regiments, and having had some experience of Service, would fill them up with useful men. I so plainly perceive the expence of this Campaign will exceed any calculation hitherto made, that I am particularly anxious to strike off every unnecessary charge. You will therefore, Sir, be pleased to favor me with the Commands of the Congress as to the mode of the reduction if it should appear to be necessary, that no Time may be lost when that necessity appears.

Yesterday we had an Account that the Light House was set on Fire—by whom and under what orders, I have not yet learn'd: But we have reason to believe it has been done by some of our Irregulars.

You will please to present me to the Congress with the utmost Duty and respect, and believe me to be, Sir, etc.

To BRIGADIER GENERAL JOHN THOMAS

When Washington was appointed Commander in Chief, Congress commissioned John Thomas one of eight brigadier generals. In Massachusetts he was assigned to the command of the right wing of the army and stationed at Roxbury and Dorchester. Aggrieved because he was outranked by General Seth Pomeroy, Thomas threatened to resign. Washington's letter, with its high appeal to patriotism, made him undergo a change of mind. Since Pomeroy was unable to serve anyhow, that change of mind was not too difficult to achieve.

Cambridge, July 23, 1775

Sɪʀ: The Retirement of a general Officer possessing the Confidence of his Country and the Army at so critical a Period, appears to me to be big with fatal Consequences both to the Publick Cause and his own Reputation. While it is unexecuted

I think it my Duty to use this last Effort to prevent it; and after suggesting those reasons which occur to me against your Resignation, your own Virtue and good sense must decide upon it. In the usual contests of Empire and Ambition, the conscience of a soldier has so little share, that he may very properly insist upon his claims of Rank, and extend his pretensions even to Punctilio; but in such a cause as this, where the Object is neither Glory nor extent of territory, but a defence of all that is dear and valuable in Life, surely every post ought to be deemed honorable in which a Man can serve his Country. What matter of triumph will it afford our enemies, that in less than one month, a spirit of Discord should shew itself in the highest Ranks of the Army, not to be extinguished by any thing less than a total desertion of Duty? How little reason shall we have to boast of American Union and Patriotism, if at such a time and in such a cause smaller and partial considerations cannot give way to the great and general Interest. These remarks can only affect you as a member of the great American body, but as an inhabitant of Massachusetts Bay, your own Province and the other Colonies have a peculiar and unquestionable claim to your Services, and in my opinion you cannot refuse them without relinquishing in some degree that Character For publick Virtue and Honor which you have hitherto supported. If our Cause is just, it ought to be supported, but where shall it find support, if Gentlemen of merit and experience, unable to conquer the prejudices of a competition, withdraw themselves in an hour of Danger. I admit, Sir, that your claims and services have not had due respect, it is by no means a singular case; worthy men of all Nations and Countries have had reason to make the same complaint, but they did not for this abandon the publick Cause, they nobly stifled the dictates of resentment, and made their enemies ashamed of their injustice. And can America shew no such instances of magnanimity? For the sake of your bleeding Country, your devoted Province, your charter rights, and by the memory of those brave men who have already fell in this great cause, I conjure you to banish from your mind every suggestion of anger and disappointment; your country will do ample justice to your merits, they already do it, by the Sorrow and regret expressed on the occasion; and the sacrifice you are called to make, will in the judgment of every good man and lover of his Country, do you more real Honor than the most distinguished Victory. You possess the confidence and affection of the troops of this Province particularly; many of them are not capable of judging the propriety and reasons of your Conduct, should they esteem themselves authorized by your example to leave the service, the consequences may be fatal and irretrievable. There is reason to fear it from the personal attachments of the men to their officers and the obligations that are supposed to arise from those attachments.

But, Sir, the other Colonies have also their claims upon you, not only as a Native of America, but an Inhabitant of this Province. They have made common cause with it, they have sacrificed their trade, loaded themselves with Taxes, and are ready to spill their Blood, in Vindication of the Rights of Massachusetts Bay, while all the security and profit of a neutrality has been offered them. But no arts or temptations could seduce them from your side, and leave you a prey to a cruel and perfidious Ministry. Sure these reflections must have some weight with a mind as generous and considerate as yours. How will you be able to answer it to your Country and your own conscience, if the step you are about to take should lead to a division of the Army or the loss and ruin of America be ascribed to measures which your counsels and conduct could have prevented? Before it is too late, I entreat, Sir, you would weigh well the greatness of the stake, and upon how much smaller circumstances the fate of Empires has depended. Of your own Honor and reputation you are the best and only judge; but allow me to say, that a People contending for Life and Liberty, are seldom disposed to look with a favorable eye upon either men or measures, whose passions, interests or consequences will clash with those inestimable objects. As to myself, Sir, be assured, that I shall with pleasure do all in my power to make your situation both easy and honorable, and that the sentiments here expressed flow from a clear opinion that your duty to your Country, your Posterity, and yourself, most explicitly require your Continuance in the Service. The order and rank of the commissions is under the consideration of the Continental Congress, whose determination will be re-

ceived in a few days. It may argue a want of respect to that
august Body not to wait the decision. But at all events, I shall
flatter myself, that these reasons with others which your own
good judgment will suggest, will strengthen your mind against
those impressions which are incident to humanity, and laudable to a certain degree, and that the result will be your resolution to assist your Country and friends in this day of distress.
That you may reap the full reward of Honor, and publick esteem which such a Conduct deserves is the sincere wish of, Sir,
Yours, &c.—

To GEORGE WILLIAM FAIRFAX

*Washington's estimates of the Americans killed, missing and
wounded at Bunker Hill are at variance with his own and the
figures given by the Congress of Massachusetts. The latter show
thirty fewer killed and missing and twenty-six fewer wounded.*

Camp at Cambridge about 5 Miles from Boston,
July 25, 1775

DEAR SIR: On the other side you will receive a Copy of
my last, dated at Philadelphia the 31st of May, and to which I
refer.

I shall say very little in this Letter, for two Reasons; first, because I have received no Letter from you since the one dated in
June 1774, and therefore (having wrote often) can have nothing to answer; but principally, because I do not know whether
it may ever get to your hands: If it should, the principal, indeed only, design is to cover the seconds of those Bills forwarded in my last.

You will, I presume, before this Letter gets to hand, hear of
my appointment to the command of the Continental Army. I
arrived at this Camp the 2d Instant.

You must, no doubt, also have heard of the engagement on
Bunker's Hill the 17th Ultimo; but as, I am persuaded, you
will have a very erroneous account transmitted, of the loss sus-

tained on the side of the Provincials, I do assure you, upon my
Word, that our loss, as appears by the Returns made me since
I came here, amounts to no more than 139, killed 36 missing
and 278 Wounded; nor had we, if I can credit the most solemn
assurances of the Officers that were in the Action, above 1,500
Men engaged on that day. The loss on the side of the Ministerial Troops, as I am informed from good Authority, consisted
of 1,043 killed and wounded, whereof 92 were Officers.

Inclosed I send you a second Address from the Congress to
the Inhabitants of Great Britain; as also a Declaration, setting
forth the Causes and necessity of their taking up Arms. My
affectionate & respectful compliments to Mrs. Fairfax concludes
me, Dear Sir, Your etc.

To JOHN AUGUSTINE WASHINGTON

*Because the British within the city of Boston were cut off
from communication with the countryside, their supply of provisions had grown scarce. Washington realized that their transports had brought all the reinforcements to be expected for a
considerable time and hence he sought to force the enemy to
venture out of Boston. If the siege were pressed, he might draw
the English garrison into a general and perhaps even a decisive action. It was then that Washington made the frighten-
ing discovery that his supply of powder was so scant that it
allowed but nine cartridges to a man!*

Camp at Cambridge, about 5 miles from Boston,
July 27, 1775

DEAR BROTHER: On the 2nd Inst. I arrived at this place,
after passing through a great deal of delightful Country, covered with grass, (although the Season has been dry) in a very
different manner to what our Lands in Virginia are.

I found a mixed multitude of People here, under very little
discipline, order, or Government. I found the enemy in possession of a place called Bunker's Hill, on Charles Town Neck,

strongly Intrenched, and Fortifying themselves; I found part of our Army on two Hills, (called Winter and Prospect Hills) about a Mile and a quarter from the enemy on Bunker's Hill, in a very insecure state; I found another part of the Army at this Village; and a third part at Roxbury, guarding the Entrance in and out of Boston. My whole time, since I came here, has been Imployed in throwing up Lines of Defence at these three several places; to secure, in the first Instance, our own Troops from any attempts of the Enemy; and, in the next, to cut off all Communication between their troops and the Country; For to do this, and to prevent them from penetrating into the Country with Fire and Sword, and to harass them if they do, is all that is expected of me; and if effected, must totally overthrow the designs of Administration, as the whole Force of Great Britain in the Town and Harbour of Boston can answer no other end, than to sink her under the disgrace and weight of the expense. Their Force, including Marines, Tories, &c., are computed, from the best accounts I can get, at about 12,000 Men; ours, including Sick absent, &c., at about 16,000; but then we have a Cemi Circle of Eight or Nine Miles, to guard to every part of which we are obliged to be equally attentive; whilst they, situated as it were in the Center of the Cemicircle, can bend their whole Force (having the entire command of the Water), against any one part of it with equal facility; This renders our Situation not very agreeable, though necessary; however, by incessant labour (Sundays not excepted), we are in a much better posture of defence than when I first came. The Inclosed, though rough, will give you some small Idea of the Situation of Boston, and Bay on this side; as also of the Post they have Taken in Charles Town Neck, Bunker's Hill, and our Posts.

By very authentick Intelligence lately received out of Boston (from a Person who saw the returns), the number of Regulars (including I presume the Marines) the morning of the Action on Bunker's Hill amounted to 7533 Men; their killed and wounded on that occasion amounted to 1043, whereof 92 were Officers. Our loss was 138 killed, 36 Missing, and 276 Wounded.

The Enemy are sickly, and scarce of Fresh provisions, Beef, which is chiefly got by slaughtering their Milch Cows in Boston, sells from one shilling to 18d. Sterling per lb.; and that it may not get cheaper, or more plenty, I have drove all the Stock, within a considerable distance of this place, back into the Country, out of the Way of the Men of war's Boats; In short, I have, and shall continue to do, every thing in my power to distress them. The Transports are all arrived and their whole Reinforcement is Landed, so that I can see no reason why they should not if they ever attempt it, come boldly out and put the matter to Issue at once; if they think themselves not strong enough to do this, they surely will carry their Arms (having Ships of War and Transports ready) to some other part of the Continent, or relinquish the dispute; the last of which the Ministry, unless compelled will never agree to do. Our Works, and those of the Enemy are so near and quite open between that we see every thing that each other is doing. I recollect nothing more worth mentioning. I shall therefore conclude with my best wishes, and love to my Sister and Family, and Compliments to any enquiring Friends, your most affectionate brother.

To THE COMMITTEE OF SAFETY OF NEW HAMPSHIRE

When the full realization of the critical lack of powder was brought home to him, Washington immediately sent out appeals for more and more ammunition. "The smallest quantities are not beneath notice," he pleads, and this becomes his theme in document after document, indicating, perhaps more than anything else, the colonists' total unpreparedness for the struggle.

Camp at Cambridge, August 4, 1775

GENTN.: Your Public Capacity and the hope that you will be both able and willing to give us some Assistance, has led me to make this Application; The Situation of the Army as to Amunition is by no Means what it ought to be, we have great Reason to expect the Enemy very soon intend to bombard our Lines, and our Stock of Powder is so small, as in a great Degree to make our heavy Artillery useless: I must therefore request you will exert yourselves to forward what ever can be spared from your Province as soon as Possible. The Necessity is great, the cause is of the last Importance; I am therefore persuaded I need use no Arguments to quicken your Zeal, The smallest Quantities are not beneath Notice, as a considerable Stock may be formed from various Collections; Lead and Flints are also very scarce, you will therefore furnish all you can spare. Next to making the Provisions, its being seasonable is of great Importance, every Hour in our present Situation is Critical.

Should there be any Arrivals in any Part of your Province with this Necessary Article, I must request you to forward all that can Possibly be spared out of it.

I am Gentn. very Respectfully, etc.

To THE NEW YORK LEGISLATURE

The war profiteer was active even in Washington's time. After almost a century and three-quarters, it is evident that the "effectual measures to prevent the like in the future" are even in our time still to be found.

Camp at Cambridge, August 8, 1775

GENTN: It must give great concern to any Considerate Mind, that, when this whole Continent, at a vast Expense of Blood and Treasure, is endeavouring to Establish Liberties on the most secure and Solid Foundations, not only by a laudable Opposition of Force to Force, but denying itself the usual advantages of Trade; there are men among us so basely sordid as to Counteract all our Exertions, for the sake of a little Gain. You cannot but have heard that the Disstresses of the Ministerial Troops, for fresh Provisions and many other Necessaries, at Boston, were very great; It is a Policy, Justifiable by all the

Laws of War, to endeavour to increase them; Desertions, Discouragement, and a Dissatisfaction with the Service, besides weakening their strength, are some of the Natural Consequences of such a Situation; and, if continued, might afford the fairest Hope of Success, without further Effusion of human Blood. A vessel cleared lately out of New York for St. Croix, with fresh Provisions and other Articles, has just gone into Boston, instead of pursuing her Voyage to the West Indies; I have endeavoured to discover the Name of the Captain or Owner, but, as yet, without success; The Owner (it is said) went to St. Croix before the Vessel, from which and her late arrival, I make no doubt you will be able to discover and expose the Villain. And, if you could fall upon some effectual Measures, to prevent the like in future, it would be doing a Signal Service to our Common Country.

I have been endeavouring, by every means in my Power, to discover the future Intentions of our Enemy here I find a General Idea prevailing thro' the Army and in the Town of Boston, that the Troops are soon to leave the Town and go to some other Part of the Continent. New York is the Place generally mentioned as their Destination. I should think a Rumour or Suggestion of this kind worthy of very little Notice, if it was not confirmed by some corresponding Circumstances. But a four Weeks total Inactivity, with all their Reinforcements arrived and recruited; the daily Diminution, by Desertions, Sickness and small Skirmishes, induce an Opinion, that any Effort they propose to make, will be directed elsewhere.

I thought it proper just to hint to you what is probably intended; you will then consider what Regard is to be paid to it, and what steps will be proper for you to take, if any. I am, with great Respect & Regard, etc.

To LIEUTENANT GENERAL THOMAS GAGE

It was not unusual for the opposing commanders to communicate with each other by letter during the height of a campaign. Washington's attitude toward prisoners of war was

*here set forth so that the enemy could not mistake his willing-
ness to exercise lenience or severity, depending on the example
given by the British.*

Head Quarters, Cambridge, August 11, 1775

SIR: I understand that the Officers engaged in the Cause
of Liberty and their Country, who by the Fortune of War have
fallen into your Hands, have been thrown, indiscriminately,
into a common Gaol appropriated for Felons; That no Consideration has been had for those of the most respectable Rank,
when languishing with Wounds, and Sickness; that some have
been even amputated, in this unworthy Situation.

Let your Opinion, Sir, of the Principle which Actuates them,
be what it may, they suppose they act from the noblest of all
Principles, a Love of Freedom, and their Country: But political
Opinions I conceive are foreign to this Point; the Obligations
arising from the Rights of Humanity, and Claims of Rank are
universally binding, and extensive (except in case of Retaliation): These I should have hoped, would have dictated a more
tender Treatment of those Individuals, whom Chance or War
had put in your Power. Nor can I forbear suggesting its fatal
Tendency, to widen that unhappy Breach, which you, and
those Ministers under whom you act, have repeatedly declared
you wish'd to see forever closed.

My Duty now makes it necessary to apprize you, that for the
future I shall regulate my Conduct towards those Gentlemen,
who are or may be in our Possession, exactly by the Rule you
shall observe towards those of ours, now in your Custody.

If Severity and Hardship mark the Line of your Conduct
(painful as it may be to me) your Prisoners will feel its Effects:
But if Kindness and Humanity are shewn to ours, I shall with
Pleasure consider those in our Hands, only as unfortunate, and
they shall receive from me that Treatment, to which the unfortunate are ever intitled.

I beg to be favoured with an Answer, as soon as possible, and
am Sir, etc.

To LIEUTENANT GENERAL THOMAS GAGE

Within nine days, Washington wrote for the second time to his adversary in rigidly formal language, but with firmness. Several such communications to and from Generals Howe, Cornwallis and Carleton are preserved. For the most part they dealt with the treatment and exchange of prisoners of war.

Head Quarters, Cambridge, August 20, 1775

Sir: I addressed you on the 11th. Instant in Terms, which gave the fairest Scope for the Exercise of that Humanity, and Politeness, which were supposed to form a Part of your Character. I remonstrated with you on the unworthy Treatment, shewn to the officers and Citizens of America, whom the Fortune of War, Chance, or a mistaken Confidence, had thrown into your Hands.

Whether British or American Mercy, Fortitude, and Patience are most preeminent, whether our virtuous Citizens, whom the Hand of Tyranny has forced into Arms to defend their Wives, their Children, and their Property, or the mercenary Instruments of lawless Domination, avarice and Revenge, best deserve the Appellation of Rebels, and the Punishment of that Cord, which your affected Clemency has forborne to inflict: whether the Authority, under which Fact, is usurped, or founded upon the genuine Principles of Liberty, were altogether foreign to the Subject. I purposely avoided all political Disquisition; nor shall I now avail myself of those Advantages, which the sacred Cause of my Country of Liberty, and human Nature, give me over you: Much less shall I stoop to Retort and Invective. But the Intelligence you say you have received from our Army requires a Reply. I have taken Time, Sir, to make strict Inquiry, and find it has not the least Foundation in Truth. Not only your Officers and Soldiers have been treated with a Tenderness, due to Fellow-Citizens, and Brethren, but even those execrable Parricides, whose Counsels and

Aid have deluged their Country with Blood, have been protected from the Fury of a justly-enraged People. Far from compelling or permitting their Assistance, I am embarrassed with the Numbers, who crowd to our Camp, animated with the purest Principles of Virtue, and Love of their Country. You advise me to give free operation to Truth, to punish misrepresentation and Falsehood. If Experience stamps Value upon Counsel, yours must have a Weight, which few can claim. You best can tell, how far the Convulsion, which has brought Such Ruin on both Countries and shaken the mighty Empire of Britain to its Foundation, may be traced to these malignant Causes.

You affect, Sir, to despise all Rank, not derived from the same Source with your own, I cannot conceive one more honourable, than that, which flows from the uncorrupted Choice of a brave and free People, the purest Source, and original Fountain of all Power. Far from making it a Plea for Cruelty, a mind of true Magnanimity, and enlarged Ideas would comprehend, and respect it.

What may have been the ministerial Views, which have precipitated the present Crisis, Lexington, Concord, and Charles Town can best declare. May that God, to whom you then appealed, judge between America, and you. Under his Providence, those who influence the Councils of America, and all the other Inhabitants of the united Colonies at the Hazard of their Lives are determined to hand down to Posterity those just and invaluable Privileges, which they received from their Ancestors.

I shall now, Sir, close my Correspondence with you, perhaps forever. If your Officers, our Prisoners, receive a Treatment from me, different from what I wish to shew them, they and you will remember the Occasion of it. I am, sir, etc.

To MAJOR GENERAL PHILIP SCHUYLER

The plan for an expedition into Canada which had engaged Washington's thoughts for several days had really been considered ever since letters from General Schuyler had warned against danger from the upper part of New York state and the

Canadian border. Both General Ethan Allen, in command at Ticonderoga, and Colonel Benedict Arnold, who claimed authority there by virtue of his commission from the Massachusetts Committee of Safety, wanted to lead a foray into Canada, which was weakly garrisoned, especially in the key province of Quebec. Allen boasted he could take Montreal with 1,500 men. General Carleton, the British commander, had no more than 600 troops under him, according to Allen. At first Congress was against such an invasion, but later approved it, when it seemed that the Canadians were becoming resentful of British rule and were ready to abandon their neutrality and declare open hostility, as were many Indians. Weighing these considerations, Washington planned to send 1,000 or 1,200 men by way of the Kennebec River to penetrate to Quebec, while Schuyler would divert the entire British force in the vicinity of Montreal and St. Johns. Schuyler agreed to the plan and went to Ticonderoga to prepare its launching.

Head Quarters, Cambridge, August 20, 1775

DEAR SIR: Since my last of the 15th Inst. I have been favoured with yours of the 6th.—I am much concerned to find the Supplies ordered have been so much delayed. By this Time, I hope, Colonel McDougall, whose Zeal is unquestionable, has joined you with every Thing necessary for prosecuting your Plan.

Several of the Delegates from Philadelphia, who have visited our Camp, assure me, that Powder is forwarded to you, and the daily arrivals of that Article give us Reason to hope we shall soon have a very ample supply. Animated with the Goodness of our Cause, and the best wishes of your Countrymen, I am sure you will not let any Difficulties not insuperable, damp your Ardour. Perseverence and spirit have done Wonders in all Ages. In my last (a Copy of which is inclosed) I sent you an account of the Arrival of several St. Francis Indians in our Camp, and their friendly Dispositions. You have also a Copy of the Resolution of Congress, by which you will find it is their Intention only to seek a Neutrality of the Indian

Nations, unless the ministerial Agents should engage them in Hostilities or enter into an offensive Alliance with them. I have been therefore embarrassed in giving them an answer when they have tendered their services and assistance. As your Situation enables you best to know the Motions of the Governour and the Agent, I proposed to him to go Home by Way of Ticonderoga, referring him to you for an answer, which you will give according to the Intelligence you have had, and the Judgment you have formed of the Transactions among the Indians; but as he does not seem in any Hurry to leave our Camp, your answer by the Return of this Express may possibly reach me before he returns and alter his Rout; Four of his Company still remain in our Camp, and propose to stay some Time with us. The Design of this Express is to communicate to you a Plan of an Expedition, which has engaged my Thoughts for several Days. It is to penetrate into Canada by Way of Kennebeck River, and so to Quebeck by a Rout ninety miles below Montreal. I can very well spare a Detachment for this Purpose of one Thousand or twelve Hundred Men, and the Land Carriage by the Rout proposed is too inconsiderable to make an objection. If you are resolved to proceed, which I gather from your last Letter is your Intention, it would make a Diversion that would distract Carlton, and facilitate your Views. He must either break up and follow this Party to Quebeck, by which he will leave you a free Passage, or he must suffer that important Place to fall into our Hands, an Event, which would have a decisive Effect and Influence on the publick Interests. There may be some Danger that such a sudden Incursion might alarm the Canadians and detach them from that Neutrality, which they have hitherto observed: but I should hope that with suitable Precautions and a strict Discipline preserved, any apprehensions and Jealousies might be removed. The few whom I have consulted upon it approve it much; but the final Determination is deferred until I hear from you. You will therefore by the Return of this Messenger inform me of your ultimate Resolution.—If you mean to proceed, acquaint me as particularly as you can with the Time and Force, what late Accounts you have had from Canada, and your Opinion as to the Sentiments of the Inhabitants, as well as those of the

Indians upon a Penetration into their Country; what Number of Troops are at Quebeck, and whether any Men of War with all other Circumstances which may be material in the Consideration of a Step of such Importance. Not a Moments Time is to be lost in the Preparations for this Enterprize if the Advices received from you favour it. With the utmost Expedition the Season will be considerably advanced, so that you will dismiss the Express as soon as possible. While the three New-Hampshire Companies remain in their present Station, they will not be considered as composing a Part of the continental Army; but as a Militia under the Direction and Pay of the Colony whose Inhabitants they are, or for whose Defence they are stationed: so that it will not be proper for me to give any Orders respecting them. We still continue in the same Situation as to the Enemy as when I wrote you last; but we have had six and an half Tons of Powder from the Southward which is a very seasonable Supply. We are not able to learn any Thing further of the Intentions of the Enemy, and they are too strongly posted for us to attempt any Thing upon them at present.

My best Wishes attend you, and believe me with much Truth and Regard, etc.

To JOSEPH PALMER

Because there were long interludes of inaction, Washington was obliged to suffer the advice of amateur strategists and others who, though they may have been well informed, were impatient and hypercritical. Typical of Washington's earnestness in listening patiently and then following his own judgment is this letter to a citizen.

Cambridge, August 22, 1775

SIR: In answer to your favor of yesterday I must inform you, that I have often been told of the advantages of Point Alderton with respect to its command of the shipping going in and out of Boston Harbor; and that it has, before now, been the object of my particular enquiries—That I find the Accts. differ, exceedingly, in regard to the distance of the Ship Channel—and that, there is a passage on the outer side of the light House Island for all Vessels except Ships of the first Rate.

My knowledge of this matter would not have rested upon enquiries only, if I had found myself at any time since I came to this place, in a condition to have taken such a post. But it becomes my duty to consider, not only what place is advantageous, but what number of Men are necessary to defend it; how they can be supported in case of an attack; how they may retreat if they cannot be supported; and what stock of Ammunition we are provided with for the purpose of self defence, or annoyance of the enemy. In respect to the first, I conceive our defence must be proportioned to the attack of Genl. Gage's whole force (leaving him just enough to Man his Lines on Charles Town Neck and Roxbury); and with regard to the Second, and most important object, we have only 184 Barrls. of Powder in all, which is not sufficient to give 30 Musket Cartridges a Man, and scarce enough to serve the Artillery in any brisk action a single day.

Would it be prudent then in me, under these Circumstances, to take a Post 30 Miles distant from this place when we already have a Line of Circumvaleation at least Ten Miles in extent, any part of which may be attacked (if the Enemy will keep their own Council) without our having one hours previous notice of it?—Or is it prudent to attempt a Measure which necessarily would bring on a consumption of all the Ammunition we have, thereby leaving the Army at the Mercy of the Enemy, or to disperse; and the Country to be ravaged, and laid waste at discretion?—To you Sir who is a well wisher to the cause, and can reason upon the effects of such a Conduct, I may open myself with freedom, because no improper discoveries will be made of our Situation: but I cannot expose my weakness to the Enemy (tho' I believe they are pretty well informed of every thing that passes) by telling this, and that man who are daily pointing out this—that—and t'other place, of all the motives that govern my actions, Notwithstanding, I know what will be the consequence of not doing it—Namely, that I shall be accused of inattention to the publick Service—and perhaps with want of spirit to prosecute it—but this shall have no effect upon my mind, and I will steadily (as far as my judgment will assist me) pursue such measures as I think most conducive to the Interest of the cause, and rest satisfied of any obloquy that shall be thrown conscious of having discharged my duty to the best of my abilities.

I am much obliged to you, however, as I shall be to every Gentleman, for pointing out any measure which is thought conducive to the publick good, and chearfully follow any advice which is not inconsistent with, but corrispondant to, the general Plan in view, and practicable under such particular circumstances as govern in cases of the like kind.

In respect to point Alderton, I was no longer ago than Monday last, talking to Genl. Thomas on this head and proposing to send Colo. Putnam down to take the distances &c, but considered it could answer no end but to alarm, and make the Enemy more vigilant, unless we were in condition to possess the Post to effect, I thought it as well to postpone the matter a while. I am, Sir, &c.

GENERAL ORDERS

The troops' addiction to cider became a problem worthy of the attention of the Commander in Chief.

Head Quarters, Cambridge, August 28, 1775

Parole Essex. Countersign Falmouth.

As the extraordinary duty necessary for some days past, prevents the mustering Genl. Sullivans Brigade this morning: The General appoints Friday morning next for that purpose, and orders that Brigade to be relieved from all but the ordinary Camp duty of their particular encampments Thursday morning that they may have that day to prepare for their mustering.

As nothing is more pernicious to the health of Soldiers, nor more certainly productive of the bloody-flux; than drinking

New Cyder: The General in the most possitive manner commands, the entire disuse of the same, and orders the Quarter
Master General this day, to publish Advertisements, to acquaint the Inhabitants of the surrounding districts, that such
of them, as are detected bringing new Cyder into the Camp,
after Thursday, the last day of this month, may depend on having their casks stove.

To THE INHABITANTS OF THE ISLAND
OF BERMUDA

*Washington's appeal to the citizens of Bermuda was virtually
an invitation to join in support of the cause of Independence
by expropriating the material stored on their island for use
against the colonists. Such an act would most likely involve the
Bermudians in a war with the Mother Country and the Continental Armies were hardly in a position to offer support. Yet
Washington suggested that course in the name of virtue.*

Camp at Cambridge 3 Miles from Boston,
September 6, 1775

GENTN: In the great Conflict, which agitates this Continent, I cannot doubt but the Assertors of Freedom and the
Rights of the Constitution, are possessed of your most favorable
Regards and Wishes for Success. As Descendents of Freemen
and Heirs with us of the same Glorious Inheritance, we flatter
ourselves that tho' divided by our Situation, we are firmly
united in Sentiment; the Cause of Virtue and Liberty is Confined to no Continent or Climate, it comprehends within its
capacious Limits, the Wise and good, however dispersed and
separated in Space or distance. You need not be informed, that
Violence and Rapacity of a tyrannick Ministry, have forced the
Citizens of America, your Brother Colonists, into Arms; We
equally detest and lament the Prevalence of those Councils,
which have led to the Effusion of so much human Blood and
left us no Alternative but a Civil War or a base Submission.

The wise disposer of all Events has hitherto smiled upon our virtuous Efforts; Those Mercenary Troops, a few of whom lately boasted of Subjugating this vast Continent, have been check'd in their earliest Ravages and are now actually encircled in a small Space; their Arms disgraced, and Suffering all the Calamities of a Siege. The Virtue, Spirit, and Union of the Provinces leave them nothing to fear, but the Want of Ammunition, The applications of our Enemies to foreign States and their Vigilance upon our Coasts, are the only Efforts they have made against us with Success. Under those Circumstances, and with these Sentiments we have turned our Eyes to you Gentlemen for Relief, We are informed there is a very large Magazine in your Island under a very feeble Guard; We would not wish to involve you in an Opposition, in which from your Situation, we should be unable to support you:—We knew not therefore to what Extent to sollicit your Assistance in availing ourselves of this Supply;—but if your Favor and Friendship to North America and its Liberties have not been misrepresented, I persuade myself you may, consistent with your own Safety, promote and further this Scheme, so as to give it the fairest prospect of Success. Be assured, that in this Case, the whole Power and Execution of my Influence will be made with the Honble. Continental Congress, that your Island may not only be Supplied with Provisions, but experience every other Mark of Affection and Friendship, which the grateful Citizens of a free Country can bestow on its Brethren and Benefactors. I am &c.

To THE INHABITANTS OF CANADA

Uncertainty as to the reception the troops under General Philip Schuyler and Colonel Benedict Arnold would be given during their Canadian expedition prompted Washington to appeal directly to the citizens of Canada for a united American effort against despotism.

September, 1775

FRIENDS AND BRETHREN: The unnatural Contest between the English Colonies, and Great Britain has now risen to such a Height, that Arms alone must decide it.

The Colonies, confiding in the Justice of their Cause and the purity of their intentions, have reluctantly appealed to that Being, in whose hands are all Human Events: He has hitherto smiled upon their virtuous Efforts: The Hand of Tyranny has been arrested in its Ravages, and the British Arms, which have shone with so much Splendor in every part of the Globe, are now tarnished with disgrace and disappointment. Generals of approved experience, who boasted of subduing this great Continent, find themselves circumscribed within the limits of a single City and its Suburbs, suffering all the shame and distress of a Siege. While the Freeborn Sons of America, animated by the genuine principles of Liberty and Love of their Country, with increasing Union, Firmness and discipline, repel every attack and despise every Danger.

Above all we rejoice that our Enemies have been deceived with Regard to you: They have persuaded themselves, they have even dared to say, that the Canadians were not capable of distinguishing between the Blessings of Liberty and the Wretchedness of Slavery; that gratifying the Vanity of a little Circle of Nobility would blind the Eyes of the people of Canada. By such Artifices they hoped to bend you to their Views; but they have been deceived: Instead of finding in you that poverty of Soul and baseness of Spirit, they see with a Chagrin equal to our Joy, that you are enlightened, generous, and Virtuous; that you will not renounce your own Rights, or serve as Instruments to deprive your Fellow subjects of theirs. Come then, my Brethern, Unite with us in an indissoluble Union. Let us run together to the same Goal. We have taken up Arms in Defence of our Liberty, our Property; our Wives and our Children: We are determined to preserve them or die. We look forward with pleasure to that day not far remote (we hope) when the Inhabitants of America shall have one Sentiment and the full Enjoyment of the blessings of a Free Government.

Incited by these Motives and encouraged by the advice of many Friends of Liberty among you, the Great American Congress have sent an Army into your Province, under the command of General Schuyler; not to plunder but to protect you; to animate and bring forth into Action those sentiments of Freedom you have declared, and which the Tools of dispositism would extinguish through the whole Creation. To co-operate with this design and to frustrate those cruel and perfidious Schemes, which would deluge our Frontier with the Blood of Women and Children, I have detached Colonel Arnold into your Country, with a part of the Army under my Command. I have enjoined upon him, and I am certain that he will consider himself, and act as in the Country of his Patrons and best Friends. Necessaries and Accommodations of every kind which you may furnish, he will thankfully receive, and render the full Value. I invite you therefore as Friends and Brethren, to provide him with such supplies as your Country affords; and I pledge myself not only for your safety and security, but for ample Compensation. Let no Man desert his habitation. Let no Man flee as before an Enemy.

The cause of America and of liberty is the cause of every virtuous American Citizen Whatever may be his Religion or his descent, the United Colonies know no distinction, but such as Slavery, Corruption and Arbitrary Domination may create. Come then ye generous Citizens, range yourselves under the Standard of general Liberty, against which all the force and Artifice of Tyranny will never be able to prevail. I am, etc.

To THE MAJOR AND BRIGADIER GENERALS

This call for a conference to discuss an attack upon Boston indicates Washington's willingness to take counsel and his forthrightness in stating the problem to be considered against the background of pitifully meager resources.

Camp at Cambridge, September 8, 1775

GENTLEMEN: As I mean to call upon you in a day or two for your opinions upon a point of a very Interesting nature to the well being of the Continent in general, and this Colony in particular; I think it proper, indeed an incumbent duty on me previous to this meeting, to intimate to the end and design of it, that you may have time to consider the matter with that deliberation and attention which the Importance of it requires.

It is to know whether, in your judgment, we cannot make a successful attack upon the Troops in Boston, by means of Boats, coöperated by an attempt upon their Lines at Roxbury. The success of such an Enterprize depends, I well know, upon the all wise disposer of Events, and is not within the reach of human wisdom to foretell the Issue; but, if the prospect is fair, the undertaking is justifiable under the following, among other reasons which might be assigned.

The Season is now fast approaching when warm, and comfortable Barracks must be erected for the Security of the Troops, against the inclemency of the Winter; large and costly provision must be made in the article of Wood, for the Supply of the Army; and after all that can be done in this way, it is but too probable that Fences, Woods, Orchards, and even Houses themselves, will fall Sacrifices to the want of Fuel, before the end of the Winter. A very considerable difficulty, if not expence, must accrue on acct. of Cloathing for the Men now ingaged in the Service, and if they do not inlist again, this difficulty will be Increased to an almost insurmountable degree. Blankets I am inform'd are now much wanted, and not to be got, how then shall we be able to keep Soldiers to their duty, already impatient to get home, when they come to feel the Severity of Winter without proper Covering? If this Army should not Incline to engage for a longer term than the first of January, what then is to be the consequence, but that you must either be obliged to levy new Troops and thereby have two Setts (or partly so) in pay at the same time, or, by disbanding one set before you get the other, expose the Country to desolation, and the Cause perhaps to irretrievable Ruin. These things are not unknown to the Enemy, perhaps it is the very ground they are building on, if they are not waiting a reinforcement; and if they are waiting for succours, ought it not to give a Spur to the attempt? Our Powder (not much of which would be consumed in such an enterprize) without any certainty of Supply, is daily wasting. and to sum up the whole, in spite of every saving that can be made, the expence of supporting this Army will so far exceed any Idea that was form'd in Congress of it, that I do not know what will be the consequences.

These among many other reasons which might be assigned, induce me to wish a speedy finish of the dispute; but, to avoid these evils we are not to loose sight of the difficulties, the hazard, and the loss that may accompany the attempt, nor, what will be the probable consequences of a failure.

That every circumstance for and against this measure may be duely weighted, that there may be time for doing of it, and nothing of this Importance resolved on but after mature deliberation, I give this previous notice of the Intention of calling you together on Monday next, at Nine o'clock, at which time you are requested to attend at head Quarters. It is unnecessary I am perswaded, to recommend Secrecy, as the Success of the Enterprize, (if undertaken) must depend in a great measure upon the suddenness of the stroke. I am with the greatest esteem, etc.

To JOHN AUGUSTINE WASHINGTON

A more optimistic note is sounded in Washington's letter to his brother. Hope for the success of the Canadian expedition, just setting forth, makes Washington count in advance the benefits to be derived from the fall of Montreal and Quebec.

Camp at Cambridge, September 10, 1775

DEAR BROTHER: So little has happened since the date of my last, that I should scarce have given you the trouble of reading this Letter, did I not imagine that it might be some satisfaction to you to know that we are well and in no fear or dread of the Enemy. Being, in our own opinion at least, very securely Intrenched, and wishing for nothing more than to see the Enemy out of their strong holds, that the dispute may come to an Issue.

The inactive state we lye in is exceedingly disagreeable, especially as we can see no end to it, having had no advices lately from Great Britain to form a judgment upon.

In taking possession about a fortnight ago, of a Hill within point blank (Cannon) shott of the Enemy's Lines on Charles Town Neck we expected to bring on a general Action, especially as we had been threatened by reports from Boston several days before, that they (that is the Enemy) intended an Attack upon our Intrenchments, nothing, however, followed but a severe Cannonade for a day or two, and a Bombardment afterwards for the like time; which, however, did us no other damage, than to kill two or three men, and wound as many more. Both are now at an end, as they found that we disregarded their Fire and continued our Works 'till we had got them compleated.

Unless the Ministerial Troops in Boston are waiting for reinforcements, I cannot devise what they are staying there after; and why (as they affect to despise the Americans) they do not come forth, and put an end to the contest at once. They suffer greatly for want of fresh Provisions, notwithstanding they have pillaged several Islands of a good many Sheep and Cattle. They are also scarce of Fuel, unless (according to the acct. of one of their Deserters) they mean to pull down Houses for Firing. In short, they are, from all accts. suffering all the Inconveniencies of a Siege. It is true, by having the entire Command of the Sea, and a powerful Navy; and moreover, as they are now beginning to take all Vessells indiscriminately, we cannot stop their Supplies through that Channel; but their Succours in this way hath not been so powerful as to enable them to give the Common Soldiers much fresh meat as yet. By an Acct. from Boston of the 4th Instt. the Cattle lately brought in there, sold at publick auction from Fifteen to £34.10 Sterg. apiece; and the Sheep from 30/ to 36/ each; and that Fowls and every other Species of Fresh Provisions went in proportion. The expence of this, one would think, must soon tire them were it not that they intend to fix all the Expence of this War upon the Colonies, if they can, I suppose we shall add.

I am just sending off a Detachment of 1000 Men to Quebec, by the way of Kennebec River, to co-operate with General Schuyler who by this is, I expect, at or near St. Johns, on the North end of Lake Champlain; and may, for ought I know have determined the Fate of his Army and that of Canada, as he left Crown point the 31st of last Month for the Isle-au-Noix, (within 12 Miles of St. Johns, where Govr. Carleton's principal force lay.) If he should succeed there, he will soon after be in Montreal without opposition; and if the Detachment I am sending (though late in the season,) from hence should be able to get posession of Quebec, the Ministrys Plan, in respect to that Government will turn out finely.

I have only to add my love to my Sister and the little ones, and that I am with the greatest truth, Dr. Sir. Yr. Most Affecte. Bror.

To COLONEL BENEDICT ARNOLD

Eleven hundred men, selected for the expedition into Canada, were encamped on Cambridge Common awaiting orders to march. Colonel Benedict Arnold had been chosen as their leader on Washington's insistence. How much trust the Commander in Chief had in him can be seen in this letter and special set of instructions. Arnold set out with great enthusiasm. His ambition to be the sole head of this exploit had been satisfied and now he certainly need have no apprehensions about his authority, since he carried with him Washington's blessings. If all went according to plan, the column under his command should reach Quebec by the middle of October.

Camp at Cambridge, September 14, 1775

SIR: You are intrusted with a Command of the utmost Consequence to the Interest and Liberties of America. Upon your Conduct and Courage and that of the Officers and Soldiers detached on this Expedition, not only the Success of the present Enterprize, and your own Honour, but the Safety and Welfare of the Whole Continent may depend. I charge you, therefore, and the Officers and Soldiers, under your Command, as you value your own Safety and Honour and the Favour and Esteem of your Country, that you consider yourselves, as marching, not through an Enemy's Country; but that of our Friends and Brethren, for such the Inhabitants of Canada, and the Indian Nations have approved themselves in this unhappy Contest between Great Britain and America. That you check by every Motive of Duty and Fear of Punishment, every Attempt to plunder or insult any of the Inhabitants of Canada. Should any American Soldier be so base and infamous as to injure any Canadian or Indian, in his Person or Property, I do most earnestly enjoin you to bring him to such severe and exemplary Punishment as the Enormity of the Crime may require. Should it extend to Death itself it will not be disproportional to its Guilt at such a Time and in such a Cause: But I hope and trust, that the brave Men who have voluntarily engaged in this Expedition, will be governed by far different Views. that Order, Discipline and Regularity of Behaviour will be as conspicuous, as their Courage and Valour. I also give it in Charge to you to avoid all Disrespect to or Contempt of the Religion of the Country and its Ceremonies. Prudence, Policy, and a true Christian Spirit, will lead us to look with Compassion upon their Errors without insulting them. While we are contending for our own Liberty, we should be very cautious of violating the Rights of Conscience in others, ever considering that God alone is the Judge of the Hearts of Men, and to him only in this Case, they are answerable. Upon the whole, Sir, I beg you to inculcate upon the Officers and Soldiers, the Necessity of preserving the strictest Order during their March through Canada;

to represent to them the Shame, Disgrace and Ruin to themselves and Country, if they should by their Conduct, turn the Hearts of our Brethren in Canada against us. And on the other Hand, the Honours and Rewards which await them, if by their Prudence and good Behaviour, they conciliate the Affections of the Canadians and Indians, to the great Interests of America, and convert those favorable Dispositions they have shewn into a lasting Union and Affection. Thus wishing you and the Officers and Soldiers under your Command, all Honour, Safety and Success, I remain Sir, etc.

INSTRUCTIONS TO
COLONEL BENEDICT ARNOLD

1st. You are immediately on their March from Cambridge to take the Command of the Detachment from the Continental Army again Quebec, and use all possible Expedition, as the Winter Season is now advancing and the Success of this Enterprize, (under God) depends wholly upon the Spirit with which it is pushed, and the favorable Disposition of the Canadians and Indians.

2nd. When you come to Newbury Port, you are to make all possible Inquiry, what Men of War or Cruizers there may be on the Coast, to which this Detachment may be exposed on their Voyage to Kennebeck River: and if you should find that their is Danger of your being intercepted, you are not to proceed by Water, but by Land, taking Care on the one Hand, not to be diverted by light and vague Reports, and on the other, not to expose the Troops rashly to a Danger, which by many judicious Persons has been deemed very considerable.

3rd. You are by every Means in your Power, to endeavour to discover the real Sentiments of the Canadians towards our Cause, and particularly as to this Expedition, ever bearing in Mind, that if they are averse to it and will not co-operate, or at least willingly acquiesce, it must fail of Success. In this Case you are by no Means to prosecute the Attempt; the Expence of the Expedition, and the Disappointment are not to be put in Competition with the dangerous Consequences which may ensue, from irritating them against us, and detaching them from that Neutrality which they have adopted.

4th. In Order to cherish those favorable Sentiments to the American Cause that they have manifested, you are as soon as you arrive in their Country, to disperse a Number of the Addresses you will have with you, particularly in those Parts, where your Rout shall lay, and observe the strictest Discipline and good Order, by no Means suffering any Inhabitant to be abused, or in any Manner injured, either in his Person or Property, punishing with examplary Severity every Person who shall trangress, and making ample Compensation to the Party injured.

5th. You are to endeavour on the other Hand to conciliate the affections of those People and such Indians as you may meet with by every Means in your Power, convincing them that we come, at the Request of many of their Principal People, not as Robbers or to make War upon them; but as the Friends and Supporters of their Liberties, as well as ours: And to give Efficacy to these Sentiments, you must carefully inculcate upon the Officers and Soldiers under your Command that not only the Good of their Country and their Honour, but their Safety depends upon the Treatment of these People.

6th. Check every Idea, and crush in it's earliest stage every attempt to plunder even those who are known to be Enemies to our Cause. It will create dreadful Apprehensions in our Friends, and when it is once begun, none can tell where it will stop. I, therefore again most expressly order, that it be discouraged and punished in every Instance without Distinction.

7th. Whatever King's Stores you shall be so fortunate as to possess yourself of, are to be secured for the Continental Use, agreeable to the Rules and Regulations of War published by the Honourable Congress. The Officers and Men may be assured that any extraordinary services performed by them will be suitably rewarded.

8th. Spare neither Pains or Expence to gain all possible Intelligence on your March, to prevent Surprizes and Accidents of every Kind, and endeavour, if possible, to correspond with General Schuyler, so that you may act in Concert with him. This, I think, may be done by Means of the St. Francis Indians.

9th. In case of an Union with General Schuyler, or if he should be in Canada upon your Arrival there, you are by no Means to consider yourself as upon a separate and independent Command; but are to put yourself under him and follow his Directions. Upon this Occasion, and all others, I recommend most earnestly to avoid all Contention about Rank. In such a Cause every Post is honourable in which a Man can serve his Country.

10th. If Lord Chatham's Son should be in Canada and in any Way fall in your Power, you are enjoined to treat him with all possible Deference and Respect. You cannot err in paying too much Honour to the Son of so illustrious a Character and so true a Friend to America. Any other Prisoners who may fall into your Hands, you will treat with as much Humanity and kindness, as may be consistent with your own Safety and the publick Interest. Be very particular in restraining not only your own Troops, but the Indians from all Acts of Cruelty and Insult, which will disgrace the American Arms, and irritate our Fellow Subjects against us.

11th. You will be particularly careful, to pay the full Value for all Provisions or other Accommodations which the Canadians may provide for you on your March. By no Means press them or any of their Cattle into your Service; but amply compensate those who voluntarily assist you. For this Purpose you are provided with a Sum of Money in Specie, which you will use with as much Frugality and Oeconomy as your necessities and good Policy will admit, keeping as exact an account as possible of your Disbursements.

12th. You are by every Opportunity to inform me of your Progress, your Prospects and Intelligence, and upon any important Occurrence to dispatch an Express.

13th. As the Season is now far advanced, you are to make all possible Dispatch, but if unforseen Difficulties should arise or if the Weather shou'd become so severe as to render it hazardous to proceed in your own Judgment and that of your principal Officers, (whom you are to consult) In that Case you are to return, giving me as early Notice as possible, that I may give you such Assistance as may be necessary.

14th. As the Contempt of the Religion of a Country by ridiculing any of its Ceremonies or affronting its Ministers or Votaries has ever been deeply resented, you are to be particularly careful to restrain every Officer and Soldier from such Imprudence and Folly and to punish every Instance of it. On the other Hand, as far as lays in your ower, you are to protect and support the free Exercise of the Religion of the Country and the undisturbed Enjoyment of the rights of Conscience in religious Matters, with your utmost Influence and Authority. Given under my Hand, at Head Quarters, Cambridge, this 14th Day of September one Thousand seven Hundred and seventy-five.

To THE PRESIDENT OF CONGRESS

Perhaps the most pressing problem with which Washington was confronted at this time was the defective organization of the army. Arrangements were on so temporary a basis as to have little effect on molding a fighting force. When the term of his enlistment ran out, a soldier merely packed up and departed, regardless of the stage of the battle. Uncertainty about pay aggravated the situation, and lack of clothing, housing and supplies inflamed it. Always reluctant to complain to Congress, Washington nonetheless here offers the alternatives for remedying these faults or suffering a dissolution of the entire army.

Camp at Cambridge, September 21, 1775

SIR: I have been in daily expectation of being favored with the Commands of the Honorable Congress on the Subjects of my two last Letters. The Season advances so fast that I cannot any longer defer laying before them such farther measures as require their immediate attention and in which I wait their direction.

The mode in which the present Army has been collected, has occasioned some Difficulty in procuring the Subscription of both Officers and Soldiers to the Continental Articles of War. Their principal Objection has been, that it might subject them to longer Service than that for which they engaged under their several Provincial Establishments. It is in vain to attempt to reason away the Prejudices of a whole Army, often instill'd and in this Instance at least encourged, by the Officers from private and narrow Views. I have therefore foreborn pressing them as I did not experience any such Inconvenience from their adherence to former Rules, as would warrant the Risque of entering into a Contest upon it: more especially as the restraints necessary for the Establishment of essential Discipline and Subordination, indisposed their Minds to every change, and made it both Duty and Policy to introduce as little Novelty as possible. With the present Army I fear such a Subscription is impracticable: But the Difficulty will cease with this Army.

The Connecticut and Rhode Island Troops stand engaged to the 1st. December only, and none longer than to the 1st. January. A Dissolution therefore, of the present Army will take place unless some early Provision is made against such an Event. Most of the General Officers are of Opinion the greater part of them may be re-inlisted for the Winter or another Campaign, with the Indulgence of a Furlough to visit their Friends, which, may be regulated so as not to endanger the Service. How far it may be proper to form the new Army entirely out of the Old for another Campaign, rather than from the Contingents of the several Provinces, is a Question which involves in it too many Considerations of Policy and Prudence for me to undertake to decide. It appears to be impossible to draw it from any other source than the Old Army this Winter; and as the Pay is ample, I hope a sufficient number will engage in the Service for that Time at least, but there are various Opinions of the Temper of the Men on the Subject, and there may be great Hazard in deferring the Tryal too long.

In the Continental Establishment no Provision has been made for the Pay of Artificers, distinct from that of common Soldiers; Whereas under the Provincial, such as found their own Tools were allowed 1/ per Day advance and particular Artizans more. The Pay of the Artillery also now differs from that of the Province. The Men have less, the Officers more, and for some Ranks no Provision is made, as the Congress will please to observe by the list which I have the Honor to inclose.

These particulars, tho' inconsiderable, are the source of much complaint and Dissatisfaction, which I endeavour to compose in the best manner I am able.

By the returns of the Rifle Companies and that Battalion, they appear to exceed their Establishment very considerably. I doubt my Authority to pay these extra men, without the directions of the Congress, but it would be deemed a great Hardship wholly to refuse them, as they have been encouraged to come.

The necessities of the Troops having required Pay, I directed those of Massachusetts should receive a Months pay, on being mustered and returning a proper Roll, but a Claim was immediately made for Pay by Lunar Months, and several Regiments have declined taking up their Warrants on this Account.

As this Practice was entirely new to me, tho' said to be warranted by former usage, the matter here now waits the Determination of the Hon. Congress. I find in Connecticut and Rhode Island, this Point was settled by Callender Months, in Massachusetts tho' mentioned in Congress, it was left undetermined, which is also the case in New Hampshire. The inclosure No. 2 is a Petition from the Subalterns, respecting their Pay. Where there are only two of them in a company, I have considered one as an Ensign and ordered him Pay as such, as in the Forces of Connecticut: I must beg leave to recommend this Petition to the Favor of the Congress, as I am of Opinion the allowance is inadequate to their rank and Service and is one great source of that Familiarity between the Officers and Men, which is incompatible with Subordination and Discipline. Many valuable Officers of these ranks, finding themselves unable to support the character and appearance of Officers, I am informed will retire, as soon as the Term of Service is expired, if there is no Alteration.

For the better regulation of Duty, I found it necessary to settle the rank of the Officers and to number the Regiments, and as I had not received the commands of the Congress upon the Subject, and the exigence of the Service forbade any farther Delay, the General Officers were considered as having no Regiments. An Alteration which I understand is not pleasing to some of them, but appeared to me and others to be proper, when it was considered, that by this means the whole Army is put upon one Footing and all particular Attachments dissolved.

Among many other Considerations, which the approach of Winter will demand, that of clothing appears to be one of the most important. So far as regards the Preservation of the Army from cold, they may be deemed in a state of nakedness. Many of the men have been without Blankets the whole campaign and those which have been in use during the Summer, are so much worn as to be of little Service. In order to make a Suitable Provision in these Articles, and at the same time to guard the Public against Imposition and expence, it seems necessary to determine the mode of continuing the Army,—for should Troops be clothed under the present Engagement and at the Expiration of the Term of Service decline renewing it, a Sett of unprovided men may be sent to supply their Places.

I cannot suppose it unknown to the Hon. Congress, that in all Armies it is an established Custom to make an Allowance of Provisions according to their Rank; as such an Allowance formed no Part of the Continental Establishment, I have hitherto forborn, to issue the Orders for that purpose, but as it is the received Opinion of such Members of the Congress, as I have had, an Opportunity of consulting, as well as throughout the Army, that it must be deemed as a Matter of Course and implied in the Establishment of the Army, I have directed the following Proportion of Rations, being the same allowed in the American Armies last War, Vizt.

Rations, Major General 15, Brigadier General 12, Colonel 6, Lieutenant Colonel 5, Major 4, Captain 3, Subaltern 2, Staff 2.

If these should not be approved by the Hon: Congress they will be pleased to signify the Alterations they would have made in the whole or in Part.

I am now to inform the Hon: Congress, that encouraged by the repeated Declarations of the Canadians and Indians and urged by their requests; I have detached Colonel Arnold with 1000 men to penetrate into Canada by Way of Kennebeck River, and if possible to make himself Master of Quebec. By this manœuvre, I propose either to divert Carlton from St. Johns, which would leave a free Passage to General Schuyler, or if this did not take Effect, Quebec in its present defenseless State must fall into our Hands an easy Prey. I made all possible

Inquiry as to the Distance, the Safety of the Rout and the Danger of the Season being too far advanced, but found nothing in either to deter me from proceeding, more especially, as it met with very General Approbation from all whom I consulted upon it.

That nothing might be omitted, to enable me to judge of its Propriety and probable Consequences, I communicated it by Express to General Schuyler, who approved of it in such Terms, that I resolved to put it into immediate Execution. They have now left this Place 7 Days and if favoured with a good Wind, I hope soon to hear of their being safe in Kennebeck River.

For the Satisfaction of the Congress, I have inclosed a copy of the proposed rout No. 3.

I also do myself the Honor of inclosing a Manifesto, which I caused to be printed here and of which Colo: Arnold has taken a suitable Quantity with him; This is the Inclosure No. 4. I have also forwarded a Copy of his Instructions No. 5 from all which I hope, the Congress will have a clear view of the Motives, Plan and intended Execution of the Enterprize, and that I shall be so happy as to meet with their approbation in it. I was the more induced to make this Detachment, as it is my clear Opinion, formed on a careful Observation of the Movements of the Enemy and corroborated by all the Intelligence we receive from the Deserters, some of whom we have every Day, that the Enemy have no Intention to come out until they are reinforced. They have been wholly employed for some time past, in procuring Materials for Barracks, Fuel and making other Preparations for Winter; these Circumstances with the Constant Additions to their Works, which are apparently defensive, have led me to the above Conclusion and enabled me to spare this Body of Men where I hope they will be usefully and successfully employed.

The State of Inactivity in which this Army has lain for some Time past, by no Means corresponds with my Wishes, by some decisive stroke to relieve my Country from the heavy Expences its subsistence must create.

After frequently reconnoitring the Situation of the Enemy in the Town of Boston, collecting all possible Intelligence and digesting the whole, a surprize did not appear impracticable though hazardous. I communicated it to the General Officers some Days before I called them to Council, that they might be prepared with their Opinions. The Result I have the Honor of sending in the inclosure No. 6. I cannot say that I have wholly laid it aside, but new Events may occasion New Measures. Of this I hope the Hon Congress can need no Assurance, that there is not a Man in America, who more earnestly Wishes such a Termination of the Campaign, as to make the Army no longer necessary.

The Season advances so fast, that I have given Orders to prepare Barracks and other Accomodations for the Winter. The great Scarcity of Tow Cloth in this Country, I fear, will totally disappoint us in our expectations of procuring Hunting Shirts. Govr. Cooke informs me, few or none to be had in Rhode Island, and Govr. Trumbull gives me little Encouragement to expect many from Connecticut.

I have filled up the Office of Quarter Master General, which the Congress was pleased to leave to me to by the Appointment of Major Mifflin, which I hope and believe will be universally acceptable.

It gives me great Pain to be obliged to sollicit the Attention of the Hon. Congress to the State of the Army, in Terms which imply the Slightest Apprehension of being neglected: But my Situation is inexpressibly distressing to see the Winter fast approaching upon a naked Army, The time of their Service within a few Weeks of expiring, and no Provision yet made for such important Events. Added to this the Military Chest is totally exhausted. The Paymaster has not a single Dollar in Hand. The Commissary General assures me he has strained his Credit to the utmost for the Subsistence of the Army:—The Quarter Master General is precisely in the same situation, and the greater part of the Army in a State not far from mutiny, upon the Deduction from their stated Allowance. I know not to whom to impute this Failure, but I am of opinion, if the Evil is not immediately remedied and more Punctuality observed in future, the Army must absolutely break up. I hoped I had expressed myself so fully on this Subject both by Letter and to those members of the Hon: Congress who have Honored the Camp with a Visit, that no Disappointment could possibly happen.

I therefore hourly expected Advices from the Pay Master, that he had received a fresh Supply in Addition to the 172,000 Dollars delivered him in August; And thought myself warranted to assure the Public Creditors, that in a few Days they should be satisfied, but the Delay has brought Matters to such a Crisis, as admits of no farther uncertain Expectation. I have therefore sent off this Express with orders to make all possible Dispatch. It is my most earnest request that he may be returned with all possible Expedition, unless the Honr. Congress have already forwarded what is so indispensibly necessary. I am with the most respectful regard &ca.

To JOHN AUGUSTINE WASHINGTON

The stalemate at Boston continued. The British were unwilling to risk penetration into the country, convinced that their forces were insufficient to insure success. The war council of the Continental Armies debated the expediency of an attack on the city, even though the harbor would soon be blocked, with winter so near, and the British could not expect reinforcements. The matter was referred to Congress, which, in turn, passed the decision back, after long debate, to Washington, who deferred action until the results of the Canadian expedition under Colonel Arnold would be known.

Camp at Cambridge, October 13, 1775

Dear Brother: Your favour of the 12th. Ulto. came safe to hand a few days ago; by it I gladly learnt that your Family were recover'd of the two complaints which had seized many of them, and confind my Sister. I am very glad to hear also, that the Convention had come to resolutions of Arming the People, and preparing vigorously for the defence of the Colony; which, by the latest accts. from England will prove a salutary

Measure. I am also pleasd to find that the Manufactury of Arms and Ammunition have been attended to with so much care; a plenty of these and unanimity and Fortitude among ourselves must defeat every attempt that a diabolical Ministry can Invent to Inslave this great Continent. In the Manufacturing of Arms for Publick use great care should be taken to make the bores of the same size, that the same Balls may answer, otherwise great disadvantages may arise from a mixture of Cartridges.

The Enemy by their not coming out, are, I suppose, afraid of us; whilst their Situation renders any attempts of ours upon them in a manner Impracticable. Nothing new has happend since my last worth communicating; since finishing of our own Lines of Defence we, as well as the Enemy, have been busily Imployed in putting our Men under proper cover for the Winter. Our advanced Works, and theirs, are within Musket Shott of each other; we are obliged to Submit to an almost daily Cannonade without returning a Shott from our scarcity of Powder, which we are necessitated to keep for closer Work than Cannon Distance whenever the red Coat gentry pleases to step out of their Intrenchments. Seeing no prospect of this I sent a Detachment, about a Month ago into Canada by the way of Kennebec River under the Command of a Colo. Arnold, this Detachment consisted of 1000 Men and was Order'd to possess themselves of Quebec if possible, but at any rate to make a diversion in favour of General Schuyler who by this is in possession I expect of Montreal and St. Johns, as I am not altogether without hopes Colo. Arnold may be [possessed] of the Capital. If so, what a pretty hand the Ministry have made of their Canada Bill, and the Diabolical Scheme which was constructed upon it. I have also, finding we were in no danger of a visit from our Neighbours, fitted, and am fitting out, several Privateers with Soldiers (who have been bred to the Sea) and have no doubt of making Captures of several of their Transports, some of which have already fallen into our hands laden with Provisions.

I am obliged to you for your advice to My Wife, and for your Intention of visiting of her; seeing no great prospect of returning to my Family and Friends this Winter I have sent

an Invitation to Mrs. Washington to come to me, altho' I fear
the Season is too far advanced (especially if she should, when
my Letters get home, be in New Kent, as I believe the case will
be) to admit this with any tolerable degree of convenience. I
have laid a state of the difficulties, however which must attend
the journey before her and left it to her own choice. My Love
to my Sister and the little ones are sincerely tenderd and I am
with true regard Yr. Most Affecte. Brother.

To MAJOR GENERAL PHILIP SCHUYLER

*Ethan Allen's misfortune, to which Washington refers with
a note of censure, befell him when he crossed the St. Lawrence
River below Montreal. He was defeated and taken prisoner by
the British because he had miscalculated the odds against him.
The whole undertaking was badly planned, insufficiently
manned and carelessly executed, and yet was on the verge of
success. Allen was sent in irons by way of Quebec to England,
where he was kept in captivity for three years and then exchanged.*

Camp at Cambridge, October 26, 1775

DEAR SIR: Your several Favors of the 12th. and 14th. Inst.
came safely to Hand, though not in the proper Order of Time,
with their several Inclosures. You do me Justice in believing
that I feel the utmost Anxiety for your Situation, that I sympa-
thize with you in all your Distresses, and shall most heartily
share in the Joy of your Success. My Anxiety extends itself to
poor Arnold, whose Fate depends upon the Issue of your Campaign. Besides your other Difficulties, I fear, you have those
of the Season added, which will increase every Day. In the
Article of Powder, we are in Danger of suffering equally with
you. Our Distresses on this Subject are mutual; but, we hope,
they are short-lived, as every Measure of Relief has been pursued which human Invention could suggest. When you write
General Montgomery, be pleased to convey my best Wishes

and Regards to him. It has been equally unfortunate for our Country and yourself, that your ill-Health has deprived the active Part of your Army of your Presence. God Almighty restore you and crown you with Happiness and Success.

Colonel Allen's Misfortune will, I hope, teach a Lesson of Prudence and Subordination to others, who may be too ambitious to outshine their General Officers, and regardless of Order and Duty, rush into Enterprizes, which have unfavorable Effects to the Publick, and are destructive to themselves. Dr. Franklin, Mr. Lynch, and Col. Harrison Delegates from the Congress, have been in the Camp for several Days, in Order to settle the Plan of continuing and supporting the Army. This Commission extended to your Department; but upon Consideration, it appeared so difficult to form any rational Plan, that nothing was done upon that Head. If your Time and Health will admit I should think it highly proper to turn your Thoughts to this Subject, and communicate the Result to the Congress, as early as possible. We have had no Event of any Consequence in our Camp for some Time, our whole Attention being taken up with Preparations for the Winter, and forming the new Army, in which many Difficulties occur. The Enemy expect considerable Reinforcements this Winter and from all Accounts are garrisoning Gibralter and other Places with foreign Troops, in order to bring the former Garrisons to America. The Ministry have begun the Destruction of our Sea Port Towns, by burning a flourishing Town of about 300 Houses to the Eastward, called Falmouth. This they Effected with every Circumstance of Cruelty and Barbarity, which Revenge and Malice could suggest. We expect every Moment to hear other Places have been attempted and have been better prepared for their Reception.

The more I reflect upon the Importance of your Expedition, the greater is my Concern, least it should sink under insuperable Difficulties. I look upon the Interests and Salvation of our bleeding Country in a great Degree to depend upon your Success. I know you feel it's Importance as connected not only with your own Honour and Happiness; but the publick Wellfare, so that you can want no Incitements to press on, if it be possible. My anxiety suggests some Doubts, which your better

Acquaintance with the Country will enable you to remove. Would it not have been practicable to pass St John's, leaving Force enough for a Blockade; or if you could not spare the Men, passing it wholly, possessing yourselves of Montreal, and the surrounding Country? Would not St. John's have fallen of Course or what would have been the probable Consequence? Believe me, dear General, I do not mean to imply the smallest Doubt of the Propriety of your Operations, or of those of Mr. Montgomery, for whom I have a great Respect.—I too well know the absurdity of judging upon a military Operation, when you are without the Knowledge of it's concomitant Circumstances. I only mean it as a matter of Curiosity, and to suggest to you my imperfect Idea on the subject. I am with the utmost truth and Regard, etc.

To THE PRESIDENT OF CONGRESS

As winter approached, Washington became gravely concerned about supplies, the waning numbers and discipline of his troops, the spread of smallpox and the still undeterminable intentions of the enemy.

Cambridge, November 28, 1775

SIR: I had the Honor of writing to you the 19th instant, I have now to inform you that Henry Knox Esqr. is gone to New York, with orders to forward to this place, what cannon and ordinance can be there procured. From thence he will proceed to General Schuyler on the same Business, as you will see by the inclosed Copy of Instructions, which I have given him. It would give me much satisfaction that this Gentleman, or any other whom you may think qualified, was appointed to the command of the Artillery Regiment. In my Letter to you of the 8th. Instant, I have expressed myself fully on this Subject, which I beg leave to recommend to your immediate attention, as the formation of that Corps will be at a stand, until I am honored with your Instructions thereon.

The Vessel laden with wine, which I advised you was wrecked on this coast, proves to have been the property of a Thomas Salter of Philadelphia, the papers relative to her and cargo were sent to Robert Morris Esqr who can give you every information thereon. The Schooner with the Dry Goods from Boston to Halifax is given up to the Committee of Safety at Beverly, who will dispose of her and Cargo, agreeable to the decision of a Court of Admiralty and the Schooner carried into Portsmouth by Captain Adams proves to be a friends and of course is discharged.

There are two persons engaged to go to Nova Scotia, on the Business recommended in your last, by the best information we have from thence, the Stores &c. have been withdrawn sometime; should this not be the case, It is next to an impossibility to attempt any thing there in the present unsetled and precarious state of the Army. Colonel Enos is arrived and under arrest, he acknowledges he had no Orders for coming away, his Trial cannot come on, until I hear from Col. Arnold, from whom there is no Account since I wrote you last.

From what I can collect, by my inquiries amongst the Officers, It will be impossible to get the men to inlist for the continuance of the War, which will be an insuperable Obstruction to the formation of the two Battalions of Marines on the plan resolved on in Congress. As it can make no difference I propose to proceed on the new Arrangement of the Army and when completed, enquire out such Officers and Men as are best qualified for that service, and endeavor to form these Battalions out of the whole; This appears to me the best method and will I hope meet the approbation of Congress. As it will be very difficult for the Men to work when the hard frost sets in, I have thought it necessary (tho' of little use at present) to take possession of Cobble Hill, for the benefit of any future Operations. It was effected without the least opposition from the Enemy the 23d Instant: Their inactivity on this Occasion is what I can not account for; It is probable they are meditating a Blow some where. About 300 Men, Women and Children of the poor Inhabitants of Boston, came out to Point Shirley last Friday, they have brought their Household furniture, but unprovided of every other necessary of Life: I have recommended them to the attention of the Committee of the Honorable Council of this Province, now sitting at Water Town.

The number inlisted since my last are 2540 men. I am very sorry to be necessitated to mention to you the egregious want of Public Spirit which reigns here; instead of pressing to be engaged in the cause of their Country, which I vainly flattered myself would be the case, I find we are likely to be deserted at a most critical time; Those that have Inlisted, must have a furlough, which I have been Obliged to grant to 50 at a time from each Regiment. The Connecticut Troops upon whom I reckoned are as backward, indeed if possible more so than the people of this colony, our situation is truly Alarming, and of this General Howe is well apprized, It being the common topick of conversation when the People left Boston last Friday; no doubt when he is reinforced he will avail himself of the Information.

I am making the best disposition I can for our defence having thrown up, besides the Works on Cobble Hill, several redoubts, Half Moons &ca. along the Bay; And I fear I shall be under the necessity of calling in the Militia and Minute Men of the Country to my Assistance. I say I fear it, because by what I can learn from the Officers in the Army belonging to this Colony, it will be next to an impossibility to keep them under any degree of Descipline, and that it will be very difficult to prevail on them to remain a moment longer than they chuse themselves; It is a mortifying reflection to be reduced to this dilemma, there has been nothing wanting on my part to infuse a proper Spirit amongst the Officers, that they may exert their Influence with the Soldiery. You see by a fortnights recruiting amongst men with Arms in their Hands, how little has been the success.

As the small Pox is now in Boston, I have used the precaution of prohibiting such as lately came out from coming near our Camp. General Burgoyne I am informed will soon embark for England. I think the risque too great to write you by Post, whilst it continues to pass thro' New York, it is certain that a post has been intercepted the begining of last Month, as they sent out several Letters from Boston with the Post mark at Baltimore on them, this goes by Captain Joseph Blewer who promises to deliver it carefully unto you.

You doubtless will have heard ere this reaches, of General Montgomery having got Possession of Montreal, I congratulate you thereon, he has troubles with his Troops as well as I have— all I can learn of Colo: Arnold is that he is near Quebec, I hope Montgomery will be able to proceed to his Assistance I shall be very uneasy until I hear they are joined. My best respects to Congress, etc. I have the Honor, etc.

To GOVERNOR JONATHAN TRUMBULL

The defection of the Connecticut troops was only sympto-matic of the declining morale of the whole army. It was, in this case, not merely a question of laying down arms and going home; worse still, it was the grave matter of taking leave with arms and ammunition that could be ill spared. Strong as were the measures advocated by Washington to put an end to this steady trickling away of his ranks, they were unavailing, as this letter to the Governor of Connecticut shows.

Cambridge, December 2, 1775

SIR: The reason of my giving you the trouble of this, is the late extraordinary and reprehensible conduct of some of the Connecticut Troops. Sometime ago, apprehending that some of them might incline to go home when their time of enlistment should be up, I applied to the Officers of the several Regiments, to know whether it would be agreeable to the men, to continue till the 1st. of January, or until a sufficient number of other forces could be raised to supply their Place; who Informed me that they believed the whole of them would readily stay, till that could be effected. Having discovered last week, that they were very uneasy to leave the Service, and determined upon it; I thought it expedient, to summon the General Officers at Head Quarters, and Invited a Delegation of the General

Court, to be present, that Suitable measures might be adopted for the defence and Support of our lines; the result was, that three thousand of the Minute Men and Militia of this Province, and two thousand men from New Hampshire, should be called in by the 10th. Instant for that purpose. With this determination the Connecticut Troops were made acquainted, and requested and ordered to remain here, as the time of most of them would not be out before the 10th., when they would be relieved. Notwithstanding this, yesterday morning, most of them resolved to leave the Camp; many went off, and the utmost Vigilance and Industry were used to apprehend them; several got away with their Arms and Amunition. I have inclosed you a list of the names of some of them in Genl. Putnam's Regiment only who escaped; and submit to your judgment, whether some example should not be made of these men, who have basely deserted the Cause of their Country at this critical Juncture, when the Enemy are receiving Reinforcement.

To COLONEL BENEDICT ARNOLD

Washington's confidence in Colonel Benedict Arnold grew with the early tidings of success in Canada. The expedition had pressed forward, well ahead of schedule, in spite of the failure of Colonel Enos, who commanded the rear division. Enos turned back with 300 men because of what he thought was an insufficiency of provisions. He was court-martialed and acquitted. Because of his failure of nerve, 200 of Arnold's soldiers starved to death and 200 had to be sent back to the colonies because of illness. Nonetheless, a good fragment of Arnold's force reached Quebec on November 9th and on November 12th General Richard Montgomery's reinforcements came within sight of Montreal, which was surrendered the next day virtually without a struggle. British General Guy Carleton escaped. The news of the fall of Montreal was most heartening to Washington, since this was the first actual success of the Continental arms.

Cambridge, December 5, 1775

DEAR SIR: Your Letter of the 8th. Ulto. with a Postscript of the 14th. from Point Levi, I have had the Pleasure to receive. It is not in the Power of any Man to command Success; but you have done more—you have deserved it, and before this, I hope, have met with the Laurels which are due to your Toils, in the Possession of Quebec. My Thanks are due, and sincerely offered to you, for your enterprizing and persevering Spirit. To your brave Followers I likewise present them. I was not unmindful of you or them in the Establishment of a new Army. One out of 26 Regiments (lately General Putnam's) you are appointed to the Command of and I have ordered all the Officers with you, to the one or the other, of these Regiments, in the Rank they now bear that in Case they choose to continue in Service, and no Appointments take Place, where they now are, no Disappointment may follow. Nothing very material has happened in this Camp since you left it. Finding we were not likely to do much in the Land Way, I fitted out several Privateers, or rather armed Vessels, in Behalf of the Continent, with which we have taken several Prizes to the Amount, it is supposed, of £15,000 Sterling. One of them a valuable Store-Ship (but no Powder in it) containing a fine Brass Mortar 13 Inch, 2000 Stands of Arms, Shot &c., &c.

I have no Doubt but a Junction of your Detachment with the Army under General Montgomery, is effected before this. If so, you will put yourself under his Command and will, I am persuaded, give him all the Assistance in your Power, to finish the glorious Work you have begun. That the Almighty may preserve and prosper you in it, is the sincere and fervent Prayer of, Dr. Sir, &c.

P. S. You could not be more surprised than I was at Enos's Return with the Division under his Command. I immediately put him under Arrest, and had him tried for quitting the Detachment without your Orders. He is acquitted, on the Score of Provision.

To JOSEPH REED

While Washington was bound to inaction in front of Boston, Congress was torn by dissensions and each of the colonies was maneuvering for political advantage. The New England delegates were jealous of the Southern representatives and resisted their appointments. A powerful group sought reconciliation with Britain, while others were for total severance. The conflict of interests raged while the army in the field was denied powder, clothing, supplies and the means to fight for the Independence that was so wordily debated by the wire-pulling delegates. Washington, in this letter to Joseph Reed, member of the Pennsylvania Assembly, studiously avoids involvement in these behind-the-lines tempests.

Cambridge, December 15, 1775

DEAR SIR: Since my last, I have had the pleasure of receiving your favours of the 28th ultimo, and the 2d instant. I must again express my gratitude for the attention shown Mrs. Washington at Philadelphia. It cannot but be pleasing, although it did, in some measure, impede the progress of her journey on the road. I am much obliged to you for the hints contained in both of the above letters, respecting the jealousies which you say are gone abroad. I have studiously avoided in all letters intended for the public eye, I mean for that of the Congress, every expression that could give pain or uneasiness; and I shall observe the same rule with respect to private letters, further than appears absolutely necessary for the elucidation of facts. I cannot charge myself with incivility, or, what in my opinion is tantamount, ceremonious civility, to the gentlemen of this colony; but if such my conduct appears, I will endeavor at a reformation, as I can assure you, my dear Reed, that I wish to walk in such a line as will give most general satisfaction. You know, that it was my wish at first to invite a certain number of gentlemen of this colony every day to dinner, but

189

unintentionally I believe by anybody, we somehow or other missed of it. If this has given rise to the jealousy, I can only say that I am sorry for it; at the same time I add, that it was rather owing to inattention, or, more properly, too much attention to other matters, which caused me to neglect it. The extracts of letters from this camp, which so frequently appear in the Pennsylvania papers, are not only written without my knowledge, but without my approbation, as I have always thought they must have a disagreeable tendency; but there is no restraining men's tongues, or pens, when charged with a little vanity, as in the accounts given of, or rather by, the riflemen.

With respect to what you have said of yourself, and your situation, to what I have before said on this subject I can only add, that whilst you leave the door open to my expectation of your return, I shall not think of supplying your place. If ultimately you resolve against coming, I should be glad to know it, as soon as you have determined upon it. The Congress have resolved well in respect to the pay of and advance to the men; but if they cannot get the money-signers to despatch their business, it is of very little avail; for we have not at this time money enough in camp to answer the commissary's and quartermaster's accounts, much less to pay and advance to the troops. Strange conduct this!

The accounts which you have given of the sentiments of the people respecting my conduct, is extremely flattering. Pray God, I may continue to deserve them, in the perplexed and intricate situation I stand in. Our enlistment goes on slow. By the returns last Monday, only five thousand nine hundred and seventeen men are engaged for the ensuing campaign; and yet we are told, that we shall get the number wanted, as they are only playing off to see what advantages are to be made, and whether a bounty cannot be extorted either from the public at large, or individuals, in case of a draft. Time only can discover this. I doubt the measure exceedingly. The fortunate capture of the store-ship has supplied us with flints, and many other articles we stood in need of; but we still have our wants. We are securing our approach to Letchmore's Point, unable upon any principle whatever to account for their silence, unless it be to lull us into a fatal security to favour some attempt they may have in view about the time of the great change they expect will take place the last of this month. If this be the drift, they deceive themselves, for, if possible, it has increased my vigilance, and induced me to fortify all the avenues to our camps, to guard against any approaches upon the ice.

If the Virginians are wise, that arch-traitor to the rights of humanity, Lord Dunmore, should be instantly crushed, if it takes the force of the whole colony to do it; otherwise, like a snow ball, in rolling, his army will get size, some through fear some through promises, and some from inclination, joining his standard. But that which renders the measure indispensably necessary is the Negroes. For if he gets formidable, numbers will be tempted to join, who will be afraid to do it without. I am exceeding happy to find that that villain Connolly is seized; I hope if there is any thing to convict him, that he will meet with the punishment due to his demerit and treachery.

We impatiently wait for accounts from Arnold. Would to God we may hear he is in Quebec, and that all Canada is in our possession. My best respects to Mrs. Reed. I am, &c.

P. S. The smallpox is in every part of Boston. The soldiers there who have never had it, are, we are told, under innoculation, and considered as a security against any attempt of ours. A third shipload of people is come out to Point Shirley. If we escape the smallpox in this camp, and the country around about, it will be miraculous. Every precaution that can be is taken, to guard against this evil, both by the General Court and myself.

To SIR WILLIAM HOWE

Word of the treatment accorded Ethan Allen as a captive of the British reached Washington. Strange to say, the very man who had seized Allen at Montreal, General Prescott, became a prisoner in the hands of the Americans. Aroused, Washington invoked the "Law of Retaliation" unless he would receive positive assurance of humane treatment for one of his officers. Howe's answer reminded Washington that his com-

mand did not reach to Canada and that he resented the "insulting" allusion to the British ministry and himself.

Camp Cambridge, December 18, 1775

SIR: We have just been informed of a Circumstance, which, were it not so well Authenticated, I should scarcely think credible; It is that Col: Allen, who with his small party, was defeated and taken Prisoner near Montreal, has been treated, without regard to decency, humanity, or the Rules of War; That he has been thrown into Irons and suffers all the Hardships inflicted upon common Felons.

I think it my Duty Sir, to demand and do expect from you an Ecclaireissement on this Subject; at the same Time I flatter myself, from the Character which Mr. Howe bears, as a man of Honor, Gentleman and Soldier, that my demand will meet with his Approbation: I must take the Liberty also of Informing you, that I shall consider your silence, as a confirmation of the Truth of the report; And further assuring you that whatever Treatment Colonel Allen receives; whatever fate he undergoes, such exactly shall be the Treatment and Fate of Brigadier Prescot, now in our Hands.

The Law of Retaliation, is not only justifiable, in the Eyes of God and Man, but absolutely a duty, which in our present circumstances we owe to our Relations, Friends and Fellow Citizens.

Permit me to add Sir, that we have all here the highest regard and reference for your great personal, Qualities and Attainments, and that the Americans in general esteem it not as the least of their Misfortunes, that the name of Howe; a name so dear to them, should appear at the Head of the Catalogue of the Instruments, employed by a wicked Ministry for their destruction.

With due Respect I have the Honor to be, etc.

P. S.: If an Exchange of Prisoners taken on each Side, in this unnatural Contest, is agreeable to General Howe, he will please to Signify as much, to his Most Obedient.

To JOSEPH REED

Beginning on an ironic note, with which he derides British justice, Washington grows deadly serious in describing his "feelings under our present circumstances." One difficulty follows another, and, worst of all, the desertions go on at an accelerated rate, but the basic problem remains: to forge an army that will not be disbanded while another is in the process of being organized.

Cambridge, January 4, 1776

DEAR SIR: Since my last I have received your obliging favours of the 19th and 23d ulto., and thank you for the articles of intelligence therein contained, as I also do for the buttons which accompanied the last letter, although I had got a set better, I think, made at Concord. I am exceeding glad to find that things wear a better face in Virginia than they did some time ago; but I do not think that any thing less than the life or liberty will free the colony from the effects of Lord Dunmore's resentments and villainies.

We are at length favored with a sight of his Majesty's most gracious speech, breathing sentiments of tenderness and compassion for his deluded American subjects; the echo is not yet come to hand; but we know what it must be, and as Lord North said, and we ought to have believed (and acted accordingly) we now know the ultimatum of British justice. The speech I send you. A volume of them was sent out by the Boston gentry, and, farcical enough, we gave great joy to them (the red coats I mean) without knowing or intending it; for on that day, the day which gave being to the new army (but before the proclamation came to hand), we had hoisted the union flag in compliment to the United Colonies. But, behold, it was received in Boston as a token of the deep impression the speech had made upon us, and as a signal of submission. So we learn by a person out of Boston last night. By this time I presume they begin to think it strange, that we have not made a formal surrender of our lines. Admiral Shuldham is arrived at Boston. The 55th and the greatest part, if not all, of the 17th regiment, are also got in there. The rest of the 5 regiments from Ireland were intended for Halifax and Quebec; those for the first, have arrived there, the others we know not where they are got to.

It is easier to conceive than to describe the situation of my mind for some time past, and my feelings under our present circumstances. Search the vast volumes of history through, and I much question whether a case similar to ours is to be found; to wit, to maintain a post against the flower of the British troops for six months together, without ———, and at the end of them to have one army disbanded and another to raise within the same distance of a reinforced enemy. It is too much to attempt. What may be the final issue of the last manœuvre, time only can tell. I wish this month was well over our heads. The same desire of retiring into a chimney-corner seized the troops of New Hampshire, Rhode Island, and Massachusetts (so soon as their time expired), as had worked upon those of Connecticut, notwithstanding many of them made a tender of their services to continue, till the lines could be sufficiently strengthened. We are now left with a good deal less than half raised regiments, and about five thousand militia, who only stand ingaged to the middle of this month; when, according to custom, they will depart, let the necessity of their stay be never so urgent. Thus it is, that for more than two months past, I have scarcely immerged from one difficulty before I have [been] plunged into another. How it will end, God in his great goodness will direct. I am thankful for his protection to this time. We are told that we shall soon get the army completed, but I have been told so many things which have never come to pass, that I distrust every thing.

I fear your fleet has been so long in fitting, and the destination of it so well known, that the end will be defeated, if the vessels escape. How is the arrival of French troops in the West Indies, and the hostile appearance there, to be reconciled with that part of the King's speech, wherein he assures Parliament, "that as well from the assurances I have received, as from the general appearance of affairs in Europe, I see no probability that the measures, which you may adopt, will be interrupted by disputes with any foreign power"? I hope the Congress will not think of adjourning at so important and critical a juncture as this. I wish they would keep a watchful eye to New York. From Captain Sears' account (now here) much is to be apprehended from that quarter.

A fleet is now fitting out at Boston, consisting of five transports and two bomb-vessels, under convoy of the Scarborough and Fowey men-of-war. Three hundred, some say, others more, troops are on board, with flat-bottomed boats. It is whispered, as if designedly, that they are intended for Newport; but it is generally believed that they are bound either to Long Island or Virginia; the other transports are taking in water and a good deal of bisquet is baking, some say for the shipping to lay in Nantasket Road, to be out of the way of ice, whilst others think a more important move is in agitation. All, however, is conjecture. I heartily wish you, Mrs. Reed and family, the compliments of the season, in which the ladies here and family join.

To THE PRESIDENT OF CONGRESS

In all his concern for raising an adequate, stable army, there was always the consideration of expense. Here Washington tried to balance the cost of maintenance of his troops against the value of placing New York, the Hudson River and Long Island in a state of defense.

Cambridge, January 11, 1776

SIR: Every Account I have out of Boston, confirms the Embarkation of Troops as mentioned in my last, which from the Season of the Year and other circumstances must be destined for some expedition to the Southward of this. I have therefore thought it prudent to send Major General Lee to New York, I have given him Letters recommentory to Governor

Trumbull, and to the Committee of Safety of New York, there are good hopes that in Connecticut he will get many Volunteers, who I have some reason to think, will accompany him on this expedition, without more expence to the Continent than their maintenance, but should it be otherwise and that they will expect pay, I think it is a trifling consideration when put in competition with the importance of the object, which is to put the City of New York such parts of the North River and long Island as to him shall seem proper, in that state of defence, which the Season of the Year and circumstances will admit of so as, if possible to prevent the Enemy forming a lodgment in that Government, which I am afraid contains too many persons disaffected to the cause of Liberty and America. —I have also wrote to Lord Stirling to give all the Assistance that he can with the Troops under his Command in the Continental Service, provided it does not interfere with any Orders, he may receive from Congress relative to them.

I hope the Congress will approve of my Conduct in sending General Lee upon this Expedition. I am sure I mean it well as experience teaches us, that it is much easier to prevent an Enemy from posting themselves, than it is to dislodge them after they have got possession.

The Evening of the 8th. instant a party of our men under the command of Major Knowlton were ordered to go and burn some houses which lay at the foot of Bunkers Hill and at the head of Charles Town they were also ordered to bring of the Guard which we expected consisted of an officer and thirty men. they crossed the Mill dam about half after eight O'Clock, and gallantly executed their design having burnt eight Houses, and brought with them a Serjeant and 4 privates of the 10th regiment, there was but one man more there, who making some resistance they were obliged to dispatch. The Gun that killed him was the only one, that was discharged by our men, tho' several hundred were fired by the Enemy from within their Works; but in so confused a manner, that not one of our people was hurt. Our Inlistments go on very heavily. I am &ca.

To COLONEL BENEDICT ARNOLD

Colonel Benedict Arnold undertook to storm Quebec. The last-minute defection of all but 300 of General Montgomery's troops deprived him of the strength to bring his long march to a successful conclusion. Fewer than 10,000 men were engaged on the American side in the attack, and it was doomed. Montgomery was killed; Arnold's leg was broken in the assault and half his troops surrendered to General Carleton. The failure at Quebec stunned Washington. He forthwith raised three regiments and sent them north in the hope of salvaging the expedition. In the face of his bitter disappointment, Washington here reaffirmed his affection for and trust in Arnold, who was promoted to the rank of Brigadier General.

Cambridge, January 27, 1776

DEAR SIR: On the 17th. Inst. I received the melancholy Account of the unfortunate Attack on the City of Quebec, attended with the Fall of General Montgomery and other brave officers and Men, and of your being wounded. This unhappy Affair affects me in a very sensible Manner and I sincerely condole with you upon the Occasion; but in the Midst of Distress, I am happy to find, that suitable Honors were paid to the Remains of Mr. Montgomery; and our Officers and Soldiers, who have fallen into their Hands, treated with Kindness and Humanity.

Having received no Intelligence later than the Copy of your Letter of the 2nd. to General Wooster, I would fain hope, that you are not in a worse situation, than you were; tho' I confess I have greatly feared that those Misfortunes would be succeeded by others, on Account of your unhappy Condition and the dispirited State of the Officers and Men. If they have not, I trust when you are joined by three Regiments now raising in this and the Governments of Connecticut and New Hampshire, and two others, ordered by the Congress from Pennsylvania, and the Jerseys, with the Men already sent off by Colonel Warner, that these Misfortunes will be done away, and Things resume a more favourable and promising Appearance than ever. I need not mention to you the great Importance of this Place, and the consequent Possession of all Canada, in the scale of American Affairs. You are well apprized of it. To whomsoever it belongs, in their Favour probably, will the Ballance turn. If it is in ours, Success, I think will most certainly crown our virtuous Struggles. If it is in theirs, the Contest at best, will be doubtful, hazardous and bloody. The glorious Work must be accomplished in the Course of this Winter, otherwise it will become difficult; most probably, impracticable: for Administration knowing that it will be impossible ever to reduce us to a State of Slavery and arbitrary Rule without it, will certainly send a large Reinforcement there in the Spring. I am fully convinced that your Exertions will be invariably directed to this grand Object, and I already view the approaching Day, when you and your brave Followers will enter this important Fortress with every Honor and Triumph, attendant on Victory, and Conquest. Then will you have added the only Link wanting in the great Chain of continental Union, and render the Freedom of your Country secure.

Wishing you a speedy Recovery, and the Possession of those Laurels, which your Bravery and Perseverance justly merit, I am. etc.

To JOSEPH REED

Washington, while denouncing the bombardment and burning of Norfolk, Virginia, by Lord Dunmore, here pays tribute to Tom Paine by commenting on "the sound doctrine and unanswerable reasoning contained in the pamphlet 'Common Sense'."

Cambridge, January 31, 1776

DEAR SIR: In my last, (date not recollected) by Mr. John Adams, I communicated my distresses to you on account of my want of your assistance. Since this I have been under some concern at doing of it, lest it should precipitate your return before you were ripe for it, or bring on a final resignation which I am unwilling to think of, if your return can be made convenient and agreeable. True it is, that from a variety of causes my business has been, and now is, multiplied and perplexed; whilst the means of execution is greatly contracted. This may be a cause for my wishing you here, but no inducement to your coming, if you hesitated before.

I have now to thank you for your favors of the 15th, 16th, and 20th inst., and for the several articles of intelligence, which they convey. The account given of your navy, at the same time that it is exceedingly unfavorable to our wishes, is a little provoking to me, inasmuch as it has deprived us of a necessary article which otherwise would have been sent hither; but which a kind of fatality, I fear, will for ever deprive us of. In the instance of New York, we are not to receive a particle of what you expected would be sent from thence; the time and season passing away, as I believe the troops in Boston also will, before the season for taking the field arrives. I dare say they are preparing for it now, as we have undoubted intelligence of Clinton's leaving Boston with a number of troops (by different accounts, from four or five hundred to ten companies of grenadiers, and nine of light infantry), believed to be designed for Long Island, or New York, in consequence of assurances from Governor Tryon of powerful aid from the Tories there.

I hope my countrymen (of Virginia) will rise superior to any losses the whole navy of Great Britain can bring on them, and that the destruction of Norfolk, and the threatened devastation of other places, will have no other effect, than to unite the whole country in one indissoluble band against a nation which seems to be lost to every sense of virtue, and those feelings which distinguish a civilized people from the most barbarous

savages. A few more of such flaming arguments, as were exhibited at Falmouth and Norfolk, added to the sound doctrine
and unanswerable reasoning contained in the pamphlet *Common Sense,* will not leave numbers at a loss to decide upon the
propriety of a separation.

By a letter of the 21st instant from Wooster, I find, that
Arnold was continuing the blockade of Quebec on the 19th,
which, under the heaviness of our loss there, is a most favorable
circumstance, and exhibits a fresh proof of Arnold's ability and
perseverance in the midst of difficulties. The reinforcements
ordered to him will, I hope, complete the entire conquest of
Canada this winter; and but for the loss of the gallant chief,
and his brave followers, I should think the rebuff rather favorable than otherwise; for had the country been subdued by such
a handful of men, it is more than probable, that it would have
been left to the defence of a few, and rescued from us in the
spring. Our eyes will now be open not only to the importance
of holding it, but to the numbers which are requisite to that
end. In return for your two beef and poultry vessels from New
York, I can acquaint you that our Commodore Manly has just
taken two ships from White Haven to Boston, with coal and
potatoes, and sent them into Plymouth, and fought a tender
(close by the light house where the vessels were taken), long
enough to give his prizes time to get off, in short, till she
thought it best to quit the combat, and he to move off from the
men-of-war, which were spectators of this scene.

In my last I think I informed you of my sending General
Lee to New York, with the intention of securing the Tories
of Long Island, &c. and to prevent, if possible, the King's troops
from making a lodgment there; but I fear the Congress will
be duped by the representations from that government, or yield
to them in such a manner as to become marplots to the expedition.

The city seems to be entirely under the government of Tryon
and the captain of the man-of-war.

Mrs. Washington desires I will thank you for the picture
sent her. Mr. Campbell, whom I never saw to my knowledge,
has made a very formidable figure of the Commander-in-chief,
giving him a sufficient portion of terror in his countenance.

Mrs. Washington also desires her compliments to Mrs. Reed, as I do, and, with the sincerest regard and affection, I remain, dear Sir, your most obedient servant.

To THE PRESIDENT OF CONGRESS

Washington is driven to the necessity of suggesting to Congress that bounties be offered for recruits to avoid disbanding one army while raising another in the midst of a campaign.

Cambridge, February 9, 1776

SIR: The purport of this Letter, will be directed to a single Object; through you I mean to lay it before Congress, and at the same time that I beg their serious attention to the subject, to ask pardon for intruding an opinion, not only unasked, but in some measure repugnant to their Resolves.

The disadvantages attending the limited, Inlistment of Troops, is too apparent to those who are eye witnesses of them, to render any animadversions necessary; but to Gentlemen at a Distance, whose attention is engross'd by a thousand important objects, the case may be otherwise.

That this cause precipitated the fate of the brave and much to be lamented Genl. Montgomery, and brought on the defeat which followed thereupon, I have not the most distant doubt of, for had he not been apprehensive of the Troops leaving him at so important a crisis, but continued the Blockade of Quebec, a capitulation, from the best account I have been able to collect, must inevitably have followed, and, that we were not obliged at one time to dispute these Lines under disadvantageous Circumstances (proceeding from the same cause, to wit, The Troops disbanding of themselves, before the Militia could be got in) is to me a matter of wonder and astonishment; and proves, that General Howe was either unacquainted with our Situation, or restrained by his Instructions from putting any thing to a hazard 'till his reinforcements should arrive.

The Instance of General Montgomery I mention it because

it is a striking one; for a number of others might be adduced; proves, that instead of having Men to take advantage of Circumstances, you are in manner compell'd, Right or Wrong, to make Circumstances, yield to a Secondary consideration. Since the first of December I have been devising every means in my power to secure these Incampments, and though I am sensible that we never have, since that Period, been able to act upon the Offensive, and at times not in a condition to defend, yet the cost of marching home one set of Men; bringing in another, the havock and waste occasioned by the first; the repairs necessary for the Second, with a thousand incidental charges and Inconveniencies which have arisen, and which it is scarce possible either to recollect or describe, amounts to near as much as the keeping up a respectable body of Troops the whole time, ready for any emergency, would have done. To this may be added that you never can have a well Disciplined Army.

To bring Men well acquainted with the Duties of a Soldier, requires time; to bring them under proper discipline and Subordination, not only requires time, but is a Work of great difficulty; and in this Army, where there is so little distinction between the Officers and Soldiers, requires an uncommon degree of attention. To expect then the same Service from Raw, and undisciplined Recruits as from Veteran Soldiers, is to expect what never did, and perhaps never will happen. Men who are familiarized to danger, meet it without shrinking, whereas those who have never seen Service often apprehend danger where no danger is. Three things prompt Men to a regular discharge of their Duty in time of Action: natural bravery, hope of reward, and fear of punishment. The two first are common to the untutor'd, and the Disciplin'd Soldiers; but the latter, most obviously distinguishes the one from the other. A Coward, when taught to believe, that if he breaks his Ranks, and abandons his Colours, will be punished with Death by his own party, will take his chance against the Enemy; but the Man who thinks little of the one, and is fearful of the other, Acts from present feelings regardless of consequences.

Again, Men of a days standing will not look forward, and from experience we find, that as the time approaches for their discharge they grow careless of their Arms, Ammunition, Camp utensils &ca. nay even the Barracks themselves have felt uncommon marks of Wanton depredation, and lays us under fresh trouble, and additional expence, in providing for every fresh sett; when we find it next to impossible to procure such Articles, as are absolutely necessary in the first Instance. To this may be added the Seasoning which new Recruits must have to a Camp, and the loss, consequent therefrom. But this is not all, Men engaged for a short, limited time only, have the Officers too much in their power; for to obtain a degree of popularity, in order to induce a second Inlistment, a kind of familiarity takes place which brings on a relaxation of Discipline, unlicensed furloughs, and other Indulgences, incompatable with order and good Government, by which means, the latter part of the time for which the Soldier was engaged, is spent in undoing what you were aiming to inculcate in the first.

To go into an enumeration of all the Evils we have experienced in this late great change of the Army, and the expence incidental to it, to say nothing of the hazard we have run, and must run, between the discharging of one Army and Inlistment of another (unless an Inormous expence of Militia is incurred) would greatly exceed the bounds of a Letter; what I have already taken the liberty of saying, will serve to convey a general Idea of the matter, and, therefore I shall with all due deference, take the freedom to give it as my opinion, that if the Congress have any reason to believe, that there will be occasion for Troops another year, and consequently of another inlistment, they would save money, and have infinitely better Troops if they were, even at the bounty of twenty, thirty or more Dollars to engage the Men already Inlisted ('till January next) and such others as may be wanted to compleat to the Establishment, for and during the War.—I will not undertake to say that the Men may be had upon these terms, but I am satisfied that it will never do to let the matter alone as it was last year, till the time of service was near expiring. The hazard is too great in the first place. In the next the trouble and perplexity of disbanding one Army and raising another at the same Instant, and in such a critical situation as the last was, is scarcely in the power of Words to describe, and such as no man, who has experienced it once, will ever undergo again.

If Congress should differ from me in Sentiment upon this point, I have only to beg that they will do me the justice to believe, that I have nothing more in view than what to me appears necessary to advance the public weal, although in the first Instance it will be attended with a capital expence; and, that I have the Honor to be etc.

To JOSEPH REED

Joseph Reed, just elected to the Pennsylvania Assembly, had been Washington's secretary. To him Washington confides the irksomeness of his situation. Goaded by criticism and hampered by the inertia of Congress, his forces depleted by half through illness and furloughs, the remainder insufficiently armed and clothed, he must even conceal the true state of affairs from his own officers. Against the sniping of "chimney-corner heroes," he can only reaffirm his unwavering faith in the cause of Independence and, more immediately, in the urgency of an assault on Boston.

Cambridge, February 10, 1776

DEAR SIR: Your obliging favors of the 28th ult. and 1st inst. are now before me, and claim my particular thanks for the polite attention you pay to my wishes in an early and regular communication of what is passing in your quarter.

If my dear sir, you conceive, that I took any thing wrong or amiss, that was conveyed in any of your former letters, you are really mistaken. I only meant to convince you, that nothing would give more real satisfaction, than to know the sentiments, which are entertained of me by the public, whether they be favorable or otherwise; and I urged as a reason, that the man, who wished to steer clear of shelves and rocks, must know where they lay I know—but to declare it, unless to a friend, may be an argument of vanity—the integrity of my own heart. I know the unhappy predicament I stand in; I know that much is expected of me; I know, that without men, without arms, without ammunition, without any thing fit for the accommodation of a soldier, little is to be done; and, which is mortifying, I know, that I cannot stand justified to the world without exposing my own weakness, and injuring the cause, by declaring my wants, which I am determined not to do, further than unavoidable necessity brings every man acquainted with them.

If, under these disadvantages, I am able to keep above water, (as it were) in the esteem of mankind, I shall feel myself happy; but if, from the unknown peculiarity of my circumstances, I suffer in the opinion of the world, I shall not think you take the freedom of a friend, if you conceal the reflections that may be cast upon my conduct. My own situation feels so irksome to me at times, that, if I did not consult the public good, more than my own tranquillity, I should long ere this have put every thing to the cast of a Dye. So far from my having an army of twenty thousand men well armed &c., I have been here with less than one half of it, including sick, furloughed, and on command, and those neither armed nor clothed, as they should be. In short, my situation has been such, that I have been obliged to use art to conceal it from my own officers. The Congress, as you observe, expect, I believe, that I should do more than others,—for whilst they compel me to enlist men without a bounty, they give 40 dollars to others, which will, I expect, put a stand to our enlistments; for notwithstanding all the publick virtue which is ascrib'd to these people, there is no nation under the sun, (that I ever came across) pay greater adoration to money than they do—I am pleas'd to find that your Battalions are cloathed and look well, and that they are filing off for Canada. I wish I could say that the troops here had altered much in Dress or appearance. Our regiments are little more than half compleat, and recruiting nearly at a stand—In all my letters I fail not the mention of Tents, and now perceive that notice is taken of yr. application. I have been convinced, by General Howe's conduct, that he has either been very ignorant of our situation (which I do not believe) or that he has received positive orders (which, I think, is natural to conclude) not to put anything to the hazard till his reinforcements arrive; otherwise there has [not] been a time since the first of December, that we must have fought like men to have maintained these Lines, so great in their extent.

The party to Bunker's Hill had some good and some bad men engaged in it. One or two courts have been held on the conduct of part of it. To be plain, these people—among friends—are not to be depended upon if exposed; and any man will fight well if he thinks himself in no danger. I do not apply this to these people only. I suppose it to be the case with all raw and undisciplined troops. You may rely upon it, that transports left Boston six weeks ago with troops; where they are gone, unless driven to the West Indies, I know not. You may also rely upon General Clinton's sailing from Boston about three weeks ago, with about four or five hundred men; his destination I am also a stranger to. I am sorry to hear of the failures you speak of from France. But why will not Congress forward part of the powder made in your province? They seem to look upon this as the season for action, but will not furnish the means. But I will not blame them. I dare say the demands upon them are greater than they can supply. The cause must be starved till our resources are greater, or more certain within ourselves.

With respect to myself, I have never entertained an idea of an accommodation, since I heard of the measures, which were adopted in consequence of the Bunker's Hill fight. The king's speech has confirmed the sentiments I entertained upon the news of that affair; and if every man was of my mind, the ministers of Great Britain should know, in a few words, upon what issue the cause should be put. I would not be deceived by artful declarations, nor specious pretences; nor would I be amused by unmeaning propositions; but in open, undisguised, and manly terms proclaim our wrongs, and our resolution to be redressed. I would tell them, that we had borne much, that we had long and ardently sought for reconciliation upon honorable terms, that it had been denied us, that all our attempts after peace had proved abortive, and had been grossly misrepresented, that we had done every thing which could be expected from the best of subjects, that the spirit of freedom beat too high in us to submit to slavery, and that, if nothing else could satisfy a tyrant and his diabolical ministry, we are determined to shake off all connexions with a state so unjust and unnatural. This I would tell them, not under covert, but in words as clear as the sun in its meridian brightness.

I observe what you say, in respect to the ardor of the chimney-corner heroes. I am glad their zeal is in some measure abated, because if circumstances will not permit us to make an attempt upon B[oston], or if it should be made and fail, we shall not appear altogether so culpable. I entertain the same opinion of the attempt now, which I have ever done. I believe an assault would be attended with considerable loss, and I believe it would succeed, if the men should behave well. As to an attack upon B[unker's] Hill, (unless it could be carried by surprise,) the loss, I conceive, would be greater in proportion than at Boston; and, if a defeat should follow, it would be discouraging to the men, but highly animating if crowned with success. Great good, or great evil, would consequently result from it. It is quite a different thing to what you left, being by odds the strongest fortress they possess, both in rear and front.

The Congress have ordered all captures to be tried in the courts of admiralty of the different governments to which they are sent, and some irreconcilable difference arising between the resolves of Congress, and the law of this colony, respecting the proceedings, or something or another which always happens to procrastinate business here, has put a total stop to the trials, to the no small injury of the public, as well as the great grievance of individuals. Whenever a condemnation shall take place, I shall not be unmindful of your advice respecting the hulls, &c. Would to heaven the plan you speak of for obtaining arms may succeed. The acquisition would be great, and give fresh life and vigor to our measures, as would the arrival you speak of; our expectations are kept alive, and if we can keep ourselves so, and spirits up another summer, I have no fears of wanting the needful after that. As the number of our Inlisted men were too small to undertake any offensive operation, if the circumstances of weather, &c, should favor, I ordered in (by application to this Govt., Connecticut and New Hampshire) as many regiments of militia as would enable us to attempt something in some manner or other.—they were to have been here by the first of the month, but only a few straggling companies are yet come in. The Bay towards Roxbury has been froze up once or twice pretty hard, and yesterday single persons might have crossed, I believe, from Letchmore's Point, by picking their way;—a thaw, I fear, is again approaching.

We have had the most laborious piece of work at Lechmore's Point, on account of the frost, that ever you saw. We hope to get it finished on Sunday. It is within as commanding a distance of Boston as Dorchester Hill, though of a different part. Our vessels now and then pick up a prize or two. Our Commodore (Manly) was very near being catched about eight days ago but happily escaped with vessel and crew after running ashore, scuttling, and defending her.

I recollect nothing else worth giving you the trouble of, unless you can be amused by reading a letter and poem addressed to me by Mrs. or Miss Phillis Wheatley. In searching over a parcel of papers the other day, in order to destroy such as were useless, I brought it to light again. At first, with a view of doing justice to her great poetical genius, I had a great mind to publish the poem; but not knowing whether it might not be considered rather as a mark of my own vanity, than as a compliment to her, I laid it aside, till I came across it again in the manner just mentioned. I congratulate you upon your election, although I consider it as the *coup de grace* to my expectation of ever seeing you resident in this camp again. I have only to regret the want of you, if that should be the case; and I shall do it the more feelingly, as I have experienced the good effects of your aid. I am, with Mrs. Washington's compliments to Mrs. Reed, and my best respects, added, dear Sir, your most obedient and affectionate servant.

To THE PRESIDENT OF CONGRESS

At last, nine months after Washington had taken command, supplies began to arrive. Colonel Henry Knox had brought by ox team from Ticonderoga and Crown Point fifty cannon, mortars and howitzers. New York sent ammunition; reinforce-

ments were made available. Dorchester Heights was stormed and taken after a severe cannonade. There was great confusion among the British in Boston as the artillery barrage fell from two sides on the city with devastating effect. Hasty preparations were made for evacuation.

Cambridge, March 7, 1776

SIR: On the 26th Ulto, I had the Honor of addressing you, and then mentioned, that we were making preparations for taking possession of Dorchester Heights. I now beg leave to Inform you, that a Council of General Officers having determined a previous Bombardment and Cannonade expedient and proper, in order to harrass the Enemy and divert their attention from that Quarter, on Saturday, Sunday and Monday nights last, we carried them on from our posts at Cobble Hill, Leechmore's point and Lam's Dam. Whether they did the Enemy any considerable and what Injury, I have not yet heard, but have the pleasure to acquaint you, that they greatly facilitated our schemes, and would have been attended with success equal to our most sanguine expectations, had it not been for the unlucky bursting of two thirteen and Three Ten Inch Mortars, among which was the Brass one, taken in the ordinance Brig. To what cause to attribute this Misfortune I know not, whether to any defect in them, or to the inexperience of the Bombardiers. But to return, on Monday Evening as soon as our firing commenced, a considerable detachment of our men, under the command of Brigadier General Thomas, crossed the Neck and took possession of the two Hills, without the least Interruption or annoyance from the Enemy, and by their great Activity and Industry before the morning advanced the Works so far, as to be secure against their Shot. They are now going on with such expedition that in a little time I hope they will be complete, and enable our Troops stationed there, to make a vigorous and obstinate stand. during the whole Canonade, which was incessant the two last Nights we were fortunate enough to lose but two Men, one a Lieutenant by a cannon Ball's taking off his Thigh, the other a private by the explosion of a Shell which also slightly wounded four or five more.

Our taking possession of Dorchester Heights is only preparatory to taking post on Nuke Hill and the points opposite the south end of Boston. It was absolutely necessary that they should be previously fortifyed, in order to cover and command them. As soon as the works on the former are finished and complete, measures will be immediately adopted for securing the latter and making them as strong and defensible as we can. Their contiguity to the Enemy, will make them of much Importance and of great service to us.

As mortars are essential and indespensibly necessary for carrying on our Operations and the prosecution of our plans, I have applied to two Furnaces to have some thirteen Inch ones cast with all expedition imaginable, and am encouraged to hope from the accounts I have had, that they will be able to do it; when they are done, and a proper supply of Powder obtained, I flatter myself from the posts we have just taken, and are about to take, that it will be in our power to force the Ministerial Troops to an attack, or to dispose of 'em in some way that will be of advantage to us. I think from these posts, they will be so galled and annoyed, that they must either give us battle, or quit their present possessions. I am resolved that nothing on my part shall be wanting to effect the one or the other.

It having been the general Opinion, that the Enemy would attempt to dislodge our People from the Hills, and force their Works, as soon as they were discovered, which probably might have brought on a general Engagement, It was thought advisable that the Honorable Council should be applied to, to order in the Militia from the neighbouring and adjacent Towns. I wrote them on the Subject, which they most readily complied with; and in justice to the Militia, I cannot but inform you, that they came in at the appointed time, and manifested the greatest alertness and determined resolution to have acted like men engaged in the cause of Freedom.

When the Enemy first discovered our works in the morning, they seemed to be in great confusion, and from their movements to have intended an attack.

It is much to be wished, that it had been made. The event I think must have been fortunate, and nothing less than success and victory on our side, as our Officers and men appeared Impatient for the appeal, and to have possessed the most animated Sentiments and determined Spirit.

On Tuesday evening a considerable number of their Troops embarked on board their Transports and fell down to the Castle, where part of them landed before dark; one or two of the Vessels got a ground and were fired at by our People with a Field piece, but without any Damage. What was the design of this embarkation and landing, I have not been able to learn; It would seem as if they meant an attack, for it is most probable, that if they make one on our Works at Dorchester at this time, that they will first go to the Castle and come from thence. If such was their design, a violent storm that night and which lasted 'till Eight O'Clock the next day, rendered the execution of it impracticable. It carried one or two of their Vessels a shore, which have since got off.

In case the Ministerial Troops had made an Attempt to dislodge our Men from Dorchester Hills, and the number detached upon the occasion, had been so great as to have afforded a probability of a successful attack's being made upon Boston, on a signal given from Roxbury for that purpose, agreeable to a settled and concerted plan; Four thousand chosen men who were held in readiness, were to have embarked at the mouth of Cambridge River in two divisions; The first under the command of Brig. Genl. Sullivan, the second under Brig. Genl. Greene, the whole to have been commanded by Major General Putnam. The first division was to land at the Powder House and gain possession of Bacon Hill and Mount Horam. The second at Barton's Point or a little South of it, and after securing that post, to join the other division and force the Enemy's Works and Gates for letting in the Roxbury Troops. Three floating batteries were to have proceeded and gone in Front of the other Boats, and kept up a heavy fire on that part of the Town where our men were to land. How far our views would have succeeded, had an Opportunity offered for attempting the Execution, is impossible for me to say. Nothing but experiment could determine with precision. The Plan was thought to be well digested and as far as I could judge from the cheerfulness and alacrity which distinguished the Officers and men who were to engage in the enterprize, I had reason to hope for a favourable and happy Issue.

The Militia which were ordered in, from the Adjacent Towns, brought with them three days Provisions. They were only called upon to Act under the Idea of an Attack's being immediately made, and were all discharged this Afternoon.

I beg leave to remind Congress that three Major Generals are essential and necessary for this Army, and that by General Lee's being called from hence to the command in Canada, the left Division is without one. I hope they will fill up the Vacancy by the Appointment of another. General Thomas is the first Brigadier, stands fair in point of Reputation and is esteemed a brave and good Officer. If he is promoted, there will be a vacancy in the Brigadier Generals, which it will be necessary to supply by the appointment of some other Gentleman, that shall be agreeable to Congress. But justice requires me to mention that William Thompson Esquire of the Rifle Regiment is the first Colonel of this department, and as far as I have had an Opportunity of Judging, is a good Officer and a man of Courage. What I have said of these two Gentlemen, I conceive to be my duty, at the same time acknowledging whatever promotions are made will be satisfactory to me.

March 9th. Yesterday evening a Captain Irvine, who escaped from Boston the night before, with Six of his crew, came to Head Quarters and gave the following Intelligence "That our Bombardment and Cannonade caused much surprize in Town, as many of the Soldiery said they never heard or thought we had Mortars or Shells"

"That several of the Officers acknowledged they were well and properly directed. That they occasioned much distress and confusion; that the Cannon Shot, for the greatest part went thro' the Houses and he was told, that one took of the Legs and Arms of 6 men lying in the Barracks on the Neck; That a Soldier who came from the Lines there on Tuesday Morning Informed him, that 20 men had been wounded the night before; It was also reported that others had been hurt, and one of the Light Horse torn to pieces by the explosion of a Shell, this was afterwards contradicted; That early on Tuesday Morning—Admiral Shuldam discovering the Works our People were throwing up on Dorchester Heights, immediately sent an Express to General Howe to inform him, that it was necessary that they should be attacked and dislodged from thence, or he would be under the necessity of withdrawing the Ships from the Harbour under his command; That preparations were directly made for that purpose as it was said, and from twelve to two OClock, about 3000 men embarked on board the Transports which fell down to the Castle, with a design of Landing on that part of Dorchester next to it, and attacking the Works at 5 O'Clock next morning; That Lord Piercy was appointed to command, and that it was generally believed the attempt would have been made, had it not been for the Violent Storm which happened that night, as I have mentioned before; That he heard several of the privates and one or two Serjeants say, as they were embarking that it would be another Bunker Hill affair. He further Informs that the Army is preparing to leave Boston, and that they will do it in a day or two; That Transports necessary for their embarkation were getting ready with the utmost expedition; That there had been great movements and confusion amongst the Troops the night and day preceeding his coming out, in hurrying down their Cannon, Artillery and other Stores to the Wharfs with the utmost precipitation, and were putting them on board the Ships in such haste that no account or memorandum was taken of them; That more of their cannon were removed from their works and embarked and embarking. That he heard a Woman say, which he took to be an Officer's wife, that she had seen Men go under ground at their Lines on the neck without returning; That the Ship he commanded was taken up, places fitted and fitting for Officers to lodge and several Shot, Shells and Cannon already on board. That the Tories were to have the Liberty of going where they pleased, If they could get Seamen to man the Vessels, of which there was great scarcity. On that account many Vessels could not be carried away, and would be burnt. That many of the Inhabitants apprehended the Town would be destroyed, and that their destination is Halifax.

The Account given by Capt. Irvine as to the embarkation

and their being about to leave the Town I believe true, there are other corroborating circumstances and it seems fully confirmed by a paper,—signed by four of the Select Men of the Town, (a Copy of which I have the honor to enclose you) which was brought out Yesterday evening by a Flag and delivered Colonel Learned by Major Bassett of the 10th Regiment, who desired it might be given me as soon as possible: I advised with such of the General Officers upon the Occasion as I could immediately Assemble and we determined it right, as it was not addressed to me, or any one else, nor authenticated by the signature of General Howe or any other Act Obliging him to a performance of the promise mentioned on his part, that I should give it no Answer, at the same time, that a Letter should be returned as going from Col. Learned signifying his having laid it before me with the reasons assigned for not answering it.—A Copy of this is also sent you.

To night I shall have a Battery thrown up on Nuke Hill (Dorchester point) with a design of acting as circumstances may require. It being judged adviseable to prosecute our plans of Fortification, as we intended before this Information from the Select Men came.

It being agreed on all hands that there is no probability of stopping them, if they determine to go, I shall order look outs to be kept upon all the Headlands, to discover their Movements and course, and moreover direct Commodore Manly and his little Squadron to dog them, as well for the same purpose, as for picking up any of their Vessels that may chance to depart their Convoy; from their loading with such precipitancy, It's presumable they'l not be in the best condition for Sea.

If the Ministerial Troops evacuate the Town and leave it standing, I have thoughts of taking measures for fortifying the entrance into the harbour, If it shall be thought proper and the situation of Affairs will admit of it.

Notwithstanding the report from Boston that Hallifax is the place of their Destination, I have no doubt but that they are going to the Southward of this, and I apprehend to New York. Many reasons lead me to this Opinion, It is in some measure corroborated by their sending an express Ship there

which on Wednesday Week got on shore and bilged at Cape
Cod. The Dispatches if written were destroyed when she was
boarded; she had a parcel of Coal and about 4000 Cannon
Shot, six Carriage Guns, 1 or 2 Swevils and three Barrels of
Powder. I shall hold the Riflemen and other parts of our
Troops in readiness to march at a Moments warning and Govern my movements by the events that happen, or such Orders
as I may receive from Congress, which I beg may be ample and
forwarded with all possible expedition.

On the 6th. Instant a Ship bound from London with Stores
for the Ministerial Army, consisting of coal, porter and Krout,
fell in with our Armed Vessels, four of them in Company
and was carried into Portsmouth. She had a long passage and
of course brought no papers of a late date. The only Letters of
Importance or the least interesting that were found I have
enclosed.

I beg leave to mention to Congress that Money is much
wanted. The Militia from these Governments engaged 'till the
1st of April are then to be paid, and if we march from hence,
the Expence will be considerable must be defrayed and cannot
be accomplished without it. the necessity of making the earliest
remittance for these purposes is too obvious for me to add
more.

When I wrote that part of this Letter which is anteceedent
to this date, I fully expected It would have gone before now by
Col. Bull; not deeming it of sufficient importance to send a
special Messenger, but he deferred his return from time to time
and never set off 'till to day.

These reasons I hope will excuse the delay and be received
as a proper apology for not transmitting it sooner. I have the
honor etc.

To THE PRESIDENT OF CONGRESS

*The British decision to abandon Boston had to be postponed
because embarkation was delayed by adverse winds. Meanwhile
terror and vandalism spread in Boston. An order for the confiscation of goods to be taken on the transports was the signal*

for widespread looting by a mob. Washington, still groping for information as to the enemy's activities and intentions, could only guess at the destination of the British transports, once they weighed anchor. On the belief that they would sail for New York, he began to make plans for the defense of that city.

Cambridge, March 13, 1776

SIR: In my letter of the 7th. and 9th. Instant, which I had the honor of Addressing you, I mentioned the Intelligence I had received respecting the embarkation of the Troops from Boston and fully expected before this, that the Town would have been entirely evacuated. Altho' I have been deceived and was rather premature in the Opinion I had then formed I have little reason to doubt but the event will take place in a very short time, as other Accounts which have come to hand since, the sailing of a great number of Transports from the Harbour to Nantasket Road and many circumstances corresponding therewith seem to confirm & render it unquestionable.

Whether the Town will be destroyed is a matter of much uncertainty, but it would seem from the destruction they are making of sundry pieces of furniture, of many of their Waggons, Carts &ca. which they cannot take with 'em, as it is said, that it will not; For if they intended it, the whole might be involved in one general ruin.

Holding it of the last importance in the present contest, that we should secure New York and prevent the Enemy from possessing it, and conjecturing they have views of that sort and their embarkation to be for that purpose, I judged it necessary under the situation of things here, to call a Council of General Officers to consult of such measures as are expedient to be taken at this interesting conjuncture of Affairs. A copy of the proceedings I have the honor to inclose you.

Agreeable to the Opinion of the Council, I shall detach the Rifle Regiment to morrow under the Command of Brigadier General Sullivan with orders to repair to New York, with all possible expedition, which will be succeeded the day after by the other five in one Brigade, they being all that it was thought advisable to send from hence until the Enemy shall have quitted the Town. Immediately upon their departure, I shall send forward Major General Putnam and will follow myself with the remainder of the Army as soon as I have it in my power; leaving here only such a number of men as circumstances may seem to require.

As the badness of the roads at this Season will greatly retard the March of our men, I have by advice of the General Officers wrote to Governor Trumbull by this express to use his utmost exertions for throwing a reinforcement of two Thousand Men into New York from the Western parts of Connecticut, and to the Commanding Officer there, to apply to the Provincial Convention or Committee of Safety of New Jersey, for a thousand more, for the same purpose, to oppose the Enemy and prevent their getting possession, in case they arrive before our Troops get there, of which there's a probability unless they are impeded by Contrary Winds. This Measure, tho it will be attended with considerable expence, I flatter myself will meet the Approbation of Congress. The Lines in Boston and on Boston Neck point out the propriety and suggest the necessity of keeping them from gaining possession and making a Lodgement. Should their destination be further southward or for Halifax for the purpose of going into Canada, the March of our Troops to New York, will place them nearer the scene of Action and more convenient for affording succours.

We have not taken post on Nuke [Nook's] Hill and fortified it, as mentioned we should in my last. On hearing that the Enemy were about to retreat and leave the Town, It was thought imprudent and unadvisable to force them with too much precipitation, that we might gain a little time and prepare for a March. To morrow Evening we shall take possession of it unless they are gone. As New York is of such importance; prudence and policy require, that every precaution that can be devised, should be adopted to frustrate the designs which the Enemy may have of obtaining possession of it. To this End I have ordered Vessels to be provided and held ready at Norwich for the embarkation and Transportation of our Troops thither. This I have done with a view not only of expediting their arrival, as it will save several days marching but also that they may be fresh and fit for intrenching and throwing up Works of defence, as soon as they got there, If they do meet the Enemy to contend with, for neither of which would they be in a proper condition after a long and fatiguing March in bad roads. If Wallace with his Ships should be apprized of the measure and attempt to prevent it by stopping up the Harbour at New London, they can but pursue their March by Land.

You will be pleased to observe, that it is the Opinion of the General Officers, If the Enemy abandon the Town, that it will be unnecessary to employ or keep any of this Army for its defence, and that I have mentioned on, that event's happening, I shall immediately repair to New York with the remainder of the Army not now detached, leaving only such a Number of Men here as circumstances may seem to require. What I partly allude to is, that as it will take a considerable time for the removal of such a large body of men, as the Divisions must precede each other in such order as to allow intermediate time sufficient for 'em to be covered and provided for on the route, and many things done previous to the march of the whole for securing and forwarding such necessaries, as can not be carried Immediately, (if proper to be carried at all) That some directions might be received from Congress, as to the number which they may judge necessary to be kept here for these or any other purposes. I could wish to have their commands upon the Subject and in time, as I may be under some degree of embarrassment as to their views.

Congress having been pleased to appoint Col. Thompson a Brigadier General, there is a Vacancy for a Colonel in the Regiment he commanded, to which I would beg leave to recommend the Lieut. Col. Hand. I shall also take the Liberty of recommending Captain Hugh Stevenson of the Virginia Riflemen to succeed Col. Hand & to be appointed in his place as Lieut. Col. (there being no Major, Magaw the late one being appointed Lt. Col. of one of the Pennsylvania Battalions and gone from hence) He is in my Opinion the fittest person in this Army for it, as well as the oldest Captain in the service, having distinguished himself at the Head of a Rifle Company all the last War and highly merited the approbation of his superior officers.

Col. Mifflin Informed me to day, of his having received Tent Cloths from Mr. Barrett of Philadelphia to the amount of 7,500£ of Pennsylvania Currency and applied for a Warrant for Payment of it. But our Fund being low & many demands against it, which must be satisfied and our calls for Money will be exceedingly great, I could not grant it, thinking it might be convenient for payment to be made in Philadelphia by your order, on the Treasury there. I have the Honor &ca.

To THE PRESIDENT OF CONGRESS

Washington entered Boston and received a joyous welcome. Actual damage caused by the bombardment and the haste with which the British had abandoned the city in an atmosphere of panic was less than he had anticipated. Apparently looting had been checked and a considerable store of munitions and supplies fell into his hands. Because of the threat of smallpox, the occupation by the main body of Washington's troops was not accomplished until three days after the capitulation of the city.

Head Quarters, Cambridge, March 19, 1776

SIR: It is with the greatest pleasure I inform you that on Sunday last the 17th. Instant, about 9th O'Clock in the forenoon the Ministerial Army evacuated the Town of Boston, and that the Forces of the United Colonies are now in actual Possession thereof. I beg leave to congratulate you Sir, and the Honorable Congress on this happy event, and particularly as it was effected without endangering the Lives and property of the remaining unhappy Inhabitants.

I have great reason to imagine their flight was precipitated by the appearance of a Work which I had ordered to be thrown up last Saturday night, on an eminence at Dorchester, which lay nearest to Boston Neck called Newks Hill. The Town although it has suffered greatly, is not in so bad a state as I expected to find it, and I have a particular pleasure in being able to inform you Sir, that your House has received no damage worth mentioning, your furniture is in tolerable Order and the family pictures are all left entire and untouched. Captn. Cazneau takes charge of the whole until he receives further Orders from you.

As soon as the Ministerial Troops had quited the Town, I ordered a Thousand men (who had had the small pox) under command of General Putnam, to take possession of the Heights, which I shall fortify in such a manner, as to prevent their return, should they attempt it; but as they are still in the Harbour, I thought it not prudent to march off with the main body of the Army, until I should be fully satisfied they had quited the Coast. I have therefore only detached five Regiments besides the Rifle Battalion to New York, and shall keep the remainder here 'till all suspicion of their return ceases.

The situation in which I found their Works, evidently discovered that their retreat was made with the greatest precipitation. They have left their Barracks and other works of wood at Bunkers Hill &ca. all standing, and have destroyed but a small part of their Lines. They have also left a number of fine pieces of Cannon, which they first spiked up, also a very large Iron Mortar; and (as I am informed) they have thrown another over the end of your Wharf—I have employed proper Persons to drill the Cannon, and doubt not I shall save the most of them.

I am not yet able to procure an exact List of all the Stores they have left. As soon as it can be done I shall take care to transmit it to you. From an estimate already made, by the Quarter Master General, of what he has discovered, they will amount to 25 or 30,000£.

Part of the Powder mentioned in yours of the 6th Instant has already arrived; The remainder I have ordered to be stop'd on the Road as we shall have no occasion for it here. The Letter to General Thomas I immediately sent to him; he desired leave for three or four days to settle some of his private affairs after which he will set out for his Command in Canada. I am happy that my Conduct in intercepting Lord Dunmore's Letter is approved of by Congress. I am etc.

PROCLAMATION

The day after his army had taken complete possession of Boston, Washington issued the following Proclamation. His first concern was to maintain order, particularly in the relationship between his soldiers and the inhabitants of the city. Since the British fleet was still within striking distance, Washington ordered the construction of defenses at the harbor and cleared those which had been built by the enemy as protection against his troops. The transports, however, soon vanished from the coast. The first great triumph of the Revolutionary Army was hailed by Congress with a vote of thanks and a gold medal for the deliverer of Boston.

March 25, 1776

Whereas the ministerial army has abandoned the town of Boston, and the forces of the United Colonies under my command are in possession of the same; I have therefore thought it necessary for the preservation of peace, good order, and discipline, to publish the following orders, that no person offending therein may plead ignorance as an excuse for their misconduct.

All officers and soldiers are hereby ordered to live in the strictest peace and amity with the inhabitants; and no inhabitant, or other person, employed in his lawful business in the town is to be molested in his person or property, on any pretence whatever.

If any officer or soldier shall presume to strike, imprison, or otherwise ill-treat any of the inhabitants, he may depend on being punished with the utmost severity; and if any officer or soldier shall receive any insult from any of the inhabitants, he is to seek redress in a legal way, and no other.

Any non-commissioned officer or soldier, or others under my command, who shall be guilty of robbing or plundering in the town, are to be immediately confined, and will be most rigidly punished. All officers are therefore ordered to be very vigilant in the discovery of such offenders, and report their names and crime to the commanding officer in the town, as soon as may be.

The inhabitants and others are called upon to make known to the Quartermaster-general, or any of his deputies, all stores belonging to the ministerial army, that may be remaining or secreted in the town; any person or persons whatsoever, that shall be known to conceal any of the said stores, or appropriate them to his or their own use, will be considered as an enemy to America, and treated accordingly.

The selectmen and other magistrates of the town are desired to return to the Commander-in-chief the names of all or any person or persons, they may suspect of being employed as spies upon the Continental army, that they may be dealt with accordingly.

All officers of the Continental army are enjoined to assist the civil magistrates in the execution of their duty, and to promote peace and good order. They are to prevent, as much as possible, the soldiers from frequenting tippling-houses, and strolling from their posts. Particular notice will be taken of such officers as are inattentive and remiss in their duty; and, on the contrary, such only as are active and vigilant will be entitled to future favor and promotion.

To JOHN AUGUSTINE WASHINGTON

The habit of writing to his brothers, John Augustine and Lund, followed throughout the war, provided Washington with the opportunity to set down a record of major and minor events as they occurred, summarized for family consumption, without self-consciousness or any formality whatever. Here he gives a noteworthy résumé of the siege and capture of Boston. Over and over again he emphasizes his conviction that unity of purpose, above everything else, will assure victory.

Cambridge, March 31, 1776

DEAR BROTHER: Your Letter of the 24th. Ulto. was duely forwarded to this Camp by Colo. Lee, and gave me the pleasure of hearing that you, my Sister and family were well. After your Post is established to Fredericksburg the Intercourse by Letter may become regular and certain (and whenever time, little of which God knows I have for friendly corrispondance, will permit, I shall be happy in writing to you). I cannot call to mind the date of my last to you, but this I recollect, that I have written more Letters to than I have received from you.

The Want of Arms, Powder &ca., is not peculiar to Virginia, this Country of which doubtless, you have heard such large and flattering Accounts, is more defficient of each than you can conceive, I have been here Months together with what will scarcely be believed; not 30 rounds of Musket Cartridges a Man; have been obliged to submit to all the Insults of the Enemy's Cannon for want of Powder, keeping what little we had for Pistol distance. Another thing has been done, which added to the above, will put it in the power of this Army to say what perhaps none other with justice ever could. We have maintain'd our Ground against the Enemy, under the above want of Powder, and we have disbanded one Army and recruited another, within Musket Shot of two and Twenty Regiments, the Flower of the British Army, when our strength have been little if any, superior to theirs; and, at last, have beat them, in a shameful and precipitate manner out of a place the strongest by Nature on this Continent, and strengthend and fortified in the best manner and at an enormous Expence.

As some Acct. of the late Manouvres of both Armies, may not be unacceptable, I shall, hurried as I always am, devote a little time to it.

Having received a small supply of Powder then; very inadequate to our wants, I resolved to take possession of Dorchester Point, laying East of Boston; looking directly into it; and commanding (absolutely) the Enemy's Lines on the Neck (Boston) To effect this, which I knew would force the Enemy to an Ingagement, or subject them to be enphiladed by our Cannon, it was necessary, in the first Instance to possess two heights (those mentioned in Genl. Burgoyne's Letter to Lord Stanley in his Acct. of the Battle of Bunkers Hill), which had the entire command of it. The grd. at this time being froze upwards of two feet deep, and as impenetrable as a Rock, nothing could be attempted with Earth; we were obligd, therefore to provide an amazing quantity of chandeliers and Fascines for the Work, and on the Night of the 4th, after a previous severe

Cannonade and Bombardment for three Nights together to divert the Enemy's attention from our real design, we removed every material to the spot under Cover of Darkness, and took full possession of those heights without the loss of a single Man.

Upon their discovery of the Works next Morning, great preparations were made for attacking them, but not being ready before the Afternoon and the Weather getting very tempestuous, much blood was Saved, and a very important blow (to one side or the other) prevented. That this remarkable Interposition of Providence is for some wise purpose, I have not a doubt; but as the principal design of the Manouvre was to draw the Enemy to an Ingagement under disadvantages, as a premeditated Plan was laid for this purpose, and seemed to be succeeding to my utmost wish, and as no Men seem'd better disposed to make the appeal than ours did upon that occasion, I can scarce forbear lamenting the disappointment, unless the dispute is drawing to an accommodation, and the Sword going to be Sheathed.

But to return, the Enemy thinking (as we have since learnt) that we had got too securely posted, before the Second Morning to be much hurt by them, and apprehending great annoyance from our new Works resolved upon a retreat, and accordingly Imbark'd in as much hurry, precipitation and confusion as ever Troops did the 17th, not taking time to fit their transports, but leaving King's property in Boston to the amount, as is supposed, of thirty or £40,000 in Provisions, Stores, &ca. Many Pieces of Cannon, some Mortars, and a number of Shot, Shells &ca. are also left; and Baggage-Waggons, Artillery Carts &ca. which they have been Eighteen Months preparing to take the Field with, were found destroyed, thrown into the Docks, and drifted upon every shore. In short, Dunbar's destruction of Stores after Genl. Braddock's defeat, which made so much noise, affords but a faint Idea of what was to be met with here.

The Enemy lay from the 17th. to the 27th. In Nantasket and King's Roads, abt. Nine Miles from Boston, to take in Water (from the Islands thereabouts surrounded by their shipping) and to fit themselves for Sea. Whither they are now bound, and where their Tents will be next pitched, I know not; but as New York and the Hudson's River are the most important objects they can have in view, as the latter secures the communication with Canada, at the same time that it seperates the Northern and Southern Colonies; and the former is thought to abound in disaffected Persons, who only wait a favourable oppertunity, and support, to declare themselves openly, it became equally important for us to prevent their gaining Possession of these advantages; and, therefore, as soon as they Imbarked I detachd a Brigade of Six Regiments to that Government, so soon as they Sailed, another Brigade compos'd of the same number, and to morrow another of Five will March. In a day or two more I shall follow myself and be in New York ready to receive all but the first.

The Enemy left all their Works standing in Boston, and on Bunker's hill, and formidable they are, the Town has shared a much better Fate than was expected, the damage done to the Houses being nothing equal to report, but the Inhabitants have sufferd a good deal by being plunder'd by the Soldiery at their departure. All those who took upon themselves the Style, and title of Government Men in Boston, in short, all those who have acted an unfriendly part in this great Contest have Shipped themselves off in the same hurry, but under still greater disadvantages than the King's Troops have done; being obliged to Man their own Vessels (for Seamen could not be had for the Transports for the Kings use) and submit to every hardship that can be conceiv'd. One or two have done, what a great many ought to have done long ago, committed Suicide. By all Accts. there never existed a more miserable set of Beings, than these wretched Creatures now are; taught to believe that the Power of Great Britain was superior to all opposition, and that foreign aid (if not) was at hand, they were even higher, and more insulting in their opposition than the Regulars. When the Order Issued therefore for Imbarking the Troops in Boston, no Electric Shock, no sudden Clap of thunder. In a word the last Trump, could not have struck them with greater Consternation. they were at their Wits' end, and conscious of their black ingratitude chose to commit themselves in the manner I have above describ'd to the Mercy of the Waves at a tempestuous Season rather than meet their offended Countrymen. but with this declaration the choice was made that if they thought the most abject submission would procure them Peace they never would have stir'd.

I believe I may, with great truth affirm, that no Man perhaps since the first Institution of Armys ever commanded one under more difficult Circumstances, than I have done, to enumerate the particulars would fill a volume, many of my difficulties and distresses were of so peculiar a cast that in order to conceal them from the Enemy, I was obliged to conceal them from my friends, indeed from my own Army, thereby subjecting my Conduct to interpretations unfavourable to my Character, especially by those at a distance, who could not, in the smallest degree be acquainted with the Springs that govern'd it. I am happy however, to find, and to hear from different Quarters, that my reputation stands fair, that my Conduct hitherto has given universal Satisfaction, the Addresses which I have received, and which I suppose will be published, from the General Court of this Colony the same as our Genl. Assembly and from the Selectmen of Boston upon the evacuation of the Town and my approaching departure from the Colony, exhibits a pleasing testimony of their approbation of my conduct, and of their personal regard, which I have found in various other Instances; and wch, in retirement, will afford many comfortable reflections.

The share you have taken in these Publick disputes is commendable and praiseworthy; it is a duty we owe our Country; a claim posterity has on us. It is not sufficient for a Man to be a passive friend and well-Wisher to the Cause. This, and every other Cause of such a Nature, must inevitably perish under such an opposition, every person should be active in some department or other, without paying too much attention to private Interest. It is a great stake we are playing for, and sure we are of winning if the Cards are well managed. Inactivity in some, disaffection in others, and timidity in many, may hurt the Cause; nothing else can, for Unanimity will carry us through triumphantly, in spite of every exertion of Great Britain, if link'd together in one indissoluble Bond; this they now know, and are practising every stratagem which Human Invention can divise, to divide us, and unite their own People, upon this principle it is, the restraining Bill is past, and Commissioners are coming over. The devise to be sure is shallow, the covering thin, But they will hold out to their own People that the Acts (complain'd of) are repealed, and Commissioners sent to each Colony to treat with us, neither of which will we attend to &ca. this upon weak Minds among us will have its effect, they wish for reconciliation; or in other Words they wish for Peace without attending to the Conditions.

General Lee, I expect, is with you before this. He is the first Officer in Military knowledge and experience we have in the whole Army. He is zealously attach'd to the Cause, honest and well meaning, but rather fickle and violent I fear in his temper. however as he possesses an uncommon share of good Sense and Spirit I congratulate my Countrymen upon his appointment to that Department. The appointment of Lewis I think was also judicious, for notwithstanding the odium thrown upon his Conduct at the Kanhawa I always look'd upon him as a Man of Spirit and a good Officer; his experience is equal to any one we have. Colo. Mercer would have supplied the place well, but I question (as a Scotchman) whether it would have gone glibly down. Bullet is no favourite of mine, and therefore I shall say nothing more of him, than that his own opinion of himself always kept pace with what others pleas'd to think of him; if any thing, rather run a head of it.

As I am now nearly at the end of my Eighth page, I think it time to conclude, especially as I set out with prefacing, the little time I had for friendly Corrispondences. I shall only add therefore my Affectionate regards to my Sister and the Children, and Compliments to any enquiring friends and that I am with every Sentiment of true Affection, your Loving Brother and faithful friend.

To BENJAMIN FRANKLIN

Washington left Boston for New York on April 4th and ar-rived on the 13th. The "Honorable Commissioners" to whom he refers were Benjamin Franklin, Samuel Chase and Charles Carroll of Carrolton, who had been sent to Canada to persuade the Canadians to join their fortunes with those of the colonists.

The mission failed, Franklin returned a sick man and the Com-
missioners recommended abandonment of the entire plan. Even
worse was the failure of the military campaign against Quebec.
Arnold and the remnants of his expedition, shattered by defeat,
by the cold, by hunger and by smallpox, finally broke in panic
and collapsed.

New York, May 20, 1776

Dear Sir I do myself the pleasure to Transmit you the Inclosed Letter which I received yesterday with several others in the condition this is and containing similar Intelligence— the rest I forwarded to Congress immediately on receipt. They had passed thro the hands of some of the Committees in the Eastern Governments by whom they were opened.

On the morning of the 17 Inst with much concern and surprize I received the melancholy account of our Troops being Obliged to raise the Seige of Quebec with the loss of their Cannon, a number of small Arms, provisions &c.

I had hoped before this misfortune, that the Troops there wou'd have maintained their posts, and on the Arrival of the two Brigades detached from hence, consisting of Ten Regiments (the last of which was at Albany under Genl Sullivan when the account came) the Blockade bravely kept up for a long time by a handfull of men against a victorious Enemy superior in numbers, wou'd terminate in a favourable and happy Issue, the reduction of Quebec and our consequent possession of the Important Country to which It belongs—to what cause to ascribe the sad disaster, I am at loss to determine, but hence I shall know the events of War are exceedingly doubtfull, and that Capricious fortune often blasts our most flattering hopes.

I feel this important and Interesting event, not a little heighten'd by Its casting up, just on your entrance and that of the other Honorable Commissioners in that Country—tho your presence may conduce to the public good in an essential manner, yet I am certain you must experience difficulties and embarrassments of a peculiar nature—perhaps in a little Time, Things may assume a more promising appearance than the present is, and your difficulties in some degree be done away.

Wishing your Councils under the guidance of a kind providence and a tender of my respectfull Compliments to the Gentn who accompany you, I have the honor etc.

To JOHN AUGUSTINE WASHINGTON

The vote of the Virginia Convention, to which Washington here refers, gave instructions to their delegates to the Continental Congress to declare the colonies free and independent states and absolved from any allegiance to Great Britain. When carried out, these instructions led to the adoption of the Declaration of Independence on July 4th. Washington's caution—"if the foundation is badly laid, the superstructure must be bad" —is characteristic, and his warning against a patched-up Constitution gives additional evidence of his calm foresight at a critical moment.

Philadelphia, May 31, 1776

DEAR BROTHER: Since my arrival at this place, where I came at the request of Congress, to settle some matters relative to the ensuing Campaign I have received your Letter of the 18th. from Williamsburg, and think I stand indebted to you for another, which came to hand some time ago, in New York.

I am very glad to find that the Virginia Convention have passed so noble a vote, and with so much unanimity, things have come to that pass now, as to convince us, that we have nothing more to expect from the justice of G. Britain; also, that she is capable of the most delusive Arts, for I am satisfied that no Commissioners ever were design'd, except Hessians and other Foreigners; and that the Idea was only to deceive, and throw us off our guard; the first it has too effectually accomplished, as many Members of Congress, in short, the representation of whole Provences, are still feeding themselves upon the dainty food of reconciliation; and tho' they will not allow that the expectation of it has any influence upon their judgments (with respect to their preparations for defence) it is but too obvious that it has an operation upon every part of their conduct and is a clog to their proceedings, it is not in the nature of things to be otherwise, for no Man, that entertains a hope of seeing this dispute speedily, and equitably adjusted by Commissioners, will go to the same expence and run the same hazards to prepare for the worst event as he who believes that he must conquer, or submit to unconditional terms, and its concomitants, such as Confiscation, hanging, &c., &c.

To form a new Government, requires infinite care, and unbounded attention; for if the foundation is badly laid the superstructure must be bad, too much time therefore, cannot be bestowed in weighing and digesting matters well. We have, no doubt, some good parts in our present constitution; many bad ones we know we have, wherefore no time can be misspent that is imployed in separating the Wheat from the Tares. My fear is, that you will all get tired and homesick, the consequence of which will be, that you will patch up some kind of Constitution as defective as the present; this should be avoided, every Man should consider, that he is lending his aid to frame a Constitution which is to render Million's happy, or Miserable, and that a matter of such moment cannot be the Work of a day.

I am in hopes to hear some good Accts from No. Carolina. If Clinton has only part of his force there, and not strongly Intrenched, I should think Genl. Lee will be able to give a very good acct. of those at Cape Fare. Surely Administration must intend more than 5000 Men for the Southern district, otherwise they must have a very contemptable opinion of those Colonies, or have great expectation of assistance from the Indians, Slaves, and Tories. We expect a very bloody Summer of it at New York and Canada, as it is there I expect the grand efforts of the Enemy will be aim'd; and I am sorry to say that we are not, either in Men, or Arms, prepared for it; however, it is to be hoped, that if our cause is just, as I do most religiously believe it to be, the same Providence which has in many Instances appear'd for us, will still go on to afford its aid.

Your Convention is acting very wisely in removing the disaffected, Stock, &ca., from the Counties of Princess Anne and

Norfolk; and are much to be commended for their attention
to the Manufacture of Salt, Salt Petre, Powder &ca. No time,
nor expense should be spared to accomplish these things.

Mrs. Washington is now under Innoculation in this City;
and will, I expect, have the Small pox favourably, this is the
13th day, and she has very few Pustules; she would have wrote
to my Sister but thought it prudent not to do so, notwithstanding there could be but little danger in conveying the Infection
in this manner. She joins me in love to you, her, and all the
little ones. I am, with every Sentiment of regard, etc.

To THE PRESIDENT OF CONGRESS

*Having urged upon Congress the establishment of a quarter-
master's department and a Board of War and Ordnance, Washington's victory in persuading the delegates to create a War
Office, the forerunner of the War Department, deserves a place
on what he calls the "Historic Page." An editor cannot resist
quoting his justification of the institution of the War Office:
"This like other great Works in its first Edition, may not be
entirely free from Error. Time will discover its Defects and
experience suggest the Remedy, and such further Improvements as may be necessary; but it was right to give it a Beginning."*

New York, June 20, 1776

SIR: I am now to acknowledge the receipt of your Favours of the 14th and 18th. instant, and the interesting resolves
contained in them, with which I have been honored.

The several matters recommended to my attention, shall be
particularly regarded, and the directions of Congress, and your
requests complied with, in every instance, as far as is in my
power.

The Institution of a War Office is certainly an Event of great
importance, and in all probability will be recorded as such in
the Historic Page. The Benefits derived from it, I flatter myself

will be considerable tho' the plan, upon which it is first formed may not be entirely perfect. This like other great Works in its first Edition, may not be entirely free from Error. Time will discover its Defects and experience suggest the Remedy, and such further Improvements as may be necessary; but it was right to give it a Beginning.

The Recommendation to the Convention of New York for restraining and punishing disaffected Persons, I am hopeful will be attended with salutary consequences, and the prohibition against exporting Provisions appears to have been a measure founded in sound Policy, lest proper supplies should be wanted wherewith to subsist our Armies.

I have transmitted General Schuyler, the resolves about the Indians, and the others on which he is to act, and have requested his strict attention and exertions in order to their being carried into Execution with all possible Dispatch.

I note your request respecting Mr. Hancock; he shall have such Directions as may be necessary for conducting his Office and I am happy he will have so early a remittance for paying the Troops in his Department.

The Silver and Paper Money designed for Canada will be highly serviceable, and I hope will be the means of reestablishing our Credit there in some degree with the Canadians, and also encourage our Men, who have complained in this Instance; when it arrives, I will send it forward under a proper Guard.

I have communicated to General Gates the Resolve of Congress for him to repair to Canada, and directed him to view Point au Fere, that a Fortress may be erected if he shall judge it necessary; he is preparing for his command and in a few days will take his Departure for it: I would, fain hope his arrival there will give our Affairs, a complexion different from what they have worn for a long Time past, and that many essential Benefits will result from it.

The kind attention Congress have shewn to afford the Commander in Chief here every assistance, by resolving that recommendatory Letters be written to the conventions of New Jersey, New York and the Assembly of Connecticut, to Authorize him to call in the militias in cases of exigency, claims my thankful acknowledgments and I trust, if carried into execution, will produce many advantages, in case It may be expedient to call in early reinforcements; the delays Incident to the ordinary mode may frequently render their aid too late and prove exceedingly Injurious.

I this Evening received Intelligence of the 19th. instt. from Captn. Pond of the Armed Sloop Schuyler, of his having taken, about 50 miles from this on the Sôuth side of Long Island, a Ship and a Sloop bound to Sandy Hook: The Ship from Glasgow with a Company of the 22d Regiment, had been taken before by one of Commodore Hopkins Fleet, who took the Soldiers out and ordered her to Rhode Island, after which she was retaken by the Cerberus and put under the convoy of the Sloop. As Captain Pond informs, there were five Commissioned Officers, Two Ladies and four Privates on board; they are not yet arrived at Head Quarters; inclosed is an Invoice of what they have on Board.

General Wooster having expressed an inclination and wish to wait on Congress, I have given him permission, not having any occasion for him here. he sets out this morning.

I have been up to view the grounds about Kings Bridge, and find them to admit of many Places well calculated for defence, and esteeming it a Pass of the utmost importance have ordered Works to be laid out and shall direct part of the two Battalions from Pennsylvania, to set about the erection immediately, and will add to their Numbers several of the Militia, when they come, in to expedite them with all possible Dispatch; their consequences, as they will keep open the Communication with the Country, requires the most speedy completion of them. I have the Honor to be &c.

GENERAL ORDERS

The omissions at the beginning and end of this communication to his officers and troops refer to minor assignments, the duties of sentries, the allotment of tents, leaves of absence, a court-martial verdict of acquittal for a soldier who was absent without permission and a warning to safeguard arms and ammunition against spoilage by rain. It is for his eloquence in call-

ing upon a citizens' army to defend freedom that this fragment of a few paragraphs from a set of General Orders is preserved.

Head Quarters, New York, July 2, 1776

. . . The time is now near at hand which must probably determine, whether Americans are to be, Freemen, or Slaves; whether they are to have any property they can call their own; whether their Houses, and Farms, are to be pillaged and destroyed, and they consigned to a State of Wretchedness from which no human efforts will probably deliver them. The fate of unborn Millions will now depend, under God, on the Courage and Conduct of this army—Our cruel and unrelenting Enemy leaves us no choice but a brave resistance, or the most abject submission; this is all we can expect—We have therefore to resolve to conquer or die: Our own Country's Honor, all call upon us for a vigorous and manly exertion, and if we now shamefully fail, we shall become infamous to the whole world. Let us therefore rely upon the goodness of the Cause, and the aid of the supreme Being, in whose hands Victory is, to animate and encourage us to great and noble Actions—The Eyes of all our Countrymen are now upon us, and we shall have their blessings, and praises, if happily we are the instruments of saving them from the Tyranny meditated against them. Let us therefore animate and encourage each other, and shew the whole world, that a Freeman contending for LIBERTY on his own ground is superior to any slavish mercenary on earth.

The General recommends to the officers great coolness in time of action, and to the soldiers a strict attention and obedience with a becoming firmness and spirit.

Any officer, or soldier, or any particular Corps, distinguishing themselves by any acts of bravery, and courage, will assuredly meet with notice and rewards; and on the other hand, those who behave ill, will as certainly be exposed and punished— The General being resolved, as well for the Honor and Safety of the Country, as Army, to shew no favour to such as refuse, or neglect their duty at so important a crisis. . . .

To THE MASSACHUSETTS LEGISLATURE
OR COMMITTEE OF SAFETY OF THE STATE

Washington's first official announcement of the Declaration of Independence was made part of a letter devoted to a request for measures of defense against a British incursion aimed at the state of New York and the Great Lakes.

New York, July 9, 1776

GENTN.: You will perceive by the inclosed Declaration, which I have the honor to transmit you, that Congress of late have been employed in deliberating on Matters of the utmost Importance. Impelled by Necessity and a Repetition of Injuries unsufferable, without the most distant prospect of relief, they have asserted the Claims of the American Colonies to the rights of Humanity and declared them, Free and Independent States. . . .

GENERAL ORDERS

The order to read the Declaration of Independence to all the brigades is preceded by the approval of a sentence of thirty-nine lashes each to two soldiers for desertion, the issuance of passes, the pay of $33.33 per month to chaplains and the request that "every officer and man will endeavour to live, and act, as becomes a Christian Soldier defending the dearest Rights and Liberties of his country." (Omitted here)

Head Quarters, New York, July 9, 1776

. . . The Hon. The Continental Congress, impelled by the dictates of duty, policy and necessity, having been pleased to dissolve the Connection which subsisted between this Country, and Great Britain, and to declare the United Colonies of North America, free and independent STATES: The several brigades are to be drawn up this evening on their respective Parades, at Six OClock, when the declaration of Congress, shewing the grounds and reasons of this measure, is to be read with an audible voice.

The General hopes this important Event will serve as a fresh incentive to every officer, and soldier, to act with Fidelity and Courage, as knowing that now the peace and safety of his Country depends (under God) solely on the success of our arms: And that he is now in the service of a State, possessed of sufficient power to reward his merit, and advance him to the highest Honors of a free Country.

The Brigade Majors are to receive, at the Adjutant Generals Office, several of the Declarations to be delivered to the Brigadiers General, and the Colonels of Regiments.

The Brigade Majors are to be excused from farther attendance at Head Quarters, except to receive the Orders of the day, that their time and attention may be withdrawn as little as possible, from the duties of their respective brigades.

GENERAL ORDERS

Growing disaffection and irritation among his troops made Washington take notice of the petty jealousies which threatened the morale of his entire army. He warned against personal disagreements and small intrigues, and called upon his men to realize that equality and justice are the means by which an army, and a nation, can be welded into a unit devoted to a common, noble cause.

Head Quarters, New York, August 1, 1776

Parole Paris. Countersign Reading.

It is with great concern, the General understands, that Jealousies &c. are arisen among the troops from the different Provinces, of reflections frequently thrown out, which can only tend to irritate each other, and injure the noble cause in which we are engaged, and which we ought to support with one hand and one heart. The General most earnestly entreats the officers, and soldiers, to consider the consequences; that they can no way assist our cruel enemies more effectually, than making division among ourselves; That the Honor and Success of the army, and the safety of our bleeding Country, depends upon harmony and good agreement with each other; That the Provinces are all United to oppose the common enemy, and all distinctions sunk in the name of an American; to make this honorable, and preserve the Liberty of our Country, ought to be our only emulation, and he will be the best Soldier, and the best Patriot, who contributes most to this glorious work, whatever his Station, or from whatever part of the Continent, he may come: Let all distinctions of Nations, Countries, and Provinces, therefore be lost in the generous contest, who shall behave with the most Courage against the enemy, and the most kindness and good humour to each other—If there are any officers, or soldiers, so lost to virtue and a love of their Country as to continue in such practices after this order; The General assures them, and is directed by Congress to declare, to the whole Army, that such persons shall be severely punished and dismissed the service with disgrace.

To THE OFFICERS AND SOLDIERS OF THE PENNSYLVANIA ASSOCIATORS

Washington's miscalculation, by some seven years, of the duration of the war—"the Fate of our Country depends in all human probability, on the Exertion of a few Weeks"—is one of his rare expressions of optimism during this period. Generally he was more inclined, out of caution, to err on the side of pessimism.

Head Quarters, August 8, 1776

GENTLEMEN: I had fully resolved to have paid you a Visit in New Jersey if the movements of the Enemy, and some intelligence indicating an early attack, had not induced me to suspend it.

Allow me therefore, to address you in this Mode, as fellow Citizens and fellow Soldiers engaged in the same Glorious Cause; to represent to you, that the Fate of our Country depends in all human probability, on the Exertion of a few Weeks; That it is of the utmost importance, to keep up a respectable Force for that time, and there can be no doubt that success will Crown our Efforts, if we firmly and resolutely determine, to conquer or to die.

I have placed so much confidence, in the Spirit and Zeal of the Associated Troops of Pennsylvania, that I cannot persuade myself an impatience to return Home, or a less honourable Motive will defeat my well grounded expectation, that they will do their Country essential Service, at this critical time, when the Powers of Despotism are all combined against it, and ready to strike their most decisive Stroke. If I could allow myself to doubt your Spirit and Perseverance, I should represent the ruinous Consequences of your leaving the Service, by setting before you, the discouragement it would give the Army, the confusion and shame of our Friends, and the still more galling triumph of our Enemies. But as I have no such doubts, I shall only thank you for the Spirit and Ardor you have shewn, in so readily marching to meet the Enemy, and am most confident you will crown it by a Glorious Perseverance. The Honor and safety of our bleeding Country, and every other motive that can influence the brave and heroic Patriot, call loudly upon us, to acquit ourselves with Spirit. In short, we must now determine to be enslaved or free. If we make Freedom our choice, we must obtain it, by the Blessing of Heaven on our United and Vigorous Efforts.

I salute you Gentlemen most Affectionately, and beg leave to remind you, that Liberty, Honor, and Safety are all at stake,

and I trust Providence will smile upon our Efforts, and establish us once more, the Inhabitants of a free and happy Country.
I am, etc.

To LUND WASHINGTON

*Rumors of peace proposals circulated and grew fantastically
in the colonies. In a General Order Washington denounced
them as false, and here, in his letter to his brother, he analyzes
these rumors calmly and with his usual common sense.*

New York, August 19, 1776

DEAR LUND: Very unexpectedly to me, another revolving
Monday is arrived before an Attack upon this City, or a movement of the Enemy; the reason of this is incomprehensible,
to me. True it is (from some late informations) they expect
another arrival of about 5000 Hessians; but then, they have
been stronger than the Army under my Command; which will
now, I expect, gain strength faster than theirs, as the Militia are
beginning to come in fast, and have already augmented our
numbers in this City and the Posts round about, to about 23,000
Men. The Enemy's numbers now on the Island and in the
Transports which lay off it, are by the lowest Accts. 20,000 Men
by the greatest 27,000 to these the expected (5000) Hessians are
to be added.

There is something exceedingly misterious in the conduct of
the Enemy. Lord Howe takes pains to throw out, upon every
occasion, that he is the Messenger of Peace; that he wants to
accomodate matters, nay, has Insinuated, that he thinks himself
authorized to do it upon the terms mentioned in the last Petition to the King of G. Britain. But has the Nation got to that,
that the King, or his Ministers will openly dispense with Acts
of Parliament. And if they durst attempt it, how is it to be
accounted for that after running the Nation to some Millions
of Pounds Sterlg. to hire and Transport Foreigners, and before
a blow is struck, they are willing to give the terms proposed by

Congress before they, or we, had encountered the enormous expence that both are now run to. I say, how is this to be accounted for but from their having received some disagreeable advices from Europe; or, by having some Manouvre in view which is to be effected by procrastination. What this can be the Lord knows, we are now passed the Middle of August and they are in possession of an Island only, which it never was in our power, or Intention to dispute their Landing on. this is but a small step towards the Conquest of this Continent. . . .

GENERAL ORDERS

As the British began to land on Long Island, Washington exhorted his men to be ready for a final test against the invaders. Apparently their plan was to have part of their force take possession of the Heights of Brooklyn and another land above New York City. From Staten Island 20,000 of their men embarked to attack Long Island and points on the Hudson, while 15,000 marched against Bergen Point and Perth Amboy. Brooklyn was vital to the defense of New York. Washington immediately sent six battalions to Brooklyn and crossed over himself on the day following the issuance of this General Order. Because General Nathanael Greene had fallen ill at the last moment, his command on Long Island was taken over by General Israel Putnam.

Head Quarters, New York, August 23, 1776

Parole Charlestown.   Countersign Lee.

The Commissary General is directed to have five days Bread baked, and ready to be delivered: If the Commissary should apply to the commanding officers of regiments, for any Bakers, they are to furnish them without waiting for a special order.

The General was sorry yesterday to find, that when some troops were ordered to march, they had no provisions, notwithstanding the Orders that have been issued. The men must march, if the service requires it, and will suffer very much if not provided: The General therefore directs, all the Troops to have two days hard Bread, and Pork, ready by them; and desires the officers will go through the encampment, and quarters, to see that it be got and kept.

The General would be obliged to any officer, to recommend to him, a careful, sober person who understands taking care of Horses and waiting occasionally. Such person being a Soldier will have his pay continued, and receive additional wages of twenty Shillings pr Month—He must be neat in his person, and to be depended on for his honesty and sobriety.

The officers of the militia are informed, that twenty-four Rounds are allowed to a man, and two Flints; that the Captains of each Company should see that the Cartridges fit the bore of the gun; they then are to be put up in small Bundles; All the Cartridges except six; writing each mans name on his bundle, and keep them safely 'till the Alarm is given, then deliver to each man his bundle; the other six to be kept for common use. In drawing for ammunition, the commanding officers should, upon the regimental parade, examine the state of their regiments, and then draw for Cartridges, and Flints, agreeable to the above regulation. Capt. Tilton will assist them in their business, and, unless in case of alarm, they are desired not to draw for every small number of men, who may be coming in.

The Enemy have now landed on Long Island, and the hour is fast approaching, on which the Honor and Success of this army, and the safety of our bleeding Country depend. Remember officers and Soldiers, that you are Freemen, fighting for the blessings of Liberty—that slavery will be your portion, and that of your posterity, if you do not acquit yourselves like men: Remember how your Courage and Spirit have been dispised, and traduced by your cruel invaders; though they have found by dear experience at Boston, Charlestown and other places, what a few brave men contending in their own land, and in the best of causes can do, against base hirelings and mercenaries— Be cool, but determined; do not fire at a distance, but wait for orders from your officers—It is the General's express orders that if any man attempt to skulk, lay down, or retreat without Orders he be instantly shot down as an example, he hopes no such

Scoundrel will be found in this army; but on the contrary, every one for himself resolving to conquer, or die, and trusting to the smiles of heaven upon so just a cause, will behave with Bravery and Resolution: Those who are distinguished for their Gallantry, and good Conduct, may depend upon being honorably noticed, and suitably rewarded: And if this Army will but emulate, and imitate their brave Countrymen, in other parts of America, he has no doubt they will, by a glorious Victory, save their Country, and acquire to themselves immortal Honor. . . .

To THE PRESIDENT OF CONGRESS

While General Putnam was taking over command of the defense of Long Island, the enemy, reinforced by two brigades of Hessians from Staten Island, was approaching in force under General William Howe and Sir Henry Clinton. As artillery fire began on land, a cannonade from a British ship opened against Red Hook. Terror struck the citizens of New York as the musket fire was heard across the river. Washington rushed to the scene of action and had to watch while his troops, hemmed in between the British and Hessians, fought against hopeless odds and suffered frightful casualties. Surrounded, some Americans fought their way out. Washington, witnessing the disaster and torn with agony, made a decision upon which a great portion of his fame as a military strategist rests. It was to retreat and retreat and retreat, until he could turn on his enemy and fight again.

Head Quarters, New York, September 8, 1776

Sir: Since I had the Honor of addressing you on the 6th. instant, I have called a Council of the General Officers, in order to take a full and comprehensive view of our Situation and thereupon form such a plan of future defence, as may be immediately pursued and subject to no other Alteration than a change of Operations on the Enemy's side may occasion. Before the landing of the Enemy on Long Island, the point of Attack could not be known or any satisfactory Judgment formed of their Intentions. It might be on Long Island, on Bergen or directly on the City, this made it necessary to be prepared for each, and has occasioned an Expence of Labour which now seems useless and is regretted by those who form a Judgment from after Knowledge. But I trust, men of discernment will think differently and see that by such Works and preparations we have not only delayed the Operations of the Campaign, till it is too late to effect any capital Incursion into the Country, but have drawn the Enemy's forces to one point and obliged them to decline their plan, so as to enable us to form our defence on some Certainty. It is now extremely obvious, from all Intelligence, from their movements and every other circumstance, that having landed their whole Army on Long Island (except about 4000, on Staten Island) they mean to enclose us on the Island of New York by taking post in our Rear, while the Shipping effectually secure the Front, and thus either by cutting off our communication with the Country, oblige us to fight them on their own Terms, or surrender at discretion, or by a brilliant Stroke endeavour to cut this Army in pieces and secure the Collection of Arms and Stores which they well know we shall not be soon able to replace.

Having therefore their System unfolded to us, it became an important consideration how it could be most successfully opposed. On every side there is a Choice of difficulties and every Measure on our part (however painful the reflection is from experience) to be formed with some Apprehension that all our Troops will not do their duty.

In deliberating on this Question it was impossible to forget, that History, our own experience, the advice of our ablest Friends in Europe, the fears of the Enemy, and even the Declarations of Congress demonstrate, that on our Side the War should be defensive. It has even been called a War of Posts. That we should on all Occasions avoid a general Action, or put anything to the Risque, unless compelled by a necessity, into which we ought never to be drawn.

The Arguments on which such a System was founded were deemed unanswerable and experience has given her sanction. With these views, and being fully persuaded that it would be presumption to draw out our Young Troops into open ground, against their Superiors both in number and Discipline; I have never spared the Spade and Pick Ax; I confess I have not found that readiness to defend even strong Posts, at all hazards, which is necessary to derive the greatest benefit from them. The honor of making a brave defence does not seem to be a sufficient stimulus, when the success is very doubtful, and the falling into the Enemy's hands probable. But I doubt not this will be gradually attained. We are now in a strong Post, but not an Impregnable one, nay acknowledged by every man of Judgment to be untenable, unless the Enemy will make the Attack upon Lines, when they can avoid it and their Movements indicate that they mean to do so. To draw the whole Army together in order to arrange the defence proportionate to the extent of Lines and works, would leave the Country open to an Approach and put the fate of this Army and its Stores on the hazard of making a successful defence in the City, or the Issue of an Engagement out of it. On the other hand to abandon a City, which has been by some deemed defensible and on whose Works much Labour has been bestowed, has a tendency to dispirit the Troops and enfeeble our Cause. It has also been considered as the Key to the Northern Country. But as to this I am fully of opinion, that by Establishing of strong posts at Mont Washington on the upper part of this Island and on the Jersey side opposite to it, with the Assistance of the Obstructions already made and which may be improved in the Water, that not only the navigation of Hudson's River but an easier and better communication, may be effectually secured between the Northern and Southern States. This I believe every one acquainted with the situation of the Country will readily agree to, and will appear evident to those who have an Opportunity of recuring to good maps. These and the many other consequences, which will be involved in the determination of our next measure, have given our Minds full employ and led every one to form a Judgement, as the various objects presented themselves to his view. The post at Kings Bridge is naturally strong and is pretty well fortified the Heights about it are commanding and might soon be made more so.

These are important Objects and I have attended to them

accordingly. I have also removed from the City all the Stores and Ammunition, except what was absolutely Necessary for its defence and made every other Disposition that did not essentially enterfere with that Object, carefully keeping in view, until it should be absolutely determined on full consideration, how far the City was to be defended at all events. In resolving points of such Importance, many circumstances peculiar to our own Army, also occur; being Provided only for a Summers Campaign, their Cloaths, Shoes and Blanketts will soon be unfit for the change of weather which we every day feel. At present we have not Tents for more than ⅔ds., many of them old and worn out, but if we had a Plentiful supply the season will not admit of continuing in them much longer.

The case of our Sick is also worthy of much consideration, their number by the returns form at least ¼th. of the Army: Policy and humanity require they should be made as comfortable as possible. With these and many other circumstances before them, the whole Council of General Officers, met Yesterday, in order to adopt some general line of Conduct to be pursued at this important crisis; I intended to have procured their seperate opinions on each point, but time would not admit I was Obliged to collect their sense more generally than I could have wished; We all agreed that the Town was not tenable if the Enemy was resolved to bombard and Cannonade it: But the difficulties attending a removal operated so strongly, that a Course was taken between abandoning it totally and concentring our whole strength for its defence; nor were some a little influenced in their Opinion, to whom the determination of Congress was known, against an Evacuation totally; suspecting that Congress wished it to be maintained at every hazard, It was concluded to arrange the Army under three Divisions 5000 to remain for the defence of the City, 9000 to remove to Kingsbridge, as well to Possess and secure those Posts, as to be ready to Attack the Enemy, who are moving Eastward on long Island, if they should attempt to land on this side; The remainder to occupy the intermediate space and support either, that the sick should be immediately removed to Orange Town—and Barracks prepared at Kingsbridge with all expedition, to cover the Troops; there were some Generals in whose Judgments great confidence is to be reposed, that were for an immediate removal from the City, urging the great danger of one part of our Army being cut off, before the other can support it, The extremities being at least 16 Miles apart; that our Army when collected is inferior to the Enemy; that they can move with their whole force to any point of Attack and consequently must succeed, by weight of numbers, if they have only a part to oppose them; that by removing from hence we deprive the Enemy of the Advantage of their Ships, which will make at least one half of the force to attack the Town; that we keep them at bay, but put nothing to the hazard and at all events keep an Army together, which can be recruited another Year; that the unspent Stores will also be preserved, and in this case the heavy Artillery can be secured.—But they were overruled by a Majority, who thought for the present a part of our force might be kept here and attempt to maintain the City a while longer. I am sensible a retreating Army is incircled with difficulties, that the declining an Engagement subjects a General to reproach and that the common Cause may be in some measure affected by the discouragements which it throws over the minds of many; nor am I insensible of the contrary effects, if a brilliant stroke could be made with any Probability of success, especially after our loss upon Long Island: but when the fate of America may be at stake on the Issue; when the Wisdom of cooler moments and experienced Men have decided that we should protract the War if Possible; I cannot think it safe or wise to adopt a different System, when the season for Action draws so near a close. That the Enemy mean to Winter in New York there can be no doubt; that with such an Armament they can drive us out is equally clear. The Congress having resolved, that it should not be destroyed, nothing seems to remain but to determine the time of their taking Possession It is our Interest and wish to prolong it, as much as possible, provided the delay does not affect our further measures. The Militia of Connecticut is reduced from 8000 to less than 2000 and in a few days will be merely nominal; the arrival of some Maryland Troops &c. from the flying Camp, has in a great degree supplied the loss of Men, but the Ammunition they have carried away will be a loss sensibly felt. The impulse for going home was so irrisistable, it answered no purpose to oppose it, tho' I could not discharge, I have been obliged to acquiesce; and it affords one more melancholy Proof how delusive such dependences are.

Inclosed I have the Honor to transmit a General Return of the Army, the first I have been able to obtain for a considerable time; Also a report from Captain Newel from our Works at Horn's Hook, or Hell Gate; their situation is extremely low and the sound so very narrow that the Enemy have 'em much within their Command. I have &ca.

To JOHN AUGUSTINE WASHINGTON

The Battle of Long Island cost the Continental Army nearly 2,000 killed, wounded and missing. The British losses were 380. The British fleet, anchored off Staten Island, could be seen when the fog lifted once to be preparing to come up the bay. If it did so, the remnants of Washington's army on Long Island would be trapped. Washington decided to evacuate all his remaining troops, numbering 9,000 men, under cover of fog and darkness and in absolute silence. The creak of an oar could have given them away. One by one, the boats were loaded with men and supplies and ferried to the New York side. Washington crossed the river with the last of his men. So successful was the silent abandonment of Brooklyn that only a few pieces of equipment fell into the hands of the enemy. It was a feat without parallel in military history.

Heights of Haerlem, September 22, 1776

DEAR BROTHER: My extreame hurry for some time past has rendered it utterly impossible for me to pay that attention to the Letters of my Friends which Inclination, and natural affection always Inclines me to. I have no doubt therefore of meeting with their excuse, tho' with respect to yourself, I have had no Letter from you since the date of my last saving the one of Septr. the 1st.

With respect to the Attack and Retreat from Long Island

the public Papers would furnish you with accts. nearly true. I shall only add, that in the former we lost about 800 Men, more than three fourths of which were taken Prisoners. This misfortune happened in a great measure by two Detachments of our People who were Posted in two Roads leading thro' a Wood in order to intercept the Enemy in their March, suffering a Surprize, and making a precipitate Retreat, which enabled the Enemy to lead a great part of their force against the Troops Commanded by Lord Sterling which formed a third detachment; who behaved with great bravery and resolution.

As to the Retreat from the Island, under the Circumstances we then were, it became absolutely necessary, and was effected without loss of Men, and with but very little baggage. A few heavy Cannon were left, not being movable, on acct. of the Grounds being soft and Miry, thro' the heavy and incessant Rains which had fallen. The Enemys loss in killed we could never ascertain, but have many reasons to believe that it was pretty considerable, and exceeded ours a good deal; our Retreat from thence as I said before was absolutely necessary, the Enemy having landed the main body of their Army to Attack us in Front while their Ships of War were to cut off all communication with the City, from whence resources of Men, Provisions &ca. were to be drawn.

Having made this Retreat, not long after we discovered by the movements of the Enemy and the information we received from Deserters and others, that they declin'd attacking our Lines in the City, and were forming a plan to get in our Rear with their Land Army, by crossing the Sound above us, and thereby to cut off all Intercourse with the Country and every necessary supply. The Ships of War were to coöperate, possess the North River, and prevent succours from the Jerseys, &c. This Plan appearing probable and but too practicable in its execution, it became necessary to guard agt. the fatal consequences that must follow if their scheme was affected; for which purpose I caused a removal of a part of our Stores, Troops, &ca. from the City, and a Council of General Officers determined on Thursday the 12th. that it must be entirely abandoned; as we had, with an Army weaker than theirs, a line of Sixteen or 18 Miles to defend, to keep open our Communication with the

Country, besides the defence of the City. We held up however every show and appearance of defence till our Sick and all our Stores could be brought away; the evacuation being resolved on every exertion in our power was made to baffle their designs, and effect our own. The sick were numerous (amounting to more than the fourth part of our whole Army) and an object of great Importance, happily we got them away; but before we could bring off all our Stores on Sunday Morning Six or Seven Ships of War which had gone up the East River some few days before began a most severe and heavy Canonade to scour the Ground and effect a Landing of their Troops. Three Ships of War also ran up the North River that Morning above the City, to prevent our Boats and Small Craft carrying away our Baggage &ca.

I had gone the Evening before to the Main body of our Army which was Posted about these Heights and the Plains of Harlem, where it seemed probable from the movements, and disposition of the Enemy they meant to Land and make an Attack the next Morning. However the Event did not happen. Immediately on hearing the Cannonade I rode with all possible expedition towards the place of Landing, and where Breast Works had been thrown up to secure our Men, and found the Troops that had been posted there to my great surprize and Mortification, and those ordered to their support (consisting of Eight Regiments) notwithstanding the exertions of their Generals to form them, running away in the most shameful and disgraceful manner. I used every possible effort to rally them but to no purpose, and, on the appearance of a small part of the Enemy (not more than 60 or 70) they ran off without firing a Single Gun. Many of our heavy Cannon wd. inevitably have fallen into the Enemy's hands as they landed so soon, but this scandalous conduct occasioned a loss of many Tents, Baggage and Camp Equipage, which would have been easily secured had they made the least opposition.

The Retreat was made with the loss of a few men only. We Incamp'd, and still are on, the Heights of Harlem which are well calculated for Defence against their approaches. On Monday Morning they advanced in sight in several large body, but attempted nothing of a general Nature, tho' there were smart skirmishes between their advanced parties and some Detachments from our lines which I sent out. In these our Troops behaved well, putting the Enemy to flight in open Ground, and forcing them from Posts they had seized two or three times. A Sergeant who deserted from them says they had as he was told 89 Wounded and Missing besides Slain, but other accts. make the wounded much greater.

· Our loss in killed and Wounded was about 60; but the greatest loss we sustained was in the death of Lt. Colo. Knowlton, a brave and Gallant officer. Majr. Leitch of Weedon's Regiment had three Balls through his Side, and behaved exceedingly well, he is in a fair way of recovery. Nothing material has happend since this; the Enemy it is said are bringing up their heavy Cannon, so that we are to expect another attack soon, both by Land and Water, as we are upon the Hudson, (or North River) at the place where we have attempted to stop the Navigation by sinking obstructions in the River and erecting Batteries.

The Dependance which the Congress has placed upon the Militia, has already greatly injured, and I fear will totally ruin our Cause. Being subject to no controul themselves they introduce disorder among the Troops you have attempted to discipline while the change in their living brings on sickness; this makes them Impatient to get home, which spreads universally, and introduces abominable Desertions. In short, it is not in the power of Words to describe the task I have to act. £50,000 should not induce me again to undergo what I have done. Our Numbers by Sickness, desertion, &ca. is greatly reduced. I have been trying these 4 or 5 days to get a return but have not yet succeeded. I am sure however we have not more than 12 or 14,000 Men fit for duty, whilst the Enemy (who it is said are very healthy) cannot have less than near 25,000. My sincere love to my Sister and the Family and Compliments to any enquiring Friends concludes me, etc.

To LUND WASHINGTON

With some 14,000 men under command, Washington was faced with the dilemma of holding New York and facing exter-

mination or retreating up the Hudson into a trap. There was strong Tory sentiment in the city and the British had a substantial fifth column working in their behalf. Washington wanted to abandon New York and thought even of burning it as well. Congress overruled him. The best he could do was to move his Headquarters northward on Manhattan Island to Harlem. From there, "never was in such an unhappy, divided state since I was born," he wrote to his brother in weariness and despair.

Col. Morris's, on the Heights of Harlem,
September 30, 1776

DEAR LUND: Your letter of the 18th, which is the only one received and unanswered, now lies before me. The amazement which you seem to be in at the unaccountable measures which have been adopted by [Congress] would be a good deal increased if I had time to unfold the whole system of their management since this time twelve months. I do not know how to account for the unfortunate steps which have been taken but from that fatal idea of conciliation which prevailed so long—fatal, I call it, because from my soul I wish it may [not] prove so, though my fears lead me to think there is too much danger of it. This time last year I pointed out the evil consequences of short enlistments, the expenses of militia, and the little dependence that was to be placed in them. I assured [Congress] that the longer they delayed raising a standing army, the more difficult and chargeable would they find it to get one, and that, at the same time that the militia would answer no valuable purpose, the frequent calling them in would be attended with an expense, that they could have no conception of. Whether, as I have said before, the unfortunate hope of reconciliation was the cause, or the fear of a standing army prevailed, I will not undertake to say; but the policy was to engage men for twelve months only. The consequence of which, you have had great bodies of militia in pay that never were in camp; you have had immense quantities of provisions drawn by men that never rendered you one hour's service (at least usefully), and this in the most profuse and wasteful way. Your stores have been expended, and every kind of military [discipline?] destroyed by them; your numbers fluctuating, uncertain, and forever far short of report—at no one time, I believe, equal to twenty thousand men fit for duty. At present our numbers fit for duty (by this day's report) amount to 14,759, besides 3,427 on command, and the enemy within stone's throw of us. It is true a body of militia are again ordered out, but they come without any conveniences and soon return. I discharged a regiment the other day that had in it fourteen rank and file fit for duty only, and several that had less than fifty. In short, such is my situation that if I were to wish the bitterest curse to an enemy on this side of the grave, I should put him in my stead with my feelings; and yet I do not know what plan of conduct to pursue. I see the impossibility of serving with reputation, or doing any essential service to the cause by continuing in command, and yet I am told that if I quit the command inevitable ruin will follow from the distraction that will ensue. In confidence I tell you that I never was in such an unhappy, divided state since I was born. To lose all comfort and happiness on the one hand, whilst I am fully persuaded that under such a system of management as has been adopted, I cannot have the least chance for reputation, nor those allowances made which the nature of the case requires; and to be told, on the other, that if I leave the service all will be lost, is, at the same time that I am bereft of every peaceful moment, distressing to a degree. But I will be done with the subject, with the precaution to you that it is not a fit one to be publicly known or discussed. If I fall, it may not be amiss that these circumstances be known, and declaration made in credit to the justice of my character. And if the men will stand by me (which by the by I despair of), I am resolved not to be forced from this ground while I have life; and a few days will determine the point, if the enemy should not change their plan of operations; for they certainly will not—I am sure they ought not—to waste the season that is now fast advancing, and must be precious to them. I thought to have given you a more explicit account of my situation, expectation, and feelings, but I have not time. I am wearied to death all day with a variety of perplexing circumstances—disturbed at the conduct of the militia, whose behavior and want of discipline has done great injury to the other troops, who never had officers, except in a few instances, worth the bread they eat. My time, in short, is so much engrossed that I have not leisure for corresponding, unless it is on mere matters of public business. . . .

To THE MASSACHUSETTS LEGISLATURE

The cat-and-mouse game Washington played with his pursuer, Lord Howe, the entire length of Manhattan and through Westchester, until he established Headquarters at White Plains, was a presage of the strategy he would have to use in the miraculous retreat across New Jersey in the beginning of the winter. Meanwhile his army was nearing dissolution and his only hope of replenishing it was through new levies of militia, the most unsatisfactory of troops, his experience had taught him.

White Plains, November 6, 1776

GENTN: The Situation of our affairs is critical and truly alarming; the dissolution of our Army is fast approaching and but little, if any, prospect of levying a New One, in a reasonable time; A large part of it, under the denomination of new Levies, are now on the eve of their departure, and this at a time when the Enemy have a very numerous and formadable force, watching an opportunity to execute their plans and to spread ruin and devastation among us. Impressed with the importance of these Matters, I this day laid them before a Council of Genl. Officers, with a view of Obtaining their opinion upon the same; and of the Measures, which in their judgment, should be immediately adopted; The result was, that I should apply to several of the States for supplies of Militia, and that your Honble. Assembly, should be requested to furnish, as soon as possible, 4,000. as their Quota, to be properly accoutred and equipped with every necessary, to supply the place of those, who are now here under General Lincoln, and who, I fear, will not be pre-vail'd upon to stay longer than the time they engaged for, at first. The hope and probability of raising a New Army, within a convenient time, are so little, and the consequences so evi-dently alarming, if a Sufficient force is not kept up to counter-act the designs of the Enemy in the mean time; that the Council and myself have unanimously agreed, that the Militia should be engaged, if possible, to continue till the first of March, un-less their Return can be sooner dispensed with. We flatter our-selves by that time, if not long before, such an Army will be levied, as to render any future claims upon them, unless in cases of the most pressing emergency, altogether unnecessary.

From the experience, I have had, of your past exertions in times of difficulty, I know that nothing, in your power to effect, will be wanting, and with the greatest confidence I trust, that the present requisition will have your most ready approba-tion and Compliance; being in some degree anticipated by the inquiry you have directed to be made into the state of our affairs, and whether any farther aid will be necessary. I have the Honor etc.

To THE PRESIDENT OF CONGRESS

The loss of Forts Washington and Lee was not so great a dis-aster as it seemed at the time. Now the Continental Army was free to engage in a war of maneuver, and Washington could exercise his masterly strategy of retreat. First he stopped west of the Hackensack River, then he moved on to Newark, and the famous retreat across New Jersey began. It was a step-by-step falling back from one position to another until the Delaware was reached and crossed. The opposing armies were always within short distances of each other; but for the clashes at Princeton and Trenton, there was little real action. Constantly Washington hoped for reinforcements for his utterly inade-quate army of 3,000 men fit for duty, but Congress was deaf to his pleas. It must have been Howe's and Cornwallis' enormous respect for Washington's generalship that deterred them from attacking this pitifully weak force and wiping it out altogether.

Trenton, December 5, 1776

SIR: As nothing but necessity obliged me to retire before the Enemy, and leave so much of the Jerseys unprotected, I conceive it to be my duty, and it corrisponds with my Inclination, to make head against them, so soon as there shall be the least probability of doing it with propriety; that the Country might in some Measure be covered, I left two Brigades (consisting of the five Virginia Regiments and that of Delaware, containing in the whole abt. 1200 Men fit for Duty, under the Command of Lord Sterling and Genl. Stephen) at Princeton, till the Baggage and stores could cross the Delaware, or the Troops under their respective Commands forced from that place. I shall now, having removed the greatest part of the above Articles, face about with such Troops as are here fit for Service and March back to Princeton and there govern myself by Circumstances and the movements of General Lee. At any event, the Enemy's progress may be retarded by this Means if they Intend to come on, and the People's fears in some measure quieted if they do not; sorry I am to observe however, that the frequent calls upon the Militia of this State, the want of exertion in the principal Gentlemen of the Country, or a fatal supiness and insensibility of danger, (till it is too late to prevent an evil, that was not only foreseen but foretold) have been the causes of our late disgraces. If the Militia of this State had step'd forth in Season, (and timely notice they had) we might have prevented the Enemy's crossing the Hackensack, although (without some previous notice of the time, and place) it was impossible to have done this at the No. River. We might with equal probability of success, have made a stand at Brunswick on the Rariton; but as both these Rivers were fordable (in a variety of places knee deep only) it required many Men to defend the passes, and these we had not. At Hackensack our force was insufficient, because part was at Elizabeth Town, Amboy and Brunswick, guarding a coast which I thought most exposed to danger; and at Brunswick, because I was disappointed in my expectation of Militia, and because on the day of the approach of the

Enemy and probably the reason of it, [why the attack was made] the term of the Jersey and Maryland Brigade's Service expired and neither of them would stay an hour longer.

These, among ten thousand other Instances, might be adduced to shew the disadvantages of short Enlistments, and the little dependance upon Militia in times of real danger; but as yesterday cannot be recalled, I will not dwell upon a subject which no doubt has given much uneasiness to Congress, as well as severe pain and mortification to me.

My first wish is, that Congress may be convinced [from experience] of the [indispensable necessity] propriety of relying as little as possible upon Militia, and of the necessity of raising a larger standing Army than they have voted, the saving in the Article of Stores, Provisions and in a thousand other things by having nothing to do with Militia, [unless in cases of extraordinary emergency and such as could not be expected in the common course of events,] would amply support a large Army which (well officered) would daily be improving instead of [allways] continuing a destructive, expensive and disorderly Mob.

I am clearly of opinion, that if 40,000 Men had been kept in constant pay since the first Commencement of Hostilities, and the Militia had been excused doing duty during that Period, the Continent would have saved Money. When I reflect on the losses we have sustain'd for want of good Troops, the certainty of this is placed beyond a doubt in my Mind. In such case the Militia, who have been Harrassed and tired by repeated calls upon them, and Farming, and Manufactures in a Manner suspended would, upon any emergency have run with alacrity to Arms, whereas the cry now is, they may as well be ruind one way as another, and with difficulty are obtained. I mention these things to shew that in my opinion, if any dependance is placed on Militia another year, the Congress will deceive themselves. When danger is a little remov'd from them, they will not turn out at all. When it comes home to them, the well affected, instead of flying to Arms to defend themselves, are busily employed in removing their Family's and Effects, while the disaffected are concerting measures to make their Submission, and spread terror and dismay all around, to induce others to follow the example; daily experience and abundant proofs warrant this Information.

I shall this day reinforce Lord Stirling with 1200 Men, which will make his Numbers about 2400, to morrow I mean to repair to Princeton myself and shall order the Pennsylvania Troops (who are not yet arrivd except part of the German Battalion, and a Company of Light Infantry), on to the same place.

By my last advices the Enemy are still at Brunswick and the Account adds that General Howe was expected at Elizabeth Town with a Reinforcement, to erect the King's Standard and demand a submission of this state. I can only give this as a Report, brot. from the Enemy's Camp by some of the Country People. I have &c.

To JOHN AUGUSTINE WASHINGTON

Washington confides to his brother his despair over the military situation and his bitterness over the conduct of the citizens of New York, New Jersey and Pennsylvania. To disaffection and dwindling enlistments are attributed the predicament in which he found himself during and after his withdrawal from White Plains.

Camp, near the Falls of Trenton, December 18, 1776

DEAR BROTHER: In the number of Letters I write, the recollection of any particular one is destroyed, but I think my last to you was by Colo. Woodford from Hackensack. Since that period and a little before, our Affairs have taken an adverse turn but not more than was to be expected from the unfortunate Measures, which had been adopted for the establishment of our Army.

The Retreat of the Enemys Army from the White Plains led me to think that they would turn their thoughts to the Jerseys, if no further, and induced me to cross the North River with some of the Troops, in order if possible to oppose them. I expected to have met at least 5000 Men of the Flying Camp and Militia; instead of which I found less than one half and no disposition in the Inhabitants to afford the least aid. This being perfectly well known to the Enemy, they threw over a large body of Troops, which pushed us from place to place till we were obliged to cross the Delaware with less than 3000 Men fit for duty owing to the dissolution of our force by short Inlistments; the Enemy's numbers, from the best Accts. exceeding Ten and by some 12,000 Men.

Before I removed to the South Side of the River, I had all the Boats, and other Vessels brought over, or destroyed from Philadelphia upwards for 70 Miles, and, by guarding the Fords have as yet, baffled all their attempts to cross. But, from some late movement of theirs, I am left in doubt whether they are moving off for Winter Quarters or making a feint to throw us off our guard.

Since I came on this side, I have been join'd by about 2000 of the City Militia, and understand that some of the Country Militia (from the back Counties,) are on their way; but we are in a very disaffected part of the Provence, and between you and me, I think our Affairs are in a very bad situation; not so much from the apprehension of Genl. Howe's Army, as from the defection of New York, Jerseys, and Pennsylvania. In short, the Conduct of the Jerseys has been most Infamous. Instead of turning out to defend their Country and affording aid to our Army, they are making their submissions as fast as they can. If they the Jerseys had given us any support, we might have made a stand at Hackensack and after that at Brunswick, but the few Militia that were in Arms, disbanded themselves [or slunk off in such a manner upon the appearance of danger as to leave us quite unsupported and to make the best shifts we could without them] and left the poor remains of our Army to make the best we could of it.

I have no doubt but that General Howe will still make an attempt upon Philadelphia this Winter. I see nothing to oppose him a fortnight hence, as the time of all the Troops, except those of Virginia (reduced almost to nothing,) and Smallwood's Regiment of Maryland, (equally as bad) will expire in less than that time. In a word my dear Sir, if every nerve is not strain'd to recruit the New Army with all possible expedition, I think the game is pretty near up, owing, in a great measure, to the insidious Arts of the Enemy, and disaffection of the Colonies before mentioned, but principally to the accursed policy of short Inlistments, and placing too great a dependence on the Militia the Evil consequences of which were foretold 15 Months ago with a spirit almost Prophetick.

Before this reaches you, you will no doubt have heard of the Captivity of Genl. Lee; this is an additional misfortune, and the more vexatious, as it was by his own folly and Imprudence (and without a view to answer any good) he was taken, going three Miles out of his own Camp [for the sake of a little better lodging] and with 20 of the Enemy to lodge, a rascally Tory rid in the Night to give notice of it to the Enemy who sent a party of light Horse that seized and carried him with every mark of triumph and indignity.

You can form no Idea of the perplexity of my Situation. No Man, I believe, ever had a greater choice of difficulties and less means to extricate himself from them. However under a full persuasion of the justice of our Cause I cannot [but think the prospect will brighten, although for a wise purpose it is, at present hid under a cloud] entertain an Idea that it will finally sink tho' it may remain for some time under a Cloud.

My love, and sincere regards attend my Sister and the Family and Compliments to [our friends at Fairfield] all enquiring friends. With every Sentiment of friendship, as well as love, I am etc.

To THE PRESIDENT OF CONGRESS

Washington, in a rare outbreak of impatience, lectures Congress on the seriousness of his army's condition. For three months he had waited in vain for the delegates to decide on his request for artillery reinforcements. Having received no reply, he took it upon himself to recruit three battalions and went even further by asking for summary authority. After setting forth in penetrating analysis exactly what faced him, he justified his demand by the forthright words: "desperate dis-

eases require desperate remedies." On December 27, 1776, one day after the totally unexpected victory at Trenton, Congress conferred upon him dictatorial powers.

Camp above Trenton Falls, December 20, 1776

Sir: I have waited with much Impatience to know the determinations of Congress on the Propositions made some time in October last for augmenting our Corps of Artillery, and establishing a Corps of Engineers; the time is now come, when the 1st cannot be delayed without the greatest injury to the safety of these States, and therefore under the Resolution of Congress bearing date the 12th. Instt. at the repeated Instance of Colo. Knox, and by the pressing advice of all the General Officers (now here) I have ventured to order three Battalions of Artillery to be immediately recruited; this is two less than Colo. Knox recommends, as you will see by his Plan Inclos'd but then this scheme comprehends all the United States whereas some of the States have Corps already established and these three Battalions are indispensibly necessary for the operations in this Quarter ([including] comprehending the Northern department). The pay of our Artillerests bearing no proportion with that in the English or French Service, the Murmering and dissatisfaction thereby occasioned, and the absolute impossibility, as I am told, of getting them upon the old terms, and the unavoidable necessity of obtaining them at all events, have Induced me (also by advice) to promise Officers, and Men that their pay should be augmented 25 pr. Ct., or that their ingagements shall become null and void; this may appear to Congress premature, and unwarrantable; but Sir, if they view our Situation in the light it strikes their officers, they will be convinced of the Utility of the Measure, and that the Execution could not be delayed till after their Meeting at Baltimore; In short, the present exigency of our Affairs will not admit of delay, either in Council or the Field, for well convinc'd I am, that if the Enemy go into Quarters at all, it will be for a short Season; but I rather think the design of Genl. Howe is to possess himself of Phila. this winter, if possible (and in truth I do not see what is to hinder [prevent] him, as 10 days more will put an end to the existence of our Army); that one great point, is to keep us as much harrassed as possible, with a view to injure the Recruiting Service, and prevent a Collection of Stores, and other necessaries for the next Campaign, I am as clear in as I am of my existence; if therefore in the short Interval we have to provide, and make these great and arduous preparations, every matter that in its nature is self evident, is to be refer'd to Congress, at the distance of 130 or 140 Miles, so much time must necessarily elapse, as to defeat the end in view.

It may be said that this is an application for powers that are too dangerous to be Intrusted. I can only add, that desperate diseases require desperate Remedies; and with truth declare, that I have no lust after power but wish with as much fervency as any Man upon this wide extended Continent, for an opper-tunity of turning the Sword into a plow share. But my feelings as an Officer and a Man, have been such as to force me to say that no person ever had a greater choice of difficulties to con-tend with than I have; it is needless to add that short Inlist-ments, and a mistaken dependance upon Militia, have been the Origin of all our Misfortunes and the great accumulation of our Debt.

We find Sir, that the Enemy are daily gathering strength from the disaffected; this Strength like a Snow ball by rolling, will Increase, unless some means can be devised to check, effec-tually, the progress of the Enemy's Arms; Militia may, possibly, do it for a little while; but in a little while also, the Militia of those States which have been frequently called upon will not turn out at all or with so much reluctance and sloth as to amount to the same thing. Instance New Jersey! Witness Pennsylvania! Could any thing but the River Delaware have sav'd Philadelphia? Can any thing (the exigency of the case indeed may justify it), be more destructive to the recruiting Service than giving 10 Dollars Bounty for Six Weeks Service of the Militia; who come in you cannot tell how, go, you can-not tell when; and act, you cannot tell where; consume your Provisions, exhaust your Stores, and leave you at last in a criti-cal moment. These Sir are the Men I am to depend upon Ten days hence,—this is the Basis on which your Cause will and

must for ever depend, till you get a large standing Army, sufficient of itself to oppose the Enemy. I therefore beg leave to give
it as my humble opinion that 88 Battalions are by no means
equal to the opposition you are to make, and that not a Moment's time is to be lost in raising a greater number; not less
in my opinion, and the opinion of my Officers than 110; it may
be urged, that it will be found difficult enough to compleat the
first Number, this may be true, and yet the Officers of 110 Battalions will recruit many more Men than those of 88. In my
judgment this is not a time to stand upon expence; our funds
are the only objects of Consideration. The State of New York
have added one (I wish they had made it two) Battalions to
their quota. If any good Officers offer to raise Men upon Continental pay and establishment in this Quarter, I shall encourage
them to do so, and Regiment them when they have done it. If
Congress disapprove of this proceeding, they will please to
signify it, as I mean it for the best.

It may be thought that, I am going a good deal out of the
line of my duty to adopt these Measures, or advise thus freely;
A Character to loose, an Estate to forfeit, the inestimable Blessing of liberty at Stake, and a life devoted, must be my excuse.

I have heard nothing of the light Horse from Virginia, nor
the Regiment from the Eastern Shore; I wish to know what
Troops are to [Act in] furnish the different departments and
to have those from the Southward (design'd for this place)
order'd on as fast as they shall be raised, the Routs should be
pointed out by which they are to March. Assistant Commissaries and Quarter Masters upon the Communication to supply
their Wants; the first or second Officer of each Battalion to forward them and the other to come on, receive, and form them at
their place of destination. Unless this is immediately set about,
the Campaign, if it should be closed, will be opened in the
Spring before we have any Men in the Field. Every exertion
should be used to procure Tents. A Clothier General should be
appointed without loss of time for Supplying the Army with
every Article in that way. He should be a Man of Business and
Abilities. A Commissary of Prisoners must be appointed [to
attend the Army]; for want of an Officer of this kind the [busi-
ness of that department] Exchange of Prisoners has been con-

ducted in a most shameful [and injurious] Manner. We have
had them from all Quarters push'd into our Camps at the most
critical junctures and without the least previous notice. We
have had them actually travelling through the different States
in all directions, by certificates from Committees without any
kind of Controul; and have had Instances of some going into
the Enemy's Camp without my privity or knowledge, after passing in the manner before mentioned. There may be other Officers necessary, which [I dont] my recollection at this time does
not furnish [and which when thought of] but must be provided; for this Sir you may rely on, that the Commanding Officer under the present establishment is obliged to attend to the
business of so many different departments as to render it impossible to conduct that of his own with the attention necessary,
than which nothing can be more Injurious.

In a former Letter, I intimated my opinion of the necessity
of having a Brigadier for every three Regiments, and a Majr.
Genl. to (at most) every three Brigades. I think no time is to
be lost in making the Appointments, that the arrangement
may be consequent; this will not only aid the Recruiting Service but will be the readiest means of forming and disciplining
the Army afterwards; which, in the short time we have to do
it, is of amazing consequence. I have labourd ever since I have
been in the Service to discourage all kinds of local attachments,
and distinctions of Country, denominating the whole by the
greater name of American; but I found it impossible to overcome prejudices, and under the New Establishment I conceive
it best to stir up an Emulation in order to do which, would it
not be better for each State to furnish (tho not appoint) their
own Brigadiers; this if known to be part of the Establishment
might get rid of [prevent] a good deal of contention and jealousy, and would, I believe, be the means of promotion going
forward with more satisfaction and quiet in the higher officers.

Whilst I am speaking of Promotion, I cannot help giving it
as my opinion that if Congress thinks proper to confirm what
I have done with respect to the Corps of Artillery, that Colo.
Knox (at present at the head of that department, but [who]
without Promotion will resign) ought to be appointed to the
Command of it with the rank and pay of Brigadier. I have also

to mention, that for want of some establishment in the department of Engineers, agreeable to the plan laid before Congress
in October last Colo. Putnam who was at the head of it, has
quitted, and taken a Regiment in the State of Massachusetts. I
know of no other Man tolerably well qualified for the conducting of that business. None of the French Gentlemen whom I
have seen with appointments in that way, appear to me to know
anything of the Matter. There is one in Philadelphia whom I
am told is clever, but him I have never seen. I must also once
more beg leave to mention to Congress the admisability [ex-
pediency] of letting Promotion go [be] in a Regimental line;
the want of this, has already driven some of the best Officers
[that were] in your Army out of the Service; from repeated, and
strict enquiry I am convinced you can adopt no mode of promotion that will be better receivd, or [that will] give more general satisfaction, I wish therefore to have it anounced.

The casting of Cannon is a matter that ought not to be one
moment delayed, and therefore I shall send Colo. Knox to put
this in a Train, as also to have travelling Carriages and Shott
provided, Elaboratories to be established, one at Hartford and
another in York, Magazines of Provisions should also be laid
in; these I shall fix with the Commissary, as our great loss last
year proceeded from a Want of Teams, I shall direct the Quarter Master Genl. to furnish a certain number to each Regiment
to answer the common purposes thereof, that the Army may be
enabled to remove from place to place differently from what
we have done, or could do, this Campaign. Ammunition Carts,
and proper Carts for Intrenching Tools should also be provided, and I shall direct about them accordingly; above all, a
Store of Small Arms should be provided or Men will be of little
use; the Consumption, and waste of these this year has been
great; Militia, Flying Campmen &ca. coming in without, were
obliged to be furnished, or become useless; Many of these threw
their Arms away, some lost them, whilst others deserted and
took them along. In a word, altho' I used every precaution to
preserve them, the loss has been great, and this will forever be
the case in such a Mixed and irregular Army as ours has been.

If no part of the Troops already Imbark'd at New York, have
appeard in Virginia their destination, doubtless, must be to

some other Quarter, and that State must, I should think, be freed from any Invasion, if Genl. Howe can be effectually opposed in this. I therefore Inclose a Memorandum given me by Brigr. Stephen of Virginia, which Congress will please to adopt in whole, in part, or reject, as may be consistent with their Plans, and Intelligence.

That division of the Army, late under the command of Genl. Lee, now Genl. Sullivan, is just upon the point of joining us; a strange kind of fatality has attended it! they had Orders on the 17th of Novr. to join, now more than a Month! Genl. Gates with four Eastern Regiments are also near at hand; three others from those States were coming on by his order by the way of Peakskill, and had joined Genl. Heath, whom I had ordered on with Parsons's Brigade to join me, leaving Clintons Brigade and some Militia (that were at Forts Montgomery and Constitution) to guard those important passes of the Highlands; but the Convention of the State of New York seeming to be much alarmed at Heath's coming away, a fleet appearing off New London, and some part of the Enemy's Troops retiring towards Brunswick, induced me to countermand the Order for the march of Parsons's Brigade, and to direct the three Regiments from Tyconderoga to Halt at Morris Town, in Jersey; where I understand about 800 Militia had collected, in order to inspirit the Inhabitants and as far as possible cover that part of the Country; I shall send Genl. Maxwell this day to take the Command of them, and if to be done, to harrass and annoy the Enemy in their Quarters and cut off their Convoys.

The care and vigilance which was used in securing the Boats on this River has hitherto baffled every attempt of the Enemy to Cross, but from concurring reports, and appearances they are waiting for Ice to afford them a passage.

Since writing the foregoing I have receiv'd a Letter from Govr. Cooke of Rhode Island of which the Inclosed is a Copy, previous to this, and immediately upon the first Intelligence obtain'd of a Fleets going, through the Sound, I dispatch'd orders to Genls. Spencer and Arnold to proceed immediately [without the least] delay to the Eastward. The first I presume is gone, the latter not getting my Letter till he came to a place called Easton was, by advice of Genl. Gates who also met my

Letter at the same place, induced to come on hither before he proceeded to the Eastward. Most of our Brigadiers are laid up, not one has come on with the division under Genl. Sullivan but [are] left sick at different places on the Road. By Accts. from the Eastward, a large body of Men had assembled in Rhode Island from the States of Massachusetts and Connecticut; I presume (but I have no advice of it) that the Militia ordered from the first, to Rendezvous at Danbury (6000 in number) under the Command of Major Genl Lincoln for the purpose of supplying the Places of the disbanded Men of that State in the Continental Army will now be ordered to Rhode Island. In speaking of Genl Lincoln I should not do him justice were I not to add that he is a Gentleman well worthy of Notice in the Military Line. He commanded the Militia from Massachusetts last Summer, or Fall Rather, and much to my satisfaction, having prov'd himself on all occasions an active, spirited, sensible Man. I do not know whether it is his wish to remain in the Military Line, or whether, if he should, any thing under the Rank he now holds in the State he comes from, would satisfy him; how far an appointment of this kind might offend the Continental Brigadiers I cannot undertake to say; many there are, over whom he ought not to be placed, but I know of no way to discriminate. Brigadier Read of New Hampshire [does] not I presume mean to continue in Service, he ought not, as I am told by the Severity of the small Pox he is become both blind and deaf. I am &c.

P. S. Genls. Gates and Sullivan have this Instant come in, by them I learn, that few or no Men are recruited out of the Regiments coming on with them; and that, there is very little reason to expect that these Regiments will be prevaild upon to continue after their term of Service expires. If Militia then do not come in the consequences are but too evident.

To THE PRESIDENT OF CONGRESS

A dwindling army which had been falling back for weeks suddenly turned about on Christmas night of 1776 and dealt a staggering blow to its pursuer. First Washington marshaled all the barges and flatboats he could find. Manned by Glover's Marblehead regiment, they were ferried through the driving ice of the Delaware in the darkness of night and in the utmost secrecy with 2,400 men and virtually all the artillery left in the Continental arsenal. The frozen river delayed the crossing, scheduled for midnight, until dawn. Half the troops, under General Sullivan, pushed toward Trenton by a lower road, while Washington led his men on the nine-mile march along the Penn Town Road. Washington reached Trenton at 8 o'clock and began the surprise attack. Three minutes later Sullivan's guns began to fire. The Hessian line broke in panic; more than a thousand prisoners were taken and the British fell back toward Princeton. The news of the victory, coming when the army was dispirited and the citizens in the depths of despair, was electric. A ray of hope had at last broken through the clouds of gloom.

Head Quarters, Newton, December 27, 1776

SIR: I have the pleasure of Congratulating you upon the success of an enterprize which I had formed against a Detachment of the Enemy lying in Trenton, and which was executed yesterday Morning. The Evening of the 25th I ordered the Troops intended for this Service [which were about 2400] to parade back of McKonkey's Ferry, that they might begin to pass as soon as it grew dark, imagining we should be able to throw them all over, with the necessary Artillery, by 12 O'Clock, and that we might easily arrive at Trenton by five in the Morning, the distance being about nine Miles. But the Quantity of Ice, made that Night, impeded the passage of the Boats so much, that it was three O'Clock before the Artillery could all get over, and near four, before the Troops took up their line of march.

This made me despair of surprising the Town, as I well knew we could not reach it before the day was fairly broke, but as I was certain there was no making a Retreat without being discovered, and harrassed on repassing the River, I determined to push on at all Events. I form'd my detachments into two divisions one to March by the lower or River Road, the other by the upper or Pennington Road. As the Divisions had nearly the same distance to March, I ordered each of them, immediately upon forcing the out Guards, to push directly into the Town, that they might charge the Enemy before they had time to form. The upper Division arrived at the Enemys advanced post, exactly at Eight O'Clock, and in three Minutes after, I found, from the fire on the lower Road that, that Division had also got up. The out Guards made but small Opposition, tho' for their Numbers, they behaved very well, keeping up a constant retreating fire from behind Houses. We presently saw their main Body formed, but from their Motions, they seemed undetermined how to act. Being hard pressed by our Troops, who had already got possession of part of their Artillery, they attempted to file off by a road on their right leading to Princetown, but perceiving their Intention, I threw a body of Troops in their Way which immediately checked them. Finding from our disposition that they were surrounded, and that they must inevitably be cut to pieces if they made any further Resistance, they agreed to lay down their Arms. The Number, that submitted in this manner, was 23 Officers and 886 Men. Col. Rall. the commanding Officer with seven others were found wounded in the Town. I dont exactly know how many they had killed, but I fancy not above twenty or thirty, as they never made any regular Stand. Our loss is very trifling indeed, only two Officers and one or two privates wounded. I find, that the Detachment of the Enemy consisted of the three Hessian Regiments of Lanspatch, Kniphausen and Rohl amounting to about 1500 Men, and a Troop of British Light Horse, but immediately upon the beginning of the Attack, all those who were, not killed or taken, pushed directly down the Road towards Bordentown. These would likewise have fallen into our hands, could my plan have been compleatly carried into Execution. Genl. Ewing was to have crossed before day at Trenton Ferry, and taken possession of the Bridge leading out of Town, but the Quantity of Ice was so great, that tho' he did every thing in his power to effect it, he could not get over.

This difficulty also hindered General Cadwallader from crossing, with the Pennsylvania Militia, from Bristol, he got part of his Foot over, but finding it impossible to embark his Artillery, he was obliged to desist. I am fully confident, that could the Troops under Generals Ewing and Cadwallader have passed the River, I should have been able, with their Assistance, to have driven the Enemy from all their posts below Trenton. But the Numbers I had with me, being inferior to theirs below me, and a strong Battalion of Light Infantry at Princetown above me, I thought it most prudent to return the same Evening, with my prisoners and the Artillery we had taken. We found no Stores of any Consequence in the Town. In justice to the Officers and Men, I must add, that their Behaviour upon this Occasion, reflects the highest honor upon them. The difficulty of passing the River in a very severe Night, and their march thro' a violent Storm of Snow and Hail, did not in the least abate their Ardour. But when they came to the Charge, each seemed to vie with the other in pressing forward, and were I to give a preference to any particular Corps, I should do great injustice to the others. Colonel Baylor, my first Aid de Camp, will have the honor of delivering this to you, and from him you may be made acquainted with many other particulars; his spirited Behaviour upon every Occasion, requires me to recommend him to your particular Notice. I have the honor &ca.

P. S. Inclosed you have a particular List of the Prisoners, Artillery and other Stores.

To ROBERT MORRIS

Even after his heartening victory at Trenton, Washington, short of money, had to appeal for financial help by means of private credit. Robert Morris's response was immediate and generous. The day after the request was made, $50,000 was dispatched to Trenton by Morris.

Trenton, December 31, 1776

SIR: Our Affairs are at present in a most delicate, tho' I hope a fortunate Situation: But the great and radical Evil which pervades our whole System and like an Ax at the Tree of our Safety, Interest and Liberty here again shews its hateful Influence. Tomorrow the Continental Troops are all at Liberty. I wish to push our Success to keep up the Pannick and in order to get their Assistance have promised them a Bounty of 10 Dollars if they will continue for one Month. But here again a new Difficulty presents itself we have not Money to pay the Bounty, and we have exhausted our Credit by such frequent Promises that it has not the Weight we could wish. If it be possible, Sir, to give us Assistance do it; borrow Money where it can be done we are doing it upon our private Credit; every Man of Interest and every Lover of his Country must strain his Credit upon such an Occasion.

No Time my dear Sir is to be lost. I am, etc.

The Bearer will escort the Money.

To THE PRESIDENT OF CONGRESS

Washington advanced into New Jersey, with Morristown as his first objective. At Princeton a sudden encounter with British troops marching toward Trenton ended with an enemy loss of 500 men and another threat had been overcome. Although Philadelphia had been made considerably safer than it had been before the victory at Trenton, Congress packed up and fled in panic to Baltimore, and from there took up where it had left off in its criticisms of Washington, in spite of the dictatorial powers they had conferred on him after his Trenton coup.

Pluckamin, January 5, 1777

Sir: I have the honor to inform you, that since the date of my last from Trenton I have remov'd with the Army under my Command to this place. The difficulty of crossing the Delaware on Acct. of the Ice made our passage over it tedeous, and gave the Enemy an oppertunity of drawing in their Several Cantonments, and assembling their whole Force at Princeton. Their large Picquets, advanc'd towards Trenton; their great preparations, and some Intelligence I had received, added to their knowledge that the first of Janry. brought on a dissolution of the best part of our Army, gave me the strongest reasons to conclude that an attack upon us was meditating.

Our Situation was most critical and our strength [force] small; to remove immediately, was again destroying every dawn of hope which had begun to revive in the breasts of the Jersey Militia, and to bring those Troops which had first cross'd the Delaware, and were laying at Crosswixs under Genl. Cadwallader, and those under Genl. Mifflin at Bordenton (amounting in the whole to abt. 3600) to Trenton, was [to] bringing of them to an exposed place; one or the other however, was unavoidable; the latter was preferred, and these Troops [they] orderd to join us at Trenton which they did by a Night March on the first Instt.

On the Second, according to my expectation, the Enemy began to advance upon us, and after some skirmishing, the head of their Column reach'd Trenton about 4 O'Clock whilst their rear was as far back as Maidenhead; they attempted to pass Sanpinck Creek (which runs through Trenton) at different places, but finding the Fords guarded, halted, and kindled their Fires. We were drawn up on the other Side of the Creek. In this Situation we remaind till dark canonading the Enemy, and receiving the Fire of their Field pieces, which did us but little damage.

Having by this time discovered that the Enemy were greatly Superior in Numbers, and that their drift [design] was to surround us. I orderd all our Baggage to be removd silently to Burlington soon after dark, and at twelve O'Clock (after renewing our Fires, and leaving Guards at the Bridge in Trenton, and other passes on the same stream above March'd by a round about road to Princeton where I knew they could not have much force left, and might have Stores. One thing I was sure of, that it would avoid the appearance of a Retreat, which (was of Consequence) or to run the hazard of the whole Army's being cut of was unavoidable whilst we might, by a fortunate stroke withdraw Genl. Howe from Trenton, give some reputation to our Arms; happily we succeeded. We found Princeton about Sunrise with only three Regiments of Infantry and three

Troops of Light Horse in it, two of which were upon their March for Trenton; these three Regiments (especially the two first) made a gallant resistance and in killed, wounded and Prisoners must have lost near 500 Men upwards of one hundred of them were left dead in the Field, and with what I have with me, and what was taken in the pursuit, and carried across the Delaware, there are near 300 Prisoners, 14 of wch. are Officers, all British.

This piece of good fortune, is counterballanced by the loss of the brave and worthy Genl. Mercer, [Cols Hazlet and Potter, Captn. Neal of the Artillery, Captn. Fleming, who commanded the 1st Virginia Regiment and four and five] and several other valuable Officers who [with 25 or 30 Privates] were slain in the Field and have since died of their Wounds. Our whole loss cannot be ascertained, as many who were in pursuit of the Enemy (who were chased three or four Miles) are not yet come in. Our Slain in the Field was about 30.

The rear of the Enemy's army laying at Maidenhead (not more than five or Six Miles from Princeton) were up with us before our pursuit was over, but as I had the precaution to destroy the Bridge over Stony Brooke (about half a Mile from the Field of Action) they were so long retarded there, as to give us time to move of in good order for this place. We took two Brass Field pieces from them, but for want of Horses could not bring them of. We also took some Blankets, Shoes, and a few other trifling Articles, Burnt the Hay and destroyed such other things as the Shortness of the time would admit of.*

My original plan when I set out from Trenton was to have pushed on to Brunswick, but the harrassed State of our own Troops (many of them having had no rest for two Nights and a day) and the danger of loosing the advantage we had gained

---

* Sparks notes that in both the actions at Trenton and Princeton General Washington encouraged the troops by his presence in the most exposed situations. An officer who was in these engagements wrote from Morristown (January 7): "Our army love their General very much, but they have one thing against him, which is the little care he takes of himself in any action. His personal bravery, and the desire he has of animating his troops by example, make him fearless of danger. This occasions us much uneasiness. But Heaven, which has hitherto been his shield, I hope will still continue to guard so valuable a life."

by aiming at too much, Induced me, by the advice of my Officers, to relinquish the attempt but in my judgment Six or Eight hundred fresh Troops upon a forcd March would have destroyed all their Stores, and Magazines; taken (as we have since learnt) their Military Chest containing 70,000 £ and put an end to the War. The Enemy from the best Intelligence I have been able to get, were so much alarmed at the apprehension of this, that they March'd immediately to Brunswick without Halting (except at the Bridges, for I also took up those on Millstone on the different routs to Brunswick) and got there before day.

From the best Information I have received, Genl. Howe has left no Men either at Trenton or Princeton; the truth of this I am endeavouring to ascertain that I may regulate my movements accordingly. The Militia are taking Spirit, and, I am told, are coming in fast from this State; but I fear those from Philadelphia will scarce Submit to the hardships of a Winter Campaign much longer, especially as they very unluckily sent their Blankets with their Baggage to Burlington; I must do them the justice however to add, that they have undergone more fatigue and hardship than I expected Militia (especially Citizens) would have done at this Inclement Season. I am just moving to Morristown where I shall endeavour to put them under the best cover I can, hitherto we have lain without any, many of our poor Soldiers quite bearfoot and ill clad in other respects. I am &c.

PROCLAMATION

With the new authority vested in him by Congress, Washington began to shape the army according to his own ideas. He demanded absolute allegiance, both military and civilian, as this Proclamation shows. Thus the year of 1777 began a little more hopefully. The army was being organized on the basis of enlistment for the duration of the war, and now Washington could look forward to the maintenance of a force that could be properly trained and would remain in the field long enough to see an engagement, a campaign and even the whole war through to the end.

Whereas several persons, inhabitants of the United States of America, influenced by inimical motives, intimidated by the threats of the enemy, or deluded by a Proclamation issued the 30th of November last, by Lord and General Howe, stiled the King's Commissioners for granting pardons, &c. (now at open war, and invading these states), have been so lost to the interest and welfare of their country, as to repair to the enemy, sign a declaration of fidelity, and in some instances have been compelled to take oaths of allegiance to and engage not to take up arms, or encourage others so to do, against the King of Great-Britain; And whereas it has become necessary to distinguish between the friends of America and those of Great-Britain, inhabitants of these States; and that every man who receives protection from, and as a subject of any State, (not being conscientiously scrupulous against bearing arms), should stand ready to defend the same against hostile invasion; I do therefore, in behalf of the United States, by virtue of the powers committed to me by Congress, hereby strictly command and require every person, having subscribed such declaration, taken such oath, and accepted such protection and certificates from Lord and General Howe or any person under their authority forthwith to repair to Head-Quarters, or to the quarters of the nearest general officer of the Continental Army, or Militia, (until further provision can be made by the Civil Authority,) and there deliver up such protections, certificates and passports, and take the oath of allegiance to the United States of America. Nevertheless hereby granting full Liberty to all such as prefer the interest and protection of Great-Britain to the freedom and happiness of their country, forthwith to withdraw themselves and families within the enemy's lines; and I do hereby declare, that all and every person, who may neglect or refuse to comply with this order, within Thirty days from the date hereof, will be deemed adherents to the King of Great-Britain, and treated as common enemies of the American States.

Given at Head-Quarters, Morris-Town, January 25, 1777.

To ROBERT MORRIS

Robert Morris had written Washington, begging him to give the brighter side of the picture for the effect it would have on Congress and the people. Washington answers with his customary candor, offering the bare facts as the only explanation of his conduct and his judgment.

Morristown, March 2, 1777

DEAR SIR: Your favour of the 27th. Ultimo came to my hands last Night. The freedom with which you have communicated your sentiments on several matters therein contained, is highly pleasing to me. For be assured, Sir, that nothing would add more to my satisfaction, than an unreserved Correspondence with a Gentleman of whose Abilities and attachment to the Cause we are contending for, I entertain so high an Opinion as I do of yours. Letters, however, being liable to various accidents, makes a communication of thoughts that way, rather unsafe: But, as this will be conveyed by a Gentleman on whom I can depend, I shall not scruple to disclose my Mind, and situation, more freely than I otherwise should do.

The Reasons, my good Sir, which you assign for thinking General Howe cannot move forward with his Army are good, but not conclusive. It is a descriptive evidence of the difficulties he has to contend with, but no proof that they cannot be surmounted. It is a view of one side of the Picture, against which let me enumerate the advantages on the other, and then determine how we would act in his situation.

General Howe cannot, by the best intelligence I have been able to get, have less than 10,000 Men in the Jerseys and on board of Transports at Amboy: Ours does not exceed 4,000: His are well disciplined, well Officered, and well appointed: Ours raw Militia, badly Officered, and under no Government. His numbers cannot, in any short time, be augmented: Ours must very considerably, and by such Troops as we can have some reliance on, or the Game is at an End. His situation with respect to Horses and Forage is bad, very bad, I believe; but will it be better? No; on the contrary, worse, and therefore, an inducement, if no other, to shift Quarters. General Howe's informants are too numerous, and too well acquainted with all these circumstances, to suffer him to remain in ignorance of them. With what propriety, then, can he miss so favourable an opportunity of striking a capital stroke against a City, from whence we derive so many advantages, the carrying of which would give such eclat to his Arms and strike such a damp upon ours? Nor is his difficulty of moving so great as is imagined. All the heavy Baggage of the Army; their Salt Provisions and Flour; their Stores, &ca. might go round by Water; whilst their superior numbers would enable them to make a sweep of the Horses for many Miles round about them (not already taken off by us).

In addition to all this, his coming himself to Brunswick, his bringing Troops which cannot be Quartered, and keeping them on Ship board at Amboy, with some other corroborating circumstances did induce a firm belief in me that he would move, and towards Philadelphia. I candidly own, I expected it would have happened before the expiration of my proclamation; the longer it is delayed, the better for us, and, happy shall I be, if I am deceived.

My Opinions upon these several matters are only known to those who have a right to be informed: As much as possible, I have endeavoured to conceal them from every one else; and that no hasty remove of the public Stores should take place thereby communicating an Alarm; it was, that I early recommended this measure, and have since been urging it, well knowing, that a measure of this kind, set hastily about when the Enemy were advancing, would give unfavourable impressions, and be attended with bad consequences. To deceive Congress, or you, through whose hands my Letters to them are to pass, with false appearances and assurances, would, in my judgment, be criminal and make me responsible for consequences. I endeavour, in all those Letters, to state matters as they appear to my judgment, without adding to, or diminishing aught from the Picture: From others my sentiments are pretty much hid.

I wish, with all my heart, that Congress had gratified General Lee in his request. If not too late, I wish they would do it still. I can see no possible evil that can result from it; some good I think might. The request to see a Gentleman or two, came from the General not from the Commissioners; there could have been no harm, therefore, in hearing what he had to say on any subject, especially as he had declared, that his own personal Interest was deeply concerned. The Resolve to put in close confinement Lieutenant Colonel Campbell and the Hessian Field Officers, in Order to retaliate General Lee's punishment upon them, is, in my Opinion, injurious in every point of view, and must have been entered into without due attention to the consequences. Does Congress know how much the Balance of Prisoners is against us? That the Enemy have, at least, 300 Officers of ours in their possession, and we not fifty of theirs; That Generals Thompson and Waterbury are subject to be recalled at any time? Do they imagine that these Officers will not share the Fate of Campbell &c.? Or possibly, by receiving very different treatment mixed with artful insinuations, have their resentments roused to Acts highly injurious to our Cause. It is much easier to raise a ferment of this kind than to allay it. Do they know that every Artifice is now practising to prepossess the Hessians, with an Idea of our mal-treatment of their Country men (in our possession) that we are treating of them as Slaves; Nay, that we mean to Sell them? And will not the close confinement of their first Officers be adduced as strong evidence of this? Congress, therefore, should be cautious how they adopt measures, which cannot be carried into execution without involving a train of evils that may be fatal in their consequences. In a Word, common prudence dictates the necessity of duly attending to the circumstances of both Armies, before the style of Conquerors is assumed by either; and sorry, I am to add, that this does not appear to be the case with us; Nor is it in my power to make Congress fully sensible of the real situation of our Affairs, and that it is with difficulty (if I may use the expression) that I can, by every means in my power, keep the Life and Soul of this Army together. In a word, when they are at a distance, they think it is but to say Presto begone, and everything is done. They seem not to have any conception of the difficulty and perplexity attending those who are to execute. Indeed, Sir, your observations on the want of many capital Characters in that Senate, are but too just. However, our cause is good and I hope Providence will support it.

If the Resolve of Congress respecting General Lee, strikes you in the same point of view it has done me, I could wish you would signify as much to that Body, as I really think they are fraught with every evil. We know that the Meeting of a Committee of Congress and Lord Howe, stop'd the Mouths of many disaffected People. I believe the Meeting solicited by General Lee would have the same effect. But the other matter relative to the confinement of the Officers, is what I am particularly anxious about, as I think it will involve much more than Congress has an idea of, and that they surely will repent adhering to their unalterable Resolution.

I have wrote you a much longer Letter than I expected to have done when I sat down; and yet, if time would permit, I could enlarge greatly on the subject of it; but, at present, shall beg pardon for taking up so much of your time, and only assure you that I am, etc.

To RICHARD HENRY LEE

The beginnings of Benedict Arnold's frustration and resentment are to be traced to his disappointment over the advancement of five major generals, all his juniors in service, while he was being ignored. Washington here anticipates that such a slight will drive him out of the army.

Morristown, March 6, 1777

DEAR SIR: I am anxious to know whether General [Benedict] Arnold's non-promotion was owing to accident or design; and the cause of it. Surely a more active, a more spirited, and sensible officer, fills no department in your army. Not seeing him then in the list of major generals, and no mention made of him, has given me uneasiness, as it is not to be presumed (being the oldest brigadier) that he will continue in service under such a slight. I imagine you will lose two or three other very good officers, by promoting your's, or any one's, over them.

My public letters will give you the state of matters in this quarter, and my anxiety to be informed of the reason of Arnold's non-promotion, gives you the trouble of this letter, being, very sincerely, etc.

GENERAL ORDERS

As in every army, gambling was a pastime and a vice among Washington's troops. To counteract its spread, the Commander in Chief issued a pious order which amounted to no more than a hope that his soldiers would resort to more elevating pursuits. Gambling continued.

Head-Quarters, Morristown, May 8, 1777

Parole New York. Countersign Albany.

As few vices are attended with more pernicious consequences, in civil life; so there are none more fatal in a military one, than that of GAMING; which often brings disgrace and ruin upon officers, and injury and punishment upon the Soldiery: And reports prevailing, which, it is to be feared are too well founded, that this destructive vice has spread its baneful influence in the army, and, in a peculiar manner, to the prejudice of the recruiting Service,—The Commander in chief, in the most pointed and explicit terms, forbids ALL officers and soldiers, playing at cards, dice or at any games, except those of EXERCISE, for diversion; it being impossible, if the practice be allowed, at all, to discriminate between innocent play, for amusement, and criminal gaming, for pecuniary and sordid purposes.

Officers, attentive to their duty, will find abundant employment, in training and disciplining their men—providing for them—and seeing that they appear neat, clean and soldier-like—Nor will any thing redound more to their honor—afford them more solid amusement—or better answer the end of their appointment, than to devote the vacant moments, they may have, to the study of Military authors.

The Commanding Officer of every corps is strictly enjoined to have this order frequently read, and strongly impressed upon the minds of those under his command. Any officer, or soldier, or other person belonging to, or following, the army, either in camp, in quarters, on the recruiting service, or elsewhere, presuming, under any pretence, to disobey this order, shall be tried by a General Court Martial.

The General Officers, in each division of the army, are to pay the strictest attention to the due execution thereof.

The Adjutant General is to transmit copies of this order, to the different departments of the army: Also to cause the same to be immediately published in the Gazettes of each State, for the information of officers, dispersed on the recruiting service.

To MAJOR GENERAL BENEDICT ARNOLD

Congress had appointed Benedict Arnold to the command of the militia in Philadelphia and along the western bank of the Delaware River. Because Washington had seen General Howe making preparations to move in force from New Brunswick toward the Delaware, he ordered his army into battle formation, but waited for developments. At first the British activity was interpreted as an expedition against Philadelphia, but later was seen to be a feint. The question was whether to risk a general action along the Raritan or wait for the march toward the Delaware before beginning to harass the British rear. On June 19th General Howe abandoned the venture and returned to New Brunswick. Washington's policy of watchful waiting proved to be wise and profitable.

Head Quarters, Camp at Middle Brook, June 17, 1777

DEAR SIR: I have received your favour of the 16th. Instant. You mention a want of intelligence respecting my Situation and that of the Enemy. As to mine, the main body of our army are encamped at Middle Brook, and a considerable body under Genl. Sullivan at Sourland Hills. The position here is very Strong, and with a little labour, which will be bestowed upon it, will be rendered a great deal more so. The passes in the Mountains are for the most part extremely difficult, and cannot be attempted with any degree of propriety. Our right is our most accessible and weakest part, but two or three redoubts will render it as secure as could be wished. The Enemy are Strongly posted, having their right at Brunswick, and their left at Somerset. Besides being well fortified on their right, they have the Rariton all along their front, and Millstone, on their left.

In this situation an attack upon them would not be warranted by a Sufficient prospect of success, and might be attended with the most ruinous consequences. My design therefore is, to collect all the force that can properly be drawn from other quarters to this post, so as to reduce the security of this Army to the greatest possible certainty, and to be in a condition of embracing any fair opportunity that may offer to make an advantageous attack upon them. In the mean time, I intend by light bodies of Militia, countenanced by a few Continental Troops, to harrass them and weaken their numbers by continual Skirmishes.

I have ordered all the Continental Troops at Peeks Kill, except the number requisite for the security of the post, to hasten on to this Army, and shall draw a part of General Sullivans Troops to reinforce our right; leaving the rest at and about Sourland Hills, to gall the flank and rear of the Enemy; with Orders, in case of any movement towards us, to endeavour to form a junction, or if this should not be practicable, to fall briskly upon their rear or flank.

The views of the Enemy must be to destroy this Army and

get possession of Philadelphia. I am, however, clearly of opinion, that they will not move that way, till they have endeavoured to give a severe blow to this Army. The risk would be too great to attempt to cross a river, when they must expect to meet a formidable opposition in front, and would have such a force as ours in their rear; They might possibly be successful, but the probability would be infinitely against them. Should they be imprudent enough to do it, I shall keep close upon their heels, and do every thing in my power to make the project fatal to them. But besides the argument for their intending, in the first place, a stroke at this Army, drawn from the policy of the measure, every appearance coincides to confirm the opinion. Had they designed for the Delaware in the first instance, they would probably have made a secret rapid march for it, and not halted, as they have done, to awaken our attention, and give us time to prepare for obstructing them. Instead of that, they have only advanced to a position necessary to facilitate an attack upon our right, which is the part they have the greatest likelihood of injuring us in; and added to this consideration, they have come out as light as possible, leaving all their baggage, provisions, boats and bridges at Brunswick; which plainly contradicts the Idea for pushing for the Delaware.

It is an happy circumstance, that such an animation prevails among the people. I would wish to let it operate and draw as many as possible together, which will be a great discouragement to the Enemy, by Showing that the popular Spirit is at such a height, and at the same time, will inspire the people themselves with confidence in their own Strength, by discovering to every individual the zeal and Spirit of his neighbours. But after they have been collected a few days, I would have the greatest part of them dismissed, as not being immediately wanted, desiring them to hold themselves in readiness for any sudden call, and concerting Signals with them, at the appearance of which they are to fly to Arms. I would have every means taken to engage a couple thousand of them for a Month, or as much more as they can be induced to consent to. In this case they will be able to render essential Service, both by an addition of Strength for the present, and by lessening the fatigue and duty of the Continental Army, which will tend to preserve them both in health and Spirits.

You will forward on all the Continental Troops by a safe route, as fast as they arrive. But you need send over no more of the Militia, 'till further orders. I approve of your fortifying such places, as you judge most likely to frustrate any attempt of the Enemy to pass the river. I am etc.

P. S. We have been so crowded with business at Head Quarters that I have not been able to write fully to Congress. I should therefore be glad you would communicate the purport of this Letter to them.

To JOSEPH REED

Washington's steadfastness of purpose, in the face of criticism and even flagrant efforts to undermine his authority, is attested in this letter to Joseph Reed. The "one great end in view" dominated his strategy and made him persevere, convinced to the point of heroic obstinacy that the cause of Independence was beyond compromise of any kind.

Middle Brook, June 23, 1777

DEAR SIR: Your favors of the 12th. and 18th. Instt. are both before me; and, on two Accts. have given me concern; first, because I much wish'd to see you at the head of the Cavalry, and secondly by refusing of it, my arrangements have been a good deal disconcerted. As your motives for refusing the appointment are, no doubt, satisfactory to yourself, and your determination fixed, it is unnecessary to enter upon a discussion of the point; I can only add, I wish it had been otherwise, especially as I flatter myself, that my last would convince you, that you still held the same place in my Affection that you ever did. If Inclination, or a desire of rendering those aids to the Service which your abilities enable you to do, shd. lead you to the Camp, it is unnecessary for me I hope to add, that I should be extremely happy in seeing you one of my Family whilst you remain in it.

The late Coalition of Parties in Pensylvania is a most fortunate Circumstance; that, and the spirited manner in which the Militia of this State turnd out upon the late Maneuvre of the Enemy has, in my opinion, given a greater shock to the Enemy than any Event which has happend in the course of this dispute, because it was altogether unexpected, and gave the decisive stroke to their enterprize on Philadelphia.

The hint you have given respecting the Compliment due to the Executive powers of Pensylvania I thank you for, but can assure you I gave General Mifflin no direction respecting the Militia that I did not conceive, nay that I had not been told, by Congress, he was vested with before; for you must know that Genl. Mifflin at the particular Instance, and by a resolve of Congress, had been detained from his duty in this Camp near a Month to be in readiness to draw out the Militia if occasion should require it, and only got here the day before I receivd such Intelligence as convinced me that the Enemy were upon the point of moving; In consequence of which I requested him to return, and without defining his duty, desired he would use his utmost endeavours to carry the designd opposition into effect; conceiving that a previous plan had been laid by Congress, or the State of Pensa., so far as respected the mode of drawing the Militia out; the action of them afterward, circumstances alone could direct, I did not pretend to give any order about it.

It gives me pleasure to learn from your Letter that the reasons assigned by me to Genl. Arnold for not attacking the Enemy in their Situation between the Raritan and Millstone met with the approbation of those who were acquainted with them. We have some among Us, and I dare say Generals, who wish to make themselves popular at the expence of others; or, who think the cause is not to be advanc'd otherwise than by fighting; the peculiar circumstances under which it is to be done, and the consequences which may follow, are objects too trivial for their attention, but as I have one great end in view, I shall, maugre all the strokes of this kind, steadily pursue the means which, in my judgment, leads to the accomplishment of it, not doubting but that the candid part of Mankind, if they are convinc'd of my Integrity, will make proper allowances for my inexperience, and Frailties. I will agree to be loaded with all the obloquy they can bestow; if I commit a wilful error.

If General Howe has not maneuvred much deeper than most People seem disposed to think him capable of, his Army is absolutely gone of panic struck; but as I cannot persuade myself into a belief of the latter, notwithstanding it is the prevailing opinion of my Officers, I cannot say that the move I am about to make towards Amboy accords altogether with my opinion, not that I am under any other apprehension than that of being obliged to loose Ground again, which would indeed be no small misfortune as the Spirits of our Troops, and the Country, is greatly reviv'd (and I presume) the Enemys not a little depress'd, by their late retrogade motions.

By some late Accts. I fancy the British Grenadiers got a pretty severe peppering yesterday by Morgans Rifle Corp; they fought, it seems, a considerable time within the distance of, from twenty, to forty yards; and from the concurring Acct. of several of the Officers, more than an hundred of them must have fallen. Had not there been some mistake in point of time for Marching the several Brigades that were ordered upon that Service, and particularly in delivering an Order to Genl. Varnum, I believe the Rear of Genl. Howe's Troops might have been a little roughfer handled than they were, or if an Express who was sent to Genl. Maxwell the Evening before had reachd him in time, to cooperate upon the Enemy's Flank, for which purpose he was sent down the day before with a respectable force, very good consequences might have resulted from it; however it is too late to remedy these mistakes now, and my Paper tells me I can add no more than to assure you that I am, etc.

To MAJOR GENERAL PHILIP SCHUYLER

As the weeks and months passed, the conflict settled into a war of attrition. Activity in New Jersey was confined to skirmishes and forays. But from the north the British Lieutenant Colonel John Burgoyne had marched from Canada and taken

Ticonderoga. This loss created a furore in Congress. The excitement was fanned by the anger of the New England delegates, who took advantage of the misfortune to criticize General Schuyler, commander of the Northern Department. Motivated more by political opportunism than by shock at the loss, the delegates hoped to elevate their favorite, Major General Horatio Gates, over Schuyler. Washington, aloof from such intrigue, knew little of these political manipulations. Congress finally succeeded in displacing Schuyler and appointing Gates.

Clove,* July 15, 1777

DEAR SIR: I last night received your favour of the 10th. Instt. Amidst the unfortunate reverse that has taken place in our affairs, I am happy to hear Genl. St. Clair and his Army are not in the hands of the Enemy. I really feared they had become prisoners.

The evacuation of Ticonderoga and Mount Independence is an event of Chagrine and Surprise, not apprehended, nor within the compass of my reasoning. I know not upon what principle it was founded, and I should suppose it still more difficult to reconcile, if the Garrison amounted to five thousand Men, in high spirits, healthy, well supplied with Provision and Ammunition, and the Eastern Militia marching to their Succour, as you mention in your Letter of the 9th. to the Council of Safety of New York. This stroke is severe indeed, and has distressed us much. But Notwithstanding things at present have a dark and gloomy aspect, I hope a Spirited Opposition will check the progress of General Burgoyne's Arms and that the confidence derived from his success, will hurry him into measures, that will in their consequences be favourable to us. We should never despair, our Situation before has been unpromising and has changed for the better, so I trust, it will again. If new difficulties arise, we must only put forth New Exertions and proportion our Efforts to the exigency of the times.

It is with pleasure I find you are so well provided with Ammunition. I confess, I was induced to believe, from your Letter

* Orange County, N. Y.

of the 9th. that you were all but destitute of this necessary Article, which occasioned me to order immediate Supplies from other posts, where it is probable it will be equally wanted. As you are not unacquainted with our Resources and Military Supplies, I could wish your requisitions only to extend to Articles essential and absolutely wanted. A redundancy of Stores is not only unnecessary, but supplying them is frequently the means of disfurnishing other posts. At this time the Ammunition sent from Peeks Kill could be but illy spared.

As the operations of this Army are uncertain, depending much upon Genl. Howe's, which still remains to be known. I think it will be expedient that you should send down to New Windsor and Fishkill, all the Vessels and Craft you may not have occasion for at Albany, to be in readiness for transporting a part of our force up the River, in case the situation of Affairs should require it, and Circumstances will admit. I should suppose his movement will be up the River, to Cooperate with Mr. Burgoyne and with a view, if possible, of concentring their forces. This Idea has led me to advise what I have, respecting the Vessels, and more particularly, as carrying our Troops by Water, will not only facilitate their arrival but fit them more for immediate Service, than marching by Land in cases of Emergency.

I observe you mention the evacuation of Fort George, as a necessary Act. For my own part, I cannot determine upon the propriety of such a measure, being totally unacquainted of its strength and situation, and of the Grounds adjoining. But there are Gentlemen here, who seem to consider it extremely defensible and of great importance. They say, that a spirited, brave, judicious Officer with two or three hundred good Men, together with the Armed Vessels you have built, would retard Genl. Burgoyne's passage across the Lake for a considerable time, if not render it impracticable, and oblige him to take a much more difficult and circuitous route. As I have mentioned above, I cannot say one thing or another upon the Subject from my unacquaintance with the place, and therefore only mean to submit it to your consideration, hoping that whatever is best will be pursued in this and every other instance. I am etc.

To MAJOR GENERAL JOHN SULLIVAN

Quick to rebuke his men for any violation of civilians' rights and property, Washington here denounces wanton seizure and destruction of noncombatants' goods.

Pompton Plains, July 25, 1777

DEAR SIR: It is with no small concern, I am constrained to inform you, that I am constantly receiving Complaints from the People living contiguous to the road, of great abuses committed by the Division under your command in their march thro the Country. From their accounts, they have experienced the most wanton and insufferable injuries. Fences destroyed without the least apparent necessity, and a great number of Horses seized and taken away. In a word, according to them, they have suffered the most flagrant violation of their property. perhaps their representations may be rather exaggerated beyond the bounds of strict truth. But I cannot but observe, that the Officers in the Quarter Master Generals Department have informed me, that more accounts have been presented to them for Injuries done by your Division and of greater amount, than by the whole Army besides, and those carry too a degree of authenticity with them, being certified in many instances under the Officers hands. At the same time, that you are sensible how destressing such a conduct is to the Inhabitants, you well know it is highly disgraceful and unworthy of the cause in which we are engaged. Add to this, that it has a fatal and obvious tendency to prejudice their minds and to disaffect them. I must request, in the most earnest manner, your attention to this matter and to prevent in future, by every exertion in your power, the like proceedings. point out the scandal and impropriety of it to your Officers and urge them, as they regard their honour and reputation, to use their endeavours to restrain such unwarrantable practices. I am etc.

To THE NEW YORK COUNCIL OF SAFETY

From Ticonderoga Lieutenant General Burgoyne moved on to Fort Edward. The British plan was to effect a meeting between Howe and Burgoyne at Albany. Howe, abandoning this undertaking, marched on toward Philadelphia, and as a consequence the Battles of Brandywine and Germantown ensued. After the loss of Ticonderoga, General Philip Schuyler evacuated Fort Edward and retreated across the Hudson to a point about thirty miles above Albany. Meanwhile a detachment of British soldiers was sent to Bennington, Vermont, to procure horses and supplies; they were surrounded and defeated by the Green Mountain militia. Burgoyne then encamped at Saratoga. A skirmish with Benedict Arnold, now a brigadier general, cost the British severe losses, most of which were inflicted by Morgan's sharpshooters. Again Burgoyne attacked, and Arnold counterattacked until he forced a retreat. General Horatio Gates, coming up with 20,000 men, surrounded Burgoyne at Saratoga and forced him to surrender in mid-October.

Head Quarters, Philadelphia, August 4, 1777

SIR: I have been duly honored by your several favors of the 25th, 27th and 30th of July.

The Misfortune at Ticonderoga, has given a very disagreeable turn to our affairs, and has thrown a gloom upon the happy prospect, which the Campaign, previous to that event, afforded. But I am in great hopes, the ill consequences of it will not continue long to operate; and that the jealousies and alarms, which so sudden and unexpected an event, has produced in the minds of the People, both of your State and to the Eastward, will soon Subside and give Place to the more rational dictates of self-preservation, and a regard to the common good. In fact, the worst effect of that event, is, that it has Served to produce those distrusts and apprehensions; for, if the Matter were cooly and dispassionately considered, there would be found nothing so formidable in Mr. Burgoyne and the force under him, with all his Successes, as to countenance the least degree of despondency; and experience would shew, that even moderate exertions of the States, more immediately interested, would be Sufficient, to check his career, and, perhaps, convert the advantages he has gained, into his ruin. But, while people continue to view what has happened, through the Medium of Suspicion and fear, there is no saying, to what length an enterprising man may push his good fortune. I have the fullest confidence that no endeavours of the Council will be wanted, to bring your State, (with the distresses of which I am deeply affected) to every effort it is capable of making, in its present mutilated Situation; and, they may rely upon it, no means in my Power Shall be unemployed, to co-operate with them, in the danger that presses upon the State, and, through it, threatens the Continent. If I do not give as effectual Aid as I could wish, to the Northern Army, it is not for want of inclination, nor from being too little impressed with the importance of doing it; It is because the State of affairs in this Quarter will not possibly admit of it. It would be the heighth of impolicy, to weaken ourselves too much here, in order to increase our Strength there; and it must certainly be considered more difficult, as well as of greater moment, to controul the main Army of the Enemy, than an inferior and, I may say, dependent one; for it is pretty obvious, that if Genl. Howe can be completely kept at bay, and prevented effecting his principal purposes, the Successes of Mr. Burgoyne, whatever they may be, must be partial and temporary.

Nothing that I can do shall be wanting, to rouse the Eastern States and excite them to those exertions, which the exigency of our Affairs so urgently demands. I lament, that they have not yet done more; that so few of their Militia have come into the field, and that those few have behaved so inconsistent with the duty they owe their Country, at this critical period. But I have, nevertheless, great reliance upon those States, I know they are capable of powerful efforts, and that their attachment to the cause, notwithstanding they may be a little tardy, will not allow them long to withold their aid, at a time when their own Safety, that of a Sister State, and in a great measure the Safety of the

Continent calls for their greatest zeal and activity. I flatter myself, the presence of Generals Lincoln and Arnold, in the Northern Department, will have a happy effect upon them. Those Gentlemen possess much of their Confidence, particularly the former, than whom there is, perhaps, no man from the State of Massachusetts who enjoys more universal esteem and popularity; and, in addition to that, they may both be considered, as very valuable Officers.

You intimate a wish, that some Assistance could be drawn from the Southern States at this time. But, while things remain in their present posture, and appearances, however illusory they may prove, afford the Strongest reason to keep their force at home, to counteract the Seeming intentions of General Howe, I could neither ask nor expect them, to detach any part of it to the Succour of the Northern States, who are so well able to defend themselves, against the force they now have to oppose.

I hope an exaggerated Idea of the Enemy's force may have no injurious influence on our measures. There is no circumstance I am acquainted with, that induces me to believe General Burgoyne can have more than Six or Seven thousand men; and, if the force left in Canada is so considerable, as the information you send me makes it, he cannot have even so many. The representations of Prisoners and deserters, in this respect, are of little validity; their knowledge is always very limited, and their intention, particularly the former, is very often bad. Beyond what regards the State of their own Companys, no attention is due to what they say. The number of Regiments your informant mentions, agrees with other Accounts, but in the number of men in each Company he gives the establishment, not, I am persuaded, the actual State. The British Army in Canada last Campaign, though they Suffered little by action, must have decreased materially by Sickness and other Casualties; and, if the recruits, both from England and Germany, bore any proportion to those which have reinforced General Howe, the State of their Regiments must be greatly inferior to what your information Supposes. Reasoning by analogy, as far as it will apply, I cannot imagine the British regiments can exceed 250 Men each, fit for the field, or that the foreign troops can amount to much more than 3000 Men.

The appointment of General Clinton to the Government of your State, is an event, that, in itself, gives me great pleasure, and very much abates the regret I should otherwise feel for the loss of his Services in the Military line. That Gentleman's Character is Such, as will make him peculiarly useful at the head of your State, in a Situation so alarming and interesting, as it at present experiences. For the future, agreeably to your desire, I shall direct my applications to him. I have the honor &ca.

To THE PRESIDENT OF CONGRESS

When Admiral Howe's fleet anchored in the Delaware, Washington marched to defend Philadelphia. When it turned to sea, he ordered his troops back toward the Hudson, and then had to about-face because Howe's ships appeared in Chesapeake Bay and troops were disembarked at the Head of Elk. Washington took up a position at Chadd's Ford on Brandywine Creek on the direct road to Philadelphia. To Washington it was a battleground chosen for a holding engagement in his over-all strategy of retreat to prevent the destruction of the Continental Army. To Howe, Brandywine seemed the key to Philadelphia, as indeed it turned out to be. General Sullivan, in command of the American right wing, was outflanked, and Washington, in the center, was forced to fight a rearguard action while falling back toward Chester. Again the main body of the army was saved by retreat, with disaster imminent, after suffering casualties of an estimated 1,200, among them the young Lafayette, who was severely wounded in the leg.

At Midnight, Chester, Setember 11, 1777

SIR: I am sorry to inform you, that in this day's engagement, we have been obliged to leave the enemy masters of the field. Unfortunately the intelligence received of the enemy's advancing up the Brandywine, and crossing at a ford about six miles above us, was uncertain and contradictory, notwithstanding all my pains to get the best. This prevented my making a disposition, adequate to the force with which the Enemy attacked us on the right; in consequence of which the troops first engaged, were obliged to retire before they could be reinforced. In the midst of the attack on the right, that body of the Enemy which remained on the other side of Chad's Ford, crossed it, and attacked the division there under the command of General Wayne and the light troops under General Maxwell who, after a severe conflict, also retired. The Militia under the command of Major Genl. Armstrong, being posted at a ford, about two miles below Chad's, had no opportunity of engaging. But though we fought under many disadvantages, and were from the causes, above mentioned obliged to retire, yet our loss of men is not, I am persuaded, very considerable, I believe much less than the enemy's. We have also lost about seven or eight pieces of cannon, according to the best information I can at present obtain. The baggage having been previously moved off, is all secure, saving the men's Blankets, which being at their backs, many of them doubtless are lost.

I have directed all the troops to Assemble behind Chester, where they are now arranging for this Night. Notwithstanding the misfortune of the day, I am happy to find the troops in good spirits; and I hope another time we shall compensate for the losses now sustained. The Marquis La Fayette was wounded in the leg, and Genl. Woodford in the hand. Divers other Officers were wounded and some Slain, but the number of either cannot now be ascertained. I have &ca.

P. S. It has not been in my power to send you earlier intelligence; the present being the first leisure moment I have had since the action.

GENERAL ORDERS

After recording approval of sentences of a General Court-Martial, issuing orders for distribution of canisters to the troops and urging the Engineers to build works in front of the encampment (omitted here from these General Orders), Washington, close to the end of his tether, exhorts his army "to contend for all that is dear to us."

Head Quarters, at Wentz's, Worcester Township,
October 3, 1777

. . . .The Commander in Chief has the satisfaction to inform the army, that at the southward, the Continental Frigate Randolph, lately fell in with a fleet of five sail of the enemy's ships, and took four of them, one of them mounting 20 guns, and another 8, all richly laden. At the northward every thing wears the most favourable aspect, every enterprise has been successful, and in a capital action, the left wing only of General Gates's army maintained it's ground, against the main body of the enemy; commanded by General Burgoyne in person; our troops behaving with the highest spirit and bravery, during the whole engagement; which lasted from one o'clock 'till dark. In short, every circumstance promises success in that quarter, equal to our most sanguine wishes. This surely must animate every man, under the General's immediate command. This army, the main American Army, will certainly not suffer itself to be out done by their northern Brethren; they will never endure such disgrace; but with an ambition becoming freemen, contending in the most righteous cause, rival the heroic spirit which swelled their bosoms, and which, so nobly exerted, has procured them deathless renown. Covet! my Countrymen, and fellow soldiers! Covet! a share of the glory due to heroic deeds! Let it never be said, that in a day of action, you turned your backs on the foe; let the enemy no longer triumph. They brand you with ignominious epithets. Will you patiently endure that reproach? Will you suffer the wounds given to your Country to go unrevenged? Will you resign your parents, wives, children and friends to be the wretched vassals of a proud, insulting foe? And your own necks to the halter? General Howe promised protection to such as submitted to his power; and a few dastard souls accepted the disgraceful boon. But his promises were deceitful; the submitting and resisting had their property alike plundered and destroyed. But even these empty promises have come to an end; the term of Mercy is expired, General Howe has, within a few days proclaimed, all who had not then submitted, to be beyond the reach of it, and has left us no choice but Conquest or Death. Nothing then remains, but nobly to contend for all that is dear to us. Every motive that can touch the human breast calls us to the most vigorous exertions. Our dearest rights, our dearest friends, and our own lives, honor, glory and even shame, urge us to the fight. And My fellow Soldiers! when an opportunity presents, be firm, be brave; shew yourselves men, and victory is yours.

The Colonels or commanding officers are to see that every regiment be drawn up this afternoon, the rolls called, and these orders distinctly read to them.

Every officer who commands a troop or company, in the several regiments and corps in the continental army, must immediately make out his muster rolls to the first of October, that the whole army may be mustered with the utmost expedition. Such officers, as have heretofore neglected a due attention, to making a regular return of their muster rolls, will be answerable for any future neglect.

To MAJOR GENERAL WILLIAM HEATH

After Brandywine, the Continental Army under Washington was hastily reorganized and concentrated at Schuylkill Falls. With Philadelphia in danger, Congress again took flight, and Cornwallis entered the city, unopposed, on September 26th. Washington's strategy now was to maintain lines between the British Army and Fleet, to prevent communication and reinforcements. General Howe's troops were encamped at Germantown, against which Washington executed a surprise attack on October 4th. Were it not for a dense fog and the confusion among his undisciplined soldiers, what had been in the beginning a victory might not have ended in a dismal defeat. As it was, the trained British troops decided the outcome. The Americans lost 1,000 men and the British only half as many. After the Battle of Germantown, with the British in control of the Delaware, and after they reduced Forts Mifflin and Mercer and had Red Bank in their hands, Howe took firm possession of Philadelphia. The Continental Army had to seek winter quar-

ters and chose Valley Forge, in Chester County, twenty miles
from Philadelphia, on the west bank of the Schuylkill River.

Camp Pawlins Mill, October 8, 1777

DEAR SIR: I have lately recd. a letter from the secretary of
the Board of War in which he complains that you have drawn
Arms for the full Complement of Henly's, Lee's and Jackson's
Regiments when there is scarce any chance of their being compleated, I therefore desire if the matter is so, that you may return all the supernumerary Arms into the Magazine at Springfield or Brookfield. As you will undoubtedly have heard many
and various Reports of the late Action upon the 4th. I will
briefly relate the Circumstances. Having recd. certain, information of the Situation of the Enemy at Germantown, it was
thought that a favorable oppertunity presented itself of giving
them a stroke by way of surprise. We accordingly marched all
the Night of 3d. and arrived at the town a little after day
Break. We attacked upon two quarters upon both of which we
were successful, but it was so exceedingly foggy that we could
neither see the Confusion into which the Enemy were thrown,
neither could each of our Wings form a judgment of the advantage which the other had gained. We continued the attack for
two Hours and then retired to our Camp bringing off all our
Artillery. We unhappily did not know how near we were to
gaining a compleat Victory till the Affair was all over. We were
informed that Genl. Howe was so dubious of the issue of the
day that he had given orders to retreat to Chester in case of
accident. The oposition was warm, our killed and wounded
amount to near four hundred, from the best Account we can obtain that of the Enemy much more considerable. Genl. Agnew
certainly killed and it is said General Grant and Sir William
Erskine badly wounded. All Accounts from people who have
left the Philada. since the Action agree that great Numbers of
wounded have been carried in. We have lost no Officer of distinction but Genl. Nash of North Carolina. The Enemy had
possessed themselves of Billingsport upon the Jersey shore, from
whence they could have annoyed our Shipping which protect

the Chevaux de friese, but they abandoned it immediately after the Action, from whence I conclude that they cannot spare the detachments. I am, etc.

To JOHN AUGUSTINE WASHINGTON

Still waiting for reinforcements from the north, rapid prepa-
rations had to be made to defend Forts Mercer and Mifflin and
Red Bank against the onslaughts of the British. Fort Mifflin
withstood a withering bombardment for six days, but was
finally overwhelmed after the garrison was reduced to ruins
and all but a handful of its defenders slaughtered. Alexander
Hamilton, sent to General Gates and Governor Clinton at Al-
bany, could only persuade them to send troops too few in num-
ber and too late in arrival to avert the disaster. When they did
arrive, ten days too late, as Washington wrote his brother, they
did not even have shoes. To find ways of covering their feet, a
reward of ten dollars was offered for any adequate substitute
that could be improvised.

Camp at White Marsh 12 miles from Philadelphia,
November 26, 1777

DEAR BROTHER: Your letters of the 26th. of Octr. and 7th. inst. have come safe to hand; by the last it would appear that a letter which I wrote you about the 18th. of October had not reached you, which I am exceeding sorry for as, to the best of my recollection I wrote you very fully on the posture of our affairs, and should be exceedingly concerned if it should have fallen into the hands of the Enemy, or some disaffected rascal, who would make an improper use of it. In that letter which upon second thoughts I put under cover to Col. Lewis, open, as I had not time to write two, that he might also be apprized of our situation. I enclosed one to my sister, thanking her for the nice and elegant stockings she was obliging enough to send me, accompanied by an affectionate letter written I think in June; but which with the Stockings, never got to my hands till about the 15th. of last month. If those letters of mine to you and her, have miscarried which I shall be exceedingly sorry for; I shall be obliged to you now to thank my sister for the present, and assure her that I shall set great store by them, and will wear them for her sake.

Red Bank or Fort Mercer being little more than an aid to Fort Mifflin was evacuated about 4 days ago, upon a large body of troops being thrown over the river for the purpose of reducing it. So soon as I got information of the design, I also detached pretty largely in hopes of saving the Fort; but the Enemy having a small distance to go, and great convenience of crossing, whilst we were deficient in the latter, and had a circuitous rout to march by: it was found impracticable; and now I have only to lament my having made the detachments, as by intelligence, the Enemy are recrossing to Philadelphia, and may in our divided state fall upon us with their whole force; which would not gibe well with our present circumstances. I have however ordered them back with all possible expedition, and shall look for them in a couple of days. When they arrive, with the assistance of some of the Northern Troops, which have joined us within these few days from Genl. Gates, we shall be on a more respectable footing, than we have been the whole campaign: but unfortunately, before this junction happened the Enemy had fortified themselves so strongly that it is now impossible to attack them with the least hopes of success. They have also by removing the obstructions in the river, got up their shipping to the City and of consequence their provisions, stores &c., had the reinforcement from the Northward arrived but ten days sooner it would I think have put it in my power to have saved Fort Mifflin which defended the Cheveaux de Frieze, and consequently have rendered Philadelphia a very ineligable situation for them this winter. They have also received a reinforcement from New York, but not quite so large I believe as ours. With truth I believe I may add, that till within these few days, I have never (notwithstanding the numbers given me by the world, and which it was not my interest to contradict) had as many Men in the field, under my immediate command, as Genl. Howe has had under his; although we have fought him twice, and prevented him hitherto from obtaining other advantages than that of possessing himself of the City; which but for the eclat it is attended with, brings no solid advantage to their arms. The Militia which have been called upon in aid of our Troops; (Continental I mean) have come out in such a manner, that before you could get a second class of them, the first were always gone; by which means although the sound of them was great; you never could increase your real numbers, and strength.

The attack upon Red Bank, als. Fort Mercer, sometime ago, followed by the loss of at least 400 Hessians killed and wounded with their leader Count Donop, as also the burning of the Augusta Man of War of 64 Guns, and the Merlin Sloop of 18, is true. Indeed the number of Men lost at the Attack of Fort Mercer is said to be much more than 400. That many we are sure of. At different times during the siege of Fort Mifflin they lost many men. The above ships however were not destroyed by either Fire Rafts, or our Galleys. The first took fire by accident, and blew up. The other getting aground and apprehending danger from the explosion of the Augusta, was set fire to by the crew and abandoned, both these things though happened during the attack on the Fort.

My love attends my sister, the young married couple, and the rest of your family. My Compliments to all friends; and with sincere regard I am, etc.

P. S. I expect part of the Troops which I sent to Jerseys, back tonight, and the residue in a day or two.

GENERAL ORDERS

On the day his army straggled into winter quarters at Valley Forge, Washington weighed the considerations of security and shelter for his eleven to twelve thousand men. He urged his soldiers to surmount their difficulties and discouragements and solemnly promised to share their hardships. The troops were famished, clothed in rags, sick and without shelter, even though provisions and apparel were scattered on the roads, in the fields and woods, immovable, however, because of a complete breakdown of commissary and transport. Teams and money to pay teamsters were lacking.

Head Quarters, at the Gulph, December 17, 1777

Parole Warwick. Countersigns Woodbridge, Winchester.

The Commander in Chief with the highest satisfaction expresses his thanks to the officers and soldiers for the fortitude and patience with which they have sustained the fatigues of the Campaign. Altho' in some instances we unfortunately failed, yet upon the whole Heaven hath smiled on our Arms and crowned them with signal success; and we may upon the best grounds conclude, that by a spirited continuance of the measures necessary for our defence we shall finally obtain the end of our Warfare, Independence, Liberty and Peace. These are blessings worth contending for at every hazard. But we hazard nothing. The power of America alone, duly exerted, would have nothing to dread from the force of Britain. Yet we stand not wholly upon our ground. France yields us every aid we ask, and there are reasons to believe the period is not very distant, when she will take a more active part, by declaring war against the British Crown. Every motive therefore, irresistably urges us, nay commands us, to a firm and manly perseverance in our opposition to our cruel oppressors, to slight difficulties, endure hardships, and contemn every danger. The General ardently wishes it were now in his power, to conduct the troops into the best winter quarters. But where are these to be found? Should we retire to the interior parts of the State, we should find them crowded with virtuous citizens, who, sacrificing their all, have left Philadelphia, and fled thither for protection. To their distresses humanity forbids us to add. This is not all, we should leave a vast extent of fertile country to be despoiled and ravaged by the enemy, from which they would draw vast supplies, and where many of our firm friends would be exposed to all the miseries of the most insulting and wanton depredation. A train of evils might be enumerated, but these will suffice. These considerations make it indispensibly necessary for the army to take such a position, as will enable it most effectually to prevent distress and to give the most extensive security; and in that position we must make ourselves the best shelter in our power. With activity and diligence Huts may be erected that will be warm and dry. In these the troops will be compact, more secure against surprises than if in a divided state and at hand to protect the country. These cogent reasons have determined the General to take post in the neighbourhood of this camp; and influenced by them, he persuades himself, that the officers and soldiers, with one heart, and one mind, will resolve to surmount every difficulty, with a fortitude and patience, be coming their profession, and the sacred cause in which they are engaged. He himself will share in the hardship, and partake of every inconvenience.

To morrow being the day set apart by the Honorable Congress for public Thanksgiving and Praise; and duty calling us devoutely to express our grateful acknowledgements to God for the manifold blessings he has granted us. The General directs that the army remain in it's present quarters, and that the Chaplains perform divine service with their several Corps and brigades. And earnestly exhorts, all officers and soldiers, whose absence is not indispensibly necessary, to attend with reverence the solemnities of the day.

To THE PRESIDENT OF CONGRESS

With the utmost sternness Washington lays before Congress the desperate plight of his ragged army at Valley Forge. Mutiny had broken out and had been suppressed. Offensive action was unthinkable and the outlook for future campaigns dismal indeed. The apathy of Congress, responsible for a condition in which the entire camp "had not a single hoof of any kind to Slaughter, and not more than 25. Barls of Flour!" forced the Commander to speak bluntly of the alternatives: "starve, dissolve or disperse."

Valley Forge, December 23, 1777

Sɪʀ: Full as I was in my representation of matters in the Commys. departmt. yesterday, fresh, and more powerful reasons oblige me to add, that I am now convinced, beyond a doubt that unless some great and capital change suddenly takes place in that line, this Army must inevitably be reduced to one or other of these three things. Starve, dissolve, or disperse, in order to obtain subsistence in the best manner they can; rest assured Sir this is not an exaggerated picture, but [and] that I have abundant reason to support what I say.

Yesterday afternoon receiving information that the Enemy, in force, had left the City, and were advancing towards Derby with apparent design to forage, and draw Subsistance from that part of the Country, I order'd the Troops to be in readiness, that I might give every opposition in my power; when, behold! to my great mortification, I was not only informed, but convinced, that the Men were unable to stir on Acct. of Provision, and that a dangerous Mutiny begun the Night before, and [which] with difficulty was suppressed by the spirited exertion's of some officers was still much to be apprehended on acct. of their [for] want of this Article.

This brought forth the only Comy. in the purchasing Line, in this Camp; and, with him, this Melancholy and alarming truth; that he had not a single hoof of any kind to Slaughter, and not more than 25. Barls. of Flour! From hence form an opinion of our Situation when I add, that, he could not tell when to expect any.

All I could do under these circumstances was, to send out a few light Parties to watch and harrass the Enemy, whilst other Parties were instantly detached different ways to collect, if possible, as much Provision as would satisfy the present pressing wants of the Soldiery. But will this answer? No Sir: three or four days bad weather would prove our destruction. What then is to become of the Army this Winter? and if we are as often without Provisions now, as with it [them], what is to become of us in the Spring, when our force will be collected, with the aid

perhaps of Militia, to take advantage of an early Campaign before the Enemy can be reinforced? These are considerations
of great magnitude, meriting the closest attention, and will,
when my own reputation is so intimately connected, and to be
affected by the event, justifie my saying that the present Commissaries are by no means equal to the execution [of the Office]
or that the disaffection of the People is past all belief. The misfortune however does in my opinion, proceed from both causes,
and tho' I have been tender heretofore of giving any opinion,
or lodging complaints, as the change in that departmt. took
place contrary to my judgment, and the consequences thereof
were predicted; yet, finding that the inactivity of the Army,
whether for want of provisions, Cloaths, or other essentials, is
charged to my Acct., not only by the common vulgar, but those
in power, it is time to speak plain in exculpation of myself;
with truth then I can declare that, no Man, in my opinion, ever
had his measures more impeded than I have, by every department of the Army. Since the Month of July, we have had no
assistance from the Quarter Master Genl. and to want of assistance from this department, the Commissary Genl. charges
great part of his deficiency; to this I am to add, that notwithstanding it is a standing order (and often repeated) that the
Troops shall always have two days Provisions by them, that
they may [might] be ready at any sudden call, yet, no oppertunity has scarce[ly] ever yet happened [offered] of taking
advantage of the Enemy that has not been either totally obstructed or greatly impeded on this Acct., and this tho' the
great and crying evil is not all. Soap, Vinegar and other Articles allowed by Congress we see none of nor have [we] seen
[them] I believe since the battle of brandywine; the first indeed we have now little occasion of [for] few men having more
than one Shirt, many only the Moiety of one, and Some none
at all; in addition to which as a proof of the little benefit received from a Cloathier Genl., and at the same time as a further proof of the inability of an Army under the circumstances
of this, to perform the common duties of Soldiers (besides a
number of Men confind to Hospitals for want of Shoes, and
others in farmers Houses on the same Acct.) we have, by a field
return this day made no less than 2898 Men now in Camp un-

fit for duty because they are bare foot and otherwise naked and by the same return it appears that our whole strength in continental Troops (Including the Eastern Brigades which have joined us since the surrender of Genl. Burgoyne) exclusive of the Maryland Troops sent to Wilmington amount to no more than 8200 In Camp fit for duty. Notwithstanding which, and that, since the 4th Instt. our Numbers fit for duty from the hardships and exposures they have undergone, particularly on Acct. of Blankets (numbers being [having been] obliged and [still are to] do set up all Night by fires, instead of taking comfortable rest in a natural [and common] way) have decreased near 2000 Men. we find Gentlemen without knowing whether the Army was really going into Winter Quarters or not (for I am sure no resolution of mine would warrant the remonstrance) reprobating the measure as much as if they thought Men [the Soldiery] were made of Stocks or Stones and equally insensible of frost and Snow and moreover, as if they conceived it [easily] practicable for an inferior Army under the disadvantages I have describ'd our's to be wch. is by no means exagerated to confine a superior one (in all respects well appointed, and provided for a Winters Campaign) within the City of Phila., and [to] cover from depredation and waste the States of Pensa., Jersey, &ca. but what makes this matter still more extraordinary in my eye is, that these very Gentn. who were well apprized of the nakedness of the Troops, from occular demonstration [who] thought their own Soldiers worse clad than others, and advised me, near a Month ago, to postpone the execution of a Plan, I was about to adopt (in consequence of a resolve of Congress) for seizing Cloaths, under strong assurances that an ample supply would be collected in ten days agreeably to a decree of the State, not one Article of wch., by the bye, is yet come to hand, should think a Winters Campaign and the covering these States from the Invasion of an Enemy so easy [and practicable] a business. I can assure those Gentlemen that it is a much easier and less distressing thing to draw remonstrances in a comfortable room by a good fire side than to occupy a cold bleak hill and sleep under frost and Snow without Cloaths or Blankets; however, although they seem to have little feeling for the naked, and distressed Soldier, I feel super-abundantly for them, and from my Soul pity those miseries, wch. it is neither in my power to relieve or prevent.

It is for these reasons therefore I have dwelt upon the Subject, and it adds not a little to my other difficulties, and distress, to find that much more is expected of me than is possible to be performed, and that upon the ground of safety and policy, I am obliged to conceal the true State of the Army from Public view and thereby expose myself to detraction and Calumny.

The Honble. Comee of Congress went from Camp fully possessed of my Sentiments respecting the Establishment of this Army, the necessity of Auditors of Accts, appointment of Officers, new arrangements, &ca. I have no need therefore to be prolix on these Subjects, but refer to them after adding a word or two to shew, first, the necessity of some better provision for binding the Officers by the tye of Interest to the Service (as No day, nor scarce an hour passes without the offer of a resignd Commission) otherwise I much doubt the practicability of holding the Army together much longer. In this I shall, probably, be thought more sincere, when I freely declare that I do not, myself, expect to derive the smallest benefit from any establishment that Congress may adopt, otherwise than as a Member of the Community at large in the good which I am perswaded will result from the measure by making better Officers and better Troops, and Secondly to point out the necessity of making the Appointments, arrangements, &ca. without loss of time. We have not more than 3 Months to prepare a great deal of business in; if we let these slip, or waste, we shall be labouring under the same difficulties all next Campaign as we have done this, to rectifie mistakes and bring things to order. Military arrangements and movements in consequence, like the Mechanism of a Clock, will be imperfect, and disorderd, by the want of a part; in a very sensible degree have I experienced this in the course of the last Summer, Several Brigades having no Brigadiers appointed to them till late and some not at all; by which means it follows that an additional weight is thrown upon the Shoulders of the Commander in chief to withdraw his attention from the great line of his duty. The Gentlemen of the Comee. when they were at Camp talk'd of an expedient for adjusting these matters, which I highly approved and wish to see adopted namely, that two or three Members of the Board of War or a Comee of Congress should repair immediately to Camp where the best aid can be had and with the Commanding Officer, or a Comee of his appointing [ment] prepare and digest the most perfect plan that can be devised for correcting all abuses, making new arrangements, considering what is to be done with the weak and debelitated regiments (if the States to wch they belong, will not draft men to fill them, for as to enlisting Soldiers it seems to me to be totally out of the question) together with many other things that would occur in the course of such a conference, and after digesting matters in the best manner they can to submit the whole to the ultimate determination of Congress. If this measure is approved of I would earnestly advise the immediate execution of it and that the Comy. General of Purchases whom I rarely see, may be directed to form Magazines without a Moments delay, in the Neighbourhood of this Camp in order to secure Provision for us in case of bad weather; the Quarter Mr. Genl. ought also to be busy in his department; in short there is as much to be done in preparing for a Campaign as in the active part of it; in fine, every thing depends upon the preparation that is made in the several departments in the course of this Winter and the success, or misfortunes of next Campaign will more than probably originate with our activity, or supineness this Winter. I am &ca.

To MAJOR GENERAL HORATIO GATES

What has come to be known as the Conway Cabal was really a political and military conspiracy in which Major General Thomas Conway played a subordinate role. On the political side it was an effort of a New England bloc to gain dominance in Congress. On the military, it was a plot to undermine Washington and bring about his downfall, so that he could be superseded by the personally ambitious Generals Gates, Mifflin, Pickering and others. The entire intrigue collapsed when the Treaty of Alliance with France was signed and the fortunes of war turned at last in favor of Washington's armies.

Valley Forge, January 4, 1778

SIR: Your Letter of the 8th. Ulto. came to my hands a few days ago; and, to my great surprize informed me, that a Copy of it had been sent to Congress, for what reason, I find myself unable to acct.; but, as some end doubtless was intended to be answered by it, I am laid under the disagreeable necessity of returning my answer through the same channel, lest any Member of that honble. body, should harbour an unfavourable suspicion of my having practiced some indirect means, to come at the contents of the confidential Letters between you and General Conway.

I am to inform you then, that Colo. Wilkenson, in his way to Congress in the Month of Octobr. last, fell in with Lord Stirling at Reading, and, not in confidence that I ever understood, inform'd his Aid de Camp Majr. McWilliams that General Conway had written thus to you,

Heaven has been determined to save your Country; or a weak General and bad Counsellors would have ruined it.

Lord Stirling from motives of friendship, transmitted the acct. with this remark.

The inclosed was communicated by Colonl. Wilkinson to Majr. McWilliams, such wicked duplicity of conduct I shall always think it my duty to detect.

In consequence of this information, and without having any thing more in view than merely to shew that Gentn. that I was not unapprized of his intrieguing disposition, I wrote him a Letter in these Words.

Sir. A Letter which I received last night contained the following paragraph.

In a Letter from Genl. Conway to Genl. Gates he says, "Heaven has been determined to save your Country; or a weak General and bad Counsellors would have ruined it."

I am Sir &ca.

Neither this Letter, nor the information which occasioned it, was ever, directly, or indirectly communicated by me to a single Officer in this Army (out of my own family) excepting the Marquis de la Fayette, who, having been spoken to on the Subject by Genl. Conway, applied for, and saw, under injunctions of secrecy, the Letter which contained Wilkenson's information; so desirous was I, of concealing every matter that could, in its consequences, give the smallest Interruption to the tranquility of this Army, or afford a gleam of hope to the enemy by dissentions therein.

Thus Sir, with an openess and candour which I hope will ever characterize and mark my conduct have I complied with your request; the only concern I feel upon the occasion (finding how matters stand) is, that in doing this, I have necessarily been obliged to name a Gentn. whom I am perswaded (although I never exchanged a word with him upon the Subject) thought he was rather doing an act of Justice, than committing an act of infidility; and sure I am, that, till Lord Stirlings Letter came to my hands, I never knew that General Conway (who I viewed in the light of a stranger to you) was a corrispondant of yours, much less did I suspect that I was the subject of your confidential Letters; pardon me then for adding, that so far from conceiving that the safety of the States can be affected, or in the smallest degree injured, by a discovery of this kind, or, that I should be called upon in such solemn terms to point out the author, that I considered the information as coming from yourself; and given with a friendly view to forewarn, and consequently forearm me, against a secret enemy; or, in other words, a dangerous incendiary; in which character, sooner or later, this Country will know Genl. Conway. But, in this, as in other matters of late, I have found myself mistaken. I am, etc.

To REVEREND WILLIAM GORDON

To put an end to many rumors of his resignation, some as part of the plot by the rival faction to undermine him and others growing out of war weariness and a desire for any kind of change after a succession of adversities, Washington wrote to Reverend Gordon voicing his determination to complete his task.

Valley-forge, February 15, 1778

DEAR SIR: Since my last to you abt. the end of Jany. I have been favourd with your Letter of the 12th. of that Month, which did not reach my hands 'till within these few days. The question there put was, in some degree, solved in my last. But to be more explicit, I can assure you that no person ever heard me drop an expression that had a tendency to resignation. the same principles that led me to embark in the opposition to the Arbitrary Claims of Great Britn. operate with additional force at this day; nor is it my desire to withdraw my Services while they are considered of importance in the present contest; but to report a design of this kind, is among the Arts wch those who are endeavouring to effect a change, are practising, to bring it to pass. I have said, and I still do say, that there is not an Officer in the Service of the United States that would return to the sweets of domestic life with more heart felt joy than I should; but I would have this declaration, accompanied by these Sentiments, that while the public are satisfied with my endeavours I mean not to shrink in the cause; but, the moment her voice, not that of faction, calls upon me to resign, I shall do it with as much pleasure as ever the weary traveller retired to rest. This my dear Doctor, you are at liberty to assert; but in doing it, I would have nothing formal. All things will come right again and soon recover their proper tone as the design is not only seen thro but reprobated.

With sincere esteem and regard I am etc.

P. S. Mrs. Washington who is now with me joins in best respects to Mrs. Gordon.

To BRYAN FAIRFAX

Bryan Fairfax was a Virginian who had lived for a time in England because he could find no real accord with the political views of his own independent colony. Upon making application for a second visit to the Mother Country, he was asked to sub-

mit to certain restrictions. This he could not conscientiously do, and, accordingly, he returned to Virginia for the duration of the war. To him, Washington, with all respect and candor, expressed his distrust of England and his own revolutionary, political creed.

Valley forge, March 1, 1778

DEAR SIR: Your favor of the 8th. of Decr. came safe to my hands after a considerable delay in its passage. The sentiments you have expressed of me in this Letter are highly flattering, meriting my warmest acknowledgements, as I have too good an Opinion of your sincerity and candour to believe that you are capable of unmeaning professions and speaking a language foreign from your Heart. The friendship I ever professed, and felt for you, met with no diminution from the difference in our political Sentiments. I know the rectitude of my own intentions, and believing in the sincerity of yours, lamented, though I did not condemn, your renunciation of the creed I had adopted. Nor do I think any person, or power, ought to do it, whilst your conduct is not opposed to the general Interest of the people and the measures they are pursuing; the latter, that is our actions, depending upon ourselves, may be controuled, while the powers of thinking originating in higher causes, cannot always be moulded to our wishes.

The determinations of Providence are all ways wise; often inscrutable, and though its decrees appear to bear hard upon us at times is nevertheless meant for gracious purposes; in this light I cannot help viewing your late disappointment; for if you had been permitted to have gone to england, unrestrained even by the rigid oaths which are administred on those occns. your feelings as a husband, Parent, &ca. must have been considerably wounded in the prospect of a long, perhaps lasting seperation from your nearest relatives. What then must they have been if the obligation of an oath had left you without a Will? Your hope of being instrumental in restoring Peace would prove as unsubstantial as mist before the Noon days Sun and would as soon dispel: for believe me Sir great Britain understood herself perfectly well in this dispute but did not comprehend America. She meant as Lord Campden in his late speech in Parlt. clearly, and explicitly declared, to drive America into rebellion that her own purposes might be more fully answered by it but take this along with it, that this Plan originating in a firm belief, founded on misinformation, that no effectual opposition would or could be made, they little dreamt of what has happened and are disappd. in their views; does not every act of administration from the Tea Act to the present Session of Parliament declare this in plain and self evidt. Characters? Had the Comrs. any powers to treat with America? If they meant Peace, would Lord Howe have been detaind in England 5 Months after passing the Act? Would the powers of these Comrs. have been confined to mere acts of grace, upon condition of absolute submission? No, surely, No! they meant to drive us into what they termed rebellion, that they might be furnished with a pretext to disarm and then strip us of the rights and privileges of Englishmen and Citizens. If they were actuated by principles of justice, why did they refuse indignantly to accede to the terms which were humbly supplicated before hostilities commenced and this Country deluged in Blood; and now make their principal Officers and even the Comrs. themselves say, that these terms are just and reasonable; Nay that more will be granted than we have yet asked, if we will relinquish our Claim to Independency. What Name does such conduct as this deserve? and what punishment is there in store for the Men who have distressed Millions, involved thousands in ruin, and plunged numberless families in inextricable woe? Could that wch. is just reasonable now, have been unjust four Years ago? If not upon what principles, I say does Administration act? they must either be wantonly wicked and cruel, or (which is only anr. mode of describing the same thing) under false colours are now endeavouring to deceive the great body of the people, by industriously propagating a belief that G. B. is willing to offer any, and that we will accept of no terms; thereby hoping to poison and disaffect the Minds of those who wish for peace, and create feuds and dissentions among ourselves. In a word, having less dependance now, in their Arms than their Arts, they are practising such low and dirty tricks, that Men of Sentiment and honr. must blush at their Villainy, among other manœuvres, in this way they are counterfeiting Letters, and publishing them, as intercepted ones of mine to prove that I am an enemy to the present measures, and have been led into them step by step still hoping that Congress would recede from their present claims. I am, etc.

THOUGHTS UPON A PLAN OF OPERATION FOR CAMPAIGN 1778

A memorandum drawn up for consideration by Congress, this document bears no date and may have been written and submitted earlier in the year. It indicates how pitiably small were the forces Washington could count upon and how modest his estimates had to be in relation to the immensity of his task. Here he again asserts his basic military and political philosophy: "... the Spirit, and willingness of the People must, in a great measure, take place of coercion."

In our present situation, and under our present prospects, there appears to be but one of three things that we either can do, or ought to attempt. First, by a collected force, to aim at the destruction of the Enemy in Philadelphia. Secondly, by dividing it, to attempt something against New York whilst Troops are left to cover this Country; and thirdly, by doing neither, lay quiet in a secure Camp and endeavour by every possible means to train and discipline our Army; thereby making our numbers (tho'. small) as formidable as possible. The first is, undoubtedly, the most desirable object, if within the reach of possibility; the Second, is also an important one, if practicable upon rational grounds; the third, we certainly have in our power to accomplish, if it is advisable.

Each of them deserves mature consideration, and should be placed in every point of light, that human wisdom can view them. The two first requires the aid of Militia; will be attended with considerable expence; great waste of Military Stores, and Arms, and will call for great supplies of Provisions; which, probably, are not within our reach. the third would be giving the Enemy time to receive their reinforcements, spread their baneful influence more extensively and be a means of disgusting our own People by our apparent inactivity; but to judge accurately of points of this magnitude, let each case be considered seperately, and the advantages, and disadvantages, with the number of Men necessary for their execution, be fairly stated and canvassed, without having much regard to popular opinions.

By the first of June we may, I should suppose, count upon 17,000 Continental Troops fit for duty in this State, Including those upon the North River, and at Albany; and I think we shall not over rate the Enemy in Philadelphia if we place them at 10,000 exclusive of Marines and Seamen. How many men, then, and what measures, are necessary, to attempt any thing with a prospect of success against this number of Troops in that City? are questions that naturally lead me into a consideration of the

FIRST PLAN

Out of the aforesaid Number of 17000 Continental Troops, not less than two thousand, I should suppose, even with the aid of Militia can maintain our Posts and Forts on the North River, and secure the important communication with the Eastern States; from whence, most of our Supplies must come; this reduces the Number to 15,000; and two methods of attack presenting themselves for consideration, to wit, by regular approaches, and Blockade, I will make a few observations on each:

The Attack by regular approaches simply, and unconnected with a Blockade, would require the least number of Men, because they would be more compact, and their operations more confined; but even here, not less I shd. think than 20,000 Men (which will be a call upon the Militia for 5000) would be sufficient to afford Detachments, carry on the Works, and resist a Sortee of the Enemy's whole force. In case of good behaviour in the Troops on both sides (and we have little room to doubt it on theirs) what time will it probably take to carry the Lines? What expence of Ammunition? What will our probable loss be? and what shall we gain by it, their retreat being open, easy, and secure by water and their Stores removed. A Quantity of Goods might be found there, belonging to Individuals, whose property would deserve confiscation, and that would be all; except the honor of driving them from the City.

To attempt to reduce the City, or rather Troops in it, by a Blockade, it is indispensably necessary to possess Billingsport, with Troops sufficient to hold it against any number not much short of the Enemy's whole force; for which reason, I should think much less than 5000 Men at the Fort, and in the Jerseys, wd. not Answer the purpose of holding the place, and cutting off their communication with that shore. Another strong body should be in the Neighbourhood of Derby; as nearly opposite to Billingsport as possible, and strongly Fortified; 2500 or three thousand may be sufficient for this Post after it is fortified because it could be supported from the main body. These two Posts should, at all events stop the Passage of Ships; or the end of taking them would not, by any means be answered. 18,000 Men might then lay in Front of the Enemy's Lines, between the two Rivers, and secure themselves in Lines, or by Redoubts, and act as circumstances may dictate. A Bridge of Communication to be thrown over the Schuylkill, at the most convenient place to this position; and the Galleys to take post as low in the Delaware, and as much upon the left Flank of this position, as Possible. A Number of Boats in their Rear for the purpose of a speedy transportation of Troops across that River if need be. Posts thus taken, and held, would, in time, starve the Town; or open a door to some other mode of attack, which might prove successful, and more expeditious. This plan at the lowest computation, requires (in aid of the 15,000 Continental Troops) Ten, or 11,000 Militia.

SECOND PLAN

To carry this into execution, there must be a seperation of our Force, and an aid of Militia. Not less than five or Six thousand Troops should go from this Army to join those on the North River; and act in concert with the Militia, as the success of this enterprize would depend in a great measure upon the well timing of matters, and celerity in the execution, hints and false appearances should favor the idea of an Attack upon Philadelphia; in order, if possible, to draw the attention from and Weaken New York and its dependencies. A body of 1000 Jersey Militia, including those now at Elizabeth Town, should Assemble without fail, at that place, on the 10th day of June. A Number of Boats should also be collected there and two or three field Pieces (of Iron Cannon) with a view of detaining the Troops upon Staten Island; or making a descent thereon, if they should be removed; or very considerably weakened. these Men to be draughted to serve at least two Months after they arrive at the place of Rendezvous, the day above mentioned.

Alike number of Connecticut Militia to assemble (unincumbered with Baggage) at Norwalk; on the same day; and to be provided, if possible, with whale Boats sufficient for the Transportation of at least 800 Men; these Men and Boats, to move down towards East Chester as the Enemys lines at Kings bridge are approached by the Main body from the highlands; or to act from thence against Long Island or York Island as circumstances may require.

Previous to any movements of this Kind, a corrispondance to be settled with Staten Island, and Long Island, to discover what effect these operations, when they take place, will have upon the Troops upon those Islands.

The Militia from the States of New York and Connecticut, now at the Posts in the High-lands to be increased to two thousand; where of, five hundred only may be drawn from Connecticut (as they are called upon for a thousand to Rendezvous at Norwalk and are also to furnish Rhode Island with Men); these Troops are also to Assemble at Fishkill on the 10th. of June with as little Baggage as possible. All the Militia are to serve two Months from the date of their arrival, and to bring Arms &ca. with them.

The Quarter Master Genl., and Commissaries of Provisions, and Military Stores, are to make ample provision in their respective departments under the best colourable pretences to deceive. the heavy Brass field pieces, and largest Howitzers should be drawn to that Quarter in the same manner, and under like false appearances. Ponton's should be provided for throwing a Bridge across Harlem River, if need be. A number of Boats should also be provided at the Post in the Highlands, Numbered, and the Number of Men which each will carry precisely ascertained; and the whole under skilful Officers, to favor an Imbarkation with regularity and dispatch, if occasion should require it. Sheep skins and Nails to be provided for Mufling the oars. A redoubt to be thrown up at Kings Ferry to secure the passage of Boats from the Enemy's armed Vessells. and good Horses for Transportation of the Artillery. A Number of Teams should also be provided for the purpose of Transporting Provisions, Forage and Stores with the Army to Kings Bridge; and this to be done under pretence of transporting Provisions &ca. to the Army in this State. The Commissary of Provns. should also, under the Idea of providing for the Troops, on their March from the North River to this Camp, lay in a stock at Morristown, and Sufferans; and a small qty. at Bound brook.

These several Orders being given, and the alarm communicated to Philadelphia, creating proper jealousies there; and matters upon the No. River, &c. being in a proper Train, the Troops from here, for that Service may be put in motion in three divisions: the first may be crossed at Bordenton by the Boats and Galleys giving oblique hints that they are bound to Billingsport after being joined by the Troops which cross above, but nevertheless are to halt there, till the effect of the discovery in Phila. of the real movement, is known; and then advance, or (in case the Enemy should attempt to throw a body of Men across to So. Amboy by Land) oppose them in conjunction with the Militia, to the utmost. and, that as great a body of Militia may be drawn forth, in case of such an event, as possible, without having them out upon uncertainty and expence let a Beacon be fixed at the noted Tree near Princeton, to be answered by others on adjacent heights, and fired by order from the Commanding Officer at Bordenton; upon which the Militia who are to be first previously notified of the intention, are immediately to Assemble at Cranbury under cover of the Continental Troops with four days Provins. and by Arms, and obstructions in the roads, give every possible opposition to the March of the Enemy.

The Second division which is also to March at the sametime,

may take the Rout by Trenton (under pretence of not interfering with the first division at Bordenton thence) by Somerset Court House, Springfield, great-falls, Peramous, Kakeate, &ca. to Kings Ferry.

The third division, also Marching at the sametime and throwing out the same Ideas may advance by the way of Coryells, Morristown, Pompton, Sufferans &ca. to Kings Ferry where Boats are to meet and transport them. These movements may be countenanced, and covered, by the whole Army advancing to the white Marsh or edgehill. The Rout of each of the two last divisions to be precisely pointed out, and their Marches and halting days assignd that it may be known to an hour when they will arrive at the North River; the day before which the Troops at New Windsor &ca. are to take Post at some proper Incampment on the other side, to be marked out by proper hands; from whence, after a little refreshment, and arrangement, the whole are to advance, and take post near the Enemy's Lines, and Works at Kings bridge. This, undoubtedly, will draw the Enemy's whole force to that place, or nearly so, leaving the City of New York Staten, and long Island, bare of Troops; to remedy this, the Shipping will, unquestionably, be disposed of to the best advantage; but whether they can afford effectual cover to those places, or not, is a matter of doubt. If they can, no disadvantage to them will follow their withdrawing the Troops from those Posts. If they cannot, their force becomes divided; their attention distracted, by a care for different objects; and easy descents may be made on the two Islands whilst the City itself through conscious security may be liable to surprize by a rapid move of the Boats from Peekskill to Philips or that Neighbourhood, for Troops to imbark, and run down under cover of a dark Night, upon the ebb tide, with mufled oars.

If nothing can be effected by the surprize, or a Coup de Main, it remains to be considered how far the Works are to be carried by regular approaches; and what may be the consequences of spending so much time as must be involved in the operation. To advance by regular approaches to Fort Independance will, I conceive, be tedious and laborious, on acct. of the roughness of the ground, and must also be expensive in the article of Am-

munition. A Bridge should be in readiness to throw over Harlem River; but unless the City, or Fort Washington could be
previously possessed; or there should be force of Men and Artillery sufficient to besiege Forts Independance and Washington
at the sametime, Troops on the Island might be endangered
without answering any valuable purpose, as the Enemy could
draw their supplies by Water under cover of Night, maugre
any post we could take there.

If upon the whole then our operations are to be confined to
regular approaches, first to Fort Independance, then to Fort
Washington, and lastly to the City, it is incumbent on us to
consider, what time it will take to effect these, and what will
be the probable loss on our side in the operation's. The first
depends upon the nature of the Ground, and the skill with
which the Works are conducted. and the second, from the time,
and manner of them. But, a matter of no small moment, is, to
judge with some degree of accuracy, of the effect that these
operations of ours will have upon the Enemy in Philada. To
suppose that General Howe will lay quiet there till his reinforcements arrive, if he thinks New York in danger is to suppose what I have not the smallest conception of; and therefore
I rather believe that he will pursue one or the other of these
two measures; either to reinforce it strongly, leaving a bare
Garrison in Philadelphia, or weakly, with some of his most indifferent Regimts. (fit enough however for Garrison duty); and
with the Flower of his Troops, aim a stroke at this Army, and
our Stores; and endeavour by vigorous exertions, to spread Terror and dismay through the State. If he should adopt the first
measure, what chance shall we have of success at New York?
and what good will result from the Manœuvre? unless, fortunately it should be a means of transferring the War to New
York, thereby disconcerting General Howe's plans, and placing things in a more eligable situation by removing him from
a Country of supplies, and ourselves to a Country of support,
on the other hand, if he should pursue the secd. Plan, prove
successful, and the enterprize on New York unfortunate, will
not the World condemn the undertaking as ill judged, and impolitic, it being a well known fact, that little is to be expected
from the spirit of the People of this state, in case of such a Ma-

nœuvre of the British Troops, and much to be apprehended from their disaffection.

THE THIRD PLAN

Has advantages and disadvantages attending it, on the one hand, no advantage is attempted to be taken of the Enemy, in their weakest State, but they suffered to remain in peace, boasting their powers and expectation, and spreading their baneful influence far and wide, till their reinforcements enabled them to take the field with some degree of eclat; and, if considerable, to form new expeditions, to which may be added the disgust, and dissatisfaction of the Public and their concomitant evils. On the other hand, we are also getting strength in the Continental line, by recruits, Draughts, &ca., and shall have time to train and discipline our Officers and Men; making the number even if it should prove small, formidable. We shall have leizure to appoint our Officers, arrange the Army, and recover from the disordered State we are now in for want of these and knowing upon what establishment the Army will be placed. We should, moreover, be able to form our Magazines, examine into the State of our Provisions, and know how far it would be in our power to feed, and supply a promiscuous number before they were assembled, avoiding a considerable expence and infinite waste, which must be incurred with Militia in order to attempt that which must be precarious in the Issue; and ruinous if it failed. We Could also make this a strong and formidable Post; too formidable to attack, and too dangerous for the Enemy to leave in their Rear, if they should incline to advance into the Country.

More reasons might be urged for, and against the three Plan's here proposed, much also might be said on the state of our currency, badness of our credit, the temper of our People, their expectations, and their fear of seeing one capital place after another fall into the hands of the Enemy, without an attempt to rescue them. The blockade of our Ports, high prices of Commodities &c. are also worthy of great attention; but, as these are matters which must have occurr'd to every one, before whom these considerations are proper to be laid, there needs no particular discussion of them, in this place although in the ultimate determination, they are worthy of the closest attention; for altho reason and sound policy (founded on a due regard to circumstances) must be the basis of our opinions, yet popular expectations should always be complied with where injury in the execution is not too apparent; especially in such a contest as the one we are engaged in, where the Spirit, and willingness of the People must, in a great measure, take place of coercion.

General Sullivan might (to use Gen. Howe's phraze) make demonstration of a descent upon Rhode Island, which would prevent any succour from that Quarter to New York, or expose the Garrison there exceedingly.

To MAJOR GENERAL BENEDICT ARNOLD

More evidence of Washington's affection for Benedict Arnold and "approbation of your conduct." Washington's misplaced trust in a man he had sponsored and defended was perhaps the severest personal disappointment he had to endure during the entire war.

Valley Forge, May 7, 1778

DEAR SIR: A gentleman in France having very obligingly sent me three sets of epaulettes and sword-knots. two of which, professedly, to be disposed of to any friends I should choose, I take the liberty of presenting them to you and General Lincoln, as a testimony of my sincere regard and approbation of your conduct. I have been informed, by a brigade major of General Huntington, of your intention of repairing to camp shortly; but notwithstanding my wish to see you, I must beg that you will run no hazard by coming out too soon. I am &c.

To JOHN AUGUSTINE WASHINGTON

Washington's emphasis on national government, "the super-structure of all," in relation to local governments is consistent with those convictions which were later to align him with the Federalists. Having only recently learned through private sources that France had signed a Treaty of Alliance with the United States, the Commander in Chief could turn his mind to thoughts of the political structure of the nation. The first and foremost concern was Independence. Now France had provided the first ray of hope after almost three years of disaster and retreat, with the winter in Valley Forge the last test of the courage of desperation. It was indeed great, glorious news.

Valley-forge, May, 1778

DEAR BROTHER: Your letter of the 27th. of Mar. from Bushfield came safe to hand, and gave me the pleasure of hearing, or rather inferring (for you are not explicit) that my Sister and the rest of your family were well. I thank you for your intelligence respecting the pamphlet of forged Letters which Colo. Lee has, and said to be written by me; not one sentence of which you may rely on it, did I ever write; although so many little family circumstances are interspersed through the whole performance to give it the air of authenticity. The Arts of the enemy, and the low dirty tricks which they are daily practising is an evincing proof that they are lost to all Sense of virtue and honor, and that they will stick at nothing however incompatible with truth and manliness to carry their points. They have lately forged, and industriously circulated, a resolve for Congress, purporting (after reciting with great propriety, and plausibility, the inconveniencies of short enlistments) that all Soldiers who have been drafted for periods short of the War, shall nevertheless continue in Service during it; and by their emissaries have endeavoured, and effected the injury of the Service by this means, alarming the fears of the Soldiery and Country.

I am mistaken if we are not verging fast to one of the most important periods that ever America saw; doubtless before this reaches you, you will have seen the Draughts of two Bills intended to be enacted into Laws, and Lord North's Speech upon the occasion; these our accts. from Phila. say, will be immediately followed by the Commissioners; and Lord Amherst, Adml. Keppel, and General Murray are said to be the Commissioners. These Gentlemen I presume, are to move in a civil and Military Line, as Genl. Howe is certainly recalled, and report adds, Lord Howe also. Be this as it may, it will require all the skill, the wisdom, and policy, of the first abilities of these States, to manage the helm, and steer with judgment to the haven of our wishes through so many Shelves and Rocks, as will be thrown in our way. This, more than ever, is the time for Congress to be replete with the first characters in every State, instead of having a thin Assembly, and many States totally unrepresented, as is the case at present. I have often regretted the pernicious (and what appears to me, fatal) policy of having our able Men engaged in the formation of the more local Governments, and filling Officers in their respective States, leaving the great national concern, on wch. the superstructure of all, and every of them does absolutely depend, and without which none can exist, to be managed by Men of more contracted abilities, indeed those at a distance from the Seat of War live in such perfect tranquility that they conceive the dispute to be at an end in a manner, and those near hand it, are so disaffected that they only serve as embarrassments; between the two, therefore, time Slips away without the necessary means for opening the Campaign in time, or with propriety.

Your accts. of the high prices of fresh Provisions in Philadelphia are true, but it affects the Inhabitants more than the Soldiery, who have plenty of Salt Meat, Pease &ca.

Since I began this Letter, authentic accts. have come to my hands of France having declared the United States free and Independant, and guaranteeing to them all the Territory formerly ceeded by them to Great Britain. My acct. (from the Gentleman who was going on to Congress with the Treaty) adds, that France have done this in the most generous manner, and to our utmost wish. This is great, 'tis glorious News. and must put the Independency of America out of all manner of dispute. and accts. for the gentle gales which have succeeded rude Boreas, of late. A publication of this important intelligence will no doubt be directed by Congress and diffused through the Continent as speedily as possible, I shall add nothing further therefore on the Subject.

It would have been a happy circumstance if the several States had been industrious in pushing their recruits into the field, early; but I see little prospect of it at present, if ever. My love and best wishes, in which Mrs. Washington joins me attend My Sister and the rest of your family and with great truth I subscribe myself Yr., etc.

To ROBERT MORRIS

Great rejoicing swept the army at Valley Forge when, on May 5th, Washington made the official announcement of the signing of the Treaty of Alliance with France. There was a parade; artillery salutes were fired; an amnesty for all prisoners of the day was declared; uniforms were gaily decorated with flowers; rum was issued to all troops; an outdoor banquet, attended by Washington, was the occasion for toasts to victory and for some glowing oratory. The friend to whom Washington refers was Isaac Governeur, and his gift was a dozen bottles of wine. The Commander's optimism about the general situation is characteristically tempered with caution.

Valley-forge, May 25, 1778

DEAR SIR: Your favor of the 9th Inst informed me of the acceptable present which your friend Mr Governeur (of Curracoa) was pleased to intend for me, and for which he will, through you. accept my sincere thanks, these are also due to you my good sir, for the kind Communication of the matter, and for the trouble you have had in ordering the Wine forward.

I rejoice most sincerely with you, on the glorious change in our prospects, Calmness and serenity, seems likely to succeed in some measure, those dark and tempestuous clouds which at times appeared ready to overwhelm us, The game, whether well or ill played hitherto, seems now to be verging fast to a favourable issue, and cannot I think be lost, unless we throw it away by too much supineness on the one hand, or impetuosity on the other, God forbid that either of these should happen at a time when we seem to be upon the point of reaping the fruits of our toil and labour, A stroke, and reverse, under such circumstances, would be doubly distressing.

My best respects in which Mrs. Washington joins, are offered to your Lady, and with sincere thanks for your kind wishes, etc.

To THE PRESIDENT OF CONGRESS

Sir William Howe, having lost prestige in England because of his inability to defeat the despised and inferior forces of the Continental Army, tendered his resignation and was superseded in command at Philadelphia by Sir Henry Clinton. Because war between France and England was impending and for that reason Philadelphia might become untenable, the British decided to evacuate the city and concentrate their forces in New York. Their march across New Jersey was marked by constant harassment in the rear. When they encamped at Monmouth Court House, Washington decided to attack, ordering General Charles Lee to advance. Instead Lee, contrary to plan, began a retreat. In a frenzy of anger at Lee, Washington rallied the demoralized troops and renewed the offensive. But under cover of night, the British were able to start on the move again toward the Hudson and arrived at Sandy Hook on June 30th. General Lee was arrested, held for court-martial, found guilty of all charges, sentenced to suspension from command for one year and ultimately was dismissed from the service.

English Town, July 1, 1778

SIR: I embrace the first moment of leisure, to give Congress a more full and particular account of the movements of the Army under my command, since its passing the Delaware, than the situation of our Affairs would heretofore permit.

I had the honor to advise them, that on the appearance of the enemy's intention to march thro' Jersey becoming serious, I had detached General Maxwells Brigade, in conjunction with the Militia of that State, to interrupt and impede their progress, by every obstruction in their power; so as to give time to the Army under my command to come up with them, and take advantage of any favorable circumstances that might present themselves. The Army having proceeded to Coryell's ferry and crossed the Delaware at that place, I immediately sent off Colo. Morgan with a select Corps of 600 Men to reinforce General Maxwell, and marched with the main Body towards Princetown.

The slow advance of the Enemy had greatly the air of design, and led me, with others, to suspect that General Clinton desirous of a general Action was endeavouring to draw us down, into the lower Country, in order by a rapid movement to gain our Right, and take possession of the strong Grounds above us. This consideration, and to give the troops time to repose and refresh themselves from the fatigues they had experienced from rainy and excessive hot Weather, determined me to halt at Hopewell Township, about five Miles from Princetown, where we remained till the Morning of the 25th. On the proceeding day I made a second detachment of 1500 chosen troops under Brigadier Genl. Scott, to reinforce those already in the vicinity of the Enemy, the more effectually to annoy and delay their march. The next day the Army moved to Kingston, and having received intelligence that the Enemy were prosecuting their Rout towards Monmouth Court House, I dispatched [a third detachment of] a thousand select Men, under Brigadier General Wayne, and sent the Marquis de la Fayette to take the command of the whole advanced Corps, including Maxwells Brigade and Morgans light Infantry; with orders to take the first fair opportunity of attacking the Enemy's Rear. In the evening of the same day, the whole Army marched from Kingston where our Baggage was left, with intention to preserve a proper distance for supporting the advanced Corps, and arrived at Cranberry early the next morning. The intense heat of the Weather, and a heavy storm unluckily coming on made it impossible to resume our march that day without great inconvenience and injury to the troops. Our advanced Corps, being differently circumstanced, moved from the position it had held the night before, and took post in the evening on the Monmouth Road, about five Miles from the Enemy's Rear; in expectation of attacking them the next morning on their march. The main Body having remained at Cranberry, the advanced Corps was found to be too remote, and too far upon the Right to be supported either in case of an attack upon, or from the Enemy, which induced me to send orders to the Marquis to file off by his left towards English Town, which he accordingly executed early in the Morning of the 27th.

The Enemy, in Marching from Allen Town had changed their disposition and placed their best troops in the Rear, consisting of all the Grenadiers, Light Infantry, and Chasseurs of the line. This alteration made it necessary to increase the number of our advanced Corps; in consequence of which I detached Major General Lee with two Brigades to join the Marquis at English Town, on whom of course the command of the whole devolved, amounting to about five thousand Men. The main Body marched the same day and encamped within three Miles of that place. Morgans Corps was left hovering on the Enemy's right flank and the Jersey Militia, amounting at this time to about 7 or 800 Men under General Dickinson on their left.

The Enemy were now encamped in a strong position, with their right extending about a Mile and a half beyond the Court House, in the parting of the Roads leading to Shrewsbury and Middletown, and their left along the Road from Allen Town to Monmouth, about three miles on this side the Court House. Their Right flank lay on the skirt of a small-wood, while their left was secured by a very thick one, and a Morass running towards their rear, and their whole front covered by a wood, and for a considerable extent towards the left with a Morass. In this situation they halted till the morning of the 28th.

Matters being thus situated, and having had the best information, that if the Enemy were once arrived at the Heights of Middletown, ten or twelve Miles from where they were, it would be impossible to attempt any thing against them with a prospect of success I determined to attack their Rear the moment they should get in motion from their present Ground.

I communicated my intention to General Lee, and ordered him to make his disposition for the attack, and to keep his Troops constantly lying upon their Arms, to be in readiness at the shortest notice. This was done with respect to the Troops under my immediate command.

About five in the Morning General Dickinson sent an Express, informing that the Front of the Enemy had began their march, I instantly put the Army in motion, and sent orders by one of my Aids to General Lee to move on and attack them, unless there should be very powerful Reason's to the contrary; acquainting him at the same time, that I was marching to support him and for doing it with the greater expedition and convenience, should make the men disincumber themselves of their packs and Blankets.

After marching about five Miles, to my great surprise and mortification, I met the whole advanced Corps retreating, and, as I was told, by General Lee's orders, without having made any opposition, except one fire given by a party under the command of Colo. Butler, on their being charged by the Enemy's Cavalry, who were repulsed. I proceeded immediately to the Rear of the Corps, which I found closely pressed by the Enemy, and gave directions for forming part of the retreating troops, who by the brave and spirited conduct of the Officers, and aided by some pieces of well served Artillery, checked the Enemy's advance, and gave time to make a disposition of the left wing and second line of the Army upon an eminence, and in a wood a little in the Rear covered by a morass in front. On this were placed some Batteries of Cannon by Lord Stirling who commanded the left Wing, which played upon the Enemy with great effect, and seconded by parties of Infantry detached to oppose them, effectually put a stop to their advance.

General Lee being detached with the advanced Corps, the command of the Right Wing, for the occasion, was given to General Greene. For the expedition of the march, and to counteract any attempt to turn our Right, I had ordered him to file off by the new Church two miles from English Town, and fall into the Monmouth Road, a small distance in the Rear of the Court House, while the rest of the Column moved directly on towards the Court House. On intelligence of the Retreat, he marched up and took a very advantageous position on the Right.

The Enemy by this time, finding themselves warmly opposed in front made an attempt to turn our left Flank; but they were bravely repulsed and driven back by detached parties of Infantry. They also made a movement to our Right, with as little success, General Greene having advanced a Body of Troops with Artillery to a commanding piece of Ground, which not only disappointed their design of turning our Right, but severely infiladed those in front of the left Wing. In addition to this, General Wayne advanced with a Body of Troops and kept up so severe and well directed a fire that the Enemy were soon compelled to retire behind the defile where the first stand in the beginning of the Action had been made.

In this situation, the Enemy had both their Flanks secured by thick Woods and Morasses, while their front could only be approached thro a narrow pass. I resolved nevertheless to attack them, and for that purpose ordered General Poor with his own and the Carolina Brigade, to move round upon their Right, and General Woodford upon their left, and the Artillery to gall them in front: [The Troops advanced with great spirit to execute their orders] But the impediments in their way prevented their getting within reach before it was dark. They remained upon the Ground, they had been directed to occupy, during the Night, with intention to begin the attack early the next morning, and the Army continued lying upon their Arms in the Field of Action, to be in readiness to support them. In the meantime the Enemy were employed in removing their wounded, and about 12 OClock at Night marched away in such silence, that tho' General Poor lay extremely near them, they effected their Retreat without his Knowledge. They carried off all their wounded except four Officers and about Fifty privates whose wounds were too dangerous to permit their removal.

The extreme heat of the Weather, the fatigue of the Men from their march thro' a deep, sandy Country almost entirely destitute of Water, and the distance the Enemy had gained by marching in the Night, made a pursuit impracticable and fruitless. It would have answered no valuable purpose, and would have been fatal to numbers of our Men, several of whom died the preceeding day with Heat.

Were I to conclude my account of this day's transactions without expressing my obligations to the Officers of the Army in general, I should do injustice to their merit, and violence to my own feelings. They seemed to vie with each other in manifesting their Zeal and Bravery. The Catalogue of those who distinguished themselves is too long to admit of particularising individuals; I cannot however forbear mentioning Brigadier General Wayne whose good conduct and bravery thro' the whole action deserves particular commendation.

The Behaviour of the troops in general, after they recovered from the first surprise occasioned by the Retreat of the advanced Corps, was such as could not be surpassed.

All the Artillery both Officers and Men that were engaged, distinguished themselves in a remarkable manner.

Inclosed Congress will be pleased to receive a Return of the killed, wounded and missing. Among the first were Lieut. Colo. Bunner of Penna. and Major Dickinson of Virginia, both Officers of distinguished merit and much to be regretted. The Enemys slain left on the Field and buried by us, according to the Return of the persons assigned to that duty were four Officers and Two hundred and forty five privates. In the former number was the Honble. Colo Monckton. Exclusive of these they buried some themselves, as there were several new Graves [on and] near the field of Battle. How many Men they may have had wounded cannot be determined; but from the usual proportion to the slain, the number must have been considerable. There were a few prisoners taken. [Nor can the amount of the Prisoners taken be ascertained, as they were sent off in small parties, as they were captured, and the returns not yet made.]

The peculiar Situation of General Lee at this time requires that I should say nothing of his Conduct. He is now in arrest. The Charges against him, with such Sentence as the Court Martial may decree in his Case, shall be transmitted for the approbation or disapprobation of Congress as soon as it shall have passed.

Being fully convinced by the Gentlemen of this Country that the Enemy cannot be hurt or injured in their embarkation at

Sandy Hook the place to which they are going, and being unwilling to get too far removed from the North River, I put the Troops in motion early this morning and shall proceed that way, leaving the Jersey Brigade, Morgan's Corps and other light parties (the Militia being all dismissed) to hover about them, countenance desertion and to prevent their depredations, as far as possible. After they embark the former will take post in the Neighbourhood of Elizabeth Town. The latter rejoin the Corps from which they were detached. I have the Honor etc.

To BRIGADIER GENERAL THOMAS NELSON

The French fleet, under the command of Count d'Estaing, consisted of twelve ships of the line and six frigates, with 4,000 soldiers aboard. The British Fleet was blocked in the bay by this armada. Unfortunately, the entrance to Sandy Hook was too shallow to admit the larger ships. So d'Estaing sailed for Newport, Rhode Island, where, in concert with General Sullivan on land, an attempt was to be made to dislodge the British. The fleet of Lord Howe arrived on the scene, but a severe storm prevented a decisive engagement. D'Estaing set sail for Boston with his storm-battered fleet and all thought of an offensive against the British in Rhode Island had to be abandoned. After alluding to the maneuvers of the French fleet, Washington here comments on the strange circumstances that brought both armies back to the point from which they had set out two years earlier, and attributes the change in his fortunes to the hand of Providence.

Camp at the White-plains, August 20, 1778

MY DEAR SIR: In what terms can I sufficiently thank you for your polite attention to me, and agreeable present? and, which is still more to the purpose, with what propriety can I deprive you of a valuable, and favourite Horse? You have pressed me once, nay twice, to accept him as a gift; as a proof of my sincere attachment to, and friendship for you, I obey, with this assurance, that from none but a Gentn. for whom I have the highest regard, would I do this, notwithstanding the distressed situation I have been in for want of one.

I am heartily disappointed at a late resolution of Congress for the discontinuance of your Corps, because I pleased myself with the prospect of seeing you, and many other Gentn. of my acquaintance from Virginia, in Camp. As you had got to Philadelphia, I do not think the saving, or difference of expense (taking up the matter even upon that ground, which under present circumstances I think a very erroneous one) was by any means an object suited to the occasion.

The arrival of the French Fleet upon the Coast of America is a great, and striking event; but the operations of it have been injured by a number of unforeseen and unfavourable circumstances, which, tho they ought not to detract from the merit, and good intention of our great Ally, has nevertheless lessened the importance of their Services in a great degree. The length of the passage in the first instance was a capital misfortune, for had even one of common length taken place, Lord Howe with the British Ships of War and all the Transports in the River Delaware must, inevitably, have fallen; and Sir Harry must have had better luck than is commonly dispensed to Men of his profession, under such circumstances, if he and his Troops had not shared (at least) the fate of Burgoyne. The long passage of Count D'Estaing was succeeded by an unfavourable discovery at the hook, which hurt us in two respects; first in a defeat of the enterprize upon New York; the Shipping, and Troops at that place; and next, in the delay that was used in ascertaining the depth of Water over the Bar; which was essential to their entrance into the Harbour of New York, and lastly, after the enterprize upon Rhode Island had been planned, and was in the moment of execution, that Lord Howe with the British Ships should interpose, merely to create diversion, and draw the French fleet from the Island was again unlucky, as the Count had not return'd on the 17th. to the Island, tho drawn of from it the 10th; by which means the Land operations were retarded, and the whole subject to a miscarriage in case of the arrival of Byrons Squadron.

I do not know what to make of the enemy at New York;

whether their stay at that place is the result of choice, or the effect of necessity, proceeding from an inferiority in the Fleet, want of Provision, or other Causes, I know not, but certain it is that, if it is not an act of necessity it is profoundly misterious unless they look for considerable reinforcements and are waiting the arrival of them to commence their operations, time will shew.

It is not a little pleasing, nor less wonderful to contemplate, that after two years Manœuvring and undergoing the strangest vicissitudes that perhaps ever attended any one contest since the creation both Armies are brought back to the very point they set out from and, that that, which was the offending party in the beginning is now reduced to the use of the spade and pick axe for defence. The hand of Providence has been so conspicuous in all this, that he must be worse than an infidel that lacks faith, and more than wicked, that has not gratitude enough to acknowledge his obligations, but, it will be time enough for me to turn preacher, when my present appointment ceases; and therefore, I shall add no more on the Doctrine of Providence; but make a tender of my best respects to your good Lady; the Secretary and other friends and assure you that with the most perfect regard I am etc.

P. S. Since writing the foregoing, I have been favoured with your Letter of the 25th. Ulto. from Baltimore, and 9th. Instt. from Philadelphia. The method you propose to take with the Public Horses in your volunteer Corps will be very proper and agreeable to me.

To MARQUIS DE LAFAYETTE

Ever since the Battle of Brandywine, the friendship between Washington and Lafayette had been growing with mutual affection. Until the end of Washington's life a warm correspondence was maintained and always with complete trust and a kind of brotherly sharing of confidences. In giving Lafayette consent to visit Count d'Estaing and offering to satisfy General Sullivan on its propriety, Washington referred obliquely to the feud between them. Lafayette had been with Sullivan in the land operation of the Rhode Island misadventure. D'Estaing was offended because Sullivan had made his move on land a day before schedule and even failed to notify him. When the Count sailed with his fleet for Boston, Sullivan felt that he had been abandoned. The irritation between the commanders by land and sea of the ill-fated expedition continued for long after, and was only smoothed over by the intervention of Congress and Washington's tact in appealing to Sullivan for harmony.

Fredericksburg in the State of New York,
September 25, 1778

MY DEAR MARQUIS: Since my last to you, I have been honoured with your several favors of the 1st., 3d., and 21st. of this Month. The two first came to hand before I left the White plains, and the last at this place. I should not have delayed acknowledging the receipt of the 1st. and 3d. till this time, (thereby neglecting to pay that just tribute of respect which is due to you) but for the close attention I was obliged to bestow on the Committee of Arrangement while they remained in Camp; To the March of the Troops since, and, to the several Posts which I found myself under a necessity of visiting in my way to this Incampment.

The Sentiments of affection and attachment which breathe so conspicuously in all your Letters to me, are at once pleasing and honourable; and afford me abundant cause to rejoice at the happiness of my acquaintance with you. Your love of liberty; The just sense you entertain of this valuable blessing, and your Noble, and disinterested exertions in the cause of it, added to the innate goodness of your heart, conspire to render you dear to me; and I think myself happy in being linked with you in bonds of strictest friendship.

The ardent Zeal which you have displayed during the whole course of the Campaign to the Eastward, and your endeavours to cherish harmony among the officers of the allied powers, and to dispel those unfavourable impressions which had begun to take place in the Minds of the unthinking (from Misfortunes which the utmost stretch of human foresight could not avert) deserves, and now receives, my particular, and warmest thanks. I am sorry for Monsr. Touzards loss of an arm, in the Action on Rhode Island; and offer my thanks to him, thro you, for his gallant behaviour on that day.

Could I have conceived, that my Picture had been an object of your Wishes, or in the smallest degree worthy of your Attention, I should, while Mr. Peale was in the Camp at Valley forge, have got him to have taken the best Portrait of me he could, and presented it to you; but I really had not so good an opinion of my own worth, as to suppose that such a compliment would not have been considered as a greater instance of my Vanity, than a mean of your gratification; and therefore, when you requested me to set for Monsr. Lanfang I thought it was only to obtain the outlines and a few shades of my features, to have some Prints struck from.

If you have entertained thoughts My dear Marquis of paying a visit to your Court; To your Lady; and to your friends this Winter, but waver on acct. of an expedition into Canada; friendship induces me to tell you, that I do not conceive that the prospect of such an operation is so favourable at this time as to cause you to change your views. Many circumstances, and events must conspire, to render an enterprize of this kind practicable and advisable. The Enemy in the first place, must either withdraw wholly, or in part from their present Posts, to leave us at liberty to detach largely from this Army. In the next place, if considerable reinforcements should be thrown into that Country, a Winter's expedition would become impracticable, on acct. of the difficulties which will attend the March of a large body of Men with the necessary apparatus, Provisions, Forage and Stores at that inclement Season. In a word, the chances are so much against the undertaking that they ought not to induce you to lay aside your other purpose; in the prosecution of which you shall have every aid, and carry with you every honourable testimony of my regard, and entire approbation of your conduct, that you can wish; but as it is a compliment which is due, so am I perswaded you would not wish to dispense with the form, of signifying your desires to Congress on the subject of your Voyage and absence.

I come now in a more especial manner to acknowledge the receipt of your obliging favor of the 21st. by Majr. Dubois, and to thank you for the important intelligence therein contained.

I do most cordially congratulate with you on the glorious defeat of the British Squadron undr. A. Keppel, an event which reflects the highest honor on the good conduct and bravery of Monsr. d'Orvilliers, and the offrs. of the Fleet under his Command; at the same time that it is to be considered, I hope, as the happy presage of a fortunate and glorious War to his Most Christian Majesty. A confirmation of the act. I shall impatiently wait, and devoutly wish for. If the Spaniards, under this favourable beginning, would unite their Fleet to that of France, together they would soon humble the pride of haughty Britain; and no longer suffer her to reign Sovereign of the Seas, and claim the privilege of giving law to the Main.

I should be very happy in havg. you with the grand Army again, but the present designs of the enemy are wrapped in such impervious darkness, that I scarce know what measures to pursue to counteract them; and therefore have thrown the Army into a position to move either to Boston, or to our Posts in the highlands with equal celerity. If they do not mean to quit the United States altogether, there is but two objects, I conceive, that they can have in view, namely, the Fleet at Boston, and the Posts just mentioned the last of which is the security of our communication between the Eastern and Southern States, and consequently of those supplies of Flour, on which the French Fleet, and our Troops to the Eastward, depend.

The Current stream of Intelligence from the Enemys Army point to an evacuation of New York; but, there is no ground on which to form a decisive judgment of this matter; my own opinion is, that they have not, at this time, any fixed object or plan; but are waiting orders from their Court, preparing in the mean while either to evacuate the City wholly or in part as they shall be directed. You have my free consent to make the Count D'Estaing a visit, and may Signify my entire approbation of it to Genl. Sullivan, who I am glad to find has moved you out of a Cul de Sac. It was my advice to him long ago to have no detachments in that situation, let particular places be never so much unguarded and exposed from the want of Troops. Immediately upon my removal from the White plains to this Ground the Enemy threw a body of Troops into the Jerseys, but for what purpose, unless to make a grand forage, I have not been able, yet, to learn. They advanced some Troops at the same time from their lines at Kings bridge, towards our old Incampment at the plains, stripping the Inhabitants not only of their Provision and forage, but even the Cloathes on their backs and witht. discrimination.

The information my dear Marquis, which I beg'd the favor of you to obtain, was not, I am perswaded, to be had thro the Channel of the Officers of the French Fleet, but by application to your fair Lady, to whom I should be happy in an oppertunity of paying my homage in Virginia, when the War is ended, if she could be prevailed upon to quit, for a few Months, the gaieties, and splendor of a Court, for the rural amusements of an humble Cottage. I shall not fail to inform Mrs. Washington of your polite attention to her. The Gentlen. of my family are sensible of the honr. you do them by your kind enquiries and join with me in a tender of best regards, than whom none can offer them with more sincerity, and affection than I do. With every Sentiment you can wish, I am, etc.

To MAJOR GENERAL PHILIP SCHUYLER

In the autumn of 1778, Washington and his armies were kept in an awkward state of inactivity and suspense. There could be only surmises concerning the intentions of the enemy, and since few of the guesses proved accurate, virtually no decisions were made. Washington shifted his Headquarters between Fredericksburg and Fishkill, in New York State, and could do little more than maintain his army and speculate on his next step. Most of all he gave consideration to the prospects of an expedition into Canada. His letter to General Schuyler, edited by Alexander Hamilton, manifests his caution and thoroughness and his military realism. If he could eliminate Fort Niagara, the threat of Indian warfare would be minimized, since this post was the stronghold of the most savage warriors on the frontier.

Fredericksburg, November 20[–21], 1778

MY DEAR SIR: Congress seem to have a strong desire to undertake an Expedition against Canada. The practicability, of it depends, upon the employment the Enemy intend to give us on the Sea board next Campaign, on their strength in Canada, the State of our resources, and other circumstances, some of which are too much buried in obscurity, others too much in the field of conjecture to form any decisive opinion of at this time; But there is not a moment to spare in preparing for such an event, if, hereafter, it should be found expedient to undertake it.

In your Letter of the 9th. Ulto., which you did me the favor of writing upon this Subject, you are opposed to an Enterprize against Canada by the way of Co'os, and assign cogent reasons for not making it a principal dependance. You are also against the rout by Oswego; but as an Expedition that way had not been suggested, you do not touch upon the reasons; but recomd. the common rout by the way of Lake Champlain; and a Winter Expedition if the Ice will admit of it.

In general, Winter Campaigns are destructive to Troops; and nothing but pressing necessity, and the best state of preparation can justify them. I fear neither the State of our Provisions, the condition of our Men, nor the situation of our Officers (whose distresses on acct. of the uncommonly high prices of every necessary of life, are a source of general discontent and indifference to the Service) would warrant the undertaking; even if the state of the Lakes, and the force of Canada, should invite the Measure. I am clear also that neither force nor Stratagem, can give us a well grounded hope of a decisive Superiority in Naval strength, upon Lake Champlain, where the Enemy are, at present, so powerful.

Your scheme for preparing Materials for building two large Ships upon this Lake is plausible, and if only one or two were entrusted with the Secret, practicable. But when fifty Men are to be consulted, before the measure can be adopted; When a number of these, (inattentive to the importance of keeping Military Manœuvres secret) make matter of incautious, if not common conversation of the Plans in contemplation, and a knowledge of them by that means gets into the hands of the Enemy's emissaries, who are industrious in acquiring, and diligent in communicating every piece of useful information, I say when this is the case, I can entertain but little hope of success from a project of this kind.

If from these considerations, a Winters Expedition is found impracticable, or unadvisable; If the conquest of the Enemy's Fleet on lake Champlain is not to be accomplished by force, nor by stratagem; And if an Enterprize by the way of Co'os is inadmissible as a primary object.

1st. What door is left open for an Expedition against Canada?

2d. How far is there a moral certainty of extending the American Arms into that Country in the course of next Campaign?

3d. And how far short of the entire conquest, and annexation of Canada to the Union, would give permanent peace and security to the Frontiers of these States?

In considering these points, and such others as may hereafter occur, it will be necessary to take the matter up in two points of view; presuming in the one case, that the Enemy will evacuate the United States. in the other, that they mean to retain New York and Rhode Island as Garrison Towns. In discussing them with that freedom and candor which I [mean] to do, you will readily perceive that [it is my] wish to enter into an unlimited, and confidential corrispondance with you on this subject. Where then, in addition to the above queries,

4th. Lie the difficulties of an Expedition against Canada by the way of Lake Ontario?

5th. Why did General Amherst take this rout (when lake Champlain was open, free, and so much more direct) if he did not foresee that some apparent advantages were to be derived from it?

6th. What resources can be drawn from the State of New York towards the support of an Expedition of this kind?

7th. At what places would it be necessary to establish Posts between Albany and Oswego, for the support of the communication, and Security of Convoys? and

8th. How many Men will be required at each Post for the above purposes? and at Oswego?

I mean to hazard my thoughts upon a Plan of operations for next Campaign, if the Enemy should evacuate these States and leave us at liberty but being unacquainted with the Country, and many other matters essentially necessary to form a right judgment upon so extensive a project I am sensible that it will be very defective and shall consider it as the part of friendship in you, to observe upon every part of my plan, with the utmost freedom.

I have already laid it down as a position, that unless a Winters Expedition can be undertaken with Success (opposed to which, in addition to the reasons already assigned, the want of Provisions I find is an almost insuperable bar) or the Fleet at St. Johns can by some means or other be destroyed, [the] door into Canada [by way of Lake Champlain] is effectually closed; I am further of opinion that the distance of Land Carriage by the way of Co'os for Flour, Stores &ca. is too great to expect that a sufficient body of Troops can be introduced through that rout to answer singly any valuable purpose; [and] I am [therefore], naturally, [led] to turn my thoughts to the Rout by the way of Oswego though the same kind of difficulties but not in so great a degree, present themselves here, as on the other Lake.

If I am not mistaken with respect to the Water carriage from Schenectady to Oswego, by the help of finesse, and false appearances, a pretty large stride may be taken towards obtaining a Naval superiority on lake Ontario before the real design would be unfolded.

The plan I would adopt shd. be this. By inuendos and oblique hints [I would endeavour to inculcate an idea] that we were determined to acquire the Mastery of lake Champlain; and to give currency to this belief, I would have the Saw Mills about Fort Ann and Fort Edwd. set to Work to prepare plank for Batteaux, and such kind of Armed Vessels as may be proper for lake Ontario. I would go further, and tho it should be inconvenient, and expensive, I would build the Batteaux, and bring the Timber for larger Vessels to some place or places that might serve to confirm an Idea of this kind. A Plan of this sort if well conceived and digested, and executed [with secrecy], might I think deceive, so far as to draw the attention of the Enemy to Lake Champlain, at the expence of Ontario; especially as part of my plan is to advance a respectable body of Troops at a proper Season to Co'os, for purposes which will be mentioned hereafter.

In the Spring, when every thing is ripe for execution, and the real design can no longer be concealed, I would advance with the utmost celerity (consistent with proper caution) to Oswego; in the Batteaux which have been provided (apparently) for Champlain, transporting the Armed Vessels in pieces to the same place. But here I am to ask if this is practicable? My knowledge of the Water Communication from Schenectady to Oswego, is not sufficiently accurate to form a decided opinion upon the possibility of this Measure; and if it is not to be effected, my plan in part fails; and we can only provide the Materials under false colours, and depend upon out building the Enemy to obtain the superiority of the Lake. Whether [the superiority can be obtained in this manner] I am [not well] able to determine, tho it is very necessâry to be known, as it is the corner Stone of the superstructure. Much will depend upon the practicability of the Enemys getting Vessels, or materials for vessels from lake Champlain or Montreal to the navigation above la galette; because I [proceed] upon the principle, that if we can deceive them effectually, their whole attention will be drawn to the more interior parts of the Country, and of course their Ship Carpenters, and Materials for Ship building, will be imployed that way.

The foregoing is a summary of my [Capital] movement; to facilitate wch. I would, as has been before observed, advance a body of Men from the Co'os. The motions of these should be regulated precisely by those of the [main] army, establishing Posts as they go, for the purposes of retreat (in case of necessity) and to protect convoys if the [main] Army should be able to penetrate Canada as far as Montreal.

Several advantages will be derived from the advance of a body of Troops by the way of Co'os; first, strengthening the belief, that we mean to enter by the way of St. John's; Secondly it will serve to distract the Enemy in their Councils and measures, [and] either divide their force and render them weak at all points, or by keeping them collected, expose the interior, or exterior part of the Country to a Successful and fortunate blow, from one or the other of these bodies, and will, [in the third place], open a communication for ample supplies of live Cattle, if we should have occasion for them for Troops in Canada.

Under this plan, it is not only possible, but to be expected, that the Enemy, if they should come at the knowledge of our real designs would oppose their whole Naval force to our Troops on lake Ontario, and their Land force against those by the way of Co'os. In this case I should be glad of solutions to the questions wch follow.

9th. Is there any practicable rout from Johnson Hall or any other part of the Mohawk River, or from the upper parts of Hudsons River, to a River emptying itself into the St. Lawrence a little above la galette, by which we could avoid lake Ontario and the Armed Vessels on those Waters altogether? and If this is not to be effected, and a superiority on the lake [is] despaired of, then, [I should wish to be informed.]

10th. Whether Niagara can be approached with an Army and the necessary apparatus by a rout which will avoid this Lake?

11th. What will be the distance of the March from Fort Schuyler? the kind of Country thro which it is to [be made]? and the difficulties that are to be expected? and lastly

12th. The advantages, and disadvantages of Maintaining that Post, after possessing it? Canada remaining in the hands of the Enemy.

For the more certain reduction of Niagara, and for the Peace and safety of the Frontiers of Pensylvania and Virginia, a part of my plan is to advance a body of Troops from Pittsburg by the way of Alligany, la beauf (or French Creek) and Prisquile to the above Post, if it be practicable, of which I am not certain, as the Enemy have Armed Vessels on lake Erie and I am ignorant of the kind of Country between Prisquile and Niagara, in case it is to be attempted by a Land March. But admitting the impracticability of this, an Expedition to Detroit which Congress meditated last Fall, and still have in contemplation, will keep the Indians in that Quarter employed, and prevent them from affording succour to the Garrison at Niagara. The preparations necessary to the one [will] answer for the other; while the one to Niagara may be [concealed] under the Idea of going to Detroit.

Although, under the present appearance of things, it is a matter of very great doubt whether we shall be in circumstances to prosecute a project of this kind, I have, nevertheless, given orders for Magazines of Provisions to be laid in at Albany and on Connecticut River from the lower Co'os to No. 4; and have ordered the Saw Mills abt. Fort Ann &ca. to be set to Work, and shall be obliged to you for your advice to Colo. Lewis on this occasion.

If it should fall in your way to ascertain with precision, the Number and strength of the Vessels upon Lake Ontario, and down to la galette, and the force of the Garrisons at Niagara, Oswegatchie &ca., I shall thank you; and must beg leave to remind you of the mode you suggested to procure intelligence from Canada in the course of the Winter, as it is of infinite importance to be well informed of the strength, expectation, and preparation of the Enemy; and to receive the acct. through different Channels is also essential, to avoid deception.

I shall be very happy to see you at the head Quarters of the Army in your way to Philadelphia whenever it happens. Governor Clinton wrote me that he should be at Albany in the course of a few days; as I have implicit confidence in him it will be quite agreeable to me that you should converse largely with him upon the sevl. matters herein contained, and then furnish me with your observations upon my Plan, and the most effectual means of carrying it, or some other into execution; with the necessary preparations to be made during the Winter. With the greatest esteem, etc.

21st., P. S. Since writing this Letter I have seen a very intelligent Man who was many years a liver at and about Detroit.

He was sent Prisoner in May last from that Post to Quebec, and from Quebec escaped the 7th. of October. He has given me a very accurate acct. of the Enemys' Naval force on the two Lakes (Erie and Ontario) at the time he was in that Country but I should still be glad to see how far other Accts. corrispond with his and whether they have made any late progress in ship building since that period. He is particular also in his acct. of the strength of the Garrisons of Michilamakinack, Detroit, Niagara, and Oswegatchie as they stood in the Spring, and adds that at the time he passed down the River, the Enemy were removing Cannon from Oswegatchie to Buck Island which place he understood they meant to fortify. When he left Canada Genl. Haldiman with most of the Troops were at the Mouth of the Sorrel, very busy in fortifying that Post and strengthening themselves above on that River, the received opinion in the Country being that an Expedition would be undertaken.

To BENJAMIN FRANKLIN

This testimonial to Lafayette for Benjamin Franklin, then United States Minister to the French Court, was followed by a letter from Congress to the Marquis which announced that the plan for a Canadian expedition had been abandoned.

Philadelphia, December 28, 1778

SIR: The Marquis de la fayette having served with distinction as Major General in the Army of the United States, two Campaigns, has been determined by the prospects of an European War to return to his native Country.

It is with pleasure that I embrace the oppertunity of introducing to your personal acquaintance a Gentn. whose merit cannot have left him unknown to you by reputation. The generous motives which first induced him to cross the Atlantic; The tribute which he paid to gallantry at Brandy-wine; his success in Jersey before he had recovered of his Wound, in an affair where he commanded Militia against British Grenadiers; the brilliant retreat by which he eluded a combined manœuvre of the whole British force in the last Campaign; his services in the enterprize against Rhode Island, are such proofs of his Zeal, military ardour and talents as have endeared him to America, and must greatly recommend him to his Prince.

Coming with so many titles to claim your esteem, it were needless for any other purpose than to endulge my own feelings to add that I have a very particular friendship for him, and that whatever services you may have it in your power to render him will confer an obligation on one who has the honor to be etc.

To LUND WASHINGTON

Washington, as a man of property, here appraises the market value of his assets in crops and Negroes. His scruples about selling slaves center upon the question of timing in terms of highest profit. To him, as to most slave-owners, the moral problem was evaded by the simple rationalization that the state of slavery existed and that a mere change of ownership need not make it more "irksome, provided husband and wife, and Parents and children are not separated from each other."

Middle Brook, February 24[–26], 1779

DEAR LUND: I wrote to you by the last post, but in so hasty a manner as not to be so full and clear as the importance of the subject might require. In truth, I find myself at a loss to do it to my own satisfaction [even?] in this hour of more leisure and thought, because it is a matter of much importance and requires a good deal of judgment and foresight to time things in such a way as to answer the purposes I have in view.

The advantages resulting from the sale of my Negroes, I have very little doubt of; because, as I observed in my last, if we should ultimately prove unsuccessful (of which I am under no apprehension unless it falls on us as a punishment for our want of public, and indeed private virtue) it would be a matter of very little consequence to me, whether my property is in Negroes, or loan office Certificates, as I shall neither ask for, nor expect any favor from his most gracious Majesty, nor any person acting under his authority; the only points therefore for me to consider, are, first, whether it would be most to my interest, in case of a fortunate determination of the present contest, to have Negroes, and the Crops they will make; or the sum they will now fetch and the interest of the money. And, secondly, the critical moment to make this sale.

With respect to the first point (if a Negro man will sell at, or near one thousand pounds, and woman and children in proportion) I have not the smallest doubt on which side the balance, placed in the scale of interest, will preponderate: My scruples arise from a reluctance in offering these people at public vendue, and on account of the uncertainty of timeing the sale well. In the first case, if these poor wretches are to be held in a state of slavery, I do not see that a change of masters will render it more irksome, provided husband and wife, and Parents and children are not separated from each other, which is not my intentions to do. And with respect to the second, the judgment founded in a knowledge of circumstances, is the only criterion for determining when the tide of depreciation is at an end; for like the flux and reflux of the water, it will no sooner have got to its full ebb or flow, but an immediate turn takes place, and every thing runs in a contrary direction. To hit this critical moment then, is the point; and a point of so much nicety, that the longer I reflect upon the subject, the more embarrassed I am in my opinion; for if a sale takes place while the money is in a depreciating state, that is, before it has arrived at the lowest ebb of depreciation; I shall lose the difference, and if it is delayed, 'till some great and important event shall give a decisive turn in favor of our affairs, it may be too late. Notwithstanding, upon a full consideration of the whole matter; if you have done nothing in consequence of my last letter, I wou'd have you wait 'till you hear further from me on this subject. I will, in the meanwhile, revolve the matter in my mind more fully, and may possibly be better able to draw some more precise conclusions than at present, while you may be employed in endeavouring to ascertain the highest prices Negroes sell at, in different parts of the Country, where, and in what manner it would be best to sell them, when such a measure is adopted, (which I think will very likely happen in the course of a few months.)

Inclosed is my Bond for conveyance of the Land purchased of the Ashfords &c. It is as well drawn as I can do it, and I believe it to be effectual.

To JOHN JAY

In offering his spirited denial of the charges and innuendoes of General Horatio Gates, whose antagonism to his Commander persisted after the collapse of the Conway Cabal, Washington takes advantage of the occasion in his letter to John Jay to review the facts and also summarize the general military situation. He refers to the plan for operations in the Indian campaign, explains the reasons for abandoning the Canadian expedition and refutes the criticism of the divided state of the army by showing the disposition of the four divisions of his troops, and the strategic reasons therefor. In so doing, he provides a general résumé of the army's status in the spring of 1779, when, after months of inaction, both armies were engaged in a war of maneuver. This letter was composed as a collaboration with Alexander Hamilton.

Head Quarters, Middle brook, April 14, 1779

DEAR SIR: I have received your several favours of the 2d., 3rd. and 28th. of March and 6th. of April. I thank you for them all, but especially for the last, which I consider as a distinguishing mark of your confidence and friendship.

Conscious that it is the aim of my actions to promote the public good, and that no part of my conduct is influenced by personal enmity to individuals, I cannot be insensible to the artifices employed by some men to prejudice me in the public esteem. The circumstance of which you have obliged me with the communication is among a number of other instances of the unfriendly views which have governed a certain Gentleman from a very early period. Some of these have been too notorious, not to have come to your knowledge; others from the manner in which, they have been conveyed to me, will probably never be known except to a very few. But you have perhaps heard enough and observed enough yourself to make any further explanation from me unnecessary.

The desire, however which it is natural I should feel to preserve the good opinion of men of sense and virtue, conspiring with my wish to cultivate your friendship in particular, induces me to trouble you with a state of some facts which will serve to place the present attack in its proper light. In doing this, I shall recapitulate and bring into one view a series of transactions, many of which have been known to you, but some of which may possibly have escaped your memory.

An opinion prevailing, that the enemy were like shortly to evacuate these states, I was naturally led to turn my thoughts to a plan of operations against Canada in case that event should take place. A winter campaign before the enemy could have an opportunity of reinforcing and putting themselves in a more perfect state of defence, appeared to promise the most certain and speedy success and the route by Co'os offered itself as most direct and practicable. In this I fully agreed with General Gates and some other Gentlemen, whom I consulted on the occasion, and on [the 12th. of Septr.] last I wrote to Congress accordingly; submitting it to them whether it would be advisable to be laying up magazines opening a road and making other preparations for the undertaking. They approved the project and authorized me to carry it into execution. I the more readily entered into it, from a consideration, that if circumstances should not permit us to carry on the enterprise, the preparations towards it could easily be converted into another channel, and made serviceable to our Operations elsewhere, without any material addition of expense to the Continent. [because provisions, which would compose the principal part of the expence were at all events to be purchased on Connecticut River the only doubt being whether it should be used in an Expedition against Canada or transported to Boston; circumstances to determine this; with truth it may be added, that excepting the articles of provisions and forage which, as before observed, would have been bot. if no Expedn. by way of Co'os had been in contemplation, the "incredible" expence mentioned by Genl. Gates in his letter of Mar. 4th. amounted to the purchase of a few pairs of Snow Shoes, and some leather for Mocosons only. If any other expence has been incurred it is unknown to me; must have been by his order, and he alone answerable for it.]

In [October] following, Congress entered into arrangements with the Marquis De la Fayette for co-operating with the Court of France, in an expedition against [that Country.] In this scheme, one body of troops was to proceed from Co'os and penetrate by way of the River St. Francis; others, forming a junction at Niagara were to enter Canada by that Route; and while these were operating in this manner, a French fleet and a body of french troops were to go up the River St. Laurence and take possession of Quebec. You are well acquainted with the opposition I gave this plan and my reasons at large for it. From what has since happened, they seem to have met the full approbation of Congress. The ideas I held up were principally these; that we ought not to enter in any contract with a foreign power, unless we were sure we should be able to fulfil our engagements; that it was uncertain whether the enemy would quit the states or not, and, in case they did not, it would be impracticable to furnish the aids which we had stipulated; that, even if they should leave us, it was very doubtful whether our resources would be equal to the supplies required; that therefore it would be impolitic to hazard a contract of the kind and better to remain at liberty to act as future conjunctures should point out. I recommended nevertheless, as there were powerful reasons to hope the enemy might go away, that eventual preparations should be made to take advantage of it, to possess ourselves of Niagara and other posts in that quarter for the security of our frontiers and to carry our views still further, with respect to a conquest of Canada, if we should find ourselves able to prosecute such an enterprise. This, Congress in a subsequent resolve, approved and directed to be done. It was not the least motive with me for recommending it, that operations of this nature seemed to be a very favourite object with that honourable body. The preparations on Hudson's river were undertaken in consequence.

Upon a nearer view of our finances and resources, and when it came to be decided, that the enemy would continue for some time longer to hold the posts, they were in possession of; in the course of the conferences with which I was honored by the Committee of Congress in Philadelphia, I suggested my doubts of the propriety of continuing our Northern preparations upon so extensive a plan as was at first determined. The Committee were of opinion with me that the state of our currency and supplies in general would oblige us to act on the defensive next campaign, except so far as related to an expedition into the Indian country for chastizing the savages and preventing their depredations on our back settlements, and that though it would be extremely desirable to be prepared for pushing our operations further, yet our necessities, exacting a system of œconomy, forbade our launching into much extra expence for objects which were remote and contingent. This determination having taken place, all the Northern preparations were discontinued except such as were necessary towards the intended Indian expedition.

Things were in this situation, when I received a Letter from General Bayley [(living at Co'os)] expressing some fears for the safety of the Magazine at Co'os, in consequence of which I directed the stores to be removed lower down the Country. This I did to prevent a possibility of accident, though I did not apprehend they were in much danger. Some time afterwards, I received the letter, No. 1, from General Gates expressing similar fears; to which I returned him the answer of the 14th. of february transmitted by him to Congress, [No. 2]. Knowing that preparations had been making at Albany, and unacquainted with their true design he very precipitately concluded from a vague expression in that letter, that the intention of attacking Canada was still adhered to, but that I had changed the plan and was going by way of Lake Champlain, or Ontario. Either of these routes he pronounces impracticable and represents that by Co'os, as the only practicable one. He goes still further and declares, that "in the present state of our army and

the actual situation of our magazines to attempt a serious invasion of Canada by whatever route would prove unsuccessful
unless the fleet of our allies, should at the same time co-operate
with us by sailing up the River St. Laurence." Though I differ with him as to the impracticability of both the other routes,
I venture to go a step beyond him respecting our ability to
invade Canada and am convinced that in our present circumstances, and with the enemy in front, we cannot undertake a
serious invasion of [that Country] at all, even with the aid of
an allied fleet. You will perceive Sir, that I have uniformly
made the departure of the enemy from these states an essential
condition to the invasion of Canada; and that General Gates
has intirely mistaken my intentions. Hoping that I had embarked in a scheme, which our situation would not justify, he
eagerly seizes the opportunity of exposing my supposed errors
to Congress; and in the excess of his intemperate zeal to injure
me, exhibits himself in a point of view, from which I imagine
he will derive little credit. The decency of the terms in which
he undertakes to arraign my conduct both to myself and to
Congress and the propriety of the hasty appeal he has made
will I believe appear at least questionable to every man of
sense and delicacy.

The last paragraph of the extract, with which you favour me
is a pretty remarkable one. I shall make no comments, further
than as it implies a charge of neglect on my part, in not writing
to him but once since december. From the beginning of last
Campaign to the middle of December, about 7 Months; I have
copies of near fifty letters to him and about forty originals from
him. I think it will be acknowledged the correspondence was
frequent enough during that period; and, if it has not continued in the same proportion since, the only reason was that
the season of the year, the troops being in Winter quarters and
Genl. Gs. situation at Boston unfruitful of events and unproductive of any military arrangements between us, afforded very
little matter for epistolary intercourse; and I flatter myself it
will be readily believed, that I am sufficiently occupied with
the necessary business of my station, and have no need of increasing it, by multiplying letters without an object. If you
were to peruse, my Dear Sir, the letters which have passed be-

tween General Gates and myself for a long time back, you
would be sensible that I have no great temptation to court his
correspondence when the transacting of public business does
not require it. An air of design, a want of candor in many instances and even of politeness give no very inviting complexion
to the correspondence on his part. As a specimen of this, I send
you a few letters and extracts, which, at your leisure, I shall
be glad you will cast your eye upon.

Last fall it was for some time strongly suspected that the
enemy would transport the whole or the greatest part of their
force Eastward and combine one great land and sea operation
against the french fleet in Boston harbour. On this supposition,
as I should go in person to Boston, the command next in importance was the posts on the North River. This properly
would devolve on General Gates; but, from motives of peculiar
scrupulousness as there had been a difference between us, I
thought it best to know whether it was agreeable to him; before I directed his continuance. By way of compliment, I wrote
him a letter containing the extract, No. 3, expecting a cordial
answer and chearful acceptance. I received the evasive and unsatisfactory reply No. 4. A few days after this, upon another
occasion I wrote him the letter No. 5, to which I received the
extraordinary answer, No. 6, which was passed over in silence.

The plan of operations for the campaign being determined,
a commanding officer was to be appointed for the Indian expedition. This command according to all present appearances
will [probably be] of the second, if not of the first, importance
for the campaign. The officer conducting it, has a flattering
prospect of acquiring more credit than can be expected by any
other this year and he has the best reason to hope for success.
General Lee from his situation, was out of the question: General Schuyler, who, by the way, would have been most agreeable to me, was so uncertain of continuing in the army that I
could not appoint him: General Putnam, I need not mention.
I therefore made the offer of it, [for the appointmt. could no
longer be delayed] to General Gates who was next in seniority,
though perhaps I might have avoided it, if I had been so disposed, from his being in a command by the special appointment of Congress. My letter to him on the occasion you will

find in No. 7. I believe you will think it was conceived in very candid and polite terms and merited a different answer from the one given to it in No. 8.

I discovered very early in the war symptoms of coldness and constraint in General Gates behavior to me. These increased as he rose into greater consequence; but we did not come to a direct breach, 'till the beginning of last year. This was occasioned, by a correspondence, which I thought rather made free with me between General Gates and Conway, which accidentally came to my knowledge. The particulars of this affair you will find delineated in the packet herewith indorsed "papers respecting General Conway." Besides the evidence contained in them of the genuineness of the offensive correspondence, I have other proofs still more convincing, which, having been given me in a confidential way, I am not at liberty to impart.

After this affair subsided, I made a point of treating Genl. Gates with all the attention and cordiality in my power, as well from a sincere desire of harmony, as from an unwillingness to give any cause of triumph to our enemies from an appearance of dissension among ourselves. I can appeal to the world and to the whole Army whether I have not cautiously avoided every word or hint that could tend to disparage General Gates in any way. I am sorry his conduct to me has not been equally generous and that he is continually giving me fresh proofs of malevolence and opposition. It will not be doing him injustice to say, that, besides the little underhand intrigues, which he is frequently practising, there has hardly been any great military question, in which his advice has been asked, that it has not been given in an equivocal and designing manner, apparently calculated to afford him an opportunity of censuring me on the failure of whatever measure might be adopted.

When I find that this Gentleman does not scruple to take the most unfair advantages of me; I am under a necessity of explaining his conduct to justify my own. This and the perfect confidence I have in you have occasioned me to trouble you with so free a communication of the state of things between us. I shall still be as passive as a regard to my own character will permit. I am however uneasy as General —— has endeavoured to impress Congress with an unfavourable idea of me, and as

I only know this in a private confidential way, that I cannot take any step to remove the impression, if it should be made.

I am aware Sir, of the delicacy of your situation; and I mean this letter only for your own private information; You will therefore not allow yourself to be embarrassed by its contents, but with respect to me pass it over in silence.

With the truest Esteem and personal Regard, I am, etc.

P. S. General Gates in his Letter of the [30th. of Septr.] disapproves the divided state of our army, what he says being in general terms might seem plausible enough, but [by no means applies to the case in hand.] The Army was then in four divisions. Three brigades of the right wing and one from the second line under General Putnam had been stationed in the Highlands in conjunction with the garrison of West Point for the immediate defence of the passes there. The remaining two brigades of that wing, under Baron De Kalb were encamped on Fishkill plains 7 or 8 Miles from the town within less than a days march of the fort. At Fredericksburgh were three brigades of the second line under Lord Stirling, about two days march from the Fort. General Gates with the [left] wing of five brigades was at Danbury [abt. 14] miles from Fredericksburgh. The manœuvring on our flanks, of which General Gates speaks by way of the North River or the sound, must have had for object either the Highland passes or the army itself. Had they attempted those passes the force immediately on the spot and close in its vicinity, was sufficient from the nature of the ground to withstand their whole force; and the rest of the Army from the time necessarily exhausted in military operations, would in all probability have been up in time to succour that part. Without gaining those passes they could not get at the army at all on the right; and in doing it, if they could have effected it, the army would have had abundant time to collect and defend itself. To advance by land in our front would have been chimerical: they would have had a much greater distance to approach us, than the whole distance from one extremity of our force to the other; and we should have had all the leisure we could desire to assemble at any point we thought proper. Had they attempted our left flank at Danbury by way of the sound, we might either, if we had judged it expedient, have brought up the other corps to support the one there, or, if it found itself pressed for want of time, it had only to fall back upon Fredericksburgh and there our whole force would have concentred with ease to oppose the enemy to the greatest advantage. The truth was, there was not at that time, the least probability they should attempt [an] Army [which had been the whole Summer inviting them out of their strong hold] nor did I think there was much, they would molest the forts; yet it would certainly have been imprudent to have risked the security of either. When the enemy was in the Jerseys the change then made in the disposition gave still greater security to the different objects for which we had to provide, by drawing a greater force to the point threatened. The intention of the disposition I have described was to push a part of our force as far Eastward as possible for the aid and protection of the French fleet, in case the enemy had directed their force against that; at the same time, I did not choose to lose sight of the North river and therefore kept a sufficient force near enough to secure it. The conciliating these two objects, produced that division of our army, of which General Gates complains. No man however was more vehement in supposing the French fleet would be the object of the enemy's operations than himself; and this he so emphatically inculcated in several of his letters, that I thought it necessary in answer to one of the 6th. of October, to write him as contained in mine of the 7th; both of which are also herewith No. 9 and 10. [I am, &c.]

SPEECH TO THE DELAWARE CHIEFS

In consonance with his policy to win the Indian tribes by persuasion or to render them harmless to the cause of Independence by force if necessary, Washington delivered this speech to the friendly Delaware chiefs as both a plea and a warning.

Head Quarters, Middle Brook, May 12, 1779

BROTHERS: I am happy to see you here. I am glad the long Journey you have made, has done you no harm; and that you are in good health: I am glad also you left All our friends of the Delaware Nation well.

Brothers: I have read your paper. The things you have said are weighty things, and I have considered them well. The Delaware Nation have shown their good will to the United States. They have done wisely and I hope they will never repent. I rejoice in the new assurances you give of their friendship. The things you now offer to do to brighten the chain, prove your sincerity. I am sure Congress will run to meet you, and will do every thing in their power to make the friendship between the people of these States, and their Brethren of the Delaware nation, last forever.

Brothers: I am a Warrior. My words are few and plain; but I will make good what I say. 'Tis my business to destroy all the Enemies of these States and to protect their friends. You have seen how we have withstood the English for four years; and how their great Armies have dwindled away and come to very little; and how what remains of them in this part of our great Country, are glad to stay upon Two or three little Islands, where the Waters and their Ships hinder us from going to destroy them. The English, Brothers, are a boasting people. They talk of doing a great deal; but they do very little. They fly away on their Ships from one part of our Country to an other; but as soon as our Warriors get together they leave it and go to some other part. They took Boston and Philadelphia, two of our greatest Towns; but when they saw our Warriors in a great body ready to fall upon them, they were forced to leave them.

Brothers: We have till lately fought the English all alone. Now the Great King of France is become our Good Brother and Ally. He has taken up the Hatchet with us, and we have sworn never to bury it, till we have punished the English and made them sorry for All the wicked things they had in their

Hearts to do against these States. And there are other Great Kings and Nations on the other side of the big Waters, who love us and wish us well, and will not suffer the English to hurt us.

Brothers: Listen well to what I tell you and let it sink deep into your Hearts. We love our friends, and will be faithful to them, as long as they will be faithful to us. We are sure our Good brothers the Delawares will always be so. But we have sworn to take vengeance on our Enemies, and on false friends. The other day, a handful of our young men destroyed the settlement of the Onondagas. They burnt down all their Houses, destroyed their grain and Horses and Cattle, took their Arms away, killed several of their Warriors and brought off many prisoners and obliged the rest to fly into the woods. This is but the beginning of the troubles which those Nations, who have taken up the Hatchet against us, will feel.

Brothers: I am sorry to hear that you have suffered for want of necessaries, or that any of our people have not dealt justly by you. But as you are going to Congress, which is the great Council of the Nation and hold all things in their hands, I shall say nothing about the supplies you ask. I hope you will receive satisfaction from them. I assure you, I will do every thing in my power to prevent your receiving any further injuries, and will give the strictest orders for this purpose. I will severely punish any that shall break them.

Brothers: I am glad you have brought three of the Children of your principal Chiefs to be educated with us. I am sure Congress will open the Arms of love to them, and will look upon them as their own Children, and will have them educated accordingly. This is a great mark of your confidence and of your desire to preserve the friendship between the Two Nations to the end of time, and to become One people with your Brethen of the United States. My ears hear with pleasure the other matters you mention. Congress will be glad to hear them too. You do well to wish to learn our arts and ways of life, and above all, the religion of Jesus Christ. These will make you a greater and happier people than you are. Congress will do every thing they can to assist you in this wise intention; and to tie the knot of friendship and union so fast, that nothing shall ever be able to loose it.

Brothers: There are some matters about which [I do not open my Lips, because they belong to Congress, and not to us warriors; you are going to them, they will tell you all you wish to know.

Brothers: When you have seen all you want to see, I will then wish you a good Journey to Philadelphia. I hope you may find there every thing your hearts can wish, that when you return home you may be able to tell your Nation good things of us. And I pray God he may make your Nation wise and Strong, that they may always see their own] true interest and have courage to walk in the right path; and that they never may be deceived by lies to do any thing against the people of these States, who are their Brothers and ought always to be one people with them.

To JOHN ARMSTRONG

To John Armstrong, Delegate to Congress from Pennsylvania, Washington confided his views on the obstructionist tactics of Congress in the face of the critical plight of the army. The "Person" referred to in the postscript was Major General John Sullivan, who was in command of the Indian expedition.

Head Qrs., Middle brook, May 18, 1779

DEAR SIR: I have received your favor of the 10th Instt. and thank you for it. Never was there an observation founded in more truth than yours of my having a choice of difficulties. I cannot say that the resolve of Congress which you allude to has increased them; but with propriety I may observe it has added to my embarrassment in fixing on them inasmuch as It gives me powers without the means of execution when these ought to be co-equal at least. The cries of the distressed, of the fatherless and the Widows, come to me from all quarters. The

States are not behind hand in making application for assistance notwithstanding scarce any one of them, that I can find, is taking effectual measures to compleat its qouta of Continental Troops, or have even power or energy enough to draw forth their Militia; each complains of neglect because it gets not what it asks; and conceives that no other suffers like itself because they are ignorant of what others experience, receiving the complaints of their own people only. I have a hard time of it and a disagreeable task. To please every body is impossible; were I to undertake it I should probably please no body. If I know myself I have no partialities. I have from the beginning, and I will to the end pursue to the best of my judgment and abilities one steady line of conduct for the good of the great whole. This will, under all circumstances administer consolation to myself however short I may fall of the expectations of others. But to leave smaller matters, I am much mis-taken if the resolve of Congress hath not an eye to something far beyond our abilities; they are not, I conceive, sufficiently acquainted with the state and strength of the Army, of our resources, and how they are to be drawn out. The powers given may be beneficial, but do not let Congress deceive them-selves by false expectations founded on a superficial view of the situation and circumstances of things in general and their own Troops in particular; for in a word, I give it to you as my opinion, that if the reinforcement expected by the enemy should arrive, and no effectual measures be taken to compleat our Battalions, and stop the further depreciation of our Money I do not see upon what ground we are able, or mean to continue the contest. We now stand upon the brink of a precipice from whence the smallest help plunges us headlong. At this moment, our Money does but pass; at what rate I need not add because unsatisfied demands upon the treasury afford too many unequivocal and alarming proofs to stand in need of illustration. Even at this hour every thing is in a manner, at a stand for want of this money (such as it is) and because many of the States instead of passing laws to aid the several depart-ments of the Army have done the reverse, and hampered the transportation in such a way as to stop the Supplies wch. are indispensably necessary and for want of wch. we are embarrassed exceedingly. This is a summary of our affairs in Genl. to which I am to add that the Officers unable any longer to support themselves in the Army are resigning continually, or doing what is even worse, spreading discontent and possibly the seeds of Sedition.

You will readily perceive my good Sir that this is a confidential letter and that however willing I may be to disclose such matters and such sentiments to particular friends who are entrusted with the government of our great national concerns, I shall be extremely unwilling to have them communicated to any others, as I should feel much compunction if a single word or thought of mine was to create the smallest despair in our own people or feed the hope of the enemy who I know pursue with avidity every track which leads to a discovery of the Sentiments of Men in Office. Such (Men in Office I mean) I wish to be impressed, deeply impressed with the importance of close attention and a vigorous exertion of the means for extricating our finances from the deplorable Situation in which they now are. I never was, much less reason have I now, to be affraid of the enemys Arms; but I have no scruple in declaring to you, that I have never yet seen the time in which our affars in my opinion were at so low an ebb as the present and witht. a speedy and capital change we shall not be able in a very short time to call out the strength and resources of the Country. The hour therefore is certainly come when party differences and disputes should subside; when every Man (especially those in Office) should with one hand and one heart pull the same way and with their whole strength. Providence has done, and I am perswaded is disposed to do, a great deal for us, but we are not to forget the fable of Jupiter and the Countryman. I am, etc.

P. S. I am not insensible of the propriety of the observn. contained in the P. S. to your Letter and can assure you that the Person you allude to was not appointed from motives of partiality or in a hasty manner; after long and cool deliberation, a due consideration of characters and circumstances; and some regard to military rules and propriety I could do no better. I must work with such means as I have. You know I presume that the comd. was offered Genl. Gtes who declined the acceptance of it.

To MARQUIS DE LAFAYETTE

Apprehensive over a British expedition up the Hudson, Washington hastily prepared the defenses of the Highlands, with his main strength at the turn of the river commanded by the two forts at West Point and Constitution Island. Measures were taken to fortify Stony Point and Verplanck's Point, but before they could be completed, a force under command of Sir Henry Clinton took possession of Stony Point. Washington moved his Headquarters to New Windsor, in order to be near West Point, the key to the entire defense of the river. Ten days later, "Mad Anthony" Wayne stormed and captured Stony Point by bayonet assault in what is still considered one of the most brilliantly conceived and executed military achievements of the war. In the meantime, General Sullivan's campaign against the Six Nations, in Central New York State, was crowned with success and the power of the Indian Confederacy was broken.

New Windsor, July 4, 1779

MY DEAR MARQS: Since my last which was written (to the best of my recollection for not having my Papers with me I can not have recourse to dates) in March, both Armies continued quiet in their Winter cantonments till about the first of May when a detachmt. of abt. 2000 of the Enemy under the command of General Matthews conveyed by Sir George Collier made a sudden invasion of a Neck of land comprehending Portsmouth and Suffolk in Virginia, and after plundering and destroying the property (chiefly private) in those places and stealing a number of Negroes returned to New York the moment they found the Country rising in Arms to oppose them.

This exploit was immediately followed by a movement of Sir Henry Clinton up the North River the beginning of June. what the real object of this expedition was, I cannot with certainty inform you. Our Posts in the highlands were supposed to be his aim because they were of importance to us, and consonant to his former plan for prosecuting the War; but whether upon a nearer approach he found them better provided and more difficult of access than he expected, or whether his only view was to cut off the communication between the East and West side of the River below the highlands I shall not undertake to decide; certain it is however that he came up in full force, disembarked at Kings ferry and there began to fortify the points on each side which to all intents and purposes are Islands and by nature exceedingly strong.

This movement of the enemy and my solicitude for the security of our defences on the River, induced me to March the Troops which were cantoned at Middle brook, immediately to their support and for the further purpose of strengthening the defences by additional Works. in this business I have been employed near three weeks, while the enemy have not been idle in establishing themselves as above. They have reinforced their main army with part of the garrison at Rhode Island.

General Sullivan commands an Expedition against the Six Nation's which aided by Butlar and Brandt, with their Tory Friends, and some force from Canada have greatly infested our Frontrs. He has already Marched to the Susquehanna with about 4000 Men, all Continental Soldiers and I trust will destroy their Settlements and extirpate them from the Country which more than probably will be effected by their flight as it is not a difficult matter for them to take up their Beds and Walk.

We have received very favourable Accts. from South Carolina, by wch. it appears that the British Troops before Charles town have met with a defeat and are in a very perilous situation. We have this matter from such a variety of hands that it scarcely admits of a doubt and yet no official information is received of it.

When my dear Marquis shall I embrace you again? Shall I ever do it? or have the charms of the amiable and lovely Marchioness, or the smiles and favors of your Prince withdrawn you from us entirely? At all times, and under all circumstances, I have the honor to be with the greatest regard, personal attachment and affection, Yr., etc.

To GOVERNOR THOMAS JEFFERSON

While congratulating Thomas Jefferson on his appointment as Governor of Virginia, Washington first alludes to the success of Colonel George Rogers Clark's undertaking to push the frontier farther west; he refers to the defenses of the Highlands and to what might be called a British punitive expedition carried out wantonly against Connecticut, aided and abetted by the former Governor of New York, now General Tryon. Convoyed up Long Island Sound, his troops landed near New Haven, plundered that town, moved to Fairfield and laid it in ashes and then devastated Norwalk while committing unwarranted atrocities. Thwarted from carrying their march of destruction to New London, the British ravagers returned to Huntington Bay, Long Island.

Head Quarters, New Windsor, July 10, 1779

SIR: On the 4th Instant I had the Honor to receive your Letter of the 19th of June. Your Excellency will permit me to offer you my sincere congratulations upon your appointment to the Government of Virginia.

I thank you much for the accounts Your Excellency has been pleased to transmit me of the successes of Cols. Clarke and Shelby. They are important and interesting, and do great honor to the Officers and Men engaged in the Enterprises. I hope these successes will be followed by very happy consequences. If Colo Clarke could by any means gain possession of Detroit, it would in all probability effectually secure the friendship or at least the neutrality of most of the Western Indians.

I have no doubt of the propriety of the proceedings against Governor Hamilton, Dejean and Lamothe. Their cruelties to our unhappy people who have fallen into their hands and the measures they have pursued to excite the savages to acts of the most wanton barbarity, discriminate them from common prisoners, and most fully authorize the treatment decreed in their case.

Your Excellency will have heard of the Enemy's movements up Hudson's river. It was generally supposed from the force in which they came, and from a variety of Other circumstances that our posts in the Highlands were their Object; however they did not attempt them. They took post themselves on Verplanks and Stoney points on the opposite sides of the River, where they have established very strong Garrisons, and from their peninsular and indeed almost insular forms, it will be very difficult if practicable to dislodge them. The taking of these positions was, among other considerations, to distress and cut off our best communication between the States East and West of the River. Since they have done this, Genl. Clinton with the main body of his Army has fallen down the River to Philipsbourg and the Country above Kings bridge. They seem determined to prosecute the system of War, threatened by the Commissioners and afterwards sanctioned by Parliament on a discussion of the point. And a Detachment sent up the Sound last week disembarked, plundered New Haven, burnt some Houses there and at East Haven, reimbarked and on the 7th relanded and burnt almost the Town of Fairfield, except a few Houses. The Militia upon these occasions considering their number and the sudden manner in which they assembled, behaved with great spirit. Genl. Tryon it is said commands these disgraceful expeditions. I have the Honor, etc.

P. S. The Enemy have burnt Norwalk, another Town on the sound.

THOUGHTS ON A BRITISH ATTEMPT
ON WEST POINT

These unfinished notations provide an insight into the manner in which Washington tried to anticipate enemy action and the steps he had to consider to block it. More and more his reliance on West Point as the bulwark by which the Hudson could be held becomes central in his plans for the maintenance of total defense against an enemy whose strategy he could only surmise.

July, 1779

The Enemy may operate four ways if they have received any considerable reinforcement, which they will choose, is difficult, at this moment, to decide on

viz.

They may attack the Fort, and consequently the Army, which is here for its defence.

or,

If the Army is their object, it may be struck at as unconnected with, and independent of, the Fort. in any situation, and under every Circumstance.

or,

If the Fort is the object, and they want to draw the Army from it. or the Army is the object, but the situation of it is disliked on account of the Mountains and defiles wch. environs this post, and its present Incampment.

They may,

In order to obtain advantages by effecting one or the other of the above ends operate upon our right flank and by harrassing the Country, menacing Philadelphia, or endangering our communication and indeed Stores at Easton and else where West of this Post draw us into the low lands.

or

For semilar purposes but more especially with a view of drawing us further from our supplies thereby lengthening our communication and rendering it more expensive, difficult and hazardous they may operate upon our left flank and more to the Eastward.

Let us consider then the most probable operation of the enemy in each of these cases.

First

The Post at West point, and consequently the Army, which is involved with it. Taking it for granted that the enemy will never attempt works of this kind by assault (unless it is by surprise, which it is our business to guard against) I shall suppose their operations will be by regular approaches and to avoid the consequences of a division of force (unless they are stronger than I conceive them to be) will endeavour with their whole force to possess the heights, and establish themselves on one side of the River first, and the East side of the two being most likely because it is most difficult for us to be supplied on and by an entire land carriage from their present posts at Kings Ferry easiest if not the safest for them. If they operate on that side it appears to me that they must depend upon a Land transportation of supplies from Verplanks point or Peekskill landing through the Continental Village as water carriage might be rendered precarious, difficult and hazardous. after having made a sufficient lodgment on the East side, erected batteries secured and amply supplied them with provisions and stores they will in order to compleat the Investiture and reduction of the Post remove their whole force to the West side.

or

Vice versa, they may begin their operations on the West and afterwards establish Posts on the East, or if the business can be done without may confine their operations to the West-side wholly as less dangerous. In this case I conceive their first movement will be to old Fort Clinton as a secure lodgment and protection to the Water communication that far, and within a short distance of the first heights which will be necessary for them to possess, to commence their approaches.

In these cases what is the proper line of Conduct for us to observe?

The first great point, is by every possible means to discover the real design of the enemy, and distinguish feints from serious movements. and neglecting the Party intended for the feint unless it can be easily cut off oppose our whole force except what ought to be in the Redoubts to the enemy's which will be found most efficatious upon their flank and rear, in order to gain these it will be necessary if there can be any previous knowledge of the time of their intended movement to advance. . .

To MARQUIS DE LAFAYETTE

In the letter in which he first used the words "after our Swords and Spears have given place to the plough share and pruning hook," Washington reaffirms his love and friendship for Lafayette in glowing terms and gives him such information as he has concerning the British movements and intentions. Lafayette had gone to France to persuade Count Charles de Vergennes, then Minister of Foreign Affairs, to equip an armada for a re-invasion of Canada. Vergennes saw Canada more as a liability than an asset, and vetoed what he considered Lafayette's quixotic scheme.

West-point, September 30, 1779

My Dear Marqs: A few days ago I wrote you a letter in much haste. the cause a sudden notification of Monsr. Gerards having changed the place of his embarkation from Boston (as was expected) to Philadelphia, and the hurry Monsir. de la Colombe was in to reach the latter before the Minister should have left it. Since that, I have been honourd with the company of the Chevr. de la Luzerne, and by him was favour'd with your obliging letter of the 12th. of June which filled me with equal pleasure and surprise; the latter at hearing that you had not received one of the many letters I had written to you, since you left the American Shore. I cannot at this time charge my memory with the precise dates of these letters but the first, which ought and I expected would have reached you at Boston and I much wished it to do so because it contained a Letter from me to Doctr Franklin expressive of the Sentiments I en-

tertained of your Services and merit was put into the hands
of a Captn. McQueen of Charles Town, who was to Sail from
Phila. soon after. In March I wrote you once or twice, and
in June or the first of July following, (when it was reported
that Monsr. Gerard was about to leave us I took the liberty of
committing to his care another of my lettrs. to you,) which
sevl. efforts though they may have been unsuccessful will exhibit no bad specimen of my having kept you constantly in
remembrance and a desire of giving you proofs of it.

It gave me infinite pleasure to hear from yourself of the favourable reception you met with from your Sovereign, and of
the joy which your safe arrival in France had diffused among
your friends. I had no doubt but that this wou'd be the case;
to hear it from yourself adds pleasure to the acct. and here My
dear friend let me congratulate you on your new, honourable
and pleasing appointment in the Army commanded by the
Count de Vaux which I shall accompy. with an assurance that
none can do it with more warmth of Affection, or sincere joy
than myself. Your forward zeal in the cause of liberty; Your
singular attachment to this infant World; Your ardent and
persevering efforts, not only in America but since your return
to France to serve the United States; Your polite attention to
Americans, and your strict and uniform friendship for me,
has ripened the first impressions of esteem and attachment
which I imbibed for you into such perfect love and gratitude
that neither time nor absence can impair which will warrant
my assuring you, that whether in the character of an Officer
at the head of a Corps of gallant French (if circumstances
should require this) whether as a Major Genl. commanding
a division of the American Army; Or whether, after our Swords
and Spears have given place to the plough share and pruning
hook, I see you as a private Gentleman, a friend and Companion, I shall welcome you in all the warmth of friendship
to Columbia's shore; and in the latter case, to my rural Cottage,
where homely fare and a cordial reception shall be substituted
for delicacies and costly living. this from past experience I
know you can submit to; and if the lovely partner of your
happiness will consent to participate with us in such rural entertainment and amusemts. I can undertake in behalf of Mrs.

Washington that she will do every thing in her power to make
Virginia agreeable to the Marchioness. My inclination and endeavours to do this cannot be doubted when I assure you that
I love everybody that is dear to you. consequently participate
in the pleasure you feel in the prospt. of again becoming a
parent and do most Sincerely congratulate you and your Lady
on this fresh pledge she is about to give you of her love.

I thank you for the trouble you have taken, and your polite
attention in favouring me with a Copy of your letter to Congress; and feel as I am perswaded they must do, the force of
such ardent zeal as you there express for the interest of this
Country. The propriety of the hint you have given them must
carry conviction and I trust will have a salutary effect; tho'
there is not, I believe, the same occasion for the admonition
now, there was some months ago; many late changes have taken
place in that honourable body which has removed in a very
great degree, if not wholly, the discordant spirit which it is said
prevailed in the Winter, and I hope measures will also be taken
to remove those unhappy and improper differences which have
extended themselves elsewhere to the prejudice of our affairs
in Europe.

You enquire after Monsr. de la Colombe, and Colo. Neville;
the first (who has been with Baron de Kalb) left this a few days
ago, as I have already observed, for Phila., in expectation of
a passage with Monsr. Gerard. Colo. Neville called upon me
about a Month since and was to have dined with us the next
day but did not come, since which I have not seen him, nor do
I know at this time where he is; he had then but just returned
from his own home; and it was the first time I had seen him
since he parted with you at Boston. It is probable he may be
with the Virginia Troops which lye at the mouth of Smiths
clove abt. 30 Miles from hence.

I have had great pleasure in the visit which the Chevalier
de la Luzerne and Monsr. Marbois did me the honor to make
at this Camp; for both of whom I have imbibed the most favourable impressions, and thank you for the honourable mention you made of me to them. The Chevr. till he had announced himself at Congress, did not choose to be received in
his public character. If he had, except paying him Military

honors, It was not my intention to depart from that plain and simple manner of living which accords with the real Interest and policy of Men struggling under every difficulty for the attainment of the most inestimable blessing of life, Liberty; the Chevalier was polite enough to approve my principle, and condescended to appear pleased with our Spartan living. In a word he made us all exceeding happy by his affability and good humour, while he remained in Camp.

You are pleased my dear Marquis to express an earnest desire of seeing me in France (after the establishment of our Independancy) and do me the honour to add, that you are not singular in your request. let me entreat you to be perswaded, that to meet you anywhere after the final accomplishment of so glorious an event would contribute to my happiness; and that, to visit a country to whose generous aid we stand so much indebted, would be an additional pleasure; but remember my good friend, that I am unacquainted with your language. that I am too far advanced in years to acquire a knowledge of it. and that to converse through the medium of an interpreter upon common occasions, especially with the Ladies must appr. so extremely aukward, insipid, and uncouth, that I can scarce bear it in idea. I will therefore hold myself disengaged for the present and when I see you in Virginia, we will talk of this matter and fix our plans.

The declaration of Spain in favour of France has given universal joy to every Whig, while the poor Tory droops like a withering flower under a declining Sun.

We are anxiously expecting to hear of great and important events on your side the Atlantic. At prest. the immagination is left in the wide field of conjecture. Our eyes one moment are turned to an Invasion of England. then of Ireland. Minorca, Gibralter, &ca. In a word we hope every thing, but know not what to expect or where to fix.

The glorious successes of Count DEstaing in the West Indies at the sametime that it adds dominion to France and fresh lustre to her Arms is a source of new and unexpected misfortune to our tender and generous parent and must serve to convince her of the folly of quitting the substance in pursuit of a shadow; and as there is no experience equal to that which is bought I trust she will have a superabundance of this kind of knowledge and be convinced as I hope all the World, and every tyrant in it will that the best and only safe road to honour, glory, and true dignity, is justice.

We have such repeated advices of Count D'Estaings being in these Seas that (though I have no official information of the event) I cannot help giving entire credit to the report and looking for his arrival every moment and am preparing accordingly. The enemy at New York also expect it, and to guard agt. the consequences as much as it is in their power to do, are repairing and strengthening all the old fortifications and adding New ones in the vicinity of the City; their fear however does not retard an embarkation which was making (and generally believed) to be for the West Indies or Charles Town. It still goes forward, and by my intelligence will consist of a pretty large detachment. About 14 days ago one british Regiment (the 44th. compleated) and 3 Hessian Regiments were embarked and are gone, as is supposed, to Hallifax. Under convoy of Admiral Arbuthnot about the 20th. of last month the Enemy recd. a reinforcement consisting of two new raised Scotch Regts. some drafts and a few Recruits amounting altogether to about 3000 Men and a few days ago Sir Andw. Hammond arrived with (as it is said) abt. 2000 more; many of these new Troops died on their passage and since landing, the rest are very sickly as indeed their whole Army is while ours keeps remarkably healthy.

The Operations of the enemy this campaign have been confined to the establishment of works of defence. taking a post at Kings ferry, and burning the defenceless towns of New haven, Fairfield, Norwalk, &ca. on the sound within reach of their Shipping where little else was, or could be opposed to them than the cries of distressed Women and helpless children; but these were offered in vain; since these notable exploits they have never stepped out of their Works or beyond their lines. How a conduct of this kind is to effect the conquest of America the wisdom of a North, a Germaine, or Sandwich best can tell. it is too deep and refined for the comprehension of common understandings and general run of politicians.

Colo. Fleury who I expect will have the honour of presenting this letter to you, and who acted an important and honourable part in the event, will give you the particulars of the assault and reduction of Stony point the capture of the G. consg. of 600 men with their Colours, Arms, Baggage, Stores, 15 pieces of valuable ordnance, &ca. He led one of the columns; struck the colours of the garrison with his own hands; and in all respects behaved with that intrepidity and intelligence which marks his conduct upon all occasions.

Since that event we surprized and took Paulus hook a very strong fortified post of the enemys, opposite to the city of New York and within reach of the batteries of that place. The garrison consisting of about 160 Men with the colors were brought off, but none of the stores could be removed on acct. of its insular situation and the difficulty of removing them; the first of these enterprizes was made under the command of General Wayne; the other was conducted by Majr. Lee of the light Horse both of whom have acquired much honor by their gallant behaviour in the respective attacks.

By my last advices from Genl. Sullivan of the 9th. Instt. I am led to conclude that ere this he has completed the entire destruction of the whole Country of the Six nations, excepting so much of it as is inhabited by the Oneidas who have always lived in amity with us; and a few towns belonging to the Cayugas and Onondago's who were disposed to be friendly. At the time these advices came away he had penetrated to the heart of their settlements after having defeated in a general engagement the united force of Indians, Tories, and regulars from Niagara. Burnt between 15 and 20 Towns, destroyed their Crops and every thing that was to be found. He was then advancing to the exterior Towns with a view to complete the desolation of the whole Country, and Remove the cruel inhabitants of it to a greater distance, who were then fleeing in the utmost confusion, consternation and distress towards Niagara, distant 100 Miles through an uninhabited wilderness; experiencing a little of that distress, but nothing of those cruelties which they have exercised on our unhappy frontier Settlers, who (Men, Women and Children) have been deliberately murdered, in a manner shocking to humanity.

But to conclude, you requested from me a long letter, I have given you one; but methinks my dear Marquis, I hear you say, there is reason in all things; that this is too long. I am clearly in sentiment with you, and will have mercy on you in my next. But at present must pray your patience a while longer, till I can make a tender of my most respectful compliments to the Marchioness. Tell her (if you have not made a mistake, and offered your own love instead of hers to me) that I have a heart susceptable of the tenderest passion, and that it is already so strongly impressed with the most favourable ideas of her, that she must be cautious of putting loves torch to it; as you must be in fanning the flame. But here again methinks I hear you say, I am not apprehensive of danger. My wife is young, you are growing old and the atlantic is between you. All this is true, but know my good friend that no distance can keep anxious lovers long asunder, and that the Wonders of former ages may be revived in this. But alas! will you not remark that amidst all the wonders recorded in holy writ no instance can be produced where a young Woman from real inclination has prefered an old man. This is so much against me that I shall not be able I fear to contest the prize with you, yet, under the encouragement you have given me I shall enter the list for so inestimable a Jewell.

I will now reverse the scene, and inform you, that Mrs. Washington (who set out for Virginia when we took the field in June) often has in, her letters to me, enquired if I had heard from you, and will be much pleased at hearing that you are well, and happy. In her name (as she is not here) I thank you for your polite attention to her; and shall speak her sense of the honor confered on her by the Marchioness.

When I look back to the length of this letter I am so much astonished and frightened at it myself, that I have not the courage to give it a careful reading for the purpose of correction. You must therefore receive it with all its imperfections, accompanied with this assurance that though there may be many incorrections in the letter, there is not a single defect in the friendship of my dear Marquis Yr., etc.

To COMTE D'ESTAING

After Count d'Estaing's failure at Rhode Island, he sailed his fleet to the West Indies, where he achieved a minor success in taking St. Vincent's and Grenada. After thus partially redeeming himself, he set forth for the coast of Georgia. In spite of Washington's emphasis on his plans for d'Estaing's participation in an all-out attack on New York as his "first and capital" object, the French Admiral chose to co-operate with the Southern Army, under General Benjamin Lincoln, in an attempt to recapture Savannah. After a siege of three weeks, a rush was made on October 9th to storm the British redoubts, but the combined French and American assault was repulsed with heavy losses. D'Estaing himself was wounded and Count Pulaski, the gallant Polish volunteer who had risen to the rank of brigadier general, was killed. The Americans retreated across the Savannah River to South Carolina and the French dragged themselves back to their ships.

West Point, October 4, 1779

SIR: On receiving advice, that your Excellency had been seen in a latitude, which indicated your approach to our Coasts, and supposing it possible you might direct your course this way, I did myself the honor to write you a letter on the 13th. September, and stationed an Officer in Monmouth County, to meet you with it on your arrival at the Hook. In that letter I explained the situation and force of the enemy, and took the liberty to propose some preliminary movements, on which the successive operations would materially depend. In the uncertainty of your coming, and having little more than conjecture on which to found an expectation of it, these were all the measures I was then authorized to take. But, I have just received dispatches from Congress, acquainting me with your arrival at Georgia, and your intention, after accomplishing your object, to proceed this way. I have, in consequence; called upon the

373

neighbouring States for a reinforcement of Militia, and am taking every other measure in my power, to prepare for a co-operation, with all the dispatch and Vigor our circumstances will permit.

I beg leave to inclose a Copy of the above mentioned letter, and the substance of the intelligence since received. Your Excellency will observe that only two detachments of troops have sailed from New York; one consisting of three German and one British Regiment for Hallifax or Quebec, and the other composed of Grenadiers, Light Infantry and one British Regiment, supposed to be destined to the southern States. I have not received any account of the debarkation of the Hallifax detachment and I believe it has prosecuted its Voyage. One of the transports has been taken and carried into Philadelphia with 160 Men on board. She reports Hallifax to have been her destination. I have reason to believe, from some information recently obtained, that the latter detachment has returned; these however are not altogether authentic, but I am the more inclined to give them credit, as I think it probable they were bound to South Carolina, and in their way may have heard of your Excellency's arrival in that quarter, which would naturally occasion their return to New York.

The Enemy's force in New York and its dependencies, supposing the return of the above detachment, I now estimate at fourteen thousand. Their fleet consists of the Russel of 74. The Europe of 64, the Renown of 50, the Roebuck 44 and a few smaller Frigates. Your Excellency will perceive that their affairs are in a fluctuating state, and therefore many changes may have taken place since my last advices.

From the advanced Season of the Year, every instant of time is infinitely precious, and must be even more so to your Excellency than to us. This makes it to be lamented, that it had not been possible to preconcert a plan before your arrival. The force under your command, and the time you can devote to this business, are essential points in determining what can with propriety be undertaken, and the first steps, will be of great consequence to all the succeeding ones. To enable you the better to regulate your own movements, I shall expose to you our prospects, and the different plans which present themselves to me, with the obstacles attending each.

New York is the first and capital object, upon which every other is dependant. The loss of the Army and Fleet there, would be one of the severest Blows the English Nation could experience. Rhode Island would fall of course. But your Excellency will be sensible, that the reduction of fourteen thousand Men concentred upon a small Island, with the assistance of fortifications, is an enterprise of no inconsiderable difficulty; and requires a vigorous exertion of our resources, in conjunction with your force, to give it a sufficient probability of success. Not less than 30,000 Men will, in my opinion, be adequate to the operation, and we cannot collect the numbers necessary on our part, in addition to what we already have in the field, in less than three Weeks from this time. The interval, between your arrival and that period, must for the most part be spent in a state of inactivity on our side, unless you judge it proper to direct your attention to an attempt upon Rhode Island.

The knowledge you have of this place, will enable you, better than me, to decide on the eligibility of this project. The Garrison there is respectable, and as I am informed, secured by a Chain of Redoubts and Retrenchments from one flank of the Island to the other, which would be exceedingly formidable to an Assault. The town however may be burnt, and with it, the Enemy's magazines, which it is probable would speedily reduce them to a surrender. Your Excellency is a better judge than I am of the time which would be exhausted in the enterprise, but I should imagine it might require at least four Weeks for its accomplishment. If you should think proper to pursue this plan, we have a Body of two thousand troops now ready at Rhode Island, and can march thither any additional number you deem necessary for a cooperation. But in order to this, I must request you will give me previous notice of your intention.

Success, in this attempt, would be favourable to our ulterior operations against New York, but a failure would be attended with the reverse, as it would damp the spirits of the Country and diminish its exertions. Another inconvenience would attend it, which is, that without a division of your force to continue the Blockade of New York, the Fleet now there would make its escape. Indeed, in any plan, a division of your force will be indispensable; Rhode Island and the Sound must be blockaded, otherwise the Garrison there will form a junction with the main Body at New York, which would be so great an accession of force, as would render the success of our operations improbable, and the Frigates and smaller Vessels may find a passage through the Sound, and elude your Excellency in that way: But the difference is this: In the latter case, two or three fifty Gun Ships and as many Frigates will answer the purpose: in the former, some of your Ships of the line must be left at New York, to have a superiority to the two that are there aided by the Frigates.

In case of the attempt upon Rhode Island, the only expedient, to avoid a division of your ships of the line, will be, to remain with the whole at New York, and send your troops round under the protection of your Frigates. Your Excellency is the best judge with what propriety a movement of this kind can be hazarded.

In either event, it appears to me advisable, that you should first enter the Bay of New York with a part at least of your Fleet, and as suddenly as possible to intercept the troops on Staten Island and the Garrisons up the River, as the capture of these will materially facilitate the reduction of the remaining force; and I take the liberty strongly to recommend, that a proper detachment may without loss of time block up the sound and the port of Rhode Island. I have taken measures for furnishing you with pilots, one of them accompanies this letter but I have directed three or four to be stationed with Major Lee at Monmouth to put off to your Excellency on your first appearance. Among these is one ——— who is acquainted with the navigation of the North River in its present state, and will be able to take up the Frigates which I had the honour to request might proceed into Haverstraw Bay.

I have written to Congress, to recommend the assembling all our Frigates and armed Vessels to act in conjunction with the fleet under your command.

With candour and freedom have I exposed to your Excellency my sentiments and expectations: and I entreat you will honor me with a similar communication of your views and intentions. Nothing will give me greater pleasure, than to concur with these, to the utmost of our Ability.

I have not concealed the difficulties in the way of a cooperation, because I thought it my duty fully to apprise you of them. I am persuaded you will ascribe what I have said, to the proper motive, and to that caution which ought always to influence enterprizes pregnant with such interesting consequences. You will not impute them to an unwillingness to exert the resources of the Country, or to a distrust of the event; for I assure your Excellency, I feel the importance of this generous and seasonable succour, and have the highest hopes of its utility to the common cause, and a termination glorious to the allied Arms. I rejoice in the opportunity it affords, nor is the prospect of acting, in immediate conjunction with your Excellency, one of the least flattering circumstances. I shall with the greatest alacrity concur in the execution of any plan which shall be thought advancive of the Interest and Glory of the two Nations, and may add to the Laurels you have already reaped in so distinguished a manner.

I hope soon to have the pleasure of assuring you personally of those sentiments of respectful attachment with which, I have the Honor, etc.

P. S. Mr. Holker, soon after your Excellency left Boston, communicated to me your desire to have the navigation of Hell Gate ascertained. I have taken the greatest pains to answer your views, and the result of my inquiries is, that never more than a fifty Gun Ship has gone thro' that passage, and this with difficulty and hazard. A large ship it is believed could not pass. The reasons are not a want of depth of Water, but the extreme narrowness of the Channel, the rapidity of the current, Whirlpools and Rocks. The least mis-steerage will precipitate the Vessels on the Banks and Shoals on either side, and the power which the Current and Whirlpools have upon larger Vessels, would make it almost impossible to keep them in their proper course. The only time when this passage is practicable for ships of any burthen, is at the height of flood tide.

I have since writing the foregoing learned that the **Renown**

of 50 Guns and not the Raisonable of 64 conveyed the detachment to Hallifax. We may therefore suppose that the Raisonable is in the Harbour of New York.

To THE PRESIDENT OF CONGRESS

*The constant diminution of his troops by the expiration of
short-term enlistments made Washington an advocate of an annual draft. Of the total 27,099 soldiers at his disposal, large-
scale deductions had to be anticipated. As evidence of the
shortage of supplies, Washington here cites the case of available blankets, of which there were 4,900 for his entire army.
Unless levies of troops could be assured, and they adequately
equipped, Washington insists that no plan of operation could
be formulated with any degree of certainty.*

Head Quarters, West Point, November 18, 1779

SIR: As the present Campaign is advancing towards a
conclusion, and the Councils of the British Cabinet, so far as
they have come to my knowledge, are far from recognizing our
Independence and pointing to an honourable peace. I have
thought, it might not be amiss for me to lay before Congress a
state of the army (notwithstanding it is frequently transmitted
the Treasury Board, I believe, by a return of the Muster Rolls,
and to the War Office Monthly in a more general view) as it is
with Congress to decide on the expediency of making it more
respectable, or of fixing its amount to any particular point. The
return I have the honor to inclose, is an abstract taken from the
muster Rolls of the Troops of each State in Octor. (South Carolina and Georgia excepted) and contains a compleat view, not
only of the whole strength of the forces of each, and of the Independent Corps &c. at that time, but of the different periods
for which they stood engaged. I conceived a return of this sort
might be material, and accordingly directed it to be made, the
better to enable Congress to govern their views and requisitions
to the several States. They will perceive by this, that our whole

force including all sorts of Troops, non Commissioned Officers and privates, Drummers and Fifers, supposing every man to have existed and to have been in service at that time, a point however totally inadmissible, amounted to 27,099: That of this number, comprehending, 410 Invalids, 14,998 are stated as engaged for the War: that the remainder, by the expiration of Inlistments, will be decreased by the 31st of December 2051, by the last of March 6,426, by the last of April (including the Levies) 8,181, by the last of June, 10,158: by the last of Septr. 10,709: by different periods (I believe shortly after) 12,157. As I have observed, it cannot be supposed that the whole of the Troops borne upon the Muster Rolls, were either in service, or really in existence, for it will ever be found for obvious reasons, that the amount of an army on Paper, will greatly exceed its real strength. Hence there are other deductions than those enumerated above, and which must equally operate against the Troops of every class; and I must further beg leave to observe, that besides these several deductions, there are of necessity, very considerable and constant drafts of men from the regiments for Artificers, Armourers, Matrosses, Waggoners, the Quarter Masters Department &c, so that we cannot estimate our operating force in the Field, with any propriety or justice, by any means as high, as it may appear at first view on Paper. This point might be more fully illustrated, by referring to the column of present fit for duty, in all general returns, and comparing it with the total amount. Nor is there any reason to expect, that these large and heavy drafts from the regiments will cease; but on the contrary it is much to be feared, from the increased and increasing difficulties in getting men, that they will be still greater.

Having shown what would be the ultimate and greatest possible amount of our force at the several periods above mentioned, according to the abstract of the Muster Rolls for October, supposing every man borne upon them to have been then, and that they would remain in service, agreeable to the terms noted in the abstract, which however is by no means supposeable, as already observed; I shall take the liberty with all possible deference, to offer my sentiments on the only mode that appears to me competent, in the present situation of things, to placing and keeping our Battalions on a respectable footing, if

Congress judge the measure essential; and I trust in doing this, it will not be deemed that I have exceeded my duty. If it should my apology must be, that it proceeded from a desire to place the business of raising the Levies we may have occasion to employ in future on a more regular and certain system, than has been adopted, or at least put in practice; and from which the Public will derive the greatest benefits from their service.

In the more early stages of the contest, when Men might have been inlisted for the War, no man, as my whole conduct and the uniform tenor of my letters will evince, was ever more opposed to short inlistments than I was, and while there remained a prospect of obtaining Recruits upon a permanent footing in the first instance as far as duty and a regard to my station would permit, I urged my sentiments in favor of it. But the prospect of keeping up an Army by voluntary inlistments being changed, or at least standing on too precarious and uncertain a footing to depend on, for the exigency of our affairs, I took the liberty in February 1778 in a particular manner, to lay before the Committee of Arrangement then with the Army at Valley Forge, a plan for an Annual draft, as the surest and most certain if not the only means left us, of maintaining the army on a proper and respectable ground. And more and more confirmed in the propriety of this opinion, by the intervention of a variety of circumstances unnecessary to detail, I again took the freedom of urging the plan to the Committee of conference in January last; and having reviewed it in every point of light and found it right, or at least the best that has occurred to me, I hope I shall be excused by Congress, in offering it to them and in time for carrying it into execution for the next year, if they should conceive it necessary for the States to compleat their Quotas of Troops.

The plan I would propose, is, that each State be informed by Congress annually, of the real deficiency of its Troops, and called upon to make it up, or such less specific number, as Congress may think proper, by a draft. That the men drafted join the Army by the 1st of January and serve 'till the first of January in the succeeding year. That from the time the drafts join the Army, the Officers of the States from which they come, be authorised and directed to use their endeavours to inlist them for the War under the bounties to the Officers themselves, and the recruits, granted by the Act of the 23d of January last, Viz Ten Dollars to the Officer for each recruit, and two hundred to the recruits themselves: That all State, County and Town bounties to drafts, if practicable, be intirely abolished, on account of the uneasiness and disorders they create among the Soldiery, the desertions they produce, and for other reasons which will readily occur; That on or before the first of October annually, an abstract or return similar to the present one, be transmitted to Congress to enable them to make their requisitions to each State with certainty and precision. This I would propose as a general plan to be pursued, and I am persuaded it is, or one nearly similar to it, will be found, the best now in our power, as it will be attended with the least expence to the Public, will place the service on the footing of order and certainty, and will be the only one that can advance the general interest to any great extent. If the plan is established, besides placing the service on the footing of more order and certainty, than it will ever otherwise be, we shall I should hope, by the exertions of the Officers, be able to increase the number of our Troops on permanent engagements for the War, especially if we should be so fortunate as to be in a condition to hold out to the drafts, that would engage, a certainty of their receiving the bounty Cloathing stipulated by the Public to be furnished the Troops, and which is so essential to the interest of both. Cloathing is now become a superior temptation, and if we were in circumstances to hold it out, and the drafts were sure that they would obtain it, as they inlisted, and that it would be regularly furnished as it became due; there are good grounds to believe from what has been experienced, and the reports of the Officers, that many would readily engage for the War. From these considerations, and as it is so highly essential to the advancement of the Public interest, both as we regard the issue of the contest, and œconomy in men and money, I would hope, that every practicable measure will be pursued to get ample and compleat supplies of Cloathing. And I will take the liberty to add, that the diminution of the Army, by the expiration of the inlistments of a part of the Troops, according to the foregoing state, should not in my opinion, lessen the calculations and estimates of supplies in any degree; but that they should be made under the idea of the whole of the Battalions being complete. When this is done, events may and some probably will occur, by which the supplies, as they do not depend upon internal manufacturers may be diminished, and scarcely any can arise, which can make them burthensome on our hands. A want will and must from the nature of things, be attended with very injurious consequences at least. A full quantity with none at all, but with almost innumerable interesting benefits. Besides the prospect we should have of gaining recruits for the War by having good supplies of Cloathing, which as already observed, is become a first inducement to service. We shall as has ever been the case, be obliged to make some issues to the drafts, as well from principles of humanity, as to get their service. I have been thus long on the subject of ample supplies of Cloathing, as it is scarcely to be conceived the distresses and disadvantages, that flow from a deficiency. For instance, nothing can be more injurious or discouraging, than our having only four thousand nine hundred Blankets to distribute to the whole Army, and so of many other Articles in but little better proportion.

The advantages of a well digested, general Uniform system for levying recruits and bringing them to the Army at a particular time, to serve to a fixed period are obvious. We may then form our plans of operation with some degree of certainty, and determine with more propriety and exactness, on what we may or may not be able to do; and the periods for joining and serving, which I have taken the liberty to mention, appear to me the most proper for a variety of considerations. It being in January when it is proposed that the recruits shall join, and when the Enemy cannot operate, they will get seasoned and accustomed in some measure to a Camp life before the Campaign opens, and will have four or five months to acquire discipline and some knowledge of maneuvres, without interruption; and their service being extended to the same time in the succeeding year, the Public will have all the benefits, that can be derived from their aid, for a whole Campaign. According to the plan on which the business has been conducted, the Public incurs a very heavy expence, on account of the recruits (all that the one proposed is liable to) and scarcely receives any benefit from them. The Levies that have been raised, have come to the Army so irregularly, that the aid they were intended to give, has never been received, or at least but to a very limited and partial extent; and the time for which they were engaged, has been spent in gaining a seasoning to Camp, and discipline, when they ought to have been in the field, or they must have been sent there raw and untutored (a circumstance which may lead in some critical moment before an Enemy to most fatal consequences) and the greater part of it has been spent in Winter Quarters. The Abstract with its remarks, will show Congress when the recruits for this Campaign joined, and of what little importance their aid could have been, if the Enemy had not been prevented by the occurrence of a variety of distant events, as providential as they were fortunate for us, from pursuing the vigorous measures there was but too much reason to believe they would have otherwise been capable of, and on which it seemed they had determined. I have the honor, etc.

P. S. From several parts of my letter Congress will conclude, that it must have been intended to have reached them before this. The fact was so, the greater part of it having been drafted early in Septr.; but unfortunately from the dispersed situation of the Troops, I could not obtain the Abstract of the Muster Rolls to shew their state, with any degree of precision, till within these four days.

GENERAL ORDERS

The court-martial charges against Benedict Arnold had their origin as far back as 1778, when he was in command of Philadelphia, where strong Tory elements were firmly established under whose influence he had fallen. Congress had directed Arnold, and Washington had confirmed the order, that no goods or merchandise should be sold or moved without its authority. Arnold, because of the extravagant way in which he lived, with mounting personal expenses, began private speculation on a grand scale with public monies. He had been courting Margaret Shippen, whose family were less than sympathetic to the American cause. Complaints against Arnold's behavior began to accumulate, but none of them ever questioned his gallantry and achievements as an officer of the Continental Army. In March a report filed by a joint congressional committee absolved Arnold of all charges, but Congress itself overruled its own committee and in April ordered a court-martial. Under the circumstances, Arnold's bitterness was understandable; he was on the verge of vindication, only to have to face trial by edict of Congress acting against the recommendation of its members in committee. One postponement after another only added to Arnold's irritation and frustration. Finally the court-martial convened at Morristown. Eight charges were reduced to four, and on two of these he was entirely exonerated. On the other two he drew a mere reprimand, which was tempered by praise of his previous record. Instead of feeling that he had gotten off lightly, Arnold nursed a deep resentment against what he considered the perpetrators of an unmerited injustice. He requested, and received from Washington, a leave of absence from the army for the summer.

Head Quarters, Morristown, Thursday, April 6, 1780

Parole Syntax. Countersigns Tanner, Thrasher.

At a General Court Martial whereof Major General Howe was President, held on the 1st. of June last at Middle Brook and afterwards at Morristown from the 23rd. of December to the 26th. of January, in consequence of a resolution of the Honorable the Congress, for the trial of Major General Arnold on the following Articles contained in the proceedings of the Executive Council of the State of Pennsylvania at the City of Philadelphia the 3rd. of February 1779. Vizt.,

First. "That while in the Camp of General Washington at Valley Forge last spring, he gave permission to a Vessel belonging to persons then voluntarily residing in this City, with the enemy, and of disaffected characters to come into a Port of the United States without the knowledge of the authority of the State or of the Commander in Chief tho' then present.

2nd. In having shut up the Shops and stores on his arrival in the City, so as even to prevent officers of the army from purchasing, while he privately made considerable purchases for his own benefit as is alledged and believed.

3rd. In imposing menial offices upon the sons of Freemen of this State, when called for by the desire of Congress, to perform militia duty, and when remonstrated to hereupon, justifying himself in writing upon the ground of having power so to do. For that when a citizen assumed the character of a soldier, the former was intirely lost in the latter, and that it was the duty of the militia to obey every order of his Aids (not a breach of the laws and constitution) as his (the General's) without judging of the propriety of them.

4th. The appropriating the waggons of this State, when called forth upon a special emergency last autumn, to the transportation of private property and that of Persons who voluntarily remained with the enemy last winter, and were deemed disaffected to the Interests and Independence of America."

The Court passed the following sentence:

The Court having considered the several charges exhibited against General Arnold, the evidence produced on the trial and his defence are of opinion with respect to the first charge: That he gave permission for a vessel to leave a port in possession of the enemy, to enter into a port in the United States; which permission circumstanced as he was, they are clearly of opinion he had no right to give, being a breach of article 5th., section 18th. of the rules and articles of war.

Respecting the 2nd. charge, that altho' it has been fully proved that the shops and stores were shut by General Arnold's orders on his arrival at Philadelphia, they are of opinion that he was justifiable in the order, by the resolution of Congress of the 5th. of June 1778, and His Excellency, the Commander in Chief's instructions of the 18th. of June 1778. And with respect to the latter part of the same charge, "The making considerable purchases while the shops and stores were shut," they are clearly of opinion that it is entirely unsupported and they do fully acquit General Arnold of it.

They do acquit General Arnold of the third charge.

Respecting the 4th. charge, it appears to the court that General Arnold made application to the Deputy Quarter Master General to supply him with waggons to remove property then in imminent danger from the enemy; that Waggons were supplied him by the Deputy Quarter Master General on this application which had been drawn from the state of Pennsylvania for the public service; and it also appears that General Arnold intended this application as a private request, and that he had no design of employing the waggons otherwise than at this private expence, nor of defrauding the public, nor injuring or impeding the public service; but considering the delicacy attending the high station in which the General acted, and that requests from him might operate as commands, they are of opinion the request was imprudent and improper and that therefore it ought not to have been made.

The Court in consequence of their determinations respecting the first and last charges exhibited against Majr. General Arnold, do sentence him to receive a reprimanded from His Excellency the Commander in Chief.

The Honorable the Congress have been pleased to confirm the foregoing sentence by the following resolution lately received.

In Congress, February 12th., 1780

Congress resumed the consideration of the proceedings of the court martial on the trial of Major General Arnold, and the same being gone through; A motion was made . . . that the sentence of the court be confirmed.

The Commander in Chief would have been much happier in an occasion of bestowing commendations on an officer who has rendered such distinguished services to his Country as Major General Arnold; but in the present case a sense of duty and a regard to candor oblige him to declare,.that he considers his conduct in the instance of the permit as peculiarly reprehensible, both in a civil and military view, and in the affair of the waggons as "Imprudent and improper."

The Honorable the Congress having been pleased by their proclamation of the 11th. of last month to appoint wednesday the 22nd. instant to be set apart and observed as a day of Fasting Humiliation and Prayer for certain special purposes therein mentioned, and recommended that there should be no labor or recreations on that day; The same is to be observed accordingly thro'out the Army and the different Chaplins will prepare discourses suited to the several objects enjoined by the said Proclamation.

To MARQUIS DE LAFAYETTE

Lafayette returned from France in April and arrived at Washington's Headquarters in Morristown on May 12th with the news that a fleet with a contingent of troops under Count de Rochambeau might soon be expected. After a day's visit, Lafayette went on to Philadelphia to receive the acclaim of Congress for his contributions to the cause of Independence. Three days after his departure from Morristown, Washington wrote Lafayette, giving his views of the best procedure for these anticipated French naval and land reinforcements. He would have them move directly to Sandy Hook and await developments. If the British did not bring up troops from the south, a concerted attack upon New York by the Americans from the Hudson Valley and the French from the harbor might bring capitulation. If, however, Sir Henry Clinton should come up from the south, then the French fleet could move on Rhode Island.

Head Quarters, Morris Town, May 16, 1780

My Dear Marquis: Since you left me, I have more fully reflected on the plan which it will be proper for the French fleet and army to pursue, on their arrival upon the Coast and it appears to me in the present situation of the enemy at New York, that it ought to be our first object to reduce that post and that it is of the utmost importance not to lose a moment in repairing to that place. I would therefore advise you to write to the Count De Rochembeau and Monsr. De Ternay in the following spirit, urging them in the strongest terms to proceed both Fleet and Army with all possible expedition to Sandy Hook, where they will be met with further advices, of the precise situation strength and disposition of the enemy and of our army, and with proposals for their future movements; unless they should have received authentic accounts that the fleet and troops now operating in the Southern states have evacuated them and formed a junction at New York. In this case; if they arrive at Rhode Island, they can disembark their troops, dispose of their sick and wait till a more definitive plan can be concerted or if they arrive off Cape Henry they can proceed directly to Rhode Island and make the same arrangements. But in case they should not have received the accounts above mentioned of the evacuation of the Southern states and junction at New York, and should proceed directly to Sandy Hook as is recommended, they can send their sick and every thing of which they wish to be disencumbered to Rhode Island.

The reasons for proceeding immediately to New York in the present situation of the enemy there are these: Their whole effective land force in regular troops is about 8000 men to which may be added about 4000 refugees and such of the militia as they would be able by persuasion or force to engage; but on the militia they can I sould suppose place [no great] dependence. Their naval force is one ship of 74 guns and three or four small frigates. If the arrival of the French succour should find them in this situation, the Fleet can enter the harbour of New York without difficulty, and this is a point on which the success of the whole enterprise absolutely turns. By stopping at Rhode Island, if they arrive there or by passing from Cape Henry to Rhode Island the most precious time will be lost which will multiply the chances to the enemy of concentrating their force, of receiving a naval reinforcement from England or the West Indies of increasing their precautions to obstruct the Channel and their preparations for the defence of their posts. By gaining possession of the Harbour and cutting off its communications the present garrison at New York would be unable to resist the efforts of the combined forces; and together with their ships must in all probability fall into our hands. On the contrary if they have time to concenter all their sea and land force on the Continent at New York, the enterprise against that place becomes extremely arduous has much less prospect of success and will at least exhaust the whole campaign to bring it to a favourable issue.

The enemy have in the expedition under Sir Henry Clinton about seven thousand land troops, three ships of the line one fifty gun two forty four and some smaller frigates. If these ships were added to the force at New York, they would I apprehend be sufficient to exclude the French Squadron, unless aided by a vigorous cooperation by land towards Sandy Hook; and the garrison increased to fourteen or fifteen thousand regular troops would present immense difficulties in the way of its reduction.

I observed that the French Squadron would find no difficulty in entering the Port of New York, with the present naval force of the enemy there. The only possible obstacle to this is the obstructions the enemy are preparing; but I am inclined to hope these will be ineffectual and will be easily removed. They last fall made an attempt of the kind on the expectation of Count D'Estaing, but it failed from the depth of the water and rapidity of the current. Pilots for the harbour can be ready at Black point in the Jerseys from which they can go on Board the fleet at its first appearance.

I would wish you to place these things in the fullest light to the French Commanders, by way of recommendation, leaving it to them to act according to the condition of the fleet and troops, with respect to health and other essential matters, and if they prefer it to go immediately to Rhode Island from Cape Henry, or if they arrive at the former place in the first instance, to wait till a definitive plan is adopted. But I think every reason points to the mode here recommended.

You will be sensible, my Dear Sir, that we can at present only touch upon preliminary measures. The plan for ultimate operations must be the result of mature deliberation, a full view of our resources and must be formed in conjunction with the General and Admiral of the French forces.

I refer Mr. Galvan to you for instructions; but I send you a letter to Governor Jefferson of Virginia to give him any assistance he may require and to correspond with him on the state of Southern affairs. His own discretion and the information he will get on the spot must chiefly govern him. He cannot be dispatched too soon.

I request you in writing to the Count De Rochembeau and

Mr De Ternay to assure them of all my respect and consideration of the high sense I entertain of this distinguished mark of
His Christian Majesty friendship to these States, and of the
happiness I anticipate in a personal acquaintance and co-operation with Gentlemen, whose reputations have inspired me with
the greatest esteem for their talents and merit. You will add
that I will do every thing on my part to give success to the intended operations, and that I flatter myself they will be attended with the happiest consequences.

I cannot forbear recalling your attention to the importance
of doing every thing possible to engage the Count De Guichen
to come upon this Coast without delay. The more I reflect upon
it the more essential it appears. With this addition to our present plan we should have reason to flatter ourselves with every
thing; without it we have a great deal to apprehend, and instead of the happiest, the worst consequences may insue to the
common cause. I am etc.

P. S. I am just informed that a Gentleman called your Aide
De Camp and the Consul of France at Boston have had a duel
in which the latter has been mortally wounded. Tis probable
the Gentleman supposed to be your Aide is the Chevalier De
Fayolles. If so it may perhaps throw him into embarrassments
which may put it out of his power to execute the intended Commission, which makes it prudent to think of some other person.

To PRESIDENT JOSEPH REED

*In his appeal to Pennsylvania through the President of its
Executive Council for more and more co-operation in the matter of the critical need for food and transportation, Washington, because the situation was desperate, used almost desperate
terms. The future of the United States hung on Pennsylvania's
compliance, he insisted. Within three days, the State Legislature passed an act for procuring supplies for the Continental
Army.*

Morris Town, May 28, 1780

DEAR SIR: I am much obliged to you for your favour of the 23. Nothing could be more necessary than the aid given by your state towards supplying us with provision. I assure you, every Idea you can form of our distresses, will fall short of the reality. There is such a combination of circumstances to exhaust the patience of the soldiery that it begins at length to be worn out and we see in every line of the army, the most serious features of mutiny and sedition. All our departments, all our operations are at a stand, and unless a system very different from that which has for a long time prevailed, be immediately adopted throughout the states our affairs must soon become desperate beyond the possibility of recovery. If you were on the spot my Dear Sir, if you could see what difficulties surround us on every side, how unable we are to administer to the most ordinary calls of the service, you would be convinced that these expressions are not too strong, and that we have every thing to dread. Indeed I have almost ceased to hope. The country in general is in such a state of insensibility and indifference to its interests, that I dare not flatter myself with any change for the better.

The Committee of Congress in their late address to the several states have given a just picture of our situation. I very much doubt its making the desired impression, and if it does not I shall consider our lethargy as incurable. The present juncture is so interesting that if it does not produce correspondent exertions, it will be a proof that motives of honor public good and even self preservation have lost their influence upon our minds. This is a decisive moment; one of the most [I will go further and say the most] important America has seen. The Court of France has made a glorious effort for our deliverance, and if we disappoint its intentions by our supineness we must become contemptible in the eyes of all mankind; nor can we after that venture to confide that our allies will persist in an attempt to establish what it will appear we want inclination or ability to assist them in.

Every view of our own circumstances ought to determine us to the most vigorous efforts; but there are considerations of another kind that should have equal weight. The combined fleets of France and Spain last year were greatly superior of those of the enemy: The enemy nevertheless sustained no material damage, and at the close of the campaign have given a very important blow to our allies. This campaign the difference between the fleets from every account I have been able to collect will be inconsiderable, indeed it is far from clear that there will not be an equality. What are we to expect will be the case if there should be another campaign? In all probability the advantage will be on the side of the English and then what would become of America? We ought not to deceive ourselves. The maritime resources of Great Britain are more substantial and real than those of France and Spain united. Her commerce is more extensive than that of both her rivals; and it is an axiom that the nation which has the most extensive commerce will always have the most powerful marine. Were this argument less convincing the fact speaks for itself; her progress in the course of the last year is an incontestible proof.

It is true France in a manner created a Fleet in a very short space and this may mislead us in the judgment we form of her naval abilities. But if they bore any comparison with those of great Britain how comes it to pass, that with all the force of Spain added she has lost so much ground in so short a time, as now to have scarcely a superiority. We should consider what was done by France as a violent and unnatural effort of the government, which for want of sufficient foundation, cannot continue to operate proportionable effects.

In modern wars the longest purse must chiefly determine the event. I fear that of the enemy will be found to be so. Though the government is deeply in debt and of course poor, the nation is rich and their riches afford a fund which will not be easily exhausted. Besides, their system of public credit is such that it is capable of greater exertions than that of any other nation. Speculatists have been a long time foretelling its downfall, but we see no symptoms of the catastrophe being very near. I am persuaded it will at least last out the war, and then, in the opinion of many of the best politicians it will be a national advantage. If the war should terminate successfully the crown will have acquired such influence and power that it may attempt any thing, and a bankruptcy will probably be made the ladder to climb to absolute authority. Administration may perhaps wish to drive matters to this issue; at any rate they will not be restrained by an apprehension of it from forcing the resources of the state. It will promote their present purposes on which their all is at stake and it may pave the way to triumph more effectually over the constitution. With this disposition I have no doubt that ample means will be found to prosecute the war with the greatest vigor.

France is in a very different position. The abilities of her present Financier have done wonders. By a wise administration of the revenues aided by advantageous loans he has avoided the necessity of additional taxes. But I am well informed, if the war continues another campaign he will be obliged to have recourse to the taxes usual in time of war which are very heavy, and which the people of France are not in a condition to endure for any duration. When this necessity commences France makes war on ruinous terms; and England from her individual wealth will find much greater facility in supplying her exigencies.

Spain derives great wealth from her mines, but not so great as is generally imagined. Of late years the profits to government is essentially diminished. Commerce and industry are the best mines of a nation; both which are wanting to her. I am told her treasury is far from being so well filled as we have flattered ourselves. She is also much divided on the propriety of the war. There is a strong party against it. The temper of the nation is too sluggish to admit of great exertions, and tho' the Courts of the two kingdoms are closely linked together, there never has been in any of their wars a perfect harmony of measures, nor has it been the case in this; which has already been no small detriment to the common cause.

I mention these things to show that the circumstances of our allies as well as our own call for peace; to obtain which we must make one great effort this campaign. The present instance of the friendship of the Court of France is attended with every circumstance that can render it important and agreeable; that can interest our gratitude or fire our emulation. If we do our duty we may even hope to make the campaign decisive on this Continent. But we must do our duty in earnest, or disgrace and ruin will attend us. I am sincere in declaring a full persuasion, that the succour will be fatal to us if our measures are not adequate to the emergency.

Now my Dear Sir, I must observe to you, that much will depend on the State of Pennsylvania. She has it in her power to contribute without comparison more to our success than any other state; in the two essential articles of flour and transportation. New York, Jersey, Pensylvania and Maryland are our flour countries: Virginia went little on this article the last crop [and her resources are call'd for to the southward]. New York by legislative coercion has already given all she could spare for the use of the army. Her inhabitants are left with scarcely a sufficiency for their own subsistence. Jersey from being so long the place of the army's residence is equally exhausted. Maryland has made great exertions; but she can still do something more. Delaware may contribute handsomely in proportion to her extent. But Pennsylvania is our chief dependence. From every information I can obtain she is at this time full of flour. I speak to you in the language of frankness and as a friend. I do not mean to make any insinuations unfavourable to the state. I am aware of the embarrassments the government labours under, from the open opposition of one party and the underhand intrigues of another. I know that with the best dispositions to promote the public service, you have been obliged to move with circumspection. But this is a time to hazard and to take a tone of energy and decision. All parties but the disaffected will acquiesce in the necessity and give their support. The hopes and fears of the people at large may be acted upon in such a manner as to make them approve and second your views.

The matter is reduced to a point. Either Pensylvania must give us all the aid we ask of her, or we can undertake nothing. We must renounce every idea of cooperation, and must confess to our allies that we look wholly to them for our safety. This will be a state of humiliation and bitterness against which the feelings of every good American ought to revolt. Your's I am convinced will; nor have I the least doubt that you will employ all your influence to animate the Legislature and the people at large. The fate of these states hangs upon it. God grant we may be properly impressed with the consequences.

I wish the Legislature could be engaged to vest the executive with plenipotentiary powers. I should then expect every thing practicable from your abilities and zeal. This is not a time for formality or ceremony. The crisis in every point of view is extraordinary and extraordinary expedients are necessary. [I am decided in this opinion.]

I am happy to hear that you have a prospect of complying with the requisitions of Congress for specific supplies; that the spirit of the city and state seems to revive and the warmth of party decline. These are good omens of our success. Perhaps this is the proper period to unite.

I am obliged to you for the renewal of your assurances of personal regard; my sentiments for you, you are so well acquainted with as to make it unnecessary to tell you with how much esteem etc.

I felicitate you on the increase of your family. Mrs. Washington does the same and begs her particular respects and congratulations to Mrs. Reed, to which permit me to add mine.

To JOHN AUGUSTINE WASHINGTON

In the bitterness of his disappointment over the failure of Congress to establish a policy by which he could be provided with troops and supplies, Washington laments to his brother that not a single recruit had been added to his army since his appeal in the fall. The States and Congress, always hoping for an early peace, were lulled into apathy year after year, with the result that the needs of the Army were subordinated to the manipulations of politicians and career hunters. At this time, to add to his despair, Washington was kept in a constant state of uncertainty and tension by the enemy's feints and trial maneuvers. Most of all, he was concerned about a possible attack on the Highlands and West Point as he watched the concentration of a British army on the east bank of the Hudson River.

Morris-Town, June 6 [—July 6,] 1780

MY DEAR BROTHER: Your letter of the 10th. of March came safe, but was rather long on its passage. I have also received the other letter refered to, dated at Mt. Vernon last fall. I do not at this time recollect the date of my last letter to you, because, however agreeable it may be to me, I have little leizure for private corrispondencies being, in a manner, wearied to death by the multiplicity of public matters I am obliged to attend to. I can only say, and I say it with much truth, that I derive much pleasure in hearing from you, although it is not in my power to response as often as I could wish.

I am glad to find that you did not dispose of your land. the Paper currency of this Continent has, for sometime past, been upon too fluctuating a scale to receive in return for real property, unless it was to be bartered off immediately for something else of permanent value. To say when the hour of apreciation will arrive, is (if not beyond the reach of human ken) very difficult; it depends upon a variety of causes; more virtue; more exertion; more œconomy and a better knowledge of our true situation. While the interested man, who makes every thing yield to his lust for gain, the Speculator, which is only another term for the same thing, and the disaffected, though acting upon different principles to effect the same end, are practising every art that human craft and cunning can devise to counteract the struggles of the virtuous part of the community I think our money is upon too unstable a footing and fluctuating to part with Land for, when the latter we are certain will become more valuable every day. It ever was my opinion, though candor obliges me to confess it is not consistent with national policy, to have my property as much as possible in Lands. I have seen no cause to change this opinion; but abundant reason to confirm me in it; being persuaded that a few years Peace will inundate these States with emigrants and of course enhaunce the price of Land. far above the comn. Intt. of Money.

July 6th. 1780

I begun this letter, and had written nearly thus far when advice came to me that the enemy had landed at Elizabeth Town point, and was advancing in force upon us. Unable as we were to oppose them, I thought it best to put on a good countenance and advance towards them; which being done; and the partial engagements which followed being published, makes it unnecessary for me to detail them again. It is to be lamented, bitterly lamented, and in the anguish of Soul I do lament, that our fatal and accursed policy should bring the 6th. of June upon us and not a single recruit to the Army, tho' the consequences were foretold last Fall, and pressed with as much precision as if the opinion had been the result of inspiration; but it has ever been our conduct and misfortune to Slumber and Sleep while we should be deligent in preparation; and when pressed by irresistable necessity and when we can delay no longer, then to bring ourselves to the brink of destruction by expensive and temporary expedients. In a word, we have no system, and seem determined not to profit by experience. We are, during the winter, dreaming of Independence and Peace, without using the means to become so. In the Spring, when our Recruits should be with the Army and in training, we have just discovered the necessity of calling for them. and by the Fall, after a distressed, and inglorious campaign for want of them, we begin to get a few men, which come in just time enough to eat our Provisions, and consume our Stores without rendering any service; thus it is, one year Rolls over another, and with out some change, we are hastening to our Ruin.

To tell a person at the distance of three or 400 Miles that an Army reduced almost to nothing (by the expiration of short enlistments) should, sometimes, be five or Six days together without Bread, then as many without Meat, and once or twice, two or three without either; that the same Army should have had numbers of Men in it with scarcely cloaths enough to cover their nakedness, and a full fourth of it without even the shadow of a blanket severe as the Winter was, and that men under these circumstances were held together, is hardly within the bounds of credibility, but is nevertheless true, it is no difficult matter therefore under this view of things (which is not sufficiently coloured to the life) to form some idea of my situation.

The States, under an expectation of hourly succour from France, are now called upon in pointed and pressing terms for Men and Supplies to co-operate with them; but in what manner they will give them; when they will arrive, and what may be the result, the womb of time only can reveal, I cannot. Our whole re-inforcement as yet is about 250 Men.

The Enemy after leaving the Jerseys, made demonstrations towards our Posts in the Highlands (on the North River) as if a visit was intended them; this occasioned my moving that way; but after hovering upon the Water for two or three days, in the River, they debarked on the East side of it, and are foraging that Ground which we ought to preserve if we had the power to accomplish it; meanwhile we lye on the West side of the River, distant from it abt. 18 Miles, with a view of refreshing our Troops, waiting the arrival of the French-fleet, and our own Reinforcements. My affectionate regards are presented to my Sister and all the family. with much truth I can assure that I am Yrs., etc.

MEMORANDUM FOR CONCERTING A PLAN OF OPERATIONS

In the five years of the Revolutionary War up to the summer of 1780, Washington was frequently faced with the question of whether an offensive against New York might be feasible. This time the urgings of Lafayette for positive action strongly influenced his deliberations. The following memorandum indicates that Washington had begun to overcome his misgivings, but nonetheless it gives evidence of his caution and the margin of safety he demanded.

Head Quarters, Bergen County, July 15, 1780

The Marquis de la Fayette will be pleased to communicate the following Genl. ideas to Monsr. the Count de Rochambeau and the Chevalr de Terney as the Sentimts. of the underwritten.

1st. In any operation, and under all circumstances a decisive Naval superiority is to be considered as a fundamental principle, and the basis upon which every hope of success must ultimately depend.

2d. The advantages of possessing the Port of New York by the Squadron of France have been already enumerated to Monsr. the Count de Rochambeau, and the Chevr. de Terney, and is so obvious, as not to need recapitulation; delay in the execution of this enterprize may defeat all our projects, and render the Campaign inactive, and inglorious.

3d. To render our operations nervous and rapid, it is essential for us to be Masters of the Navigation of the No. River and of the Sound. Without this our Land transportation will be great; our expences enormous, and our progress slow, if not precarious, for want of Forage, &ca. &ca.

4th. With these Ideas, and upon this grd., it is conceived that many advantages will result from the French Squadrons taking possession of the inner [sic] of the harbor between Staten Island and the City of New York; and detachg. a frigate or two above the Cheveaux de Frieze [in the North River opposite Fort Washington] for the purpose of opening the Navigation of the River; shortening the Transportation by Land on the upper and lower communication, and bringing the enemy to an explanation respecting Staten Island. Shipping so near the Town would, at the same time they coverd the frigates in the N. Rivr. keep the Garrison in Check, and be more likely to facilitate other movements of the army than if they were to remain at the hook or below the Narrows.

5th. Our operations against the Enemy in the City of New York may commence from two points, to wit: Morrissania (or the heights near Kings-bridge), or Staten Island; both have their advantages and disadvantages; but under a full view of all circumstances the preponderancy is in favor of Morrissania; especially since the generous aid of his most Christian Majesty has come by the way of Rhode Island instead of Cape Henry, as it was expected they wd. do and touch at Sandy hook in consequence of advices lodged there.

6th. As the means for carrying on our operations are not yet sufficiently appreciated, nor is the time by which our aids will arrive sufficiently ascertained; it is impossible to be precise as to the time the American Troops can, with safety, Rendezvous at Morrissania; but as it is necessary to fix some Epoch to it, and it is hoped that it may happen by the 5th. of August, I would propose this day for the reembarkation of the French efficient force at New London (if they should have come there) and that they proceed up the Sound to Whitstown on Long Island, or to such other place on that Island, or on the Main, as circumstances may require, and the Count shall be advised of. for the operations against the enemy depending very much upon their holding all or dismantling some of their present Posts, and upon contingencies within ourselves, it is not possible, at this time, to mark out a precise plan, or determine whether our approaches to the City of New York shall be by the way of York Island, Brooklyn, or both. numbers must determine the latter and circumstances of the moment the former.

7th. It must be clearly understood and agreed between the parties that if any capitol operation is undertaken the French fleet and Land Forces will at all events continue their aid untill the success of the enterprize or until it is mutually determined to abandon it.

8th. In all matters of arrangement, accommodation &ca. not repugnant to the foregoing ideas the Marquiss (in behalf of the United States) will consult the convenience and wishes of the Count and Chevalier and will be pleased to assure them of the disposition I possess to make evy. thing as agreebl. to them as possible and of my desire to manifest on all occasions the high sense I entertain of their merits and of the generous aid they have brought us.

To MAJOR GENERAL BENEDICT ARNOLD

Washington's orders to General Benedict Arnold as the newly appointed commander of West Point are explicit. The importance of the assignment, in view of the recurring fears that an attack was imminent, suggests the confidence Arnold inspired in his chief. After months spent in petitioning Congress for a vindication from the mild findings of the court-martial and for redress of his losses in money, Arnold finally appealed directly to Washington for reinstatement in the army, with preference for a garrison post rather than command in the field. Because his leg wound unfitted him for strenuous duty, he was assigned to West Point and the sector from Fishkill to King's Ferry. His specific orders were to complete the fortifications at West Point as quickly as possible and to avert a surprise attack. Washington's judgment of men was on the whole accurate. This time he erred grievously.

Head Quarters at Peekskill, August 3, 1780

SIR: You are to proceed to West point and take the command of that post and its dependencies, in which are included all from Fishkill to Kings Ferry. The Corps of Infantry and Cavalry advanced towards the Enemy's lines on the East side of the River will [also] be under your orders and will take directions from you, and you will endeavour to obtain every intelligence of the Enemy's Motions. The Garrison of West point is to consist of the Militia of New Hampshire and Massachusetts, for which reason, as soon as the number from those States amounts to [twelve hundd] the New York Militia under the command of Colo. Malcom are to join the Main Army on the West side of the River, [and when the number from Massachusetts-bay alone shall amount to fifteen hundred Rank and file, the Militia of New Hampshire will also march to the Main Army.] Colo. James Livingstons Regiment is, till further orders, to garrison the Redoubts at Stoney and Verplanks points.

Claverac upon the North River is appointed for the place of rendezvous of the Militia of New Hampshire and Massachusetts, from whence you will have them brought down as fast as they arrive. A supply of provision will be necessary at that place, which you will order from time to time as there may be occasion.

You will endeavour to have the Works at West point carried on as expeditiously as possible by the Garrison, under the direction and superintendance of the Engineers. The Stores carefully preserved, and the provision safely deposited and often inspected, particularly the salted Meat. A certain quantity of provision has been constantly kept in each Work, to be ready against a sudden attack. Where there are Bomb proofs, they serve for Magazines; but in the smaller Works where there are none, you will have places erected sufficiently tight to preserve the provision from damage and pillage.

You will, as soon as possible, obtain and transmit an accurate Return of the Militia which have come in, and inform me regularly of their increase.

Should any Levies, from the State of New York or those to the Eastward of it, intended for the Continental Army arrive at West point, you will immediately forward them to the Lines to which they respectively belong.

The difficulties we shall certainly experience on the score of provisions render the utmost œconomy highly necessary. You will therefore attend frequently to the daily Issues, and by comparing them with your Returns, will be able to check any impositions.

To GOVERNOR THOMAS JEFFERSON

Here Washington pays his respects to the system of politics which threatened total loss to the cause of Independence. Over and over again he begs for the means by which he can persevere, and always he attributes the new nation's weakness in warfare to the temporary levies of soldiers, the obstructionist tactics of many of the States and the indifference of Congress.

Head Quarters, Orange Town, August 14, 1780

SIR: I have been honoured with Your Excellys. favour of the 22 of July and with its inclosure. With respect to appointing Officers for the Levies, Your Excellency I presume will have received before this, my Letters of the 18 and 22 Ulto, and by which You would find that I had arranged the matter, as far as the circumstances I was possessed of would admit, in consequence of your former application. But as the Officers of the 1 and 2 State Regiments were not included and they are complete, or nearly so, in their number, and your Excellency has determined that these Corps shall march to the Southward, I see no objection to their receiving a proportion of the Levies, and the less so, as it will make the Officers of the Other Regiments, who are too few, more competent to their commands. I shall write a line to this effect to Genl. Muhlenberg to day. The Levies, I find by a Copy of a Resolution of Congress of the 5th Inst. are to join the Southern Army. It is certainly much more for the public interest that these Men are to serve till Decr. 1781, than for any shorter term, and I most earnestly wish, because I am certain the interest, if not the absolute safety and existence of America demands it, that the States would at once attempt to raise a sufficient number of Levies for the War. The expence in the first instance would be very little greater than the enormous bounties now paid for a few months service, and in the end it would be found to be by far the most œconomical plan, both as to money and as to Men. To our Army's being levied on a short and temporary footing, the War has been protacted already to a period, to which I am doubtful whether it would ever have otherwise extended; to this we may ascribe near all our other misfortunes and present embarrassments, and to this the loss of our liberties and Independence, if the fatal event should take place. This system of politics has brought us very low indeed, and had we not been held up by providence and a powerful Ally, we must have submitted before this to the Yoke of bondage. A perseverance in the system may yet effect it. I beg Your Excellency to pardon this digression, which the misfortunes we have suffered and the difficulties that now surround us have led me as it were to make involuntarily. I am happy to learn by Genl. Muhlenburg that several of our Troops have escaped from Charles Town, both as it releases them from Captivity, and as it adds men of service and tried courage, without giving an equivalent for them, to our remaining force. The General mentions that he has heard 200 have returned, which I consider as a valuable acquisition; but he adds that Many of them tho' they were engaged for the War, conceive themselves discharged by reason of their captivity and escape and have gone to their homes. It is astonishing that they should have taken up such an idea, and I have directed him to pursue the most effectual measures to collect them. It is very unfortunate that the Navigation of the Bay should be so interrupted and destroyed, and as I imagine that the Enemy's frigates are now drawn from thence, I would hope that means will have been found to drive away the smaller pickerooning craft. Their continuing must be attended with great public inconvenience at least, and be highly prejudicial to the trade of Virginia and Maryland.

I informed Your Excellency of the arrival of the Armament from France, and also of Admiral Greaves's with six ships of the line on the part of the British. These added to the Ships the Enemy had before, give them a decided superiority at present over the French Squadron under the Chevr de Ternay, and keep it blocked up at Rhode Island. We expect a reinforcement to the latter, and hope it will be such as to turn the scale of superiority and that it will arrive before it is long and effect a junction, as upon the event our prospects and extensive operations must depend should we be even so fortunate as to get matters in good train on our own part. I have the Honor etc.

P. S. From the information I have received that there are many Deserters in the State; and also that many Soldiers who have been captured in the course of the War, and escaped from the Enemy, have gone to their homes and consider themselves as discharged from service. I have been induced to issue the inclosed proclamation which I request the favor of Your Excellency to have published in the News Papers.

To COLONEL NATHANIEL WADE

Except for a cryptic allusion in a letter written at 7:30 p.m. on September 25th to Major General Greene—"Transactions of a most interesting nature and such as will astonish you have just been discovered"—this message to Colonel Wade is Washington's first direct mention of Benedict Arnold's treachery. Major André, traveling under the name of John Anderson, was halted and detained on September 23rd by John Paulding, David Williams and Isaac Van Wart, on the way to New York with papers which contained enough information to insure the delivery of West Point to the British. When, on September 25th, Arnold learned of the interception of André, he quickly left his quarters and made his way by barge to the British man-o'-war Vulture *and escaped to the enemy's lines. For his perfidy Arnold was paid £6315 sterling by the British. Later he fought against the American army, and after the war lived in England, where he died in 1801. André was hanged. All the letters, communications to Congress and the General Orders written immediately after the attempted betrayal record Washington's quick reaction to the stunning blow and the measures taken by him to thwart British action. Arnold proved to be one of the very few men Washington misjudged. This, in part, accounts for the deep personal injury evident in Washington's observations on the whole sorry affair.*

Head Quarters, Robinson's House, September 25, 1780

Sir: General Arnold is gone to the Enemy. I have just now received a line from him, inclosing one to Mrs. Arnold dated on board the Vulture. From this circumstance and Colo. Lambs being detached on some business, the command of the Garrison for the present devolves on you. I request you will be as vigilant as possible, and as the Enemy may have it in contemplation to attempt some enterprise, even to night, against these Posts, I wish you to make immediately after receipt of this, the best disposition you can of your force, so as to have a proportion of men in each work on the west side of the River. You will see or hear from me further to-morrow. I am etc.

To LIEUTENANT COLONEL JOHN JAMESON

Head Quarters, Robinson's House,
September 25, 1780, O'Clock P.M.

Sir: I wish every precaution and attention to be paid to prevent Major André from making his escape. He will without doubt effect it if possible and in order that he may not have it in his power, You will send him under the care of such a party and so many Officers as to preclude him from the least opportunity of doing it. That he may be less liable to be recaptured by the Enemy, who will make every effort to gain him, He had better be conducted to this place by some upper road rather than by the route thro Crompond. I would not wish Mr André to be treated with insult, but he does not appear to stand upon the footing of a common prisoner of War and therefore he is not intitled to the usual indulgencies they receive, and is to be most closely and narrowly watched.

General Arnold before I arrived here went off to day to the Enemy, and is on board the Vulture Sloop of War. I am etc. André must not escape.

To MAJOR GENERAL WILLIAM HEATH

Robinson's House, September 26, 1780

Dr Sir: In the present situation of things I think it necessary that You should join the Army, and request that You will do it. You will come to Head Qrs: Yourself; the Route thro Litchfield will be the most eligible for You on account of security and You may direct your baggage to halt at Fish Kill for your further orders. I write to the Count de Rochambeau by this conveyance and I trust that your coming away now will not be attended with any material inconvenience to him.

I cannot conclude without informing You of an event which has happened here which will strike You with astonishment and indignation. Major General Arnold has gone to the Enemy. He had had an interview with Major André, Adjutant Genl. of the British Army, and had put into his possession a state of our Army; of the Garrison at this post; of the number of Men considered as necessary for the defence of it; a Return of the Ordnance, and the disposition of the Artillery Corps in case of an Alarm. By a most providential interposition, Major André was taken in returning to New York with all these papers in General Arnold's hand writing, who hearing of the matter kept it secret, left his Quarters immediately under pretence of going over to West point on Monday forenoon, about an hour before my arrival, then pushed down the river in the barge, which was not discovered till I had returned from West point in the Afternoon and when I received the first information of Mr. André's captivity Measures were instantly taken to apprehend him, but before the Officers sent for the purpose could reach Verplank's point, he had passed it with a Flag and got on board the Vulture Ship of War, which lay a few miles below. He knew of my approach and that I was visiting with the Marquiss, the North and Middle Redoubts, and from this circumstance was so straitned in point of time that I believe, he carried with him but very few if any material papers, tho he has a very precise knowledge of the Affairs of the post.

The Gentlemen of General Arnold's family, I have the greatest reason to believe, were not privy in the least degree to the measures he was carrying on, or to his escape. I am etc.

To THE PRESIDENT OF CONGRESS

Robinson's House in the Highlands,
September 26, 1780

SIR: I have the honor to inform Congress that I arrived here yesterday about 12 o'clock on my return from Hartford. Some hours previous to my arrival Major General Arnold went from his quarters which were at this place; and as it was supposed over the river to the garrison at West-point, whither I proceeded myself in order to visit the post. I found General Arnold had not been there during the day, and on my return to his quarters, he was still absent. In the mean time a packet had arrived from Lt. Colonel Jamison announcing the capture of a John Anderson who was endeavouring to go to New-York, with the several interesting and important papers mentioned below, all in the hand writing of General Arnold. This was also accompanied with a letter from the prisoner avowing himself to be Major John André Adjt: General of the British army, relating the manner of his capture, and endeavouring to shew that he did not come under the description of a spy. From these several circumstances, and information that the General seemed to be thrown into some degree of agitation on receiving a letter a little time before he went from his quarters, I was led to conclude immediately that he had heard of Major André's captivity, and that he would if possible escape to the enemy, and accordingly took such measures as appeared the most probable to apprehend him. But he had embarked in a barge, and proceeded down the river under a flag to the vulture ship of war, which lay at some miles below Stony and Verplank's points. He wrote me after he got on board a letter, of which the inclosed is a copy. Major André is not arrived yet, but I hope he is secure and that he will be here to-day. I have been and am taking proper precautions, which I trust will prove effectual, to prevent the important consequences which this conduct on the part of General Arnold was intended to produce. I do not know the party that took Major André; but it is said, it consisted only of a few militia, who acted in such a manner upon the occasion as does them the highest honor and proves them to be men of great virtue. They were offered, I am informed, a large sum of money for his release, and as many goods as they would demand, but without any effect. Their conduct gives them a just claim to the thanks of their country, and I also hope they will be otherwise rewarded. As soon as I know their names I shall take pleasure in transmitting them to Congress. I have taken such measures with respect to the Gentlemen of General Arnolds family as prudence dictated; but from every thing that has hitherto come to my knowledge, I have the greatest reason to believe they are perfectly innocent. I early secured, Joshua Smith, the person mentioned in the close of General Arnolds letter, and find him to have had a considerable share in this business. I have the honor etc.

To GOVERNOR GEORGE CLINTON

Head Quarters, Robinsons, September 26, 1780

DEAR SIR: I arrived here yesterday on my return from an interview with the French General and Admiral and have been witness to a scene of treason as shocking as it was unexpected. General Arnold from every circumstance had entered into a plot for sacrificing West Point. He had an interview with Major Andre the British Adjutant General last Week at Jos. Smiths where the plan was concerted; by an extraordinary concurrence of incidents, Andre was taken on his return with several papers in Arnolds handwriting that proved the treason. The latter unluckily got notice of it before I did, went immediately down the river got on board the Vulture which brought up Andre and proceeded to New York.

I found the post in the most critical condition and have been taking measures to give it security which I hope will be to night effectual. With the greatest respect etc.

P. S. Smith is also in our possession and has confessed facts sufficient to establish his guilt.

GENERAL ORDERS

Head Quarters, Orangetown,
Tuesday, September 26, 1780

Parole Smallwood. Countersigns Gist, Marion.
Watchword Intrepid.

The truly martial appearance made by the troops yesterday the order and regularity with which they made the different marches and the ease and facility they performed the several manœuvres does them the greatest Credit and affords the most flattering prospect of substantial service reputation and military glory.

Nothing can be more pleasing to the officers who feel for the honor of the Army and the Independence of America than to see the rapid progress made by the Troops in military discipline.

The good conduct of all the officers yesterday gave the general the highest satisfaction and the particular services of the Inspector General and those serving in that line deserve his particular thanks.

Treason of the blackest dye was yesterday discovered! General Arnold who commanded at Westpoint, lost to every sentiment of honor, of public and private obligation, was about to deliver up that important Post into the hands of the enemy. Such an event must have given the American cause a deadly wound if not a fatal stab. Happily the treason has been timely discovered to prevent the fatal misfortune. The providential train of circumstances which led to it affords the most convincing proof that the Liberties of America are the object of divine Protection.

At the same time that the Treason is to be regretted the General cannot help congratulating the Army on the happy discovery. Our Enemies despairing of carrying their point by force are practising every base art to effect by bribery and Corruption what they cannot accomplish in a manly way.

Great honor is due to the American Army that this is the first instance of Treason of the kind where many were to be expected from the nature of the dispute, and nothing is so bright an ornament in the Character of the American soldiers as their having been proof against all the arts and seduction of an insidious enemy.

Arnold has made his escape to the Enemy but Mr. André the Adjutant General to the British Army who came out as a spy to negotiate the Business is our Prisoner.

His Excellency the commander in Chief has arrived at Westpoint from Hartford and is no doubt taking the proper measures to unravel fully, so hellish a plot.

To COMTE DE ROCHAMBEAU

Head Quarters, near West Point, September 27, 1780

SIR: On my arrival here a very disagreeable scene unfolded itself. By a lucky accident, a conspiracy of the most dangerous nature, the object of which was to sacrifice this post, has been detected. General Arnold, who has sullied his former glory by the blackest treason, has escaped to the enemy. This is an event that occasions me equal regret and mortification; but traitors are the growth of every country and in a revolution of the present nature, it is more to be wondered at, that the catalogue is so small than that there have been found a few.

The situation of the army at this time will make General Heath's presence with us useful. I have written to him for this purpose. I hope his removal will be attended with no inconvenience to your Excellency. With the greatest regard etc.

To THE OFFICER COMMANDING AT WEST POINT AND ITS DEPENDENCIES

Head Quarters, Robinson's Farms, September 27, 1780

SIR: You will immediately make a distribution of the troops under your command to the several posts that the whole may be in a state of defence at the shortest notice. You will also have each work supplied with ten days provision wood water and stores and keep up constantly that supply; and you will take every other precaution for the security of the post. The Enemy will have acquired from General Arnold a perfect knowledge of the defences, and will be able to take their measures with the utmost precision. This makes it essential our vigilance and care should be redoubled for its preservation. You will do every thing in your power to gain information of the enemy's designs, and give me intelligence as early as possible of any movement against you. . . .

To THE BOARD OF GENERAL OFFICERS

Head Quarters, Tappan, September 29, 1780

GENTLEMEN: Major André, Adjutant General, to the British army will be brought before you for your examination. He came within our lines in the night on an interview with Major General Arnold, and in an assumed character; and was taken within our lines, in a disguised habit, with a pass under a feigned name, and with the inclosed papers concealed upon him. After a careful examination, you will be pleased, as speedily as possible, to report a precise state of his case, together with your opinion of the light, in which he ought to be considered, and the punishment, that ought to be inflicted. The Judge Advocate will attend to assist in the examination, who has sundry other papers relative to this matter, which he will lay before the Board. I have the honor, etc.

To SIR HENRY CLINTON

Head Quarters, September 30, 1780

SIR: In answer to Your Excellency's Letter of the 26th Instant, which I had the honor to receive, I am to inform You, that Major André was taken under such circumstances as would have justified the most summary proceedings against him. I determined however to refer his case to the examination and decision of a Board of General Officers, who have reported, on his free and voluntary confession and Letters; "That he came on Shore from the Vulture Sloop of war in the night of the Twenty first of September Instant on an interview with General Arnold in a private and secret manner. Secondly that he changed his dress within our lines, and under a feigned name and in a disguised habit passed our Works at Stoney and Verplanks points the Evening of the Twenty second of September Instant, and was taken the morning of the Twenty third of September Instant, at Tarry Town, in a disguised habit, being then on his way to New York, and when taken he had in his possession Several papers which contained intelligence for the Enemy. The Board having maturely considered these Facts do also report to His Excellency General Washington, that Major André Adjutant General to the British Army ought to be considered as a Spy from the Enemy, and that agreable to the Law and usage of Nations it is their opinion he ought to suffer death"

From these proceedings it is evident Major André was employed in the execution of measures very foreign to the Objects of Flags of truce and such as they were never meant to authorize or countenance in the most distant degree; and this Gentleman confessed with the greatest candor in the course of his examination, "that it was impossible for him to suppose he came on shore under the sanction of a Flag." I have the Honor etc.

GENERAL ORDERS

Head Quarters, Orangetown, Sunday, October 1, 1780

Parole Hellespont. Countersigns M., Q.
Watchword Look about.

The Board of General officers appointed to examine into the Case of Major André have reported.

1st. "That he came on shore from the Vulture sloop of War in the night of the 21st. of September last on an interview with General Arnold in a private and secret manner."

2dly. "That he changed his dress within our Lines and under a feigned name and in a disguised habit passed our works at Stoney and Vere-Planks Points the Evening of the 22d. of September last and was taken the morning of the 23d. of September last at Tarrytown in a disguised habit being then on his way to New York; and when taken he had in his possession several Papers which contain'd intelligence for the Enemy."

The Board having maturely considered these Facts do also report to his Excellency General Washington:

"That Major André Adjutant General to the British Army ought to be considered as a spy from the Enemy and that agreeable to the Law and usage of nations it is their opinion he ought to suffer Death."

The Commander in Chief directs the execution of the above Sentence in the usual way this afternoon at five o'clock precisely.

At a division General Court martial the 11th. of September last Lieutenant Colonel Commandant Sherman President, Major Albert Chapman* was tried upon the following Charges:

1st. "For Embezzling public property and endeavouring to

* Of the Fifth Connecticut Regiment. He retired in January, 1781.

induce the Quarter master of the regiment to assist him in embezzling powder for his own private use."

2d. "For making up two enormous bills against Colonel Nelson, an inhabitant of Morristown for taking up a strayed horse the property of said Nelson and that without any expence to himself."

3d "For giving a Certificate to a soldier in the 7th. regiment that he was inlisted for three years only, when he had repeatedly muster'd him for during the war and sworn to the Muster Rolls."

The Court on considering the first and third Charges against Major Chapman are of opinion the charge of Embezzling public property is not supported therefore do acquit him of it; but find him guilty of the other part of the first and third charge being a breach of Article 5th. Section 18th. of the Articles of War and do sentence him to be reprimanded in Division orders.

The General is sorry to be under the disagreeable necessity of differing in opinion with the Court; but he thinks the sentence entirely inadequate to charges of so serious a nature as those of which they find Major Chapman guilty. He is released from Arrest.

There was a mistake in entering the evening order of the 25th. ultimo: instead of the Pennsylvania division, the first Pennsylvania brigade only should have been mentioned as the second brigade did not receive marching orders 'till several hours after.

AFTER ORDERS

The Execution of Major André is postponed 'till tomorrow.

EVENING ORDERS

Major André is to be executed tomorrow at twelve o'clock precisely a Battalion of Eighty files from each wing to attend the Execution.

To THE PRESIDENT OF CONGRESS

Paramus, October 7, 1780

SIR: I had the honor on the 1st: Inst to receive Your Excellency's dispatches of the 24th Ulto. addressed to Major General Greene, and since, Your very obliging Letter of the 29th, for which I beg leave to return You my acknowledgments. I have written to Sir Henry Clinton in consequence of the former and requested him to make the desired communications. When these are received, they shall be transmitted.

I have the honor to inclose Congress a Copy of the proceedings of a Board of General Officers (No 1) in the case of Major André, Adjutant General to the British Army. This Officer was executed in pursuance of the opinion of the Board, on Monday the 2d. Inst at 12 OClock, at our late Camp at Tappan. He acted with great candor, from the time he avowed himself after his capture, untill he was executed. Congress will perceive by a Copy of a Letter I received from him of the 1st Inst, that it was his desire to be shot, but the practice and usage of war, circumstanced as he was, were against the indulgence. At the bottom of the 6th page of the proceedings, an explanatory note is added, to prevent any suspicions being entertained injurious to Colonel Sheldon, who otherwise, from the Letter addressed to him, might be supposed to have been privy to the measures between General Arnold and Major André. If it should be the pleasure of Congress to publish the case, and which I would take the liberty to suggest may not be improper, it will be necessary for the explanatory note to be annexed. Besides the proceedings, I transmit in the Inclosure No 2, Copies of Sundry Letters respecting the matter, which are all that passed on the subject, not included in the proceedings. I would not suffer Mr. Elliot and Mr. Smith to land, who came up to Dobbs's ferry agreeable to Sir Henry Clinton's Letter of the 30th of September. Genl. Robertson was permitted to come on shore and was met by Major Genl Greene, and mentioned substantially what is contained in his Letter of the 2d Instant. It might not perhaps be improper to publish the Letters or part of them in this Inclosure, as an Appendix to the proceedings of the Board of General Officers.

I had the honor to mention in my Letter of the 24th of August, that an interview was in contemplation between General Lincoln and General Phillips, to take place at Elizabeth Town, and that I should direct Mr Skinner, the Commissary to attend and endeavour to effectuate an exchange of prisoners on the principles and to the extent mentioned by Congress in their Act of the 7th. The Inclosure No 3 contains my Instructions to Mr Skinner, No 4 and 5 his Report and Major General Lincoln's of the result of the meeting, which happened on the 20th Ulto at the place appointed, and to which I beg leave to refer Congress. As it is now become certain that we cannot operate against New York this Campaign, and it was the expectation of this event's happening that prevented the release of our private prisoners; it appears to me that the exchange of those in that place, should be immediately attempted, especially as the liberation of a great many of our Officers is made to depend upon it and is otherwise wholly rejected. From these considerations I have ventured to close with the terms of Mr Lorings Letter to Mr Skinner of the 22d of Sepr, respecting the exchange of Our Officers and privates at New York and Long Island, and have written to Sir Henry Clinton accordingly. I hope Congress will approve the measure. As to the exchange proposed between the Convention and the Southern prisoners, Congress will be pleased to decide on it themselves. They have the fullest knowledge of the present, and what will be the future situation of our Affairs, and can best judge of the conduct which the public good and humanity require to be pursued in the matter. For a variety of reasons I am, and profess myself wholly incompetent to determine in the case.

I have now the pleasure to communicate the names of the Three persons who captured Major André, and who refused to release him notwithstanding the most earnest importunities and assurances of a liberal reward on his part. Their conduct merits our warmest esteem and I beg leave to add, that, I think, the public will do well to make them a handsome gratuity. They have prevented in all probability our suffering one of the severest strokes that could have been meditated against us. Their names are John Paulding, David Williams and Isaac Van Wart.

For the present I have detached the Jersey, New York and New Hampshire Brigades with Stark's to the Highland posts. They marched this morning from Orange Town and will relieve the Pennsylvania line, which was thrown in at the moment General Arnold went to the Enemy. Major Genl Greene has marched with these four Brigades and will command at West point and its dependencies, 'till a further dispostion. The main body of the Army, the forage about Orange town and the lower Country being exhausted, also moved this morning and is now arrived here. We have had a cold, wet, and tedious march on account of the feeble state of our Cattle, and have not a drop of rum to give the Troops. My intention is to proceed with them to the Country in the neighbourhood of Passaick falls. I have the honor etc.

P. S. I have added a Note at the foot of Sir Henry Clintons Letter of the 30th of Septr and one at the foot of Major Andrés Letter to me of the 1st of October, which are in the Inclosure No. 2, which, if the Letters are published I request may be published also.

To BENJAMIN FRANKLIN

During the months following the exposure of Benedict Arnold's plot, the campaign fell once more into a state of watchful waiting. Washington could only devote himself to measures designed to strengthen his forces. At any rate, the political outlook became brighter and Congress seemed a little more determined to continue the war to a successful conclusion.

Hd. Qrs., New Windsor, December 20, 1780

SIR: A few days since, by the Chevr. De Chatteleaux, I had the honor to receive your favor of the 19th. of March introductory of him, and thank you for bringing me acquainted with a gentn. of his merit, knowledge, and agreeable manners. I spent several days very happily with him, at our Camp near the great Falls of Passaic in New Jerseys before the Army seperated for its cantonments, the principle of which is at West point in the vicinity of this place where I make my own Quarters.

Disappointed of the second division of French Troops; but more especially in the expected Naval superiority which was the pivet upon wch. every thing turned, we have been compelled to spend an inactive Campaign after a flattering prospect at the opening of it, and vigorous struggles to make it a decisive one on our part. Latterly we have been obliged to become Spectators of a succession of detachments from the Army at New York, in aid of Lord Cornwallis; while our Naval weakness, and the political dissolution of a large part of our Army, puts it out of our power to counteract them at the Southward, or take advantage of them here.

The movements of Lord Cornwallis during the last Month or two have been retrogade; what turn the late reinforcements which have been sent to him may give to his Affairs, remains to be known. I have reinforc'd also, principally with Horse, but the length of the March is so much opposed to the measure, that evy. corps, in a greater or lesser degree, is ruined that encounters it.

I am happy however in assurg. you, that a better disposition never prevailed in the Legislatures of the several States than does at this time. The folly of temporary expedients are seen into and exploded, and vigorous efforts will be used to obtain a permanent Army, and carry on the War systematically, if the obstinacy of Great Britain should compel us to continue it. We want nothing but the aid of a loan to enable us to put our Finance into a tolerable train. The Country does not want resources, but we the means of drawing them forth.

It is unnecessary for me to go into a more detail acct. of our affairs, as you are doubtless officially advised of every material occurrence. I shall therefore only add my Compliments to Mr. Adams, and the strongest assurances of being, With the greatest esteem etc.

CIRCULAR TO THE NEW ENGLAND STATES

Disaffection of troops, because of inadequate pay and cloth-ing, long-endured physical suffering and months of inactivity, finally developed into a series of mutinous outbreaks. Organ-ized into platoons equipped with artillery, the mutineers planned a march on Philadelphia to seek redress of their griev-ances from Congress and actually reached Princeton and Tren-ton, where they halted to begin negotiations. When a part of the Jersey line followed the example of the Pennsylvanians, Washington ordered a detachment from West Point to march against his rebellious soldiers. At the end of the month the mutiny was quelled by a display of force, which included sev-eral executions by hanging on the spot. A general pardon was granted to those penitent troops who returned to their bat-talions.

Head Quarters, New Windsor, January 5, 1781

Sir: It is with extreme anxiety, and pain of mind, I find myself constrained to inform Your Excellency that the event I have long apprehended would be the consequence of the com-plicated distresses of the Army, has at length taken place. On the night of the 1st instant a mutiny was excited by the Non Commissioned Officers and Privates of the Pennsylvania Line, which soon became so universal as to defy all opposition; in attempting to quell this tumult, in the first instance, some Offi-cers were killed, others wounded, and the lives of several com-mon Soldiers lost. Deaf to the arguments, entreaties, and utmost efforts of all their Officers to stop them, the Men moved off from Morris Town, the place of their Cantonment, with their Arms, and six pieces of Artillery: and from Accounts just received by Genl. Wayne's Aid De Camp, they were still in a body, on their March to Philadelphia, to demand a redress of their grievances. At what point this defection will stop, or how extensive it may prove God only knows; at present the Troops at the important Posts in this vicinity remain quiet, not being acquainted with this unhappy and alarming affair; but how long they will continue so cannot be ascertained, as they labor under some of the pressing hardships, with the Troops who have revolted.

The aggravated calamities and distresses that have resulted, from the total want of pay for nearly twelve Months, for want of cloathing, at a severe season, and not unfrequently the want of provisions; are beyond description. The circumstances will now point out much more forcibly what ought to be done, than any thing that can possibly be said by me, on the subject.

It is not within the sphere of my duty to make requisitions, without the Authority of Congress, from individual States: but at such a crisis, and circumstanced as we are, my own heart will acquit me; and Congress, and the States (eastward of this) whom for the sake of dispatch, I address, I am persuaded will excuse me, when once for all I give it decidedly as my opinion, that it is in vain to think an Army can be kept together much longer, under such a variety of sufferings as ours has experienced: and that unless some immediate and spirited measures are adopted to furnish at least three Months pay to the Troops, in Money that will be of some value to them; And at the same time ways and means are devised to cloath and feed them better (more regularly I mean) than they have been, the worst that can befall us may be expected.

I have transmitted Congress a Copy of this Letter, and have in the most pressing manner requested them to adopt the measure which I have above recommended, or something similar to it, and as I will not doubt of their compliance, I have thought proper to give you this previous notice, that you may be prepared to answer the requisition.

As I have used every endeavour in my power to avert the evil that has come upon us, so will I continue to exert every means I am possessed of to prevent an extension of the Mischief, but I can neither foretell, or be answerable for the issue.

That you may have every information that an officer of rank and abilities can give of the true situation of our affairs, and the condition and temper of the Troops I have prevailed upon Brigadier Genl Knox to be the bearer of this Letter, to him I beg leave to refer your Excellency for many Matters which would be too tedious for a Letter. I have the honor etc.

To LIEUTENANT COLONEL JOHN LAURENS

Lieutenant Colonel John Laurens, son of the President of Congress, had been sent on a mission to France to obtain aid in the form of money, help for a more vigorous offensive on land and added naval power on the coast. He was successful in having six million livres put at Washington's disposal and in strengthening the alliance with promises of more land and naval detachments. As matters stood in the Southern theatre of war before Laurens' departure, the help was desperately needed. Lord Cornwallis, who had established his Headquarters at Charleston, S. C., had fought off Thomas Sumter at the head of a hastily organized band of partisans at Rocky Mount. General De Kalb, joined by General Gates, had reached Camden, and there the British succeeded in routing the Americans. De Kalb, with eleven wounds, died in the field. At about this time, Benedict Arnold, now a brigadier general in the British Army, began an incursion into Virginia. His marauders took Richmond, burned and abandoned it, and then built up a fortified stronghold at Portsmouth. Lafayette was ordered by Washington to engage and, if possible, capture Arnold in Virginia, but, although almost trapped, the traitor managed to slip away. A story, perhaps apocryphal, suggests a pre-Byronic kind of romantic cynicism in Arnold. When asked what he thought the Americans would do to him if they captured him, he is said to have replied that they would probably cut off the leg wounded at Quebec and bury it with military honors and hang the rest of him. In the bitterness of disappointment, Washington speaks: "The failure of this Expedition, (which was most flattering in the commencement of it) is much to be regretted; because a successful blow in that quarter, would, in all probabil-

ity, have given a decisive turn to our Affairs in all the Southern States." The expedition to which he refers envisaged a combined effort by Lafayette, Rochambeau and Chevalier Destouches, which had as one of its aims "seeing Arnold in Gibbets."

New Windsor, April 9, 1781

MY DEAR LAURENS: Colo. Armand, who was charged with the delivery of many letters to you from the Marquis de la Fayette, imparting to his friends and the Ministry of France your mission, unfortunately arrived at Boston after you had Sailed from that place. By him I gave you an acct. of the revolt of part of the Jersey Troops; Arnolds Expedition to Virginia, Leslies arrival at Charles Town, and such other matters as occurred after your departure.

Since that period, several interesting events have happened; some favourable, others adverse. Among the first may be reckoned Morgans brilliant action with Tarleton; among the latter the advantages gained by Lord Cornwallis over General Greene. The official accts. of these I inclose you. Cornwallis, after the defeat of Tarleton destroyed his Waggons and made a violent effort to recover his prisoners; but failing therein moved equally light and rapidly against General Greene; who (though he had formed a junction with Morgan) was obliged to retreat before him into Virginia; whether from despair of recovering his prisoners, of bringing Greene to a general Action, or because he conceived his own situation critical, I do not take upon me to determine; but the fact is, that here commenced Cornwallis's retrograde movements; and Greenes advance; from the Roanoke to the place of Action.

On the first notice of the storm which happened on the 22d. of Jany. and its effects, I intimated to the French Genl. the possibility and importance of improving the oppertunity in an attempt upon Arnold. When I received a more certn. acct. of the total loss of the Culloden and the dismasting of the Bedford two 74 Gun ships belonging to the British Fleet at Gardners bay, I immediately put in motion, under the comd. of the

Marqs. de la Fayette, as large a part of my small force here, as I could with prudence detach to proceed to the head of Elk, and made with all expedition a proposal to the Count de Rochambeau and the Chevalir. Destouches for co-operation in Virginia, with the whole of the fleet of our Allies, and a part of their land force. Before my proposition arrived, in consequence of an application to him from Philadelphia, the Chevr. Destouches had sent a Ship of the line and two or three frigates to Chesapeak bay which not only retarded the plan I had proposed (by awaiting their return) but ultimately, defeated the project, as the enemy in the mean time remasted the Bedford with those taken out of the Culloden, and following the French fleet, arrived off the Capes of Virginia before it; where a Naval combat glorious for the French (who were inferior in Ships and Guns) but unprofitable for us who were disappointed of our object was the issue.

The failure of this Expedition, (which was most flattering in the commencement of it) is much to be regretted; because a successful blow in that quarter, would, in all probability, have given a decisive turn to our Affairs in all the Southern States. Because it has been attended with considerable expence on our part, and much inconvenience to the State of Virginia, by assembling its Militia; and because the World are disappointed at not seeing Arnold in Gibbets. above all, because we stood in need of something to keep us a float, till the result of your mission is known for be assured my dear Laurens, that day does not follow night more certainly, than it brings with it some additional proof of the impracticability of carrying on the War without the aids you were directed to sollicit. As an honest and candid man; as a man whose all depends on the final and happy termination of the present contest, I assert this. While I give it decisively as my opinion, that without a foreign loan our present force (which is but the remnant of an Army) cannot be kept together this Campaign; much less will it be encreased, and in readiness for another. The observations contained in my letter to you of the 15th. of Jany. last, are verified every moment; And if France delays, a timely, and powerful aid in the critical posture of our affairs it will avail us nothing should she attempt it hereafter; for we are at this hour, suspended in the Balle; not from choice, but from hard and absolute necessity; for you may rely on it as a fact, that we cannot transport the provisions from the States in which they are Assessed to the Army, because we cannot pay the Teamsters, who will no longer work for Certificates. It is equally certain, that our Troops are approaching fast to nakedness and that we have nothing to cloath them with. That our Hospitals are without medicines, and our Sick without Nutriment, except such as well men eat. That all our public works are at a stand, and the Artificers disbanding; but why need I run into the detail, when it may be declared in a word, that we are at the end of our tether, and that now or never our deliverance must come. While Alas! how easy would it be to retort the enemys own game upon them if it could be made to comport with the genl. plan of the War to keep a superior Fleet always in these Seas and France would put us in a conditn. to be active, by advancing us money. the ruin of the enemys schemes would then be certain; the bold game they are now playing would be the mean to effect it for they would be reduced to the necessity of concentering their force at capital points, thereby giving up all the advantages they have gained in the Southern States, or be vulnerable every where.

Such of the Pensylvania line as had reassembled, and were recruited say about 1000 were ordered the middle of Feby to join the Southern Army and since the disappointment of our enterprize on Arnold I have directed the detachment under the Comd. of the Marqs. de la Fayette to proceed thither but how either can march without money or credit, is more than I can tell . . .

To THE MARQUIS DE LAFAYETTE

Still weighing the possibilities of an attempt upon New York, for its own value and because such an attack would force a diversion of enemy troops from the south, Washington characteristically made his preparations slowly and with some reliance on the rumors that the British might quit the stronghold of their own accord.

New Windsor, May 31, 1781

MY DEAR MARQS: I have just returned from Weathersfield at which I expected to have met the Count de Rochambeau and Count de Barras, but the British fleet having made its appearance off Block Island, the Admiral did not think it prudent to leave Newport. Count Rochambeau was only attended by Chevr. Chattellux; Generals Knox and Duportail were with me.

Upon a full consideration of our affairs in every point of view, an attempt upon New York with its present Garrison (which by estimation is reduced to 4500 regular Troops and about 3000 irregulars) was deemed preferable to a Southern operation as we had not the Command of the Water. The reasons which induced this determination were, the danger to be apprehended from the approaching heats, the inevitable dissipation and loss of Men by so long a March, and the difficulty of transportation; but above all, it was thought that we had a tolerable prospect of expelling the enemy or obliging them to withdraw part of their force from the Southward, which last would give the most effectual relief to those States. The French Troops are to March this way as soon as certain circumstances will admit, leaving about 200 Men at Providence with the heavy Stores and 500 Militia upon Rhode Island to secure the Works.

I am endeavouring to prevail upon the States to fill up their Battalions, for the Campaign; if they cannot do it upon better terms, and to send in ample and regular supplies of Provision. Thus you perceive it will be sometime before our plan can be ripe for execution, and that a failure on our part in Men and Supplies may defeat it; but I am in hopes that the States in this quarter will exert themselves to attain what has long been a favourite and is an important object to them.

We have rumours, but I cannot say they are well founded, that the enemy are about to quit New Yk. altogether. Should they do this we must follow them of necessity, as they can have no other view than endeavouring to sieze and secure the Southern States, if not to hold them finally, to make them the means of an advantageous Negociation of Peace.

I take it for granted that your last dispatches inform you fully of European Affairs and that you can judge from them of the probability of such an event as I have mentioned taking place. As you have no cypher by which I can write I can write to you in safety, and my letters have been frequently intercepted of late I restrain myself from mentioning many matters I wish to communicate to you.

I shall advise you every now and then of the progress of our preparations. It would be unnecessary for you to be here at present, and I am sure you would not wish to leave your charge while you are so near an enemy, or untill you could deliver them up to General Greene or to another officer capable of exercising the command which you are in. You will always remember My dear Marquis that your return to this army depends upon your own choice, and that I am with every sentiment of esteem regd. and Affecte. Yr. etc.

To GOVERNOR THOMAS JEFFERSON

Washington insists that the rumors of an impending evacuation of New York by the British deserve little credence. Under these circumstances, he takes pains to explain to Governor Jefferson, the greatest relief he can afford the hard-pressed South is to force the diversion of British troops northward. Without the command of the ocean waterway, it would be impossible to send men and supplies to help the South in its dire straits. Through the years of cautious planning for the possession of New York, the city became the symbol of victory in Washington's mind for the cause of Independence.

Head Qrs., New Windsor, June 8, 1781

DEAR SIR: I have had the honor of receiving your Excellency's favors of the 9th. and 28th. of May. The progress which the enemy are making in Virginia is very alarming not only to the State immediately invaded but to all the rest, as I strongly suspect, from the most recent European intelligences, that they are endeavouring to make as large seeming conquests as possible that they may urge the plea of uti possidetis in the proposed mediation. Your Excellency will be able to judge of the probability of this conjecture from the Circular letter of the President of Congress of the 1st. Inst.

Were it prudent to commit a detail of our plans and expectations to paper I could convince Your Excellency by a variety of reasons that my presence is essential to the operations which have lately been concerted between the French Commanders and myself and which are to open in this quarter provided the British keep possession of New York. There have lately been rumours of an evacuation of that place, but I do not place confidence in them.

Should I be supported by the Neighbouring States in the manner which I expect, the enemy will, I hope, be reduced to the necessity of recalling part of their force from the Southward to support New York or they will run the most eminent risque of being expelled with a great loss of Stores from that Post which is to them invaluable, while they think of prosecuting the War in America, and should we, by a lucky coincidence of Circumstances, gain a Naval superiority their ruin would be inevitable. The prospect of giving relief to the Southern States by an operation in this quarter, was the principal inducement for undertaking it. Indeed we found upon a full consideration of our Affairs in every point of view, that, without the command of the Water it would be next to impossible for us to transport the Artillery, Baggage, and Stores of the Army to so great a distance and besides, that we should loose at least one third of our force by desertion, Sickness, and the heats of the approaching Season even if it could be done.

Your Excellency may probably ask whether we are to remain here for the above reasons should the enemy evacuate New York and transfer the whole War to the Southward? To that I answer that we must, in such case, follow them at every expence, and under every difficulty and loss; but that while we remain inferior at Sea, and there is a probability of giving relief by diversion (and that perhaps sooner than by sending reinforcements immediately to the point in distress) good policy dictates the trial of the former.

Give me leave before I take leave of your Excellency in your public capacity to Express the obligations I am under for the readiness and Zeal with which you have always forwarded and supported every measure which I have had occasion to recommend thro' you, and to assure you that I shall esteem myself honored by a continuation of your friendship and corrispondence shou'd your Country permit you to remain in the private walk of life. I have the honor etc.

CIRCULAR TO THE STATES

After years of weighing hazards and months of minute planning, the attempt on New York was suddenly abandoned. Washington removed his Headquarters from the Hudson, ferried his troops to the west bank and began the march at their head toward Virginia. The decision, so long delayed, was made with the realization that the best hope of success would be to destroy British strength in the South. Because of new increments of enemy troops, many of them German mercenaries, Washington again advocated the establishment of a permanent army as one of the first objectives of the United States.

Head Quarters, Kings Ferry, August 21, 1781

SIR: I feel myself unhappy in being obliged to inform you, that the Circumstances in which I find myself at this late Period, have induced me to make an Alteration of the main Object which was at first adopted, and has hitherto been held in View, for the Operations of this Campaign. It gives me pain to say, that the Delay in the several States to comply with my Requisitions of the 24th of May last, on which in a great Measure depended the Hopes of our Success in that Attempt, has been one great and operative Reason to lead to this Alteration. Other Circumstances, it is true, have had their Weight in this Determination, and it may in the Course of Events, prove happy to the States, that this Deviation from our main Design has been adopted.

The Fleet of the Count de Grasse, with a Body of French Troops on Board, will make its first Appearance in the Chesapeak; which, should the Time of the Fleets Arrival prove favorable, and should the Enemy under Lord Cornwallis hold their present Position in Virginia, will give us the fairest Opportunity to reduce the whole British Force in the South, and to ruin their boasted Expectations in that Quarter: to effect this desirable Object, it has been judged expedient, taking into Consideration our own present Circumstances, with the Scituation of the Enemy in New York and at the Southward, to abandon the Seige of the former, and to march a Body of Troops, consisting of a Detachment from the American Army, with the whole of the French Troops, immediately to Virginia. With this Detachment, which will be very considerable, I have determined to march myself. The American Troops are already on the West Side of the Hudson, and the French Army will arrive at Kings Ferry this Day. When the whole are crossed, our March will be continued with as much Dispatch as Circumstances will admit. The American army which will remain in this Department, excepting two light Companys and some few Detachments, consists of the two New Hampshire Regiments, Ten of Massachusetts five of Connecticut Infantry, with Sheldons Legion, Cranes Artillery, the State Troops and Militia, which with proper Exertions of the States, will it is expected, be sufficient to hold the Enemy in Check at New York and prevent their Ravages on the Frontier. The Command, during my Absence is given to Major General Heath, who will have the Honor to communicate with the States, on every Occasion which may require their Attention.

As the Enemys Force in New York has been for some Time past very considerable, and it is reported with a good Degree of Certainty, that they have lately received a very respectable Reinforcement of German Recruits from Europe, it will be necessary still to send forward a great Part, if not the whole of the Militia requested from your State, in the same Manner as 'tho no Alteration had taken Place in our Measures. You will therefore continue to send on at least 400 Men from your State to the

Order of Genl Heath, with as much Dispatch as possible, unless you should be informed from him that this Number need not be compleated.

On this Occasion, I cannot omit to repeat to you my Opinion, of the absolute Importance of filling your Continental Battalions to their compleat Numbers, for the War, or three Years. Not only our past Experience for a Course of Years, but our present Scituation should strongly inforce the Necessity of this Measure. Every Campaign teaches us the increasing Difficulty and Expence of procuring short-termed Levies, and their decreasing Utility in the Field. The large Reinforcements which the Enemy have this Campaign sent to America, strongly indicates their Expectations of the Continuance of the War; should that be the Case, the best Way to meet them is certainly with a permanent Force. but, should the War be drawing towards a Close, a permanent and respectable Army will give us the happiest Prospects of a favorable Peace. In every View, a permanent Army, should be the great Object of the States to obtain, as they regard sound Policy, Prudence or Economy. I have the Honor etc.

GENERAL ORDERS

On August 3rd Count de Grasse, with a fleet of twenty-five to thirty ships of the line and a substantial body of troops, left San Domingo for Chesapeake Bay, where he arrived on the 26th. Washington, on the march from the Hudson, had passed through New Jersey, Pennsylvania and Delaware, while Rochambeau, starting from White Plains, joined forces with the American commander close to the Delaware River. As a diversionary measure, the British ordered Benedict Arnold to attack and ravage New London in his native state of Connecticut. The sacking and burning of New London, the last of Arnold's infamous acts against his own country, were carried out with savage vindictiveness. After all the damage was done, he returned safely to his fleet and subsequently sailed for England. The armies of Washington and Rochambeau, marching down the Chesapeake, could now effect a junction with Lafayette's troops and attempt to bottle up Lord Cornwallis on the York River, so that he could not retreat by land or replenish his supplies from the country.

Head Quarters, Head of Elk, September 6, 1781

It is with the highest pleasure and satisfaction the Commander in Chief announces to the Army the arrivals of the Count de Grasse in the Chesapeake with a very formidable Naval and Land force; at the same time he felicitates them on this auspicious occasion he anticipates the glorious Events which may be expected from the combined Operations now in contemplation. As no circumstance cou'd possibly have happened more opportunely in point of time, no prospect cou'd ever have promised more important successes, and nothing but our want of exertions can probably blast the pleasing prospects before us. The General calls upon all the gallant Officers, the brave and faithful soldiers he has the honor to command to exert their utmost abilities in the cause of their Country and to share with him (with their usual alacrity) the difficulties, dangers and glory of the present Enterprize. The Commanding Officers of Corps are to cause abstracts to be immediately made for a Months pay of their respective Commands, excluding any infamous characters who may have been so far left to the sense of Honor, the pride of their professions and the love of their Country as to desert the standard of freedom at this critically interesting period, those men only are to be comprehended who are present with their several Corps.

Major Platt is appointed Division Inspector to the Division Commanded by Major General Lincoln and is to be respected and obeyed accordingly.

To MAJOR GENERAL NATHANAEL GREENE

Fully aware of his dangerous predicament, Lord Cornwallis at first thought of retreat through the Carolinas; then, realizing that he was hemmed in, he gathered his troops within York-

town itself to prepare for siege. He was also made acutely aware that he had been cut off from any possibility of falling back through North Carolina to Charleston by General Greene's victory at Eutaw Springs. On the day on which Washington wrote the following letter to General Greene, the combined French and American forces, numbering 12,000, marched from Williamsburg to Yorktown and encamped within two miles of the half-encircled British garrison.

Headquarters, Williamsburg, September 28, 1781

DEAR SIR: I am very sorry to observe in your Letter of the 6th. Augst., a Complaint, that you have heard nothing from me since the 1st June; many Letters have been written to you since that Time, some of very particular Importance. This failure gives me Reason to fear some foul play on the Route.

The last I wrote to you was from Philadelphia, the 4th, of the instant Month, informing that the Plan of our Campaign was totally changed from the Attack of N York, which had been in Contemplation, and that I was then so far as that Place, advanced with my Troops, to commence a combined Operation against Lord Cornwallis in Virginia, with the french Fleet, wch. was expected to arrive in the Chesapeake. I likewise informed, that Admiral Hood, with 13 Ships of the Line, had arrived at N York, and joined the force already there under Adml. Graves, and that I had not heard of the Arrival of Count De Grasse.

I have now to inform that I left Phila. on the 5th instt. The same Day, on my Rout, I met the agreeable News of the Arrival of Admiral D Grasse in the Chesapeak on the 26th Augst. with a formidable Fleet of 28 Ships of the Line and 4 frigates, and that he had landed 3000 Troops, who had formed their Junction with the Marquis. All possible Expedition was made to hurry on our Troops, Artillery, and Stores, which, I have the Satisfaction to inform you, have nearly all safely arrived at and near this Place, with less Accident or Disaster, than might have been expected. I arrived myself, preceding the Troops, on the 14th. and very soon paid a Visit to the french Admiral on Board his Ship, to make our Arrangements for the Enterprize; which were most happily effected, and settled to mutual Satisfaction. The Admiral has taken his Position, for our Water Security, to facilitate our Transportation, and to block the Enemy. Our Operations are fast drawing to a Point of Commencement, and by the 1st Octo. I hope to open Trenches upon the Enemy's Works.

While these Things are takg place on our Side, the Enemy are not idle on their Part. Lord Cornwallis has collected his Troops on York River, and taken two posts. One in York, the other in Gloucester; where he is fortifying with great Assiduity, and seems resolved to defend himself against our Siege with great Obstinacy. By Accounts, thro Deserters, and other ways, I fear we shall have little Hope to starve him into a Surrender; my greater Hope is, that he is not well provided with Artillery and Military Stores for such Defence, not having had in Contemplation, the Situation to which he is now reduced. By Information from N York, I collect, that Admiral Digby, with (probably) 10 Ships of the Line from Europe, is arrived On the Coast, and joined the British Squadron already here; this Junction, if formed, will probably make the English Fleet consist of 30 Ships of Line, besides 50, and 40s, and a Number of Frigates, which will bring the two Fleets upon too near an Equality. Tis said also from N York, that a large Embarkation of their Troops is formed, and on Board Transports, and that Sir Hy Clinton himself is with them; their Views undoubtedly look Southward.

The Count de Grasse has, most happily and critically, effected a Junction with the Count de Barras from Newport, the conjoined Fleet are now in a good Position within the Capes of Chesapeak Bay, makg in Number 36 Capital Ships of the Line, four large french Frigates, with some smaller Ships, captured from the English, on Board one of which was Ld Rawdon, who had embarked for England; two British Frigates, the Iris and Richmond, which had been peeping into the Bay, have also been captured, and now form part of the [mutilated]. Thus you have a particular Detail of Circumstances so far as this Time, as to future prospects and Operations, should we have Success in the present Operations, it is impossible for me to decide in favor of your Wishes, expressed in your Letter of the 6th. Augst. If the Fleet remains so long as the Completion of the present Object, it is all I can expect from present Appearances. I hope, however, if nothing further is obtained, that we may be aided in our Transportation towards the Point of your Wishes.

Colo Steward, who is on his Way to your Camp, favors the Conveyance of this. Colo Morris, is now ill, and with me, will be detained a few Days; by him you may expect to have further and particular Accounts of our Progress, with a confidential, verbal Communication of our future prospects, Views and Expectations.

I am informed, by circuitous Means, of a very severe Action which took place on the 8th. between your Army and the British under Comd. of Colo Stewart, so many particulars are mentioned as give me Reason to believe these Reports are grounded in Fact. I wait impatiently for your Dispatches. With very great Esteem etc.

To THE PRESIDENT OF CONGRESS

By October 1st the encirclement of Yorktown was complete. Washington and Rochambeau commanded the troops on land which controlled the garrison, and de Grasse's fleet held the sea approaches. Short of food, the defenders sent out foraging parties, which were attacked and routed. The siege was now on in earnest.

Head Quarters, Camp before York, October 1, 1781

Sir: Last Evening I was honored with your Excellency's Favor of the 21st ulto., with its Inclosure. The Intelligence it contains respectg the British Fleet, is very agreable, and will be immediately transmitted to the Count de Grasse.

In my last, which bore Date the 23d ulto. I informed, that our Preparations for a near Investment of the Enemy at York, were fast ripening to a Point. I have now to acquaint [your

Excellency] that I marched from Williamsburg with the whole Army, on the 28th and approached within about two Miles of the Enemy at York, at which Distance a Shew was made of some Opposition [on our Left]. But, upon the Count Rochambeau, who Commands that Part of the Army, his Moving a few peices of field Artillery under Direction of the Baron Viominil, and giving a few Shots, the Enemy retired. On the 29th. the American Troops moved forward and took their Ground in front of the Enemys Works on their Left; no Opposition, except a few scattered Shots from a small Work, by Moor's Mill, on Wormleys Creek and a Battery on the Left of Pigeon Quarter. A small fire all Day from our Rifle Men and the Enemy's Jagers. 30th. in the Morng we discovered, that the Enemy had evacuated all their Exterior Line of Works, and withdrawn themselves to those near the Body of the Town. By this Means we are in possession of very advantageous Grounds, which command, in a very near Advance, almost the whole Remaing. Line of their Defence. All the Expedition that our Circumstances will admit, is using, to bring up our heavy Artillery and Stores, and to open our Batteries, this Work I hope will be executed in a few Days, when our Fire will begin with great Vigor.

The Investment of the Enemy is now fully compleated, and drawn very near to their Lines, except on the River above the Town, where their Communication is still open; to prevent this and to compleat the Blockade a Request is gone to the Count de Grasse, desiring him, to push, if he thinks it practicable, One or more Ships above the Town; this, if effected will answer, many very valuable Purposes.

The Position of the Count de Grasse, is judiciously taken: the Main fleet keeping their Station in Lynn Haven Bay and Detachments made to secure the Rivers; the Determination of the Count is favorably disposed to comply with our Wishes in every necessary Co-operation.

I shall continue to keep Congress advised of such Occurrences as are worthy the Communication. With the Highest Regard etc.

To PRESIDENT THOMAS McKEAN

A cannonade against the fortifications of Yorktown began on October 6th. The town itself was under fire on the 9th and the barrage continued with increasing damage for four days. Then one assault after another struck at the outer ramparts. Alexander Hamilton led the first advance; the French, under Lafayette, another; Rochambeau's men, still another; and the British batteries were silenced. Washington could now write, with a little less than his customary caution: "I think in all human probability Lord Cornwallis must fall into our hands."

Camp before York, October 6, 1781

SIR: I feel myself peculiarly obliged and honored by your Excellency's interesting communication of the 26th Ulto. That America must place her principal dependence upon her own exertions I have always foreseen and have ever endeavoured to inculcate, and I flatter myself that from the wise system of policy which has been of late adopted and which Congress seem determined to pursue our internal means will be so improved and applied, that with the assistance of our most generous Allies, tho' not operating immediately with us hereafter we shall be enabled to bring matters to a happy and glorious conclusion.

I am not apt to be sanguine, but I think in all human probability Lord Cornwallis must fall into our hands. The smallness of Digby's reinforcement and the deduction from the enemy's former naval strength by the loss of the Terrible and the condemnation of two other Ships of the line leaves them so vastly inferior that I think they will not venture upon a relief.

It is to be wished that your Excellency's plan could be adopted, but there are reasons which operate forcibly against Count de Grasse's dividing his fleet. By grasping at too much we might loose a stake which nothing but the most adverse stroke of fortune can take out of our hands, and which if we attain will give a most fatal stab to the power of Great Britain in America.

I hope your Excellency will excuse my short and imperfect answers to your very full letters. The variety of matter which engages my attention must be my apology. My public dispatch will inform your Excellency of our progress up to this date. With the greatest esteem and respect etc.

To THE PRESIDENT OF CONGRESS

Under incessant bombardment and wave after wave of infantry charges, the Yorktown garrison held out until October 17th. Lack of food, sickness and exhaustion, the steady loss of men, wounded and dead, and the utter hopelessness of his position forced Lord Cornwallis at ten in the morning to ask for a parley with Washington. Under cover of a flag of truce, a letter was dispatched, asking for a twenty-four-hour armistice.

Head Quarters Before York, October 16, 1781

SIR: I had the honor to inform your Excellency in my last, of the 12th. instant, that we had the evening before opened our second parallel. The 13th. and 14th. we were employed in compleating it. The Engineers having deemed the two Redoubts on the left of the enemy's line sufficiently injured by our shot and shells to make them practicable, it was determined to carry them by assault on the evening of the 14th. The following disposition was accordingly made. The Work on the enemy's extreme left to be attacked by the American Light Infantry under the command of the Marquis de la Fayette. The other by a detachment of the French Grenadiers and Chasseurs commanded by Major General the Baron Viomenil. I have the pleasure to inform your Excellency that we succeeded in both. Nothing could exceed the firmness and bravery of the Troops. They advanced under the fire of the Enemy without returning a shot and effected the business with the Bayonet only. The reports of His Excellency the Count de Rochambeau, The Marquis de la Fayette and Lt. Colonel Hamilton, copies of which I inclose, enter more particularly into a detail of the mode in which the attacks on the part of the French and American Columns were Conducted. We made prisoners in both Redoubts one Major, 2 Captains, 3 subalterns and 67 privates.

The Works which we have carried are of vast importance to us. From them we shall enfilade the enemy's whole line and I am in hopes we shall be able to command the communication from York to Gloucester. I think the Batteries of the second parallel will be in sufficient forwardness to begin to play in the course of this day.

The enemy last night made a sortie for the first time. They entered one of the French and one of the American Batteries on the second parallel which were unfinished. They had only time to thrust the points of their Bayonets into four pieces of the French and two of the American Artillery and break them off, but the spikes were easily extracted. They were repulsed the moment the supporting Troops came up, leaving behind them seven or eight dead and six prisoners. The French had four officers and twelve privates killed and wounded, and we had one serjeant mortally wounded.

I inclose your Excellency a Return of the killed and wounded of both Armies up to the present time. It is much smaller than might have been expected. I have the honor etc.

To CHARLES, EARL CORNWALLIS

Answering Lord Cornwallis' appeal for a truce, Washington demanded that the British proposals be committed to writing and sent to the American lines. Two hours would be granted for suspension of hostilities from the time of the delivery of his letter for an answer from the enemy. This was accepted, but Cornwallis' proposals were at first unsatisfactory. Washington countered with his own set of conditions and submitted terms of capitulation, with an ultimatum that they be signed by 11 o'clock on the morning of the 19th.

Camp before York, October 17, 1781

My Lord: I have had the Honor of receiving Your Lordship's Letter of this Date.

An Ardent Desire to spare the further Effusion of Blood, will readily incline me to listen to such Terms for the Surrender of your Posts and Garrisons of York and Gloucester, as are admissible.

I wish previously to the Meeting of Commissioners, that your Lordship's proposals in writing, may be sent to the American Lines: for which Purpose, a Suspension of Hostilities during two Hours from the Delivery of this Letter will be granted. I have the Honor etc.

To CHARLES, EARL CORNWALLIS

Head Quarters before York, October 18, 1781

My Lord: To avoid unnecessary Discussions and Delays, I shall at Once, in Answer to your Lordships Letter of Yesterday, declare the general Basis upon which a Definitive Treaty and Capitulation must take place. The Garrisons of York and Gloucester, including the Seamen, as you propose, will be received Prisoners of War. The Condition annexed, of sending the British and German Troops to the parts of Europe to which they respectively belong, is inadmissible. Instead of this, they will be marched to such parts of the Country as can most conveniently provide for their Subsistence; and the Benevolent Treatment of Prisoners, which is invariably observed by the Americans, will be extended to them. The same Honors will be granted to the Surrendering Army as were granted to the Garrison of Charles Town. The Shipping and Boats in the two Harbours with all their Guns, Stores, Tackling, Furniture and

Apparel, shall be delivered in their present State to an Officer of the Navy, appointed to take possession of them.

The Artillery, Arms, Accoutrements, Military Chest and Public Stores of every Denomination, shall be delivered unimpaired to the Heads of Departments, to which they respectively belong.

The Officers will be indulged in retaining their Side Arms, and the Officers and Soldiers may preserve their Baggage and Effects, with this Reserve, that Property taken in the Country, will be reclaimed.

With Regard to the Individuals in civil Capacities, whose Interests Your Lordship wishes may be attended to, until they are more particularly described, nothing definitive can be settled.

I have to add, that I expect the Sick and Wounded will be supplied with their own Hospital Stores, and be attended by British Surgeons, particularly charged with the Care of them.

Your Lordship will be pleased to signify your Determination either to accept or reject the Proposals now offered, in the Course of Two Hours from the Delivery of this Letter, that Commissioners may be appointed to digest the Articles of Capitulation, or a Renewal of Hostilities may take place. I have the Honor etc.

To THE PRESIDENT OF CONGRESS

Yorktown and Gloucester were surrendered to Washington, and the American troops took possession at noon. All the British land force became prisoners of the United States and the sea force was turned over to the French Navy under de Grasse. More than 7,000 troops gave up to the combined attacking army and navy of 16,000. Rejoicing spread through the nation, and Congress immediately voted thanks to Washington, Rochambeau and de Grasse. After more than six years of war, victory was in sight.

Head Quarters near York, October 19, 1781

SIR: I have the Honor to inform Congress, that a Reduction of the British Army under the Command of Lord Cornwallis, is most happily effected. The unremitting Ardor which actuated every Officer and Soldier in the combined Army on this Occasion, has principally led to this Important Event, at an earlier period than my most sanguine Hopes had induced me to expect.

The singular Spirit of Emulation, which animated the whole Army from the first Commencement of our Operations, has filled my Mind with the highest pleasure and Satisfaction, and had given me the happiest presages of Success.

On the 17th instant, a Letter was received from Lord Cornwallis, proposing a Meeting of Commissioners, to consult on Terms for the Surrender of the Posts of York and Gloucester. This Letter (the first which had passed between us) opened a Correspondence, a Copy of which I do myself the Honor to inclose; that Correspondence was followed by the Definitive Capitulation, which was agreed to, and Signed on the 19th. Copy of which is also herewith transmitted, and which I hope, will meet the Approbation of Congress.

I should be wanting in the feelings of Gratitude, did I not mention on this Occasion, with the warmest Sense of Acknowledgements, the very chearfull and able Assistance, which I have received in the Course of our Operations, from his Excellency the Count de Rochambeau, and all his Officers of every Rank, in their respective Capacities. Nothing could equal this Zeal of our Allies, but the emulating Spirit of the American Officers, whose Ardor would not suffer their Exertions to be exceeded.

The very uncommon Degree of Duty and Fatigue which the Nature of the Service required from the Officers of Engineers and Artillery of both Armies, obliges me particularly to mention the Obligations I am under to the Commanding and other Officers of those Corps.

I wish it was in my Power to express to Congress, how much I feel myself indebted to The Count de Grasse and the Officers of the Fleet under his Command for the distinguished Aid and Support which have been afforded by them; between whom, and the Army, the most happy Concurrence of Sentiments and Views have subsisted, and from whom, every possible Cooperation has been experienced, which the most harmonious Intercourse could afford.

Returns of the Prisoners, Military Stores, Ordnance Shipping and other Matters, I shall do myself the Honor to transmit to Congress as soon as they can be collected by the Heads of Departments, to which they belong.

Colo. Laurens and the Viscount de Noiailles, on the Part of the combined Army, were the Gentlemen who acted as Commissioners for formg and settg the Terms of Capitulation and Surrender herewith transmitted, to whom I am particularly obliged for their Readiness and Attention exhibited on the Occasion.

Colo Tilghman, one of my Aids de Camp, will have the Honor to deliver these Dispatches to your Excellency; he will be able to inform you of every minute Circumstance which is not particularly mentioned in my Letter; his Merits, which are too well known to need my observations at this time, have gained my particular Attention, and could wish that they may be honored with the Notice of your Excellency and Congress.

Your Excellency and Congress will be pleased to accept my Congratulations on this happy Event, and believe me to be With the highest Respect etc.

P. S. Tho' I am not possessed of the Particular Returns, yet I have reason to suppose that the Number of Prisoners will be between five and Six thousand, exclusive of Seamen and others.

To THE PRESIDENT AND PROFESSORS OF THE UNIVERSITY OF WILLIAM AND MARY

The surrender at Yorktown meant that Washington could divert the main body of his troops to the Hudson. A skeleton force was sent to General Greene in the Carolinas to help confine the British in Charleston. Count de Grasse led his fleet to sea on orders from his Government and Lafayette asked leave to return to France. Enemy prisoners were confined at Winchester, and Lord Cornwallis, with many of his officers, was sent to New York on parole. Washington, in receiving the acclaim of William and Mary, the second oldest university in the United States, promised relief from its burden of caring for the wounded and encouragement for its "communication of useful learning . . . and diffusion of the true principles of rational liberty."

October 27, 1781

GENTLEMEN: I accept very kindly the Address of the President and Professors of the University of William and Mary.

The Reduction of the British Force in this State, for which I feel myself highly indebted to the Noble Exertions of our Brave and Generous Allies, is a Circumstance which gives me great pleasure, not only as it affords a Return of peaceful Security to many of my fellow Citizens; but as it will, I hope, in its event be productive of more extensive good Consequences.

The Seat of Literature at Williamsburg, has ever in my View, been an Object of Veneration. As an Institution, important for its Communication of useful Learning, and conducive to the Diffusion of the true principles of rational Liberty, you may be assured, that it shall receive every encouragement and Benefaction in my Power towards its Re-Establishment.

The Sick and wounded of the Army, which my Necessities have compelled me to trouble you with, shall be removed as soon as Circumstances will permit, An Event which will be as pleasing to me, as agreeable to you.

To MAJOR GENERAL NATHANAEL GREENE

After Lord Cornwallis had surrendered at Yorktown, the war again lapsed into inactivity. The American troops marched northward in larger and larger contingents and Washington took a respite in Mount Vernon. He then went to Philadelphia, where he remained until the end of March, 1782. Successively thereafter his Headquarters were in Morristown and Pompton, New Jersey, in the spring, and Newburgh, New York, through the summer. During this time, new operations were only in the planning stage and again and again Washington weighed the chances of an assault on New York as one of the last two remaining bases in the United States, the other being at Charlestown. The enemy also maintained scattered and inconsequential garrisons in Savannah, Georgia, in Canada and in Halifax. As it became increasingly evident that the British were unwilling to reinforce their armies on the American continent, rumors of conciliation and peace overtures began to spread. On August 2nd a joint letter from Sir Guy Carleton and Admiral Robert Digby informed Washington that negotiations for peace had actually begun in Paris and that a modified Independence for the United States would be assured. Washington's doubts about British sincerity led him to suspect the kind of Independence the Mother Country had to offer. He would tolerate no conditions; Independence had to be complete or the word had no meaning.

Head Quarters, Newburgh, August 6, 1782

My DEAR SIR: In my last Letter of the 9th of July, in which I acknowledged your several favors of the 22d of April and 19th of May, I mentioned my expectation of soon meeting the Count de Rochambeau in Philadelphia, and my intention of writing you from that place in case any thing of Moment should turn up in the mean while. But as our hopes, that public Dispatches would have arrived from France before our Meeting, have been disappointed; I can only inform you that matters now rest in the same situation, as discribed in my former Letters; except with regard to the negotiations, which are said to be carrying on by the belligerent Powers in Europe.

Indeed I hardly know what to think or believe of the disposition of the Court of Britain. Certain it is the new Administration have made Overtures of Peace to the several Nations at War, apparently with a design to detach some one or another of them from the general combination; but not having succeeded in their efforts for a seperate Negotiation; how far the necessity of Affairs may carry them in their wishes for a general Pacification upon admissible terms, I cannot undertake to determine. From the former infatuation, duplicity and perverse system of british Policy; I confess I am induced, to doubt every thing; to suspect every thing. Otherwise I should suppose, from the subsequent Extract of a Letter from Sir Guy Carleton and Admiral Digby to me dated the 2nd inst; that the prospects of and negotiation for a general Peace would be very favorable.

We are acquainted, Sir, by authority, that Negotiations for a general Peace have already commenced at Paris, and that Mr. Grenville is invested with full Powers to treat with all Parties at War, and is now at Paris in the execution of his Commission. And we are likewise, Sir, further made acquainted, that his Majesty, in order to remove all obstacles to that Peace which he so ardently wishes to restore, has commanded his Ministers to direct Mr. Grenville, that the Independency of the Thirteen Provinces should be proposed by him, in the first instance, instead of making it a condition of a general Treaty; however not without the highest Confidence, that the Loyalists shall be restored to their Possessions, or a full Compensation made them for whatever Confiscations may have taken place.

These communications they say had just arrived by a Packet. They further add that Mr Laurens was enlarged from all engagements, and that Transports were prepared for conveying all American Prisoners to this Country to be exchanged here. Whatever the real intention of the Enemy may be, I think the strictest attention and exertion which have ever been practiced on our part, instead of being diminished, ought to be encreased thereby. Jealousy and precaution, at least, can do no harm, too much confidence and supineness may be pernicious in the extream.

There having been a vague report that a small embarkation of Cavalry and Infantry was to take place at New York, to relieve part of the Garrison of Charles Town, I have made use of the occasion to desire the Secretary at War, to put Armands Legion immediately in motion to join you, and have requested he will use his endeavours to have the means afforded to facilitate and expedite the Movement.

A Mail has lately been intercepted by the Enemy between Philadelphia and Trenton, in which, I am informed there were Letters from you to me, these by the time of their capture were probably of the same date as your Dispatches to Congress, wherein the Correspondence between General Leslie and yourself was enclosed. I mention these circumstances, that you may forward Duplicates in case you should judge it necessary.

You will, I imagine, have heard before this reaches you, of the arrival of M. Vaudreuil with a fleet of 13 Ships of the Line on this Coast; I can give you no particulars, as I have no Official account of his arrival.

The Army of the Count de Rochambeau having, as I advised you in my last, marched towards the Northward, at our Meeting in Philadelphia, it was concluded (upon a consideration of all circumstances) that this Corps should proceed to join the Army on the Hudson; they were at Baltimore by the last intelligence from that quarter.

Since the receipt of the Letter from the Commissioners Sir Guy Carleton and Admiral Digby; I have seen a New York Paper of the 3d. in which is a Speech of General Conway* and some other Articles, which appear to be designed to propose Independence to America on certain conditions not admissible: viz that the Legislature of America should be totally independant of the Parliament of Great Britain, but that the King of England should have the same kind of supremacy here as in Ireland. I have not information sufficient to determine whether this is the species of Independence alluded to in the Letter of the Commissioners or not. I wish my suspicions, however, may be ill founded.

Wishing you all the success and happiness you can desire yourself, I am etc.

* Maj. Gen. Henry Seymour Conway, commander in chief of the British Army.

To JAMES McHENRY

Washington's misgivings about the intentions of the British in suing for peace are expressed in this letter to James McHenry, Delegate to Congress from South Carolina. The doctrine that "there is nothing which will so soon produce a speedy and honorable Peace as a State of preparation for War" follows logically from Washington's insistence upon an unrelaxed vigilance.

Verplanks point, September 12, 1782

MY DEAR SIR: I am pained to find by your letter of the 30th Ulto., that you cannot get rid of your fever. Try change of Air; come to the Camp, anything to remove a disorder which seems to pursue you with unabating obstinacy, and may, if suffered to run on you any longer, become too powerful for Medicine. The Army has at length taken the Field, and is Encamped at this place; waiting a junction with the French Corps; which will, I expect, take effect in the course of this Week.

Our prospect of Peace is vanishing. The death of the Marquis of Rockingham has given a shock to the New Administration, and disordered its whole System. Fox, Burke, Lord John Cavendish Lord Heppel (and I believe others) have left it; Earl Shelburne takes the lead as first Lord of the Treasury; to which Office he was appointed by the King, in the instant the vacancy happened by the death of Lord Rockingham. This Nobleman, Lord Shelburne I mean, declares that, the Sun of Great Britain will set, the moment American Independency is acknowledged, and that no Man has ever heard him give an assent to the measure. On the other hand, the Duke of Richmond asserts, that the Ministry, of which Lord Shelburne is one, came into Office pledged to each other, and upon the Express condition that America should be declared Independent. that he will watch him; and the moment he finds him departing therefrom, he will quit Administration, and give it every opposition in his power. That the King will push the War as long as the Nation will find Men or Money, admits not of a doubt in my mind. The whole tenor of his conduct, as well as his last Proroguing Speech on the 11th of July, plainly indicate it; and shews in a clear point of view the impolicy of relaxation on our parts. If we are wise, let us prepare for the worst; there is nothing which will so soon produce a speedy and honorable Peace as a State of preparation for War, and we must either do this, or lay our acct. for a patched up inglorious Peace, after all the Toil, Blood, and treasure we have spent. This has been my uniform opinion, a doctrine I have endeavoured, amidst the torrent of expectation of an approaching Peace, to inculcate; the event, I am sure, will justify me in it. With much truth I am etc.

To THOMAS PAINE

The Crisis *paper to which Washington alludes, according to John C. Fitzpatrick, editor of the Bicentennial Commission's thirty-nine-volume edition of* The Writings of George Washington, *was dated May 31, 1782, and dealt with the murder of Captain Joseph Huddy and the fate of Captain Charles Asgill. In it Paine sounded a note of optimism for an impending victory for the American arms. Washington's comment on the "Period of Seven Years" has reference to Paine's mystical interpretation of the recurrence of the number seven as a portent of an early capitulation by the British: There have been seven years of war; the British demand seven years of apprenticeship from their artisans; Parliament is elected for seven years; punishment is often for seven years, etc., etc.*

The case of Captain Charles Asgill became a cause célèbre *during the last months of the war. A New Yorker, Philip White, was killed while trying to escape from Monmouth jail, where he was being taken under the accusation of having been a marauder. To avenge the death of this British sympathizer, an American prisoner of war, a Captain Joseph Huddy, was dragged out of confinement in New York and taken to Middletown, where he was hanged by a British Captain, Richard Lip-*

pincott. A clamor for punishment was raised and Washington demanded that Lippincott should be surrendered or retaliation would be exercised on a prisoner of equal rank. The British refused to give up Lippincott. To make good his threat, Washington ordered that a choice be made by a drawing by lot among the British prisoners in Lancaster, Pennsylvania. Captain Asgill, a youth of nineteen and of excellent family and character, was the unfortunate victim of the drawing. He was sentenced to be hanged. In spite of appeals and frantic denunciations, Washington had no choice but to remain firm, even though he was impressed by the lad's unimpeachable character. When, finally, Lippincott was tried by court-martial and acquitted, Washington found reason enough to place Asgill on parole and ultimately release him. The case created an international furore, and Washington's determination to see it through to its end won him little sympathy.

Head Quarters, September 18, 1782

SIR: I have the pleasure to acknowledge your favor of the 7th. instant, informg of your proposal to present me with fifty Copies of your last publication, for the Amusement of the Army.

For this Intention you have my sincere thanks, not only on my own Acco, but for the pleasure, I doubt not, the Gentlemen of the Army will receive from the perusal of your Pamphlets.

Your Observation on the Period of Seven Years, as it applies itself to and affects British Minds, are ingenious, and I wish it may not fail of its Effects in the present Instance.

The Measures and the policy of the Enemy are at present in great perplexity and Embarrassment. But I have my fears, whether their Necessities (which are the only operating motive with them) are yet arrived to that point, which must drive them unavoidably into what they will esteem disagreeable and dishonourable Terms of peace; such for Instance as an absolute, unequivocal Admission of American Independence, on the Terms upon which she can accept it.

For this Reason, added to the Obstinancy of the King, and the probable consonant principle of some of his principal Ministers, I have not so full Confidence in the Success of the present Negotiation for peace, as some Gentlemen entertain.

Should Events prove my Jealousies to be illfounded, I shall make myself happy under the Mistake, consoling myself with the Idea of havg erred on the safest Side, and enjoying with as much Satisfaction as any of my Countrymen, the pleasing Issue of our severe Contest.

The case of Capt Asgill has indeed been spun out to a great Length. But with you, I hope, that its termination will not be unfavourable to this Country. I am &c.

To BENJAMIN FRANKLIN

In expressing to Benjamin Franklin his deep abhorrence of British obstinacy, wickedness and pride, Washington consistently follows the pattern of all his thinking on the subject since he first espoused the cause of Independence. In and out of season, in defeat and in victory, total independence remained the whole meaning and purpose of the war, so far as he was concerned. It was the steadfastness of this conviction, which he never conceded could be compromised or bargained for, that shows the rocklike strength of his character.

Head Quarters, October 18, 1782

SIR: I have been honored with two Favors of your Excellency; One presented by the Count de Segur, of the 2d. of April, the other delivered by the Prince de Broglie, of the 8th. both which were rendered doubly agreeable, by the pleasure I had in receiving them from the Hands of two such amiable and accomplished Young Gentlemen.

Independent of my Esteem for your Excellency. Be assured Sir! that my respect and Regard for the french Nation at large, to whom this Country is under so great Obligations, as well as

the very favorable Impressions I have conceived for their particular Characters, will secure my warmest attention to the
persons of these distinguished young Noblemen.

I am much obliged by the political Information, which you
have taken the trouble to convey to me; but feel myself much
embarrassed in my Wish to make you a Return in kind. At
the first of the Season, the Expectations of America were much
raised, in Consequence of the Change of the British Ministry
and the Measures of Parliament; but Events have shewn, that
their Hopes have risen too high. The Death of the Marquis of
Rockingham, the Advancement of the Earl of Shelburne, and
the Delays of Negotiation, have given us very different Impressions from those we at first conceived. We now begin again
to reflect upon the persevering Obstinacy of the King, the
wickedness of his Ministry, and the haughty Pride of the Nation, which Ideas recall to our Minds very disagreeable prospects, and a probable Continuance of our present Trouble.

The military Operations of the Campaign, are drawing to a
Close, without any very important Events, on this Side the
Water, unless the Evacuation of Charlestown, which is generally expected, but not yet known to me, should take place
and form a paragraph in the Page of this Years History.

The British Fleet from the West Indies, still continues in
N York. I have not been able yet to decide on the Enemy's In-
tentions there. It is generally tho't that a detachment of their
Troops will sail with them when the fleet returns to the West
Indies, where it is conjectured their Efforts for the Winter,
will be prosecuted with Vigor. [I have the honr] etc.

To MAJOR GENERAL NATHANAEL GREENE

*The end of hostilities in the Southern States was auspicious
for the general peace that was to follow within six months.
In this letter to General Nathanael Greene, Washington at
last puts all circumspection aside and expresses, with only
slight reservation, the feeling of elation that comes when a
task is almost completed.*

Newburgh, February 6, 1783

My DEAR SIR: I have the pleasure to inform you that your Packet for Govr. Greene which came inclosed to me (in your private Letter of the 12th. of December) was forwarded in an hour after it came to my hands by a Gentleman returning to Rhode Island (Welcome Arnold Esquire); there can be no doubt therefore of its having got safe to the Governor.

It is with a pleasure which friendship only is susceptible of, I congratulate you on the glorious end you have put to hostilities in the Southern States; the honor and advantage of it, I hope, and trust, you will live long to enjoy. when this hemisphere will be equally free is yet in the womb of time to discover; a little whole, however 'tis presumed, will disclose the determinations of the British Senate with respect to Peace or War as it seems to be agreed on all hands, that the present Premeir (especially if he should find the opposition powerful) intends to submit the decision of these matters to Parliament. The Speech, the Addresses, and Debates for which we are looking in every direction, will give a data from which the bright rays of the one, or the gloomy prospect of the other, may be discovered.

If Historiographers should be hardy enough to fill the page of History with the advantages that have been gained with unequal numbers (on the part of America) in the course of this contest, and attempt to relate the distressing circumstances under which they have been obtained, it is more than probable that Posterity will bestow on their labors the epithet and marks of fiction; for it will not be believed that such a force as Great Britain has employed for eight years in this Country could be baffled in their plan of Subjugating it by numbers infinitely less, composed of Men oftentimes half starved; always in Rags, without pay, and experiencing, at times, every species of distress which human nature is capable of undergoing.

I intended to have wrote you a long letter on sundry matters but Majr. Burnett popped in unexpectedly, at a time when I was preparing for the Celebration of the day; and was just going to a review of the Troops, previous to the Fue de joy. As he is impatient, from an apprehension of the Sleighing failing. and as he can give you the occurrences of this quarter more in detail than I have time to do, I will refer you to him. I cannot omit informing you however, that I let no oppertunity slip to enquire after your Son George at Princeton, and that it is with pleasure I hear he enjoys good health, and is a fine promising boy.

Mrs. Washington joins me in most Affectionate regards, and best wishes for Mrs Greene and yourself. With great truth and sincerity and every sentiment of friendship. I am etc.

To THOMAS JEFFERSON

Because negotiations toward a preliminary treaty of peace were proceeding successfully, Jefferson canceled his departure from the United States. Early in April Congress considered his mission unnecessary and Washington's hope "you will have found the business already done" was fulfilled.

Newburgh, February 10, 1783

DEAR SIR: I have been honored with your favor of the 22d. of Jany. from Philadelpa. I feel myself much flattered by your kind remembrance of me in the hour of your departure from this Continent. and for the favourable Sentiments you are pleased to entertain of my Services for this our common Country. To merit the approbation of good and virtuous Men is the height of my ambition, and will be a full compensation for all my toils and Sufferings in the long and painful Contest we have been engaged.

It gave me great pleasure to hear that the call upon you from Congress to pass the Atlantic in the Character of one of their Ministers for Negotiating Peace, had been repeated. But I hope you will have found the business already done.

The Speech of his Britainic Majesty is strongly indicative of the Olive branch; and yet, as he observes, unforeseen events may place it out of reach. At present, the prospect of Peace absorbs, or seems to do so, every other consideration among us; and would, it is to be feared, leave us in a very unprepared state to continue the War if the Negociations at Paris should terminate otherwise than in a general pacification. but I will hope that it is the dearth of other News that fills the Mouths of every person with Peace while their Minds are employed in contemplating on the means for prosecuting the War, if necessity should drive us to it.

You will please to accept my grateful thanks for your obliging offer of Services during your stay in France. To hear frequently from you, will be an honor and very great satisfaction to Dr. Sir etc.

To THE OFFICERS OF THE ARMY

The officers encamped at Newburgh, New York, anxious over their arrears in pay and sullen with idleness, drew up a memorial to Congress, asking for the money due them. Congress, as usual, debated the matter for three months and did nothing. An anonymous paper was circulated in March, urging an end to moderation and making a call to action. A meeting was held on March 15th and Washington brought to it a prepared address analyzing the impropriety and dangers of such action, which he considered a challenge to the sovereign power of the United States. While solemnly assuring the officers that he would do everything in his power to redress their wrongs, he pleaded with them to depend upon Congress to render them justice. Even more persuasive than his enormous personal prestige and the calm reasoning of his prepared speech was the spontaneous and homely occurrence just after Washington mounted the platform. After he had read the first paragraph of the address, he paused and interpolated: "Gentlemen, you will permit me to put on my spectacles, for I not only have grown gray but almost blind in the service of my country." His speech won his audience completely. Washington's representations to Congress gained favorable action for the officers' demands, with nine states concurring.

Head Quarters, Newburgh, March 15, 1783

GENTLEMEN: By an anonymous summons, an attempt has been made to convene you together; how inconsistent with the rules of propriety! how unmilitary! and how subversive of all order and discipline, let the good sense of the Army decide.

In the moment of this Summons, another anonymous production was sent into circulation, addressed more to the feelings and passions, than to the reason and judgment of the Army. The author of the piece, is entitled to much credit for the goodness of his Pen and I could wish he had as much credit for the rectitude of his Heart, for, as Men see thro' different Optics, and are induced by the reflecting faculties of the Mind, to use different means, to attain the same end, the Author of the Address, should have had more charity, than to mark for Suspicion, the Man who should recommend moderation and longer forbearance, or, in other words, who should not think as he thinks, and act as he advises. But he had another plan in view, in which candor and liberality of Sentiment, regard to justice, and love of Country, have no part; and he was right, to insinuate the darkest suspicion, to effect the blackest designs.

That the Address is drawn with great Art, and is designed to answer the most insidious purposes. That it is calculated to impress the Mind, with an idea of premeditated injustice in the Sovereign power of the United States, and rouse all those resentments which must unavoidably flow from such a belief. That the secret mover of this Scheme (whoever he may be) intended to take advantage of the passions, while they were warmed by the recollection of past distresses, without giving time for cool, deliberative thinking, and that composure of Mind which is so necessary to give dignity and stability to measures is rendered too obvious, by the mode of conducting the business, to need other proof than a reference to the proceeding.

Thus much, Gentlemen, I have thought it incumbent on me to observe to you, to shew upon what principles I opposed the irregular and hasty meeting which was proposed to have been

held on Tuesday last: and not because I wanted a disposition
to give you every oppertunity consistent with your own honor,
and the dignity of the Army, to make known your grievances.
If my conduct heretofore, has not evinced to you, that I have
been a faithful friend to the Army, my declaration of it at this
time wd. be equally unavailing and improper. But as I was
among the first who embarked in the cause of our common
Country. As I have never left your side one moment, but when
called from you on public duty. As I have been the constant
companion and witness of your Distresses, and not among the
last to feel, and acknowledge your Merits. As I have ever considered my own Military reputation as inseperably connected
with that of the Army. As my Heart has ever expanded with
joy, when I have heard its praises, and my indignation has
arisen, when the mouth of detraction has been opened against
it, it can scarcely be supposed, at this late stage of the War, that
I am indifferent to its interests. But, how are they to be promoted? The way is plain, says the anonymous Addresser. If
War continues, remove into the unsettled Country; there establish yourselves, and leave an ungrateful Country to defend itself. But who are they to defend? Our Wives, our Children,
our Farms, and other property which we leave behind us. or,
in this state of hostile seperation, are we to take the two first
(the latter cannot be removed), to perish in a Wilderness, with
hunger, cold and nakedness? If Peace takes place, never sheath
your Swords Says he untill you have obtained full and ample
justice; this dreadful alternative, of either deserting our Country in the extremest hour of her distress, or turning our Arms
against it (which is the apparent object, unless Congress can
be compelled into instant compliance) has something so shocking in it, that humanity revolts at the idea. My God! what can
this writer have in view, by recommending such measures? Can
he be a friend to the Army? Can he be a friend to this Country? Rather, is he not an insidious Foe? Some Emissary, perhaps, from New York, plotting the ruin of both, by sowing
the seeds of discord and seperation between the Civil and Military powers of the Continent? And what a Compliment does
he pay to our Understandings, when he recommends measures
in either alternative, impracticable in their Nature?

But here, Gentlemen, I will drop the curtain, because it wd. be as imprudent in me to assign my reasons for this opinion, as it would be insulting to your conception, to suppose you stood in need of them. A moment's reflection will convince every dispassionate Mind of the physical impossibility of carrying either proposal into execution.

There might, Gentlemen, be an impropriety in my taking notice, in this Address to you, of an anonymous production, but the manner in which that performance has been introduced to the Army, the effect it was intended to have, together with some other circumstances, will amply justify my observations on the tendency of that Writing. With respect to the advice given by the Author, to suspect the Man, who shall recommend moderate measures and longer forbearance, I spurn it, as every Man, who regards that liberty, and reveres that justice for which we contend, undoubtedly must; for if Men are to be precluded from offering their Sentiments on a matter, which may involve the most serious and alarming consequences, that can invite the consideration of Mankind, reason is of no use to us; the freedom of Speech may be taken away, and, dumb and silent we may be led, like sheep, to the Slaughter.

I cannot, in justice to my own belief, and what I have great reason to conceive is the intention of Congress, conclude this Address, without giving it as my decided opinion, that that Honble Body, entertain exalted sentiments of the Services of the Army; and, from a full conviction of its merits and sufferings, will do it compleat justice. That their endeavors, to discover and establish funds for this purpose, have been unwearied, and will not cease, till they have succeeded, I have not a doubt. But, like all other large Bodies, where there is a variety of different Interests to reconcile, their deliberations are slow. Why then should we distrust them? and, in consequence of that distrust, adopt measures, which may cast a shade over that glory which, has been so justly acquired; and tarnish the reputation of an Army which is celebrated thro' all Europe, for its fortitude and Patriotism? and for what is this done? to bring the object we seek nearer? No! most certainly, in my opinion, it will cast it at a greater distance.

For myself (and I take no merit in giving the assurance,

being induced to it from principles of gratitude, veracity and justice), a grateful sence of the confidence you have ever placed in me, a recollection of the chearful assistance, and prompt obedience I have experienced from you, under every vicissitude of Fortune, and the sincere affection I feel for an Army, I have so long had the honor to Command, will oblige me to declare, in this public and solemn manner, that, in the attainment of compleat justice for all your toils and dangers, and in the gratification of every wish, so far as may be done consistently with the great duty I owe my Country, and those powers we are bound to respect, you may freely command my Services to the utmost of my abilities.

While I give you these assurances, and pledge myself in the most unequivocal manner, to exert whatever ability I am possessed of, in your favor, let me entreat you, Gentlemen, on your part, not to take any measures, which, viewed in the calm light of reason, will lessen the dignity, and sully the glory you have hitherto maintained; let me request you to rely on the plighted faith of your Country, and place a full confidence in the purity of the intentions of Congress; that, previous to your dissolution as an Army they will cause all your Accts. to be fairly liquidated, as directed in their resolutions, which were published to you two days ago, and that they will adopt the most effectual measures in their power, to render ample justice to you, for your faithful and meritorious Services. And let me conjure you, in the name of our common Country, as you value your own sacred honor, as you respect the rights of humanity, and as you regard the Military and National character of America, to express your utmost horror and detestation of the Man who wishes, under any specious pretences, to overturn the liberties of our Country, and who wickedly attempts to open the flood Gates of Civil discord, and deluge our rising Empire in Blood. By thus determining, and thus acting, you will pursue the plain and direct road to the attainment of your wishes. You will defeat the insidious designs of our Enemies, who are compelled to resort from open force to secret Artifice. You will give one more distinguished proof of unexampled patriotism and patient virtue, rising superior to the pressure of the most complicated sufferings; And you will, by the dignity of your Conduct, afford occasion for Posterity to say, when speaking of the glorious example you have exhibited to Mankind, "had this day been wanting, the World had never seen the last stage of perfection to which human nature is capable of attaining."

To THE SECRETARY FOR FOREIGN AFFAIRS

So slow were communications in 1783 that more than two months were required to bring to Washington the official notification of the General Peace which had been signed at Paris on January 20th. The news was carried in a letter written by Lafayette aboard a vessel of Count d'Estaing's fleet from the port of Cadiz to the President of Congress. It is noteworthy that Washington seeks the consent of Congress to grant the special honor of bearing the peace ratification to his comrade-in-arms and closest friend, Lafayette.

Head Quarters, March 29, 1783

MY DEAR SIR: Your obliging Letter of the 24 was delivered me the day before Yesterday and accompanied the Account of a General Peace having been concluded in Europe on the 20 of January last. Most sincerely do I accept your Congratulations on this happy Event which has already diffused a General Joy thro' every Class of People and to none more than to the Army. It will now be our own faults if we do not enjoy that happiness which we have flattered ourselves this Event would bring; to see, such measures taken as will ensure this, is all that remains for me to wish; I shall then enjoy in the bosom of my family, a felicity that will amply repay every care.

In a Letter I received by the Cutter from the Marqs. De la Fayette dated Cadiz Feby. 5th. is this passage.

Independent of my public letter to Mr. Livingston, there is a private one which he will also communicate, amongst the many favors which I have received, I would take it as a most flattering circumstance in my life to be sent to England with the ratification of the American Treaty; you know it is but an honorary Commission, that would require the attendance of a few Weeks, and if any Sedentary Minister is sent, I should have the pleasure of introducing him; this, my dear General is entirely confidential.

From hence, I suppose it is necessary for Congress to ratifie the treaty of Peace entered into by their Commissioners at Paris to give it the form and solemnity which is essential to such a work, and that the Marqs. wishes for the honor of putting the last hand to this business by being the bearer of the Ratification. How far it is consistent with our National honor, how far motives of policy make for or agst. sending a foreigner with it; or how far such a measure might disappoint the expectations of others, I pretend not to determine but if there is no impropriety, or injustice in it, I should hope that Congress would feel a pleasure in gratifying the wishes of a Man who has been such a Zealous labourer in the cause of this Country. Whether the above paragraph was only meant to bring me acquainted with what he had done, or that I might second his views, I know not, therefore, notwithstanding the injunction I have given these Sentiments.

Your Letters for Governor Clinton were forwarded by Express immediately on the rect. of them. I am &c.

To ALEXANDER HAMILTON

Washington's insistence upon the strengthening of the Confederation of States on liberal and permanent principles is the recurring motif of his letters to Alexander Hamilton as the war ended and the Commander in Chief's thoughts turned to safeguarding the fruits of victory.

Newburgh, March 31, 1783

DEAR SIR: I have duly received your favors of the 17th. and 24th. Ulto. I rejoice most exceedingly that there is an end to our Warfare, and that such a field is opening to our view as will, with wisdom to direct the cultivation of it, make us a great, a respectable, and happy People; but it must be improved by other means than State politics, and unreasonable jealousies and prejudices; or (it requires not the second sight to see that) we shall be instruments in the hands of our Enemies, and those European powers who may be jealous of our greatness in Union to dissolve the confederation; but to attain this, altho' the way seems extremely plain, is not so easy.

My wish to see the Union of these States established upon liberal and permanent principles, and inclination to contribute my mite in pointing out the defects of the present Constitution, are equally great. All my private letters have teemed with these Sentiments, and whenever this topic has been the subject of conversation, I have endeavoured to diffuse and enforce them; but how far any further essay by me might be productive of the wished for end, or appear to arrogate more than belongs to me, depends so much upon popular opinions, and the temper and dispositions of People, that it is not easy to decide. I shall be obliged to you however for the thoughts which you have promised me on this Subject, and as soon as you can make it convenient.

No Man in the United States is, or can be more deeply impressed with the necessity of a reform in our present Confederation than myself. No Man perhaps has felt the bad effects of it more sensibly; for the defects thereof, and want of Powers in Congress, may justly be ascribed the prolongation of the War, and consequently the expenses occasioned by it. More than half the perplexities I have experienced in the course of my command, and almost the whole of the difficulties and distress of the Army, have their origin here; but still the prejudices of some, the designs of others, and the mere Machinery of the Majority, makes address and management necessary to give weight to opinions which are to Combat the doctrines of those different classes of Men, in the field of Politics.

I would have been more full on this subject but the bearer (in the Clothing department) is waiting. I wish you may understand what I have written. I am etc.

To SIR GUY CARLETON

Ordered to proclaim cessation of hostilities, Sir Guy Carleton had written a formal letter to Washington, who replied that, subject to authorization from Congress, he had also proclaimed suspension of warfare at all American outposts. Under all the circumstances, one can detect a note of pride and dignity in Washington's use of the phrase "the Sovereign power of the United States" to the chief of the British forces on the American continent.

Head Quarters, April 9, 1783

SIR: I feel great satisfaction from your Excellency's Dispatches by Capt Stapleton, conveying to me the Joyful enunciation of your having received Official Accounts of the Conclusion of a general Peace, and a cessation of Hostilities.

Without official Authority from Congress, but perfectly relying on your Excellency's Communication, I can at this Time, only issue my Orders to the American Outposts to suspend all Acts of Hostilities until further Orders; this shall be instantly done; And I shall be happy in the momentary Expectation of having it in my power to publish, to the American Army, a general Cessation of all Hostilities between G Britain and America.

To your Excellency's Observations respecting particular Articles of the Peace, I am obliged to reply, that it rests with Congress to direct Measures for the Observance of all the Articles contained in the provisional Treaty. Your Excellency may be assured that as soon as I receive my Instructions from the Sovereign power of the United States, I shall rejoice, in giving every facility in my power to carry it into compleat Execution, that Article of the Treaty which respects the Restitution of all prisoners of War, being perfectly disposed to contribute to the diffusing, as much as possible, the happy Effects of this great Event.

I thank your Excellency for the Assurances you are pleased to express of your readiness to cultivate that spirit of perfect good Will and Conciliation, which you wish should take place between the King of G Britain and the United States and the Citizens and Subjects of both Countries. And I beg Sir, that you will please to accept a Tender from me of reciprocal good Will and Attention; accompanied with sincere Congratulations to your Excellency on this joyful Restoration of Peace and general Tranquility, with an earnest Wish, that, resting on the firm Basis of mutual Interest and good Will, it may prove as lasting as it is happy. I have the Honor etc.

GENERAL ORDERS

The official order for the cessation of war came on the anniversary of the Battle of Lexington, April 18, 1775, after eight years of intermittent battles but almost constantly heartbreaking struggle. Washington is careful to distinguish here between the end of hostilities and the announcement of General Peace. In view of the importance of the occasion, the General certainly has earned the right to a few rhetorical flourishes and the soldiers cannot be begrudged their extra ration of liquor.

Friday, April 18, 1783

Parole Kenalal. Countersigns Litchfield, Montreal.

The Jersey regiment gives the Guards and the Jersey battalion the fatigues tomorrow.

The Commander in Chief orders the Cessation of Hostilities between the United States of America and the King of Great Britain to be publickly proclaimed tomorrow at 12 o'clock at the Newbuilding, and that the Proclamation which will be communicated herewith, be read tomorrow evening at the head of every regiment and corps of the army. After which the Chaplains with the several Brigades will render thanks to almighty God for all his mercies, particularly for his over ruling the wrath of man to his own glory, and causing the rage of war to cease amongst the nations.

Although the proclamation before alluded to, extends only to the prohibition of hostilities and not to the annunciation of a general peace, yet it must afford the most rational and sincere satisfaction to every benevolent mind, as it puts a period to a long and doubtful contest, stops the effusion of human blood, opens the prospect to a more splendid scene, and like another morning star, promises the approach of a brighter day than hath hitherto illuminated the Western Hemisphere; on such a happy day, a day which is the harbinger of Peace, a day which compleats the eighth year of the war, it would be ingratitude not to rejoice! it would be insensibility not to participate in the general felicity.

The Commander in Chief far from endeavouring to stifle the feelings of Joy in his own bosom, offers his most cordial Congratulations on the occasion to all the Officers of every denomination, to all the Troops of the United States in General, and in particular to those gallant and persevering men who had resolved to defend the rights of their invaded country so long as the war should continue. For these are the men who ought to be considered as the pride and boast of the American Army; And, who crowned with well earned laurels, may soon withdraw from the field of Glory, to the more tranquil walks of civil life.

While the General recollects the almost infinite variety of Scenes thro which we have passed, with a mixture of pleasure, astonishment, and gratitude; While he contemplates the prospects before us with rapture; he can not help wishing that all the brave men (of whatever condition they may be) who have shared in the toils and dangers of effecting this glorious revolution, of rescuing Millions from the hand of oppression, and of laying the foundation of a great Empire, might be impressed with a proper idea of the dignifyed part they have been called to act (under the Smiles of providence) on the stage of human affairs: for, happy, thrice happy shall they be pronounced hereafter, who have contributed any thing, who have performed the meanest office in erecting this steubendous fabrick of Freedom and Empire on the broad basis of Indipendency; who have assisted in protecting the rights of humane nature and establishing an Asylum for the poor and oppressed of all nations and religions. The glorious task for which we first fleu to Arms being thus accomplished, the liberties of our Country being fully acknowledged, and firmly secured by the smiles of heaven, on the purity of our cause, and the honest exertions of a feeble people (determined to be free) against a powerful Nation (disposed to oppress them) and the Character of those who have persevered, through every extremity of hardship; suffering and danger being immortalized by the illustrious appellation of the patriot Army: Nothing now remains but for the actors of this mighty Scene to preserve a perfect, unvarying, consistency of character through the very last act; to close the Drama with applause; and to retire from the Military Theatre with the same approbation of Angells and men which have crowned all their former vertuous Actions. For this purpose no disorder or licentiousness must be tolerated, every considerate and well disposed soldier must remember it will be absolutely necessary to wait with patience untill peace shall be declared or Congress shall be enabled to take proper measures for the security of the public stores &ca.; as soon as these Arrangements shall be made the General is confident there will be no delay in discharging with every mark of distinction and honor all the men enlisted for the war who will then have faithfully performed their engagements with the public. The General has already interested himself in their behalf; and he thinks he need not repeat the assurances of his disposition to be useful to them on the present, and every other proper occasion. In the mean time he is determined that no Military neglects or excesses shall go unpunished while he retains the command of the Army.

The Adjutant General will have such working parties detailed to assist in making the preperations for a general rejoycing as the Chief Engineer with the Army shall call for, and the Quarter Master Genl. will also furnish such materials as he may want.

The Quarter Master General will without delay procure such a number of Discharges to be printed as will be sufficient for all the men enlisted for the War; he will please to apply to Head Quarters for the form.

An extra ration of liquor to be issued to every man tomorrow, to drink Perpetual Peace, Independence and Happiness to the United States of America.

SENTIMENTS ON A PEACE ESTABLISHMENT

After lying buried in manuscript form for one hundred and forty-seven years, "Sentiments on a Peace Establishment" was discovered and published by Brigadier General John McAuley Palmer, author of America in Arms. *Had it been found earlier, this document would undoubtedly have had an enormous influence on the policy of military organization in the United States. In it Washington recommended the employment of professionals for their special, highly trained services, while emphasizing at the same time the need of a citizen army. That Washington should take the position that the national militia be placed in such a "condition as that they may appear truly respectable in the Eyes of our Friends and formidable to those who would otherwise become our enemies" may seem irreconcilable with his previous attitude toward the militia. This paradox is explained by General Palmer as a preference for a well-organized over the ill-organized militia with which Washington had to deal through the whole Revolutionary War. General George C. Marshall, Chief of Staff during the Second World War and one of the most famous military organizers of modern times, frequently quoted from this document with such telling effect that it has shaped the present military organization of the Army of the United States.*

(Addressed to Alexander Hamilton)
Newburgh, May 2, 1783

SIR: A necessary absence from Camp and several unavoidable interruptions have been the occasion of, and must be my apology for with holding the inclosed thoughts on a peace establishment so long.

If they will afford any assistance, or contain any thing satisfactory, I shall think my time and labour well spent. I have the honour.

SENTIMENTS ON A PEACE ESTABLISHMENT

A Peace Establishment for the United States of America may in my opinion be classed under four different heads Vizt:

First. A regular and standing force, for Garrisoning West Point and such other Posts upon our Northern, Western, and Southern Frontiers, as shall be deemed necessary to awe the Indians, protect our Trade, prevent the encroachment of our Neighbours of Canada and the Florida's, and guard us at least from surprizes; Also for security of our Magazines.

Secondly. A well organized Militia; upon a Plan that will pervade all the States, and introduce similarity in their Establishment Manœuvres, Exercise and Arms.

Thirdly. Establishing Arsenals of all kinds of Military Stores.

Fourthly. Academies, one or more for the Instruction of the Art Military; particularly those Branches of it which respect Engineering and Artillery, which are highly essential, and the knowledge of which, is most difficult to obtain. Also Manufactories of some kinds of Military Stores.

Upon each of these, and in the order in which they stand, I shall give my sentiments as concisely as I can, and with that freedom which the Committee have authorized.

Altho' a *large* standing Army in time of Peace hath ever been considered dangerous to the liberties of a Country, yet a few Troops, under certain circumstances, are not only safe, but indispensably necessary. Fortunately for us our relative situation requires but few. The same circumstances which so effectually retarded, and in the end conspired to defeat the attempts of Britain to subdue us, will now powerfully tend to render us secure. Our *distance* from the European States in a great degree frees us of apprehension, from their numerous regular forces and the Insults and dangers which are to be dreaded from their Ambition.

But, if our danger from those powers was more imminent, yet we are too poor to maintain a standing Army adequate to our defence, and was our Country more populous and rich, still it could not be done without great oppression of the people. Besides, as soon as we are able to raise funds more than adequate to the discharge of the Debts incurred by the Revolution, it may become a Question worthy of consideration, whether the surplus should not be applied in preparations for building and equipping a Navy, without which, in case of War we could neither protect our Commerce, nor yield that Assistance to each other, which, on such an extent of Sea-Coast, our mutual Safety would require.

Fortifications on the Sea Board may be considered in two points of view, first as part of the general defence, and next, as securities to Dock Yards, and Arsenals for Ship Building, neither of which shall I take into this plan; because the first would be difficult, if not, under our circumstances, impracticable; at any rate amazingly expensive. The other, because it is a matter out of my line, and to which I am by no means competent, as it requires a consideration of many circumstances, to which I have never paid attention.

The Troops requisite for the Post of West Point, for the Magazines, and for our Northern, Western and Southern Frontiers, ought, in my opinion, to amount to 2631 Officers of all denominations included; besides the Corps of Invalids. If this number should be thought large, I would only observe; that the British Force in Canada is now powerful, and, by report, will be increased; that the frontier is very extensive; that the Tribes of Indians within our Territory are numerous, soured and jealous; that Communications must be established with the exterior Posts; And, that it may be policy and œconomy, to appear respectable in the Eyes of the Indians, at the Commencement of our National Intercourse and Traffic with them. In a word, that it is better to reduce our force hereafter, by degrees, than to have it to increase after some unfortunate disasters may have happened to the Garrisons; discouraging to us, and an inducement to the Enemy to attempt a repetition of them.

Besides these Considerations, we are not to forget, that altho' by the Treaty, half the Waters, and the free Navigation of the Lakes appertain to us, yet, in Case of a rupture with Great Britain we should in all probability, find little benefits from the Communications with our upper Posts, by the Lakes Erie and Ontario; as it is to be presumed, that the Naval superiority which they now have on those Waters, will be maintained. It follows as a Consequence then, that we should open new or improve the present half explored Communications with Detroit and other Posts on the Lakes, by the Waters of the Susquehannah Potowmack or James River, to the Ohio, from whence, with short Portages several Communications by Water may be opened with Lake Erie. To do which, posts should be established at the most convenient places on the Ohio. This would open several doors for the supply of the Garrisons on the Lakes; and is absolutely necessary for such others as may be tho't advisable to establish upon the Mississippi. The Ohio affording the easiest, as well as the safest Route to the Illinois settlements, and the whole Country below on the Mississippi, quite to our Southern boundary.

To protect the Peltry and Fur Trade, to keep a watch upon our Neighbours, and to prevent their encroaching upon our Territory undiscovered, are all the purposes that can be answered by an extension of our Posts, at this time, beyond Detroit, to the Northward or Westward: but, a strong Post on the Scioto, at the carrying place between it and the River Sandusky, which empties into Lake Erie, mentioned in Hutchins's Description of that Country Page 24, and more plainly pointed out by Evans's Map, is indispensably necessary for the security of the present Settlers, and such as probably, will *immediately* settle within those Limits. And by giving security to the Country and covering its Inhabitants, will enable them to furnish supplies to the Garrisons Westward and Northward of these settlements, upon moderate and easy Terms.

The 2,631 Men beforementioned, I would have considered to all Intents and purposes as Continental Troops; looking up to Congress for their Orders, their pay, and supplies of every kind. The Infantry of which, being 1908 and, composing four Regiments may be thrown into the following disposition.

Not having that *particular* knowledge of the situation of the Southern and Western Boundaries of the Carolinas and Georgia, which is necessary to decide on the Posts to be established in that District, the allotment of only one Regiment thereto, may be judged inadequate; should that be the case, a greater force may be established and a sufficient allowance made them.

The above establishment differs from our present one, in the following instances Vizt: The exclusion of the light Company and reducing a sergeant and 18 Privates from each of the Battalion Companies, and giving a Chaplain to each Regiment instead of a Brigade. If it should be asked why the Reduction of Non Commisd. Officers and Privates is made, while the Commissioned Officers remain the same? It may be answered, that the number of Men which compose the Infantry, will be sufficient for my Calculation, and that the situation of our Frontiers renders it convenient to divide them into so many Corps as have been mentioned, for the ease and propriety of Command. I may also say, that in my Opinion, the number of our Commissioned Officers, has always been disproportionate to the Men. And that in the detached State in which these Regiments must be employed, they cannot consistently with the good of Service be reduced.

It may also be observed, that in case of War and a necessity of assembling their Regiments in the Field, nothing more will be necessary, than to recruit 18 Men to each Compy. and give the Regiment its flank Company. Or if we should have occasion to add strength to the Garrisons, or increase the number of our Posts, we may augment 900 Men including Serjeants, without requiring more than the Officers of 4 Companies, or exceeding our present Establishment. In short, it will give us a Number of Officers well skilled in the Theory and Art of War, who will be ready on any occasion, to mix and diffuse their knowledge of Discipline to other Corps, without that lapse of Time, which, without such Provision, would be necessary to bring intire new Corps acquainted with the principles of it.

Besides the 4 Regiments of Infantry, one of Artillery will be indispensably necessary. The Invalid Corps should also be retained. Motives of humanity, Policy and justice will all combine to prevent their being disbanded. The numbers of the last will, from the nature of their composition, be fluctuating and uncertain. The establishment of the former will be as follows, Vizt:

Establishment and Disposition of four Regts. of Infantry 1908 Men including Officers

Disposition	Colonel	Lt. Colonel	Major	Captains	Lieuts.	Ensigns	Chaplain	Adjutant	P Master	Qr. Master	Surgeon	Mate	Sergt. Major	Qr. Mr. Sergt.	Drum Major	Fife Major	Sergeants	Drum & fifes	Rank & File	Total
Penobscot or St Croix or both	1	1	1	3	3	3	1	1	1	1	1	1	1	1	1	1	9	6	150	
North End of Lake Champlain				4	4	4											12	8	200	
Connecticut River near the 45th degree																	2	1	30	
Ticonderoga				1	1	1											1	1	20	
Establishment & Strength	1	1	1	8	8	8	1	1	1	1	1	1	1	1	1	1	24	16	400	477
Niagara	1		1	3	3	3	1	1	1	1	1		1		1	1	9	6	150	
Oswego																	2	1	30	
Fort Erie No. end of Lake Erie				1	1	1											1	1	20	
Detroit		1		3	3	3						1		1			9	6	150	
Streights between Lakes Huron & Superior				1	1	1											3	2	50	
Establishment & Strength	1	1	1	8	8	8	1	1	1	1	1	1	1	1	1	1	24	16	400	477

Fort Pitt....................				1	1	1	1									2	1	30	
Mouth of the Scioto..........								1								1	1	20	
Portage between Scioto & Sandusky	1	1		3	3	3			1	1						9	6	150	
Mouth of Kentucky or the Rapids..				1	1	1					1					2	1	30	
Mouth of the Ohio or near it.....												1				1	1	20	
Height at the mouth of the River Illinois....................			1	3	3	3							1	1	1	9	6	150	
Establishment & Strength...	1	1	1	8	8	8	1	1	1	1	1	1	1	1	1	24	16	400	477
To be disposed, as those who are best acquainted with the Frontiers of the Carolinas & Georgia may direct.	1	1	1	8	8	8	1	1	1	1	1	1	1	1	1	24	16	400	477
Establishment & Strength of 4 Regts....................	4	4	4	32	32	32	4	4	4	4	4	4	4	4	4	96	64	1600	1908

Establishment for one Regiment of Artillery.

| | Officers. | | | | | | | | | | | | | | | | | | | | | | | |
| | Commissioned | | | | | | Staff | | | | | | Non Commissioned | | | | | | | | | | |
Colonel	Lieut. Colonel	Major	Captains	Captn. Lieuts.	1st Lieutenants	2d. Lieutenants	Chaplain	Adjutant	Pay Mr.	Qur. Master	Surgeon	Mate	Serjt. Major	Qur. M. Serjeant	Drum Major	Fife Major	Serjeants	Corporals	Bombadiers	Gunners	Drums & fifes	Matrosses	Total
1	1	1	10	10	10	30	1	1	1	1	1	1	1	1	1	1	60	60	60	60	20	390	723

To this Regiment of Artillery should be annexed 50 or 60 Artificers, of the various kinds which will be necessary, who may be distributed in equal numbers into the different Companies and being part of the Regiment, will be under the direction and Command of the Commanding Officer, to be disposed into different services as Circumstances shall require. By thus blending Artificers with Artillery, the expence of Additional Officers will be saved; and they will Answer all the purposes which are to be expected from them, as well as if formed into a distinct Corps.

The Regiment of Artillery, with the Artificers, will furnish all the Posts in which Artillery is placed, in proportionate numbers to the Strength and importance of them. The residue, with the Corps of Invalids, will furnish Guards for the Magazines, and Garrison West Point. The importance of this last mentioned Post, is so great, as justly to have been considered, the key of America; It has been so pre-eminently advantageous to the defence of the United States, and is still so necessary in that view, as well as for the preservation of the Union, that the loss of it might be productive of the most ruinous Consequences. A Naval superiority at Sea and on Lake Champlain, connected by a Chain of Posts on the Hudson River, would effect an entire separation of the States on each side, and render it difficult, if not impracticable for them to co-operate.

Altho' the total of the Troops herein enumerated does not amount to a large number, yet when we consider their detached situation, and the extent of Country they are spread over: the variety of objects that are to be attended to, and the close inspection that will be necessary to prevent abuses or to correct them before they become habitual; not less than two General Officers in my opinion will be competent to the Duties to be required of them. They will take their Instructions from the Secretary at War, or Person acting at the Head of the Military Department, who will also assign them their respective and distinct Districts. Each should twice a Year visit the Posts of his particular District, and notice the Condition they are in, Inspect the Troops, their discipline and Police, Examine into their Wants, and see that strict justice is rendered them and to the Public, they should also direct the Colonels, at what intermediate Times they shall perform the like duties at the Posts occupied by the Detachments of their respective Regiments. The visiting General ought frequently, if not always, to be accompanied by a Skillful Engineer, who should point out such alterations and improvements as he may think necessary from time to time, for the defence of any of the Posts; which, if approved by the General, should be ordered to be carried into execution.

Each Colonel should be responsible for the Administration of his Regiment; and when present, being Commanding Officer of any Post, which is occupied by a Detachment from his Regt., he may give such directions as he may think proper, not inconsistent with the Orders of his Superior Officer, under whose general superintendence the Troops are. He will carefully exact Monthly Returns from all detachments of his Regiment; and be prepared to make a faithful report of all occurrences, when called upon by the General Officer in whose Department he may be placed and whose instructions he is at all times to receive and obey. These Returns and Reports, drawn into a General one, are to be transmitted to the Secretary at War, by the visiting General, with the detail of his own proceedings, remarks and Orders.

The three Years Men now in service will furnish the proposed Establishment, and from these, it is presumed, the Corps must in the first Instance be composed. But as the pay of an American Soldier is much greater than any other we are acquainted with; and as there can be little doubt of our being able to obtain them in time of Peace, upon as good Terms as other Nations, I would suggest the propriety of inlisting those who may come after the present three years Men, upon Terms of similarity with those of the British, or any other the most liberal Nations.

When the Soldiers for the War have frolicked a while among their friends, and find they must have recourse to hard labour for a livelyhood, I am persuaded numbers of them will reinlist upon almost any Terms. Whatever may be adopted with respect to Pay, Clothing and Emoluments, they should be clearly and unequivocally expressed and promulgated, that there may be no deception or mistake. Discontent, Desertion and frequently Mutiny, are the natural consequences of these; and it is not more difficult to know how to punish, than to prevent these inconveniencies, when it is known, that there has been delusion on the part of the Recruiting Officer, or a breach of Compact on the part of the public. The pay of the Battalion Officer's is full low, but those of the Chaplain, Surgeon and Mate are too high; and a proper difference should be made between the Non-Commissioned Officers (serjeants particularly) and Privates, to give them that pride and consequence which is necessary to Command.

At, or before the Time of discharging the Soldiers for the War, the Officers of the Army may signify their wishes either to retire, upon the Half pay, or to continue in the service; from among those who make the latter choice, the number wanted for a Peace Establishment may be selected; and it were to be wished, that they might be so blended together from the Several Lines, as to remove, as much as possible, all Ideas of State distinctions.

No Forage should be allowed in time of Peace to Troops in Garrison, nor in any circumstances, but when actually on a March.

Soldiers should not be inlisted for *less* than three Years, to commence from the date of their attestations; and the more difference there is in the commencement of their terms of Service, the better; this Circumstance will be the means of avoiding the danger and inconvenience of entrusting any important Posts to raw Recruits unacquainted with service.

Rum should compose no part of a Soldier's Ration; but Vinegar in large quantities should be issued. Flour or Bread, and a stipulated quantity of the different kinds of fresh or Salted Meat, with Salt, when the former is Issued, is all that should be contracted for.

Vegetables they can, and ought to be compelled to raise. If spruce, or any other kind of small Beer, could be provided, it ought to be given gratis, but not made part of the Compact with them. It might be provided also, that they should receive one or two days fish in a Week, when to be had; this would be a saving to the public, (the Lakes and most of the Waters of the Ohio and Mississippi abounding with Fish) and would be no disservice to the Soldier.

A proper recruiting fund should be established; from which the Regiment may always be kept complete.

The Garrisons should be changed as often as it can be done with convenience; long continuance in the same place is injurious. Acquaintances are made, Connections formed, and habits acquired, which often prove very detrimental to the service. By this means, public duty is made to yield to interested pursuits, and real abuses are the Result. To avoid these Evils, I would propose, that there should be a change made in every Regiment once a Year, and one Regiment with another every two Years.

An Ordinance for the service of Troops in Garrison, should be annexed to our present Regulations for the order and discipline of the Army. The latter should be revised, corrected and enlarged so as to form a Basis of Discipline under all circumstances for Continental Troops, and, as far as they will apply, to the Militia also: that one uniform system may pervade all the States.

As a peace establishment may be considered as a change in, if not the Commencement of our Military system, it will be the proper time, to introduce new and beneficial regulations, and to expunge all customs, which from experience have been found unproductive of general good. Among the latter I would ask, if promotion by Seniority is not one? That it is a good general rule admits of no doubt, but that it should be an invariable one, is in my opinion wrong. It cools, if it does not destroy, the incentives to Military Pride and Heroic Actions. On the one hand, the sluggard, who keeps within the verge of his duty, has nothing to fear. On the other hand, the enterprising Spirit has nothing to expect. Whereas, if promotion was the *sure* reward of Merit, *all* would contend for Rank and the service would be benefited by their Struggles for Promotion. In establishing a mode by which this is to be done, and from which nothing is to be expected, or apprehended, either from favour or prejudice, lies the difficulty. Perhaps, reserving to Congress the right inherent in Sovereignties, of making all Promotions. A Board of superior Officers, appointed to receive and examine the claims to promotions out of common course, of any Officer, whether founded on particular merit, or extra service, and to report their opinion thereon to Congress; might prove a likely means of doing justice. It would certainly give a Spur to Emulation, without endangering the rights, or just pretentions of the Officers.

Before I close my observations under this head, of a regular force, and the Establishment of Posts, it is necessary for me to observe, that, in fixing a Post at the North End of Lake Champlain I had three things in view. The Absolute Command of the entrance into the Lake from Canada. A cover to the Settlements on the New Hampshire Grants and the prevention of any illicit intercourse thro' that Channel. But, if it is known, or should be found, that the 45th Degree crosses the Lake South of any spot which will command the entrance into it, the primary object fails; And it then becomes a question whether any place beyond Ticonderoga or Crown Point is eligible.

Altho' it may be somewhat foreign to, and yet not altogether unconnected with the present subject, I must beg leave, from the importance of the object, as it appears to my mind, and for the advantages which I think would result from it to the United States, to hint, the propriety of Congress taking some early steps, by a liberal treatment, to gain the affections of the French settlements of Detroit, those of the Illinois and other back Countries. Such a measure would not only hold out great encouragement to the Inhabitants already on those lands, who will doubtless make very useful and valuable subjects of the United States; but would probably make deep and conciliatory impressions on their friends in the British settlements, and prove a means of drawing thither great numbers of Canadian Emigrants, who, under proper Regulations and establishments of Civil Government, would make a hardy and industruous race of Settlers on that Frontier; and who, by forming a barrier against the Indians, would give great security to the Infant settlement, which, soon after the close of the War, will probably be forming in the back Country.

I come next in the order I have prescribed myself, to treat of the Arrangements necessary for placing the Militia of the Continent on a respectable footing for the defence of the Empire and in speaking of this great Bulwark of our Liberties and independence, I shall claim the indulgence of suggesting whatever general observations may occur from experience and reflection with the greater freedom, from a conviction of the importance of the subject; being persuaded, that the immediate safety and future tranquility of this extensive Continent depend in a great measure upon the peace Establishment now in contemplation; and being convinced at the same time, that the only probable means of preventing insult or hostility for any length of time and from being exempted from the consequent calamities of War, is to put the National Militia in such a condition as that they may appear truly respectable in the Eyes of our Friends and formidable to those who would otherwise become our enemies.

Were it not totally unnecessary and superfluous to adduce arguments to prove what is conceded on all hands the Policy and expediency of resting the protection of the Country on a respectable and well established Militia, we might not only shew the propriety of the measure from our peculiar local situation, but we might have recourse to the Histories of Greece and Rome in their most virtuous and Patriotic ages to demonstrate the Utility of such Establishments. Then passing by the Mercinary Armies, which have at one time or another subverted the liberties of allmost all the Countries they have been raised to defend, we might see, with admiration, the Freedom and Independence of Switzerland supported for Centuries, in the midst of powerful and jealous neighbours, by means of a hardy and well organized Militia. We might also derive useful lessons of a similar kind from other Nations of Europe, but I believe it will be found, the *People of this Continent* are too well acquainted with the Merits of the subject to require information or example. I shall therefore proceed to point out some general outlines of their duty, and conclude this head with a few particular observations on the regulations which I conceive ought to be immediately adopted by the States at the instance and recommendation of Congress.

It may be laid down as a primary position, and the basis of our system, that every Citizen who enjoys the protection of a free Government, owes not only a proportion of his property, but even of his personal services to the defence of it, and consequently that the Citizens of America (with a few legal and official exceptions) from 18 to 50 Years of Age should be borne on the Militia Rolls, provided with uniform Arms, and so far accustomed to the use of them, that the Total strength of the Country might be called forth at a Short Notice on any very interesting Emergency, for these purposes they ought to be duly organized into Commands of the same formation; (it is not of *very* great importance, whether the Regiments are large or small, provided a sameness prevails in the strength and composition of them and I do not know that a better establishment, than that under which the Continental Troops now are, can be adopted. They ought to be regularly Mustered and trained, and to have their Arms and Accoutrements inspected at certain appointed times, not less than once or twice in the course of every [year] but as it is obvious, amongst such a Multitude of People (who may indeed be useful for temporary service) there must be a great number, who from domestic Circumstances, bodily defects, natural awkwardness or disinclination, can never acquire the habits of Soldiers; but on the contrary will injure the appearance of any body of Troops to which they are attached, and as there are a sufficient proportion of able bodied young Men, between the Age of 18 and 25, who, from a natural fondness for Military parade (which passion is almost ever prevalent at that period of life) might easily be enlisted or drafted to form a Corps in every State, capable of resisting any sudden impression which might be attempted by a foreign Enemy, while the remainder of the National forces would have time to Assemble and make preparations for the Field. I would wish therefore, that the former, being considered as a *denier resort,* reserved for some great occasion, a judicious system might be adopted for forming and placing the latter on the best possible Establishment. And that while the Men of this description shall be viewed as the Van and flower of the American Forces, ever ready for Action and zealous to be employed whenever it may become necessary in the service of their Country; they should meet with such exemptions, privileges or distinctions, as might tend to keep alive a true Military pride, a nice sense of honour, and a patriotic regard for the public. Such sentiments, indeed, ought to be instilled into our Youth, with their earliest years, to be cherished and inculcated as frequently and forcibly as possible.

It is not for me to decide positively, whether it will be ultimately most interesting to the happiness and safety of the United States, to form this Class of Soldiers into a kind of Continental Militia, selecting every 10th 15th or 20th. Man from the Rolls of each State for the purpose; Organizing, Officering and Commissioning those Corps upon the same principle as is now practiced in the Continental Army. Whether it will be best to comprehend in this body, all the Men fit for service between some given Age and no others, for example between 18 and 25 or some similar description, or whether it will be preferable in every Regiment of the proposed Establishment to have one additional Company inlisted or drafted from the best Men for 3, 5, or 7 years and distinguished by the name of the additional or light Infantry Company, always to be kept complete. These Companies might then be drawn together occasionally and formed into particular Battalions or Regiments under Field Officers appointed for that Service. One or other of these plans I think will be found indispensably necessary, if we are in earnest to have an efficient force ready for Action at a moments Warning. And I cannot conceal my private sentiment, that the formation of additional, or light Companies will be most consistent with the genius of our Countrymen and perhaps in their opinion most consonant to the spirit of our Constitution.

I shall not contend for names or forms, it will be altogether essential, and it will be sufficient that perfect Uniformity should be established throughout the Continent, and pervade, as far as possible, every Corps, whether of standing Troops or Militia, and of whatever denomination they may be. To avoid the confusion of a contrary practice, and to produce the happy consequences which will attend a uniform system of Service, in case Troops from the different parts of the Continent shall ever be brought to Act together again, I would beg leave to propose, that Congress should employ some able hand, to digest a Code of Military Rules and regulations, calculated immediately for the Militia and other Troops of the United States; And as it should seem the present system, by being a little simplified, altered, and improved, might be very well adopted to the purpose; I would take the liberty of recommending, that measures should be immediately taken for the accomplishment of this interesting business, and that an Inspector General should be appointed to superintend the execution of the proposed regulations in the several States.

Congress having fixed upon a proper plan to be established, having caused the Regulations to be compiled, having approved, Printed and distributed them to every General Field Officer, Captain and Adjutant of Militia, will doubtless have taken care, that whenever the system shall be adopted by the States the encouragement on the one hand, and the fines and penalties on the other will occasion an universal and punctual compliance therewith.

Before I close my remarks on the establishment of our National Militia, which is to be the future guardian of those rights and that Independence, which have been maintain'd so gloriously, by the fortitude and perseverance of our Countrymen, I shall descend a little more minutely to the interior arrangements, and sum up what I have to say on this head with the following Positions.

1st. That it appears to me extremely necessary there should

be an Adjutant General appointed in each State, with such Assistants as may be necessary for communicating the Orders of the Commander in Chief of the State, making the details, collecting the Returns and performing every other duty incident to that Office. A duplicate of the Annual Returns should always be lodged in the War Office by the 25th of Decr. in every year, for the information of Congress; with any other reports that may be judged expedient. The Adjutant Generals and Assistants to be considered as the deputies of the Inspector General, and to assist him in carrying the system of Discipline into effect.

2d. That every Militia Officer should make himself acquainted with the plan of Discipline, within a limited time, or forfeit his Commission, for it is in vain to expect the improvement of the Men, while the Officers remain ignorant, which many of them will do, unless Government will make and enforce such a Regulation.

3dly. That the formation of the Troops ought to be perfectly simple and entirely uniform, for example each Regiment should be composed of two Battalions, each Battalion to consist of 4 Companies and each Company as at present of 1 Captain, 1 Lieutenant, 1 Ensign, 5 Sergeants, 3 Corporals, 2 Music, 65 Privates.

Two Battalions should form a Regiment four Regts a Brigade and two Brigades a Division. This might be the general formation; but as I before observed, I conceive it will be eligible to select from the district forming a Regiment, the flower of the young Men to compose an additional or light Company to every Regiment, for the purposes before specified, which undoubtedly ought to be the case unless something like a Continental Militia shall be instituted. To each Division two Troops of Cavalry and two Companies of Artillery might also be annexed, but no Independent or Volunteer Companies foreign to the Establishment should be tolerated.

4thly. It is also indispensable that such a proportion of the Militia (under whatever discription they are comprehended) as are always to be held in readiness for service, nearly in the same manner the Minute Men formerly were, should be excercised at least from 12 to 25 days in a year, part of the time in

Company, part in Battalion and part in Brigade, in the latter case, by forming a Camp, their Discipline would be greatly promoted, and their Ideas raised, as near as possible, to real service; Twenty five days might be divided thus, ten days for training in squads, half Companies and Companies, ten in Battalion and five in Brigade.

5thly. While in the Field or on actual duty, there should not only be a Compensation for the time thus spent, but a full allowance of Provisions Straw, Camp Equipage &c; it is also of so great consequence that there should be, a perfect similarity in the Arms and Accoutrements, that they ought to be furnished, in the first instance by the public, if they cannot be obtained in any other way, some kind of Regimentals or Uniform Clothing (however cheap or course they may be) are also highly requisite and should be provided for such occasions. Nor is it unimportant that every Article should be stamped with the appearance of regularity; and especially that all the Articles of public property should be numbered, marked or branded with the name of the Regiment or Corps that they may be properly accounted for.

6thly. In addition to the Continental Arsenals, which will be treated of under the next head. Every State ought to Establish Magazines of its own, containing Arms, Accoutrements, Ammunitions, all kinds of Camp Equipage and Warlike Stores, and from which the Militia or any part of them should be supplied whenever they are call'd into the Field.

7thly. It is likewise much to be wished, that it might be made agreeable to Officers who have served in the Army, to accept Commands in the Militia; that they might be appointed to them so far as can be done without creating uneasiness and jealousy, and that the principle Characters in the Community would give a countenance to Military improvements, by being present at public reviews and Exhibitions, and by bringing into estimation amongst their fellow Citizens, those who appear fond of cultivating Military knowledge and who excel in the Exercise of Arms. By giving such a tone to our Establishment; by making it universally reputable to bear Arms and disgraceful to decline having a share in the performance of Military duties; in fine, by keeping up in Peace "a well regulated, and disciplined Militia," we shall take the fairest and best method to preserve, for a long time to come, the happiness, dignity and Independence of our Country.

With regard to the third Head in Contemplation, to wit. the "Establishment of Arsenals of all kinds of Military Stores." I will only observe, that having some time since seen a plan of the Secretary of War, which went fully into the discussion of this branch of Arrangement, and appeared (as well as I can, at this time recollect) to be in general perfectly well founded, little more need be said on the subject, especially as I have been given to understand the plan has been lately considerably improved and laid before Congress for their approbation; and indeed there is only one or two points in which I could wish to suggest any Alteration.

According to my recollection, five grand Magazines are proposed by the Secretary at War, one of which to be fixed at West Point. Now, as West Point is considered not only by our selves, but by all who have the least knowledge of the Country, as a post of the greatest importance, as it may in time of Peace, from its situation on the Water be somewhat obnoxious to surprise or *Coup de Main* and as it would doubtless be a first object with any Nation which might commence a War against the United States, to seize that Post and occupy or destroy the Stores, it appears to me, that we ought particularly to guard against such an event, so far as may be practicable, and to remove some part of the Allurements to enterprise, by establishing the grand Arsenals in the Interior part of the Country, leaving only to West Point an adequate supply for its defence in almost any extremity.

I take the liberty also to submit to the consideration of the Committee, whether, instead of five great Arsenals, it would not be less expensive and equally convenient and advantageous to fix three general Deposits, one for the Southern, one for the Middle and one for the Eastern States, including New York, in each of which there might be deposited, Arms, Ammunition, Field Artillery, and Camp Equipage for thirty thousand Men, Also one hundred heavy Cannon and Mortars, and all the Apparatus of a Siege, with a sufficiency of Ammunition.

Under the fourth General Division of the subject, it was proposed to consider the Establishment of Military Academies and Manufactures, as the means of preserving that knowledge and being possessed of those Warlike Stores, which are essential to the support of the Sovereignty and Independence of the United States. But as the Baron Steuben has thrown together his Ideas very largely on these Articles, which he had communicated to me previous to their being sent to the secretary at War, and which being now lodged at the War Office, I imagine have also been submitted to the inspection of the Committee, I shall therefore have the less occasion for entering into the detail, and may, without impropriety, be the more concise in my own observations.

That an Institution calculated to keep alive and diffuse the knowledge of the Military Art would be highly expedient, and that some kinds of Military Manufactories and Elaboratories may and ought to be established, will not admit a doubt; but how far we are able at this time to go into great and expensive Arrangements and whether the greater part of the Military Apparatus and Stores which will be wanted can be imported or Manufactured, in the cheapest and best manner: I leave those to whom the observations are to be submitted, to determine, as being more competent, to the decision than I can pretend to be. I must however mention some things, which I think cannot be dispensed with under the present or any other circumstances; Until a more perfect system of Education can be adopted, I would propose that Provision should be made at some Post or Posts where the principle Engineers and Artillerists shall be stationed, for instructing a certain number of young Gentlemen in the Theory of the Art of War, particularly in all those branches of service which belong to the Artillery and Engineering Departments. Which, from the affinity they bear to each other, and the advantages which I think would result from the measure, I would have blended together; And as this species of knowledge will render them much more accomplished and capable of performing the duties of Officers, even in the Infantry or any other Corps whatsoever, I conceive that appointments to vacancies in the Established Regiments, ought to be made from the candidates who shall have completed their course of Military Studies and Exercises. As it does in an essential manner qualify them for the duties of Garrisons, which will be the principal, if not only service in which our Troops can be employed in time of Peace and besides the Regiments of Infantry by this means will become in time a nursery from whence a number of Officers for Artillery and Engineering may be drawn on any great or sudden occasion.

Of so great importance is it to preserve the knowledge which has been acquired thro' the various Stages of a long and arduous service, that I cannot conclude without repeating the necessity of the proposed Institution, unless we intend to let the Science become extinct, and to depend entirely upon the Foreigners for their friendly aid, if ever we should again be involved in Hostility. For it must be understood, that a Corps of able Engineers and expert Artillerists cannot be raised in a day, nor made such by any exertions, in the same time, which it would take to form an excellent body of Infantry from a well regulated Militia.

And as to Manufactories and Elaboratories it is my opinion that if we should not be able to go largely into the business at present, we should nevertheless have a reference to such establishments hereafter, and in the meantime that we ought to have such works carried on, wherever our principal Arsenals may be fixed, as will not only be sufficient to repair and keep in good order the Arms, Artillery, Stores &c of the Post, but shall also extend to Founderies and some other essential matters.

Thus have I given my sentiments without reserve on the four different heads into which the subject seemed naturally to divide itself, as amply as my numerous avocations and various duties would permit. Happy shall I be, if any thing I have suggested may be found of use in forming an Establishment which will maintain the lasting Peace, Happiness and Independence of the United States.

CIRCULAR TO THE STATES

In the two months following the declaration of the cessation of hostilities, Washington's documents relate to General Orders on camp discipline and provisions, the discharge of troops, the distribution of honors, memorials, proclamations and the long memorandum, "Sentiments on a Peace Establishment" (the preceding item in this volume). While that document embodies his ideas for military security in almost professional terms, "Circular to the States" gives, in essence, the political philosophy, with an admixture of his military principles, by which he hopes freedom, unity, justice and community of effort among all the States can be made certain and lasting.

Head Quarters, Newburgh, June 8, 1783

SIR: The great object for which I had the honor to hold an appointment in the Service of my Country, being accomplished, I am now preparing to resign it into the hands of Congress, and to return to that domestic retirement, which, it is well known, I left with the greatest reluctance, a Retirement, for which I have never ceased to sigh through a long and painful absence, and in which (remote from the noise and trouble of the World) I meditate to pass the remainder of life in a state of undisturbed repose; But before I carry this resolution into effect, I think it a duty incumbent on me, to make this my last official communication, to congratulate you on the glorious events which Heaven has been pleased to produce in our favor, to offer my sentiments respecting some important subjects, which appear to me, to be intimately connected with the tranquility of the United States, to take my leave of your Excellency as a public Character, and to give my final blessing to that Country, in whose service I have spent the prime of my life, for whose sake I have consumed so many anxious days and watchfull nights, and whose happiness being extremely dear to me, will always constitute no inconsiderable part of my own.

Impressed with the liveliest sensibility on this pleasing occasion, I will claim the indulgence of dilating the more copiously on the subjects of our mutual felicitation. When we consider the magnitude of the prize we contended for, the doubtful nature of the contest, and the favorable manner in which it has terminated, we shall find the greatest possible reason for gratitude and rejoicing; this is a theme that will afford infinite delight to every benevolent and liberal mind, whether the event in contemplation, be considered as the source of present enjoyment or the parent of future happiness; and we shall have equal occasion to felicitate ourselves on the lot which Providence has assigned us, whether we view it in a natural, a political or moral point of light.

The Citizens of America, placed in the most enviable condition, as the sole Lords and Proprietors of a vast Tract of Continent, comprehending all the various soils and climates of the World, and abounding with all the necessaries and conveniencies of life, are now by the late satisfactory pacification, acknowledged to be possessed of absolute freedom and Independency; They are, from this period, to be considered as the Actors on a most conspicuous Theatre, which seems to be peculiarly designated by Providence for the display of human greatness and felicity; Here, they are not only surrounded with every thing which can contribute to the completion of private and domestic enjoyment, but Heaven has crowned all its other blessings, by giving a fairer oppertunity for political happiness, than any other Nation has ever been favored with. Nothing can illustrate these observations more forcibly, than a recollection of the happy conjuncture of times and circumstances, under which our Republic assumed its rank among the Nations; The foundation of our Empire was not laid in the gloomy age of Ignorance and Superstition, but at an Epocha when the rights of mankind were better understood and more clearly defined, than at any former period, the researches of the human mind, after social happiness, have been carried to a great extent, the Treasures of knowledge, acquired by the labours of Philosophers, Sages and Legislatures, through a long succession of years, are laid open for our use, and their collected wisdom may be happily applied in the Establishment of our forms of Government; the free cultivation of Letters, the unbounded extension of Commerce, the progressive refinement of Manners, the growing liberality of sentiment, and above all, the pure and benign light of Revelation, have had a meliorating influence on mankind and increased the blessings of

Society. At this auspicious period, the United States came into existence as a Nation, and if their Citizens should not be completely free and happy, the fault will be intirely their own.

Such is our situation, and such are our prospects: but notwithstanding the cup of blessing is thus reached out to us, notwithstanding happiness is ours, if we have a disposition to seize the occasion and make it our own; yet, it appears to me there is an option still left to the United States of America, that it is in their choice, and depends upon their conduct, whether they will be respectable and prosperous, or contemptable and miserable as a Nation; This is the time of their political probation, this is the moment when the eyes of the whole World are turned upon them, this is the moment to establish or ruin their national Character forever, this is the favorable moment to give such a tone to our Federal Government, as will enable it to answer the ends of its institution, or this may be the ill-fated moment for relaxing the powers of the Union, annihilating the cement of the Confederation, and exposing us to become the sport of European politics, which may play one State against another to prevent their growing importance, and to serve their own interested purposes. For, according to the system of Policy the States shall adopt at this moment, they will stand or fall, and by their confirmation or lapse, it is yet to be decided, whether the Revolution must ultimately be considered as a blessing or a curse: a blessing or a curse, not to the present age alone, for with our fate will the destiny of unborn Millions be involved.

With this conviction of the importance of the present Crisis, silence in me would be a crime; I will therefore speak to your Excellency, the language of freedom and of sincerity, without disguise; I am aware, however, that those who differ from me in political sentiment, may perhaps remark, I am stepping out of the proper line of my duty, and they may possibly ascribe to arrogance or ostentation, what I know is alone the result of the purest intention, but the rectitude of my own heart, which disdains such unworthy motives, the part I have hitherto acted in life, the determination I have formed, of not taking any share in public business hereafter, the ardent desire I feel, and shall continue to manifest, of quietly enjoying in private life, after all the toils of War, the benefits of a wise and liberal Government, will, I flatter myself, sooner or later convince my Countrymen, that I could have no sinister views in delivering with so little reserve, the opinions contained in this Address.

There are four things, which I humbly conceive, are essential to the well being, I may even venture to say, to the existence of the United States as an Independent Power:

1st. An indissoluble Union of the States under one Federal Head.

2dly. A sacred regard to Public Justice.

3dly. The adoption of a proper Peace Establishment, and

4thly. The prevalence of that pacific and friendly Disposition, among the People of the United States, which will induce them to forget their local prejudices and policies, to make those mutual concessions which are requisite to the general prosperity, and in some instances, to sacrifice their individual advantages to the interest of the Community.

These are the Pillars on which the glorious Fabrick of our Independency and National Character must be supported; Liberty is the Basis, and whoever would dare to sap the foundation, or overturn the Structure, under whatever specious pretexts he may attempt it, will merit the bitterest execration, and the severest punishment which can be inflicted by his injured Country.

On the three first Articles I will make a few observations, leaving the last to the good sense and serious consideration of those immediately concerned.

Under the first head, altho' it may not be necessary or proper for me in this place to enter into a particular disquisition of the principles of the Union, and to take up the great question which has been frequently agitated, whether it be expedient and requisite for the States to delegate a larger proportion of Power to Congress, or not, Yet it will be a part of my duty, and that of every true Patriot, to assert without reserve, and to insist upon the following positions, That unless the States will suffer Congress to exercise those prerogatives, they are undoubtedly invested with by the Constitution, every thing must very rapidly tend to Anarchy and confusion, That it is indispensable to the happiness of the individual States, that there should be lodged somewhere, a Supreme Power to regulate and govern the general concerns of the Confederated Republic, without which the Union cannot be of long duration. That there must be a faithful and pointed compliance on the part of every State, with the late proposals and demands of Congress, or the most fatal consequences will ensue, That whatever measures have a tendency to dissolve the Union, or contribute to violate or lessen the Sovereign Authority, ought to be considered as hostile to the Liberty and Independency of America, and the Authors of them treated accordingly, and lastly, that unless we can be enabled by the concurrence of the States, to participate of the fruits of the Revolution, and enjoy the essential benefits of Civil Society, under a form of Government so free and uncorrupted, so happily guarded against the danger of oppression, as has been devised and adopted by the Articles of Confederation, it will be a subject of regret, that so much blood and treasure have been lavished for no purpose, that so many sufferings have been encountered without a compensation, and that so many sacrifices have been made in vain. Many other considerations might here be adduced to prove, that without an entire conformity to the Spirit of the Union, we cannot exist as an Independent Power; it will be sufficient for my purpose to mention but one or two which seem to me of the greatest importance. It is only in our united Character as an Empire, that our Independence is acknowledged, that our power can be regarded, or our Credit supported among Foreign Nations. The Treaties of the European Powers with the United States of America, will have no validity on a dissolution of the Union. We shall be left nearly in a state of Nature, or we may find by our own unhappy experience, that there is a natural and necessary progression, from the extreme of anarchy to the extreme of Tyranny; and that arbitrary power is most easily established on the ruins of Liberty abused to licentiousness.

As to the second Article, which respects the performance of Public Justice, Congress have, in their late Address to the United States, almost exhausted the subject, they have explained their Ideas so fully, and have enforced the obligations the States are under, to render compleat justice to all the Public Creditors, with so much dignity and energy, that in my opinion, no real friend to the honor and Independency of America, can hesitate a single moment respecting the propriety of complying with the just and honorable measures proposed; if their Arguments do not produce conviction, I know of nothing that will have greater influence; especially when we recollect that the System referred to, being the result of the collected Wisdom of the Continent, must be esteemed, if not perfect, certainly the least objectionable of any that could be devised; and that if it shall not be carried into immediate execution, a National Bankruptcy, with all its deplorable consequences will take place, before any different Plan can possibly be proposed and adopted; So pressing are the present circumstances! and such is the alternative now offered to the States!

The ability of the Country to discharge the debts which have been incurred in its defence, is not to be doubted, an inclination, I flatter myself, will not be wanting, the path of our duty is plain before us, honesty will be found on every experiment, to be the best and only true policy, let us then as a Nation be just, let us fulfil the public Contracts, which Congress had undoubtedly a right to make for the purpose of carrying on the War, with the same good faith we suppose ourselves bound to perform our private engagements; in the mean time, let an attention to the chearfull performance of their proper business, as Individuals, and as members of Society, be earnestly inculcated on the Citizens of America, that will they strengthen the hands of Government, and be happy under its protection: every one will reap the fruit of his labours, every one will enjoy his own acquisitions without molestation and without danger.

In this state of absolute freedom and perfect security, who will grudge to yield a very little of his property to support the common interest of Society, and insure the protection of Government? Who does not remember, the frequent declarations, at the commencement of the War, that we should be compleatly satisfied, if at the expence of one half, we could defend the remainder of our possessions? Where is the Man to be found, who wishes to remain indebted, for the defence of his own person and property, to the exertions, the bravery, and the blood of others, without making one generous effort to repay the debt of honor and of gratitude? In what part of the Continent shall we find any Man, or body of Men, who would not blush to stand up and propose measures, purposely calculated to rob the Soldier of his Stipend, and the Public Creditor of his due? and were it possible that such a flagrant instance of Injustice could ever happen, would it not excite the general indignation, and tend to bring down, upon the Authors of such measures, the aggravated vengeance of Heaven? If after all, a spirit of disunion or a temper of obstinacy and perverseness, should manifest itself in any of the States, if such an ungracious disposition should attempt to frustrate all the happy effects that might be expected to flow from the Union, if there should be a refusal to comply with the requisitions for Funds to discharge the annual interest of the public debts, and if that refusal should revive again all those jealousies and produce all those evils, which are now happily removed, Congress, who have in all their Transaction shewn a great degree of magnanimity and justice, will stand justified in the sight of God and Man, and the State alone which puts itself in opposition to the aggregate Wisdom of the Continent, and follows such mistaken and pernicious Councils, will be responsible for all the consequences.

For my own part, conscious of having acted while a Servant of the Public, in the manner I conceived best suited to promote the real interests of my Country; having in consequence of my fixed belief in some measure pledged myself to the Army, that their Country would finally do them compleat and ample Justice; and not wishing to conceal any instance of my official conduct from the eyes of the World, I have thought proper to transmit to your Excellency the inclosed collection of Papers, relative to the half pay and commutation granted by Congress to the Officers of the Army; From these communications, my decided sentiment will be clearly comprehended, together with the conclusive reasons which induced me, at an early period, to recommend the adoption of the measure, in the most earnest and serious manner. As the proceedings of Congress, the Army, and myself are open to all, and contain in my opinion, sufficient information to remove the prejudices and errors which may have been entertained by any; I think it unnecessary to say any thing more, than just to observe, that the Resolutions of Congress, now alluded to, are undoubtedly as absolutely binding upon the United States, as the most solemn Acts of Confederation or Legislation. As to the Idea, which I am informed has in some instances prevailed, that the half pay and commutation are to be regarded merely in the odious light of a Pension, it ought to be exploded forever; that Provision, should be viewed as it really was, a reasonable compensation offered by Congress, at a time when they had nothing else to give, to the Officers of the Army, for services then to be performed. It was the only means to prevent a total dereliction of the Service, It was a part of their hire, I may be allowed to say, it was the price of their blood and of your Independency, it is therefore more than a common debt, it is a debt of honour, it can never be considered as a Pension or gratuity, nor be cancelled until it is fairly discharged.

With regard to a distinction between Officers and Soldiers, it is sufficient that the uniform experience of every Nation of the World, combined with our own, proves the utility and propriety of the discrimination. Rewards in proportion to the aids the public derives from them, are unquestionably due to all its Servants; In some Lines, the Soldiers have perhaps generally had as ample a compensation for their Services, by the large Bounties which have been paid to them, as their Officers will receive in the proposed Commutation, in others, if besides the donation of Lands, the payment of Arrearages of Cloathing and Wages (in which Articles all the component parts of the Army must be put upon the same footing) we take into the estimate, the Bounties many of the Soldiers have received and the gratuity of one Year's full pay, which is promised to all, possibly their situation (every circumstance being duly considered) will not be deemed less eligible than that of the Officers. Should a farther reward, however, be judged equitable, I will venture to assert, no one will enjoy greater satisfaction than myself, on seeing an exemption from Taxes for a limited time, (which has been petitioned for in some instances) or any other adequate immunity or compensation, granted to the brave defenders of their Country's Cause; but neither the adoption or rejection of this proposition will in any manner affect, much less militate against, the Act of Congress, by which they have offered five years full pay, in lieu of the half pay for life, which had been before promised to the Officers of the Army.

Before I conclude the subject of public justice, I cannot omit to mention the obligations this Country is under, to that meritorious Class of veteran Non-commissioned Officers and Privates, who have been discharged for inability, in consequence of the Resolution of Congress of the 23d of April 1782, on an annual pension for life, their peculiar sufferings, their singular merits and claims to that provision need only be known, to interest all the feelings of humanity in their behalf: nothing but a punctual payment of their annual allowance can rescue them from the most complicated misery, and nothing could be a more melancholy and distressing sight, than to behold those who have shed their blood or lost their limbs in the service of their Country, without a shelter, without a friend, and without the means of obtaining any of the necessaries or comforts of Life; compelled to beg their daily bread from door to door! suffer me to recommend those of this discription, belonging to your State, to the warmest patronage of your Excellency and your Legislature.

It is necessary to say but a few words on the third topic which was proposed, and which regards particularly the defence of the Republic, As there can be little doubt but Congress will recommend a proper Peace Establishment for the United States, in which a due attention will be paid to the importance of placing the Militia of the Union upon a regular and respectable footing; If this should be the case, I would beg leave to urge the great advantage of it in the strongest terms. The Militia of this Country must be considered as the Palladium of our security, and the first effectual resort in case of hostility; It is essential therefore, that the same system should pervade the whole; that the formation and discipline of the Militia of the Continent should be absolutely uniform, and that the same species of Arms, Accoutrements and Military Apparatus, should be introduced in every part of the United States; No one, (who has not learned it from experience, can conceive the difficulty, expence, and confusion which result from a contrary system, or the vague Arrangements which have hitherto prevailed.

If in treating of political points, a greater latitude than usual has been taken in the course of this Address, the importance of the Crisis, and the magnitude of the objects in discussion, must be my apology: It is, however, neither my wish or expectation, that the preceding observations should claim any regard, except so far as they shall appear to be dictated by a good intention, consonant to the immutable rules of Justice; calculated to produce a liberal system of policy, and founded on whatever experience may have been acquired by a long and close attention to public business. Here I might speak with the more confidence from my actual observations, and, if it would not swell this Letter (already too prolix) beyond the bounds I had prescribed myself: I could demonstrate to every mind open to conviction, that in less time and with much less expence than has been incurred, the War might have been brought to the same happy conclusion, if the resourses of the Continent could have been properly drawn forth, that the distresses and disappointments which have very often occurred, have in too many instances, resulted more from a want of energy, in the Continental Government, than a deficiency of means in the particular States. That the inefficiency of measures, arising from the want of an adequate authority in the Supreme Power, from a partial compliance with the Requisitions of Congress in some of the States, and from a failure of punctuality in others, while it tended to damp the zeal of those which were more willing to exert themselves; served also to accumulate the expences of the War, and to frustrate the best concerted Plans, and that the discouragement occasioned by the complicated difficulties and embarrassments, in which our affairs were, by this means involved, would have long ago produced the dissolution of any Army, less patient, less virtuous and less persevering, than that which I have had the honor to command. But while I mention these things, which are notorious facts, as the defects of our Federal Constitution, particularly in the prosecution of a War, I beg it may be understood, that as I have ever taken a pleasure in gratefully acknowledging the assistance and support I have derived from every Class of Citizens, so shall I always be happy to do justice to the unparalleled exertion of the individual States, on many interesting occasions.

I have thus freely disclosed what I wished to make known, before I surrendered up my Public trust to those who committed it to me, the task is now accomplished, I now bid adieu to your Excellency as the Chief Magistrate of your State, at the same time I bid a last farewell to the cares of Office, and all the imployments of public life.

It remains then to be my final and only request, that your Excellency will communicate these sentiments to your Legislature at their next meeting, and that they may be considered as the Legacy of One, who has ardently wished, on all occasions, to be useful to his Country, and who, even in the shade of Retirement, will not fail to implore the divine benediction upon it.

I now make it my earnest prayer, that God would have you, and the State over which you preside, in his holy protection, that he would incline the hearts of the Citizens to cultivate a spirit of subordination and obedience to Government, to entertain a brotherly affection and love for one another, for their fellow Citizens of the United States at large, and particularly for their brethren who have served in the Field, and finally, that he would most graciously be pleased to dispose us all, to do Justice, to love mercy, and to demean ourselves with that Charity, humility and pacific temper of mind, which were the Characteristicks of the Divine Author of our blessed Religion, and without an humble imitation of whose example in these things, we can never hope to be a happy Nation.

FAREWELL ORDERS TO THE ARMIES OF THE UNITED STATES

The definitive Treaty of Peace was signed in Paris on September 3, 1783. Washington at that time had established his Headquarters at Rocky Hill, a short distance from Princeton, New Jersey, and from there he took final leave of the Army.

Rock Hill, near Princeton, November 2, 1783

The United States in Congress assembled after giving the most honorable testimony to the merits of the fœderal Armies, and presenting them with the thanks of their Country for their long, eminent, and faithful services, having thought proper by their proclamation bearing date the 18th. day of October last. to discharge such part of the Troops as were engaged for the war, and to permit the Officers on furlough to retire from service from and after to-morrow; which proclamation having been communicated in the publick papers for the information and government of all concerned; it only remains for the Comdr in Chief to address himself once more, and that for the last time, to the Armies of the U States (however widely dispersed the individuals who compose them may be) and to bid them an affectionate, a long farewell.

But before the Comdr in Chief takes his final leave of those he holds most dear, he wishes to indulge himself a few moments in calling to mind a slight review of the past. He will then take the liberty of exploring, with his military friends, their future prospects, of advising the general line of conduct, which in his opinion, ought to be pursued, and he will conclude the Address by expressing the obligations he feels himself under for the spirited and able assistance he has experienced from them in the performance of an arduous Office.

A contemplation of the compleat attainment (at a period earlier than could have been expected) of the object for which we contended against so formidable a power cannot but inspire us with astonishment and gratitude. The disadvantageous circumstances on our part, under which the war was undertaken, can never be forgotten. The singular interpositions of Providence in our feeble condition were such, as could scarcely escape the attention of the most unobserving; while the unparalleled perseverance of the Armies of the U States, through almost every possible suffering and discouragement for the space of eight long years, was little short of a standing miracle.

It is not the meaning nor within the compass of this address to detail the hardships peculiarly incident to our service, or to describe the distresses, which in several instances have resulted from the extremes of hunger and nakedness, combined with the rigours of an inclement season; nor is it necessary to dwell on the dark side of our past affairs. Every American Officer and Soldier must now console himself for any unpleasant circumstances which may have occurred by a recollection of the uncommon scenes in which he has been called to Act no inglorious part, and the astonishing events of which he has been a witness, events which have seldom if ever before taken place on the stage of human action, nor can they probably ever happen again. For who has before seen a disciplined Army form'd at once from such raw materials? Who, that was not a witness, could imagine that the most violent local prejudices would cease so soon, and that Men who came from the different parts of the Continent, strongly disposed, by the habits of education, to despise and quarrel with each other, would instantly become but one patriotic band of Brothers, or who, that was not on the spot, can trace the steps by which such a wonderful revolution has been effected, and such a glorious period put to all our warlike toils?

It is universally acknowledged, that the enlarged prospects of happiness, opened by the confirmation of our independence and sovereignty, almost exceeds the power of description. And shall not the brave men, who have contributed so essentially to these inestimable acquisitions, retiring victorious from the field of War to the field of agriculture, participate in all the blessings which have been obtained; in such a republic, who will exclude them from the rights of Citizens and the fruits of their labour. In such a Country, so happily circumstanced, the pursuits of Commerce and the cultivation of the soil will unfold to industry the certain road to competence. To those hardy Soldiers, who are actuated by the spirit of adventure the Fisheries will afford ample and profitable employment, and the extensive and fertile regions of the West will yield a most happy asylum to those, who, fond of domestic enjoyments are seeking for personal independence. Nor is it possible to conceive, that any one of the U States will prefer a national bankruptcy and a dissolution of the union, to a compliance with the requisitions of Congress and the payment of its just debts; so that the Officers and Soldiers may expect considerable assistance in recommencing their civil occupations from the sums due to them from the public, which must and will most inevitably be paid.

In order to effect this desirable purpose and to remove the prejudices which may have taken possession of the minds of any of the good people of the States, it is earnestly recommended to all the Troops that with strong attachments to the Union, they should carry with them into civil society the most conciliating dispositions; and that they should prove themselves not less virtuous and useful as Citizens, than they have been persevering and victorious as Soldiers. What tho, there should be some envious individuals who are unwilling to pay the debt the public has contracted, or to yield the tribute due to merit; yet, let such unworthy treatment produce no invective or any instance of intemperate conduct; let it be remembered that the unbiassed voice of the few Citizens of the United States has promised the just reward, and given the merited applause; let it be known and remembered, that the reputation of the foederal Armies is established beyond the reach of malevolence; and let a conscientiousness of their achievements and fame still unite the men, who composed them to honourable actions; under the persuasion that the private virtues of oeconomy, prudence, and industry, will not be less amiable in civil life, than the more splendid qualities of valour, perseverance, and enterprise were in the Field. Every one may rest assured that much, very much of the future happiness of the Officers and Men will depend upon the wise and manly conduct which shall be adopted by them when they are mingled with the great body of the community. And, altho the General has so frequently given it as his opinion, in the most public and explicit manner, that, unless the principles of the federal government were properly supported and the powers of the union increased, the honour, dignity, and justice of the nation would be lost forever. Yet he cannot help repeating, on this occasion, so interesting a sentiment, and leaving it as his last injunction to every Officer and every Soldier, who may view the subject in the same serious point of light, to add his best endeavours to those of his worthy fellow Citizens towards effecting these great and valuable purposes on which our very existence as a nation so materially depends.

The Commander in chief conceives little is now wanting to enable the Soldiers to change the military character into that of the Citizen, but that steady and decent tenor of behaviour which has generally distinguished, not only the Army under his immediate command, but the different detachments and seperate Armies through the course of the war. From their good sense and prudence he anticipates the happiest consequences; and while he congratulates them on the glorious occasion, which renders their services in the field no longer necessary, he wishes to express the strong obligations he feels himself under for the assistance he has received from every Class, and in every instance. He presents his thanks in the most serious and affectionate manner to the General Officers, as well for their counsel on many interesting occasions, as for their Order in promoting the success of the plans he had adopted. To the Commandants of Regiments and Corps, and to the other Officers for their great zeal and attention, in carrying his orders promptly into execution. To the Staff, for their alacrity and exactness in performing the Duties of their several Departments. And to the Non Commissioned Officers and private Soldiers, for their extraordinary patience in suffering, as well as their invincible fortitude in Action. To the various branches of the Army the General takes this last and solemn opportunity of professing his inviolable attachment and friendship. He wishes more than bare professions were in his power, that he were really able to be useful to them all in future life. He flatters himself however, they will do him the justice to believe, that whatever could with propriety be attempted by him has been done, and being now to conclude these his last public Orders, to take his ultimate leave in a short time of the military character, and to bid a final adieu to the Armies he has so long had the honor to Command, he can only again offer in their behalf his recommendations to their grateful country, and his prayers to the God of Armies. May ample justice be done them here, and may the choicest of heaven's favours, both here and hereafter, attend those who, under the divine auspices, have secured innumerable blessings for others; with these wishes, and this benediction, the Commander in Chief is about to retire from Service. The Curtain of seperation will soon be drawn, and the military scene to him will be closed for ever.

ADDRESS TO CONGRESS ON RESIGNING HIS COMMISSION

Washington's appearance before Congress was marked by solemn etiquette. A committee of three—Thomas Jefferson, Elbridge Gerry and James McHenry—arranged the proceedings to do honor to the retiring Commander in Chief. On the previous day, a public dinner, attended by two or three hundred men, was enlivened by many toasts. That night the Governor gave a ball in the State House, and witnesses declared that Washington did not miss a dance. After the delivery of his Address to Congress on Resigning His Commission, he bade farewell to every member of Congress individually and set off for Mount Vernon for, at first, the Christmas celebrations and then for what he thought would be the life of retirement awaiting him on his estate.

Annapolis, December 23, 1783

MR. PRESIDENT: The great events on which my resignation depended having at length taken place; I have now the honor of offering my sincere Congratulations to Congress and of presenting myself before them to surrender into their hands the trust committed to me, and to claim the indulgence of retiring from the Service of my Country.

Happy in the confirmation of our Independence and Sovereignty, and pleased with the oppertunity afforded the United States of becoming a respectable Nation, I resign with satisfaction the Appointment I accepted with diffidence. A diffidence in my abilities to accomplish so arduous a task, which however was superseded by a confidence in the rectitude of our Cause, the support of the Supreme Power of the Union, and the patronage of Heaven.

The Successful termination of the War has verified the most sanguine expectations, and my gratitude for the interposition of Providence, and the assistance I have received from my Countrymen, encreases with every review of the momentous Contest.

While I repeat my obligations to the Army in general, I should do injustice to my own feelings not to acknowledge in this place the peculiar Services and distinguished merits of the Gentlemen who have been attached to my person during the War. It was impossible the choice of confidential Officers to compose my family should have been more fortunate. Permit me Sir, to recommend in particular those, who have continued in Service to the present moment, as worthy of the favorable notice and patronage of Congress.

I consider it an indispensable duty to close this last solemn act of my Official life, by commending the Interests of our dearest Country to the protection of Almighty God, and those who have the superintendence of them, to his holy keeping.

Having now finished the work assigned me, I retire from the great theatre of Action; and bidding an Affectionate farewell to this August body under whose orders I have so long acted, I here offer my Commission, and take my leave of all the employments of public life.

Part Three

THE
PRESIDENCY

To MARQUIS DE LAFAYETTE

Now retired to his estate in Mount Vernon, Washington devoted himself to the affairs of a landed proprietor. This is not to say that he detached himself completely from matters of public concern. Two weeks before writing the following letter to Lafayette, he expressed his anxiety, in a letter to Governor Benjamin Harrison, over "the disinclination of the individual States to yield competent powers to Congress for the Federal Government, their unreasonable jealousy of that body and of one another, and the disposition which seems to pervade each of being all-wise and all-powerful within itself. . . . My political creed therefore is to be wise in the choice of Delegates, support them like Gentlemen while they are our representatives, give them competent powers for all federal purposes, support them in due exercise thereof, and lastly, to compel them to close attendance in Congress during their delegation."

In postponing a promised visit to France, Washington did not realize that he would never leave the shores of America. He was content to look forward to tranquil days at Mount Vernon, with fox-hunting as his relaxation and the management of his huge properties as his only business.

Mount Vernon, February 1, 1784

At length my Dear Marquis I am become a private citizen on the banks of the Potomac, and under the shadow of my own Vine and my own Fig-tree, free from the bustle of a camp and the busy scenes of public life, I am solacing myself with those tranquil enjoyments, of which the Soldier who is ever in pursuit of fame, the Statesman whose watchful days and sleepless nights are spent in devising schemes to promote the welfare of his own, perhaps the ruin of other countries, as if this globe was insufficient for us all, and the Courtier who is always watching the countenance of his Prince, in hopes of catching a gracious smile, can have very little conception. I am not only retired from all public employments, but I am retiring within myself; and shall be able to view the solitary walk, and tread the paths of private life with heartfelt satisfaction. Envious of none, I am determined to be pleased with all; and this my dear friend, being the order for my march, I will move gently down the stream of life, until I sleep with my Fathers.

Except an introductory letter or two, and one countermanding my request respecting plate, I have not written to you since the middle of October by Genl. Duportail. To inform you at this late hour, that the city of New York was evacuated by the British forces on the 25th. of November; that the American Troops took possession of it the same day, and delivered it over to the civil authority of the State; that good order, contrary to the expectation and predictions of Gl. Carleton, his Officers and all the loyalists, was immediately established; and that the harbour of New York was finally cleared of the British flag about the 5th. or 6th. of Decemr., would be an insult to your intelligence. And to tell you that I remained eight days in New York after we took possession of the city; that I was very much hurried during that time, which was the reason I did not write to you from thence; that taking Phila. in my way, I was obliged to remain there a week; that at Annapolis, where Congress were then, and are now sitting, I did, on the 23d. of December present them my commission, and made them my last bow, and on the Eve of Christmas entered these doors an older man by near nine years, than when I left them, is very uninteresting to any but myself. Since that period, we have been fast locked up in frost and snow, and excluded in a manner from all kinds of intercourse, the winter having been, and still continues to be, extremely severe.

I have now to acknowledge, and thank you for your favors of the 22d of July and 8th of September, both of which, altho' the first is of old date, have come to hand since my letter to you of October. The accounts contained therein of the political and commercial state of affairs as they respect America, are interesting, and I wish I could add that they were altogether satisfactory; and the agency you have had in both, particularly with regard to the free ports in France, is a fresh evidence of your unwearied endeavours to serve this country; but there is no part of your Letters to Congress My Dear Marquis, which bespeaks the excellence of your heart more plainly than that, which contains those noble and generous sentiments on the justice which is due to the faithful friends and Servants of the public; but I must do Congress the justice to declare, that as a body, I believe there is every disposition in them, not only to acknowledge the merits, but to reward the services of the army: There is a contractedness, I am sorry to add, in some of the States, from whence all our difficulties on this head, proceed; but it is to be hoped, the good sense and perseverance of the rest, will ultimately prevail, as the spirit of meanness is beginning to subside.

From a letter which I have just received from the Governor of this State* I expect him here in a few days, when I shall not be unmindful of what you have written about the bust, and will endeavour to have matters respecting it, placed on their proper basis. I thank you most sincerely My Dear Marqs. for your kind invitation to your house, if I should come to Paris. At present I see but little prospect of such a voyage, the deranged situation of my private concerns, occasioned by an absence of almost nine years, and an entire disregard of all private business during that period, will not only suspend, but may put it for ever out of my power to gratify this wish. This not being the case with you, come with Madame la Fayette and view me in my domestic walks. I have often told you, and repeat it again, that no man could receive you in them with more friendship and affection than I should do; in which I am sure Mrs. Washington would cordially join me. We unite in respectful compliments to your Lady, and best wishes for your little flock. With every sentiment of esteem, Admiration and Love, I am etc.

* Benjamin Harrison, Governor of Virginia.

To PATRICK HENRY

Washington's unsolicited tribute, as well as his appeal for recognition and aid, in behalf of the fiery author of Common Sense, *is not so much an act of generosity as a simple acknowledgment of services rendered in the cause which both served so differently but so devotedly. It is, incidentally, significant that this letter was written by perhaps the wealthiest man in America for one of its most poverty-stricken patriots.*

Mount Vernon, June 12, 1784

DEAR SIR: After a long silence, more the effect of great hurry and business, than want of inclination; permit me to recall myself to your mind, by introducing to your recollection Mr. Paine, the Author of Commonsense, the Crisis &c.

To say what effect the writings of this Gentleman has had on our public affairs at the epochas at which they were given to the world, would, to a person of your information, be altogether unnecessary; it is more for his interest, and to my present purpose to add, that he stands unrewarded for his exertions in the American cause, is poor, and I believe very much chagrined at the little notice which has been taken of him for his lucubrations.

New York, lately, has testified her sense of his merits by a donation which is very pleasing to him; and from individual States, rather than from Congress (for reasons which seem to have weight in his mind,) he wishes they might be continued in this line. If his services appear in your eyes to merit reward, I am persuaded you will endeavor to do justice to them.

I mention this matter to you equally unsollicited by, as unknown to him; for I never have heard that he has it in contemplation to bring himself before any State in the Union. Convinced as I am of the efficacy of his publications, and of the little attention shewn him for them, I could not with hold

510

this attempt to serve him, and to assure you of the esteem and regard with which I have the honor etc.

To THOMAS JEFFERSON

The project nearest Washington's interest at this time was the study and promotion of inland waterways, linked to the Potomac River, as a means of opening and expanding the western country. Thirty years earlier Washington had made preliminary surveys of the navigability of the Potomac and had submitted a report to Thomas Lee, then President of the Virginia Council. Now, after a tour west of the Appalachian Mountains on a visit to his own lands on the Ohio River, he was more than ever convinced of the feasibility of a water route up the Potomac and James Rivers to the waters of the Ohio and from there to the Great Lakes. The channeling of western trade by water transportation to the eastern seaboard could become tremendously profitable. Such a project involved not only the financing by subscription of shares, but the persuasion of the States affected by the political and commercial advantages of this undertaking. Always scrupulous about receiving money or any other material reward for the services he had rendered his country, Washington refused fifty free shares of the navigation stock and subsequently invested money on his own account.

Mount Vernon, February 25, 1785

DEAR SIR: I had the pleasure to find by the public Gazettes that your passage to France had been short, and pleasant. I have no doubt but that your reception at Court has been equally polite, and agreeable.

I have the honor to inclose you the copy of an Act which passed the Assemblies of Virginia and Maryland at the close of their respective Sessions; about the first of last month. The circumstances of these States, it is said, would not enable them to take the matter up, altogether, on public ground; but they have granted at the joint and equal expence of the two, 6666⅔ dollars for the purpose of opening a road of communication between the highest navigation of the Potomac, and the river Cheat; and have concurred in an application to the State of Pensylvania for leave to open another road from Fort Cumberland or Wills Creek, to the Yohiogany, at the three forks, or Turkey foot.

Besides these joint Acts of the States of Virginia and Maryland; the former has passed a similar law respecting the navigation of James River, and its communications with the Green brier; and have authorized the Executive to appoint Commissioners, who shall carefully examine and fix on the most convenient course for a Canal from the Waters of Elizabeth River in this State, to those passing through the State of North Carolina; and report their proceedings therein, with an estimate of the expence necessary for opening the Same, to the next General Assembly; and in case they shall find that, the best course for such canal, will require the concurrence of the State [*sic*] of North Carolina in the opening thereof, they are further authorized and instructed to signify the same to the said State, and to concert with any person or persons who may be appointed on the part thereof, the most convenient and equitable plan for the execution of such work; and to report the result to the General Assembly.

With what Success the Books will be opened, I cannot, at this early stage of the business, inform you; in general the friends of the measure are better stocked with good wishes than money; the former of which unfortunately, goes but a little way in works where the latter is necessary, and is not to be had. and yet, if this matter could be well understood, it should seem that, there would be no deficiency of the latter, any more than of the former; for certain I am, there is no speculation of which I have an idea, that will ensure such *certain* and *ample* returns of the money advanced, with a great, and encreasing interest, as the tolls arising from these navigations; the accomplishment of which, if funds can be obtained, admits of no more doubt in my mind, under proper direction, than that a ship with skilful Mariners can be carried from hence to Europe. What a misfortune therefore would it be, if a project which is big with such great political consequences, commercial advantages, and which might be made so productive to private Adventurers should miscarry; either from the inability of the two States to execute it, at the public expence, or for want of means, or the want of spirit or foresight to use them, in their citizens. Supposing a danger of this, do you think, Sir, the monied men of France, Holland, England or any other Country with which you may have intercourse, might be induced to become Adventurers in the Scheme? Or if from the remoteness of the object, this should appear ineligable to them, would they incline to lend money to one, or both of these States, if there should be a disposition in them to borrow, for this purpose? Or, to one or more individuals in them, who are able, and would give sufficient security for the repayment? At what interest, and on what conditions respecting time, payment of interest, &ca. could it be obtained?

I forsee such extensive political consequences depending on the navigation of these two rivers, and communicating them by short and easy roads with the waters of the Western territory, that I am pained by every doubt of obtaining the means for their accomplishment: for this reason, I also wish you would be so obliging as to direct your enquiries after one or more characters, who have skill in this kind of work; that if Companies should be incorporated under the present Acts, and should incline to send to France, or England for an Engineer, or Man of practical knowledge in these kinds of works, there may be a clue to the application. You will perceive tho' my dear Sir, that no engagement, obligatory or honorary can be entered into at this time, because no person can answer for the determination of the Companies, admitting their formation.

As I have accustomed myself to communicate matters of difficulty to you, and have met forgiveness for it, I will take the liberty, my good Sir, of troubling you with the rehearsal of one more, which has lately occurred to me. Among the Laws of the last Session of our Assembly, there is an Act which particularly respects myself; and tho' very flattering, is also very embarrassing to me. This Act, after honorable, flattering, and delicate recitals, directs the treasurer of the State to Subscribe towards each of the Navigations fifty Shares for my use and benefit; which it declares, is to be vested in me and my heirs forever. It has ever been my wish, and it is yet my intention, never to receive any thing from the United States, or an individual State for any Services I have hitherto rendered, or which in the course of events, I may have it in my power to render them hereafter as it is not my design to accept of any appointment from the public, which might make emoluments necessary: but how to decline this act of generosity without incurring the imputation of disrespect to my Country, and a slight of her favors on the one hand, or that of pride, or an ostentatious display of disinterestedness on the other, is the difficulty. As none of these have an existence in my breast, I should be sorry, if any of them should be imputed to me. The Assembly, as if determined that I should not act from the first impulse, made this the last act of their Session; without my having the smallest intimation or suspicion of their generous intention. As our Assembly is now to be holden once a year only, I shall have time to hit upon some expedient that will enable me to indulge the bent of my own inclination, without incurring any of the imputations before mentioned; and of hearing the sentiments of my friends upon the subject; than whose, none would be more acceptable than yours.

Your friends in our Assembly will have been able to give you so much better information of what has passed there, and of the general state of matters in this Commonwealth, that a repetition from me is unnecessary, and might be imperfect. If we are to credit News paper Accts. the flames of war are again kindled, or are about to be so, in Europe. None of the sparks, it is to be hoped will cross the Atlantic and touch the inflameable matter in these States. I pray you to believe that with sentimts. of great esteem, etc.

To DAVID HUMPHREYS

Washington's misgivings about his ability to write, his awareness of the defects of his education and his lack of time made him averse to undertaking memoirs or commentaries of any kind. His diaries, letters and public papers are totally without literary pretension, and even his spelling is a matter of convenience and haphazard improvisation. To Humphreys, Wash-

ington expands his ideas on the development of water-borne commerce and its political and economic effects on the young country.

Mount Vernon, July 25, 1785

MY DR. HUMPHREYS: Since my last to you, I have received your letter of the 15th. of January, and I believe that of the 11th. of November, and thank you for them. It always gives me pleasure to hear from you; and I should think if amusements would spare you, business could not so much absorb your time as to prevent your writing more frequently, especially as there is a regular conveyance once a month by the Packet.

As the complexion of European politics seems now (from letters I have received from the Marqs. de la Fayette, Chevrs. Chartellux, De la Luzerne, &c.,) to have a tendency to Peace, I will say nothing of war, nor make any animadversions upon the contending powers; otherwise, I might possibly have said that the retreat from it seemed impossible after the explicit declaration of the parties: My first wish is to see this plague to mankind banished from off the Earth, and the sons and Daughters of this world employed in more pleasing and innocent amusements, than in preparing implements and exercising them for the destruction of mankind: rather than quarrel about territory let the poor, the needy and oppressed of the Earth, and those who want Land, resort to the fertile plains of our western country, the second [land of] Promise, and there dwell in peace, fulfilling the first and great commandment.

In a former letter, I informed you my Dr. Humphreys, that if I had talents for it, I have not leisure to turn my thoughts to commentaries: a consciousness of a defective education, and a certainty of the want of time, unfit me for such an undertaking; what with company, letters and other matters, many of them quite extraneous, I have not been able to arrange my own private concerns so as to rescue them from that disorder'd state into which they have been thrown by the war, and to do which is become absolutely necessary for my support, whilst I remain on this stage of human action. The sentiments of your last letter on this subject gave me great pleasure; I should be pleased indeed to see you undertake this business: your abilities as a writer; your discernment respecting the principles which lead to the decision by arms; your personal knowledge of many facts as they occurred in the progress of the War; your disposition to justice, candour and impartiality, and your diligence in investigating truth, combining fit you, when joined with the vigor of life, for this task; and I should with great pleasure, not only give you the perusal of all my papers, but any oral information of circumstances, which cannot be obtained from the former, that my memory will furnish: and I can with great truth add that my house would not only be at your service during the period of your preparing this work, but (and without an unmeaning compliment I say it) I should be exceedingly happy if you would make it your home. You might have an apartment to yourself, in which you could command your own time; you wou'd be considered and treated as one of the family; and meet with that cordial reception and entertainment which are characteristic of the sincerest friendship.

To reverberate European news would be idle, and we have little of domestic kind worthy of attention: We have held treaties indeed, with the Indians; but they were so unseasonably delayed, that these people by our last accounts from the westward, are in a discontented mood, supposed by many to be instigated thereto by our late enemies, now, to be sure, fast friends; who from any thing I can learn, under the indefinite expression of the treaty hold, and seem resolved to retain possession of our western Posts. Congress have also, after a long and tedious deliberation, passed an ordinance for laying off the Western Territory into States, and for disposing of the land; but in a manner and on terms which few people (in the Southern States) conceive can be accomplished: Both sides are sure, and the event is appealed to, let time decide it. It is however to be regretted that local politics and self-interested views obtrude themselves into every measure of public utility: but to such characters be the consequences.

My attention is more immediately engaged in a project which I think big with great political, as well as commercial consequences to these States, especially the middle ones: it is, by removing the obstructions, and extending the inland navigation of our rivers, to bring the States on the Atlantic in close connexion with those forming to the westward, by a short and easy transportation: without this, I can easily conceive they will have different views, separate interests and other connexions. I may be singular in my ideas; but they are these, that to open a door to, and make easy the way for those Settlers to the westward (which ought to progress regularly and compactly) before we make any stir about the navigation of the Mississippi, and before our settlements are far advanced towards that river, would be our true line of policy. It can, I think, be demonstrated, that the produce of the western Territory (if the navigations which are now in hand succeed, and of which I have no doubt) as low down the Ohio as the Great Kanhawa, I believe to the Falls, and between the parts above and the Lakes, may be brought either to the highest shipping port on this or James river, at a less expence, with more ease, (including the return) and in a much shorter time, than it can be carried to New Orleans if the Spaniards instead of restricting, were to throw open their ports and invite our trade. But if the commerce of that country should embrace this channel, and connexions be formed; experience has taught us (and there is a very recent proof with G: Britain) how next to impracticable it is to divert it; and if that should be the case, the Atlantic States (especially as those to the westward will in a great degree fill with foreigners) will be no more to the present union, except to excite perhaps very justly our fears, than the Country of California which is still more to the westward, and belonging to another power.

Mrs. Washington presents her compliments to you, and with every wish for your happiness, I am etc.

To ROBERT MORRIS

Washington's views on the abolition of slavery are on the conservative side. On the one hand, he would like in the end to see slavery abolished by legislative procedure, and, on the other, he is concerned about property loss and the deprivation of the happiness of the Negroes under emancipation. On balance, he fears that the freeing of slaves would introduce far more evil than it would cure. In brief, his point of view on this question seems to have been determined by his own vested interests, since he was, even for his time, a large holder of human property.

Mount Vernon, April 12, 1786

DEAR SIR: I give you the trouble of this letter at the instance of Mr. Dalby of Alexandria; who is called to Philadelphia to attend what he conceives to be a vexatious lawsuit respecting a slave of his, which a Society of Quakers in the city (formed for such purposes) have attempted to liberate; The merits of this case will no doubt appear upon trial. but from Mr. Dalby's state of the matter, it should seem that this Society is not only acting repugnant to justice so far as its conduct concerns strangers, but, in my opinion extremely impolitickly with respect to the State, the City in particular; and without being able, (but by acts of tyranny and oppression) to accomplish their own ends. He says the conduct of this society is not sanctioned by Law: had the case been otherwise, whatever my opinion of the Law might have been, my respect for the policy of the State would on this occasion have appeared in my silence; because against the penalties of promulgated Laws one may guard; but there is no avoiding the snares of individuals, or of private societies. And if the practice of this Society of which Mr. Dalby speaks, is not discountenanced, none of those whose *misfortune* it is to have slaves as attendants, will visit the City if they can possibly avoid it; because by so doing they hazard their property; or they must be at the expence (and this will not always succeed) of providing servants of another description for the trip.

I hope it will not be conceived from these observations, that it is my wish to hold the unhappy people, who are the subject of this letter, in slavery. I can only say that there is not a man living who wishes more sincerely than I do, to see a plan adopted for the abolition of it; but there is only one proper and effectual mode by which it can be accomplished, and that is by Legislative authority; and this, as far as my suffrage will go, shall never be wanting. But when slaves who are happy and contented with their present masters, are tampered with and seduced to leave them; when masters are taken unawares by these practices; when a conduct of this sort begets discontent on one side and resentment on the other, and when it happens to fall on a man, whose purse will not measure with that of the Society, and he looses his property for want of means to defend it; it is oppression in the latter case, and not humanity in any; because it introduces more evils than it can cure.

I will make no apology for writing to you on this subject; for if Mr. Dalby has not misconceived the matter, an evil exists which requires a remedy; if he has, my intentions have been good, though I may have been too precipitate in this address. Mrs. Washington joins me in every good and kind wish for Mrs. Morris and your family, and I am, &c.

To DAVID HUMPHREYS

Shays' Rebellion in Massachusetts, to which Washington refers as "these commotions," was a farmers' revolt against inequalities of taxation due to inflation and consequently an increasing economic burden upon small-scale landowners and agriculturists. The Revolutionary War veteran, Captain Daniel Shays, was the eloquent leader of the outburst. The uprising succeeded in the sense that it forced the Massachusetts Legislature ultimately to pass ameliorative agrarian laws in behalf of its own people. Washington, far from the scene and really unfamiliar with the small croppers' problems, at first sensed "British-influence disseminated by the tories," but did not overlook the possibility of real grievances which might have been adjusted by simple arbitrative methods and with substantial justice to the farmers. Finally, the rebellion was suppressed, but its influence went beyond the borders of Massachusetts, for it

*helped convince Washington and many others of the need of
hastening the Convention which was to lay the foundation of
our national government.*

Mount Vernon, October 22, 1786

MY DR. HUMPHREYS: Your favor of the 24th. ulto. came
to my hands about the middle of this month. For the enclosures
it contained I pray you to receive my warmest acknowledgments
and thanks. The Poem, tho' I profess not to be a connoisseur in
these kind of writings, appears pretty in my eye, and has sentiment and elegance which must I think render it pleasing to
others.

With respect to the circular letter, I see no cause for sup-
pressing or altering any part of it, except as to the place of meeting. Philadelphia, on three accots. in my opinion must be more
convenient to the majority of the delegation, than New York.
1st. as most central. 2dly. because there are regularly established
packet-boats, well accommodated for Passengers, to it from the
Southern States; and 3dly. because it appears to me that the seat
of Congress would not be so well for this meeting. When you
have digested your thoughts for publication, in the case of
Captn. Asgill, I would thank you for a copy of them; having
arrested the account I had furnished Mr. Tilghman, with an
assurance of a more authentic one for his friend in England.

I am pleased with the choice of Delegates which was made at
your State meeting; and wish the Representatives of all the
State societies may appear at the Genl. Meeting, with as good
dispositions as I believe they will. It gives me pleasure also to
hear that so many Officers are sent to your Assembly: I am
persuaded they will carry with them more liberality of sentiments, than is to be found among any other class of Citizens.
The speech of our friend Cobb was noble, worthy of a patriot
and himself; as was the conduct of Genl. Sullivan. But for
God's sake tell me what is the cause of all these commotions:
do they proceed from licentiousness, British-influence disseminated by the tories, or real grievances which admit of redress?
If the latter, why were they delayed 'till the public mind had

become so much agitated? If the former why are not the powers of Government tried at once? It is as well to be without, as not to live under their exercise. Commotions of this sort, like snow-balls, gather strength as they roll, if there is no opposition in the way to divide and crumble them. Do write me fully, I beseech you, on these matters; not only with respect to facts, but as to opinions of their tendency and issue. I am mortified beyond expression that in the moment of our acknowledged independence we should by our conduct verify the predictions of our transatlantic foe, and render ourselves ridiculous and contemptible in the eyes of all Europe. My health (I thank you for the enquiry) is restored to me; and all under this roof join me in most affectionate regards, and in regretting that your letter has held out no idea of visiting it again this winter, as you gave us hope of doing when you left us. To all the gentn. of my acquaintance who may happen to be in your circle, I beg to be remembered with sincere regard. To assure you of the sincerity of my friendship for you, would be unnecessary; as you must I think be perfectly satisfied of the high esteem and affection with which, I am, etc.

To HENRY LEE

One of the consequences of Shays' Rebellion and the widespread discontent in the Thirteen States was that it forced a clarification of the ideas of the leaders of the nation on the immediate need for a strong Federal government to replace the now-obsolete "Articles of Confederation and Perpetual Union." Washington's thinking on this subject is plain in his writings of this time. "Influence is no Government," he wrote Henry Lee. "Let us have one by which our lives, liberties and properties will be secured. . . . There is a call for decision."

The Confederation, formed in 1777, was a league of States, not a central government, and was lacking in authority. After the end of the war such power as it had was now totally inadequate to cope with a severe economic depression, in which the national currency was virtually worthless ("Not worth a Continental"); hostility to the Government was open and highly

vocal; taxes were uncollectible and anarchy threatened. In this
atmosphere of crisis, a preliminary convention of delegates
from five States met in Annapolis in 1786 to consider some sort
of regulation of commerce and an extensive overhauling of the
Articles of Confederation by means of amendments. That
Washington was in complete accord with these troubled dele-
gates, who recommended a general convention to be summoned
the following year for the purpose of such revision, is attested
by his statement: ". . . if defective, let it [the Constitution of
the Confederation] be amended, but not suffered to be tram-
pled upon whilst it has an existence."

Mount Vernon, October 31, 1786

MY DR. SIR: I am indebted to you for your several favors
of the 1st. 11th. and 17th. of this instt: and shall reply to them
in the order of their dates; but first let me thank you for the
interesting communications imparted by them.

The picture which you have exhibited, and the accounts
which are published of the commotions, and temper of numerous bodies in the Eastern States, are equally to be lamented
and deprecated. They exhibit a melancholy proof of what our
trans-Atlantic foe has predicted; and of another thing perhaps,
which is still more to be regretted, and is yet more unaccountable, that mankind when left to themselves are unfit for their
own Government. I am mortified beyond expression when I
view the clouds that have spread over the brightest morn that
ever dawned upon any Country. In a word, I am lost in amazement when I behold what intrigue, the interested views of desperate characters, ignorance and jealousy of the minor part, are
capable of effecting, as a scourge on the major part of our fellow
Citizens of the Union; for it is hardly to be supposed that the
great body of the people, tho' they will not act, can be so short-
sighted, or enveloped in darkness, as not to see rays of a distant
sun thro' all this mist of intoxication and folly.

You talk, my good Sir, of employing influence to appease the
present tumults in Massachusetts. I know not where that influence is to be found; and if attainable, that it would be a

proper remedy for the disorders. Influence is no Government. Let us have one by which our lives, liberties and properties will be secured; or let us know the worst at once. Under these impressions, my humble opinion is, that there is a call for decision. Know precisely what the insurgents aim at. If they have real grievances, redress them if possible; or acknowledge the justice of them, and your inability to do it in the present moment. If they have not, employ the force of government against them at once. If this is inadequate, all will be convinced that the superstructure is bad, or wants support. To be more exposed in the eyes of the world, and more contemptible than we already are, is hardly possible. To delay one or the other of these, is to exasperate on the one hand, or to give confidence on the other, and will add to their numbers; for, like snow-balls, such bodies increase by every movement, unless there is something in the way to obstruct and crumble them before the weight is too great and irresistible.

These are my sentiments. Precedents are dangerous things; let the reins of government then be braced and held with a steady hand, and every violation of the Constitution be reprehended: if defective, let it be amended, but not suffered to be trampled upon whilst it has an existence.

With respect to the navigation of the Mississippi, you already know my sentiments thereon: they have been uniformly the same, and as I have observed to you in a former letter, are controverted by one consideration only of weight, and that is the operation the occlusion of it may have on the minds of the western settlers, who will not consider the subject in a relative point of view or on a comprehensive scale, and may be influenced by the demagogues of the country to acts of extravagance and desperation, under a popular declamation that their interests are sacrificed. Colo. Mason, at present, is in a fit of the gout; what [his] sentiments on the subject are, I know not, nor whether he will be able to attend the Assembly during the present Session. For some reasons, however, (which need not be mentioned) I am inclined to believe he will advocate the navigation of that river. But in all matters of great national moment, the only true line of conduct, in my opinion, is, dispassionately to compare the advantages and disadvantages of the measure proposed, and decide from the balance. The lesser evil, where there is a choice of them, should always yield to the greater. What benefits (more than we now enjoy) are to be obtained by such a Treaty as you have delineated with Spain, I am not enough of a Commercial man to give any opinion on. The China came to hand without much damage; and I thank you for your attention in procuring and forwarding of it to me. Mrs. Washington joins me in best wishes for Mrs. Lee and yourself and I am &c.

To JAMES MADISON

Eager for a "liberal and energetic Constitution," Washington addressed an appeal to James Madison for the solidarity of the Thirteen States in framing a document which would prevent them from pulling against one another. Little by little Washington's immense prestige was making itself felt in national affairs, at that time almost in chaos and in desperate need of calm thinking and wise guidance. During the three years of his retirement after the end of the war, Washington had undergone the transformation so seldom achieved in our national history by which the eminently successful soldier became the far-sighted and influential statesman.

Mount Vernon, November 5, 1786

My DEAR SIR: I thank you for the communications in your letter of the first instt. The decision of the House on the question respecting a paper emission, is portentous I hope, of an auspicious Session. It may certainly be classed among the important questions of the present day; and merited the serious consideration of the Assembly. Fain would I hope, that the great, and most important of all objects, the fœderal governmt., may be considered with that calm and deliberate attention which the magnitude of it so loudly calls for at this critical moment. Let prejudices, unreasonable jealousies, and local interest yield to reason and liberality. Let us look to our National character, and to things beyond the present period. No morn ever dawned more favourably than ours did; and no day was ever more clouded than the present! Wisdom, and good examples are necessary at this time to rescue the political machine from the impending storm. Virginia has now an opportunity to set the latter, and has enough of the former, I hope, to take the lead in promoting this great and arduous work. Without some alteration in our political creed, the superstructure we have been seven years raising at the expence of so much blood and treasure, must fall. We are fast verging to anarchy and confusion!

A letter which I have just received from Genl Knox, who had just returned from Massachusetts (whither he had been sent by Congress consequent of the commotion in that State) is replete with melancholy information of the temper, and designs of a considerable part of that people. Among other things he says,

there creed is, that the property of the United States, has been protected from confiscation of Britain by the joint exertions of all, and therefore ought to be the common property of all. And he that attempts opposition to this creed is an enemy to equity and justice, and ought to be swept from off the face of the Earth.

again

They are determined to annihillate all debts public and private, and have Agrarian Laws, which are easily effected by the means of unfunded paper money which shall be a tender in all cases whatever.

He adds

The numbers of these people amount in Massachusetts to about one fifth part of several populous Counties, and to them may be collected, people of similar sentiments from the States of Rhode Island, Connecticut, and New Hampshire, so as to constitute a body of twelve or fifteen thousand desperate, and unprincipled men. They are chiefly of the young and active part of the Community.

How melancholy is the reflection, that in so short a space, we should have made such large strides towards fulfilling the prediction of our transatlantic foe! "leave them to themselves, and their government will soon dissolve." Will not the wise and good strive hard to avert this evil? Or will their supineness suffer ignorance, and the arts of self-interested designing disaffected and desperate characters, to involve this rising empire in wretchedness and contempt? What stronger evidence can be given of the want of energy in our governments than these disorders? If there exists not a power to check them, what security has a man for life, liberty, or property? To you, I am sure I need not add aught on this subject, the consequences of a lax, or inefficient government, are too obvious to be dwelt on. Thirteen Sovereignties pulling against each other, and all tugging at the fœderal head will soon bring ruin on the whole; whereas a liberal, and energetic Constitution, well guarded and closely watched, to prevent incroachments, might restore us to that degree of respectability and consequence, to which we had a fair claim, and the brightest prospect of attaining. With sentiments of the sincerest esteem etc.

To THOMAS JEFFERSON

The Constitutional Convention, summoned to meet in Philadelphia on May 14, 1787, completed its preliminary organizational business and was ready for debate on May 25th. Seven States were then represented by fifty-five delegates, instructed to revise the Articles of Confederation. Washington was elected the presiding officer, who, because of an agreement to secrecy, kept no record of the proceedings. His own references to the gathering are scant and, when made at all, very discreet. Even while writing to Jefferson five days after the deliberations had begun, he hardly trusted himself to do more than mention them. Not until 1796 did Washington deliver the records of the Convention to the State Department, and they were not published until 1819, twenty years after his death.

Yet in that atmosphere of secrecy, the more than four months of daily sessions were characterized by a boldness and courage, manifested from the beginning, when the original instructions were ignored and the delegates set to work to prepare a wholly new Constitution.

Here Washington goes into considerable detail about matters other than the Constitutional debates: the advantages of the inland-waterway project and the internal politics of the Society of Cincinnati. Washington had been elected president of this postwar officers' organization. It began by encountering difficulties. Even before its first general meeting there were protests because of a deep-seated resentment by more democratic citizens against what was interpreted as an attempt to raise military above civil classes and institute a military caste with hereditary privileges. Washington was able to soothe the suspicions of the Society's critics by advocating a change in its Constitution, whereby the clause dealing with honorary and hereditary memberships was eliminated. For many years the Society of Cincinnati remained an exclusive officers' club of glittering respectability but little influence. A few proud descendants kept the organization fluttering as a kind of banner of aristocratic distinction.

Philadelphia, May 30, 1787

DEAR SIR: It has so happened, that the letter which you did me the honor of writing to me the 14th. of November last, did not come to my hands till the first of the present month; and at a time when I was about to set off for the Convention of the States, appointed to be holden in this City the 14th. Instt. Consequently, it has not been in my power at an earlier period, to reply to the important matters wch. are the subjects thereof. This, possibly, may be to be regretted if the house of de Coulteaux should, in the meantime, have directed its enquiries to Philadelphia, Baltimore or New York without having had the advantages which are to be derived from the extension of the inland Navigations of the Rivers Potomack and James, deliniated to them. Silence on this head may be construed into inferiority, when the fact (in my judgment) is, that Alexandria or Richmond, provided the communication with the latter can be conducted by the Green brier and Great Kanhawa (as some aver and others doubt) has infinite advantages over either of the Towns just mentioned. With respect to James River, I am not able to speak with so much precision as of the former, with which (having had opportunities to be so) I am much better acquainted. To this therefore I shall chiefly confine my observations.

In investigating the advantages of Alexandria as the most proper place for a principal deposit in the Fur Trade, I have thought it necessary to leave as little room for partiality and prejudice to operate as possible, by concealing, as far as may be, the object of the investigation. Tho' the result has been favourable to Alexandria, I trust it will be found to have arisen from such weighty considerations, as must be felt by every mind; particularly that of the Merchant whose interests on this subject must alone determine the scale. With A very superficial knowledge of the relative Geography of the places (Alexanda. Baltimore, Philada. New York) in contemplation by Monsr. Coulteaux to establish a concern in the Fur Trade to the Country yielding this Article, a meer glance at the Map must decide Alexandria in point of distance to be the most convenient spot. Hence, a considerable saving would accrue in the articles of Land carriage; an object of so much importance in the communication between places seperated by immense wildernesses, and rugged roads, as to render any comment on it to a Merchant, superfluous. But the difficulty arising from this sourse (tho' already less) will soon, in a great measure, be obviated with respect to Alexandria, by the extension of the Navigation of Potomack. The progress already made in this great National work, Not only justifies this opinion, but the most sanguine expectations wch. have been formed of its success. Granting therefore that the advantage of a greater proximity to the Fur Country, was not on the side of Alexandria, still the immense superiority which a communication almost by water, would give it, must be obvious to all who consider the case, with which the distant produce of the different, and opposite parts of the earth are mutually exchanged, by means of this element. As neither of the other places can ever enjoy this singular benefit to so great a degree, Alexandria must, of course, be the place to which the Inhabitants of the Western Country must resort with all their Commodities (unless by the other channel mentioned, Richmond should be found equal to it); and from whence they will take back their returns in foreign products with the least expence. The Act for opening a road from the highest point to which the Navigation of Potomack can be extended, to the Cheat river, must also be considered as an important circumstance in favour of Alexandria; and in the same light the Act of the last Session for opening a road to the Mouth of the little Kanhawa, from the road last mentioned, must be considered. Besides these, leave has been obtained from Pensylvania by the States of Virginia and Maryld., to open another road from Wills' Creek to the Yohiogani, by the nearest and best rout. By these Acts, great part of the Trade which has been accustomed to flow through Pittsburgh to Philadelphia must be derived in rich streams to the Potomack: for I believe it to be as true in commerce as in every thing else, that nature, however she may be opposed for a while, will soon return her regular course, neither therefore the attractive power of wealth, nor the exertions of industry, will long, it is presumed, with hold from Alexandria the advantages which nature has bestowed on her.

If the great extent of territory adjacent to the Fur Country, which Virginia possesses, in comparison with the States to wch. the other Towns belong, be viewed; Alexandria must still be consindered [*sic*] as the most proper place. The Country about the Illinois and wabash (Rivers which nearly reach the Lakes in their Course) has been long considered as the most abundant in Furs; and the completion of the Navigation of James River must, without doubt, render Richmond the most convenient for *these* of any other; if, as I have once or twice before observed, the Navigation of the Kanhawa can be improved to any good account. By those however who are not acquainted with the nature of the western waters, and the short portages between them, it may be objected that the Rivers above mentioned are too far South to meet with good Furs; but it may not be amiss to observe here, that the Rivers of lake Erie &ca. communicate to nearly, and with such ease, with those of the Ohio, as to afford the shortest and best transportation from Detroit; by which all the Furs of the upper lakes must pass; whether they go to Canada, New York, Philadelphia, Baltimore, Alexandria or Richmond; and that the routs, from thence to the two latter are thro' the territory of the United States; whereas the one to New York passes along the line, and is besides, Subject to interruptions by Ice when these are entirely free from it. These objections, particularly the latter, apply in a degree both to Philadelphia and Baltimore; because if either can avail itself of water transportation, it must be by the more Northern streams of the Ohio, with the Waters of the Susquehanna, considerably above the Monongahela, and still more so above the Great Kanhawa, the first of which communicates with the River Potomack, and the latter with that of James.

The last advantage which occurs to me in favor of Alexandria, is, that the business would be carried on there without any competition: No one having yet engaged so deeply in it, as to hold out any encouragement. I have even been informed that Waggons loaded with Furs, have sometimes passed through Alexandria to Baltimore in search of a Market; and from Winchester it is their common practice to go there with this Commodity; tho' Alexandria is much more convenient to them. On the side of New York, the most eligable Posts for this trade are in the possession of the British; and whenever they are ceded it will, I expect, be found, that the Merchants of that Nation, from their Wealth, long establishment, and consequent knowledge of the Country, will be such formidable competitors, as to draw the greater part of the Furs into Canada.

I shall now proceed to mention a person in whose skill and integrity Monsr. Coulteaux may, I think, have the fullest confidence; and tho' I am precluded in some measure from so doing by being told that it is required that he should be an American born; I shall still venture to name a Gentleman who is a native of Ireland, Colo. John Fitzgerald. The active Services of this Gentleman during the War, his long residence in the Country, and intermarriage in it (with one of the most respectable families, Digges of Maryland) all entitle him to be considered as an American. The laws of this Country know no difference between him and a Native of America. He has besides been bred to trade, is esteemed a Man of property and is at present engaged in the former in Alexandria. Lest however this should be considered as an insuperable obstacle, I shall name a second, Robert Townshend Hooe Esqr., who has every desired requisite. I shall just observe, that if the business is carried on extensively, it would probably require the various acquaintance and combined activity of each of those Gentlemen.

I come now to the other part of your letter, which concerns the Cincinnati, and here indeed I scarcely know what to say. It is a delicate, it is a perplexing subject. Not having the extract from the Encyclopedia before me, I cannot now undertake to enter into the merits of the publication. It may therefore perhaps be as much as will be expected from me, to observe that the Author appears in general to have detailed very candidly and ingenuously the motives, and inducements wch. gave birth to the Society. Some of the subsequent facts, which I cannot, however, from memory pretend to discuss with precision are thought by Gentlemen who have seen the publication to be misstated; in so much that it is commonly said, truth and falsehood are so intimately blended, that it will be difficult to sever them.

For myself, I only recollect two or three circumstances, in the narration, of which palpable mistakes seem to have insinuated themselves. Majr. L'Enfant did not arrive and bring the Eagles during the Session of the General meeting, but sometime before that Convention. The Legislature of Rhode Island never passed any Act whatever on the subject (that ever came to my knowledge) notwithstanding what Mirabeau and others had previously advanced. Nothing can be more ridiculous than the supposition of the author that the Society was instituted partly because the Country could not then pay the Army, except the assertion that the United States have now made full and compleat provision for paying not only the arrearages due to the Officers, but the half pay or commutation, at their option. From whence the Author deduces an argument for its dissolution. Though I conceive, this never had any thing to do with the Institution; yet, the Officers, in most of the States, who never have, nor I believe expect to receive one farthing of the principal or interest on their final settlement securities, would doubtless be much obliged to the Author to convince them how, and when they received a compensation for their Services. No foreigner, nor American who has been absent sometime, will easily comprehend how tender those concerned are on this point. I am sorry to say, a great many of the Officers consider me as having in a degree committed myself by inducing them to trust too much in the justice of their Country. They heartily wish no settlement had been made, because it has rendered them obnoxious to their fellow Citizens, without affording the least emolument.

For the reason I have mentioned, I cannot think it expedient for me to go into an investigation of the Writers deductions. I shall accordingly content myself with giving you some idea of the part I have acted, posterior to the first formation of the Association.

When I found that you, and many of the most respectable characters in the Country would entirely acquiesce with the Institution as altered and amended in the first General Meeting of 1784, and that the objections against the obnoxious parts were wholly done away, I was prevailed upon to accept the Presidency. Happy in finding (so far as I could learn by assiduous enquiries) that all the clamours and jealousies, which had been excited against the original association, had ceased; I judged it a proper time in the last Autumn, to withdraw myself from any farther Agency in the business, and to make my retirement compleate agreeably to my original plan. I wrote circular letters to all the State Societies, announcing my wishes, informing that I did not propose to be at the trienniel meeting, and requested not to be re-elected President. This was the last step of a public nature I expected ever to have taken. But having since been appointed by my Native State to attend the National Convention, and having been pressed to a compliance in a manner which it hardly becomes me to describe; I have, in a measure, been obliged to sacrifice my own Sentiments, and to be present in Philadelphia at the very time of the General Meeting of the Cincinnati; after which I was not at liberty to decline the Presidency without placing myself in an extremely disagreeable situation with relation to that brave and faithful class of men, whose persevering friendship I had experienced on so many trying occasions.

The business of this Convention is as yet too much in embryo to form any opinion of the result. Much is expected from it by some; but little by others; and nothing by a few. That something is necessary, all will agree; for the situation of the

General Governmt. (if it can be called a governmt.) is shaken to its foundation, and liable to be overset by every blast. In a word, it is at an end, and unless a remedy is soon applied, anarchy and confusion will inevitably ensue. But having greatly exceeded the bounds of a letter already I will only add assurances of that esteem, regard, and respect.

To HENRY KNOX

After the Constitution had been drafted and agreed upon by the delegates on September 17, 1787, Washington returned to Mount Vernon, there to wait through many months while the States deliberated on ratification. His concern about the action Virginia might take was justified by the deferment of its final, but favorable, vote which was reached by the middle of 1788, but only after nine other States had accepted it. To answer the criticism of reflective men who feared that a powerful central government would infringe on the rights of the States and the liberties of individual citizens, Washington suggests the remedy of amendments to correct defects which would only be apparent after trial. This argument foreshadows the actual adoption, two years later, of the first ten amendments in the Bill of Rights.

Mount Vernon, October 15, 1787

My Dear Sir: Your favor of the 3d. came duly to hand. The fourth day after leaving Philadelphia I reached home and found Mrs. Washington and the Family tolerably well, but the fruits of the Earth almost entirely destroyed by one of the severest droughts (in this neighborhood) that has ever been experienced. The Crops, pretty generally, have been injured in this State below the Mountains, but not to the degree that mine, and some others in a small circle around me, have suffered.

The Constitution is now before the Judgment Seat. It has, as was expected, its adversaries and supporters. Which will preponderate is yet to be decided: the former, more than probably will be most active, as the major part of them will, it is to be feared, be governed by sinister and self important motives, to which every thing in their breasts must yield. The opposition from another class of them may perhaps, (if they should be men of reflection, candour, and information) subside in the solution of the following simple questions. 1. Is the Constitution which is submitted by the Convention preferable to the Government (if it can be called one) under which we now live? 2. Is it probable that more confidence would at the time be placed in another Convention, provided the experiment should be tried, than was placed in the last one, and is it likely that a better agreement would take place therein? 3. What would be the consequences if these should not happen, or even from the delay, which must inevitably follow such an experiment? Is there not a Constitutional door open for alterations or amendments? and is it not likely that real defects will be as readily discovered after as before trial; and will not our successors be as ready to apply the remedy as ourselves if occasion should require it? To think otherwise will, in my Judgment, be ascribing more of the amor patria, more wisdom and more virtue, to ourselves, than I think we deserve.

It is highly probable that the refusal of our Govr. and Colo. Mason to subscribe to the proceedings of the Convention will have a bad effect in this State; for, as you well observe, they must not only assign reasons for the Justification of their own conduct, but it is highly probable that these reasons will be clothed in most terrific array for the purpose of alarming; some things are already addressed to the fears of the people and will no doubt have their effect. As far however as the sense of this part of the Country has been taken, it is strongly in favor of the proposed Constitution; Further I cannot speak with precision. If a powerful opposition is given to it, the weight thereof will, I apprehend, come from the South side of James River and from the Western Counties. I am, &c.

To BUSHROD WASHINGTON

"The power under the Constitution will always be in the People," wrote Washington to his nephew Bushrod. Having

scrupulously restrained himself from taking part in the debates while the Convention was in session, he now became the open advocate of ratification, but only by private influence. The public effort to win adherents after the delegates had ended their deliberations was in the able hands of Alexander Hamilton, John Jay and James Madison, who, jointly under the pseudonym of "Publius," issued eighty-five articles in a fighting defense of the Constitution within seven months. In 1788, these articles appeared in book form as The Federalist. *Washington was firmly aligned with its authors as a champion of a closely bound Union with power freely granted by the States to the Central Government.*

Mount Vernon, November 10, 1787

DEAR BUSHROD: In due course of Post, your letters of the 19th. and 26th. Ult. came to hand and I thank you for the communications therein; for a continuation in matters of importance, I shall be obliged to you. That the Assembly would afford the People an opportunity of deciding on the proposed Constitution I had scarcely a doubt, the only question with me was, whether it would go forth under favourable auspices, or receive the stamp of disapprobation. The opponents I expected, (for it ever has been that the adversaries to a measure are more active than its Friends) would endeavor to stamp it with unfavourable impressions, in order to bias the Judgment that is ultimately to decide on it, this is evidently the case with the writers in opposition, whose objections are better calculated to alarm the fears, than to convince the Judgment, of their readers. They build their objections upon principles that do not exist, which the Constitution does not support them in, and the existence of which has been, by an appeal to the Constitution itself flatly denied; and then, as if they were unanswerable, draw all the dreadful consequences that are necessary to alarm the apprehensions of the ignorant or unthinking. It is not the interest of the major part of those characters to be convinced; nor will their local views yield to arguments, which do not accord with their present, or future prospects.

A Candid solution of a single question to which the plainest understanding is competent does, in my opinion, decide the dispute: namely is it best for the States to unite, or not to unite? If there are men who prefer the latter, then unquestionably the Constitution which is offered must, in their estimation, be wrong from the words, we the People to the signature inclusively; but those who think differently and yet object to parts of it, would do well to consider that it does not lye with any one State, or the minority of the States to superstruct a Constitution for the whole. The separate interests, as far as it is practicable, must be consolidated; and local views must be attended to, as far as the nature of the case will admit. Hence it is that every State has some objection to the present form and these objections are directed to different points. that which is most pleasing to one is obnoxious to another, and so vice versa. If then the Union of the whole is a desirable object, the componant parts must yield a little in order to accomplish it. Without the latter, the former is unattainable, for again I repeat it, that not a single State nor the minority of the States can force a Constitution on the Majority; but admitting the power it will surely be granted that it cannot be done without involving scenes of civil commotion of a very serious nature let the opponents of the proposed Constitution in this State be asked, and it is a question they certainly ought to have asked themselves, what line of conduct they would advise it to adopt, if nine other States, of which I think there is little doubt, should accede to the Constitution? would they recommend that it should stand single? Will they connect it with Rhode Island? or even with two others checkerwise and remain with them as outcasts from the Society, to shift for themselves? or will they return to their dependence on Great Britain? or lastly, have the mortification to come in when they will be allowed no credit for doing so?

The warmest friends and the best supporters the Constitution has, do not contend that it is free from imperfections; but they found them unavoidable and are sensible, if evil is likely to arise there from, the remedy must come hereafter; for in the present moment, it is not to be obtained; and, as there is a Constitutional door open for it, I think the People (for it is with them to Judge) can as they will have the advantage of experi-

ence on their Side, decide with as much propriety on the alterations and amendments which are necessary [as] ourselves. I
do not think we are more inspired, have more wisdom, or possess more virtue, than those who will come after us.

The power under the Constitution will always be in the People. It is entrusted for certain defined purposes, and for a certain limited period, to representatives of their own chusing;
and whenever it is executed contrary to their Interest, or not
agreeable to their wishes, their Servants can, and undoubtedly
will be, recalled. It is agreed on all hands that no government
can be well administered without powers; yet the instant these
are delegated, altho' those who are entrusted with the administration are no more than the creatures of the people, act as
it were but for a day, and are amenable for every false step they
take, they are, from the moment they receive it, set down as
tyrants; their natures, one would conceive from this, immediately changed, and that they could have no other disposition
but to oppress. Of these things, in a government constituted
and guarded as ours is, I have no idea; and do firmly believe
that whilst many ostensible reasons are assigned to prevent the
adoption of it, the real ones are concealed behind the Curtain,
because they are not of a nature to appear in open day. I believe further, supposing them pure, that as great evils result
from too great Jealousy as from the want of it. We need look
I think no further for proof of this, than to the Constitution, of
some if not all of these States. No man is a warmer advocate for
proper restraints and wholesome checks in every department
of government than I am; but I have never yet been able to discover the propriety of placing it absolutely out of the power of
men to render essential Services, because a possibility remains
of their doing ill.

If Mr. Ronald can place the Finances of this Country upon
so respectable a footing as he has intimated, he will deserve
much of its thanks. In the attempt, my best wishes, I have nothing more to offer, will accompany him. I hope there remains
virtue enough in the Assembly of this State to preserve inviolate public treaties and private Contracts; if these are infringed,
farewell to respectability and safety in the Government.

I have possessed a doubt, but if any had existed in my breast, reiterated proofs would have convinced me of the impolicy of all commutable Taxes. If we cannot learn wisdom from experience, it is hard to say where it is to be found. But why talk of learning it; these things are mere Jobs by which few are enriched at the public expense; for whether premeditation, or ignorance, is the cause of this destructive scheme, it ends in oppression.

You have I find broke the Ice; the only advice I will offer to you on the occasion (if you have a mind to command the attention of the House) is to speak seldom, but to important Subjects, except such as particularly relate to your Constituents, and, in the former case make yourself perfectly master of the Subject. Never exceed a decent warmth, and submit your sentiments with diffidence. A dictatorial Stile, though it may carry conviction, is always accompanied with disgust. I am, &c.

To JAMES MADISON

When Massachusetts finally did ratify the Constitution, it was by a dangerously narrow margin, as Washington foresaw in his letter to Madison. Naturally, he preferred a close victory to a rejection. He realized that the example set by an unfavorable vote might be disastrous, since it would hearten the minorities in those States which were wavering and give new life to the factions still opposed to the Constitution in those States which had already voted for adoption. Victory by a close vote would at least give the Constitution a chance. New York followed the example of Massachusetts and cast its vote, also by a slender majority, for the Constitution. In both cases the determining factor was not so much the persuasive arguments in The Federalist *as the fear in the new nation of the aggression of foreign powers and a sense of weakness, acquired and grown since the end of the Revolutionary War.*

Mount Vernon, February 5, 1788

MY DEAR SIR: I am indebted to you for several of your favors, and thank you for their enclosures. The rumours of War between France and England have subsided; and the poor Patriots of Holland, it seems, are left to fight their own Battles or negotiate, in neither case with any great prospect of advantage. They must have been deceived, or their conduct has been divided, precipitate, and weak. the former, with some blunders, have, I conceive, been the causes of their misfortunes.

I am sorry to find by yours, and other accts. from Massachusetts, that the decision of its Convention (at the time of their dates) remains problematical. A rejection of the New form by that State will invigorate the opposition, not only in New York, but in all those which are to follow; at the same time that it will afford materials for the Minority in such as have adopted it, to blow the Trumpet of discord more loudly. The acceptance by a bare majority, tho' preferable to a rejection, is also to be deprecated. It is scarcely possible to form any decided opinion of the general sentiment of the people of this State, on this important subject. Many have asked me with anxious solicitude, if you did not mean to get into the Convention; conceiving it of indispensable necessity. Colo Mason, who returned only yesterday, has offered himself, I am told for the County of Stafford; and his friends add, he can be elected not only there, but for Prince William and Fauquier also. The truth of this I know not. I rarely go from home, and my visitors, who, for the most part are travellers and strangers, have not the best information.

At the time you suggested for my consideration, the expediency of a communication of my sentiments on the proposed Constitution, to any correspondent I might have in Massachusetts, it did not occur to me that Genl Lincoln and myself frequently interchanged letters; much less did I expect, that a hasty, and indigested extract of one which I had written, intermixed with a variety of other matter to Colo Chas Carter, in answer to a letter I had received from him respecting Wolf dogs, Wolves, Sheep, experiments in Farming &c &c &c. was then in the press, and would bring these sentiments to public view by means of the extensive circulation I find that extract has had. Altho' I never have concealed, and am perfectly regardless who becomes acquainted with my sentiments on the proposed Constitution, yet nevertheless, as no care had been taken to dress the ideas, or any reasons assigned in support of my opinion, I feel myself hurt by the publication; and informed my friend the Colonel of it. In answer, he has fully exculpated himself of the intention, but his zeal in the cause prompted him to distribute copies, under a prohibition (which was disregarded) that they should not go to the press. As you have seen the rude, or crude extract (as you may please to term it) I will add no more on the subject.

Perceiving that the Fœderalist, under the signature of Publius, is about to be republished, I would thank you for forwarding to me three or four Copies, one of which to be neatly bound, and inform me of the cost. Altho' we have not had many, or deep Snows yet we have since the commencement of them, had a very severe Winter; and if the cold of this day is proportionately keen with you a warm room, and a good fire will be found no bad, or uncomfortable antidote to it. With sentiments of perfect esteem etc.

To MARQUIS DE LAFAYETTE

By the middle of April, almost a year after the Convention had assembled, only six States had ratified the Constitution, with Maryland following their example at the end of the month. In the meantime, under the still-existing Confederation, commercial treaties to encourage trade with European countries were held in abeyance, but, worse still, the traffic of goods between States was snarled by contradictory legislation. To Washington, acceptance of the Constitution was basic; thereafter adjustments could be made by means of amendments. On the question whether a President, under the Constitution, could continue in office indefinitely and thus create a despotism, he did not consider a clause to provide for rotation necessary, arguing that the people themselves would be capable of deciding when the issue arose. Not until more than one hundred and fifty years later did this question present itself for the decision of the American people. As to his own availability for the office, Washington deprecated the suggestion, preferring a life of retirement.

Mount Vernon, April 28, 1788

I have now before me, my dear Marqs. your favor of the 3d of August in the last year; together with those of the 1st. of January, the 2d. of January and the 4th. of February in the present. Though the first is of so antient a date, they all come to hand lately, and nearly at the same moment. The frequency of your kind remembrance of me, and the endearing expressions of attachment, are by so much the more satisfactory, as I recognise them to be a counterpart of my own feelings for you. In truth, you know I speak the language of sincerity and not of flattery, when I tell you, that your letters are ever most welcome and dear to me.

This I lay out to be a letter of Politics. We are looking anxiously across the Atlantic for news and you are looking anxiously back again for the same purpose. It is an interesting subject to contemplate how far the war, kindled in the north of Europe, may extend its conflagrations, and what may be the result before its extinction. The Turk appears to have lost his old and acquired a new connection. Whether England has not, in the hour of her pride, overacted her part and pushed matters too far for her own interest, time will discover: but, in my opinion (though from my distance and want of minute information I should form it with diffidence) the affairs of that nation cannot long go on in the same prosperous train: in spite of expedients and in spite of resources, the Paper bubble will one day burst. And it will whelm many in the ruins. I hope the affairs of France are gradually sliding into a better state. Good effects may, and I trust will ensue, without any public convulsion. France, were her resources properly managed and her administrations wisely conducted, is (as you justly observe) much more potent in the scale of empire, than her rivals at present seem inclined to believe.

I notice with pleasure the additional immunities and facilities in trade, which France has granted by the late Royal arret to the United States. I flatter myself it will have the desired effect, in some measure, of augmenting the commercial intercourse. From the productions and wants of the two countries, their trade with each other is certainly capable of great amelioration, to be actuated by a spirit of unwise policy. For so surely as ever we shall have an efficient government established, so surely will that government impose retaliating restrictions, to a certain degree, upon the trade of Britain. at present, or under our existing form of Confederations, it would be idle to think of making commercial regulations on our part. One State passes a prohibitory law respecting some article, another State opens wide the avenue for its admission. One Assembly makes a system, another Assembly unmakes it. Virginia, in the very last session of her Legislature, was about to have passed some of the most extravagant and preposterous Edicts on the subject of trade, that ever stained the leaves of a Legislative Code. It is in vain to hope for a remedy of these and innumerable other evils, untill a general Government shall be adopted.

The Conventions of Six States only have as yet accepted the new Constitution. No one has rejected it. It is believed that the Convention of Maryland, which is now in session; and that of South Carolina, which is to assemble on the 12th of May, will certainly adopt it. It is, also, since the elections of Members for the Convention have taken place in this State, more generally believed that it will be adopted here than it was before those elections were made. There will, however, be powerful and eloquent speeches on both sides of the question in the Virginia Convention; but as Pendleton, Wythe, Blair, Madison, Jones, Nicholas, Innis and many other of our first characters will be advocates for its adoption, you may suppose the weight of abilities will rest on that side. Henry and Mason are its great adversaries. The Governor, if he opposes it at all will do it feebly.

On the general merits of this proposed Constitution, I wrote to you, some time ago, my sentiments pretty freely. That letter had not been received by you, when you addressed to me the last of yours which has come to my hands. I had never supposed that perfection could be the result of accommodation and mutual concession. The opinion of Mr. Jefferson and yourself is certainly a wise one, that the Constitution ought by all means to be accepted by nine States before any attempt should be made to procure amendments. For, if that acceptance shall not previously take place, men's minds will be so much agitated and soured, that the danger will be greater than ever of our becoming a disunited People. Whereas, on the other hand, with prudence in temper and a spirit of moderation, every essential alteration, may in the process of time, be expected.

You will doubtless, have seen, that it was owing to this conciliatory and patriotic principle that the Convention of Massachusetts adopted the Constitution in toto; but recommended a number of specific alterations and quieting explanations, as an early, serious and unremitting subject of attention. Now, although it is not to be expected that every individual, in Society, will or can ever be brought to agree upon what is, exactly, the best form of government; yet, there are many things in the Constitution which only need to be explained, in order to prove equally satisfactory to all parties. For example: there was not a member of the convention, I believe, who had the least objection to what is contended for by the Advocates for a Bill of Rights and Tryal by Jury. The first, where the people evidently retained every thing which they did not in express terms give up, was considered nugatory as you will find to have been more fully explained by Mr. Wilson and others: And as to the second, it was only the difficulty of establishing a mode which should not interfere with the fixed modes of any of the States, that induced the Convention to leave it, as a matter of future adjustment.

There are other points on which opinions would be more likely to vary. As for instance, on the ineligibility of the same person for President, after he should have served a certain course of years. Guarded so effectually as the proposed Constitution is, in respect to the prevention of bribery and undue influence in the choice of President: I confess, I differ widely myself from Mr. Jefferson and you, as to the necessity or expediency of rotation in that appointment. The matter was fairly discussed in the Convention, and to my full convictions; though I cannot have time or room to sum up the argument in this letter. There cannot, in my judgment, be the least danger that the President will by any practicable intrigue ever be able to continue himself one moment in office, much less perpetuate himself in it; but in the last stage of corrupted morals and political depravity: and even then there is as much danger that any other species of domination would prevail. Though, when a people shall have become incapable of governing themselves and fit for a master, it is of little consequence from what quarter he comes. Under an extended view of this part of the subject, I can see no propriety in precluding ourselves from the services of any man, who on some great emergency shall be deemed universally, most capable of serving the Public.

In answer to the observations you make on the probability of my election to the Presidency (knowing me as you do) I need only say, that it has no enticing charms, and no fascinating allurements for me. However, it might not be decent for me to say I would refuse to accept or even to speak much about an appointment, which may never take place: for in so doing, one might possibly incur the application of the moral resulting from that Fable, in which the Fox is represented as inveighing against the sourness of the grapes, because he could not reach them. All that it will be necessary to add, my dear Marquis, in order to show my decided predilection, is, that, (at my time of life and under my circumstances) the encreasing infirmities of nature and the growing love of retirement do not permit me to entertain a wish beyond that of living and dying an honest man on my own farm. Let those follow the pursuits of ambition and fame, who have a keener relish for them, or who may have more years, in store, for the enjoyment.

Mrs. Washington, while she requests that her best compliments may be presented to you, joins with me in soliciting that the same friendly and affectionate memorial of our constant remembrance and good wishes may be made acceptable to Madame de la Fayette and the little ones. I am &c.

P. S. May 1st. Since writing the foregoing letter, I have received Authentic Accounts that the Convention of Maryland have ratified the new Constitution by a Majority of 63 to 11.

To ALEXANDER HAMILTON

Washington's commendation of Hamilton, Jay and Madison's The Federalist *is prophetic because the book has merited "the Notice of Posterity," if more than a century and a half of vitality can be a test of its enduring qualities. "The delicate subject" to which the Squire of Mount Vernon refers at the close of this letter is one broached by Hamilton, who merely took it for granted that Washington would respond to the general call to head the new Government. Disclaiming any such ambition, Washington here insists that he has no desire for the office, but really wishes to live out his life on his estate.*

Mount Vernon, August 28, 1788

DEAR SIR: I have had the pleasure to receive your letter dated the 13th. accompanied by one addressed to Genl. Morgan. I will forward the letter to General Morgan by the first conveyance, and add my particular wishes, that he would comply with the request contained in it. Although I can scarcely imagine how the watch of a British officer, killed within their lines, should have fallen into his hands who was many miles distant from the scene of action, yet, if it so happened, I flatter myself there will be no reluctance or delay in restoring it to the family.

As the perusal of the political papers under the signature of Publius has afforded me great satisfaction, I shall certainly consider them as claiming a most distinguished place in my Library. I have read every performance which has been printed on one side and the other of the great question lately agitated (so far as I have been able to obtain them) and, without an unmeaning compliment, I will say, that I have seen no other so well calculated (in my judgment) to produce conviction on an unbiased Mind, as the Production of your triumvirate. When the transient circumstances and fugitive performances which attended this Crisis shall have disappeared, That Work will merit the Notice of Posterity; because in it are candidly and ably discussed the principles of freedom and the topics of government, which will be always interesting to mankind so long as they shall be connected in Civil Society.

The circular letter from your Convention, I presume, was the equivalent by which you obtained an acquiescence in the proposed Constitution. Notwithstanding I am not very well satisfied with the tendency of it, yet the fœderal affairs had proceeded, with few exceptions, in so good a train, that I hope the political Machine may be put in motion, without much effort or hazard of miscarrying.

On the delicate subject with which you conclude your letter, I can say nothing; because the event alluded to may never happen; and because, in case it should occur, it would be a point of prudence to defer forming one's ultimate and irrevocable decision, so long as new data might be afforded for one to act with the greater wisdom and propriety. I would not wish to conceal my prevailing sentiment from you. For you know me well enough, my good Sir, to be persuaded, that I am not guilty of affectation, when I tell you, that it is my great and sole desire to live and die, in peace and retirement on my own farm. Were it even indispensable a different line of conduct should be adopted; while you and some others who are acquainted with my heart would acquit, the world and Posterity might probably accuse me [of] inconsistency and ambition. Still I hope I shall always possess firmness and virtue enough to maintain (what I consider the most enviable of all titles) the character of an honest man, as well as prove (what I desire to be considered in reality) that I am, with great sincerity and esteem, etc.

To HENRY LEE

Virginia and New York were the tenth and eleventh States to ratify the Constitution. Only North Carolina and Rhode

Island remained outside the fold and did not enter it until a year later, when the Government created by the Constitution had already begun to function. Again Washington tried to discourage the growing sentiment in his behalf as the first President. He was convinced that someone else would perform the duties quite as well as he. The coy practice of denying candidacy until the moment was most propitious to insure nomination, as employed by many succeeding aspirants to the office, certainly cannot be charged to Washington. His sincerity and integrity were as obvious as his concern for the welfare of the country was beyond dispute.

Mount Vernon, September 22, 1788

DEAR SIR: Your letter of the 13th. instant was of so friendly and confidential a complexion, as to merit my early attention and cordial acknowledgments. I am glad Congress have at last decided upon an Ordinance for carrying the new government into execution. In my mind the place for the meeting of the new Congress was not an object of such very important consequence; but I greatly fear that the question entailed upon that body, respecting their permanent residence, will be pregnant with difficulty and danger. God grant that true patriotism and a spirit of moderation may exclude a narrow locality, and all ideas unfriendly to the Union, from every quarter.

Your observations on the solemnity of the crisis and its application to myself, bring before me subjects of the most momentous and interesting nature. In our endeavors to establish a new general government, the contest nationally considered, seems not to have been so much for glory, as existence. It was for a long time doubtful whether we were to survive as an independent Republic, or decline from our fœderal dignity into insignificant and wretched Fragments of Empire. The adoption of the Constitution so extensively, and with so liberal an acquiescence on the part of the Minorities in general, promised the former; until lately the circular letter of New York carried, in my apprehension, an unfavorable if not an insidious tendency to a contrary policy. I still hope for the best; but before you mentioned it, I could not help fearing it would serve as a Standard to which the disaffected might resort. It is now evidently the part of all honest men, who are friends to the new Constitution, to endeavor to give it a chance to disclose its merits and defects, by carrying it fairly into effect, in the first instance. For it is to be apprehended, that by an attempt, to obtain amendments before the experiment has been candidly made, "more is meant than meets the ear" that an intention is concealed, to accomplish slily, what could not have been done openly, to undo all that has been done.

If the fact so exists, that a kind of combination is forming to stifle the government in embrio; it is a happy circumstance that the design has become suspected. Preparations should be the sure attendant upon forewarning. Probably, prudence, wisdom, and patriotism were never more essentially necessary than at the present moment; and so far as it can be done in an irreproachably direct manner, no effort ought to be left unessayed to procure the election of the best possible characters to the new Congress. On their harmony, deliberation and decision every thing will depend. I heartily wish Mr. Madison was in our Assembly, as I think, with you, it is of unspeakable importance Virginia should set out in her fœderal measures under right auspices.

The principal topic of your letter is, to me, a point of great delicacy indeed; insomuch that I can scarcely, without some impropriety touch upon it. In the first place, the event to which you allude may never happen; among other reasons because, if the partiality of my fellow citizens conceive it to be a means by which the sinews of the new government would be strengthened, it will of consequence be obnoxious to those who are in opposition to it, many of whom, unquestionably will be placed among the Electors.

This consideration alone would supersede the expediency of announcing any definite and irrevocable resolution. You are among the small number of those who know my invincible attachment to domestic life, and that my sincerest wish is to continue in the enjoyment of it, solely, until my final hour. But the world would be neither so well instructed, nor so candidly disposed as to believe me uninfluenced by sinister motives, in case any circumstance should render a deviation from the line of conduct I had prescribed to myself indispensable.

Should the contingency you suggest take place, and (for argument sake alone let me say it) should my unfeigned reluctance to accept the office be overcome by a deference for the reasons and opinions of my friends; might I not, after the Declarations I have made (and Heaven knows they were made in the sincerity of my heart) in the judgment of the impartial World and of Posterity, be chargeable with levity and inconsistency; if not with rashness and ambition? Nay farther would there not even be some apparent foundation for the two former charges? Now justice to myself and tranquility of conscience require that I should act a part, if not above imputation, at least capable of vindication. Nor will you conceive me to be too solicitous for reputation. Though I prize, as I ought, the good opinion of my fellow citizens; yet, if I know myself, I would not seek or retain popularity at the expense of one social duty or moral virtue.

While doing what my conscience informed me was right, as it respected my God, my Country and myself, I could despise all the party clamor and unjust censure, which must be expected from some, whose personal enmity might be occasioned by their hostility to the government. I am conscious, that I fear alone to give any real occasion for obloquy, and that I do not dread to meet with unmerited reproach. And certain I am, whensoever I shall be convinced the good of my country requires my reputation to be put in risque; regard for my own fame will not come in competition with an object of so much magnitude. If I declined the task, it would lie upon quite another principle. Notwithstanding my advanced season of life, my encreasing fondness for agricultural amusements and my growing love of retirement augment and confirm my decided predilection for the character of a private citizen: yet it would be no one of these motives, nor the hazard to which my former reputation might be exposed, or the terror of encountering new fatigues and troubles that would deter me from an acceptance; but a belief that some other person, who had less pretence and less inclination to be excused, could execute all the duties full as satisfactorily as myself. To say more would be indiscreet; as a disclosure of a refusal beforehand, might incur the application of the Fable, in which the Fox is represented as undervaluing the grapes he could not reach. You will perceive, my dear Sir, by what is here observed (and which you will be pleased to consider in the light of a confidential communication) that my inclinations will dispose and decide me to remain as I am; unless a clear and insurmountable conviction should be impressed on my mind that some very disagreeable consequences must in all human probability result from the indulgence of my wishes.

If you return by land, I shall expect without failure the pleasure of your company. I am much indebted to you for your obliging offer of forwarding such articles as I might want from New York; though I shall not have occasion at this moment to avail myself of your goodness. Mrs. Washington offers her best Complts. to Mrs. Lee, with ardent wishes for the re-establishment of her health which, joined with my own, will conclude me. With great regard etc.

To ALEXANDER HAMILTON

After the Constitution had been ratified, Congress passed an act in September, 1788, designating the first Wednesday in January, 1789, as the day on which the people would choose electors of a President. On the first Wednesday in February the electors were to meet and make their choice, and on the first Wednesday in March, the Government would convene in New York City. To nearly everyone except Washington, his selection as the first President seemed certain, and even he was becoming half-persuaded by the powerful arguments of the country's leaders. Evidence of the gradual breaking down of his resistance is the admission to Hamilton that he faced "the dreaded Dilemma of being forced to accept or refuse." As earnestly as he wanted retirement, he could not ignore public pressure and his own genuine concern for the public weal.

Mount Vernon, October 3, 1788

DEAR SIR: In acknowledging the receipt of your candid and kind letter by the last Post; little more is incumbent upon me, than to thank you sincerely for the frankness with which you communicated your sentiments, and to assure you that the same manly tone of intercourse will always be more than barely welcome, indeed it will be highly acceptable to me. I am particularly glad in the present instance, that you have dealt thus freely and like a friend.

Although I could not help observing, from several publications and letters that my name had been sometimes spoken of, and that it was possible the Contingency which is the subject of your letter might happen; yet I thought it best to maintain a guarded silence and to seek the counsel of my best friends (which I certainly hold in the highest estimation) rather than to hazard an imputation unfriendly to the delicacy of my feelings. For, situated as I am, I could hardly bring the question into the slightest discussion, or ask an opinion even in the most confidential manner, without betraying, in my judgment, some impropriety of conduct, or without feeling an apprehension, that a premature display of anxiety might be construed into a vain-glorious desire of pushing myself into notice as a candidate. Now, if I am not grossly deceived in myself, I should unfeignedly rejoice, in case the Electors, by giving their votes in favor of some other person, would save me from the dreaded Dilemma of being forced to accept or refuse.

If that may not be, I am, in the next place, earnestly desirous of searching out the truth, and of knowing whether there does not exist a probability that the government would be just as happily and effectually carried into execution without my aid, as with it. I am truly solicitous to obtain all the previous information which the circumstances will afford, and to determine (when the determination can with propriety be no longer postponed) according to the principles of right reason, and the dictates of a clear conscience; without too great a reference to the unforeseen consequences, which may affect my person or reputation. Untill that period, I may fairly hold myself open to conviction; though I allow your sentiments to have weight in them; and I shall not pass by your arguments without giving them as dispassionate a consideration, as I can possibly bestow upon them.

In taking a survey of the subject, in whatever point of light I have been able to place it, I will not suppress the acknowledgment, my Dr. Sir that I have always felt a kind of gloom upon my mind, as often as I have been taught to expect, I might, and perhaps must ere long, be called to make a decision. You will, I am well assured, believe the assertion (though I have little expectation it would gain credit from those who are less acquainted with me) that if I should receive the appointment and if I should be prevailed upon to accept it, the acceptance would be attended with more diffidence and reluctance that I ever experienced before in my life. It would be, however, with a fixed and sole determination of lending whatever assistance might be in my power to promote the public weal, in hopes that at a convenient and early period my services might be dispensed with, and that I might be permitted once more to retire, to pass an unclouded evening after the stormy day of life, in the bosom of domestic tranquility.

But why these anticipations? if the friends to the Constitution conceive that my administering the government will be a means of its acceleration and strength, is it not probable that the adversaries of it may entertain the same ideas, and of course make it an object of opposition? That many of this description will become Electors, I can have no doubt of, any more than that their opposition will extend to any character who (from whatever cause) would be likely to thwart their measures. It might be impolitic in them to make this declaration previous to the Election; but I shall be out in my conjectures if they do not act conformably thereto, and that the seeming moderation by which they appear to be actuated at present is neither more or less than a finesse to lull and deceive. Their plan of opposition is systematized, and a regular intercourse, I have much reason to believe between the Leaders of it in the several States is formed to render it more effectual. With sentiments of sincere regard &c.

To SAMUEL VAUGHAN

The choice had been made and Washington could do nothing else but accept. The election took place, in accordance with the act of 1788, on March 4th and his term began on that date. Actually, the electoral votes were counted early in April, because of the delay in gathering a quorum of Congress, and they were unanimous for Washington. In his letter to Samuel Vaughan, three weeks before official notification, the only stipulation Washington makes, characteristically, is one of complete independence. A government relying on the good will of the people, he points out, is exposed to the severest criticism, especially in its beginnings. Free of all commitments, except the fundamental one to give good government under the Constitution, Washington insists upon liberty of action and full responsibility.

Mount Vernon, March 21, 1789

My dear Sir: I have just now been favored with the receipt of your letter, dated the 10th. of October last; and would not delay to make my acknowledgments by the earliest opportunity. While I appreciate with gratitude the favorable sentiments you are pleased to express for me; I flatter myself, in the communication of the following ideas which have occurred on the subject of your letter, you will be persuaded I am influenced alone by that genuine frankness, which is most consistant with friendship and which I desire may ever be a characteristic feature in my conduct through life.

The event which I have long dreaded, I am at last constrained to believe, is now likely to happen. For that I have, during many months, been oppressed with an apprehension it might be deemed unavoidably expedient for me to go again into public life, is known to all, who know me. But from the moment, when the necessity had become more apparent, and as it were inevitable, I anticipated, in a heart filled with distress, the ten thousand embarrassments, perplexities and troubles to which I must again be exposed in the evening of a life, already nearly consumed in public cares. Among all these anxieties, I will not conceal from you, I anticipated none greater, than those that were likely to be produced by applications for appointments to the different offices, which would be created under the new Government. Nor will I conceal, that my apprehensions have already been but too well justified. Scarcely a day passes in which applications of one kind or another do not arrive. Insomuch, that had I not early adopted some general principles, I should before this time have been wholly occupied in this business. As it is, I have found the number of answers, which I have been necessitated to give in my own hand, an almost insupportable burden to me. The points in which all these answers have agreed in substance are: that should it be my lot to go again into public office, I would go into it, without being under any possible engagements of any nature whatsoever: that, so far as I know my own heart, I would not be in the remotest degree influenced, in making nominations, by motives arising from the ties of amity or blood: and that, on the other hand, three things, in my opinion, ought principally to be regarded, viz, the fitness of characters to fill offices, the comparative claims from the former merits and sufferings in service of the different candidates, and the distribution of appointments in as equal a proportion as might be to persons belonging to the different States in the Union; for without precautions of this kind, I clearly foresaw the endless jealousies, and, possibly, the fatal consequences, to which a government, depending altogether on the good will of the people for its establishment, would certainly be exposed in its early stages. Besides I thought, whatever the effect might be in pleasing or displeasing any individuals at the present moment, a due concern for my own reputation not less decisively than a sacred regard to the interest of the community, required that I should hold myself absolutely at liberty to act, while in office, with a sole reference to justice and the public good. It is true, in such a fallible state of existence I may err, and from the want of a complete knowledge of characters in my nominations: but my errors shall be such as result from the head, and not from the heart.

The hurry I am at present in will not permit me to be so particular, as I wished to have been. Nor would the limits of a letter suffice to describe the difficulty which I fear might occur in conferring important offices upon persons, however meritorious they may really be, who have resided but a little while, and are consequently but little known in America. A single disgust excited in a particular State on this account, might, perhaps, raise a flame of opposition that could not easily, if ever, be extinguished. For the fact, I apprehend, will be found to be, that there will be at least a hundred competitors for every office of any kind of importance. Indeed, the number of offices will, in our œconomical management of the affairs of the Republic, be much fewer, as I conceive, and the pretentions of those who may wish to occupy them much more forcible; than many well informed men have imagined. In all events, so much I can with truth declare, that several of the candidates, who have already come forward, have claims to the public attention and gratitude, which cannot be set aside without a palpable act of injustice. Some of them are men of unquestionable talents, who have wasted the flower of their lives, in the civil or military service of their Country: men who have materially injured their properties, and excluded themselves from obtaining a subsistance for their families by the professions they were accustomed to pursue. There are some, I may add, who have shed their blood and deserved all that a grateful Country has to bestow. Nor are they, in my judgment, incapable of reflecting lustre on the most dignified Stations.

From this simple, but just state of circumstances, you will perceive, my dear Sir, on what an ocean of troubles I am likely to be embarked. In the meantime, you will suffer me to observe, that, from the very satisfactory accounts I have been able to obtain of your Son's abilities, accomplishments and dispositions, I am thoroughly persuaded he is capable of discharging the duties of a public office, with the greatest reputation to himself and advantage to the government which might employ him. But, however, I may be convinced of his merits; or, however, I may be disposed to serve him: you will be able to comprehend, from what I have already said, a part of the serious obstacles which will oppose themselves to the success of any

Candidate, so partially known in America as he is. I have no conception of a more delicate task, than that, which is imposed by the Constitution on the Executive. It is the nature of Republicans, who are nearly in a state of equality, to be extremely jealous as to the disposal of all honorary or lucrative appointments. Perfectly convinced I am, that, if injudicious or unpopular measures should be taken by the Executive under the New Government with regards to appointments, the Government itself would be in the utmost danger of being utterly subverted by those measures. So necessary is it, at this crisis, to conciliate the good will of the People: and so impossible is it, in my judgment, to build the edifice of public happiness, but upon their affections.

Your good sense and native candour must serve me as an apology, for being thus explicit. Mrs. Washington and the family desire their most respectful compliments may be presented to you. I add no more than that you may ever count upon the friendly Sentiments and best wishes of him who has the pleasure to subscribe himself. With real esteem etc.

To CHARLES THOMSON

Charles Thomson was Secretary to the Continental Congress. It was 'he who was delegated to convey to Mount Vernon the official notification of Washington's unanimous election as the first President of the United States. The journey to New York City, begun two days later, was a triumphal procession with public festivities and unrestrained ovations along the entire route, culminating when Washington crossed the Hudson on a barge built for the occasion. Hundreds of decorated boats followed in its wake across the bay. On landing, Washington walked past cheering multitudes who threw flowers at his feet, and that night the city was brilliantly illuminated in his honor. The celebration continued for several days, while he was the guest of Governor Clinton, partly because of public exuberance and more particularly because the Inauguration was delayed until April 30th. The postponement was necessitated by a mere matter of protocol concerning the manner in which the Presi-

dent-elect should be addressed. After long debate, it was finally decided that "The President of the United States" would be proper and sufficient as a title.

Mount Vernon, April 14, 1789

SIR: I have been accustomed to pay so much respect to the opinion of my fellow-citizens, that the knowledge of their having given their unanimous suffrages in my favor, scarcely leaves me the alternative for an option. I can not, I believe, give a greater evidence of my sensibility of the honor which they have done me than by accepting the appointment.

I am so much affected by this fresh proof of my Country's Esteem and Confidence that silence can best explain my gratitude. While I realize the arduous nature of the Task which is imposed upon me, and feel my own inability to perform it, I wish however that there may not be reason for regretting the Choice, for indeed all I can promise is only to accomplish that which can be done by an honest zeal.

Upon considering how long a time some of the Gentlemen of both Houses of Congress have been at New York, how anxiously desirous they must be to proceed to business, and how deeply the public mind appears to be impressed with the necessity of doing it speedily, I can not find myself at liberty to delay my journey. I shall therefore be in readiness to set out the day after tomorrow and shall be happy in the pleasure of your company; for you will permit me to say that it is a peculiar gratification to have received the communication from you.

THE FIRST INAUGURAL ADDRESS

The Inaugural ceremony began at nine o'clock in the morning of April 30th with religious services. At noon there was a parade of troops and at 12:30 Washington, in a state coach, rode to the Senate Chamber on the site of what is now the Sub-Treasury Building on Wall Street in New York City. The oath was administered on its balcony by the Chancellor of the State *of New York. Returning to the Senate Chamber, Washington delivered the First Inaugural Address with great gravity. After pledging adherence to the Constitution, Washington renounced any desire for pecuniary reward for his services. In doing so, he followed a principle he had pursued through the entire Revolutionary War. He soon realized, however, that such a precedent would not be followed indefinitely. Accordingly, he later signed an appropriation act which stipulated the Presidential salary at $25,000 per annum.*

April 30, 1789

Fellow Citizens of the Senate and the House of Representatives.

Among the vicissitudes incident to life, no event could have filled me with greater anxieties than that of which the notification was transmitted by your order, and received on the fourteenth day of the present month. On the one hand, I was summoned by my Country, whose voice I can never hear but with veneration and love, from a retreat which I had chosen with the fondest predilection, and, in my flattering hopes, with an immutable decision, as the asylum of my declining years: a retreat which was rendered every day more necessary as well as more dear to me, by the addition of habit to inclination, and of frequent interruptions in my health to the gradual waste committed on it by time. On the other hand, the magnitude and difficulty of the trust to which the voice of my Country called me, being sufficient to awaken in the wisest and most experienced of her citizens, a distrustful scrutiny into his qualifications, could not but overwhelm with dispondence, one, who, inheriting inferior endowments from nature and unpractised in the duties of civil administration, ought to be peculiarly conscious of his own deficiencies. In this conflict of emotions, all I dare aver, is, that it has been my faithful study to collect my duty from a just appreciation of every circumstance, by which it might be affected. All I dare hope, is, that, if in executing this task I have been too much swayed by a grateful remembrance of former instances, or by an affectionate sensibility to this transcendent proof, of the confidence of my fellow-citizens; and have thence too little consulted my incapacity as well as disinclination for the weighty and untried cares before me; my error will be palliated by the motives which misled me, and its consequences be judged by my Country, with some share of the partiality in which they originated.

Such being the impressions under which I have, in obedience to the public summons, repaired to the present station; it would be peculiarly improper to omit in this first official Act, my fervent supplications to that Almighty Being who rules over the Universe, who presides in the Councils of Nations, and whose providential aids can supply every human defect, that his benediction may consecrate to the liberties and happiness of the People of the United States, a Government instituted by themselves for these essential purposes: and may enable every instrument employed in its administration to execute with success, the functions allotted to his charge. In tendering this homage to the Great Author of every public and private good, I assure myself that it expresses your sentiments not less than my own; nor those of my fellow-citizens at large, less than either. No People can be bound to acknowledge and adore the invisible hand, which conducts the Affairs of men more than the People of the United States. Every step, by which they have advanced to the character of an independent nation, seems to have been distinguished by some token of providential agency. And in the important revolution just accomplished in the system of their United Government, the tranquil deliberations and voluntary consent of so many distinct communities, from which the event has resulted, cannot be compared with the means by which most Governments have been established, without some return of pious gratitude along with an humble anticipation of the future blessings which the past seem to presage. These reflections, arising out of the present crisis, have forced themselves too strongly on my mind to be suppressed. You will join with me I trust in thinking, that there are none under the influence of which, the proceedings of a new and free Government can more auspiciously commence.

By the article establishing the Executive Department, it is made the duty of the President "to recommend to your consideration, such measures as he shall judge necessary and expedient." The circumstances under which I now meet you, will acquit me from entering into that subject, farther than to refer to the Great Constitutional Charter under which you are assembled; and which, in defining your powers, designates the objects to which your attention is to be given. It will be more consistent with those circumstances, and far more congenial with the feelings which actuate me, to substitute, in place of a recommendation of particular measures, the tribute that is due to the talents, the rectitude, and the patriotism which adorn the characters selected to devise and adopt them. In these honorable qualifications, I behold the surest pledges, that as on one side, no local prejudices, or attachments; no seperate views, nor party animosities, will misdirect the comprehensive and equal eye which ought to watch over this great assemblage of communities and interests: so, on another, that the foundations of our National policy will be laid in the pure and immutable principles of private morality; and the pre-eminence of a free Government, be exemplified by all the attributes which can win the affections of its Citizens, and command the respect of the world.

I dwell on this prospect with every satisfaction which an ardent love for my Country can inspire: since there is no truth more thoroughly established, than that there exists in the œconomy and course of nature, an indissoluble union between virtue and happiness, between duty and advantage, between the genuine maxims of an honest and magnanimous policy, and the solid rewards of public prosperity and felicity: Since we ought to be no less persuaded that the propitious smiles of Heaven, can never be expected on a nation that disregards the eternal rules of order and right, which Heaven itself has ordained: And since the preservation of the sacred fire of liberty, and the destiny of the Republican model of Government, are justly considered as deeply, perhaps as finally staked, on the experiment entrusted to the hands of the American people.

Besides the ordinary objects submitted to your care, it will remain with your judgment to decide, how far an exercise of the occasional power delegated by the Fifth article of the Constitution is rendered expedient at the present juncture by the nature of objections which have been urged against the System, or by the degree of inquietude which has given birth to them. Instead of undertaking particular recommendations on this subject, in which I could be guided by no lights derived from official opportunities, I shall again give way to my entire confidence in your discernment and pursuit of the public good: For I assure myself that whilst you carefully avoid every alteration which might endanger the benefits of an United and effective Government, or which ought to await the future lessons of experience; a reverence for the characteristic rights of freemen, and a regard for the public harmony, will sufficiently influence your deliberations on the question how far the former can be more impregnably fortified, or the latter be safely and advantageously promoted.

To the preceding observations I have one to add, which will be most properly addressed to the House of Representatives. It concerns myself, and will therefore be as brief as possible. When I was first honoured with a call into the Service of my Country, then on the eve of an arduous struggle for its liberties, the light in which I contemplated my duty required that I should renounce every pecuniary compensation. From this resolution I have in no instance departed. And being still under the impressions which produced it, I must decline as inapplicable to myself, any share in the personal emoluments, which may be indispensably included in a permanent provision for the Executive Department; and must accordingly pray that the pecuniary estimates for the Station in which I am placed, may, during my continuance in it, be limited to such actual expenditures as the public good may be thought to require.

Having thus imparted to you my sentiments, as they have been awakened by the occasion which brings us together, I shall take my present leave; but not without resorting once more to the benign parent of the human race, in humble supplication that since he has been pleased to favour the American people, with opportunities for deliberating in perfect tranquility, and dispositions for deciding with unparellelled unanimity on a form of Government, for the security of their Union, and the advancement of their happiness; so his divine blessing may be equally conspicuous in the enlarged views, the temperate consultations, and the wise measures on which the success of this Government must depend.

QUERIES ON A LINE OF CONDUCT TO BE PURSUED BY THE PRESIDENT

The questions addressed to John Jay, Alexander Hamilton and John Adams indicate Washington's uncertainty about the observance of the proprieties of his new office. The matter of additional expenses that might be incurred by entertainment and travel troubled him. The search for guidance in business and etiquette reflects creditably on Washington's attention to detail and the humility with which he approaches small as well as larger problems.

May 10, 1789

The President of the United States wishes to avail himself of your sentiments on the following points:

1st. Whether a line of conduct, equally distant from an association with all kinds of company on the one hand and from a total seclusion from Society on the other, ought to be adopted by him? and, in that case, how is it to be done?

2d. What will be the least exceptionable method of bringing any system, which may be adopted on this subject, before the public and into use?

3d. Whether, after a little time, one day in every week will not be sufficient for receiving visits of Compliment?

4th. Whether it would tend to prompt impertinent applications and involve disagreeable consequences to have it known, that the President will, every Morning at eight Oclock, be at leisure to give Audience to persons who may have business with him?

5th. Whether, when it shall have been understood that the President is not to give general entertainments in the manner the Presidents of Congress have formerly done, it will be practicable to draw such a line of discrimination in regard to persons, as that Six, eight or ten official characters (including in the rotation the members of both Houses of Congress) may be invited informally or otherwise to dine with him on the days fixed for receiving Company, without exciting clamours in the rest of the Community?

6th. Whether it would be satisfactory to the Public for the President to make about four great entertainmts. in a year on such great occasions as . . . the Anniversary of the Declaration of Independence . . . the Alliance with France . . . the Peace with Great Britain . . . the Organization of the general Government: and whether arrangements of these two last kinds could be in danger of diverting too much of the Presidents time from business, or of producing the evils which it was intended to avoid by his living more recluse than the Presidts. of Congress have heretofore lived.

7th. Whether there would be any impropriety in the Presidents making informal visits; that is to say, in his calling upon his Acquaintances or public Characters for the purposes of sociability or civility: and what (as to the form of doing it) might evince these visits to have been made in his private character, so as that they may not be construed into visits from the President of the United States? and in what light would his appearance rarely at Tea parties be considered?

8th. Whether, during the recess of Congress, it would not be advantageous to the interests of the Union for the President to make the tour of the United States, in order to become better acquainted with their principal Characters and internal Circumstances, as well as to be more accessible to numbers of well-informed persons, who might give him useful information and advices on political subjects?

9th. If there is a probability, that either of the arrangements may take place, which will eventually cause additional expences, whether it would not be proper that those ideas should come into contemplation, at the time when Congress shall make a permanent provision for the support of the Executive?

Remarks

On the one side no augmentation can be effected in the pecuniary establishment which shall be made in the first instance, for the support of the Executive. On the other, all monies destined to that purpose beyond the actual expenditures, will be left in the Treasury of the United States or sacredly applied to the promotion of some national objects.

Many things which appear of little importance in themselves and at the beginning, may have great and durable consequences from their having been established at the commencement of a new general government. It will be much easier to commence the administration, upon a well adjusted system, built on tenable grounds, than to correct errors or alter inconveniences after they shall have been confirmed by habit. The President in all matters of business and etiquette, can have no object but to demean himself in his public character, in such a manner as to maintain the dignity of Office, without subjecting himself to the imputation of superciliousness or unnecessary reserve. Under these impressions, he asks for your candid and undisguised Opinions.

To BENJAMIN FRANKLIN

Franklin was eighty-four years old when this letter was written. Seven months later, on April 17, 1790, he died. As there is no record of any further correspondence between them, this tribute may well have been the last of Washington's few communications to Benjamin Franklin.

New York, September 23, 1789

DEAR SIR: The affectionate congratulations on the recovery of my health, and the warm expressions of personal friendship which were contained in your favor of the 16th instant, claim my gratitude. And the consideration that it was written when you were afflicted with a painful malady, greatly increases my obligation for it.

Would to God, my dear Sir, that I could congratulate you upon the removal of that excruciating pain under which you labour! and that your existence might close with as much ease to yourself, as its continuance has been beneficial to our Country and useful to mankind! Or, if the United wishes of a free people, joined with the earnest prayers of every friend to Science and humanity could relieve the body from pains or infirmities, you could claim an exemption on this score. But this cannot be, and you have within yourself the only resource to which we can confidently apply for relief: a *Philosophic mind.*

If to be venerated for benevolence: If to be admired for talents: If to be esteemed for patriotism: if to be beloved for philanthropy, can gratify the human mind, you must have the pleasing consolation to know that you have not lived in vain; And I flatter myself that it will not be ranked among the least grateful occurrences of your life to be assured that so long as I retain my memory, you will be thought on with respect, veneration and Affection by Your sincere friend etc.

THANKSGIVING PROCLAMATION

The first of the now traditional Presidential Thanksgiving Proclamations set aside the last Thursday in November as the occasion for the offering of prayer and expressions of gratitude by all the people of the nation.

City of New York, October 3, 1789

Whereas it is the duty of all Nations to acknowledge the providence of Almighty God, to obey his will, to be grateful for his benefits, and humbly to implore his protection and favor, and Whereas both Houses of Congress have by their joint Committee requested me "to recommend to the People of the United States a day of public thanks-giving and prayer to be observed by acknowledging with grateful hearts the many signal favors of Almighty God, especially by affording them an opportunity peaceably to establish a form of government for their safety and happiness."

Now therefore I do recommend and assign Thursday the 26th. day of November next to be devoted by the People of these States to the service of that great and glorious Being, who is the beneficent Author of all the good that was, that is, or that will be. That we may then all unite in rendering unto him our sincere and humble thanks, for his kind care and protection of the People of this country previous to their becoming a Nation, for the signal and manifold mercies, and the favorable interpositions of his providence, which we experienced in the course and conclusion of the late war, for the great degree of tranquillity, union, and plenty, which we have since enjoyed, for the peaceable and rational manner in which we have been enabled to establish constitutions of government for our safety and happiness, and particularly the national One now lately instituted, for the civil and religious liberty with which we are blessed, and the means we have of acquiring and diffusing useful knowledge and in general for all the great and various favors which he hath been pleased to confer upon us.

And also that we may then unite in most humbly offering our prayers and supplications to the great Lord and Ruler of Nations and beseech him to pardon our national and other transgressions, to enable us all, whether in public or private stations, to perform our several and relative duties properly and punctually, to render our national government a blessing to all the People, by constantly being a government of wise, just and constitutional laws, discreetly and faithfully executed and obeyed, to protect and guide all Sovereigns and Nations (especially such as have shown kindness unto us) and to bless them with good government, peace, and concord. To promote the knowledge and practice of true religion and virtue, and the encrease of science among them and Us, and generally to grant unto all Mankind such a degree of temporal prosperity as he alone knows to be best.

FIRST ANNUAL ADDRESS TO CONGRESS

In his two terms as President of the United States, Washington delivered eight Annual Addresses to Congress. The one delivered at its opening session on January 8, 1790, marked the beginning of the long tradition of offering an account of the

state of the Union by the Chief Executive. Following the prec-
edent set by this speech, subsequent addresses at the opening
of every session for more than a century and a half have made
use of each occasion to suggest legislation for the deliberation
of the people's elected representatives. The frequently quoted
"To be prepared for War is one of the most effectual means of
preserving peace" appears in the same speech as the less-well-
known plea for the promotion of education as a means of at-
taining better government "by the enlightened confidence of
the people."

January 8, 1790

Fellow Citizens of the Senate and House of Representatives: I embrace with great satisfaction the opportunity which
now presents itself, of congratulating you on the present favourable prospects of our public affairs. The recent accession of the
important State of North Carolina to the Constitution of the
United States (of which official information has been received);
the rising credit and respectability of our Country; the general and increasing good will towards the Government of the
Union, and the concord, peace, and plenty, with which we are
blessed are circumstances auspicious in an eminent degree, to
our national prosperity.

In resuming your consultations for the general good, you
cannot but derive encouragement from the reflection that the
measures of the last Session have been as satisfactory to your
Constituents, as the novelty and difficulty of the work allowed
you to hope. Still further to realize their expectations and to
secure the blessings which a Gracious Providence has placed
within our reach, will in the course of the present important
Session, call for the cool and deliberate exertion of your patriotism, firmness and wisdom.

Among the many interesting objects, which will engage your
attention, that of providing for the common defence will merit
particular regard. To be prepared for War is one of the most
effectual means of perserving peace.

A free people ought not only to be armed but disciplined; to which end a uniform and well digested plan is requisite: And their safety and interest require, that they should promote such manufactories, as tend to render them independent on others for essential, particularly for military supplies.

The proper establishment of the Troops, which may be deemed indispensable, will be entitled to mature deliberation. In the arrangements, which may be made respecting it, it will be of importance to conciliate the comfortable support of the Officers and Soldiers with a due regard to œconomy.

There was reason to hope that the pacific measures adopted with regard to certain hostile tribes of Indians would have relieved the Inhabitants of our Southern and Western frontiers from their depredations. But you will perceive from the information contained in the papers which I shall direct to be laid before you (comprehending a communication from the Commonwealth of Virginia) that we ought to be prepared to afford protection to those parts of the Union; and if necessary to punish aggressors.

The interests of the United States requires that our intercourse with other nations should be facilitated, by such provisions as will enable me to fulfill my duty in that respect, in the manner which circumstances may render most conducive to the public good: And to this end that the compensations to be made to the persons who may be employed, should according to the nature of their appointments, be defined by law; and a competent fund designated for defraying the expenses incident to the conduct of our foreign affairs.

Various considerations also render it expedient, that the terms on which foreigners may be admitted to the rights of Citizens should be speedily ascertained by a uniform rule of naturalization.

Uniformity in the Currency, Weights and Measures of the United States is an object of great importance, and will I am persuaded be duly attended to.

The advancement of Agriculture, Commerce and Manufactures by all proper means, will not I trust need recommendation. But I cannot forbear intimating to you the expediency of giving effectual encouragement as well to the introduction of new and useful inventions from abroad, as to the exertions of skill and genius in producing them at home; and of facilitating the intercourse between the distant parts of our Country by a due attention to the Post-Office and Post-Roads.

Nor am I less persuaded, that you will agree with me in opinion, that there is nothing which can better deserve your patronage than the promotion of Science and Literature. Knowledge is in every country the surest basis of public happiness. In one in which the measures of Government receive their impression so immediately from the sense of the Community as in ours it is proportionably essential. To the security of a free Constitution it contributes in various ways: By convincing those who are intrusted with the public administration, that every valuable end of Government is best answered by the enlightened confidence of the people: and by teaching the people themselves to know and to value their own rights; to discern and provide against invasions of them; to distinguish between oppression and the necessary exercise of lawful authority; between burthens proceeding from a disregard to their convenience and those resulting from the inevitable exigencies of Society; to discriminate the spirit of Liberty from that of licentiousness, cherishing the first, avoiding the last, and uniting a speedy, but temperate vigilance against encroachments, with an inviolable respect to the Laws.

Whether this desirable object will be the best promoted by affording aids to seminaries of learning already established, by the institution of a national University, or by any other expedients, will be well worthy of a place in the deliberations of the Legislature.

To THOMAS JEFFERSON

After the exchange of several letters, Washington prevailed upon Thomas Jefferson to become Secretary of State in the first Cabinet. Jefferson, then Minister to France and at the crest of his fame as the author of the Declaration of Independence and Notes on Virginia, accepted in mid-February and assumed office on March 22, 1790. With him in the Cabinet were Alexander Hamilton as Secretary of the Treasury, Henry Knox as Secre-

tary of War, Edmund Randolph as Attorney General. John Adams occupied the office which he termed "the most insignificant that ever the invention of man contrived, or his imagination conceived," namely, the Vice Presidency, and John Jay was Chief Justice. Between Hamilton and Jefferson there stretched an unbridgeable chasm. The thirty-two-year-old Hamilton was brilliant, resourceful, dominating and an administrative genius. He believed in the sanctity of property and in the sovereignty of a merchant-owner government. Jefferson, on the other hand, had decidedly antithetical political ideas; they were agrarian, for diffusion rather than centralization of power, with final authority vested in the masses of people. Opposition between them was inevitable. The contest became public when John Fenno's United States Gazette, *openly Hamiltonian, and Philip Freneau's partisanly democratic* National Gazette *fought out the issues. The struggle between two ideologies and two men, with the conflict between the Southern planters' and the Northern industrialists' economic philosophies sharpening in focus, was to have an enormous influence on the acts and policies of Washington's Administrations, and, subsequently, on the history of the dominant political parties of the United States.*

New York, January 21, 1790

DEAR SIR: I had the pleasure to receive duly your letter dated the 15th. of Decr. last; but I thought proper to delay answering or mentioning the contents of it, until after the arrival of Mr. Madison, who I understood had been with you. He arrived yesterday, and I now take the earliest opportunity of mentioning to you the result of my reflections; and the expediency of your deciding, at as early a period as may consist with your convenience, on the important subject before you.

Previous to any remarks on the nature of the Office to which you have been recently appointed, I will premise, that I feel such delicacy and embarrassment in consequence of the footing on which you have placed your final determination, as to make it necessary for me to recur to the first ground on which I rested the matter. In confidence, therefore, I will tell you plainly that

I wish not to oppose your inclinations; and that, after you shall have been made a little farther acquainted with the light in which I view the Office of Secretary of State, it must be at your option to determine relative to your acceptance of it, or continuance in your Office abroad.

I consider the successful Administration of the general Government as an object of almost infinite consequence to the present and future happiness of the Citizens of the United States. I consider the Office of Secretary for the Department of State as very important on many accts: and I know of no person, who, in my judgment, could better execute the Duties of it than yourself. Its duties will probably be not quite so arduous and complicated in their execution as you might have been led at the first moment to imagine. At least, it was the opinion of Congress, that, after the division of all the business of a domestic nature between the Departments of the Treasury, War and State that those wch. would be comprehended in the latter might be performed by the same Person, who should have the charge of conducting the Department of foreign Affairs. The experiment was to be made; and if it shall be found that the fact is different, I have little doubt that a farther arrangement or division of the business in the Office of the Department of State will be made, in such manner as to enable it to be performed, under the superintendence of one man, with facility to himself, as well as with advantage and satisfaction to the Public. These observations, however, you will be pleased to remark are merely matters of opinion. But, in order that you may be the better prepared to make your ultimate decision on good grounds, I think it necessary to add one fact, which is this, so far as I have been able to obtain information from all quarters, your late appointment has given very extensive and very great satisfaction to the Public. My original opinion and wish may be collected from my nomination.

As to what you mention in the latter part of your letter, I can only observe, I do not know that any alteration is likely to take place in the Commission from the United States to the Court of France. The necessary arrangements with regard to our intercourse with Foreign Nations have never yet been taken up on a great scale by the Government: because the Department which comprehended Affairs of that nature has never been properly organized, so as to bring the business well and systematically before the Executive. If you shd. finally determine to take upon yourself the duties of the Department of State, it would be highly requisite for you to come on immediately, as many things are required to be done while Congress is in Session rather than at any other time; and as, in that case, your presence might doubtless be much better dispensed with after a little time than at the present moment. Or, in all events, it will be essential that I should be informed of your conclusive option, so that, if you return to France, another Person may be, at as early a day as possible, nominated to fill the Department of State. With sentiments of the highest regard etc.

SECOND ANNUAL ADDRESS TO CONGRESS

Eleven months to the day after the First Annual Address to Congress, Washington appeared before the same body to deliver a message which announced the imminent admission of Kentucky as a State and the establishment of the Judiciary System. Recommendations for the militia, a mint, the Post Office and Post Roads were made with optimism for their adoption. Economic conditions had improved beyond the most sanguine expectations. The panic year of 1786 was being forgotten as if it had been a bad dream; revenues were higher, and altogether the infant nation gave signs of a flourishing childhood and a sturdy maturity.

December 8, 1790

Fellow citizens of the Senate and House of Representatives: In meeting you again I feel much satisfaction in being able to repeat my congratulations on the favorable prospects which continue to distinguish our public Affairs. The abundant fruits of another year have blessed our Country with plenty, and with the means of a flourishing commerce. The progress of public credit is witnessed by a considerable rise of American

Stock abroad as well as at home. And the revenues allotted for this and other national purposes, have been productive beyond the calculations by which they were regulated. This latter circumstance is the more pleasing as it is not only a proof of the fertility of our resources, but as it assures us of a further increase of the national respectability and credit; and let me add, as it bears an honorable testimony to the patriotism and integrity of the mercantile and marine part of our Citizens. The punctuality of the former in discharging their engagements has been exemplary.

In conforming to the powers vested in me by acts of the last Session, a loan of three millions of florins, towards which some provisional measures had previously taken place, has been completed in Holland. As well the celerity with which it has been filled, as the nature of the terms, (considering the more than ordinary demand for borrowing created by the situation of Europe) gives a reasonable hope that the further execution of those powers may proceed with advantage and success. The Secretary of the Treasury has my directions to communicate such further particulars as may be requisite for more precise information.

Since your last Sessions, I have received communications by which it appears, that the District of Kentucky, at present a part of Virginia, has concurred in certain propositions contained in a law of that State; in consequence of which the District is to become a distinct member of the Union, in case the requisite sanction of Congress be added. For this sanction application is now made. I shall cause the papers on this very important transaction to be laid before you. The liberality and harmony, with which it has been conducted will be found to do great honor to both the parties; and the sentiments of warm attachment to the Union and its present Government expressed by our fellow citizens of Kentucky cannot fail to add an affectionate concern for their particular welfare to the great national impressions under which you will decide on the case submitted to you.

It has been heretofore known to Congress, that frequent incursions have been made on our frontier settlements by certain banditti of Indians from the North West side of the Ohio. These with some of the tribes dwelling on and near the Wabash have of late been particularly active in their depredations; and being emboldened by the impunity of their crimes, and aided by such parts of the neighboring tribes as could be seduced to join in their hostilities or afford them a retreat for their prisoners and plunder, they have, instead of listening to the humane overtures made on the part of the United States, renewed their violences with fresh alacrity and greater effect. The lives of a number of valuable Citizens have thus been sacrificed, and some of them under circumstances peculiarly shocking; whilst others have been carried into a deplorable captivity.

These aggravated provocations rendered it essential to the safety of the Western Settlements that the aggressors should be made sensible that the Government of the Union is not less capable of punishing their crimes, than it is disposed to respect their rights and reward their attachments. As this object could not be effected by defensive measures it became necessary to put in force the Act, which empowers the President to call out the Militia for the protection of the frontiers. And I have accordingly authorized an expedition in which the regular troops in that quarter are combined with such drafts of Militia as were deemed sufficient. The event of the measure is yet unknown to me. The Secretary of war is directed to lay before you a statement of the information on which it is founded, as well as an estimate of the expence with which it will be attended.

The disturbed situation of Europe, and particularly the critical posture of the great maritime powers, whilst it ought to make us more thankful for the general peace and security enjoyed by the United States, reminds us at the same time of the circumspection with which it becomes us to preserve these blessings. It requires also that we should not overlook the tendency of a war and even of preparations for a war, among the Nations most concerned in active Commerce with this Country, to abridge the means, and thereby at least enhance the price of transporting its valuable productions to their proper markets. I recommend it to your serious reflexion how far and in what mode, it may be expedient to guard against embarrassments from these contingencies, by such encouragements to our own Navigation as will render our commerce and agriculture less dependent on foreign bottoms, which may fail us in the very moments most interesting to both of these great objects. Our fisheries, and the transportation of our own produce offer us abundant means for guarding ourselves against this evil.

Your attention seems to be not less due to that particular branch of our trade which belongs to the Mediterranean. So many circumstances unite in rendering the present state of it distressful to us, that you will not think any deliberations misemployed, which may lead to its relief and protection.

The laws you have already passed for the establishment of a Judiciary System have opened the doors of Justice to all descriptions of persons. You will consider in your wisdom, whether improvements in that system may yet be made; and particularly whether a uniform process of execution on sentences issuing, from the federal Courts be not desireable through all the states.

The patronage of our commerce, of our merchants and Seamen, has called for the appointment of Consuls in foreign Countries. It seems expedient to regulate by law the exercise of that Jurisdiction and those functions which are permitted them, either by express Convention, or by a friendly indulgence in the places of their residence. The Consular Convention too with his most Christian Majesty has stipulated in certain cases, the aid of the national authority to his Consuls established here. Some legislative provision is requisite to carry these stipulations into full effect.

The establishment of the Militia; of a mint; of Standards of weights and measures; of the Post Office and Post Roads are subjects which (I presume) you will resume of course, and which are abundantly urged by their own importance.

Gentlemen of the House of Representatives: The sufficiency of the Revenues you have established for the objects to which they are appropriated, leaves no doubt that the residuary provisions will be commensurate to the other objects for which the public faith stands now pledged. Allow me, moreover, to hope that it will be a favorite policy with you not merely to secure a payment of the Interest of the debt funded, but, as far and as fast as [the] growing resources of the Country will permit, to exonerate it of the principal itself. The appropriation you have made of the Western Lands explains your dispositions on this subject: And I am persuaded the sooner that valuable fund can be made to contribute along with other means to the actual reduction of the public debt, the more salutary will the measure be to every public interest, as well as the more satisfactory to our Constituents.

Gentlemen of the Senate and House of Representatives: In pursuing the various and weighty business of the present Session I indulge the fullest persuasion that your consultations will be equally marked with wisdom, and animated by the love of your Country. In whatever belongs to my duty, you shall have all the co-operation which an undiminished zeal for its welfare can inspire. It will be happy for us both, and our best reward, if by a successful administration of our respective trusts we can make the established Government more and more instrumental in promoting the good of our fellow Citizens, and more and more the object of their attachment and confidence.

PROCLAMATION

The ambitious, unprecedented plan for a national capital evolved by Major Pierre Charles L'Enfant, the French architect, had Washington's wholehearted approval and support. Unfortunately, speculative greed in holding real estate for inflated prices within the zone of the then-named Federal City created serious difficulties and unforeseeable delays. L'Enfant's insistence on the removal of the house of so influential a citizen as Daniel Carroll, because it obstructed a planned avenue, was said to have led to the troubles which ultimately were the architect's undoing. The uncompromising artist would brook no interference in his grand scheme and even overcame the objections of so capable an architect as Jefferson himself to so large a project. In the end L'Enfant was dismissed. Nonetheless, his pioneer large-scale venture in city planning was carried through as he envisioned it and became the capital that we know today.

Philadelphia, January 24, 1791

Whereas the General assembly of the state of Maryland by an act passed on the 23d. day of December in the year 1788 intitled "an act to cede to Congress a district of 10 miles square in this state for the seat of the government of the U. S." did enact that the representatives of the said state in the house of representatives of the Congress of the U. S. appointed to assemble at New York on the 1st. Wednesday of March then next ensuing, should be; and they were thereby authorised and required on the behalf of the sd state to cede to the Congress of the U. S. any district in the said state not exceeding ten miles square which the Congress might fix upon and accept for the seat of government of the U. S.

And the general assembly of the commonwealth of Virginia by an act passed on the 3d day of December 1789 and intitled "an Act for the cession of ten miles square, or any lesser quantity of territory within this state, to the U. S. in Congress assembled, for the permanent seat of the General government" did enact that a tract of country not exceeding ten miles square, or any lesser quantity, to be located within the limits of the sd state and in any part thereof as Congress might by law direct, should be, and the same was thereby for ever ceded and relinquished to the Congress and government of the U. S. in full and absolute right, and exclusive jurisdiction as well of soil, as of persons residing or to reside thereon, pursuant to the tenor and effect of the 8th section of the first article of the constitution of government of the U. S.

And the Congress of the U. S. by their act passed the 16th day of July 1790 and intitled "an act for establishing the temporary and permanent seat of the government of the U. S." authorised the President of the U. S. to appoint three commissioners to survey, under his direction, and by proper metes and bounds to limit a district of territory, not exceeding ten miles square, on the river Potomac, at some place between the mouths of the Eastern branch, and Connogochegue, which district so to be located and limited, was accepted by the said act of Congress as the district for the permanent seat of the government of the U. S.

Now therefore in pursuance of the powers to me confided, and after duly examining and weighing the advantages and disadvantages of the several situations within the limits aforesd, I do hereby declare and make known that the location of one part of the sd district of ten miles square shall be found by running four lines of experiment in the following manner, that is to say, running from the Court house of Alexandria in Virginia due South West half a mile, and thence a due South East course till it shall strike Hunting creek to fix the Beginning of the sd four lines of experiment.

Then beginning the first of the sd four lines of experiment at the point on Hunting creek where the sd South East course shall have struck the same, and running the sd first line due North West ten miles: thence the second line into Maryland due North East ten miles: thence the third line due South East ten miles: and thence the fourth line due South West ten miles to the beginning on Hunting creek.

And the sd four lines of experiment being so run, I do hereby declare and make known that all that part within the sd four lines of experiment which shall be within the state of Maryland and above the Eastern branch, and all that part within the same four lines of experiment which shall be within the commonwealth of Virginia and above a line to be run from the point of land forming the upper cape of the mouth of the Eastern branch due South West, and no more, is now fixed upon and directed to be surveyed defined, limited and located for a part of the sd district accepted by the sd act of Congress for the permanent seat of the government of the U. S. (Hereby expressly reserving the direction of the survey and location of the remaining part of the said district to be made hereafter contiguous to such part or parts of the present location as is, or shall be agreeable to law.)

And I do accordingly direct the sd Commissioners, appointed agreeably to the tenor of the sd act to proceed forthwith to run the sd lines of experiment, and the same being run, to survey, and by proper metes and bounds to define and limit the part within the same which is herein before directed for immediate location and acceptance, and thereof to make due report to me under their hands and seals.

THIRD ANNUAL ADDRESS TO CONGRESS

On balance, the Third Annual Address to Congress was favorable in its appraisals and recommendations. Washington minimized the hostility of the Indians on the western border and the discontents aroused by the excise laws. Actually, the dangers of Indian uprisings had grown. General Harmar's expedition had failed and Major General Arthur St. Clair had superseded him in command. The succession was less than an improvement. St. Clair's army was wiped out, and another had to be recruited. It was not until three years afterward that "Mad Anthony" Wayne subdued the tribesmen and brought about the Treaty of 1795 which insured peace for many years. As Washington was to learn soon enough, the rumblings over the excise laws were not merely vocal protests. The violence of the Whiskey Rebellion was soon to become a major crisis in the nation.

October 25, 1791

Fellow Citizens of the Senate and House of Representatives:

I meet you, upon the present occasion, with the feelings which are naturally inspired by a strong impression of the prosperous situation of our common Country, and by a persuasion equally strong that the labours of the present Session, which has just commenced, will, under the guidance of a spirit no less prudent than patriotic, issue in measures, conducive to the stability and increase of national prosperity.

Numerous as are the Providential blessings which demand our grateful acknowledgments; the abundance with which another year has again rewarded the industry of the husbandman is too important to escape recollection.

Your own observations, in your respective situations, will have satisfied you of the progressive state of Agriculture, Manufactures, Commerce and Navigation: In tracing their causes, you will have remarked, with particular pleasure, the happy effects of that revival of confidence, public as well as private, to which the Constitution and Laws of the United States have so eminently contributed: And you will have observed, with no less interest, new and decisive proofs of the increasing reputation and credit of the Nation. But you nevertheless, cannot fail to derive satisfaction from the confirmation of these circumstances, which will be disclosed, in the several official communications, that will be made to you in the course of your deliberations.

The rapid subscriptions to the Bank of the United States, which completed the sum allowed to be subscribed, in a single day, is among the striking and pleasing evidences which present themselves, not only of confidence in the Government, but of resource in the community.

In the interval of your recess due attention has been paid to the execution of the different objects which were specially provided for by the laws and Resolutions of the last Session.

Among the most important of these is the defence and security of the Western Frontiers. To accomplish it on the most humane principles was a primary wish.

Accordingly, at the same time that treaties have been provisionally concluded, and other proper means used to attach the wavering, and to confirm in their friendship, the well-disposed tribes of Indians; effectual measures have been adopted to make those of a hostile description sensible that a pacification was desired upon terms of moderation and justice.

These measures having proved unsuccessful, it became necessary to convince the refractory of the power of the United States to punish their depredations. Offensive operations have therefore been directed; to be conducted however, as consistently as possible with the dictates of humanity. Some of these have been crowned with full success, and others are yet depending. The expeditions which have been completed were carried on under the authority, and at the expense of the United States by the Militia of Kentucke; whose enterprise, intripidity and good conduct, are entitled to peculiar commendation.

Overtures of peace are still continued to the deluded Tribes, and considerable numbers of individuals belonging to them, have lately renounced all further opposition, removed from their former situations, and placed themselves under the immediate protection of the United States.

It is sincerely to be desired that all need of coercion, in future, may cease; and that an intimate intercourse may succeed; calculated to advance the happiness of the Indians, and to attach them firmly to the United States.

In order to do this it seems necessary: That they should experience the benefits of an impartial administration of justice. That the mode of alienating their lands the main source of discontent and war, should be so defined and regulated, as to obviate imposition, and, as far as may be practicable, controversy concerning the reality, and extent of the alienations which are made. That commerce with them should be promoted under regulations tending to secure an equitable deportment towards them, and that such rational experiments should be made, for imparting to them the blessings of civilization, as may, from time to time suit their condition. That the Executive of the United States should be enabled to employ the means to which the Indians have been long accustomed for uniting their immediate Interests with the preservation of Peace. And that efficatious provision should be made for inflicting adequate penalties upon all those who, by violating their rights, shall infringe the Treaties, and endanger the peace of the Union.

A System corrisponding with the mild principles of Religion and Philanthropy towards an unenlightened race of Men, whose happiness materially depends on the conduct of the United States, would be as honorable to the national character as conformable to the dictates of sound policy.

The powers specially vested in me by the Act laying certain duties on distilled spirits, which respect the subdivisions of the districts into Surveys, the appointment of Officers, and the assignment of compensations, have likewise been carried into effect. In a matter in which both materials and experience were wanting to guide the calculation, it will be readily conceived that there must have been difficulty in such an adjustment of the rates of compensation as would conciliate a reasonable competency with a proper regard to the limits prescribed by the law. It is hoped that the circumspection, which has been used will be found in the result to have secured the last of the two objects; but it is probable, that with a view to the first, in some instances, a revision of the provision will be found adviseable.

The impressions with which this law has been received by the community, have been, upon the whole, such as were to be expected among enlightened and well-disposed Citizens, from the propriety and necessity of the measure. The novelty, however of the tax, in a considerable part of the United States, and a misconception of some of its provisions, have given occasion, in particular places to some degree of discontent. But it is satisfactory to know that this disposition yields to proper explanations and more just apprehensions of the true nature of the law. and I entertain a full confidence, that it will, in all, give way to motives which arise out of a just sense of duty, and a virtuous regard to the public welfare.

If there are any circumstances, in the law, which consistently with its main design, may be so varied as to remove any well intentioned objections, that may happen to exist, it will consist with a wise moderation to make the proper variations. It is desirable on all occasions, to unite with a steady and firm adherence to constitutional and necessary Acts of Government, the fullest evidence of a disposition, as far as may be practicable, to consult the wishes of every part of the Community, and to lay the foundations of the public administration in the affection of the people.

Pursuant to the authority contained in the several Acts on that subject, a district of ten miles square for the permanent seat of the Government of the United States has been fixed, and announced by proclamation; which district will comprehend lands on both sides of the River Potomack, and the towns of Alexandria and George Town. A City has also been laid out agreeably to a plan which will be placed before Congress: And as there is a prospect, favoured by the rate of sales which have already taken place, of ample funds for carrying on the necessary public buildings, there is every expectation of their due progress.

The completion of the Census of the Inhabitants, for which provision was made by law, has been duly notified (excepting in one instance in which the return has been informal, and another in which it has been omitted or miscarried) and the returns of the Officers, who were charged with this duty, which will be laid before you, will give you the pleasing assurance that the present population of the United States borders on four Millions of persons.

It is proper also to inform you that a further loan of two millions and a half of Florins has been completed in Holland; the terms of which are similar to those of the one last announced, except as to a small reduction of charges. Another on like terms, for six Millions of Florins, had been set on foot under circumstances that assured immediate completion.

Gentlemen of the Senate:

Two treaties, which have been provisionally concluded with the Cherokees and Six Nations of Indians, will be laid before you for your consideration and ratification.

Gentlemen of the House of Representatives:

In entering upon the discharge of your legislative trust, you must anticipate with pleasure, that many of the difficulties, necessarily incident to the first arrangements of a new Government, for an extensive Country, have been happily surmounted by the zealous, and judicious exertions of your predecessors, in co-operation with the other branch of the legislature. The important objects, which remain to be accomplished, will, I am persuaded, be conducted upon principles equally comprehensive, and equally well calculated for the advancement of the general weal.

The time limited for receiving subscriptions to the loans proposed by the Act making provision for the debt of the United States having expired, statements from the proper department will, as soon as possible, apprize you of the exact result. Enough, however is already known, to afford an assurance that the views of that Act have been substantially fulfilled. The subscription in the domestic debt of the United States, has embraced by far the greatest proportion of that debt; affording at the same time proof of the general satisfaction of the public Creditors with the System which has been proposed to their acceptance, and of the spirit of accommodation to the convenience of the Government with which they are actuated. The subscriptions in the debts of the respective States, as far as the provisions of the law have permitted, may be said to be yet more general. The part of the debt of the United States, which remains unsubscribed, will naturally engage your further deliberations.

It is particularly pleasing to me to be able to announce to you, that the revenues which have been established, promise to be adequate to their objects; and may be permitted, if no unforeseen exigency occurs, to supercede, for the present, the necessity of any new burthens upon our Constituents.

An Object which will claim your early attention, is, a provision for the current service of the ensuing year, together with such ascertained demands upon the Treasury as require to be immediately discharged; and such casualties as may have arisen in the execution of the public business, for which no specific appropriations may have yet been made; of all which a proper estimate will be laid before you.

Gentlemen of the Senate,
    and of the House of Representatives:
I shall content myself with a general reference to former communications for several objects, upon which the urgency of other affairs has hitherto postponed any definite resolution. Their importance will recall them to your attention; and I trust that the progress already made in the most arduous arrangements of the Government, will afford you leisure to resume them with advantage.

There are, however, some of them of which I cannot forbear a more particular mention. These are, the Militia; the Post-Office and Post-roads; the Mint; Weights and Measures; a provision for the sale of the vacant lands of the United States.

The first is certainly an object of primary importance,

whether viewed in reference to the national security, to the satisfaction of the community, or to the preservation of order. In connection with this, the establishment of competent Magazines and Arsenals, and the fortification of such places as are peculiarly important and vulnerable, naturally present them-selves to consideration. The safety of the United States, under Divine protection, ought to rest on the basis of systematic and solid arrangements; exposed as little as possible to the hazard of fortuitous circumstances.

The importance of the Post-Office and Post-Roads, on a plan sufficiently liberal and comprehensive, as they respect the expedition, safety and facility of communication, is increased by the instrumentality in diffusing a knowledge of the laws and proceedings of the government; which, while it contributes to the security of the people, serves also to guard them against the effects of misrepresentation and misconception. The establishment of additional cross-posts, especially to some of the important points in the Western and Northern parts of the Union, cannot fail to be of material Utility.

The disorders in the existing currency, and especially the scarcity of small change, a scarcity so peculiarly distressing to the poorer classes, strongly recommend the carrying into immediate effect the resolution already entered into concerning the establishment of a Mint. Measures have been taken, pursuant to that Resolution, for procuring some of the most necessary Artists, together with the requisite Apparatus.

An uniformity in the weights and measures of the Country is among the important objects submitted to you by the Constitution, and if it can be derived from a standard at once invariable and universal, must be no less honorable to the public Councils than conducive to the public convenience.

A provision for the sale of the vacant lands of the United States is particularly urged, among other reasons, by the important considerations that they are pledged as a fund for reimbursing the public debt; that if timely and judiciously applied, they may save the necessity of burthening our citizens with new taxes for the extinguishment of the principal; and that being free to discharge the principal but in a limited proportion no opportunity ought to be lost for availing the public of its right.

To JAMES MADISON

This handwritten letter to James Madison provides early evidence of Washington's authorship of The Farewell Address, delivered on September 19, 1796 (See page 627). Here are to be found the general ideas ultimately incorporated into the valedictory, expanded and amplified there, but set down in essence for Madison's consideration four years and four months before the historic Address was read. The contention among some historians and the legend that has grown concerning Hamilton's "ghosting" of the document disregard Washington's own thoughts on the subject nurtured for almost five years, as well as his written words before and up to the time The Farewell Address was edited into its final form.

Mount Vernon, May 20, 1792

My dear Sir: As there is a possibility if not a probability, that I shall not see you on your return home; or, if I should see you, that it may be on the road and under circumstances which will prevent my speaking to you on the subject we last conversed upon; I take the liberty of committing to paper the following thoughts, and requests.

I have not been unmindful of the sentiments expressed by you in the conversations just alluded to: on the contrary I have again, and again revolved them, with thoughtful anxiety; but without being able to dispose my mind to a longer continuation in the Office I have now the honor to hold. I therefore still look forward to the fulfilment of my fondest and most ardent wishes to spend the remainder of my days (which I can not expect will be many) in ease and tranquility.

Nothing short of conviction that my deriliction of the Chair of Government (if it should be the desire of the people to continue me in it) would involve the Country in serious disputes respecting the chief Magestrate, and the disagreeable consequences which might result therefrom in the floating, and divided opinions which seem to prevail at present, could, in any wise, induce me to relinquish the determination I have formed: and of this I do not see how any evidence can be obtained previous to the Election. My vanity, I am sure, is not of that cast as to allow me to view the subject in this light.

Under these impressions then, permit me to reiterate the request I made to you at our last meeting, namely, to think of the proper time, and the best mode of anouncing the intention; and that you would prepare the latter. In revolving this subject myself, my judgment has always been embarrassed. On the one hand, a previous declaration to retire, not only carries with it the appearance of vanity and self importance, but it may be construed into a manœuvre to be invited to remain. And on the other hand, to say nothing, implys consent; or, at any rate, would leave the matter in doubt, and to decline afterwards might be deemed as bad, and uncandid.

I would fain carry my request to you farther than is asked above, although I am sensible that your compliance with it must add to your trouble; but as the recess may afford you leizure, and I flatter myself you have dispositions to oblige me, I will, without apology desire (if the measure in itself should strike you as proper, and likely to produce public good, or private honor) that you would turn your thoughts to a Valadictory address from me to the public; expressing in plain and modest terms: that having been honored with the Presidential Chair, and to the best of my abilities contributed to the Organization and Administration of the government. that having arrived at a period of life when the private Walks of it, in the shade of retirement, becomes necessary, and will be most pleasing to me; and the spirit of the government may render a rotation in the Elective Officers of it more congenial with their ideas of liberty and safety, that I take my leave of them as a public man; and in bidding them adieu (retaining no other concern than such as will arise from fervent wishes for the prosperity of my Country) I take the liberty at my departure from civil, as I formerly did at my military exit, to invoke a continuation of the blessings of Providence upon it; and upon all those who are the supporters of its interests, and the promoters of harmony, order and good government.

That to impress these things it might, among other things be observed, that we are all the Children of the same country; a Country great and rich in itself; capable, and promising to be, as prosperous and as happy as any the Annals of history have ever brought to our view. That our interest, however, deversified in local and smaller matters, is the same in all the great and essential concerns of the Nation. That the extent of our Country, the diversity of our climate and soil, and the various productions of the States consequent to both, are such as to make one part not only convenient, but perhaps indispensably necessary to the other part; and may render the whole (at no distant period) one of the most independant in the world. That the established government being the work of our own hands, with the seeds of amendment engrafted in the Constitution, may by wisdom, good dispositions, and mutual allowances; aided by experience, bring it as near to perfection as any human institution ever aproximated; and therefore, the only strife among us ought to be, who should be foremost in facilitating and finally accomplishing such great and desirable objects; by giving every possible support, and cement to the Union. That however necessary it may be to keep a watchful eye over public servants, and public measures, yet there ought to be limits to it; for suspicions unfounded, and jealousies too lively, are irritating to honest feelings; and oftentimes are productive of more evil than good.

To enumerate the various subjects which might be introduced into such an Address would require thought; and to mention them to you would be unnecessary, as your own judgment will comprehend all that will be proper; whether to touch, specifically, any of the exceptionable parts of the Constitution may be doubted. All I shall add therefore at present, is, to beg the favor of you to consider: 1st. the propriety of such an Address. 2d. if approved, the several matters which ought to be contained in it; and 3d. the time it should appear: that is, whether at the declaration of my intention to withdraw from the service of the public; or to let it be the closing Act of my

Administration; which, will end with the next Session of Congress (the probability being that that body will continue sitting until March,) when the House of Representatives will also dissolve.

'Though I do not wish to hurry you (the cases not pressing) in the execution of either of the publications beforementioned, yet I should be glad to hear from you generally on both; and to receive them in time, if you should not come to Philadelphia until the Session commences, in the form they are finally to take. I beg leave to draw your attention also to such things as you shall conceive fit subjects for Communication on that occasion; and, noting them as they occur, that you would be so good as to furnish me with them in time to be prepared, and engrafted with others for the opening of the Session. With very sincere and Affectionate regard etc.

PROCLAMATION

The imposition of excise taxes in 1791 and 1792 was the signal for an outbreak of violence in western Pennsylvania. The Whiskey Rebellion was attributed by some to the formation of the so-called Democratic Societies, which had their origins in Kentucky and were opposed by Washington, more under the influence of Hamilton than of Jefferson. It is more likely that the insurrection was economic in its inception and simply broke into violence because a special group felt aggrieved against what was thought burdensome taxation. At any rate, Presidential proclamations were ignored, Federal officers were attacked, buildings were burned and mob rule swayed over a large section of the State. Washington, determined that the law of the nation must be observed and executed, sent in the militia and he himself hurried to the scene. The rebellion was subdued with virtually no casualties and three years later Washington granted an amnesty to the rebels.

September 15, 1792

Whereas certain violent and unwarrantable proceedings have lately taken place tending to obstruct the operation of the laws of the United States for raising a revenue upon spirits distilled within the same, enacted pursuant to express authority delegated in the constitution of the United States; which proceedings are subversive of good order, contrary to the duty that every citizen owes to his country, and to the laws, and of a nature dangerous to the very being of a government:

And whereas such proceedings are the more unwarrantable, by reason of the moderation which has been heretofore shewn on the part of the government, and of the disposition which has been manifested by the Legislature (who alone have authority to suspend the operation of laws) to obviate causes of objection, and to render the laws as acceptable as possible: And whereas it is the particular duty of the Executive "to take care that the laws be faithfully executed;" and not only that the duty, but the permanent interests and happiness of the people require, that every legal and necessary step should be pursued, as well to prevent such violent and unwarrantable proceedings, as to bring to justice the infractors of the laws and secure obedience thereto.

Now therefore I GEORGE WASHINGTON, President of the United States, do by these presents most earnestly admonish and exhort all persons whom it may concern, to refrain and desist from all unlawful combinations and proceedings whatsoever having for object or tending to obstruct the operation of the laws aforesaid; inasmuch as all lawful ways and means will be strictly put in execution for bringing to justice the infractors thereof and securing obedience thereto.

And I do moreover charge and require all Courts, Magistrates and Officers whom it may concern, according to the duties of their several offices, to exert the powers in them respectively vested by law for the purposes aforesaid, hereby also enjoining and requiring all persons whomsoever, as they tender the welfare of their country, the just and due authority of government and the preservation of the public peace, to be aiding and assisting therein according to law.

FOURTH ANNUAL ADDRESS TO CONGRESS

Four months before taking the oath of office for his second term as President, Washington rendered to Congress the following address on the achievements and program of his Administration. Anxiety about Indian affairs was balanced by reassurances on the prosperous condition of the Treasury. The Whiskey Rebellion is alluded to only obliquely as an obstruction to the operation of the law, which must be obeyed, offenders against it being brought to justice within Constitutional and legal limits. Washington urges revision of the judiciary system and argues for the circulation of political information on an ever-wider scale. The mint is in operation; Kentucky has adopted a Constitution; provisions are being made for reducing the public debt.

November 6, 1792

Fellow-Citizens of the Senate, and of the House of Representatives: It is some abatement of the satisfaction, with which I meet you on the present occasion, that in felicitating you on a continuance of the National prosperity, generally, I am not able to add to it information that the Indian hostilities, which have for some time past distressed our North Western frontier, have terminated.

You will, I am persuaded, learn, with no less concern than I communicate it, that reiterated endeavors, toward effecting a pacification, have hitherto issued only in new and outrageous proofs of persevering hostility, on the part of the tribes with whom we are in contest. An earnest desire to procure tranquillity to the frontier; to stop the further effusion of blood; to arrest the progress of expense; to forward the prevalent wish of the Nation, for peace, has led, through various channels, to strenuous efforts, to accomplish these desirable purposes: In making which efforts, I consulted less my own anticipations of the event, or the scruples, which some considerations were calculated to inspire, than the wish to find the object attainable; or if not attainable, to ascertain unequivocally that such is the case.

A detail of the measures, which have been pursued, and of their consequences, which will be laid before you, while it will confirm to you the want of success, thus far, will, I trust, evince that means as proper and as efficacious as could have been devised, have been employed. The issue of some of them, indeed, is still depending; but a favourable one, though not to be despaired of, is not promised by anything that has yet happened.

In the course of the attempts which have been made, some valuable citizens have fallen victims to their zeal for the public service. A sanction commonly respected even among savages, has been found, in this instance, insufficient to protect from Massacre the emissaries of peace. It will, I presume, be duly considered whether the occasion does not call for an exercise of liberality towards the families of the deceased.

It must add to your concern, to be informed, that besides the continuation of hostile appearances among the tribes North of the Ohio, some threatening symptoms have of late been revived among some of those south of it.

A part of the Cherokees, known by the name of Chickamagas, inhabitating five Villages on the Tennesee River, have been long in the practice of committing depredations on the neighbouring settlements.

It was hoped that the treaty of Holstin, made with the Cherokee nation in July 1791, would have prevented a repetition of such depredations. But the event has not answered this hope. The Chickamagas, aided by some Banditti of another tribe in their vicinity, have recently perpetrated wanton and unprovoked hostilities upon the Citizens of the United States in that quarter. The information which has been received on this subject will be laid before you. Hitherto defensive precautions only have been strictly enjoined and observed.

It is not understood that any breach of Treaty, or aggression whatsoever, on the part of the United States, or their Citizens, is even alleged as a pretext for the spirit of hostility in this quarter.

I have reason to believe that every practicable exertion has been made (pursuant to the provision by law for that purpose) to be prepared for the alternative of a prosecution of the war, in the event of a failure of pacific overtures. A large proportion of the troops authorized to be raised, has been recruited, though the number is still incomplete. And pains have been taken to discipline and put them in condition for the particular kind of service to be performed. A delay of operations (besides being dictated by the measures which were pursuing towards a pacific termination of the war) has been in itself deemed preferable to immature efforts. A statement from the proper department with regard to the number of troops raised, and some other points which have been suggested, will afford more precise information, as a guide to the legislative consultations; and among other things will enable Congress to judge whether some additional stimulus to the recruiting service may not be adviseable.

In looking forward to the future expense of the operations, which may be found inevitable, I derive consolation from the information I receive, that the product of the revenues for the present year, is likely to supersede the necessity of additional burthens on the community, for the service of the ensuing year. This, however, will be better ascertained in the course of the Session; and it is proper to add, that the information alluded to proceeds upon the supposition of no material extension of the spirit of hostility.

I cannot dismiss the subject of Indian affairs without again recommending to your consideration the expediency of more adequate provision for giving energy to the laws throughout our interior frontier, and for restraining the commission of outrages upon the Indians; without which all pacific plans must prove nugatory. To enable, by competent rewards, the employment of qualified and trusty persons to reside among them, as agents, would also contribute to the preservation of peace and good neighbourhood. If, in addition to these expedients, an eligible plan could be devised for promoting civilization among the friendly tribes, and for carrying on trade with them, upon a scale equal to their wants, and under regulations calculated to protect them from imposition and extortion, its influence in cementing their interests with our's could not but be considerable.

The prosperous state of our Revenue has been intimated. This would be still more the case, were it not for the impediments, which in some places continue to embarrass the collection of the duties on spirits distilled within the United States. These impediments have lessened, and are lessening in local extent, and as applied to the community at large, the contentment with the law appears to be progressive.

But symptoms of increased opposition having lately manifested themselves in certain quarters, I judged a special interposition on my part, proper and adviseable; and under this impression, have issued a proclamation, warning against all unlawful combinations and proceedings, having for their object or tending to obstruct the operation of the law in question, and announcing that all lawful ways and means would be strictly put in execution for bringing to justice the infractors thereof, and securing obedience thereto.

Measures have also been taken for the prosecution of offenders: and Congress may be assured, that nothing within Constitutional and legal limits, which may depend on me, shall be wanting to assert and maintain the just authority of the laws. In fulfilling this trust, I shall count intirely upon the full cooperation of the other departments of Government, and upon the zealous support of all good Citizens.

I cannot forbear to bring again into the view of the Legislature the subject of a revision of the Judiciary System. A representation from the Judges of the Supreme Court, which will be laid before you, points out some of the inconveniences that are experienced. In the course of the execution of the laws, considerations arise out of the structure of that System, which, in some cases, tend to relax their efficacy. As connected with this subject, provisions to facilitate the taking of bail upon processes out of the Courts of the United States, and supplementary definition of Offences against the Constitution and laws of the Union, and of the punishment for such Offences, will, it is presumed, be found worthy of particular attention.

Observations on the value of peace with other Nations are unnecessary. It would be wise, however, by timely provisions, to guard against those acts of our own Citizens, which might tend to disturb it, and to put ourselves in a condition to give that satisfaction to foreign Nations which we may sometimes have occasion to require from them. I particularly recommend to your consideration the means of preventing those aggressions by our Citizens on the territory of other nations, and other infractions of the law of Nations, which, furnishing just subject of complaint, might endanger our peace with them. And in general, the maintenance of a friendly intercourse with foreign powers will be presented to your attention by the expiration of the law for that purpose, which takes place, if not renewed, at the close of the present session.

In execution of the Authority given by the legislature, measures have been taken for engaging some artists from abroad to aid in the establishment of our mint; others have been employed at home. Provision has been made for the requisite buildings, and these are now putting into proper condition for the purposes of the establishment. There has also been a small beginning in the coinage of half-dismes; the want of small coins in circulation calling the first attention to them.

The regulation of foreign Coins in correspondency with the principles of our national coinage, as being essential to their due operation, and to order in our money concerns, will, I doubt not, be resumed and completed.

It is represented that some provisions in the law, which establishes the Post-Office, operate, in experiment, against the transmission of newspapers to distant parts of the Country. Should this, upon due inquiry, be found to be the case, a full conviction of the importance of facilitating the circulation of political intelligence and information, will, I doubt not, lead to the application of a remedy.

The adoption of a Constitution for the State of Kentucky has been notified to me. The Legislature will share with me in the satisfaction which arises from an event interesting to the happiness of the part of the Nation to which it relates, and conducive to the general Order.

It is proper likewise to inform you, that since my last communication on the subject, and in further execution of the Acts severally making provision for the public debt, and for the reduction thereof, three new loans have been effected, each for three millions of Florins. One at Antwerp, at the annual interest of four and one half per Cent, with an Allowance of four per Cent in lieu of all charges; and the other two at Amsterdam, at the annual interest of four per Cent, with an allowance of five and one half per Cent in one case, and of five per Cent in the other in lieu of all charges. The rates of these loans, and the circumstances under which they have been made, are confirmations of the high state of our Credit abroad.

Among the objects to which these funds have been directed to be applied, the payment of the debts due to certain foreign Officers, according to the provision made during the last Session, has been embraced.

Gentlemen of the House of Representatives: I entertain a strong hope that the state of the national finances is now sufficiently matured to enable you to enter upon a Systematic and effectual arrangement for the regular redemption and discharge of the public debt, according to the right which has been reserved to the Government. No measure can be more desireable, whether viewed with an eye to its intrinsic importance, or to the general sentiment and wish of the Nation.

Provision is likewise requisite for the reimbursement of the loan which has been made for the Bank of the United States, pursuant to the eleventh section of the Act by which it is incorporated. In fulfilling the public stipulations in this particular, it is expected a valuable saving will be made.

Appropriations for the current service of the ensuing year, and for such extraordinaries as may require provision, will demand, and, I doubt not, will engage your early attention.

Gentlemen of the Senate and of the House of Representatives: I content myself with recalling your attention, generally, to such objects, not particularized in my present, as have been suggested in my former communications to you.

Various temporary laws will expire during the present Session. Among these, that which regulates trade and intercourse with the Indian Tribes, will merit particular notice .

The results of your common deliberations, hitherto, will, I trust, be productive of solid and durable advantages to our Constituents; such as, by conciliating more and more their ultimate suffrage, will tend to strengthen and confirm their attachment to that constitution of Government, upon which, under Divine Providence, materially depend their Union, their safety and their happiness.

Still further to promote and secure these inestimable ends, there is nothing which can have a more powerful tendency, than the careful cultivation of harmony, combined with a due regard to stability, in the public Councils.

SECOND INAUGURAL ADDRESS

With what is the briefest Inaugural Address delivered by a President of the United States, Washington began his second term in office. His often-asserted reluctance again to undertake the duties and cares of the Presidency were overcome at last by pressures and persuasions from all sides. The four sentences of this speech make up in solemnity what they lack in spacious promises.

[Philadelphia,] March 4, 1793

Fellow-Citizens: I am again called upon by the voice of my Country to execute the functions of its Chief Magistrate. When the occasion proper for it shall arrive, I shall endeavour to express the high sense I entertain of this distinguished honor, and of the confidence which has been reposed in me by the people of United America.

Previous to the execution of any official act of the President, the Constitution requires an Oath of Office. This Oath I am now about to take, and in your presence, that if it shall be found during my administration of the Government I have in any instance violated willingly, or knowingly, the injunction thereof, I may (besides incurring Constitutional punishmt) be subject to the upbraidings of all who are now witnesses of the present solemn Ceremony.

QUESTIONS PROPOSED TO BE SUBMITTED TO THE JUDGES OF THE SUPREME COURT

France had declared war on Great Britain and Spain. By the Treaty of 1778 the United States was still an ally of France and might be called upon to live up to the guarantee to the French of her possessions in the West Indies. Washington's proclamation of neutrality on April 22, 1793, immediately stirred a violent division of opinion. To one faction, his statement of policy was read in the light of a royal edict; it was too great an assumption of power; it was a manifestation of partiality toward England and hostility toward the French who had been so co-operative in our Revolutionary struggle. To another faction, it was a declaration of abhorrence of the doctrines of the French Revolution and thus deserved support as a conservative measure. Hamilton, who saw no resemblance whatever between the Revolutions in France and America, was for it. Jefferson, regarding the cause of France as sacred and also wanting to keep America out of war, could not give it his whole-hearted approval. Yet he carried out its provisions to the letter.

Edmond Charles Genet, appointed Minister from France to the United States, landed at Charleston and forthwith began, without even offering his credentials to Jefferson, to commission, arm and equip privateers to prey on British shipping in the West Indies trade. The Girondist aroused wild popular acclaim. At first, Jefferson, sympathetic to Revolutionary France and eager to approve a movement that arose from the people, welcomed Genet, but later was less enthusiastic. Hamilton, more conservative, was antagonistic from the beginning. With more zeal than tact, Genet presumed to question Washington's authority and went further and further in defiance of the Government's policy of neutrality. He only succeeded in bringing about a request for his recall, with Jefferson's concurrence. Genet had overplayed his popularity. His maneuvers to embroil the United States failed and he was suspended as a Minister by his Government.

The following questions give evidence of Washington's scrupulous search for information before he came to a decision on matters of fateful consequence.

July 18, 1793

I. Do the treaties between the United States and France give to France or her Citizens a right, when at war with a power with whom the United States are at peace, to fit out originally in and from the ports of the United States vessels armed for war, with or without commission?

II. If they give such a right, does it extend to all manner of armed vessels, or to particular kinds only? if the latter, to what kinds does it extend?

III. Do they give to France, or her Citizens, in the case supposed, a right to refit or arm anew vessels, which before their coming within any port of the United States were armed for war, with or without commission?

IV. If they give such a right, does it extend to all manner of armed Vessels, or to particular kinds only? If the latter, to what kinds does it extend? Does it include an augmentation of force, or does it only extend to replacing the Vessel in statu quo?

V. Does the 22d article of the treaty of commerce, in the case supposed, extend to vessels armed for war on account of the Government of a power at war with France, or to merchant armed vessels belonging to the subjects or Citizens of that power, (viz) of the description of those which, by the English are called Letters of Marque Ships, by the French Batiments armés en marchandize et en guerrè?

VI. Do the treaties aforesaid prohibit the United States from permitting, in the case supposed, the armed vessels belonging to a power at war with France, or to the Citizens or Subjects of such power to come within the ports of the United States, there to remain as long as they may think fit, except in the case of their coming in with prizes made of the Subjects or property of France?

VII. Do they prohibit the United States from permitting, in the case supposed, vessels armed on account of the Government of a power at war with France, or vessels armed for merchandise and war, with or without commission on account of the Subjects or Citizens of such power, or any vessels other than those commonly called privateers, to sell freely whatsoever they may bring into the ports of the United States and freely to purchase in and carry from the ports of the U S goods, merchandize, and commodities, except as excepted in the last question?

VIII. Do they oblige the United States to permit France, in the case supposed, to sell in their ports the prizes which she or her Citizens may have made of any power at war with her, the Citizens or Subjects of such power; or exempt from the payment of the usual duties, on Ships and merchandize, the prizes so made, in the case of their being to be sold within the ports of the United States?

IX. Do those treaties, particularly the Consular Convention, authorize France, as of right, to erect Courts within the Jurisdiction of the United States, or the trial and condemnation of prizes made by armed Vessels in her service?

X. Do the laws and usages of Nations authorize her, as of right, to erect such Courts for such purpose?

XI. Do the laws of neutrality, considered relatively to the treaties of the United States with foreign powers, or independently of those treaties, permit the United States in the case supposed, to allow France or her Citizens the privilege of fitting out originally in and from the ports of the United States, vessels armed and commissioned for war, either on account of the Government, or of private persons, or both?

XII. Do those laws permit the United States to extend the like privilege to a power at war with France?

XIII. Do the laws of neutrality, considered as aforesaid, permit the United States, in the case supposed, to allow to France or her Citizens the privilege of refitting or arming anew, vessels, which before their coming within the United States, were armed and commissioned for war? May such privileges include an augmentation of the force of such Vessels?

XIV. Do those laws permit the United States to extend the like privilege to a power at war with France?

XV. Do those laws, in the case supposed, permit Merchant Vessels of either of the powers at war, to arm in the Ports of the United States, without being commissioned? May this privilege be rightfully refused?

XVI. Does it make any difference in point of principle, whether a vessel be armed for war, or the force of an armed vessel be augmented, in the ports of the United States, with means procured in the United States or with means brought into them by the party who shall so arm or augment the force of such vessel? If the first be unlawful, is the last lawful?

XVII. Do the laws of neutrality, considered as aforesaid, authorize the United States to permit France, her Subjects or Citizens, the sale within their ports of prizes made of the Subjects or property of a power at war with France, before they have been carried into some port of France and there condemned, refusing the like privilege to her enemy?

XVIII. Do those laws authorize the United States to permit to France the erection of Courts within their territory and jurisdiction for the trial and condemnation of prizes, refusing that privilege to a power at war with France?

XIX. If any armed vessel of a foreign power at war with another, with whom the United States are at peace, shall make prize of the subjects or property of its enemy within the territory or jurisdiction of the United States, have not the United States a right to cause restitution of such prizes? Are they bound, or not by the principles of Neutrality to do so, if such prize shall be within their power?

XX. To what distance, by the laws and usages of Nations, may the United States exercise the right of prohibiting the hostilities of foreign powers at war with each other, within Rivers, Bays, and Arms of the Sea, and upon the Sea along the coasts of the United States?

XXI. Have vessels armed for war, under commission from a foreign power a right without the consent of the United States to engage within their jurisdiction Seamen or Soldiers for the service of such vessels, being Citizens of that power or of another foreign power, or Citizens of the United States?

XXII. What are the Articles, by name, to be prohibited to both or either party?

XXIII. To what does the reparation permitted in the 19th Article of the treaty with France go?

XXIV. What may be done as to vessels armed in our ports before the President's proclamation? and what as to the prizes they made before and after?

XXV. May we, within our own ports, sell ships to both parties, prepared merely for merchandise? may they be pierced for guns?

XXVI. May we carry either or both kinds to the ports of the belligerent powers for sale?

XXVII. Is the principle that free bottoms make free goods, and enemy bottoms make enemy goods, to be considered as now an established part of the law of Nations?

XXVIII. If it is not, are nations with whom we have no treaties, authorized by the law of Nations to take out of our vessels enemy passengers, not being soldiers, and their baggage?

XXIX. May an armed vessel belonging to any of the belligerent powers follow immediately merchant-vessels, enemies, departing from our ports, for the purpose of making prizes of them? If not, how long ought the former to remain after the latter has sailed? And what shall be considered as the place of departure, from which the time is to be counted? And how are the facts to be ascertained?

FIFTH ANNUAL ADDRESS TO CONGRESS

Here, in the light of a bewildered public opinion over the policy of neutrality, the intrigues of Genet, English aggressions and a sense of indebtedness to France, Washington reports on the measures taken and proposed to protect the rights and interests of the United States, while advancing peaceful relations with foreign countries. Over and over again he emphasizes the need for complete defense as the best guarantee of peace, saying: "There is a rank due to the United States among Nations, which will be withheld, if not absolutely lost, by the reputation of weakness. If we desire to avoid insult, we must be able to repel it. . . ."

Philadelphia, December 3, 1793

Fellow Citizens of the Senate, and of the House of Representatives: Since the commencement of the term, for which I have been again called into office, no fit occasion has arisen for expressing to my fellow Citizens at large, the deep and respectful sense, which I feel, of the renewed testimony of public approbation. While on the one hand, it awakened my gratitude for all those instances of affectionate partiality, with which I have been honored by my Country; on the other, it could not prevent an earnest wish for that retirement, from which no private consideration should ever have torn me. But influenced by the belief, that my conduct would be estimated according to its real motives; and that the people, and the authorities derived from them, would support exertions, having nothing personal for their object, I have obeyed the suffrage which commanded me to resume the Executive power; and I humbly implore that Being, on whose Will the fate of Nations depends, to crown with success our mutual endeavours for the general happiness.

As soon as the War in Europe had embraced those Powers, with whom the United States have the most extensive relations; there was reason to apprehend that our intercourse with them might be interrupted, and our disposition for peace, drawn into question, by the suspicions, too often entertained by belligerent Nations. It seemed therefore to be my duty to admonish our Citizens of the consequences of a contraband trade, and of hostile Acts to any of the parties; and to obtain by a declaration of the existing legal state of things, an easier admission of our right to the immunities, belonging to our situation. Under these impressions the Proclamation, which will be laid before you, was issued.

In this posture of affairs, both new and delicate, I resolved to adopt general rules, which should conform to the Treaties, and assert the priviledges, of the United States. These were reduced into a system, which will be communicated to you. Although I have not thought myself at liberty to forbid the Sale of the prizes, permitted by our treaty of Commerce with France to be brought into our ports; I have not refused to cause them to be restored, when they were taken within the protection of our territory; or by vessels commissioned, or equipped in a warlike form within the limits of the United States.

It rests with the wisdom of Congress to correct, improve or enforce this plan of procedure; and it will probably be found expedient, to extend the legal code, and the Jurisdiction of the Courts of the United States, to many cases, which, though dependent on principles already recognized, demand some further provisions.

Where individuals shall within the United States, array themselves in hostility against any of the powers at war; or enter upon Military expeditions, or enterprizes within the jurisdiction of the United States; or usurp and exercise judicial authority within the United States; or where the penalties on violations of the law of Nations may have been indistinctly marked, or are inadequate; these offences cannot receive too early and close an attention, and require prompt and decisive remedies.

Whatsoever those remedies may be, they will be well administered by the Judiciary, who possess a long established course of investigation, effectual process, and Officers in the habit of executing it. In like manner; as several of the Courts have doubted, under particular circumstances, their power to liberate the vessels of a Nation at peace, and even of a citizen of the United States, although seized under a false colour of being hostile property; and have denied their power to liberate certain captures within the protection of our territory; it would seem proper to regulate their jurisdiction in these points. But if the Executive is to be the resort in either of the two last mentioned cases, it is hoped, that he will be authorized by law, to have facts ascertained by the Courts, when, for his own information, he shall request it.

I cannot recommend to your notice measures for the fulfilment of our duties to the rest of the world, without again pressing upon you the necessity of placing ourselves in a condition of compleat defence, and of exacting from them the fulfilment of their duties towards us. The United States ought not to endulge a persuasion, that, contrary to the order of human events, they will for ever keep at a distance those painful appeals to arms, with which the history of every other nation abounds. There is a rank due to the United States among Nations, which will be withheld, if not absolutely lost, by the reputation of weakness. If we desire to avoid insult, we must be able to repel it; if we desire to secure peace, one of the most powerful instruments of our rising prosperity, it must be known, that we are at all times ready for War.

The documents, which will be presented to you, will shew the amount, and kinds of Arms and military stores now in our Magazines and Arsenals: and yet an addition even to these supplies cannot with prudence be neglected; as it would leave nothing to the uncertainty of procuring a warlike apparatus, in the moment of public danger. Nor can such arrangements, with such objects, be exposed to the censure of jealousy of the warmest friends of Republican Government. They are incapable of abuse in the hands of the Militia, who ought to possess a pride in being the depositary of the force of the Republic, and may be trained to a degree of energy, equal to every military exigency of the United States. But it is an inquiry, which cannot be too solemnly pursued, whether the act "more effectually to provide for the National defence by establishing an uniform Militia throughout the United States" has organized them so as to produce their full effect; whether your own experience in the several States has not detected some imperfections in the scheme; and whether a material feature in an improvement of it, ought not to be, to afford an opportunity for the study of those branches of the Military art, which can scarcely ever be attained by practice alone?

The connexion of the United States with Europe, has become extremely interesting. The occurrences, which relate to it, and have passed under the knowledge of the Executive, will be exhibited to Congress in a subsequent communication.

When we contemplate the war on our frontiers, it may be truly affirmed, that every reasonable effort has been made to adjust the causes of dissension with the Indians, North of the Ohio. The Instructions given to the Commissioners evince a moderation and equity proceeding from a sincere love of peace, and a liberality, having no restriction but the essential interests and dignity of the United States. The attempt, however, of an amicable negotiation having been frustrated, the troops have marched to act offensively. Although the proposed treaty did not arrest the progress of military preparation; it is doubtful, how far the advance of the Season, before good faith justified active movements, may retard them, during the remainder of the year. From the papers and intelligence, which relate to this important subject, you will determine, whether the deficiency in the number of Troops, granted by law, shall be compensated by succours of Militia; or additional encouragements shall be proposed to recruits. An anxiety has been also demonstrated by the Executive, for peace with the Creeks and the Cherokees. The former have been relieved with Corn and with clothing, and offensive measures against them prohibited during the recess of Congress. To satisfy the complaints of the latter, prosecutions have been instituted for the violences committed upon them. But the papers, which will be delivered to you, disclose the critical footing on which we stand in regard to both those tribes; and it is with Congress to pronounce what shall be done.

After they shall have provided for the present emergency, it will merit their most serious labours, to render tranquillity with the Savages permanent, by creating ties of interest. Next to a rigorous execution of justice on the violators of peace, the establishment of commerce with the Indian nations in behalf of the United States, is most likely to conciliate their attachment. But it ought to be conducted without fraud, without extortion, with constant and plentiful supplies; with a ready market for the commodities of the Indians, and a stated price for what they give in payment, and receive in exchange. Individuals will not pursue such a traffic, unless they be allured by the hope of profit; but it will be enough for the United States to be reimbursed only. Should this recommendation accord with the opinion of Congress, they will recollect, that it cannot be accomplished by any means yet in the hands of the Executive.

Gentlemen of the House of Representatives

The Commissioners, charged with the settlement of Accounts between the United and individual States, concluded their important functions, within the time limited by Law; and the balances, struck in their report, which will be laid before Congress, have been placed on the Books of the Treasury.

On the first day of June last, an instalment of one million of florins became payable on the loans of the United States in Holland. This was adjusted by a prolongation of the period of reimbursement, in nature of a new loan, at an interest at five per cent for the term of ten years; and the expences of this operation were a commission of three pr Cent.

The first instalment of the loan of two millions of dollars from the Bank of the United States, has been paid, as was directed by Law. For the second, it is necessary, that provision should be made.

No pecuniary consideration is more urgent, than the regular redemption and discharge of the public debt: on none can delay be more injurious, or an œconomy of time more valuable.

The productiveness of the public revenues hitherto, has continued to equal the anticipations which were formed of it; but it is not expected to prove commensurate with all the objects, which have been suggested. Some auxiliary provisions will, therefore, it is presumed, be requisite; and it is hoped that these may be made, consistently with a due regard to the convenience of our Citizens, who cannot but be sensible of the true wisdom of encountering a small present addition to their contributions, to obviate a future accumulation of burthens.

But here, I cannot forbear to recommend a repeal of the tax on the transportation of public prints. There is no resource so firm for the Government of the United States, as the affections of the people guided by an enlightened policy; and to this primary good, nothing can conduce more, than a faithful representation of public proceedings, diffused, without restraint, throughout the United States.

An estimate of the appropriations, necessary for the current service of the ensuing year, and a statement of a purchase of Arms and Military stores made during the recess, will be presented to Congress.

Gentlemen of the Senate, and of the House of Representatives

The several subjects, to which I have now referred, open a wide range to your deliberations; and involve some of the choicest interests of our common Country. Permit me to bring to your remembrance the magnitude of your task. Without an un-prejudiced coolness, the welfare of the Government may be haz-arded; without harmony, as far as consists with freedom of Sentiment, its dignity may be lost. But, as the Legislative pro-ceedings of the United States will never, I trust, be reproached for the want of temper or candour; so shall not the public hap-piness languish, from the want of my strenuous and warmest cooperations.

SIXTH ANNUAL ADDRESS TO CONGRESS

The "self-created societies," to which Washington here refers as being responsible for fomenting resistance to the law in the Whiskey Rebellion, were the so-called Democratic Societies. He was convinced that they were abetted by Genet's agitation and had no place in the political life of the young nation, since they represented a challenge to authority and a threat to a strong centralized government. Jefferson did not share the President's views, but insisted that these Societies, born of a popular move-ment toward more and more democracy, deserved support. That the Chief Executive was influenced by the counsel of Hamilton, who was inclined to distrust such movements, is an oversimplified explanation of Washington's attitude toward such problems as were created by the Democratic Societies and the whole question of neutrality. Neutrality, to him, was part of his concept of total Independence, and so consistently did he cling to it that his fear of "foreign entanglements" became the basis for the traditional policy of the nation well into the twen-tieth century.

United States, November 19, 1794

Fellow Citizens of the Senate and of the House of Rep-resentatives: When we call to mind the gracious indulgence of Heaven, by which the American People became a nation; when we survey the general prosperity of our country, and look for-ward to the riches, power, and happiness, to which it seems destined; with the deepest regret do I announce to you, that during your recess, some of the citizens of the United States have been found capable of an insurrection. It is due, however, to the character of our government, and to its stability, which cannot be shaken by the enemies of order, freely to unfold the course of this event.

During the session of the year one thousand seven hundred and ninety, it was expedient to exercise the legislative power, granted by the constitution of the United States, "to lay and collect excises." In a majority of the States, scarcely an objection was heard to this mode of taxation. In some, indeed, alarms were at first conceived, until they were banished by reason and patriotism. In the four western counties of Pennsylvania, a prejudice, fostered and embittered by the artifice of men, who labored for an ascendency over the will of others, by the guidance of their passions, produced symptoms of riot and violence. It is well known, that Congress did not hesitate to examine the complaints which were presented, and to relieve them, as far as justice dictated, or general convenience would permit, But the impression, which this moderation made on the discontented, did not correspond, with what it deserved. The arts of delusion were no longer confined to the efforts of designing individuals.

The very forbearance to press prosecutions was misinterpreted into a fear of urging the execution of the laws; and associations of men began to denounce threats against the officers employed. From a belief, that by a more formal concert, their operation might be defeated, certain self-created societies assumed the tone of condemnation. Hence, while the greater part of Pennsylvania itself were conforming themselves to the acts of excise, a few counties were resolved to frustrate them. It was now perceived, that every expectation from the tenderness which had been hitherto pursued, was unavailing, and that further delay could only create an opinion of impotency or irresolution in the government. Legal process was, therefore, delivered to the marshal, against the rioters and delinquent distillers.

No sooner was he understood to be engaged in this duty, than the vengeance of armed men was aimed at his person, and

the person and property of the inspector of the revenue. They
fired upon the marshal, arrested him, and detained him for
some time, as a prisoner. He was obliged, by the jeopardy of his
life, to renounce the service of other process, on the west side of
the Allegeny mountain; and a deputation was afterwards sent
to him to demand a surrender of that which he had served. A
numerous body repeatedly attacked the house of the inspector,
seized his papers of office, and finally destroyed by fire, his
buildings, and whatsoever they contained. Both of these officers, from a just regard to their safety, fled to the seat of government; it being avowed, that the motives to such outrages were
to compel the resignation of the inspector, to withstand by
force of arms the authority of the United States, and thereby to
extort a repeal of the laws of excise, and an alteration in the
conduct of government.

Upon the testimony of these facts, an associate Justice of the
Supreme Court of the United States notified to me, that "in the
counties of Washington and Allegeny, in Pennsylvania, laws of
the United States were opposed, and the execution thereof obstructed by combinations, too powerful to be suppressed by the
ordinary course of judicial proceedings, or by the powers vested
in the marshal of that district." On this call, momentous in the
extreme, I sought and weighed, what might best subdue the
crisis. On the one hand, the judiciary was pronounced to be
stripped of its capacity to enforce the laws; crimes, which
reached the very existence of social order, were perpetrated
without controul, the friends of government were insulted,
abused, and overawed into silence, or an apparent acquiescence; and the yield to the treasonable fury of so small a portion of the United States, would be to violate the fundamental
principle of our constitution, which enjoins that the will of the
majority shall prevail. On the other, to array citizen against citizen, to publish the dishonor of such excesses, to encounter the
expense, and other embarrassments of so distant an expedition,
were steps too delicate, too closely interwoven with many affecting considerations, to be lightly adopted. I postponed, therefore, the summoning of the militia immediately into the field.
But I required them to be held in readiness, that if my anxious
endeavours to reclaim the deluded, and to convince the malig-

nant of their danger, should be fruitless, military force might be prepared to act, before the season should be too far advanced.

My Proclamation of the 7th of August last was accordingly issued, and accompanied by the appointment of Commissioners, who were charged to repair to the scene of insurrection. They were authorized to confer with any bodies of men, or individuals. They were instructed to be candid and explicit, in stating the sensations, which had been excited in the Executive, and his earnest wish to avoid a resort to coercion. To represent, however, that without submission, coercion *must* be the resort; but to invite them, at the same time, to return to the demeanor of faithful citizens, by such accommodations as lay within the sphere of the executive power. Pardon, too, was tendered to them by the government of the United States, and that of Pennsylvania, upon no other condition, than a satisfactory assurance of obedience to the laws.

Although the report of the commissioners marks their firmness and abilities, and must unite all virtuous men, by shewing, that the means of conciliation have been exhausted, all of those who had committed or abetted the tumults, did not subscribe the mild form, which was proposed, as the atonement; and the indications of a peaceable temper were neither sufficiently general, nor conclusive, to recommend or warrant, a further suspension of the march of the militia.

Thus, the painful alternative could not be discarded. I ordered the militia to march, after once more admonishing the insurgents, in my proclamation of the 25th of September last.

It was a task too difficult to ascertain with precision, the lowest degree of force, competent to the quelling of the insurrection. From a respect, indeed, to œconomy, and the ease of my fellow citizens belonging to the militia, it would have gratified me to accomplish such an estimate. My very reluctance to ascribe too much importance to the opposition, had its extent been accurately seen, would have been a decided inducement to the smallest efficient numbers. In this uncertainty, therefore, I put in motion fifteen thousand men, as being an army, which, according to all human calculation, would be prompt, and adequate in every view; and might perhaps, by rendering resistance desperate, prevent the effusion of blood. Quotas had been assigned to the states of New-Jersey, Pennsylvania, Maryland, and Virginia; the governor of Pennsylvania having declared on this occasion, an opinion which justified a requisition to the other states.

As commander in chief of the militia, when called into the actual service of the United States, I have visited the places of general rendezvous, to obtain more exact information, and to direct a plan for ulterior movements. Had there been room for a persuasion, that the laws were secure from obstruction; that the civil magistrate was able to bring to justice such of the most culpable, as have not embraced the proffered terms of amnesty, and may be deemed fit objects of example; that the friends to peace and good government were not in need of that aid and countenance, which they ought always to receive, and I trust, ever will receive, against the vicious and turbulent; I should have caught with avidity the opportunity of restoring the militia to their families and home. But succeeding intelligence has tended to manifest the necessity of what has been done; it being now confessed by those who were not inclined to exaggerate the ill-conduct of the insurgents, that their malevolence was not pointed merely to a particular law; but that a spirit, inimical to all order, has actuated many of the offenders. If the state of things had afforded reason for the continuance of my presence with the army, it would not have been withholden. But every appearance assuring such an issue, as will redound to the reputation and strength of the United States, I have judged it most proper, to resume my duties at the seat of government, leaving the chief command with the governor of Virginia.

Still, however, as it is probable, that in a commotion like the present, whatsoever may be the pretence, the purposes of mischief and revenge may not be laid aside; the stationing of a small force for a certain period in the four western counties of Pennsylvania will be indispensable; whether we contemplate the situation of those, who are connected with the execution of the laws; or of others who may have exposed themselves by an honorable attachment to them.

Thirty days from the commencement of this session, being

the legal limitation of the employment of the militia, Congress cannot be too early occupied with this subject.

Among the discussions, which may arise from this aspect of our affairs, and from the documents which will be submitted to Congress, it will not escape their observation, that not only the inspector of the revenue, but other officers of the United States in Pennsylvania have, from their fidelity in the discharge of their functions, sustained material injuries to their property. The obligation and policy of indemnifying them are strong and obvious. It may also merit attention, whether policy will not enlarge this provision to the retribution of other citizens, who, though not under the ties of office, may have suffered damage by their generous exertions for upholding the constitution and the laws. The amount, even if all the injured were included, would not be great; and on future emergencies, the government would be amply repaid by the influence of an example, that he, who incurs a loss in its defence shall find a recompense in its liberality.

While there is cause to lament, that occurrences of this nature should have disgraced the name, or interrupted the tranquillity of any part of our community, or should have diverted to a new application, any portion of the public resources, there are not wanting real and substantial consolations for the misfortune. It has demonstrated, that our prosperity rests on solid foundations; by furnishing an additional proof, that my fellow citizens understand the true principles of government and liberty: that they feel their inseparable union: that notwithstanding all the devices which have been used to sway them from their interest and duty, they are now as ready to maintain the authority of the laws against licentious invasions, as they were to defend their rights against usurpation. It has been a spectacle, displaying to the highest advantage, the value of Republican Government, to behold the most and least wealthy of our citizens standing in the same ranks as private soldiers; pre-eminently distinguished by being the army of the constitution; undeterred by a march of three hundred miles over rugged mountains, by the approach of an inclement season, or by any other discouragement. Nor ought I to omit to acknowledge the efficacious and patriotic co-operation, which I have experienced from the chief magistrates of the states, to which my requisitions have been addressed.

To every description, indeed, of citizens let praise be given. But let them persevere in their affectionate vigilance over that precious depository of American happiness, the constitution of the United States. Let them cherish it too, for the sake of those, who from every clime are daily seeking a dwelling in our land. And when in the calm moments of reflection, they shall have retraced the origin and progress of the insurrection, let them determine, whether it has not been fomented by combinations of men, who, careless of consequences, and disregarding the unerring truth, that those who rouse, cannot always appease a civil convulsion, have disseminated, from an ignorance or perversion of facts, suspicions, jealousies, and accusations of the whole government.

Having thus fulfilled the engagement, which I took, when I entered into office, "to the best of my ability to preserve, protect, and defend the constitution of the United States," on you, Gentlemen, and the people by whom you are deputed, I rely for support.

In the arrangements, to which the possibility of a similar contingency will naturally draw your attention, it ought not to be forgotten, that the militia laws have exhibited such striking defects, as could not have been supplied but by the zeal of our citizens. Besides the extraordinary expense and waste, which are not the least of the defects, every appeal to those laws is attended with a doubt of its success.

The devising and establishing of a well regulated militia, would be a genuine source of legislative honor, and a perfect title to public gratitude. I, therefore, entertain a hope, that the present session will not pass, without carrying to its full energy the power of organizing, arming, and disciplining the militia; and thus providing, in the language of the constitution, for calling them forth to execute the laws of the union, suppress insurrections, and repel invasions.

As auxiliary to the state of our defence, to which Congress can never too frequently recur, they will not omit to enquire whether the fortifications, which have been already licensed by law, be commensurate with our exigencies.

The intelligence from the army, under the command of general Wayne, is a happy presage to our military operations against the hostile Indians north of the Ohio. From the advices which have been forwarded, the advance which he has made must have damped the ardor of the savages, and weakened their obstinacy in waging war against the United States. And yet, even at this late hour, when our power to punish them cannot be questioned, we shall not be unwilling to cement a lasting peace, upon terms of candor, equity, and good neighborhood.

Towards none of the Indian tribes have overtures of friendship been spared. The Creeks in particular are covered from encroachment by the interposition of the General Government and that of Georgia. From a desire also to remove the discontents of the Six Nations, a settlement, meditated at Presqu'isle on Lake Erie, has been suspended; and an agent is now endeavoring to rectify any misconception, into which they may have fallen. But I cannot refrain from again pressing upon your deliberations, the plan which I recommended at the last session, for the improvement of harmony with all the Indians within our limits, by the fixing and conducting of trading houses, upon the principles then expressed.

Gentlemen of the House of Representatives: The time, which has elapsed, since the commencement of our fiscal measures, has developed our pecuniary resources, so as to open a way for a definitive plan for the redemption of the public debt. It is believed, that the result is such, as to encourage Congress to consummate this work, without delay. Nothing can more promote the permanent welfare of the nation, and nothing would be more grateful to our constituents. Indeed whatsoever is unfinished of our system of public credit, cannot be benefited by procrastination; and as far as may be practicable, we ought to place that credit on grounds which cannot be disturbed, and to prevent that progressive accumulation of debt which must ultimately endanger all governments.

An estimate of the necessary appropriations, including the expenditures into which we have been driven by the insurrection, will be submitted to Congress.

Gentlemen of the Senate, and of the House of Representatives: The mint of the United States has entered upon the coinage of the precious metals; and considerable sums of defective coins and bullion have been lodged with the director by individuals. There is a pleasing prospect that the institution will, at no remote day, realize the expectation which was originally formed of its utility.

In subsequent communications, certain circumstances of our intercourse with foreign nations, will be transmitted to Congress. However, it may not be unseasonable to announce that my policy in our foreign transactions has been, to cultivate peace with all the world; to observe treaties with pure and absolute faith; to check every deviation from the line of impartiality; to explain what may have been misapprehended, and correct what may have been injurious to any nation; and having thus acquired the right, to lose no time in acquiring the ability, to insist upon justice being done to ourselves.

Let us unite, therefore, in imploring the Supreme Ruler of nations, to spread his holy protection over these United States: to turn the machinations of the wicked to the confirming of our constitution: to enable us at all times to root out internal sedition, and put invasion to flight: to perpetuate to our country that prosperity, which his goodness has already conferred, and to verify the anticipations of this government being a safe guard to human rights.

To ELEANOR PARKE CUSTIS

Washington's advice to the lovelorn comes as a relief to the solemnity of his writings at a time of growing factionalism. Nelly Custis, granddaughter of Mrs. Washington, was a great favorite with the President. Wooed by Lawrence Lewis of Mount Vernon and young Carroll of Carrollton, she finally decided on the former and married him on Washington's birthday, February 22, 1799, the year of his death.

Philadelphia, January 16, 1795

[DEAR NELLIE:] Your letter, the receipt of which I am now acknowledging, is written correctly and in fair characters, which is an evidence that you command, when you please, a fair hand. Possessed of these advantages, it will be your own fault if you do not avail yourself of them, and attention being paid to the choice of your subjects, you can have nothing to fear from the malignancy of criticism, as your ideas are lively, and your descriptions agreeable. Let me touch a little now on your Georgetown ball, and happy, thrice happy, for the fair who were assembled on the occasion, that there was a man to spare; for had there been 79 ladies and only 78 gentlemen, there might, in the course of the evening, have been some disorder among the caps; notwithstanding the apathy which one of the company entertains for the "youth" of the present day, and her determination "never to give herself a moment's uneasiness on account of any of them." A hint here; men and women feel the same inclinations to each other now that they always have done, and which they will continue to do until there is a new order of things, and you, as others have done, may find, perhaps, that the passions of your sex are easier raised than allayed. Do not therefore boast too soon or too strongly of your insensibility to, or resistance of, its powers. In the composition of the human frame there is a good deal of inflammable matter, however dormant it may lie for a time, and like an intimate acquaintance of yours, when the torch is put to it, that which is within you may burst into a blaze; for which reason and especially too, as I have entered upon the chapter of advices, I will read you a lecture drawn from this text.

Love is said to be an involuntary passion, and it is, therefore, contended that it cannot be resisted. This is true in part only, for like all things else, when nourished and supplied plentifully with aliment, it is rapid in its progress; but let these be withdrawn and it may be stifled in its birth or much stinted in its growth. For example, a woman (the same may be said of the other sex) all beautiful and accomplished, will, while her hand and heart are undisposed of, turn the heads and set the circle in which she moves on fire. Let her marry, and what is the consequence? The madness ceases and all is quiet again. Why? not because there is any diminution in the charms of the lady, but because there is an end of hope. Hence it follows, that love may and therefore ought to be under the guidance of reason, for although we cannot avoid first impressions, we may assuredly place them under guard; and my motives for treating on this subject are to show you, while you remain Eleanor Parke Custis, spinster, and retain the resolution to love with moderation, the propriety of adhering to the latter resolution, at least until you have secured your game, and the way by which it may be accomplished.

When the fire is beginning to kindle, and your heart growing warm, propound these questions to it. Who is this invader? Have I a competent knowledge of him? Is he a man of good character; a man of sense? For, be assured, a sensible woman can never be happy with a fool. What has been his walk in life? Is he a gambler, a spendthrift, or drunkard? Is his fortune sufficient to maintain me in the manner I have been accustomed to live, and my sisters do live, and is he one to whom my friends can have no reasonable objection? If these interrogatories can be satisfactorily answered, there will remain but one more to be asked, that, however, is an important one. Have I sufficient ground to conclude that his affections are engaged by me? Without this the heart of sensibility will struggle against a passion that is not reciprocated; delicacy, custom, or call it by what epithet you will, having precluded all advances on your part. The declaration, without the most indirect invitation of yours, must proceed from the man, to render it permanent and valuable, and nothing short of good sense and an easy unaffected conduct can draw the line between prudery and coquetry. It would be no great departure from truth to say, that it rarely happens otherwise than that a thorough-paced coquette dies in celibacy, as a punishment for her attempts to mislead others, by encouraging looks, words, or actions, given for no other purpose than to draw men on to make overtures that they may be rejected.

This day, according to our information, gives a husband to

your elder sister, and consummates, it is to be presumed, her fondest desires. The dawn with us is bright, and propitious, I hope, of her future happiness, for a full measure of which she and Mr. Law have my earnest wishes. Compliments and congratulations on this occasion, and best regards are presented to your mamma, Dr. Stuart and family; and every blessing, among which a good husband when you want and deserve one, is bestowed on you by yours, affectionately.

To ALEXANDER HAMILTON

(Private, and perfectly confidential)

The treaty negotiated by John Jay with Great Britain detonated the highly explosive political factionalism in the United States. The anti-Federalists denounced it as an abject surrender to the country from which they had just wrested their independence. The Federalists countered with the defense that the Treaty achieved all the new nation had the right to hope for, namely, the promise of peace. The document stipulated the date on which the British would relinquish their Western outposts and insured an even flow of trade to the West Indies, then an important center of export. Washington, Hamilton and Jay were excoriated by the inflamed and highly partisan antagonists to the treaty. Hamilton was not then in the Cabinet, having resigned as Secretary of the Treasury. Nonetheless, he played a prominent role in framing it. By the end of Washington's second Administration, the furore over the Treaty of Amity, Commerce and Navigation died down altogether.

Philadelphia, July 3, 1795

My dear Sir: The treaty of Amity, Commerce and Navigation, which has lately been before the Senate, has, as you will perceive, made its public entry into the Gazettes of this city. Of course the merits, and demerits of it will (especially in its unfinished state) be freely discussed.

It is not the opinion of those who were determined (before it was promulgated) to support, or oppose it, that I am sollicitous to obtain; for these I well know rarely do more than examine the side to which they lean; without giving the reverse the consideration it deserves; possibly without a wish to be apprised of the reasons, on which the objections are founded. My desire is to learn from dispassionate men, who have knowledge of the subject, and abilities to judge of it, the genuine opinion they entertain of each article of the instrument; and the result of it in the aggregate. In a word, placed on the footing the matter now stands, it is, more than ever, an incumbent duty on me, to do what propriety, and the true interest of this country shall appear to require at my hands on so important a subject, under such delicate circumstances.

You will be at no loss to perceive, from what I have already said, that my wishes are, to have the favorable, and unfavorable side of each article stated, and compared together; that I may see the bearing and tendency of them: and, ultimately, on which side the balance is to be found.

This treaty has, I am sensible, many relations, which, in deciding thereon, ought to be attended to; some of them too are of an important nature. I know also, that to judge with precision of its commercial arrangements, there ought likewise to be an intimate acquaintance with the various branches of commerce between this Country and Great Britain as it now stands; as it will be placed by the treaty; and as it may affect our present, or restrain our future treaties with other nations. All these things I am persuaded you have given as much attention to as most men; and I believe that your late employment under the General government afforded you more opportunities of deriving knowledge therein, than most of them who had not studied and practiced it scientifically, upon a large and comprehensive scale.

I do not know how you may be occupied at present; or how incompatible this request of mine may be to the business you have in hand. All I can say is, that however desirous I may be of availing myself of your sentiments on the points I have enumerated, and such others as are involved in the treaty, and the resolution of the Senate; (both of which I send you, lest they should not be at hand) it is not my intention to interrupt you in that business; or, if you are disinclined to go into the investigation I have requested, to press the matter upon you: for of this you may be assured, that with the most unfeigned regard, and with every good wish for your health and prosperity I am etc.

PS. Admitting that his B: Majesty will consent to the suspension of the 12th. article of the treaty, is it necessary that the treaty should again go to the Senate? or is the President authorized by the resolution of that body to ratify it without?

SEVENTH ANNUAL ADDRESS

Washington could report a brighter outlook to Congress at the end of 1795. He announced the treaty effected by General Anthony Wayne with the Indians northwest of the Ohio River, one with the Emperor of Morocco and still another with the Dey and Regency of Algiers. Negotiations with Madrid were progressing satisfactorily and the Treaty of Amity, Commerce and Navigation with Great Britain was all but signed. Domestically, general happiness and prosperity prevailed, and even the last of the late insurrectionists in Pennsylvania had been granted a Presidential amnesty. Concluding on a plea for temperate discussion and mutual forbearance on all national questions, this speech leaves the impression of a benign, aging statesman anxious only for the tranquillity of retirement.

United States, December 8, 1795

Fellow-Citizens of the Senate, and House of Representatives: I trust I do not deceive myself, while I indulge the persuasion, that I have never met you at any period, when more than at present, the situation of our public affairs has afforded just cause for mutual congratulation; and for inviting you, to join with me, in profound gratitude to the Author of all good, for the numerous, and extraordinary blessings we enjoy.

The termination of the long, expensive and distressing war in which we have been engaged with certain Indians North west of the Ohio, is placed in the option of the United States, by a treaty, which the Commander of our Army has concluded, provisionally, with the hostile tribes in that Region.

In the adjustment of the terms, the satisfaction of the Indians was deemed an object worthy no less of the policy, than of the liberality of the United States, as the necessary basis of durable tranquility. This object, it is believed, has been fully attained. The articles agreed upon, will immediately be laid before the Senate, for their consideration.

The Creek and Cherokee Indians, who alone of the Southern tribes had annoyed our frontier, have lately confirmed their pre-existing treaties with us; and were giving evidence of a sincere disposition to carry them into effect, by the surrender of the prisoners and property they had taken: But we have to lament, that the fair prospect in this quarter, has been once more clouded by wanton murders, which some Citizens of Georgia are represented to have recently perpetrated on hunting parties of the Creeks; which have again subjected that frontier to disquietude and danger; which will be productive of further expense; and may occasion effusion of blood. Measures are pursuing to prevent, or mitigate, the usual consequences of such outrages; and with the hope of their succeeding, at least to avert general hostility.

A letter from the Emperor of Morocco, announces to me his recognition of our Treaty made with his father, the late Emperor; and, consequently the continuance, of peace with that Power. With peculiar satisfaction I add, that information has been received from an Agent, deputed on our part to Algiers, importing, that the terms of a Treaty with the Dey and Regency of that country, had been adjusted in such a manner, as to authorise the expectation of a speedy peace; and the restoration of our unfortunate fellow-citizens from a grievous captivity.

The latest advises from our Envoy at the Court of Madrid, give moreover, the pleasing information, that he had received assurances of a speedy, and satisfactory conclusion of his negociation. While the event, depending upon unadjusted particulars, cannot be regarded as ascertained, it is agreeable to cherish the expectation of an issue, which securing amicably, very essential interests of the United States, will at the same time lay the foundation of lasting harmony with a power, whose friendship we have uniformly, and sincerely desired to cultivate.

Though not before officially disclosed to the House of Representatives, you, Gentlemen, are all apprized, that a Treaty of Amity, Commerce and Navigation has been negotiated with Great Britain; and that the Senate have advised and consented to its ratification, upon a condition which excepts part of one article. Agreeably thereto, and to the best judgment I was able to form of the public interest, after full and mature deliberation, I have added my sanction. The result on the part of His Britannic Majesty, is unknown. When received, the subject will, without delay be placed before Congress.

This interesting summary of our affairs, with regard to the foreign powers, between whom and the United States controversies have subsisted, and with regard also to those of our Indian neighbours, with whom we have been in a state of enmity or misunderstanding, opens a wide field for consoling and gratifying reflections. If by prudence and moderation on every side the extinguishment of all the causes of external discord, which have heretofore menaced our tranquillity, on terms compatible with our national rights and honor, shall be the happy result; how firm and how precious a foundation will have been laid for accelerating, maturing and establishing the prosperity of our country!

Contemplating the internal situation, as well as the external relations of the United States, we discover equal cause for contentment and satisfaction. While many of the nations of Europe, with their American Dependencies, have been involved in a contest unusually bloody, exhausting and calamitous; in which the evils of foreign war have been aggravated by domestic convulsion and insurrection; in which many of the arts most useful to society have been exposed to discouragement and decay; in which scarcity of subsistence has embittered other sufferings; while even the anticipations of a return of the blessings of peace and repose, are alloyed by the sense of heavy and accumulating burthens, which press upon all the departments of industry, and threaten to clog the future springs of Government: Our favored country, happy in a striking contrast, has enjoyed general tranquility; a tranquility the more satisfactory, because maintained at the expense of no duty. Faithful to ourselves, we have violated no obligation to others. Our Agriculture, Commerce and Manufactures, prosper beyond former example; the molestations of our trade (to prevent a continuance of which, however, very pointed remonstrances have been made) being over-balanced by the aggregate benefits which it derives from a Neutral position. Our population advances with a celerity, which exceeding the most sanguine calculations, proportionally augments our strength and resources, and guarantees our future security. Every part of the union displays indications of rapid and various improvement, and with burthens so light as scarcely to be perceived; with resources fully adequate to our present exigencies; with Governments founded on genuine principles of rational liberty, and with mild and wholesome laws; is it too much to say, that our country exhibits a spectacle of national happiness never surpassed if ever before equalled?

Placed in a situation every way so auspicious, motives of commanding force impel us, with sincere acknowledgment to heaven, and pure love to our country, to unite our efforts to preserve, prolong, and improve, our immense advantages. To co-operate with you in this desirable work, is a fervent, and favorite wish of my heart.

It is a valuable ingredient in the general estimate of our welfare, that the part of our country, which was lately the scene of disorder and insurrections, now enjoys the blessings of quiet and order. The misled have abandoned their errors, and pay the respect to our Constitution and laws which is due from good citizens, to the public authorities of the society. These circumstances, have induced me to pardon, generally, the offenders here referred to; and to extend forgiveness to those who had been adjudged to capital punishment. For though I shall always think it a sacred duty, to exercise with firmness and energy, the Constitutional powers with which I am vested, yet it appears to me no less consistent with the public good, than it is with my personal feelings, to mingle in the operations of government, every degree of moderation and tenderness, which the national justice, dignity and safety may permit.

Gentlemen: Among the objects which will claim your attention in the course of the session, a review of our Military establishment is not the least important. It is called [for] by the events which have changed, and may be expected still further to change, the relative situation of our frontiers. In this review, you will doubtless allow due weight to the considerations, that the questions between us, and certain foreign powers, are not yet finally adjusted; that the war in Europe is not yet terminated; and that our Western Posts, when recovered, will demand provision for garrisoning and securing them. A statement of our present military force will be laid before you by the department of war.

With the review of our army establishment, is naturally connected that of the Militia. It will merit inquiry, what imperfections in the existing plan, further experience may have unfolded. The subject is of so much moment, in my estimation, as to excite a constant solicitude that the consideration of it may be renewed, till the greatest attainable perfection shall be accomplished. Time is wearing away some advantages for forwarding the object, while none better deserves the persevering attention of the public councils.

While we indulge the satisfaction, which the actual condition of our Western borders so well authorizes, it is necessary that we should not lose sight of an important truth, which continually receives new confirmations, namely, that the provisions heretofore made with a view to the protection of the Indians, from the violences of the lawless part of our frontier inhabitants are insufficient. It is demonstrated that these violences can now be perpetrated with impunity. And it can need no argument to prove, that unless the murdering of Indians can be restrained, by bringing the murderers to condign punishment, all the exertions of the government to prevent destructive retaliations, by the Indians, will prove fruitless; and all our present agreeable prospects illusory. The frequent destruction of innocent women and children, who are chiefly the victims of retaliation, must continue to shock humanity; and an enormous expence to drain the Treasury of the Union.

To enforce upon the Indians the observance of Justice, it is indispensable that there shall be competent means of rendering justice to them. If these means can be devised by the wisdom of Congress; and especially if there can be added an adequate provision for supplying the necessities of the Indians on reasonable terms, (a measure the mention of which I the more readily repeat, as in all the conferences with them they urge it with solicitude) I should not hesitate to entertain a strong hope, of rendering our tranquility permanent. I add with pleasure, that the probability even of their civilization is not diminished, by the experiments which have been thus far made under the auspices of Government. The accomplishment of this work, if practicable, will reflect undecayed lustre on our national character, and administer the most grateful consolations that virtuous minds can know.

Gentlemen of the House of Representatives: The state of our revenue with the sums which have been borrowed and reimbursed, pursuant to different acts of Congress, will be submitted from the proper Department; together with an estimate of the appropriations necessary to be made for the service of the ensuing year.

Whether measures may not be advisable to reinforce the provision for the redemption of the public debt, will naturally engage your examination. Congress have demonstrated their sense to be, and it were superfluous to repeat mine, that whatsoever will tend to accelerate the honorable extinction of our Public Debt, accords as much with the true interest of our country, as with the general sense of our Constituents.

Gentlemen of the Senate, and House of Representatives: The Statements, which will be laid before you relative to the Mint, will shew the situation of that institution; and the necessity of some further Legislative provisions for carrying the business of it more completely into effect; and for checking abuses which appear to be arising in particular quarters.

The progress in providing materials for the Frigates, and in building them; the state of the fortifications of our harbours; the measures which have been pursued for obtaining proper sites for Arsenals, and for replenishing our Magazines with military stores; and the steps which have been taken towards the execution of the law for opening a trade with the Indians; will likewise be presented for the information of Congress.

Temperate discussion of the important subjects, which may arise in the course of the Session, and mutual forbearance where there is a difference of opinion, are too obvious, and necessary for the peace happiness and welfare of our country, to need any recommendation of mine.

FAREWELL ADDRESS

In a letter to James Madison, dated May 20, 1792, (See page 586) Washington had not only expressed his determination not to stand for the Presidential office again, but had asked Madison's advice as to the proper time for and the best way of making known his intentions and even sought help in the preparation of a valedictory address. He was deterred from taking this step then on two counts: one, a too-early declaration of retirement would suggest vanity; and, second, it might be looked upon as a shrewd maneuver to remain in office. He even went so far as to outline in that letter to Madison of four years earlier what became in substance the major points of The Farewell Address. Now, in the Fall of 1796, the Presidential election was approaching and a third term was in prospect. Washington, this time, would not be dissuaded. He had prepared, with the aid of Hamilton and with some revisions by John Jay, what remains one of the great documents of American history. The four-way collaboration—Washington, Madison, Jay and Hamilton—was in the President's handwriting, with many corrections, alterations and addenda. The political effect of The Farewell Address was tremendous immediately, but its enduring force derives from Washington's character; every word of it reflects his steadfastness, sincerity, courage and forthrightness. It is the seal upon his devoted career for the independence of his country.

United States, September 19, 1796

FRIENDS, AND FELLOW-CITIZENS: The period for a new election of a Citizen, to Administer the Executive government of the United States, being not far distant, and the time actually arrived, when your thoughts must be employed in designating the person, who is to be cloathed with that important trust, it appears to me proper, especially as it may conduce to a more distinct expression of the public voice, that I should now apprise you of the resolution I have formed, to decline being considered among the number of those, out of whom a choice is to be made.

I beg you, at the same time, to do me the justice to be assured, that this resolution has not been taken, without a strict regard to all the considerations appertaining to the relation, which binds a dutiful citizen to his country, and that, in with drawing the tender of service which silence in my situation might imply, I am influenced by no diminution of zeal for your future interest, no deficiency of grateful respect for your past kindness; but am supported by a full conviction that the step is compatible with both.

The acceptance of, and continuance hitherto in, the office to which your Suffrages have twice called me, have been a uniform sacrifice of inclination to the opinion of duty, and to a deference for what appeared to be your desire. I constantly hoped, that it would have been much earlier in my power, consistently with motives, which I was not at liberty to disregard, to return to that retirement, from which I had been reluctantly drawn. The strength of my inclination to do this, previous to the last Election, had even led to the preparation of an address to declare it to you; but mature reflection on the then perplexed and critical posture of our Affairs with foreign Nations, and the unanimous advice of persons entitled to my confidence, impelled me to abandon the idea.

I rejoice, that the state of your concerns, external as well as internal, no longer renders the pursuit of inclination incompatible with the sentiment of duty, or propriety; and am persuaded whatever partiality may be retained for my services, that in the present circumstances of our country, you will not disapprove my determination to retire.

The impressions, with which I first undertook the arduous trust, were explained on the proper occasion. In the discharge of this trust, I will only say, that I have, with good intentions, contributed towards the Organization and Administration of the government, the best exertions of which a very fallible judgment was capable. Not unconscious, in the outset, of the inferiority of my qualifications, experience in my own eyes, perhaps still more in the eyes of others, has strengthened the motives to diffidence of myself; and every day the encreasing weight of years admonishes me more and more, that the shade of retirement is as necessary to me as it will be welcome. Satisfied that if any circumstances have given peculiar value to my services, they were temporary, I have the consolation to believe, that while choice and prudence invite me to quit the political scene, patriotism does not forbid it.

In looking forward to the moment, which is intended to terminate the career of my public life, my feelings do not permit me to suspend the deep acknowledgment of that debt of gratitude wch. I owe to my beloved country, for the many honors it has conferred upon me; still more for the stedfast confidence with which it has supported me; and for the opportunities I have thence enjoyed of manifesting my inviolable attachment, by services faithful and persevering, though in usefulness unequal to my zeal. If benefits have resulted to our country from these services, let it always be remembered to your praise, and as an instructive example in our annals, that, under circumstances in which the Passions agitated in every direction were liable to mislead, amidst appearances sometimes dubious, viscissitudes of fortune often discouraging, in situations in which not unfrequently want of Success has countenanced the spirit of criticism, the constancy of your support was the essential prop of the efforts, and a guarantee of the plans by which they were effected. Profoundly penetrated with this idea, I shall carry it with me to my grave, as a strong incitement to unceasing vows that Heaven may continue to you the choicest tokens of its beneficence; that your Union and brotherly affection may be perpetual; that the free constitution, which is the work of your hands, may be sacredly maintained; that its Administration in every department may be stamped with wisdom and Virtue; that, in fine, the happiness of the people of these States, under the auspices of liberty, may be made complete, by so careful a preservation and so prudent a use of this blessing as will acquire to them the glory of recommending it to the applause, the affection, and adoption of every nation which is yet a stranger to it.

Here, perhaps, I ought to stop. But a solicitude for your welfare, which cannot end but with my life, and the apprehension of danger, natural to that solicitude, urge me on an occasion like the present, to offer to your solemn contemplation, and to recommend to your frequent review, some sentiments; which are the result of much reflection, of no inconsiderable observation, and which appear to me all important to the permanency of your felicity as a People. These will be offered to you with the more freedom, as you can only see in them the disinterested warnings of a parting friend, who can possibly have no personal motive to biass his counsel. Nor can I forget, as an encouragement to it, your endulgent reception of my sentiments on a former and not dissimilar occasion.

Interwoven as is the love of liberty with every ligament of your hearts, no recommendation of mine is necessary to fortify or confirm the attachment.

The Unity of Government which constitutes you one people is also now dear to you. It is justly so; for it is a main Pillar in the Edifice of your real independence, the support of your tranquility at home; your peace abroad; of your safety; of your prosperity; of that very Liberty which you so highly prize. But as it is easy to foresee, that from different causes and from different quarters, much pains will be taken, many artifices employed, to weaken in your minds the conviction of this truth; as this is the point in your political fortress against which the batteries of internal and external enemies will be most constantly and actively (though often covertly and insidiously) directed, it is of infinite moment, that you should properly estimate the immense value of your national Union to your collective and individual happiness; that you should cherish a cordial, habitual and immoveable attachment to it; accustoming yourselves to think and speak of it as of the Palladium of your political safety and prosperity; watching for its preservation with jealous anxiety; discountenancing whatever may suggest even a suspicion that it can in any event be abandoned, and indignantly frowning upon the first dawning of every attempt to alienate any portion of our Country from the rest, or to enfeeble the sacred ties which now link together the various parts.

For this you have every inducement of sympathy and interest. Citizens by birth or choice, of a common country, that country has a right to concentrate your affections. The name of AMERICAN, which belongs to you, in your national capacity, must always exalt the just pride of Patriotism, more than any appellation derived from local discriminations. With slight shades of difference, you have the same Religion, Manners, Habits and political Principles. You have in a common cause fought and triumphed together. The independence and liberty you possess are the work of joint councils, and joint efforts; of common dangers, sufferings and successes.

But these considerations, however powerfully they address themselves to your sensibility are greatly outweighed by those which apply more immediately to your Interest. Here every portion of our country finds the most commanding motives for carefully guarding and preserving the Union of the whole.

The *North,* in an unrestrained intercourse with the *South,* protected by the equal Laws of a common government, finds in the productions of the latter, great additional resources of Maratime and commercial enterprise and precious materials of manufacturing industry. The *South* in the same Intercourse, benefitting by the Agency of the *North,* sees its agriculture grow and its commerce expand. Turning partly into its own channels the seamen of the *North,* it finds its particular navigation envigorated; and while it contributes, in different ways, to nourish and increase the general mass of the National navigation, it looks forward to the protection of a Maratime strength, to which itself is unequally adapted. The *East,* in a like intercourse with the *West,* already finds, and in the progressive improvement of interior communications, by land and water, will more and more find a valuable vent for the commodities which it brings from abroad, or manufactures at home. The *West* derives from the *East* supplies requisite to its growth and comfort, and what is perhaps of still greater consequence, it must of necessity owe the secure enjoyment of indispensable outlets for its own productions to the weight, influence, and the future Maratime strength of the Atlantic side of the Union, directed by an indissoluble community of Interest as one Nation. Any other tenure by which the *West* can hold this essential advantage, whether derived from its own seperate strength, or from an apostate and unnatural connection with any foreign Power, must be intrinsically precarious.

While then every part of our country thus feels an immediate and particular Interest in Union, all the parts combined cannot fail to find in the united mass of means and efforts greater strength, greater resource, proportionably greater security from external danger, a less frequent interruption of their Peace by foreign Nations; and, what is of inestimable value! they must derive from Union an exemption from those broils and Wars between themselves, which so frequently afflict neighbouring countries, not tied together by the same government; which their own rivalships alone would be sufficient to produce, but which opposite foreign alliances, attachments and intriegues would stimulate and imbitter. Hence likewise they will avoid the necessity of those overgrown Military establishments, which under any form of Government are inauspicious to liberty, and which are to be regarded as particularly hostile to Republican Liberty: In this sense it is, that your Union ought to be considered as a main prop of your liberty, and that the love of the one ought to endear to you the preservation of the other.

These considerations speak a persuasive language to every reflecting and virtuous mind, and exhibit the continuance of the UNION as a primary object of Patriotic desire. Is there a doubt, whether a common government can embrace so large a sphere? Let experience solve it. To listen to mere speculation in such a case were criminal. We are authorized to hope that a proper organization of the whole, with the auxiliary agency of governments for the respective Sub divisions, will afford a happy issue to the experiment. 'Tis well worth a fair and full experiment With such powerful and obvious motives to Union, affecting all parts of our country, while experience shall not have demonstrated its impracticability, there will always be reason, to distrust the patriotism of those, who in any quarter may endeavor to weaken its bands.

In contemplating the causes wch. may disturb our Union, it

occurs as matter of serious concern, that any ground should have been furnished for characterizing parties by Geographical discriminations: *Northern* and *Southern; Atlantic* and *Western;* whence designing men may endeavour to excite a belief that there is a real difference of local interests and views. One of the expedients of Party to acquire influence, within particular districts, is to misrepresent the opinions and aims of other Districts. You cannot shield yourselves too much against the jealousies and heart burnings which spring from these misrepresentations. They tend to render Alien to each other those who ought to be bound together by fraternal affection. The Inhabitants of our Western country have lately had a useful lesson on this head. They have seen, in the Negociation by the Executive, and in the unanimous ratification by the Senate, of the Treaty with Spain, and in the universal satisfaction at that event, throughout the United States, a decisive proof how unfounded were the suspicions propagated among them of a policy in the General Government and in the Atlantic States unfriendly to their Interests in regard to the MISSISSIPPI. They have been witnesses to the formation of two Treaties, that with G: Britain and that with Spain, which secure to them every thing they could desire, in respect to our Foreign relations, towards confirming their prosperity. Will it not be their wisdom to rely for the preservation of [*sic*] these advantages on the UNION by wch. they were procured? Will they not henceforth be deaf to those advisers, if such there are, who would sever them from their Brethren and connect them with Aliens?

To the efficacy and permanency of Your Union, a Government for the whole is indispensable. No Alliances however strict between the parts can be an adequate substitute. They must inevitably experience the infractions and interruptions which all Alliances in all times have experienced. Sensible of this momentous truth, you have improved upon your first essay, by the adoption of a Constitution of Government, better calculated than your former for an intimate Union, and for the efficacious management of your common concerns. This government, the offspring of our own choice uninfluenced and unawed, adopted upon full investigation and mature deliberation, completely free in its principles, in the distribution of its powers, uniting security with energy, and containing within itself a provision for its own amendment, has a just claim to your confidence and your support. Respect for its authority, compliance with its Laws, acquiescence in its measures, are duties enjoined by the fundamental maxims of true Liberty. The basis of our political systems is the right of the people to make and to alter their Constitutions of Government. But the Constitution which at any time exists, 'till changed by an explicit and authentic act of the whole People, is sacredly obligatory upon all. The very idea of the power and the right of the People to establish Government presupposes the duty of every Individual to obey the established Government.

All obstructions to the execution of the Laws, all combinations and Associations, under whatever plausible character, with the real design to direct, controul counteract, or awe the regular deliberation and action of the Constituted authorities are distructive of this fundamental principle and of fatal tendency. They serve to organize faction, to give it an artificial and extraordinary force; to put in the place of the delegated will of the Nation, the will of a party; often a small but artful and enterprizing minority of the Community; and, according to the alternate triumphs of different parties, to make the public administration the Mirror of the ill concerted and incongruous projects of faction, rather than the organ of consistent and wholesome plans digested by common councils and modefied by mutual interests. However combinations or Associations of the above description may now and then answer popular ends, they are likely, in the course of time and things, to become potent engines, by which cunning, ambitious and unprincipled men will be enabled to subvert the Power of the People, and to usurp for themselves the reins of Government; destroying afterwards the very engines which have lifted them to unjust dominion.

Towards the preservation of your Government and the permanency of your present happy state, it is requisite, not only that you steadily discountenance irregular oppositions to its acknowledged authority, but also that you resist with care the spirit of innovation upon its principles however specious the pretexts. one method of assault may be to effect, in the forms of the Constitution, alterations which will impair the energy of the system, and thus to undermine what cannot be directly overthrown. In all the changes to which you may be invited, remember that time and habit are at least as necessary to fix the true character of Governments, as of other human institutions; that experience is the surest standard, by which to test the real tendency of the existing Constitution of a country; that facility in changes upon the credit of mere hypotheses and opinion exposes to perpetual change, from the endless variety of hypotheses and opinion: and remember, especially, that for the efficient management of your common interests, in a country so extensive as ours, a Government of as much vigour as is consistent with the perfect security of Liberty is indispensable. Liberty itself will find in such a Government, with powers properly distributed and adjusted, its surest Guardian. It is indeed little else than a name, where the Government is too feeble to withstand the enterprises of faction, to confine each member of the Society within the limits prescribed by the laws and to maintain all in the secure and tranquil enjoyment of the rights of person and property.

I have already intimated to you the danger of Parties in the State, with particular reference to the founding of them on Geographical discriminations. Let me now take a more comprehensive view, and warn you in the most solemn manner against the baneful effects of the Spirit of Party, generally

This spirit, unfortunately, is inseperable from our nature, having its root in the strongest passions of the human Mind. It exists under different shapes in all Governments, more or less stifled, controuled, or repressed; but, in those of the popular form it is seen in its greatest rankness and is truly their worst enemy.

The alternate domination of one faction over another, sharpened by the spirit of revenge natural to party dissention, which in different ages and countries has perpetrated the most horrid enormities, is itself a frightful despotism. But this leads at length to a more formal and permanent despotism. The disorders and miseries, which result, gradually incline the minds of men to seek security and repose in the absolute power of an Individual: and sooner or later the chief of some prevailing faction more able or more fortunate than his competitors, turns this disposition to the purposes of his own elevation, on the ruins of Public Liberty.

Without looking forward to an extremity of this kind (which nevertheless ought not to be entirely out of sight) the common and continual mischiefs of the spirit of Party are sufficient to make it the interest and the duty of a wise People to discourage and restrain it.

It serves always to distract the Public Councils and enfeeble the Public administration. It agitates the Community with ill founded jealousies and false alarms, kindles the animosity of one part against another, foments occasionally riot and insurrection. It opens the door to foreign influence and corruption, which find a facilitated access to the government itself through the channels of party passions. Thus the policy and the will of one country, are subjected to the policy and will of another.

There is an opinion that parties in free countries are useful checks upon the Administration of the Government and serve to keep alive the spirit of Liberty. This within certain limits is probably true, and in Governments of a Monarchical cast Patriotism may look with endulgence, if not with favour, upon the spirit of party. But in those of the popular character, in Governments purely elective, it is a spirit not to be encouraged. From their natural tendency, it is certain there will always be enough of that spirit for every salutary purpose. And there being constant danger of excess, the effort ought to be, by force of public opinion, to mitigate and assuage it. A fire not to be quenched; it demands a uniform vigilance to prevent its bursting into a flame, lest instead of warming it should consume.

It is important, likewise, that the habits of thinking in a free Country should inspire caution in those entrusted with its administration, to confine themselves within their respective Constitutional spheres; avoiding in the exercise of the Powers of one department to encroach upon another. The spirit of encroachment tends to consolidate the powers of all the departments in one, and thus to create whatever the form of government, a real despotism. A just estimate of that love of power, and proneness to abuse it, which predominates in the human heart is sufficient to satisfy us of the truth of this position. The necessity of reciprocal checks in the exercise of political power; by dividing and distributing it into different depositories, and constituting each the Guardian of the Public Weal against invasions by the others, has been evinced by experiments ancient and modern; some of them in our country and under our own eyes. To preserve them must be as necessary as to institute them. If in the opinion of the People, the distribution or modification of the Constitutional powers be in any particular wrong, let it be corrected by an amendment in the way which the Constitution designates. But let there be no change by usurpation; for though this, in one instance, may be the instrument of good, it is the customary weapon by which free governments are destroyed. The precedent must always greatly overbalance in permanent evil any partial or transient benefit which the use can at any time yield.

Of all the dispositions and habits which lead to political prosperity, Religion and morality are indispensable supports. In vain would that man claim the tribute of Patriotism, who should labour to subvert these great Pillars of human happiness, these firmest props of the duties of Men and citizens. The mere Politician, equally with the pious man ought to respect and to cherish them. A volume could not trace all their connections with private and public felicity. Let it simply be asked where is the security for property, for reputation, for life, if the sense of religious obligation desert the oaths, which are the instruments of investigation in Courts of Justice? And let us with caution indulge the supposition, that morality can be maintained without religion. Whatever may be conceded to the influence of refined education on minds of peculiar structure, reason and experience both forbid us to expect that National morality can prevail in exclusion of religious principle.

'Tis substantially true, that virtue or morality is a necessary spring of popular government. The rule indeed extends with more or less force to every species of free Government. Who that is a sincere friend to it, can look with indifference upon attempts to shake the foundation of the fabric.

Promote then as an object of primary importance, Institutions for the general diffusion of knowledge. In proportion as the structure of a government gives force to public opinion, it is essential that public opinion should be enlightened

As a very important source of strength and security, cherish public credit. One method of preserving it is to use it as sparingly as possible: avoiding occasions of expence by cultivating peace, but remembering also that timely disbursements to prepare for danger frequently prevent much greater disbursements to repel it; avoiding likewise the accumulation of debt, not only by shunning occasions of expence, but by vigorous exertions in time of Peace to discharge the Debts which unavoidable wars may have occasioned, not ungenerously throwing upon posterity the burthen which we ourselves ought to bear. The execution of these maxims belongs to your Representatives, but it is necessary that public opinion should cooperate. To facilitate to them the performance of their duty, it is essential that you should practically bear in mind, that towards the payment of debts there must be Revenue; that to have Revenue there must be taxes; that no taxes can be devised which are not more or less inconvenient and unpleasant; that the intrinsic embarrassment inseperable from the selection of the proper objects (which is always a choice of difficulties) ought to be a decisive motive for a candid construction of the Conduct of the Government in making it, and for a spirit of acquiescence in the measures for obtaining Revenue which the public exigencies may at any time dictate.

Observe good faith and justice towds. all Nations. Cultivate peace and harmony with all. Religion and morality enjoin this conduct; and can it be that good policy does not equally enjoin it? It will be worthy of a free, enlightened, and, at no distant period, a great Nation, to give to mankind the magnanimous and too novel example of a People always guided by an exalted justice and benevolence. Who can doubt that in the course of time and things the fruits of such a plan would richly repay any temporary advantages wch. might be lost by a steady adherence to it? Can it be, that Providence has not connected the permanent felicity of a Nation with its virtue? The experiment, at least, is recommended by every sentiment which ennobles human Nature. Alas! is it rendered impossible by its vices?

In the execution of such a plan nothing is more essential than that permanent, inveterate antipathies against particular Nations and passionate attachments for others should be excluded; and that in place of them just and amicable feelings towards all should be cultivated. The Nation, which indulges towards another an habitual hatred, or an habitual fondness, is in some degree a slave. It is a slave to its animosity or to its affection, either of which is sufficient to lead it astray from its duty and its interest. Antipathy in one Nation against another, disposes each more readily to offer insult and injury, to lay hold of slight causes of umbrage, and to be haughty and intractable, when accidental or trifling occasions of dispute occur. Hence frequent collisions, obstinate envenomed and bloody contests. The Nation, prompted by illwill and resentment sometimes impels to War the Government, contrary to the best calculations of policy. The Government sometimes participates in the national propensity, and adopts through passion what reason would reject; at other times, it makes the animosity of the Nation subservient to projects of hostility instigated by pride, ambition and other sinister and pernicious motives. The peace often, sometimes perhaps the Liberty, of Nations has been the victim.

So likewise, a passionate attachment of one Nation for another produces a variety of evils. Sympathy for the favourite nation, facilitating the illusion of an imaginary common interest, in cases where no real common interest exists, and infusing into one the enmities of the other, betrays the former into a participation in the quarrels and Wars of the latter, without adequate inducement or justification: It leads also to concessions to the favourite Nation of priviledges denied to others, which is apt doubly to injure the Nation making the concessions; by unnecessarily parting with what ought to have been retained; and by exciting jealousy, ill will, and a disposition to retaliate, in the parties from whom eql. priviledges are withheld: And it gives to ambitious, corrupted, or deluded citizens (who devote themselves to the favourite Nation) facility to betray, or sacrifice the interests of their own country, without odium, sometimes even with popularity; gilding with the appearances of a virtuous sense of obligation a commendable deference for public opinion, or a laudable zeal for public good, the base or foolish compliances of ambition corruption or infatuation.

As avenues to foreign influence in innumerable ways, such attachments are particularly alarming to the truly enlightened and independent Patriot. How many opportunities do they afford to tamper with domestic factions, to practice the arts of seduction, to mislead public opinion, to influence or awe the public Councils! Such an attachment of a small or weak, towards a great and powerful Nation, dooms the former to be the satellite of the latter.

Against the insidious wiles of foreign influence, (I conjure you to believe me fellow citizens) the jealousy of a free people ought to be constantly awake; since history and experience prove that foreign influence is one of the most baneful foes of Republican Government. But that jealousy to be useful must be impartial; else it becomes the instrument of the very influence to be avoided, instead of a defence against it. Excessive partiality for one foreign nation and excessive dislike of another, cause those whom they actuate to see danger only on one side, and serve to veil and even second the arts of influence on the other. Real Patriots, who may resist the intriegues of the favourite, are liable to become suspected and odious; while its tools and dupes usurp the applause and confidence of the people, to surrender their interests.

The Great rule of conduct for us, in regard to foreign Nations is in extending our commercial relations to have with them as little political connection as possible. So far as we have already formed engagements let them be fulfilled, with perfect good faith. Here let us stop.

Europe has a set of primary interests, which to us have none, or a very remote relation. Hence she must be engaged in frequent controversies, the causes of which are essentially foreign to our concerns. Hence therefore it must be unwise in us to implicate ourselves, by artificial ties, in the ordinary vicissi-

tudes of her politics, or the ordinary combinations and collisions of her friendships, or enmities:

Our detached and distant situation invites and enables us to
pursue a different course. If we remain one People, under an
efficient government, the period is not far off, when we may defy
material injury from external annoyance; when we may take
such an attitude as will cause the neutrality we may at any
time resolve upon to be scrupulously respected; when belligerent nations, under the impossibility of making acquisitions
upon us, will not lightly hazard the giving us provocation;
when we may choose peace or war, as our interest guided by
our justice shall Counsel.

Why forego the advantages of so peculiar a situation? Why
quit our own to stand upon foreign ground? Why, by inter-
weaving our destiny with that of any part of Europe, entangle
our peace and prosperity in the toils of European Ambition,
Rivalship, Interest, Humour or Caprice?

'Tis our true policy to steer clear of permanent Alliances,
with any portion of the foreign world. So far, I mean, as we
are now at liberty to do it, for let me not be understood as
capable of patronising infidility to existing engagements (I
hold the maxim no less applicable to public than to private
affairs, that honesty is always the best policy). I repeat it therefore, let those engagements be observed in their genuine sense.
But in my opinion, it is unnecessary and would be unwise to
extend them.

Taking care always to keep ourselves, by suitable establishments, on a respectably defensive posture, we may safely trust
to temporary alliances for extraordinary emergencies.

Harmony, liberal intercourse with all Nations, are recommended by policy, humanity and interest. But even our Commercial policy should hold an equal and impartial hand: neither seeking nor granting exclusive favours or preferences;
consulting the natural course of things; diffusing and deversify-
ing by gentle means the streams of Commerce, but forcing nothing; establishing with Powers so disposed; in order to give to
trade a stable course, to define the rights of our Merchants, and
to enable the Government to support them; conventional rules

of intercourse, the best that present circumstances and mutual opinion will permit, but temporary, and liable to be from time to time abandoned or varied, as experience and circumstances shall dictate; constantly keeping in view, that 'tis folly in one Nation to look for disinterested favors from another; that it must pay with a portion of its Independence for whatever it may accept under that character; that by such acceptance, it may place itself in the condition of having given equivalents for nominal favours and yet of being reproached with ingratitude for not giving more. There can be no greater error than to expect, or calculate upon real favours from Nation to Nation. 'Tis an illusion which experience must cure, which a just pride ought to discard.

In offering to you, my Countrymen these counsels of an old and affectionate friend, I dare not hope they will make the strong and lasting impression, I could wish; that they will controul the usual current of the passions, or prevent our Nation from running the course which has hitherto marked the Destiny of Nations: But if I may even flatter myself, that they may be productive of some partial benefit, some occasional good; that they may now and then recur to moderate the fury of party spirit, to warn against the mischiefs of foreign Intriegue, to guard against the Impostures of pretended patriotism; this hope will be a full recompence for the solicitude for your welfare, by which they have been dictated.

How far in the discharge of my Official duties, I have been guided by the principles which have been delineated, the public Records and other evidences of my conduct must Witness to You and to the world. To myself, the assurance of my own conscience is, that I have at least believed myself to be guided by them.

In relation to the still subsisting War in Europe, my Proclamation of the 22d. of April 1793 is the index to my Plan. Sanctioned by your approving voice and by that of Your Representatives in both Houses of Congress, the spirit of that measure has continually governed me; uninfluenced by any attempts to deter or divert me from it.

After deliberate examination with the aid of the best lights I could obtain I was well satisfied that our Country, under all the circumstances of the case, had a right to take, and was bound in duty and interest, to take a Neutral position. Having taken it, I determined, as far as should depend upon me, to maintain it, with moderation, perseverence and firmness.

The considerations, which respect the right to hold this conduct, it is not necessary on this occasion to detail. I will only observe, that according to my understanding of the matter, that right, so far from being denied by any of the Belligerent Powers has been virtually admitted by all.

The duty of holding a Neutral conduct may be inferred, without any thing more, from the obligation which justice and humanity impose on every Nation, in cases in which it is free to act, to maintain inviolate the relations of Peace and amity towards other Nations.

The inducements of interest for observing that conduct will best be referred to your own reflections and experience. With me, a predominant motive has been to endeavour to gain time to our country to settle and mature its yet recent institutions, and to progress without interruption, to that degree of strength and consistency, which is necessary to give it, humanly speaking, the command of its own fortunes.

Though in reviewing the incidents of my Administration, I am unconscious of intentional error, I am nevertheless too sensible of my defects not to think it probable that I may have committed many errors. Whatever they may be I fervently beseech the Almighty to avert or mitigate the evils to which they may tend. I shall also carry with me the hope that my Country will never cease to view them with indulgence; and that after forty five years of my life dedicated to its Service, with an upright zeal, the faults of incompetent abilities will be consigned to oblivion, as myself must soon be to the Mansions of rest.

Relying on its kindness in this as in other things, and actuated by that fervent love towards it, which is so natural to a Man, who views in it the native soil of himself and his progenitors for several Generations; I anticipate with pleasing expectation that retreat, in which I promise myself to realize, without alloy, the sweet enjoyment of partaking, in the midst of my fellow Citizens, the benign influence of good Laws under a free

Government, the ever favourite object of my heart, and the happy reward, as I trust, of our mutual cares, labours and dangers.

EIGHTH ANNUAL ADDRESS TO CONGRESS

The last of the Addresses to Congress recommended means for the improvement of agriculture, the establishment of a military academy and a national university, and the gradual strengthening of the Navy. Washington made a special appeal for better understanding with the French Republic and ended on a note of hope that the Government he helped to found, dedicated to the protection of liberty, would be perpetual. Farewell dinners and receptions followed the final address on the state of the Union. Washington remained in Philadelphia to attend the inauguration of the second President and his Vice President, John Adams and Thomas Jefferson, on March 4th. Then he returned to Mount Vernon in the hope of finding the freedom from public responsibility he had so long and earnestly sought.

December 7, 1796

Fellow Citizens of the Senate and House of Representatives: In recurring to the internal situation of our Country, since I had last the pleasure to Address you, I find ample reason for a renewed expression of that gratitude to the ruler of the Universe, which a continued series of prosperity has so often and so justly called forth.

The Acts of the last Session, which required special arrangements, have been, as far as circumstances would admit, carried into operation.

Measures calculated to insure a continuance of the friendship of the Indians, and to preserve peace along the extent of our interior frontier, have been digested and adopted. In the framing of these, care has been taken to guard on the one hand, our advanced Settlements from the predatory incursions of those unruly Individuals, who cannot be restrained by their Tribes;

and on the other hand, to protect the rights secured to the Indians by Treaty; to draw them nearer to the civilized state; and inspire them with correct conceptions of the Power, as well as justice of the Government.

The meeting of the deputies from the Creek Nation at Colerain, in the State of Georgia, which had for a principal object the purchase of a parcel of their land, by that State, broke up without its being accomplished; the Nation having, previous to their departure, instructed them against making any Sale; the occasion however has been improved, to confirm by a new Treaty with the Creeks, their pre-existing engagements with the United States; and to obtain their consent, to the establishment of Trading Houses and Military Posts within their boundary; by means of which, their friendship, and the general peace, may be more effectually secured.

The period during the late Session, at which the appropriation was passed, for carrying into effect the Treaty of Amity, Commerce, and Navigation, between the United States and his Britannic Majesty, necessarily procrastinated the reception of the Posts stipulated to be delivered, beyond the date assigned for that event. As soon however as the Governor General of Canada could be addressed with propriety on the subject, arrangements were cordially and promptly concluded for their evacuation; and the United States took possession of the principal of them, comprehending Oswego, Niagara, Detroit, Michelimackina, and Fort Miami; where, such repairs, and additions have been ordered to be made, as appeared indispensible.

The Commissioners appointed on the part of the United States and of Great Britain, to determine which is the river St. Croix, mentioned in the Treaty of peace of 1783, agreed in the choice of Egbert Benson Esqr. of New York, for the third Commissioner. The whole met at St. Andrews, in Passamaquoddy Bay, in the beginning of October; and directed surveys to be made of the Rivers in dispute; but deeming it impracticable to have these Surveys completed before the next Year, they adjourned, to meet at Boston in August 1797, for the final decision of the question.

Other Commissioners appointed on the part of the United States, agreeably to the seventh Article of the Treaty with Great

Britain, relative to captures and condemnations of Vessels and other property, met the Commissioners of his Britannic Majesty in London, in August last, when John Trumbull, Esqr. was chosen by lot, for the fifth Commissioner. In October following the Board were to proceed to business. As yet there has been no communication of Commissioners on the part of Great Britain, to unite with those who have been appointed on the part of the United States, for carrying into effect the sixth Article of the Treaty.

The Treaty with Spain, required, that the Commissioners for running the boundary line between the territory of the United States, and his Catholic Majesty's Provinces of East and West Florida, should meet at the Natchez, before the expiration of six Months after the exchange of the ratifications, which was effected at Aranjuez on the 25th. day of April; and the troops of his Catholic Majesty occupying any Posts within the limits of the United States, were within the same period to be withdrawn. The Commissioner of the United States therefore, commenced his journey for the Natchez in September; and troops were ordered to occupy the Posts from which the Spanish Garrisons should be withdrawn. Information has been recently received, of the appointment of a Commissioner on the part of his Catholic Majesty for running the boundary line, but none of any appointment, for the adjustment of the claims of our Citizens, whose Vessels were captured by the Armed Vessels of Spain.

In pursuance of the Act of Congress, passed in the last Session, for the protection and relief of American Seamen, Agents were appointed, one to reside in Great Britain, and the other in the West Indies. The effects of the Agency in the West Indies, are not yet fully ascertained; but those which have been communicated afford grounds to believe, the measure will be beneficial. The Agent destined to reside in Great Britain, declining to accept the appointment, the business has consequently devolved on the Minister of the United States in London; and will command his attention, until a new Agent shall be appointed.

After many delays and disappointments, arising out of the European War, the final arrangements for fulfilling the en-

gagements made to the Dey and Regency of Algiers, will, in all
present appearance, be crowned with success: but under great,
tho' inevitable disadvantages, in the pecuniary transactions,
occasioned by that War; which will render a further provision
necessary. The actual liberation of all our Citizens who were
prisoners in Algiers, while it gratifies every feeling heart, is
itself an earnest of a satisfactory termination of the whole negotiation. Measures are in operation for effecting Treaties with
the Regencies of Tunis and Tripoli.

To an active external Commerce, the protection of a Naval
force is indispensable. This is manifest with regard to Wars in
which a State itself is a party. But besides this, it is in our own
experience, that the most sincere Neutrality is not a sufficient
guard against the depredations of Nations at War. To secure
respect to a Neutral Flag, requires a Naval force, organized,
and ready to vindicate it, from insult or aggression. This may
even prevent the necessity of going to War, by discouraging
belligerent Powers from committing such violations of the
rights of the Neutral party, as may first or last, leave no other
option. From the best information I have been able to obtain,
it would seem as if our trade to the mediterranean, without a
protecting force, will always be insecure; and our Citizens exposed to the calamities from which numbers of them have but
just been relieved.

These considerations invite the United States, to look to the
means, and to set about the gradual creation of a Navy. The
increasing progress of their Navigation, promises them, at no
distant period, the requisite supply of Seamen; and their means,
in other respects, favour the undertaking. It is an encouragement, likewise, that their particular situation, will give weight
and influence to a moderate Naval force in their hands. Will it
not then be adviseable, to begin without delay, to provide, and
lay up the materials for the building and equipping of Ships of
War; and to proceed in the Work by degrees, in proportion
as our resources shall render it practicable without inconvenience; so that a future War of Europe, may not find our Commerce in the same unprotected state, in which it was found by
the present.

Congress have repeatedly, and not without success, directed

their attention to the encouragement of Manufactures. The object is of too much consequence, not to insure a continuance of their efforts, in every way which shall appear eligible. As a general rule, Manufactures on public account, are inexpedient. But where the state of things in a Country, leaves little hope that certain branches of Manufacture will, for a great length of time obtain; when these are of a nature essential to the furnishing and equipping of the public force in time of War, are not establishments for procuring them on public account, to the extent of the ordinary demand for the public service, recommended by strong considerations of National policy, as an exception to the general rule? Ought our Country to remain in such cases, dependant on foreign supply, precarious, because liable to be interrupted? If the necessary Articles should, in this mode cost more in time of peace, will not the security and independence thence arising, form an ample compensation? Establishments of this sort, commensurate only with the calls of the public service in time of peace, will, in time of War, easily be extended in proportion to the exigencies of the Government; and may even perhaps be made to yield a surplus for the supply of our Citizens at large; so as to mitigate the privations from the interruption of their trade. If adopted, the plan ought to exclude all those branches which are already, or likely soon to be, established in the Country; in order that there may be no danger of interference with pursuits of individual industry.

It will not be doubted, that with reference either to individual, or National Welfare, Agriculture is of primary importance. In proportion as Nations advance in population, and other circumstances of maturity, this truth becomes more apparent; and renders the cultivation of the Soil more and more, an object of public patronage. Institutions for promoting it, grow up, supported by the public purse: and to what object can it be dedicated with greater propriety? Among the means which have been employed to this end, none have been attended with greater success than the establishment of Boards, composed of proper characters, charged with collecting and diffusing information, and enabled by premiums, and small pecuniary aids, to encourage and assist a spirit of discovery and improvement.

This species of establishment contributes doubly to the increase of improvement; by stimulating to enterprise and experiment, and by drawing to a common centre, the results everywhere of individual skill and observation; and spreading them thence over the whole Nation. Experience accordingly has shewn, that they are very cheap Instruments, of immense National benefits.

I have heretofore proposed to the consideration of Congress, the expediency of establishing a National University; and also a Military Academy. The desirableness of both these Institutions, has so constantly increased with every new view I have taken of the subject, that I cannot omit the opportunity of once for all, recalling your attention to them.

The Assembly to which I address myself, is too enlightened not to be fully sensible how much a flourishing state of the Arts and Sciences, contributes to National prosperity and reputation. True it is, that our Country, much to its honor, contains many Seminaries of learning highly respectable and useful; but the funds upon which they rest, are too narrow, to command the ablest Professors, in the different departments of liberal knowledge, for the Institution contemplated, though they would be excellent auxiliaries.

Amongst the motives to such an Institution, the assimilation of the principles, opinions and manners of our Country men, but the common education of a portion of our Youth from every quarter, well deserves attention. The more homogeneous our Citizens can be made in these particulars, the greater will be our prospect of permanent Union; and a primary object of such a National Institution should be, the education of our Youth in the science of Government. In a Republic, what species of knowledge can be equally important? and what duty, more pressing on its Legislature, than to patronize a plan for communicating it to those, who are to be the future guardians of the liberties of the Country?

The Institution of a Military Academy, is also recommended by cogent reasons. However pacific the general policy of a Nation may be, it ought never to be without an adequate stock of Military knowledge for emergencies. The first would impair the energy of its character, and both would hazard its safety, or expose it to greater evils when War could not be avoided. Besides that War, might often, not depend upon its own choice. In proportion, as the observance of pacific maxims, might exempt a Nation from the necessity of practising the rules of the Military Art, ought to be its care in preserving, and transmitting by proper establishments, the knowledge of that Art. Whatever argument may be drawn from particular examples, superficially viewed, a thorough examination of the subject will evince, that the Art of War, is at once comprehensive and complicated; that it demands much previous study; and that the possession of it, in its most improved and perfect state, is always of great moment to the security of a Nation. This, therefore, ought to be a serious care of every Government: and for this purpose, an Academy, where a regular course of Instruction is given, is an obvious expedient, which different Nations have successfully employed.

The compensations to the Officers of the United States, in various instances, and in none more than in respect to the most important stations, appear to call for Legislative revision. The consequences of a defective provision, are of serious import to the Government. If private wealth, is to supply the defect of public retribution, it will greatly contract the sphere within which, the selection of Characters for Office, is to be made, and will proportionally diminish the probability of a choice of Men, able, as well as upright: Besides that it would be repugnant to the vital principles of our Government, virtually to exclude from public trusts, talents and virtue, unless accompanied by wealth.

While in our external relations, some serious inconveniences and embarrassments have been overcome, and others lessened, it is with much pain and deep regret I mention, that circumstances of a very unwelcome nature, have lately occurred. Our trade has suffered, and is suffering, extensive injuries in the West Indies, from the Cruisers, and Agents of the French Republic; and communications have been received from its Minister here, which indicate the danger of a further disturbance of our Commerce, by its authority; and which are, in other respects, far from agreeable.

It has been my constant, sincere, and earnest wish, in conformity with that of our Nation, to maintain cordial harmony, and a perfectly friendly understanding with that Republic. This wish remains unabated; and I shall persevere in the endeavour to fulfil it, to the utmost extent of what shall be consistent with a just, and indispensable regard to the rights and honour of our Country; nor will I easily cease to cherish the expectation, that a spirit of justice, candour and friendship, on the part of the Republic, will eventually ensure success.

In pursuing this course however, I cannot forget what is due to the character of our Government and Nation; or to a full and entire confidence in the good sense, patriotism, self-respect, and fortitude of my Countrymen.

I reserve for a special Message a more particular communication on this interesting subject.

Gentlemen of the House of Representatives: I have directed an estimate of the Appropriations, necessary for the service of the ensuing year, to be submitted from the proper Department; with a view of the public receipts and expenditures, to the latest period to which an account can be prepared.

It is with satisfaction I am able to inform you, that the Revenues of the United States continue in a state of progressive improvement.

A reinforcement of the existing provisions for discharging our public Debt, was mentioned in my Address at the opening of the last Session. Some preliminary steps were taken towards it, the maturing of which will, no doubt, engage your zealous attention during the present. I will only add, that it will afford me, heart felt satisfaction, to concur in such further measures, as will ascertain to our Country the prospect of a speedy extinguishment of the Debt. Posterity may have cause to regret, if, from any motive, intervals of tranquillity are left unimproved for accelerating this valuable end.

Gentlemen of the Senate, and of the House of Representatives: My solicitude to see the Militia of the United States placed on an efficient establishment, has been so often, and so ardently expressed, that I shall but barely recall the subject to your view on the present occasion; at the same time that I shall submit to your enquiry, whether our Harbours are yet sufficiently secured.

The situation in which I now stand, for the last time, in the midst of the Representatives of the People of the United States, naturally recalls the period when the Administration of the present form of Government commenced; and I cannot omit the occasion, to congratulate you and my Country, on the success of the experiment; nor to repeat my fervent supplications to the Supreme Ruler of the Universe, and Sovereign Arbiter of Nations, that his Providential care may still be extended to the United States; that the virtue and happiness of the People, may be preserved; and that the Government, which they have instituted, for the protection of their liberties, may be perpetual.

To THE PRESIDENT OF THE UNITED STATES

The crisis with France had not abated after Washington's retirement. With war clouds hovering, Congress had authorized President Adams to enlist a provisional army of 10,000 men. In his perplexity over military responsibility, Adams turned to Washington, and, in a letter dated June 22, 1798, asked for the ex-President's counsel. On July 3rd the Senate nominated Washington as "Lieutenant General and Commander in Chief of all the armies raised or to be raised." Again Washington's hope of rest was shattered, but he accepted on these conditions: that he should not be called into the field until actually needed; that he should receive no pay. Subsequently he added another: that his principal officers should be men in whom he could place the utmost confidence. He chose Alexander Hamilton as the actual commander. For several months Washington directed the policies of the Army from Mount Vernon. The critical phase of our relations with France passed, and Washington remained a peace-time Lieutenant General and Commander in Chief until his death.

Mount Vernon, July 13, 1798

DEAR SIR: I had the honour on the evening of the 11th. instant to receive from the hands of the Secretary of War, your favour of the 7th. announcing, that you had, with the advice and consent of the Senate appointed me "Lieutenant General and Commander in Chief of all the Armies raised, or to be raised for the Service of the U. S."

I cannot express how greatly affected I am at this New proof of public confidence, and the highly flattering manner in which you have been pleased to make the communication; at the sametime I must not conceal from you my earnest wish, that the choice had fallen on a man less declined in years, and better qualified to encounter the usual vicissitudes of War.

You know, Sir, what calculations I had made relative to the probable course of events, on my retiring from Office, and the determination I had consoled myself with, of closing the remnant of my days in my present peaceful abode; you will therefore be at no loss to conceive and appreciate, the Sensations I must have experienced, to bring my mind to any conclusion, that would pledge me, at so late a period of life, to leave Scenes I sincerely love, to enter upon the boundless field of public action, incessant trouble, and high responsibility.

It was not possible for me to remain ignorant of, or indifferent to, recent transactions. The conduct of the Directory of France towards our Country; their insidious hostility to its Government; their various practices to withdraw the affections of the People from it; the evident tendency of their Arts and those of their Agents to countenance and invigorate opposition; their disregard of solemn treaties and the laws of Nations; their war upon our defenceless Commerce; their treatment of our Minister of Peace, and their demands amounting to tribute, could not fail to excite in me corresponding sentiments with those my countrymen have so generally expressed in their affectionate Addresses to you. Believe me, Sir, no one can more cordially approve of the wise and prudent measures of your Administration. They ought to inspire universal confidence, and will no doubt, combined with the state of things, call from Congress such laws and means as will enable you to meet the full force and extent of the Crisis.

Satisfied therefore, that you have sincerely wished and endeavoured to avert war, and exhausted to the last drop, the cup of reconciliation, we can with pure hearts appeal to Heaven for the justice of our cause, and may confidently trust the final result to that kind Providence who has heretofore, and so often, signally favoured the People of these United States.

Thinking in this manner, and feeling how incumbent it is upon every person, of every description, to contribute at all times to his Countrys welfare, and especially in a moment like the present, when every thing we hold dear and Sacred is so seriously threatened, I have finally determined to accept the Commission of Commander in Chief of the Armies of the United States, with the reserve only, that I shall not be called into the field until the Army is in a situation to require my presence, or it becomes indispensable by the urgency of circumstances.

In making this reservation, I beg it to be understood that I do not mean to withhold any assistance to arrange and organize the Army, which you may think I can afford. I take the liberty also to mention, that I must decline having my acceptance considered as drawing after it any immediate charge upon the Public, or that I can receive any emoluments annexed to the appointment, before entering into a Situation to incur expence.

The Secretary of War being anxious to return, to the seat of Government, I have detained him no longer than was necessary to a full communication upon the several points he had in charge. With very great respect and consideration I had the honor etc.

LAST WILL AND TESTAMENT

Washington, apparently in good health during his retirement, attended to the manifold duties of his estate and was host to many visitors. On the 12th of December, he mounted his horse and made his accustomed rounds of Mount Vernon. Snow, which had begun to fall, covered his head and greatcoat. The following morning, Washington complained of a sore throat. That night he was shaken with chills and breathing became difficult. After having been bled copiously, but without relief, his condition became steadily worse. Other remedies were tried, but to no avail. He died quietly between ten and eleven at night, on December 14, 1799. His Last Will and Testament, one of two similar documents, the second of which he asked Mrs. Washington to destroy, was completed early in July and was recorded in Fairfax County, Virginia, on July 9, 1799.

In the name of God amen

I George Washington of Mount Vernon, a citizen of the United States, and lately President of the same, do make, ordain and declare this Instrument; which is written with my own hand and every page thereof subscribed with my name, to be my last Will and Testament, revoking all others.

Imprimus. All my debts, of which there are but few, and none of magnitude, are to be punctually and speedily paid; and the Legacies hereinafter bequeathed, are to be discharged as soon as circumstances will permit, and in the manner directed.

Item. To my dearly beloved wife Martha Washington I give and bequeath the use, profit and benefit of my whole Estate, real and personal, for the term of her natural life; except such parts thereof as are specifically disposed of hereafter: My improved lot in the Town of Alexandria, situated on Pitt and Cameron Streets, I give to her and her heirs forever, as I also do my [2] household and Kitchen furniture of every sort and kind, with the liquors and groceries which may be on hand at the time of my decease; to be used and disposed of as she may think proper.

Item Upon the decease of my wife, it is my Will and desire that all the Slaves which I hold in my own right, shall receive their freedom. To emancipate them during her life, would, tho' earnestly wished by me, be attended with such insuperable difficulties on account of their intermixture by Marriages with the Dower Negroes, as to excite the most painful sensations, if not disagreeable consequences from the latter, while both descriptions are in the occupancy of the same Proprietor; it not being in my power, under the tenure by which the Dower Negroes are held, to manumit them. And whereas among those who will receive freedom according to this devise, there may be some, who from old age or bodily infirmities, and others who on account of their infancy, that will be unable to support themselves; it is my Will and desire that all who come under the first and second description shall be comfortably cloathed and fed by my heirs while they live; and [3] that such of the latter description as have no parents living, or if living are unable, or unwilling to provide for them, shall be bound by the Court until they shall arrive at the age of twenty five years; and in cases where no record can be produced, whereby their ages can be ascertained, the judgment of the Court upon its own view of the subject, shall be adequate and final. The Negroes thus bound, are (by their Masters or Mistresses) to be taught to read and write; and to be brought up to some useful occupation, agreeably to the Laws of the Commonwealth of Virginia, providing for the support of Orphan and other poor Children. And I do hereby expressly forbid the Sale, or transportation out of the said Commonwealth, of any Slave I may die possessed of, under any pretence whatsoever. And I do moreover most pointedly, and most solemnly enjoin it upon my Executors hereafter named, or the Survivors of them, to see that *this* clause respecting Slaves, and every part thereof be religiously fulfilled at the Epoch at which it is directed to take place; without evasion, neglect or delay, after the Crops which may then be on the ground are harvested, particularly as it respects [4] the aged and infirm; Seeing that a regular and permanent fund be established for their Support so long as there are subjects requiring it; not trusting to the uncertain provision to be made by individuals. And to my Mulatto man William (calling himself William Lee) I give immediate freedom; or if he should prefer it (on account of the accidents which have befallen him, and which have rendered him incapable of walking or of any active employment) to remain in the situation he now is, it shall be optional in him to do so: In either case however, I allow him an annuity of thirty dollars during his natural life, which shall be independent of the victuals and cloaths he has been accustomed to receive, if he chuses the last alternative; but in full, with his freedom, if he prefers the first; and this I give him as a testimony of my sense of his attachment to me, and for his faithful services during the Revolutionary War.

Item To the Trustees (Governors, or by whatsoever other name they may be designated) of the Academy in the Town of Alexandria, I give and bequeath, in Trust, four thousand dollars, or in other words twenty of the shares which I [5] hold in the Bank of Alexandria, towards the support of a Free school established at, and annexed to, the said Academy; for the purpose of Educating such Orphan children, or the children of such other poor and indigent persons as are unable to accomplish it with their own means; and who, in the judgment of the Trustees of the said Seminary, are best entitled to the benefit of this donation. The aforesaid twenty shares I give and bequeath in perpetuity; the dividends only of which are to be drawn for, and applied by the said Trustees for the time being, for the uses above mentioned; the stock to remain entire and untouched; unless indications of a failure of the said Bank should be so apparent, or a discontinuance thereof should render a removal of this fund necessary; in either of these cases, the amount of the Stock here devised, is to be vested in some other Bank or public Institution, whereby the interest may with regularity and certainby be drawn, and applied as above. And to prevent misconception, my meaning is, and is hereby declared to be, that these twenty shares are in lieu of, and not in addition to, the thousand pounds given by a missive letter some years ago; in consequence whereof an an[6]nuity of fifty pounds has since been paid towards the support of this Institution.

Item Whereas by a Law of the Commonwealth of Virginia, enacted in the year 1785, the Legislature thereof was pleased (as an evidence of Its approbation of the services I had rendered the Public during the Revolution; and partly, I believe, in consideration of my having suggested the vast advantages which the Community would derive from the extension of its Inland Navigation, under Legislative patronage) to present me with one hundred shares of one hundred dollars each, in the incorporated company established for the purpose of extending the navigation of James River from tide water to the Mountains: and also with fifty shares of one hundred pounds Sterling each, in the Corporation of another company, likewise established for the similar purpose of opening the Navigation of the River Potomac from tide water to Fort Cumberland; the acceptance of which, although the offer was highly honorable, and grateful to my feelings, was refused, as inconsistent with a principle which I had adop[7]ted, and had never departed from, namely, not to receive pecuniary compensation for any services I could render my country in its arduous struggle with great Britain, for its Rights; and because I had evaded similar propositions from other States in the Union; adding to this refusal, however, an intimation that, if it should be the pleasure of the Legislature to permit me to appropriate the said shares to public uses, I would receive them on those terms with due sensibility; and this it having consented to, in flattering terms, as will appear by a subsequent Law, and sundry resolutions, in the most ample and honourable manner, I proceed after this recital, for the more correct understanding of the case, to declare:

That as it has always been a source of serious regret with me, to see the youth of these United States sent to foreign Countries for the purpose of Education, often before their minds were formed, or they had imbibed any adequate ideas of the happiness of their own; contracting, too frequently, not only habits of dissipation and extravagence, but principles unfriendly to Republican Governmt. and to the true and genuine liberties [8] of mankind; which, thereafter are rarely overcome. For these reasons, it has been my ardent wish to see a plan devised on a liberal scale which would have a tendency to sprd. systematic ideas through all parts of this rising Empire, thereby to do away local attachments and State prejudices, as far as the nature of things would, or indeed ought to admit, from our National Councils. Looking anxiously forward to the accomplishment of so desirable an object as this is (in my estimation) my mind has not been able to contemplate any plan more likely to effect the measure than the establishment of a UNIVERSITY in a central part of the United States, to which the youth of fortune and talents from all parts thereof might be sent for the completion of their Education in all the branches of polite literature; in arts and Sciences, in acquiring knowledge in the principles of Politics and good Government; and (as a matter of infinite Importance in my judgment) by associating with each other, and forming friendships in Juvenile years, be enabled to free themselves in a proper degree from those local prejudices and habi[9]tual jealousies which have just been mentioned; and which, when carried to excess, are never failing sources of disquietude to the Public mind, and pregnant of mischievous consequences to this Country: Under these impressions, so fully dilated,

Item I give and bequeath in perpetuity the fifty shares which I hold in the Potomac Company (under the aforesaid Acts of the Legislature of Virginia) towards the endowment of a UNIVERSITY to be established within the limits of the District of Columbia, under the auspices of the General Government, if that government should incline to extend a fostering hand towards it; and until such Seminary is established, and the funds arising on these shares shall be required for its support, my further WILL and desire is that the profit accruing therefrom shall, whenever the dividends are made, be laid out in purchasing Stock in the Bank of Columbia, or some other Bank, at the discretion of my Executors; or by the Treasurer of the United States for the time being under the direction of Congress; provided that Honourable body should [10] Patronize the measure, and the Dividends proceeding from the purchase of such Stock is to be vested in more stock, and so on, until a sum adequate to the accomplishment of the object is obtained, of which I have not the smallest doubt, before many years passes away; even if no aid or encouraged is given by Legislative authority, or from any other source

Item The hundred shares which I held in the James River Company, I have given, and now confirm in perpetuity to, and for the use and benefit of Liberty-Hall Academy, in the County of Rockbridge, in the Commonwealth of Virga.

Item I release exonerate and discharge, the Estate of my deceased brother Samuel Washington, from the payment of the money which is due to me for the land I sold to Philip Pendleton (lying in the County of Berkeley) who assigned the same to him the said Samuel; who, by agreement was to pay me therefor. And whereas by some contract (the purport of which was never communicated to me) between the said Samuel and his son Thornton Washington, the latter became possessed of the aforesaid Land, without [11] any conveyance having passed from me, either to the said Pendleton, the said Samuel, or the said Thornton, and without any consideration having been made, by which neglect neither the legal nor equitable title has been alienated; it rests therefore with me to declare my intentions concerning the Premises; and these are, to give and bequeath the said land to whomsoever the said Thornton Washington (who is also dead) devised the same; or to his heirs forever if he died Intestate: Exonerating the estate of the said Thornton, equally with that of the said Samuel from payment of the purchase money; which, with Interest; agreeably to the original contract with the said Pendleton, would amount to more than a thousand pounds. And whereas two other Sons of my said deceased brother Samuel, namely, George Steptoe Washington and Lawrence Augustine Washington, were, by the decease of those to whose care they were committed, brought under my protection, and in conseqe. have occasioned advances on my part for their Education at College, and other Schools, for their board, cloathing, and other incidental expences, to the amount of near [12] five thousand dollars over and above the Sums furnished by their Estate wch. Sum may be inconvenient for them, or their fathers Estate to refund. I do for these reasons acquit them, and the said estate, from the payment thereof. My intention being, that all accounts between them and me, and their fathers estate and me shall stand balanced.

Item The balance due to me from the Estate of Bartholomew Dandridge deceased (my wife's brother) and which amounted on the first day of October 1795 to four hundred and twenty five pounds (as will appear by an account rendered by his deceased son John Dandridge, who was the acting Exr. of his fathers Will) I release and acquit from the payment thereof. And the Negroes, then thirty three in number formerly belonging to the said estate, who were taken in execution, sold, and purchased in on my account in the year   and ever since have remained in the possession, and to the use of Mary, Widow of the said Bartholomew Dandridge, with their increase, it is my Will and desire shall continue, and be in her possession, without paying hire, or ma[13]king compensation for the same for the time past or to come, during her natural life; at the expiration of which, I direct that all of them who are forty years old and upwards, shall receive their freedom; all under that age and above sixteen, shall serve seven years and no longer; and all under sixteen years, shall serve until they are twenty five years of age, and then be free. And to avoid disputes respecting the ages of any of those Negroes, they are to be taken to the Court of the County in which they reside, and the judgment thereof, in this relation, shall be final; and a record thereof made; which may be adduced as evidence at any time thereafter, if disputes should arise concerning the same. And I further direct, that the heirs of the said Bartholomew Dandridge shall, equally, share the benefits arising from the Services of the said Negroes according to the tenor of this devise, upon the decease of their Mother.

Item If Charles Carter who intermarried with my niece Betty Lewis is not sufficiently secured in the title to the lots he had of me in the Town of Fredericksburgh, it is my Will and desire that my Executors shall make such conveyances [14] of them as the Law requires, to render it perfect.

Item To my Nephew William Augustine Washington and his heirs (if he should conceive them to be objects worth prosecuting) and to his heirs, a lot in the Town of Manchester (opposite to Richmond) No 265 drawn on my sole account, and also the tenth of one or two, hundred acre lots, and two or three half acre lots in the City, and vicinity of Richmond, drawn in partnership with nine others, all in the lottery of the deceased William Bryd are given; as is also a lot which I purchased of John Hood, conveyed by William Willie and Samuel Gordon Trustees of the said John Hood, numbered 139 in the Town of Edinburgh, in the County of Prince George, State of Virginia

Item To my Nephew Bushrod Washington, I give and bequeath all the Papers in my possession, which relate to my Civel and Military Administration of the affairs of this Country; I leave to him also, such of my private Papers as are worth preserving; and at the decease of my wife, and before, if she is not inclined to retain them, I give and bequeath my library of Books, and Pamphlets of every kind.

[15] Item Having sold Lands which I possessed in the State of Pennsylvania, and part of a tract held in equal right with George Clinton, late Governor of New York, in the State of New York; my share of land, and interest, in the Great Dis-

mal Swamp, and a tract of land which I owned in the County of Gloucester; withholding the legal titles thereto, until the consideration money should be paid. And having moreover leased, and conditionally sold (as will appear by the tenor of the said leases) all my lands upon the Great Kanhawa, and a tract upon Difficult Run, in the county of Loudoun, it is my Will and direction, that whensoever the Contracts are fully, and respectively complied with, according to the spirit, true intent and meaning thereof, on the part of the purchasers, their heirs or Assigns, that then, and in that case, Conveyances are to be made, agreeably to the terms of the said Contracts; and the money arising therefrom, when paid, to be vested in Bank stock; the dividends whereof, as of that also wch. is already vested therein, is to inure to my said Wife during her life; but the Stock itself is to remain, and [16] be subject to the general distribution hereafter directed.

Item To the Earl of Buchan I recommit "the Box made of the Oak that sheltered the Great Sir William Wallace after the battle of Falkirk" presented to me by his Lordship, in terms too flattering for me to repeat, with a request "to pass it, on the event of my decease, to the man in my country, who should appear to merit it best, upon the same conditions that have induced him to send it to me." Whether easy, or not, to select the man who might comport with his Lordships opinion in this respect, is not for me to say; but conceiving that no disposition of this valuable curiosity can be more eligable than the recommitment of it to his own Cabinet, agreeably to the original design of the Goldsmith Company of Edenburgh, who presented it to him, and at his request, consented that it should be transfered to me; I do give and bequeath the same to his Lordship, and in case of his decease, to his heir with my grateful thanks for the distinguished honour of presenting it to me; and more especially for the favourable sentiments [17] with which he accompanied it.

Item To my brother Charles Washington I give and bequeath the gold headed Cane left me by Doctr. Franklin in his Will. I add nothing to it, because of the ample provision I have made for his Issue. To the acquaintances and friends of my Juvenile years, Lawrence Washington and Robert Washington of Chotanck, I give my other two gold headed Canes, having my Arms engraved on them; and to each (as they will be useful where they live) I leave one of the Spy-glasses which constituted part of my equipage during the late War. To my compatriot in arms, and old and intimate friend Doctr. Craik, I give my Bureau (or as the Cabinet makers call it, Tambour Secretary) and the circular chair, and appendage of my Study. To Doctor David Stuart I give my large shaving and dressing Table, and my Telescope. To the Reverend, now Bryan, Lord Fairfax, I give a Bible in three large folio volumes, with notes, presented to me by the Right reverend Thomas Wilson, Bishop of Sodor and Man. To General de la Fayette I give a pair of finely wrought steel Pistols, taken from the enemy in the Revolutionary War. To my Sisters in law [18] Hannah Washington and Mildred Washington; to my friends Eleanor Stuart, Hannah Washington of Fairfield, and Elizabeth Washington of Hayfield, I give, each, a mourning Ring of the value of one hundred dollars. These bequests are not made for the intrinsic value of them, but as mementos of my esteem and regard. To Tobias Lear, I give the use of the Farm which he now holds, in virtue of a Lease from me to him and his deceased wife (for and during their natural lives) free from Rent, during his life; at the expiration of which, it is to be disposed as is hereinafter directed. To Sally B. Haynie (a distant relation of mine) I give and bequeath three hundred dollars. To Sarah Green daughter of the deceased Thomas Bishop, and to Ann Walker daughter of Jno. Alton, also deceased, I give, each one hundred dollars, in consideration of the attachment of their fathers to me, each of whom having lived nearly forty years in my family. To each of my Nephews, William Augustine Washington, George Lewis, George Steptoe Washington, Bushrod Washington and Samuel Washington, I give one of the Swords or Cutteaux of which I may die pos[19]sessed; and they are to chuse in the order they are named. These Swords are accompanied with an injunction not to unsheath them for the purpose of shedding blood, except it be for self defence, or in defence of their Country and its rights; and in the latter case, to keep them unsheathed, and prefer falling with them in their hands, to the relinquishment thereof.

AND NOW

Having gone through these specific devises, with explanations for the more correct understanding of the meaning and design of them; I proceed to the distribution of the more important parts of my Estate, in manner following:

First To my Nephew Bushrod Washington and his heirs (partly in consideration of an intimation to his deceased father while we were Bachelors, and he had kindly undertaken to superintend my Estate during my Military Services in the former War between Great Britain and France, that if I should fall therein, Mount Vernon (then less extensive in domain than at present) should become his property) I give and bequeath all that part thereof which is comprehen[20]ded within the following limits, viz: Beginning at the ford of Dogue run, near my Mill, and extending along the road, and bounded thereby as it now goes, and ever has gone since my recollection of it, to the ford of little hunting Creek at the Gum spring until it comes to a knowl, opposite to an old road which formerly passed through the lower field of Muddy hole Farm; at which, on the north side of the said road are three red, or Spanish Oaks marked as a corner, and a stone placed.—thence by a line of trees to be marked, rectangular to the back line, or outer boundary of the tract between Thomson Mason and myself. thence with that line Easterly (now double ditching with a Post and Rail fence thereon) to the run of little hunting Creek. thence with that run which is the boundary between the Lands of the late Humphrey Peake and me, to the tide water of the said Creek; thence by that water to Potomac River. thence with the River to the mouth of Dogue Creek. and thence with the said Dogue Creek to the place of beginning at the aforesaid ford; containing upwards of four thousand Acres, be the same more or less; together with the Mansion house [21] and all other buildings and improvements. thereon.

Second In consideration of the consanguinity between them and my wife, being as nearly related to her as to myself, as on account of the affection I had for, and the obligation I was under to, their father when living, who from his youth had attached himself to my person, and followed my fortunes through the viscissitudes of the late Revolution; afterwards devoting his time to the Superintendence of my private concerns for many years, whilst my public employments rendered it impracticable for me to do it myself, thereby affording me essential Services, and always performing them in a manner the most felial and respectful: for these reasons I say, I give and bequeath to George Fayette Washington, and Lawrence Augustine Washington and their heirs, my Estate East of little hunting Creek, lying on the River Potomac; including the Farm of 360 Acres, Leased to Tobias Lear as noticed before, and containing in the whole, by Deeds, Two thousand and Seventy seven acres, be it more or less. Which said Estate it is my Will and desire should be equitably, and advantageously divided between them, according to quantity, quality and other circumstances when [22] the youngest shall have arrived at the age of twenty one years, by three judicious and disinterested men; one to be chosen by each of the brothers, and the third by these two. In the mean-time, if the termination of my wife's interest therein should have ceased, the profits arising therefrom are to be applied for thir joint uses and benefit.

Third And whereas it has always been my intention, since my expectation of having Issue has ceased, to consider the Grand children of my wife in the same light as I do my own relations, and to act a friendly part by them; more especially by the two whom we have reared from their earliest infancy, namely: Eleanor Parke Custis, and George Washington Parke Custis. And whereas the former of these hath lately intermar-ried with Lawrence Lewis, a son of my deceased Sister Betty Lewis, by which union the inducement to provide for them both has been increased; Wherefore, I give and bequeath to the said Lawrence Lewis and Eleanor Parke Lewis, his wife, and their heirs, the residue of my Mount Vernon Estate, not already devised to my Nephew Bushrod Washington, comprehended within the fol[23]lowing description. viz: All the land North of the Road leading from the ford of Dogue run to the Gum spring as described in the devise of the other part of the tract, to Bushrod Washington, until it comes to the Stone and three red or Spanish Oaks on the knowl. thence with the rectangular line to the back line (between Mr. Mason and me) thence with that line westerly, along the new double ditch to Dogue run, by the tumbling Dam of my Mill; thence with the said run to the ford aforementioned; to which I add all the Land I possess West of the said Dogue run, and Dogue Crk. bounded Easterly and Southerly thereby; together with the Mill, Distillery, and all other houses and improvements on the premises, making together about two thousand Acres, be it more or less.

Fourth Actuated by the principal already mentioned, I give and bequeath to George Washington Parke Custis, the Grandson of my wife, and my Ward, and to his heirs, the tract I hold on four mile run in the vicinity of Alexandria, containing one thousd. two hundred acres, more or less, and my entire Square, number twenty one, in the City of Washington.

[24] Fifth All the rest and residue of my Estate, real and personal, not disposed of in manner aforesaid. In whatsoever consisting, wheresoever lying, and whensoever found, a schedule of which, as far as is recollected, with a reasonable estimate of its value, is hereunto annexed: I desire may be sold by my Executors at such times, in such manner, and in such credits (if an equal, valid, and satisfactory distribution of the specific property cannot be made without), as, in their judgment shall be most condusive to the interest of the parties concerned; and the monies arising therefrom to be divided into twenty three equal parts, and applied as follows, viz:

To William Augustine Washington, Elizabeth Spotswood, Jane Thornton, and the heirs of Ann Ashton; son, and daughters of my deceased brother Augustine Washington, I give and bequeath four parts; that is, one part to each of them.

To Fielding Lewis, George Lewis, Robert Lewis, Howell Lewis and Betty Carter, sons and daughter of my deceased Sister Betty Lewis, I give and bequeath five other parts, one to each of them.

To George Steptoe Washington, Lawrence Augustine Washington, Harriet [25] Parks, and the heirs of Thorton Washington, sons and daughter of my deceased brother Samuel Washington, I give and bequeath other four parts, one part to each of them.

To Corbin Washington, and the heirs of Jane Washington,

Son and daughter of my deceased Brother John Augustine Washington, I give and bequeath two parts; one part to each of them.

To Samuel Washington, Frances Ball and Mildred Hammond, son and daughters of my Brother Charles Washington, I give and bequeath three parts; one part to each of them. And to George Fayette Washington Charles Augustine Washington and Maria Washington, sons and daughter of my deceased Nephew Geo: Augustine Washington, I give one other part; that is, to each a third of that part.

To Elizabeth Parke Law, Martha Parke Peter, and Eleanor Parke Lewis, I give and bequeath three other parts, that is a part to each of them.

And to my Nephews Bushrod Washington and Lawrence Lewis, and to my ward, the grandson of My wife, I give and bequeath one other part; that is, a third thereof to each of them. And if it should so happen, that any of these persons whose names are here ennumerated (unknown to me) should now [26] be deceased, or should die before me, that in either of these cases, the heirs of such deceased persons shall, notwithstanding, derive all the benefits of the bequest; in the same manner as if he, or she, was actually living at the time.

And by way of advice, I recommend it to my Executors not to be precipitate in disposing of the landed property (herein directed to be sold) if from temporary causes the Sale thereof should be dull; experience having fully evinced, that the price of land (especially above the Falls of the Rivers, and on the Western Waters) have been progressively rising, and cannot be long checked in its increasing value. And I particularly recommend it to such of the Legatees (under this clause of my Will) as can make it convenient, to take each share of my Stock in the Potomac Company in preference to the amount of what it might sell for; being thoroughly convinced myself, that no uses to which the money can be applied will be so productive as the Tolls arising from this navigation when in full operation (and this from the nature of things it must be 'ere long) and more especially if that of the Shanondoah is added thereto.

[27] The family Vault at Mount Vernon requiring repairs,

and being improperly situated besides, I desire that a new one of Brick, and upon a larger Scale, may be built at the foot of what is commonly called the Vineyard Inclosure, on the ground which is marked out. In which my remains, with those of my deceased relatives (now in the old Vault) and such others of my family as may chuse to be entombed there, may be deposited. And it is my express desire that my Corpse may be Interred in a private manner, without parade, or funeral Oration.

Lastly I constitute and appoint my dearly beloved wife Martha Washington, My Nephews William Augustine Washington, Bushrod Washington, George Steptoe Washington, Samuel Washington, and Lawrence Lewis, and my ward George Washington Parke Custis (when he shall have arrived at the age of twenty years) Executrix and Executors of this Will and testament, In the construction of which it will readily be perceived that no professional character has been consulted, or has had any Agency in the draught; and that, although it has occupied [28] many of my leisure hours to digest, and to through it into its present form, it may, notwithstanding, appear crude and incorrect. But having endeavoured to be plain, and explicit in all the Devises, even at the expence of prolixity, perhaps of tautology, I hope, and trust, that no disputes will arise concerning them; but if, contrary to expectation, the case should be otherwise from the want of legal expression, or the usual technical terms, or because too much or too little has been said on any of the Devises to be consonant with law, My Will and direction expressly is, that all disputes (if unhappily any should arise) shall be decided by three impartial and intelligent men, known for their probity and good understanding; two to be chosen by the disputants, each having the choice of one, and the third by those two. Which three men thus chosen, shall, unfettered by Law, or legal constructions, declare their Sense of the Testators intention; and such decision is, to all intents and purposes to be as binding on the Parties as if it had been given in the Supreme Court of the United States.

[29] In witness of all, and of each of the things herein contained, I have set my hand and Seal, this ninth day of July, in the year One thousand seven hundred and ninety and of the Independence of the United States the twenty fourth.

Schedule of property comprehended in the foregoing Will, which is directed to be sold, and some of it, conditionally is sold; with discriptive, and explanatory notes relative thereto.

In Virginia

Loudoun County

	acres	price dollars
Difficult run	300	6,666 (a)

(a) This tract for the size of it is valuable, more for its situation than the quality of its soil, though that is good for Farming; with a considerable portion of grd. that might, very easily, be improved into Meadow. It lyes on the great road from the City of Washington, Alexandria and George Town, to Leesburgh and Winchester; at Difficult bridge, nineteen miles from Alexandria, less from the City of George Town, and not more than three from Matildaville at the Great Falls of Potomac.

There is a valuable seat on the Premises, and the whole is conditionally sold, for the sum annexed in the Schedule

Loudoun and Fauquier

Ashbys Bent	2481..	$10..	24,810 ⎫ (b)
Chattins Run	885..	8..	7,080 ⎭

(b) What the selling prices of lands in the vicinity of these two tracts are, I know not; but compared with those above the ridge, and others below them, the value annexed will appear moderate; a less one would not obtain them from me.

Berkeley

So. fork of Bullskin	1600
Head of Evans's M	453
On Wormeley's line	183

2236... 20...44.720 (c)

(c) The surrounding land, not superior in Soil, situation or properties of any sort, sell currently at from twenty to thirty dollars an Acre. The lowest price is affixed to these

Frederick
    Bought from Mercer .... 571... 20... 11.420 (d)
    (d) The observations made in the last note applies equally
to this tract tract; being in the vicinity of them, and of similar
quality, altho' it lyes in another County

Hampshire
    On Potk River above B .... 240... 15... 3.600 (e)
    (e) This tract, though small, is extremely valuable. It lyes on
Potomac River about 12 miles above the Town of Bath (or
Warm springs) and is in the shape of a horse Shoe; the river
running almost around it. Two hundred Acres of it is rich low
grounds; with a great abundance of the largest and finest Wal-
nut trees; which, with the produce of the Soil, might (by means
of the improved Navigation of the Potomac) be brought to a
shipping port with more ease, and at a smaller expence, than
that which is transported 30 miles only by land.

Gloucester
    On North River .... 400... abt... 3.600 (f)
    (f) This tract is of second rate Gloucester low grounds. It has
no improvement thereon, but lyes on navigable water, abounding in Fish and Oysters. It was received in payment of a debt
(carrying interest) and valued in the year 1789 by an impartial
Gentleman to £800. N B. it has lately been sold, and there is
due thereon, a balance equal to what is annexed the Schedule

Nansemond
    Near Suffolk ⅓ of
      1119 acres .... } .... 373.... 8... 2.984 (g)
    (g) These 373 acres are the third part of undivided purchases
made by the deceased Fielding Lewis Thomas Walker and myself; on full conviction that they would become valuable. The
land lyes on the Road from Suffolk to Norfolk; touches (if I am
not mistaken) some part of the Navigable water of Nansemond
River; borders on, and comprehends part of the rich Dismal
Swamp; is capable of great improvement; and from its situation
must become extremely valuable.

Great Dismal Swamp

My dividend thereof ....abt... 20.000 (*h*)

(*h*) This is an undivided Interest wch. I held in the Great Dismal Swamp Company; containing about 4000 acres, with my part of the Plantation and Stock thereon belonging to the Company in the sd Swamp.

Ohio River

Round bottom	587
Little Kanhawa	2314
16 Miles lowr down	2448
Opposite Big Bent	4395

9744... 10... 97.440 (*i*)

(*i*) These several tracts of land are of the first quality on the Ohio River, in the parts where they are situated; being almost if not altogether River bottoms.

The smallest of these tracts is actually sold at ten dollars an acre but the consideration therefor not received; the rest are equally valuable and will sell as high, especially that which lyes just below the litte Kanhawa and is opposite to a thick settlement on the West side the Rivr.

The four tracts have an aggregate breadth upon the River of Sixteen miles and is bounded thereby that distance.

Great Kanhawa

Near the Mouth West	10990
East side above	7276
Mouth of Cole River	2000
Opposite thereto	2950
Burning Spring	125

23341 .... 200.000 (*k*)

(*k*) These tracts are situated on the Great Kanhawa River, and the first four are bounded thereby for more than forty miles. It is acknowledged by all who have seen them (and of the tract containing 10990 acres which I have been on myself, I can assert) that there is no richer, or more valuable land in all that Region; They are conditionally sold for the sum mentioned in the Schedule; that is $200.000 and if the terms of that Sale are not complied with they will command considerably more. The tract of which the 125 acres is a moiety, was taken up by General Andrew Lewis and myself for, and on account of a bituminous Spring which it contains, of so inflamable a nature as to burn as freely as spirits, and is as nearly difficult to extinguish

Maryland

Charles County .... 600.... 6.... 3.600 (*l*)
Montgomery Do .... 519.... 12.... 6.228 (*m*)

(*l*) I am but little acquainted with this land, although I have once been on it. It was received (many years since) in discharge of a debt due to me from Daniel Jenifer Adams at the value annexed thereto, and must be worth more. It is very level, lyes near the River Potomac

(*m*) This tract lyes about 30 miles above the City of Washington, not far from Kittoctan. It is good farming Land, and by those who are well acquainted with it I am informed that it would sell at twelve or $15 pr. acre.

Pennsylvania

Great Meadows .... 234.... 6.... 1.404 (*n*)

(*n*) This land is valuable on account of its local situation and other properties. It affords an exceeding good stand on Braddocks road from Fort Cumberland to Pittsburgh, and besides a fertile soil, possesses a large quantity of natural Meadow, fit for the scythe. It is distinguished by the appellation of the Great Meadows, where the first action with the French in the year 1754 was fought.

New York

Mohawk River .... abt.1000.... 6   6.000 (*o*)

(*o*) This is the moiety of about 2000 Acs. which remains unsold of 6071 Acres on the Mohawk River (Montgomery Cty) in a Patent granted to Daniel Coxe in the Township of Coxeborough and Carolana, as will appear by Deed from Marinus Willet and wife to George Clinton (late Governor of New

York) and myself. The latter sales have been at Six dollars an acr; and what remains unsold will fetch that or more

North Westn. Territy
On little Miami.............. 839
Ditto 977
Ditto 1235

3051....5 ....15.251 (*p*)

(*p*) The quality of these lands and their Situation, may be known by the Surveyors Certificates, which are filed along with the Patents. They lye in the vicinity of Cincinnati; one tract near the mouth of little Miami, another seven and the third ten miles up the same. I have been informed that they will readily command more than they are estimated at.

Kentucky
Rough Creek 3000
Ditto adjoining 2000

5000.... 2....10.000 (*q*)

(*q*) For the description of these tracts in detail, see General Spotswoods letters, filed with the other papers relating to them. Besides the General good quality of the Land, there is a valuable Bank of Iron Ore thereon: which, when the settlement becomes more populous (and settlers are moving that way very fast) will be found very valuable; as the rough Creek, a branch of Green River affords ample water for Furnaces and forges.

Lots—viz.

City of Washington
Two, near the Capital, Sqr 634 Cost $963; and with Buildgs } .. 15000 (*r*)

No. 5. 12. 13. and 14: the 3 last, Water lots on the Eastern Branch, in Sqr. 667. containing together 34.438 sqr. feet a 12 Cts } .. 4.132 (*s*)

(*r*) The two lots near the Capital, in square 634, cost me 963$ only; but in this price I was favoured, on condition that I should build two Brick houses three Story high each: without this reduction the selling prices of those Lots would have cost me about $1350. These lots, with the buildings thereon, when completed will stand me in $15000 at least.

(s) Lots No. 5. 12. 13 & 14 on the Eastn. branch, are advantageously situated on the water, and although many lots much less convenient have sold a great deal higher I will rate these at 12 Cts. the square foot only.

Alexandria

    Corner of Pitt and Prince Stts. half an Acre;
        laid out into buildgs. 3 or 4 of wch. are let   ... 4.000 (t)
        on grd. Rent at $3 pr. foot

  (t) For this lot, though unimproved, I have refused $3500. It has since been laid off into proper sized lots for building on; three or 4 of which are let on ground Rent, forever, at three dollars a foot on the Street. and this price is asked for both fronts on Pitt and Princes Street.

Winchester

    A lot in the Town of half an Acre and another in the Commons of about 6 Acs. supposed   .... 400 (u)

  (u) As neither the lot in the Town or Common have any improvements on them, it is not easy to fix a price, but as both are well situated, it is presumed the price annexed to them in the Schedule is a reasonable valun.

Bath—or Warm Springs

    Two Well situated, and had buildings to the amt of £150   .... 800 (w)

  (w) The Lots in Bath (two adjoining) cost me, to the best of my recollection, betwn. fifty and sixty pounds 20 years ago; and the buildings thereon £150 more. Whether property there has increased or decreased in its value, and in what condition the houses are, I am ignorant. but suppose they are not valued too high

Stock

United States 6 pr Cts 3746
  . Do   defered .... 1873 ⎫ ... 2500   6.246   (x)
          3 pr Cts .... 2946 ⎭   ——

(x) These are the sums which are actually funded. And though no more in the aggregate than $7.566; stand me in at least ten thousand pounds Virginia money. being the amount of bonded and other debts due to me, and discharged during the War when the money had depreciated in that ratio, and was so settled by public authoy.

Potomack Company

     24 Shares, cost ea £100 Sterg...................20.666 (y)

(y) The value annexed to these sha: is what they have actually cost me, and is the price affixed by Law: and although the present selling price is under par, my advice to the Legatees (for whose benefit they are intended, especially those who can afford to lye out of the money) is that each should take and hold one; there being a moral certainty of a great and increasing profit arising from them in the course of a few years.

James River Company

     5 Shares, each cost $100......................... 500 (z)

(z) It is supposed that the Shares in the James River Company must also be productive. But of this I can give no decided opinion for want of more accurate informatn.

Bank of Columbia

     170 Shares, $40 each .... 6.800 ⎫
Bank of Alexandria, besides ⎫ .... 1.000 ⎬ (&)
     20 to the Free School 5   ⎭   ⎭

(&) These are nominal prices of the Shares of the Banks of Alexandria and Columbia, the selling prices vary according to circumstances. But as the Stock usually divided from eight to ten per cent per annum, they must be worth the former, at least, so long as the Banks are conceived to be Secure, though from circumstances may, some times be below it.

Stock, living, viz:

> 1 Covering horse, 5 Coh. horses; 4 riding do; Six
> brood Mares; 20 working horses and mares; 2
> Covering Jacks, and 3 young ones; 10 she Asses,
> 42 working Mules; 15 younger ones 329 head of
> horned Cattle 640 head of Sheep, and a large ⎬ 15.653
> Stock of Hogs, the pricise number unknown
> ☞ My Manager has estimated this live Stock
> at £7,000 but I shall set it down in order to make
> rd sum at

Agregate amt........ $530.000

The value of live stock depends more upon the quality than quantity of the different species of it, and
this again upon the demand, and judgment or
fancy of purchasers.

Mount Vernon ⎱
  9th. July 1799 ⎰   Go: Washington

At a Court held for the County of Fairfax the 20th. January
1800 This Last Will and Testament of George Washington
deceased late president of the United States of America, was
presented in Court by George Steptoe Washington Samuel
Washington and Lawrence Lewis, three of the Executors
therein named, who made oath thereto, and the same being
proved by the oath of Charles Little, Charles Simms and Lud-
well Lee, to be in the true handwriting of the said Testator,
as also the Schedule thereto annexed, and the said will, being
sealed and signed by him on motion, Ordered to be recorded.
and the said Executors having given Security and performed
what the Laws require, a Certificate is granted them for obtaining a probate thereof in due form.

Test.   G. Deneale, *Cl: Fx.*

INDEX